elow.

CASES AND MATERIALS

FAMILY LAW

CASES AND MATERIALS

FAMILY LAW

M. E. Rodgers
Solicitor and Senior Lecturer, Nottingham Law School

BLACKSTONE
PRESS LIMITED

First published in Great Britain 1998 by Blackstone Press Limited,
Aldine Place, London W12 8AA.   Telephone 0181–740 2277

© Nottingham Law School, Nottingham Trent University, 1998

ISBN: 1 85431 746 6

British Library Cataloguing in Publication Data
A CIP catalogue record for this book is available from the British Library.

Typeset by Style Photosetting Limited, Mayfield, East Sussex
Printed by Livesey Limited, Shrewsbury, Shropshire

FOREWORD

The books in the LLB series have been written for students studying law at undergraduate level. There are two books for each subject. The first is the *Learning Text* which is designed to teach you about the particular subject in question. However, it does much more than that. By means of Activities, Self Assessment, and End of Chapter Questions, the *Learning Text* allows you to test your knowledge and understanding as you work. Each chapter starts with 'Objectives' which indicate what you should be able to do by the end of it. You should use these Objectives in your learning — check them frequently and ask yourself whether you have attained them.

The second book is a volume of *Cases and Materials*. This is cross-referenced from the *Learning Text*. It contains the primary sources of law such as statutes and cases plus subsidiary sources such as extracts from journals, law reform papers and textbooks. This is your portable library. Although each volume can stand alone, they are designed to be complementary.

The two-volume combination aims to support your learning by challenging you to demonstrate your mastery of the principles and application of the law. They are appropriate whatever your mode of study — full-time or part-time.

CONTENTS

ACKNOWLEDGEMENTS

Nottingham Law School and the publishers would like to thank the following for permission to reproduce copyright material:

Butterworths & Co. (Publishers) Ltd for extracts from the *All England Law Reports; Halsbury's Statutes;* Gray, *Land Law;* Hayes and Williams, *Family Law: Principles, Policy and Practice.*

Cavendish Publishers Ltd for extracts from Colbey, *Child Abuse and the Law.*

CPAG for extracts from the *Child Support Handbook* (4th and 5th editions).

Department of Health, Welsh Office for extracts from *Adoption: A Service for Children.*

Haworth Press Inc, for extracts from Silberberg and Silberberg, *Abusing poor children and trying to protect them.*

Her Majesty's Stationery Office and the Government Statistical Service for extracts from *Social Trends 27; Population Trends* (1996); *Judicial Statistics in England and Wales; OPCS Updates; Children and Young People on Child Protection Registers; Adoption: The Future;* Law Commission Reports Nos 6, 170, 172, 192; *Working Together under the Children Act 1989* and *Volume 1, Court Orders.*

Incorporated Council of Law Reporting for England & Wales for extracts from the Law Reports and *Weekly Law Reports.*

Jordans for extracts from the *Family Law Reports* and *Family Law.*

Government Statistical Service for extracts from OPCS Updates and *Children and Young People on Child Protection Registers.*

Law Society's Gazette for Lloyd, 'Family Law Act 1996: pilot projects', 21 May 1997.

New Society, 'Child Abuse: finding a balance', 3 July 1987.

News International for extracts from *The Times, Sunday Times* and *The Observer.*

Office for National Statistics for *Monitor Population and Health,* 1995.

Open University for extracts from *Social Problems and Social Welfare: Interfering in People's Lives,* Unit 2, 1988.

Oyez for reproducing Form C11.

Reed Elsevier plc for extracts from Lord Mackay, 'Joseph Jackson Memorial Lecture: Perceptions of the Children Bill and Beyond', *New Law Journal*, 14 April 1989.

Registrars of the Convocations of Canterbury & York for extracts from *Putting Asunder: A Divorce Law for Contemporary Society*, 1966.

Routledge for extracts from Parry, 'The Children Act 1989, local authorities wardship and the revival of the inherent jurisdiction', *Journal of Social Welfare Law*.

Sweet & Maxwell Ltd for extracts from Cretney and Masson, *Principles of Family Law* (5th and 6th editions).

The Telegraph for Barwick, 'Judges let parents decide fate of liver boy', 25 October 1995.

Woman, 'Too Young', 7 February 1987.

TABLE OF CASES

Cases reported in full are shown in heavy type. The page at which the report is printed is shown in heavy type.

TABLE OF STATUTES

Statutes, and sections thereof, which are set out in full or in part are shown in heavy type. The page at which the statute or section is printed is shown in heavy type.

TABLE OF STATUTORY INSTRUMENTS

Statutory instruments, and sections thereof, which are set out in full or in part are shown in heavy type. The page at which the statute or section is printed is shown in heavy type.

CHAPTER ONE

THE FAMILY — WHAT?

1.1 Prevalent Family Groupings

1.1.1 HOUSEHOLDS

Projection of Households in England to 2016, **Department of the Environment, 1995**

Table 1   Household estimates and projections 1971–2016: England

Thousands

	Households						Concealed families	
	Married couple	Cohab couple	Lone parent	Other multi-person	One person	Total	Couple	Lone parent
1971	11,249	204	378	1,168	2,944	15,942	127	108
1981	11,012	500	626	1,235	3,932	17,306	83	83
1991	10,547	1,222	981	1,350	5,115	19,215	74	89
1996	10,341	1,377	1,122	1,512	5,824	20,177	67	86
2001	10,217	1,447	1,202	1,671	6,509	21,046	62	82
2006	10,118	1,499	1,243	1,852	7,185	21,897	60	83
2011	10,037	1,549	1,259	2,051	7,875	22,769	60	84
2016	9,945	1,579	1,257	2,240	8,577	23,598	60	83

2.   The peak rate of increase is projected in the first half of the 1990s (annual average of 192,000), with around 170,000 a year projected in the two decades from 1996. In the two decades to 2011 (the end-year of the 1989-based projections), a net increase of nearly 3.6 million households in England is projected; and in the quarter century from 1991 to 2016 the projected increase is nearly 4.4 million households. In considering these projected increases in households, the definition of a separate household (Annex A) is important. As defined in these projections, two or more households can live in one dwelling. The number of dwellings in the housing stock need not therefore constrain the number of separate households and the projections of the number of households do not embody implicit assumptions about new house building of the size of the dwelling stock.

Population Trends, HMSO, 1996

First marriages*: age and sex   England and Wales

Year and quarter	All ages		Persons marrying per 1,000 single population at ages					Per cent aged under 20	Mean age (years)	Median age (years)
	Number (thousands)	Rate†	16–19	20–24	25–29	30–34	35–34			
Males										
1961	308.8	74.9	16.6	159.1	182.8	91.9	39.8	6.9	25.6	24.0
1966	339.1	78.9	22.1	168.6	185.4	91.1	36.4	9.9	24.9	23.4
1971	343.6	82.3	26.1	167.7	167.3	84.6	33.8	10.1	24.6	23.4
1976	274.4	62.8	18.5	123.7	132.5	78.7	32.0	9.8	25.1	23.7
1981	259.1	51.7	11.1	94.1	120.8	70.3	31.1	7.2	25.4	24.1
1983	251.8	47.5	8.5	79.4	115.1	70.9	30.4	5.7	25.7	24.5
1984	255.5	47.1	7.6	74.1	113.4	72.8	31.4	5.0	25.9	24.7
1985	253.3	46.6	7.0	70.8	118.3	74.4	31.0	4.6	26.0	24.9
1986	253.0	44.6	6.0	63.5	104.3	73.7	30.9	3.8	26.3	25.1
1987	258.7	44.7	5.6	62.3	100.7	74.6	31.2	3.4	26.4	25.3
1988	252.8	43.1	4.9	57.5	94.1	75.1	32.1	3.0	26.7	25.6
1989	252.2	42.6	4.7	55.7	90.2	75.1	31.1	2.8	26.9	25.8
1990	241.5	40.4	4.2	49.2	84.6	70.1	31.3	2.5	27.2	26.1
1991‡	222.8	37.0	3.4	42.5	76.5	64.5	31.5	2.1	27.5	26.5
1992‡	224.2	36.7	3.0	39.4	75.1	62.0	32.0	1.7	27.9	26.8
1993‡	213.5	35.5	2.5	35.2	73.5	62.4	32.9	1.5	28.2	27.2
Females										
1961	312.3	83.0	77.0	261.1	162.8	74.6	29.8	28.7	23.1	21.6
1966	342.7	89.3	82.6	263.7	153.4	74.1	30.2	32.5	22.5	21.2
1971	347.4	97.0	92.9	246.5	167.0	75.7	30.3	31.1	22.6	21.4
1976	276.5	76.9	66.7	185.4	140.7	77.6	31.6	31.1	22.8	21.5
1981	263.4	64.0	41.5	140.8	120.2	67.0	28.7	24.0	23.1	21.9
1983	256.2	59.1	32.9	122.1	115.6	64.3	27.6	19.9	23.4	22.3
1984	260.4	58.8	30.4	115.4	117.8	67.2	28.1	17.9	23.6	22.6
1985	258.1	58.2	27.3	114.0	124.7	69.5	29.5	16.2	23.8	22.8
1986	256.8	55.7	24.1	102.4	108.8	67.1	28.6	13.9	24.1	23.1
1987	263.0	56.1	23.0	101.6	106.8	68.6	27.9	12.8	24.3	23.3
1988	256.2	54.2	19.9	95.6	102.5	71.2	29.6	11.1	24.6	23.6
1989	254.8	53.5	18.8	91.6	100.4	71.6	28.3	10.2	24.8	23.9
1990	243.8	51.0	16.3	84.7	96.7	67.2	29.1	8.9	25.2	24.3
1991‡	224.8	46.9	14.0	74.0	89.4	62.8	30.4	7.9	25.5	24.6
1992‡	225.6	46.8	12.5	71.0	90.4	63.3	30.2	6.6	25.9	25.0
1993‡	215.0	45.5	10.7	66.0	92.2	64.5	31.5	5.7	26.2	25.3

‡ Provisional

Table 22   Remarriages*: age, sex, and previous marital status   England and Wales

Year and quarter	Remarriages of divorced persons									Remarriages of widowed persons	
	All ages		Persons remarrying per 1,000 divorced population at ages				Per cent aged under 35	Mean age (years)	Median age (years)	Number (thousands)	Rate**
	Number (thousands)	Rate†	16–24	25–29	30–34	35–44					
Males											
1961	18.8	162.9	478.6	473.6	351.6	198.3	33.9	40.5	39.2	19.1	28.8
1966	26.7	192.2	737.8	522.5	403.1	244.4	40.8	39.3	37.4	18.7	28.3
1971	42.4	227.3	525.2	509.0	390.7	251.3	42.8	39.8	37.0	18.7	27.5
1976	67.2	178.8	656.8	359.7	266.8	187.9	46.7	38.4	36.0	16.9	24.7
1981	79.1	129.5	240.7	260.9	205.8	141.9	46.1	38.1	35.9	13.8	19.7
1983	79.7	109.1	194.4	203.5	172.0	124.0	41.9	38.5	36.6	12.8	18.4
1984	81.4	103.5	192.7	191.8	162.8	118.8	40.5	38.7	37.0	12.3	17.6
1985	81.4	103.1	202.6	189.7	157.0	119.2	39.8	38.9	37.3	11.7	16.8
1986	83.4	90.8	138.6	157.8	141.0	105.8	38.5	39.1	37.7	11.6	16.7
1987	82.3	84.8	125.5	155.9	136.5	97.7	38.8	39.2	37.8	10.7	15.5
1988	85.0	82.4	111.3	143.8	129.9	96.9	36.5	39.6	38.4	10.7	15.5
1989	84.0	77.3	101.7	133.5	122.5	91.0	35.5	39.9	38.7	10.4	15.1
1990	80.3	69.9	91.1	122.0	111.6	82.1	34.9	40.1	38.9	9.6	13.9
1991	74.9	61.6	79.9	108.4	99.5	72.4	34.3	40.3	39.0	9.1	13.1
1992	78.5	61.0	89.8	105.5	99.6	72.2	37.6	40.3	39.4	8.9	12.9
1993‡	77.0	59.1	81.2	96.1	94.3	70.4	32.4	40.8	39.4	8.7	12.6
Females											
1961	18.0	97.1	542.2	409.6	250.2	111.5	46.8	37.2	35.9	16.5	6.5
1966	25.1	114.7	567.8	411.2	254.8	135.9	52.4	36.2	34.3	16.8	6.3
1971	39.6	134.0	464.4	359.0	232.7	139.8	57.0	35.7	33.0	17.7	6.3
1976	65.1	122.2	458.9	272.3	188.0	124.0	59.8	34.9	32.4	17.0	5.9
1981	75.1	90.7	257.5	202.1	142.9	95.5	57.9	35.1	33.4	13.5	4.6
1983	75.9	79.0	230.0	176.0	126.4	84.9	54.5	35.4	34.0	12.2	4.1
1984	76.9	75.1	226.9	170.6	119.6	82.2	52.9	35.6	34.3	11.9	4.0
1985	77.0	75.0	231.4	169.0	117.3	82.1	52.5	35.7	34.4	11.3	3.8
1986	80.0	68.7	190.6	156.2	111.7	75.5	51.2	36.0	34.7	11.2	3.8
1987	78.2	63.7	166.3	150.7	107.7	69.6	51.2	36.1	34.7	10.6	3.6
1988	81.7	66.6	153.8	146.8	108.0	69.9	49.3	36.5	35.2	10.6	3.6
1989	81.7	60.2	140.7	141.2	104.7	67.9	48.2	36.8	35.4	10.2	3.5
1990	78.0	54.8	123.3	129.8	98.9	61.9	47.8	37.0	35.6	9.3	3.2
1991	73.4	49.0	113.0	118.5	90.1	55.3	47.4	37.1	35.6	8.5	2.9
1992	77.5	49.5	123.2	118.8	93.1	56.5	46.4	37.4	35.9	8.4	2.9
1993‡	75.9	48.0	106.4	109.7	89.3	56.3	44.9	37.7	36.2	8.3	2.9

‡ Provisional

Dissolution of Marriage: Divorce, Nullity and Judicial Separation,
Judicial Statistics, 1995

Table 5.5   Matrimonial suits: summary of proceedings in selected years since 1938

	1938	1958	1968	1978	1988	1990	1991	1992	1993	1994	1995
Dissolution of marriage:											
Petitions filed	9,970	25,584	21,036	162,450	182,804	191,615	179,103	189,329	184,471	175,510	173,966
Decrees nisi	7,621	23,456	47,959	151,533	154,788	157,344	153,258	149,126	160,625	154,241	155,739
Decrees absolute	6,092	22,195	45,036	142,726	152,139	155,239[1]	155,927	156,679	162,579	154,873	153,337
Nullity of marriage											
Petitions filed	263	655	971	1,117	604	665	619	535	634	822	881
Decrees nisi	170	496	819	959	389	430	508	369	365	705	425
Decrees absolute	158	459	758	941	494	467	417	435	410	1,017	516
Judicial separation:											
Petitions filed	71	158	233	2,611	2,925	2,900	2,588	2,434	2,251	4,358	3,349
Decrees granted	25	88	105	1,228	1,917	1,794	1,747	1,452	1,413	1,350	1,543

[1] Revised figure

Lone Parent Families, OPCS Update, 1995

Lone parent families 1971-1993

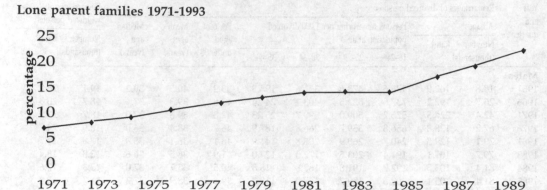

The proportion of families with dependent children headed by a lone parent increased from 8 per cent in 1971 to 22 per cent in 1993.

1.1.2   BIRTHS

Monitor Population and Health, HMSO/Government Statistical Service

Fig 1   Outcome of conceptions in England and Wales

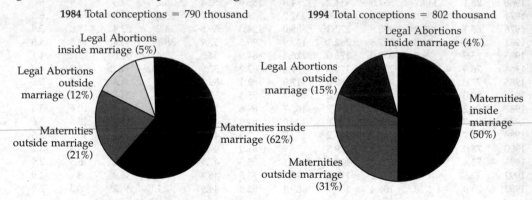

1984 Total conceptions = 790 thousand

Legal Abortions inside marriage (5%)

Legal Abortions outside marriage (12%)

Maternities outside marriage (21%)

Maternities inside marriage (62%)

1994 Total conceptions = 802 thousand

Legal Abortions inside marriage (4%)

Legal Abortions outside marriage (15%)

Maternities inside marriage (50%)

Maternities outside marriage (31%)

OPCS Update, HMSO/Government Statistical Service

Fig 3   Conceptions oustide marriage as a percentage of all conceptions, England and Wales, 1992

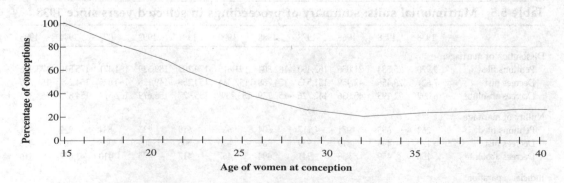

The proportion of conceptions outside marriage leading to a maternity outside marriage was 58 per cent, with 34 per cent leading to a termination. In 1992, 8 per cent of conceptions inside marriage were terminated by a legal abortion.

Women in their early thirties tended to have the lowest proportion of conceptions outside marriage (about one in four) and teenagers the highest proportion (about nine in ten). (Fig 3)

Live births outside marriage as a percentage of all live births in England and Wales by type of registration, 1983–1993

In 1993, about one third of all births in England and Wales occurred outside marriage. Three quarters of these births were jointly registered by both parents. For almost three quarters of the jointly registered births, the parents gave the same address.

Jointly registered births outside marriage by age of mother, 1983 and 1993

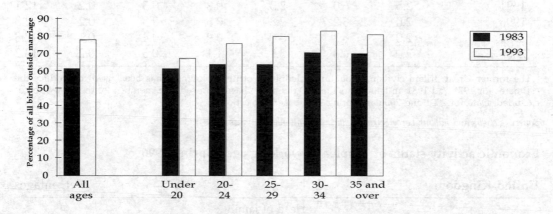

For all age groups of mother the proportion of births jointly registered increased. The greatest proportionate increase was in the 20-24 age group, which increased from 62 per cent of all births outside marriage in 1983 to 77 per cent in 1993.

1.1.3 ECONOMIC ACTIVITY

Social Trends 27, London: The Stationery Office, 1997

Labour force[1]: by gender and age

Great Britain   Millions

	16–24	25–44	45–54	55–59	60–64	65 and over	All aged 16 and over
Males							
1971	2.9	6.3	3.1	1.5	1.2	0.5	15.6
1981	3.1	7.0	2.9	1.4	0.9	0.3	15.7
1991	3.0	7.9	2.9	1.1	0.7	0.3	16.0
1996	2.4	7.9	3.3	1.1	0.6	0.3	15.6
2001	2.3	8.1	3.4	1.2	0.7	0.3	15.9
2006	2.4	7.8	3.4	1.3	0.7	0.3	16.0
Females							
1971	2.2	3.4	2.1	0.9	0.5	0.3	9.4
1981	2.6	4.4	2.1	0.9	0.4	0.2	10.6
1991	2.5	6.0	2.3	0.8	0.3	0.2	12.1
1996	2.0	6.2	2.8	0.8	0.3	0.2	12.3
2001	2.0	6.3	3.0	0.9	0.4	0.1	12.8
2006	2.1	6.3	3.1	1.1	0.5	0.2	13.3

[1] The former Great Britain civilian labour force definition of unemployment has been used to produce the estimates for 1971 and 1981; in later years the ILO definition has been used and members of the armed forces excluded. Data for 2001 and 2006 are Spring 1995-based projections.

Source: Census and Labour Force Survey, Office for National Statistics

Economic activity status of couples of working age[1], Spring 1996

United Kingdom   Percentages

	Head of family				
	Working full time	Working part time	Unemployed[2]	Inactive	All
Partner					
Working full time	31.7	1.0	0.8	2.1	35.6
Working part time	30.2	1.2	0.9	2.3	34.7
Unemployed[2]	2.1	0.1	0.7	0.2	3.1
Inactive	16.0	1.1	3.0	6.5	26.6
All	79.9	3.4	5.5	11.2	100.0

[1] Males aged 16 to 64 and females aged 16 to 59.
[2] Based on the ILO definition. See Appendix. Part 4: Unemployment — ILO definition.
Source: Labour Force Survey, Office for National Statistics

Whether a woman is economically active or not depends to some extent on the number and ages of her children. Women with a child under school age are the least likely to be in paid work (table below). As the age of the youngest child increases, women are increasingly likely to be in work, and in particular more likely to be in full-time employment.

Economic activity status of women[1]: by age of youngest dependent child, Spring 1996

United Kingdom					Percentages
	Age of youngest dependent child			No dependent children	All women aged 16–59
	0–4	5–10	11–15		
Working full time	17	22	34	47	37
Working part time	31	43	41	24	29
Unemployed[2]	5	5	4	4	5
Inactive	46	30	21	25	29
All women[1] (=100%) millions	3.1	2.2	1.5	10.2	17.0

[1] Aged 16 to 59.
[2] Based on the ILO definition. See Appendix, Part 4: Unemployment — ILO definition.
Source: Labour Force Survey, Office for National Statistics

Percentage of employees working part time: by gender and age, Spring 1996

United Kingdom			Percentages
	Males	Females	All
16–19			
In FTE[1]	97	99	98
Not in FTE[1]	12	26	19
All aged 16–19	51	65	58
20–24	11	23	17
25–44	3	42	21
45–54	3	47	25
55–59	7	54	30
60–64	16	71	38
65 and over	73	84	78
All aged 16 and over	8	45	25

[1] Full-time education.
Source: Labour Force Survey, Office for National Statistics

Employees[1]: by gender and occupation, 1991 and 1996

United Kingdom				Percentages
	Males		Females	
	1991	1996	1991	1996
Professional	10	12	8	10
Managers and administrators	16	19	8	10
Associate professional and technical	8	8	10	10
Clerical and secretarial	8	8	29	26
Personal and protective services	7	8	14	16
Sales	6	6	12	12
Craft and related	21	17	4	3
Plant and machine operatives	15	15	5	4
Other occupations	8	8	11	9
All employees	100	100	100	100

[1] At Spring each year. Excludes those who did not state their occupation.
Source: Labour Force Survey, Office for National Statistics

1.1.4 INCOME

Social Trends 27, London: The Stationery Office, 1997

Sources of gross household income: by household type, 1994–95

United Kingdom					Percentages
	Earned income[1]	Investment income[2]	Contributory cash benefits	Non-contributory cash benefits	Gross household income (=100%) (£ per week)
Retired households[3]					
Single person	—	39	45	16	137
Couple	2	52	39	7	246
Other	16	37	32	15	301
Non-retired households					
Single person	80	8	4	9	266
Lone parent					
Dependent children[4]	37	12	1	49	203
Non-dependent children only	71	9	10	10	340
Couple					
No children	87	9	3	2	498
Dependent children[4]	88	4	1	7	537
Non-dependent children only	88	6	3	3	660
Other	76	9	5	11	503
All households	73	12	8	8	381

[1] Including wages and salaries, self-employed income and income from 'fringe benefits'.
[2] Including occupational pensions and annuities and other income.
[3] Households where the combined income of retired members amounts to at least half the total gross income of the household.
[4] Children aged under 16 and those aged 16 to 18 who are not married and receiving full-time non-advanced further education. This category includes households with a mixture of dependent and non-dependent children.
Source: Family Expenditure Survey, Office for National Statistics

Relative earnings[1] of male and female partners[2], 1994–95

Great Britain	Percentages
	1994–95
Man earns over £100 more	54
Man earns £50–£100 more	11
Earnings are equal[3]	21
Woman earns £50–£100 more	4
Woman earns over £100 more	10
All couples[2]	100

[1] Gross weekly earnings from employment or self-employment.
[2] One man/one woman couples (with or without children) where both partners work full time.
[3] Equal to within £50 per week.
Source: Family Resources Survey, Department of Social Security

1.2   A Change in Direction — Where is the Law Enforced?

The English Family Court Hierarchy

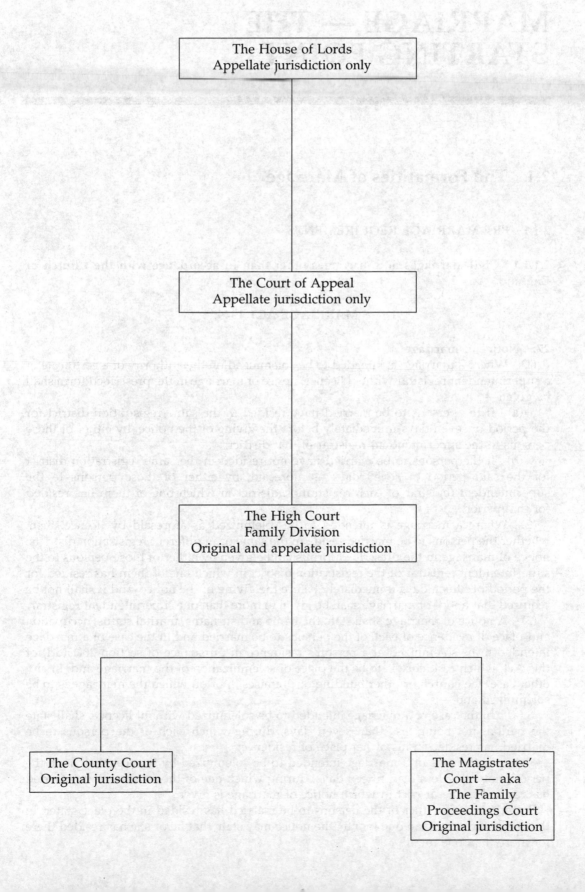

CHAPTER TWO

MARRIAGE — THE STARTING POINT

2.1 The Formalities of Marriage

2.1.1 PRE-MARRIAGE REQUIREMENTS

2.1.1.1 Civil marriages and marriages other than in accordance with the Church of England

MARRIAGE ACT 1949

27. Notice of marriage

(1) Where a marriage is intended to be solemnized on the authority of a certificate of a superintendent registrar without licence, notice of marriage in the prescribed form shall be given—

(a) if the persons to be married have resided in the same registration district for the period of seven days immediately before the giving of the notice, by either of those persons to the superintendent registrar of that district;

(b) if the persons to be married have not resided in the same registration district for the said period of seven days as aforesaid, by either of those persons to the superintendent registrar of each registration district in which one of them has resided for that period.

(2) Where a marriage is intended to be solemnized as aforesaid by licence, then, whether the persons to be married reside in the same or in different registration districts, notice of marriage in the prescribed form shall be given by either of those persons to the superintendent registrar of the registration district in which one of them has resided for the period of fifteen days immediately before the giving of the notice, and it shall not be required that notice of marriage shall be given to more than one superintendent registrar.

(3) A notice of marriage shall state the name and surname, marital status, occupation and place of residence of each of the persons to be married and in the case of a marriage intended to be solemnized at a person's residence in pursuance of section 26(1)(dd) of this Act, which residence is to be the place of solemnization of the marriage and, in any other case, the church or other building or premises in or on which the marriage is to be solemnized and—

(a) in the case of a marriage intended to be solemnized without licence, shall state the period, not being less than seven days, during which each of the persons to be married has resided in his or her place of residence;

(b) in the case of a marriage intended to be solemnized by licence, shall state the period, not being less than fifteen days, during which one of the persons to be married has resided in the district in which notice of marriage is given:

Provided that if either of the persons to be married has resided in the place stated in the notice for more than one month, the notice may state that he or she has resided there for more than one month.

(4)   The superintendent registrar shall file all notices of marriage and keep them with the records of his office, and shall subject to section 27A of this Act also forthwith enter the particulars given in every such notice, together with the date of the notice and the name of the person by whom the notice was given, in a book (in this Act referred to as 'the marriage notice book') furnished to him for that purpose by the Registrar General, and the marriage notice book shall be open for inspection free of charge at all reasonable hours.

(5)   If the persons to be married wish to be married in the presence of a registrar in a registered building for which an authorised person has been appointed, they shall, at the time when notice of marriage is given to the superintendent registrar under this section, give notice to him that they require a registrar to be present at the marriage.

31.   Marriage under certificate without licence

(1)   Where a marriage is intended to be solemnized on the authority of a certificate of a superintendent registrar without licence, the superintendent registrar to whom notice of marriage has been given shall suspend or affix in some conspicuous place in his office, for twenty-one successive days next after the day on which the notice was entered in the marriage book, the notice of marriage, or an exact copy signed by him of the particulars thereof as entered in the marriage notice book.

(2)   At the expiration of the said period of twenty-one days the superintendent registrar, on the request of the person by whom the notice of marriage was given, shall issue a certificate in the prescribed form unless—

(a)   any lawful impediment to the issue of the certificate has been shown to the satisfaction of the superintendent registrar; or

(b)   the issue of the certificate has been forbidden under the last foregoing section by any person authorised in that behalf.

(3)   Every such certificate shall set out the particulars contained in the notice of marriage and the day on which the notice was entered in the marriage notice book and shall contain a statement that the issue of the certificate has not been forbidden as aforesaid.

(4)   No marriage shall be solemnized on the production of a certificate of a superintendent registrar without licence until after the expiration of the said period of twenty-one days.

(5)   Where a marriage is to be solemnized in a registered building for which an authorised person has been appointed and no notice requiring a registrar to be present at the marriage has been given to the superintendent registrar under subsection (5) of section twenty-seven of this Act, the superintendent registrar shall, when issuing a certificate under this section, give to one of the persons to be married printed instructions in the prescribed form for the due solemnization of the marriage.

32.   Marriage under certificate by licence

(1)   Where a marriage is intended to be solemnized on the authority of a certificate of a superintendent registrar by licence, the person by whom notice of marriage is given shall state in the notice that the marriage is intended to be solemnized by licence, and the notice shall not be suspended in the office of the superintendent registrar.

(2)   Where a notice of marriage containing such a statement as aforesaid has been received by a superintendent registrar, then, after the expiration of one whole day next after the day on which the notice was entered in the marriage notice book, the superintendent registrar, on the request of the person by whom the notice was given, shall issue a certificate and a licence in the prescribed form unless—

(a)   any lawful impediment to the issue of the certificate has been shown to the satisfaction of the superintendent registrar; or

(b)   the issue of the certificate has been forbidden under section thirty of this Act by any person authorised in that behalf.

(3)   Every such certificate shall set out the particulars contained in the notice of marriage and the day on which the notice was entered in the marriage notice book, and shall contain a statement that the issue of the certificate has not been forbidden as aforesaid.

(4)   Where a marriage is to be solemnized in a registered building for which an authorised person has been appointed and no notice requiring a registrar to be present

at the marriage has been given to the superintendent registrar under subsection (5) of section twenty-seven of this Act, the superintendent registrar shall, when issuing a certificate and licence under this section, give to one of the persons to be married printed instructions in the prescribed form for the due solemnization of the marriage.

33. Period of validity of certificate and licence

(1)   A marriage maybe solemnized on the authority of a certificate of a superintendent registrar, whether by licence or without licence, at any time within three months from the day on which the notice of marriage was entered in the marriage notice book.

(2)   If the marriage is not solemnized within the said period of three months, the notice of marriage and the certificate, and any licence which may have been granted hereon, shall be void, and no person shall solemnize the marriage on the authority thereof.

2.1.1.2   Anglican or Church of England marriages

MARRIAGE ACT 1949

5.   Methods of authorising marriages

A marriage according to the rites of the Church of England may be solemnized—

(a)   after the publication of banns of matrimony;

(b)   on the authority of a special licence of marriage granted by the Archbishop of Canterbury or any other person by virtue of the Ecclesiastical Licences Act 1533 (in this Act referred to as a 'special licence');

(c)   on the authority of a licence of marriage (other than a special licence) granted by an ecclesiastical authority having power to grant such a licence (in this Act referred to as a 'common licence'); or

(d)   on the authority of a certificate issued by a superintendent registrar under Part III of this Act,

except that paragraph (a) of this section shall not apply in relation to the solemnization of any marriage mentioned in subsection (2) of section 1 of this Act.

6.   Place of publication of banns

(1)   Subject to the provisions of this Act, where a marriage is intended to be solemnized after the publication of banns of matrimony, the banns shall be published—

(a)   if the persons to be married reside in the same parish, in the parish church of that parish;

(b)   if the persons to be married do not reside in the same parish, in the parish church of each parish in which one of them resides:

Provided that if either of the persons to be married resides in a chapelry or in a district specified in a licence granted under section twenty of this Act, the banns may be published in an authorised chapel of that chapelry or district instead of in the parish church of the parish in which that person resides.

(2)   In relation to a person who resides in an extra-parochial place, the last foregoing subsection shall have effect as if for reference to a parish there were substituted references to that extra-parochial place, and as if for references to a parish church there were substituted references to an authorised chapel of that place.

(3)   For the purposes of this section, any parish in which there is no parish church or chapel belonging thereto or no church or chapel in which divine service is usually solemnized every Sunday, and any extra-parochial place which has no authorised chapel, shall be deemed to belong to any adjoining parish or chapelry.

(4)   Banns of matrimony may be published in any parish church or authorised chapel which is the usual place of worship of the persons to be married or of one of them although neither of those persons resides in the parish or chapelry to which the church or chapel belongs;

Provided that the publication of the banns by virtue of this subsection shall be in addition to and not in substitution for the publication of banns required by subsection (1) of this section.

7. Time and manner of publication of banns

(1)   Subject to the provisions of section nine of this Act, banns of matrimony shall be published on three Sundays preceding the solemnization of the marriage during morning service or, if there is no morning service on a Sunday on which the banns are to be published, during evening service.

(2)   Banns of matrimony shall be published in an audible manner and in accordance with the form of words prescribed by the rubric prefixed to the office of matrimony in the Book of Common Prayer, and all the other rules prescribed by the said rubric concerning the publication of banns and the solemnization of matrimony shall, so far as they are consistent with the provisions of this Part of this Act, be duly observed.

(3)   The parochial church council of a parish shall provide for every church and chapel in the parish in which marriages may be solemnized, a register book of banns made of durable materials and marked in the manner directed by section fifty-four of this Act for the register book of marriages, and all banns shall be published from the said register book of banns by the officiating clergyman, and not from loose papers, and after each publication the entry in the register book shall be signed by the officiating clergyman, or by some person under his direction.

(4)   Any reference in the last foregoing subsection to a parochial church council shall, in relation to an authorised chapel in an extra-parochial place, be construed as a reference to the chapel warden or other officer exercising analogous duties in the chapel or, if there is no such officer, such person as may be appointed in that behalf by the bishop of the diocese.

15. Places in which marriages may be solemnized by common licence

(1)   Subject to the provisions of this Part of this Act, a common licence shall not be granted for the solemnization of a marriage in any church or chapel other than—

(a)   the parish church of the parish, or an authorised chapel of the ecclesiastical district, in which one of the persons to be married has had his or her usual place of residence for fifteen days immediately before the grant of the licence; or

(b)   a parish church or authorised chapel which is the usual place of worship of the persons to be married or of one of them.

(2)   For the purposes of this section, any parish in which there is no parish church or chapel belonging thereto or no church or chapel in which divine service is usually solemnized every Sunday, and any extra-parochial place which has no authorised chapel, shall be deemed to belong to any adjoining parish or chapelry.

16. Provisions as to common licences

(1)   A common licence shall not be granted unless one of the persons to be married has sworn before a person having authority to grant such a licence—

(a)   that he or she believes that there is no impediment of kindred or alliance or any other lawful cause, nor any suit commenced in any court, to bar or hinder the solemnizing of the marriage in accordance with the licence:

(b)   that one of the persons to be married has had his or her usual place of residence in the parish or other ecclesiastical district in which the marriage is to be solemnized for fifteen days immediately before the grant of the licence or that the parish church or authorised chapel in which the marriage is to be solemnized is the usual place of worship of those persons or of one of them;

2.1.2   THE MARRIAGE CEREMONY

2.1.2.1   The civil ceremony

MARRIAGE ACT 1949

44. Solemnization of marriage in registered building

(3)   Where a marriage is solemnized in a registered building each of the persons contracting the marriage shall, in some part of the ceremony and in the presence of the witnesses and the registrar or authorised person, make the following declaration:—

'I do solemnly declare that I know not of any lawful impediment why I, *AB*, may not be joined in matrimony to *CD'*
and each of them shall say to the other:—
'I call upon these persons here present to witness that I, *AB*, do take thee, *CD*, to be my lawful wedded wife [*or* husband]':
  Provided that if the marriage is solemnized in the presence of an authorised person without the presence of a registrar, the persons to be married, instead of saying each to the other the last-mentioned form of words, may say:—
'I, *AB*, do take thee, *CD*, to be my wedded wife [or husband].'

MARRIAGE CEREMONY (PRESCRIBED WORDS) ACT 1996

1. Alternatives for prescribed declaration and words of contract
  (1) In section 44(3) of the Marriage Act 1949 . . . for the proviso there shall be substituted—
'(3A) As an alternative to the declaration set out in subsection (3) of this section the persons contracting the marriage may make the requisite declaration either—
    (a) by saying "I declare that I know of no legal reason why I [*name*] may not be joined in marriage to [*name*]"; or
    (b) by replying "I am" to the question put to them successively "Are you [*name*] free lawfully to marry [*name*]?";
and as an alternative to the words of contract set out in that subsection the persons to be married may say to each other "I [*name*] take you [*or* thee] [*name*] to be my wedded wife [*or* husband]".'.

2.1.2.2 Alternative venues for the ceremony

MARRIAGE ACT 1994

1. Solemnization of marriages on premises approved by local authorities
  (1) In section 26(1) of the Marriage Act 1949 (marriages which may be solemnized on authority of superintendent registrar's certificate) after paragraph (b) there shall be inserted—
'(bb) a marriage on approved premises;'.
  (2) After section 46 of that Act there shall be inserted—

'Marriages on approved premises

46A. Approval of premises
  (1) The Secretary of State may by regulations make provision for and in connection with the approval by local authorities of premises for the solemnization of marriages in pursuance of section 26(1)(bb) of this Act.
  (2) The matters dealt with by the regulations may include—
    (a) the kinds of premises in respect of which approvals may be granted;
    (b) the procedure to be followed in relation to applications for approval;
    (c) the considerations to be taken into account by a local authority in determining whether to approve any premises;
    (d) the duration and renewal of approvals;
    (e) the conditions that must or may be imposed by a local authority on granting or renewing an approval;
    (f) the determination and charging by local authorities of fees in respect of applications for the approval of premises and in respect of the renewal of approvals;
    (g) the circumstances in which a local authority must or may revoke an approval;
    (h) the review of any decision to refuse an approval or the renewal of an approval, to impose conditions on granting or renewing an approval or to revoke an approval;
    (i) the notification to the Registrar General of all approvals granted, renewed or revoked;

(j)   the keeping by local authorities of registers of approved premises;

(k)   the issue by the Registrar General of guidance supplementing the provision made by the regulations.

(3)   In this section 'local authority' means a county council, metropolitan district council or London borough council.

. . .

46B.   Solemnization of marriage on approved premises

(1)   Any marriage on approved premises in pursuance of section 26(1)(bb) of this Act shall be solemnized in the presence of—

(a)   two witnesses, and

(b)   the superintendent registrar and a registrar of the registration district in which the premises are situated.

(2)   Without prejudice to the width of section 46A(2)(e) of this Act, the Secretary of State shall exercise his power to provide for the imposition of conditions as there mentioned so as to secure that members of the public are permitted to attend any marriage solemnized on approved premises in pursuance of section 26(1)(bb) of this Act.

(3)   Each of the persons contracting such a marriage shall make the declaration and use the form of words set out in section 44(3) of this Act in the case of marriages in registered buildings in the presence of a registrar.

(4)   No religious service shall be used at a marriage on approved premises in pursuance of section 26(1)(bb) of this Act.'

. . .

MARRIAGES (APPROVED PREMISES) REGULATIONS 1995

Schedule 1   Requirements for the grant of approval   Regulation 5(1)

1.   Having regard to their primary use, situation, construction and state of repair, the premises must, in the opinion of the authority, be a seemly and dignified venue for the solemnization of marriages.

2.   The premises must be regularly available to the public for use for the solemnization of marriages.

3.   The premises must have the benefit of such fire precautions as may reasonably be required by the authority, having consulted with the fire authority, and such other reasonable provision for the health and safety of persons employed in or visiting the premises as the authority considers appropriate.

4.   The premises must have no recent or continuing connection with any religion, religious practice or religious persuasion which would be incompatible with the use of the premises for the solemnization of marriages in pursuance of section 26(1)(*bb*) of the Act.

5.   The room or rooms in which ceremonies of marriage will be solemnized if approval is granted must be identifiable by description as a distinct part of the premises.

Schedule 2. Conditions to be attached to grants of approval   Regulation 6(1)(a)

1.   The holder of the approval must ensure that there is at all times an individual with responsibility for ensuring compliance with these conditions ('the responsible person') and that the responsible person's occupation, seniority, position of responsibility in relation to the premises, or other factors (his 'qualification'), indicate that he is in a position to ensure compliance with these conditions.

2.   The responsible person or, in his absence, an appropriately qualified deputy appointed by him, shall be available on the premises for a minimum of one hour prior to each marriage ceremony and throughout each marriage ceremony.

3.   The holder must notify the authority—

(*a*)   of his name and address immediately upon him becoming the holder of an approval under regulation 7(2), and

(*b*)   of the name, address and qualification of the responsible person immediately upon the appointment of a new responsible person.

4.   The holder must notify the authority immediately of any change to any of the following—

    (*a*) the layout of the premises, as shown in the plan submitted with the approved application, or in the use of the premises,
    (*b*) the name or full postal address of the approved premises,
    (*c*) the description of the room or rooms in which marriages are to be solemnized,
    (*d*) the name or address of the holder of the approval, and
    (*e*) the name, address or qualification of the responsible person.

5. The approved premises must be made available at all reasonable times for inspection by the authority.

6. A suitable notice stating that the premises have been approved for the solemnization of marriages in pursuance of section 26(1)(bb) of the Marriage Act 1949 and identifying and giving directions to the room in which a marriage ceremony is to take place must be displayed at each public entrance to the premises for one hour prior to the ceremony and throughout the ceremony.

7. No food or drink may be sold or consumed in the room in which a marriage ceremony takes place for one hour prior to that ceremony or during that ceremony.

8. All marriage ceremonies must take place in a room which was identified as one to be used for the solemnization of marriages on the plan submitted with the approved application.

9. The room in which a marriage is solemnized must be separate from any other activity on the premises at the time of the ceremony.

10. The arrangements for and content of each marriage ceremony must meet with the prior approval of the superintendent registrar of the district in which the approved premises are situated.

11. Any reading, music, words or performance which forms part of a ceremony of marriage celebrated on the premises must be secular in nature; for this purpose any such material used by way of introduction to, in any interval between parts of, or by way of conclusion to the ceremony shall be treated as forming part of the ceremony.

12. Public access to any ceremony of marriage solemnized in approved premises must be permitted without charge.

13. Any reference to the approval of premises on any sign or notice, or on any stationery or publication, or within any advertisement may state that the premises have been approved by the authority as a venue for marriage in pursuance of section 26(1)(bb) of the Act, but shall not state or imply any recommendation of the premises or its facilities by the authority, the Registrar General or any of the officers or employees of either of them.

Wilkins, E, Encounter at Station not so Brief, *The Times*, 21 March 1996

The platform announcement came 50 years too late for the couple from *Brief Encounter* but yesterday a railway station unveiled plans to conduct marriage ceremonies.

While Celia Johnson and Trevor Howard were forced to bring their railway romance to an abrupt end, couples can now hop on a Eurostar for a Paris honeymoon after tying the knot at Ashford International station.

The 265 ceremonies, to be conducted in Ashford's first-class departure lounge, were announced when Kent County Council agreed to grant Eurostar a licence to hold civil weddings.

Couples are expected to drive to Ashford, leave their cars in the 2,000-space car park and go through Customs to the VIP area. If forgetful relatives arrive without passports, they can be granted special security clearance through the Customs point.

A local registrar will conduct the marriage and provide a portable hi-fi to play the couple's favourite tapes during the 20-minute service.

Bryne , S, Get married at your local stately home, *Sunday Times*, 27 August 1995

Couples are deserting the register office to marry in castles, hotels and even at their favourite football club.

Fewer people are getting married than at any time since the second world war, but owners of 'approved premises' for weddings report a boom since they were given the go-ahead in April under the Marriage Act.

Indeed, the freedom to marry in a hotel, stately home or football ground instead of a dull register office may yet turn round Britain's plunging marriage rate.

More than 500 locations have been granted a licence. They include some 280 hotels, 30 stately homes and 33 civic buildings as well as racecourses and university colleges.

Cretney, S., and Masson, J., Principles of Family Law, 6th edn, Sweet & Maxwell, 1996, p. 27

According to S. Byrne, *The Sunday Times*, August 27, 1995. It has also been reported that Eurostar has obtained a licence to hold weddings in the First Class Departure Lounge at Ashford International Railway station; and *The Times* (March 21, 1996), states that guests will have to go through Customs to get to the marriage room. If accurate, it is questionable whether the requirement that marriages be celebrated 'with open doors' will be honoured.

2.2 Consent

MARRIAGE ACT 1949

3. Marriages of persons under eighteen

(1) Where the marriage of a child, not being a widower or widow, is intended to be solemnized on the authority of a certificate issued by a superintendent registrar under Part III of this Act, whether by licence or without licence, the consent of the person or persons specified in subsection (1A) of this section shall be required.

Provided that—

(a) if the superintendent registrar is satisfied that the consent of any person whose consent is so required cannot be obtained by reason of absence or inaccessibility or by reason of his being under any disability, the necessity for the consent of that person shall be dispensed with, if there is any other person whose consent is also required; and if the consent of no other person is required, the Registrar General may dispense with the necessity of obtaining any consent, or the court may, on application being made, consent to the marriage, and the consent of the court so given shall have the same effect as if it had been given by the person whose consent cannot be so obtained;

(b) if any person whose consent is required refuses his consent, the court may, on application being made, consent to the marriage, and the consent of the court so given shall have the same effect as if it had been given by the person whose consent is refused.

(1A) The consents are—

(a) subject to paragraphs (b) to (d) of this subsection, the consent of—

  (i) each parent (if any) of the child who has parental responsibility for him; and

  (ii) each guardian (if any) of the child;

(b) where a residence order is in force with respect to the child, the consent of the person or persons with whom he lives, or is to live, as a result of the order (in substitution for the consents mentioned in paragraph (a) of this subsection);

(c) where a care order is in force with respect to the child, the consent of the local authority designated in the order (in addition to the consents mentioned in paragraph (a) of this subsection);

(d) where neither paragraph (b) nor (c) of this subsection applies but a residence order was in force with respect to the child immediately before he reached the age of sixteen, the consent of the person or persons with whom he lived, or was to live, as a result of the order (in substitution for the consents mentioned in paragraph (a) of this subsection).

. . .

(3) Where the marriage of a child not being a widower or widow, is intended to be solemnized after the publication of banns of matrimony then, if any person whose consent to the marriage would have been required under this section in the case of a marriage intended to be solemnized otherwise than after the publication of the banns, openly and publicly declares or causes to be declared, in the church or chapel in which

the banns are published, at the time of the publication, his dissent from the intended marriage, the publication of banns shall be void.

. . .

(5)   For the purposes of this section, 'the court' means the High Court, the county court of the district in which any applicant or respondent resides, or a court of summary jurisdiction appointed for the commission area (within the meaning of the Justices of the Peace Act 1979) which includes the place in which any applicant or respondent resides, and rules of court may be made for enabling applications under this section—

(a)   if made to the High Court, to be heard in chambers;

(b)   if made to the county court, to be heard and determined by the registrar subject to appeal to the judge;

(c)   if made to a court of summary jurisdiction, to be heard and determined otherwise than in open court,

and shall provide that, where an application is made in consequence of a refusal to give consent, notice of the application shall be served on the person who has refused consent.

(6)   Nothing in this section shall dispense with the necessity of obtaining the consent of the High Court to the marriage of a ward of court.

2.3   Consequences of Non-compliance with the Formalities

MARRIAGE ACT 1949

48.   Proof of certain matters not necessary to validity of marriages

(1)   Where any marriage has been solemnized under the provisions of this Part of this Act, it shall not be necessary in support of the marriage to give any proof—

(a)   that before the marriage either of the parties thereto resided, or resided for any period, in the registration district stated in the notice of marriage to be that of his or her place of residence.

(b)   that any person whose consent to the marriage was required by section three of this Act had given his consent;

(c)   that the registered building in which the marriage was solemnized had been certified as required by law as a place of religious worship;

(d)   that that building was the usual place of worship of either of the parties to the marriage; or

(e)   that the facts stated in a declaration made under subsection (1) of section thirty-five of this Act were correct:

nor shall any evidence be given to prove the contrary in any proceedings touching the validity of the marriage.

(2)   A marriage solemnized in accordance with the provisions of this Part of this Act in a registered building which has not been certified as required by law as a place of religious worship shall be as valid as if the building had been so certified.

49.   Void marriages

If any persons knowingly and wilfully intermarry under the provisions of this Part of this Act—

(a)   without having given due notice of marriage to the superintendent registrar;

(b)   without a certificate for marriage having been duly issued by the superintendent registrar to whom notice of marriage was given;

(c)   without a licence having been so issued, in a case in which a licence is necessary;

(d)   on the authority of a certificate which is void by virtue of subsection (2) of section thirty-three of this Act;

(e)   in any place other than the church, chapel, registered building, office or other place specified in the notice of marriage and certificate of the superintendent registrar;

(ee)   in the case of a marriage purporting to be in pursuance of section 26(1)(bb) of this Act, on any premises that at the time the marriage is solemnized are not approved premises;

(f)   in the case of a marriage in a registered building (not being a marriage in the presence of an authorised person), in the absence of a registrar of the registration district in which the registered building is situated;

(g)   in the case of a marriage in the office of a superintendent registrar, in the absence of the superintendent registrar or of a registrar of the registration district of that superintendent registrar;

(gg)   in the case of a marriage on approved premises, in the absence of the superintendent registrar of the registration district in which the premises are situated or in the absence of a registrar of that district; or

(h)   in the case of a marriage to which section 45A of this Act applies, in the absence of any superintendent registrar or registrar whose presence at that marriage is required by that section;

the marriage shall be void.

20 MARRIAGE — THE STARTING POINT

2.4 End of Chapter Assessment Question

'[M]any of the procedures [relating to marriage] are unnecessarily complex and restrict-ive.'
    Government Green Paper, Cm 531: *Registration: A Modern Service*.
    Discuss the validity of this statement.

2.5 End of Chapter Assessment Outline Answer

To answer this question you are not only required to discuss the procedures or formalities relating to marriage, but also to evaluate whether they are or are not restrictive and complex. Hence, to start, you should identify the core formalities to marriage.

Starting with the pre-marriage formality of notice, the question requires you to identify the different types of notice that can be given in relation to the various religious or civil ceremonies. These would be:

(a)   Marriage under a superintendent registrar's certificate (seven days' residence and 21 days' notice).

(b)   Marriage under a superintendent registrar's certificate and licence (15 days' residence of one party and one day's notice).

(c)   Marriage under a registrar's general licence (relevant to death bed marriages or those where the individual cannot get to the registered place for the ceremony).

(d)   Marriage after banns have been called (banns called for three successive Sundays in the parish of residence and celebration of the marriage if different).

(e)   Marriage under common licence (residence of one party of 15 days and marriage permitted when licence issued).

(f)   Special licence or 'Archbishops licence', which permits death bed marriages or marriages in churches where there is no connection for the parties.

With respect to all notice provisions, the issue of payment of fees and length of residence or time between giving notice in an area and the actual ceremony are key features. Those formalities involving the largest residence/notice period are the cheapest. Complexity arises in the sense that there are different notice periods in existence. If a couple can fit into all three categories then they may find it hard to make a choice — but this is hardly 'complex'. The notice periods appear to cater for different needs (and products) and if this is accepted, then the process is not harsh.

The question of restrictiveness is somewhat different. Unless able to afford the more expensive 'licences' couples will be restricted to marrying in the area or church where notice is given. This has been slightly ameliorated by the Marriage Act 1994. The time periods are also restrictive in the sense that they require some sort of planning of the marriage. But this should be evaluated in the light of why notice periods are needed. If the notice periods are designed to enable impediments or objections to be given, then they should be retained. However, given the general ineffectiveness of the process, you may agree that they are not really needed. To suggest this is not to agree that they are restrictive or complex.

Looking now at the formalities of the marriage ceremony itself, the requirements you should have focussed on were:

• Qualification of celebrant.
• Place of marriage.
• Wording and witnesses.
• Hours/doors.

In all but Quaker and Jewish ceremonies the law lays down requirements to meet the above.

If the celebrant, whether a civil marriage or religious, is not qualified and this is known to the parties, the marriage will be invalid. This would not appear to be too complex. As to restrictive, surely the parties will decide what type of ceremony to have in light of the celebrant they want.

The place of marriage is restricted by virtue of the type of notice given. The law has widened the scope of venues for marriages in 1994. You may argue that the nature of the regulations are too limiting — a marriage cannot be conducted on a beach, or at the top of Snowden (although a marriage can be blessed) which may be the preferred place. You may believe that these sorts of venues are inappropriate — how can other legal formalities be ensured?

Turning to the wording, the legal requirements are not draconian. It is however strange that a so-called 'simple contract' needs to have a minimum of two witnesses. The reference to 'no lawful impediment' may result in a perjury charge if there was in fact a known impediment.

Thus, these requirements can be classed as complex or restrictive since especially where wording is concerned, there is nothing to stop the rest of the ceremony being in the couple's own chosen wording.

The hours for marriage and the 'public' element of open doors, could, arguably be seen as irrelevant. If a couple wish to marry, have the necessary licence, does it matter what time the ceremony takes place? Equally is it relevant that the public can gain access when there are the required witnesses? Whilst you may believe these formalities are unnecessary, especially given the lack of sanctions if they are broken, this does not mean the requirements are complex, albeit they may be restrictive.

Finally, look at past marriage requirements — that of registration. The purpose of registration is to provide public evidence of a change in status. Marriage confers additional rights and obligations which are not otherwise available, so registration is necessary. The process of evidencing a marriage, with handwritten certificates and filing of copies is, arguably, complex but, more relevantly far too outdated.

In your conclusion you should draw all these threads together. In isolation, the requirements are not overly complex or restrictive of an individual's freedom. Taken together, a picture of more complexity may build up, but even so, it can be suggested that the Law Commission's statement does not reflect the truth of the situation when taken at face value. By broadening out the evaluation of the reason and need for the requirements, it is easier to agree that the formalities need to be changed.

CHAPTER THREE

NULLITY AND JUDICIAL SEPARATION

3.1 Void Marriages

MATRIMONIAL CAUSES ACT 1973

11. Grounds on which a marriage is void

A marriage celebrated after 31st July 1971 shall be void on the following grounds only, that is to say—

(a) that it is not a valid marriage under the provisions of the Marriages Acts 1949 to 1986 (that is to say where—

(i) the parties are within the prohibited degrees of relationship;

(ii) either party is under the age of sixteen; or

(iii) the parties have intermarried in disregard of certain requirements as to the formation of marriage);

(b) that at the time of the marriage either party was already lawfully married;

(c) that the parties are not respectively male and female;

(d) in the case of a polygamous marriage entered into outside England and Wales, that either party was at the time of the marriage domiciled in England and Wales.

For the purposes of paragraph (d) of this subsection a marriage may be polygamous although at its inception neither party has any spouse additional to the other.

3.1.1 THE PROHIBITED DEGREES

MARRIAGE ACT 1949

FIRST SCHEDULE   KINDRED AND AFFINITY

PART 1
Prohibited degrees of relationship

Mother, adoptive mother or former adoptive mother	Father, adoptive father or former adoptive father
Daughter, adoptive daughter or former adoptive daughter	Son, adoptive son or former adoptive son
Father's mother	Father's father
Mother's mother	Mother's father
Son's daughter	Son's son
Daughter's daughter	Daughter's son
Sister	Brother
Father's sister	Father's brother
Mother's sister	Mother's brother
Brother's daughter	Brother's son
Sister's daughter	Sister's son

PART II
Degrees of affinity referred to in section 1(2) and (3) of this Act

Daughter of former wife	Son of former husband
Former wife of father	Former husband of mother
Former wife of father's father	Former husband of father's mother
Former wife of mother's father	Former husband of mother's mother
Daughter of son of former wife	Son of son of former husband
Daughter of daughter of former wife	Son of daughter of former husband

PART III
Degrees of affinity referred to in section 1(4) and (5) of this Act

Mother of former wife	Father of former wife
Former wife of son	Former husband of daughter

MARRIAGE (PROHIBITED DEGREES OF RELATIONSHIP) ACT 1986

1. Marriage between certain persons related by affinity not to be void

(1) A marriage solemnized after the commencement of this Act between a man and a woman who is the daughter or granddaughter of a former spouse of his (whether the former spouse is living or not) or who is the former spouse of his father or grandfather (whether his father or grandfather is living or not) shall not be void by reason only of that relationship if both the parties have attained the age of twenty-one at the time of the marriage and the younger party has not at any time before attaining the age of eighteen been a child of the family in relation to the other party.

(2) A marriage solemnized after the commencement of this Act between a man and a woman who is the grandmother of a former spouse of his (whether the former spouse is living or not) or is a former spouse of his grandson (whether his grandson is living or not) shall not be void by reason only of that relationship.

(3) A marriage solemnized after the commencement of this Act between a man and a woman who is the mother of a former spouse of his shall not be void by reason only of that relationship if the marriage is solemnized after the death of both that spouse and the father of that spouse and after both the parties to the marriage have attained the age of twenty-one.

(4) A marriage solemnized after the commencement of this Act between a man and a woman who is a former spouse of his son shall not be void by reason only of that relationship if the marriage is solemnized after the death of both his son and the mother of his son and after both the parties to the marriage have attained the age of twenty-one.

(5) In this section 'child of the family' in relation to any person, means a child who has lived in the same household as that person and been treated by that person as a child of his family.

. . .

3.1.2 THE PARTIES ARE NOT RESPECTIVELY MALE AND FEMALE

CORBETT v CORBETT (OTHERWISE ASHLEY) [1970] 2 All ER 33

ORMROD J: The petitioner in this case, Mr Arthur Cameron Corbett, prays, in the first place, for a declaration that a ceremony of marriage which took place in Gibraltar on 10th September 1963 between himself and the respondent, then known as April Ashley, is null and void and of no effect because the respondent, at the time of the ceremony, was a person of the male sex.

The relevant facts must now be stated as concisely as possible. The respondent was born on 29th April 1935 in Liverpool and registered at birth as a boy in the name of George Jamieson, and brought up as a boy. It has not been suggested at any time in this case that there was any mistake over the sex of the child. In 1951, at the age of 16 years, he joined the Merchant Navy. Before being accepted, the respondent had what she (I shall use 'he' and 'she' and 'his' and 'her' throughout this judgment as seems convenient in the context) described in cross-examination as a 'vague medical examination', and was accepted. As George Jamieson, the respondent did one and a half voyages as a merchant seaman before being put ashore at San Francisco and admitted to hospital there, after taking an overdose of tablets. He was subsequently returned to this country and became a patient at Ormskirk Hospital.

Thereafter, the respondent came to London and did casual work in the hotel trade there, and in Jersey, until, in 1956, he went to the south of France, where he met the members of a well-known troupe of male female impersonators, normally based at the Carousel night club in Paris, and later himself became a member of the troupe. By this time, on any view of the evidence, the respondent was taking the female sex hormone, oestrogen, regularly, to encourage the development of the breasts and of a feminine type of physique. At that stage he was known as 'Toni/April'.

It will be necessary to examine the evidence relating to the taking of oestrogen in more detail later. After about four years at the Carousel night club, he was introduced to a certain Dr Burou who practised at Casablanca, and, on 11th May 1960, he underwent, at Dr Burou's hands, a so called 'sex-change operation', which consisted in the amputation of the testicles and most of the scrotum and the construction of a so-called 'artificial vagina', by making an opening in front of the anus, and turning in the skin of the penis after removing the muscle and other tissues from it, to form a pouch or cavity occupying approximately the position of the vagina in a female, that is between the bladder and the rectum. Parts of the scrotum were used to produce an approximation in appearance to female external genitalia.

Following the operation, the respondent returned to London, now calling herself April Ashley, and dressing and living as a female. In evidence she stated that, after the operation, she had had sexual relations with at least one man, using the artificial cavity quite successfully. In November 1960, about six months after the operation, the petitioner and the respondent met for the first time. He was then aged 40, married and living with his wife and four children, but sexually unhappy and abnormal.

In July 1963, the petitioner took the first steps about a marriage. He consulted a lawyer in Gibralter about it and discuss discussed financial arrangements with the respondent.

It is, I think, obvious that both of them had considerable doubts about whether they could marry, or whether they could find anyone to marry them. In fact, the lawyer in Gibralter succeeded in getting a special licence for them. They neither asked for, nor received, any legal advice as to the validity of such a marriage. The ceremony was fixed provisionally for 10th September 1963, but the respondent continued to vacillate until the morning of 10th September when she suddenly agreed to go through with it and they rushed off to Gibralter.

There was general agreement among all the doctors on the basic principles and the fundamental scientific facts. Anomalies of sex may be divided into two broad divisions, those cases which are primarily psychological in character, and those in which there are developmental abnormalities in the anatomy of the reproductive system (including the external genitalia). Two kinds of psychological abnormality are recognised, the transvestite and the transsexual. The transvestite is an individual (nearly, if not always a man) who has an intense desire to dress up in the clothes of the opposite sex. This is intermittent in character and is not accompanied by a corresponding urge to live as or pass as a member of the opposite sex at all times. Transvestite males are usually heterosexual, often married, and have no wish to cease to play the male role in sexual activity. The transsexual, on the other hand, has an extremely powerful urge to become a member of the opposite sex to the fullest extent which is possible. They give a history, dating back to early childhood, of seeing themselves as members of the opposite sex which persists in spite of their being brought up normally in their own sex. This goes on until they come to think of themselves as females imprisoned in male bodies, or vice versa, and leads to intense resentment of, and dislike for, their own sexual organs which constantly remind them of their biological sex. They are said to be 'selective historians', tending to stress events which fit in with their ideas and to suppress those which do not. Some transsexual men live, dress and work regularly as females and pass more or less unnoticed. They become adept at make-up and knowledgeable about using oestrogen, the female sex hormone, to promote the development of female-like breasts, and at dealing with such masculine attributes as facial and pubic hair. As a result of the publicity which has been given from time to time to so-called 'sex-change operations', many of them go to extreme lengths to importune doctors to perform such operations on them. The difficulties under which these people inevitably live result in various psychological conditions such as extreme anxiety and obsessional states. They do not appear to respond favourably to any known form of psychological treatment and, consequently, some serious-minded and responsible doctors are inclining to the view that such operations may provide the only way of relieving the psychological distress. Dr Randell has recommended surgical treatment in about 35 cases, mostly restricted to castration and amputation of the penis, but in a few carefully selected cases he and Professor Dewhurst and the plastic surgeon who is working with them have undertaken vagino-plasty as well, that is the construction of a so-called artificial vagina. The purpose of these operations is, of course, to help to relieve the patient's symptoms and to assist in the management of their disorder; it is not to change their patient's sex, and, in fact, they require their patients before operation to sign a form of consent which is in these terms:

I . . . of . . . do consent to undergo the removal of the male genital organs and fashioning of an artificial vagina as explained to me by . . . (surgeon). I understand it will not alter my male sex and that it is being done to prevent deterioration in my mental health.

It is clear from the account which I have given of the respondent's history that it accords very closely with this description of a male transsexual. Dr Randell considered that the respondent is properly classified as a male homosexual transsexualist. Professor Dewhurst agreed with this diagnosis and said the description 'a castrated male' would be correct.

My conclusions of fact on this part of the case can be summarised, therefore, as follows. The respondent has been shown to have XY chromosomes and, therefore, to be of male chromosomal sex; to have had testicles prior to the operation and, therefore, to be of male gonadal sex; to have had male external genitalia without any evidence of internal or external female sex organs and, therefore, to be of male genital sex; and psychologically to be a transsexual. The evidence does not establish that she is a case of Klinefelter's syndrome or some similar condition of partial testicular failure, although the possibility of some abnormality in androgenisation at puberty cannot be excluded. Socially, by which I mean the manner in which the respondent is living in the community, she is living as, and passing as, a woman more or less successfully. Her outward appearance, at first sight, was convincingly feminine, but on closer and longer examination in the witness box it was much less so. The voice, manner, gestures and attitude became increasingly reminiscent of the accomplished female impersonator. The evidence of the medical inspectors, and of the other doctors who had an opportunity during the trial of examining the respondent clinically, is that the body, in its post-operative condition, looks more like a female than a male as a result of very skilful surgery. Professor Dewhurst, after this examination, put his opinion in these words—'the pastiche of feminity was convincing'. That, in my judgment, is an accurate description of the respondent. It is common ground between all the medical witnesses that the biological sexual constitution of all individual is fixed at birth (at the latest), and cannot be changed, either by the natural development of organs of the opposite sex, or by medical or surgical means. The respondent's operation, therefore, cannot affect her true sex. The only cases where the term 'change of sex' is appropriate are those in which a mistake as to sex is made it birth and subsequently revealed by further medical investigation.

Since marriage is essentially a relationship between man and woman, the validity of the marriage in this case depends, in my judgment, on whether the respondent is or is not a woman. I think, with respect, that this is a more precise way of formulating the question than that adopted in para. 2 of the petition, in which it is alleged that the respondent is a male. The greater, of course, includes the less, but the distinction may not be without importance, at any rate in some cases. The question then becomes what is meant by the word 'woman' in the context of a marriage, for I am not concerned to determine the 'legal sex' of the respondent at large. Having regard to the essentially heterosexual character of the relationship which is called marriage, the criteria must, in my judgment, be biological, for even the most extreme degree of transsexualism in a male or the most severe hormonal imbalance which can exist in a person with male chromosomes, male gonads and male genitalia cannot reproduce a person who is naturally capable of performing the essential role of a woman in marriage. In other words, the law should adopt, in the first place, the first three of the doctors' criteria, ie the chromosomal, gonadal and genital tests, and, if all three are congruent, determine the sex for the purpose of marriage accordingly, and ignore any operative intervention. The real difficulties, of course, will occur if these three criteria are not congruent. This question does not arise in the present case and I must not anticipate, but it would seem to me to follow from what I have said that greater weight would probably be given to the genital criteria than to the other two. This problem and, in particular, the question of the effect of surgical operations in such cases of physical inter-sex, must be left until it comes for decision. My conclusion, therefore, is that the respondent is not a woman for the purposes of marriage but is a biological male and has been so since birth. It follows that the so-called marriage of 10th September 1963 is void.

I must now return briefly to counsel for the respondent's submissions. If the law were to recognise the 'assignment' of the respondent to the female sex, the question which would have to be answered is, what was the respondent's sex immediately before the operation? If the answer is that it depends on 'assignment' then, if the decision at that time was female, the respondent would be a female with male sex organs and no female ones. If the assignment to the female sex is made after the operation, then the operation has changed the sex. From this it would follow that if a 50 year old male transsexual, married and the father of children, underwent the operation, he would then have to be regarded in law as a female, and capable of 'marrying' a man! The results would be nothing if not bizarre. I have dealt, by implication, with the submission that, because the respondent is treated by society for many purposes as a woman, it is illogical to refuse to treat her as a woman for the purpose of marriage. The illogicality would only arise if marriage were substantially similar in character to national insurance and other social situations, but the differences are obviously fundamental. These submissions, in effect, confuse sex with gender. Marriage is a relationship which depends on sex and not on gender.

J v S-T (FORMERLY J) (TRANSSEXUAL: ANCILLARY RELIEF) [1997] 1 FLR 402

WARD LJ: The defendant, for whom I use the male pronoun, was born into a modest home in the north of England. He was registered at birth as a girl named Wendy. It is not disputed that at birth he had the chromosomal, gonadal and genital features of the female sex. He was never at ease in that sex and increasingly acted and dressed as a boy. Aged 14, when in trouble with the police, he gave the false name Michael which he has ever since adopted. There followed some, but it is unclear what, psychiatric intervention. We now know that he was born with a recognised gender identity dysphoria — transsexualism. By the age of 17 he was living as and had become socially accepted as a male. He was attracted by and attractive to the female sex and at the age of about 20 began the first of two quite long relationships with women. It must have been about this time that he used an improvised prosthesis to engage in sexual intercourse. It was a rigid device which he wore more or less permanently. In 1972, at the age of about 26, and whilst in the course of his second relationship, he suffered a period of severe depression, feeling trapped in a body 'that was not mine' and 'unable to go on living'. After intensive psychiatric counselling, he was given a course of in injections of testosterone which led to the development of secondary male characteristics including the growth of a beard.

Dr Fleming supported the defendant's request for his driving licence and National Insurance records to show his new name but his birth certificate could not be and was not altered. He referred the appellant for a bilateral mastectomy which was performed in December 1973. It was such a difficult operation that the defendant never underwent the further recommended surgical procedure of phalloplasty for the construction of a penis. Physically, therefore, his body was scarred from the removal of his breasts, he retained the large nipples of a woman, and, more relevantly, the genital organs of a woman but to all other intents and purposes in his attitude of mind and behaviour he was a man. To make a new start in life he moved to London and it was in the Home Counties that, in December 1977, he met the plaintiff. They began to live together and on 7 July 1977 went through a ceremony of marriage despite opposition from the plaintiff's family.

(1) Transsexuals and the matrimonial law
The landmark decision was *Corbett* v *Corbett (Otherwise Ashley)* [1971] P 83. It was, and remains, (the sensational case of the day, judgment being given in February 1970, some $3\frac{1}{2}$ years before Dr Fleming wrote his letter of 19 October 1973. It would be a surprise if he, a specialist in this field, were unaware of the implications of the case for those whom he was treating. To the knowledge of the petitioner in that case, the respondent, April Ashley, had been born a man but had undergone a 'sex-change operation', now more usually referred to as a 'gender reassignment operation', by which the external male sexual organs were removed and an artificial vagina created. Thereafter April Ashley lived as a woman capable of having, and in fact having, sexual intercourse. On Mr Corbett's application to annul their marriage, Ormrod J held, inter alia, that because marriage is essentially a union between a man and a woman, the relationship depended on sex and not on gender; that the only criteria for assessing the sexual condition of an individual were first the chromosomal factors (XY chromosomes for a male child, XX for a female child), secondly the gonadal factors (presence or absence of testes or ovaries), and thirdly the genital factors (including internal sex organs). If those three factors were congruent, that would determine the question of sex for the purpose of marriage and any psychological factors and operative interventions were to be ignored. It is interesting to note that Mr Corbett's counsel sought to persuade the court to make a declaration under RSC Ord 15, rather than the usual decree of nullity. Ormrod J observed at 109:

> The importance of this distinction is, of course, that on a decree of nullity the court has power to entertain an application for ancillary relief whereas, if a declaration order is made, there is no such power.

Because a matrimonial relationship was a legal impossibility at all times and in all circumstances, Ormrod J had considerable sympathy with the petitioner's submission that the ceremony of marriage was in fact if not in intention only a sham and the resulting 'marriage' not merely void but also meretricious, but he held that as the ecclesiastical courts did in fact grant declaratory sentences in cases of meretricious marriages, there was no discretion to withhold any decree of nullity.

This decision has held sway in this country ever since. it has been applied here to the criminal law: see *R* v *Tan and Others* [1993] QB 1053 where the Court of Appeal rejected the submission that if a person had become philosophically or psychologically or socially female, that person should be field not to be a man. Parker J held that:

> . . . both common sense and the desirability of certainty and consistency demand that the decision in *Corbett* v *Corbett* should apply for the purpose not only of marriage, but also for a charge under section 30 of the Sexual Offences Act 1956 or section 5 of the Sexual Offences Act 1967.

As things stand at this moment, the law as stated in *Corbett* has escaped the censure of the European Court of Human Rights, but counsel has argued that strong winds of change are blowing. In the *Rees* Case [1987] 2 FLR 111, the applicant was a female-to-male transsexual who, like the defendant, had undergone a bilateral mastectomy and considered himself to be and was socially accepted as a man. He complained that the refusal to amend his birth certificate was a breach of his right to respect for his private and family life, contrary to Art 8 of the European Convention for the Protection of Human Rights and Fundamental Freedoms because the certificate made manifest the discrepancy between his apparent and his legal sex, causing him embarrassment and humiliation whenever social practices required its production. The court held by a majority of 12 to 3 that there was little common ground between the Contracting States and that, generally speaking, the law appeared to be in a transitional state. Accordingly it was an area in which Contracting Parties enjoyed a wide margin of appreciation and it could not be said that the UK had not struck the requisite balance. The applicant also alleged that because he could not marry a woman, there was a breach of Art 12 providing that:

Men and women of marriageable age have the right to marry and to found a family, according to the national laws governing the exercise of this right.

On this point, the decision was unanimous. It was:

(49)   In the Court's opinion, the right to marry guaranteed by Art 12 refers to the traditional marriage between persons of opposite biological sex. This appears also from the wording of the article which makes it clear that Art 12 is mainly concerned to protect marriage as the basis of the family.

(50)   Furthermore, Art 12 lays down that the exercise of this right shall be subject to the national laws of the Contracting States. The limitations thereby introduced must riot restrict or reduce the right in such a way or to such an extent that the very essence of the right is impaired. However, the legal impediment in the United Kingdom on the marriage of persons who are not of the opposite biological sex cannot be said to have an effect of this kind.

(51)   There is accordingly no violation in the instant case of Art 12 of the Convention.

In *Cossey v UK* [1991] 2 FLR 492, similar issues arose in the case of a male-to-female transsexual who had undergone full gender reassignment surgery. She wished to marry. The court held that despite the Resolution of the European Parliament on 12 September 1989 and Recommendation 1117 adopted by the Parliamentary Assembly of the Council of Europe on 29 September 1989—both of which sought to encourage the harmonisation of laws and practices in this field—there remained the same diversity of practice as obtained at the time of the *Rees* judgment. Accordingly, there was still little common ground between the Contracting States in an area in which they enjoyed a wide margin *of* appreciation. On the alleged violation of Art 8 it was held:

. . . it cannot at present be said that a departure from the Court's earlier decision is warranted in order to ensure that the interpretation of Art 8 on the point at issue remains in line with present-day conditions . . .

As to the alleged violation of Art 12 it was held:

(45)   As to the applicant's inability to marry a woman, this does not stem from any legal impediment and, in this respect, it cannot be said that the right to marry has been impaired as a consequence of the provisions of domestic law.

As to her inability to marry a man, the criteria adopted by English law are in this respect in conformity with the concept of marriage to which the right guaranteed by Art 12 refers . . .

(46)   Although some Contracting States would now regard as valid a marriage between a person in Miss Cossey's situation and a man, the developments which have occurred to date . . . cannot be said to be evidence of any general abandonment of the traditional concept of marriage. In these circumstances instances, the Court does not consider that it is open to it to take a new approach to the interpretation of Art 12 on the point at issue. It finds, furthermore, that attachment to the traditional concept of marriage provides sufficient reasons for the continued adoption of biological criteria for determining a person's sex for the purposes of marriage, this being a matter encompassed within the power of the Contracting States to regulate by national law the exercise of the right to marry.

In *M v M* (1991) 8 FRNZ 209 in the New Zealand Family Court, Judge Aubin held that the applicant's 'core identity' was that of a woman and as her body find been brought into harmony with her psychological sex, he inclined to the view that 'however elusive the definition of "woman" may be, the applicant came within it for the purpose of and at the time of the ceremony of marriage' which he declared to be a valid one. Mr Emmerson has helpfully supplied us with a copy of the judgment of Ellis J in the Supreme Court which declared that for the purposes of the New Zealand Marriage Act 1955 where a person has undergone surgical and medical procedures that have effectively given that person the physical conformation of a person of a specified sex, there is no lawful impediment to that person marrying as a person of that sex, Ellis J held:

> Some persons have a compelling desire to be recognised and be able to behave as persons of the opposite sex. If society allows such persons to undergo therapy and surgery in order to fulfil that desire, then it ought also to allow such persons to function as fully as possible in their reassigned sex, and this must include the capacity to marry. Where two persons present themselves as having the apparent genitals of a man and a woman, they should not have to establish that each can function sexually.
>
> Once a transsexual has undergone surgery, he or she is no longer able to operate in his or her original sex. A male to female transsexual will have had the penis and testes removed, and have had a vagina-like cavity constructed, and possible breast implants, and can never appear unclothed as a male, or enter into a sexual relationship as a male, or procreate. A female to male transsexual will have had the uterus and ovaries and breast removed, have a beard growth, a deeper voice, and possibly a constructed penis and can no longer appear unclothed as a woman, or enter into a sexual relationship as a woman or procreate. There is no social advantage in the law not recognising the validity of the marriage of a transsexual in the sex of reassignment. It would merely confirm the factual reality.
>
> If the law insists that genetic sex is the pre-determinant for entry into a valid marriage, then a male to female transsexual can contract a valid marriage with a woman and a female to male transsexual can contract a valid marriage to a man. To all outward appearances, such would be same-sex marriages . . . I can see no socially adverse effects from allowing such transsexuals to marry in their adopted sex, I cannot see any harm to others, children in particular, that is not properly proscribed and manageable in accordance with the existing framework of the law.

Hollis J did not find this 'persuasive authority'. For my part, I find myself unable lightly to dismiss it. Taken with the new insight into the aetiology of transsexualism, it may be that *Corbett* would bear re-examination at some appropriate time. For present purposes, it should, however, be stressed that the judge's reasoning, and the appended submissions of counsel incorporated into the judgment, make clear that the declaration of validity will only apply in a case where there has been 'physical conformation' to the desired sex by full reconstructive surgery, including, in the case of a female-to-male transsexual, surgical construction of a penis. For that reason, that decision does not assist the defendant.

3.1.3 POLYGAMOUS MARRIAGES

HUSSAIN v *HUSSAIN* [1982] 3 All ER 369

ORMROD LJ: There is no dispute on the facts. The marriage took place on 4 August 1979 at Chirag Park Shad Bad in the District of Lahore, Pakistan, in accordance with the Muslim Laws Family, Ordinance 1961. Both parties are Muslim by religion. At all material times the husband was and is domiciled in England; the wife's ante-nuptial domicile was Pakistan.

It is common ground that under this form of marriage a husband is permitted to marry a second wife during the subsistence of the marriage, but a wife is not permitted to marry a second husband. In other words, the personal law of the wife precludes her from contracting another marriage so long as her present marriage continues.

The question in this appeal is purely one of construction of para. (d) of s. 11, and it turns on the meaning to be given to the phrase 'a polygamous marriage' in the context in which it appears.

Had the intention of Parliament been to prevent persons domiciled in England and Wales from entering into marriages under the Muslim Laws Family Ordinance, or under other similar laws which 'permit polygamy', it would have been easy to say so in so many words. On the other hand, once the position of *Hyde* v *Hyde* had been abandoned, the question of the capacity of persons domiciled in England and Wales to enter into polygamous or potentially polygamous marriages had to be considered. Actually polygamous marriages were already covered by what is now para. (b) of s. 11, but potentially polygamous marriages were not completely covered by the existing law. The spouse domiciled in England and Wales is, of course, incapable of marrying a second spouse, but if one of the spouses in the first marriage retains a domicile the law of which permits polygamy a situation could arise in which the spouse domiciled in this country becomes a party to a polygamous union. Counsel for the wife submits that s. 4 of the 1972 Act (now s. 11(d) of the 1973 Act) was passed to prevent this situation from arising. The effect would be that a marriage between a woman domiciled in England and Wales and a man domiciled in Pakistan would be a polygamous marriage because the husband has the capacity, by his personal law, to take a second wife, but not vice versa.

The language used by the draftsman is, at least, consistent with this construction. The insertion of the qualifying words at the end of the section suggests that without them the phrase 'polygamous marriage' would, or might be, confined to a marriage which was actually polygamous at its inception, ie one in which one of the spouses was already married to another spouse. The use of the word 'may' in the qualifying words suggests that the draftsman had some contingency in mind the happening of which would make a marriage between two unmarried persons polygamous, within the meaning of the provision, that is, as it is called, a potentially polygamous marriage. A marriage can only be potentially polygamous if at least one of the spouses has the capacity to marry a second spouse.

On the facts of this case the husband, by English law, is incapable of contracting a valid marriage when he is already lawfully married (para. (b)), and the wife, by Pakistan law, cannot marry another man so long as she is married to the husband, so this marriage can never become polygamous. Consequently, the marriage was not polygamous at its inception and cannot become polygamous at any time in the future. It is, therefore, not avoided by para. (d) of s. 11.

PRIVATE INTERNATIONAL LAW (MISCELLANEOUS PROVISIONS) ACT 1995

5. Validity in English law of potentially polygamous marriages

(1) A marriage entered into outside England and Wales between parties neither of whom is already married is not void under the law of England and Wales on the ground that it is entered into under a law which permits polygamy and that either party is domiciled in England and Wales.

(2) This section does not affect the determination of the validity of a marriage by reference to the law of another country to the extent that it falls to be so determined in accordance with the rules of private international law.

3.2 Voidable Marriages

MATRIMONIAL CAUSES ACT 1973

12. Grounds on which a marriage is voidable

A marriage celebrated after 31st July 1971 shall be voidable on the following grounds only, that is to say—

(a) that the marriage has not been consummated owing to the incapacity of either party to consummate it;

(b) that the marriage has not been consummated owing to the wilful refusal of the respondent to consummate it;

(c) that either party to the marriage did not validly consent to it, whether in consequence of duress, mistake, unsoundness of mind or otherwise;

(d)   that at the time of the marriage either party, though capable of giving a valid consent, was suffering (whether continuously or intermittently) from mental disorder within the meaning of the Mental Health Act 1983 of such a kind or to such an extent as to be unfitted for marriage;

(e)   that at the time of the marriage the respondent was suffering from venereal disease in a communicable form;

(f)   that at the time of the marriage the respondent was pregnant by some person other than the petitioner.

0.2.1   INCAPACITY TO CONSUMMATE/WILFUL REFUSAL TO CONSUMMATE

R v R (OTHERWISE F) [1952] 1 All ER 1194

COMMISSIONER BUSH-JAMES QC: The issue, therefore, turns on the meaning of the word 'consummate', and it is necessary from the outset to make three distinctions. The first of these distinctions is set out in clear terms by Lord Jowitt, LC, in *Baxter v Baxter* [1947] 2 All ER 886. His lordship refers to the new ground for annulment introduced by the Matrimonial Causes Act, 1937, s. 7(1)(a) (now s. 8(1) of the Act of 1950), namely, 'wilful refusal . . . to consummate', and points out that this ground, being a post-nuptial defect, differs completely from the old ecclesiastical ground of annulment, i.e., impotence, which must exist at the time of the marriage. To quote his own words ([1947] 2 All ER 889):

It is necessary, however, to beware of applying too literally to suits for nullity under the section in question in this case principles and rules relating to suits for nullity on the ground of incapacity under the old jurisdiction. In such a suit it was, and still is, necessary to prove that at the time of the marriage the particular wife or husband was incapable of consummating the marriage with the other spouse, whereas the section has introduced as a ground of nullity a cause necessarily arising after the marriage which, as Pickford, LJ, said in *Napier v Napier* [1915] P 189, was 'contrary to the principles of the ecclesiastical law as administered in the ecclesiastical courts' . . . It is clear, therefore, that in relation to the meaning of the word 'consummate', the common area covered by suits for nullity on the grounds respectively of incapacity and of wilful refusal to consummate is very small.

The second preliminary distinction to which I refer relates to the practice of withdrawal before emission, the practice known as coitus interruptus. In *Baxter v Baxter* Lord Jowitt emphasised (ibid., 888) that he was expressing no view on that practice. But from the point of view of the present case, a case on impotence, the decisions on coitus interruptus are not of direct assistance, since, whatever remedies coitus interruptus may give rise to in practice (as to which learned judges have held different views (*Grimes (otherwise Edwards) v Grimes* [1948] 2 All ER 147, *White (otherwise Berry) v White* [1948] 2 All ER 151, *Cackett (otherwise Trice) v Cackett* [1950] 1 All ER 677, *W v W* [1950] 1 Western Weekly Rep 981, British Columbia, it assumes the very point in issue in the present case, namely, whether omission is necessary to prove a man 'potent' according to the old ecclesiastical laws.

The third distinction is one which I must have in mind the whole time, and it concerns the end of marriage. It used to be said, as in Ayliffe's Parergon Juris Canonici, 2nd ed., p. 360, that

as the first cause and reason of matrimony ought to be the design of having offspring; so the second ought to be the avoiding of fornication.

But in *Baxter v Baxter* Lord Jowitt said (ibid., 890):

In any view of Christian marriage the essence of the matter . . . is that the children, if there be any, should be born into a family . . . but this is not the same thing as saying that a marriage is not consummated unless children are procreated or that procreation of children is the principal end of marriage.

He went on to emphasise the irrelevance of procreation as an end in marriage.

Bearing these three distinctions in mind, one must look at the medical evidence adduced before the court in the present case. It comes to this. The husband was able to obtain an erection and penetrate his wife, but during the conjunction of their bodies, and I use the expression advisedly, he was unable to ejaculate whether with or without spermatozoa and she was unable to enjoy an orgasm. That is the evidence, and there is no dispute of consequence concerning it. It was suggested that there was a possibility of what was termed a 'leakage' by the husband when their bodies were joined as opposed to a proper, full ejaculation with or without seed. There was no evidence on that point, nor, indeed, could there be, as neither party would have been aware of such a thing, and I must disregard it, both for being hypothetical and for the reasons, taken by way of analogy, given by Lord Jowitt in *Baxter* v *Baxter* when deploring, in relation to the statutory remedy, the attempt to make 'consummation' depend on an unwitting and unintentional hole in a contraceptive sheath. I have, therefore, to decide whether the husband or wife, physically joined together as they were from time to time, in fact consummated their marriage in the manner and the degree which would have convinced the ecclesiastical lawyers that the marriage had been consummated. It is curious that there is no direct authority on the point that I have to decide, though this is probably due to the fact that such a question would not have arisen before the advances made by medical science in investigating and explaining the intimacies of the marriage bed, and in enabling parties to give evidence thereon in a comparatively scientific way.

What, then, was 'consummation' in ecclesiastical law? The ecclesiastical laywers, in fact, used the term 'vera copula'. 'Copula', or copulation, means simply, in dictionary terms, 'sexual union' (Concise Oxford Dictionary), so that the meaning in law of vera copula must be sought elsewhere. I have referred already to Lord Jowitt's judgment in *Baxter* v *Baxter*, and it is to be noted that in that case he cited with approval a statement in Lord Stair's Institutions, 1681 ed., book I, tit. 4, para. 6, that the relevant factor is the creation of a consent.

> . . . whereby ariseth that conjugal society, which may have the conjunction of bodies as well as of minds, as the general end of the institution of marriage, is the solace and satisfaction of man.

Then there is the 'true distinction' stated by Dr Lushington in *D—e* v *A—g (falsely calling herself D—e)* (1845) 1 Rob Ecc 279 (approved in *Baxter* v *Baxter*, a case in which the wife had no uterus at all when he said (1 Rob Ecc 299):

> If there is be a reasonable probability that the lady can be made capable of a vera copula—of the natural sort of coitus, though without power of conception—I cannot pronounce this marriage void. If, on the contrary, she is not and cannot be made capable of more than an incipient, imperfect, and unnatural coitus, I would pronounce the marriage void.

Of course in *D—e* v *A—g*, the husband was capable of ejaculation, so that it may be said that in *D—e* v *A—g* there was coitus, i.e., penetration and ejaculation, and so it does not help in the present case. But examination of the passage cited shows that the learned judge was willing to treat coitus in the abstract as being identical with vera copula, i.e., as being equivalent to penetration without emission. (I emphasise that coitus in this sense has not the inference which appears in the term coitus interruptus where ejaculation is always implied.) So it may be said that a surgical operation before marriage which makes the wife incapable of bearing children does not make vera copula impossible: *L* v *L* *(otherwise D)* (1922) 38 TLR 697; though, again, I must point out that the husband in that case was, it seems, capable of ejaculation.

In *White* v *White*, a coitus interruptus case, Willmer J, points out that vera copula means merely 'conjunction of the bodies'. I do not wish to refer further to the learned judge's conclusion because he is discussing a case where ejaculation was always possible, but he indicates ([1948] 2 All ER 155) that for some cases, and I think the present case is one of them, a 'true conjunction' is achieved

. . . as soon as full entry and penetration has been achieved. What follows goes merely to the likelihood or otherwise of conception.

I have already pointed out *Baxter* v *Baxter* decided firmly that conception was not the principal end of marriage, indeed, it is well-known that a marriage might not be consummated in either the statutory or ecclesiastical sense, even though the woman has conceived from her husband with no artificial aid. It is not without interest to note, too, the case of *J* v *J* [1947] 2 All ER 43, where the Court of Appeal held that a man who, by reason of an operation before marriage, rendered himself only capable of penetration and emission, but in such a fashion that the male sperm could not leave his body, was incapable of consummation in the ecclesiastical view. But that decision was virtually overruled in *Baxter* v *Baxter*, and I do not think it affects the present case. Indeed, the comment on it in *Baxter* v *Baxter* supports my view.

Therefore, in my view, vera copula consists of erectio and intromissio. This is the view of the author in Jackson on the Formation and Annulment of Marriage from which I have derived considerable assistance. At pp. 209 and 210 the learned author says:

> Contraceptive devices do not prevent intercourse—Vera copula consists of erectio and intromissio. Once this has been achieved, the fact that consummation, in the sense of potential conception, has been made impossible by the use by one or both of the parties of contraceptives, is irrelevant. Only intercourse in the sense of vera copula is necessary to 'consummate' a marriage. 'A person is in law impotent who is incapax copulandi, apart from the question of whether he or she is incapax procreandi'.

This last remark is a quotation from Lord Dunedin in *G* v *G* [1924] AC 349, and it is to be further observed that in that case Lord Dunedin refers ([1924] AC 354) to *AB* v *CB* (1906) 8 F 603 where the marriage 'never was actually consummated' and the husband had tried 'all ordinary expedients to induce the wife to admit connection'. 'Connection' is the operative word in that sentence. In my judgment, therefore, 'connection', or the 'conjunction of bodies', or 'erectio and intromissio', is for the present purpose—the purpose of deciding what is potency in ecclesiastical law—equivalent to consummation in the ecclesiastical view interpreted in the light of modern authorities. I wish to make it clear that the fact that the husband has been able to achieve consummation in the fullest sense with another woman, as that term is probably indicated in the statute of 1937 and now in the statute of 1950, has not affected my view in the slightest, as the medical evidence demonstrates that this case is a perfect example of impotence quoad hunc or hanc. I find, in consequence, that this marriage has been consummated, and the petition fails and must be dismissed.

SINGH v *SINGH* [1971] 2 All ER 828

KARMINSKI LJ: The facts of the case are comparatively simple. Both parties, as their names suggest, are Sikhs. The wife was a girl of about 17 at the time of the ceremony of marriage, which took place before the registrar at West Bromwich on 1st October 1968. The husband was 21 years of age, and he was described as a bachelor living at West Bromwich. The wife, in accordance with what she believed to be Sikh practice and custom, had never seen the bridegroom before the actual ceremony of marriage. Following what we were told was the long-established custom of the Sikhs, the marriage was arranged by her parents.

The wife's story was that, having gone to the registry office she then saw the husband for the first time and she did not like what she saw. Her evidence was that she was told that the husband was a man of education, and handsome; but having seen him, she thought that he was neither. In the result, therefore, after the civil ceremony of marriage had been carried through she went back to her parents and refused to go on with the Sikh religious ceremony a week later. She now says that there was no marriage in law, first because she did not consent, and secondly, because she was incapable of consummating the marriage because the husband was repugnant to her. There was never any attempt at consummation. The facts of this case are not in dispute. The father gave evidence, as did an uncle of the wife. Medical evidence was given by a gynaecologist who deposed that she was physically capable of marriage and was at the time that he examined her after the ceremony a complete virgin.

There is the alternative matter of repugnance. It is true that the wife never submitted herself to the physical embraces of the husband, because after the ceremony of marriage before the registrar it does not appear that she saw him again or went near him. Having taken the view which she did, that she did not want to be married to him, it is understandable that she did not want to have sexual intercourse with him; but that again seems to be a very long way from an invincible repugnance. True, as counsel for the wife argued, invincible repugnance can have a number of forms; and he reminded us of a decided case where the wife refused to undress when she went to bed so that the husband could not have intercourse with her. But here the wife abandoned the idea of her marriage altogether, and there is nothing of a psychiatric or sexual aversion on her part which is in any way established. In my view that ground of nullity fails completely.

I have come to the conclusion, therefore, that the learned county court judge was right on both grounds, and that this appeal should be dismissed.

So far as concerns the allegation of invincible repugnance, it seems to me again that there is nothing to show that in this case. There is nothing to show that she suffered a physical repugnance to having intercourse with the husband. It seems to me that, if anything, this was a case of wilful refusal. Invincible repugnance is a lack of capacity quoad the husband. This is a case of unwillingness, and there is nothing, as I say, to show that owing to some defect in her mental or physical make-up she was unable to have intercourse with him. He might, I suppose, have cross-petitioned on the ground of her wilful refusal under s. 9(1)(a) of the Matrimonial Causes Act 1965, which provides:

> In addition to any other grounds on which a marriage is by law void or voidable, a marriage shall, subject to the next following subsection, be voidable on the ground—
> (a) that the marriage has not been consummated owing to the wilful refusal of the respondent to consummate it . . .

It seems very likely that the husband, had he been so minded, would have succeeded on a cross-petition; but the wife cannot rely on her own wilful refusal.

FORD v FORD [1987] Fam Law 17

GOODMAN J: In August 1986, the petitioner sought a decree of nullity against the respondent on the ground that the marriage had not been consummated, due to the wilful refusal of the respondent. The parties met in 1982. They had a short, casual relationship during which sexual intercourse took place on three occasions, but they never lived together. In December 1982 the respondent was arrested and in February 1983, following conviction for armed robbery, was sentenced to 5 years' imprisonment. The petitioner visited the respondent in custody and on 13 March 1984 the parties married whilst the respondent was in prison. After the ceremony, and on several subsequent occasions whilst the respondent was in custody at various prisons, the parties were left alone for about two hours in a room, where the petitioner indicated that she would be prepared to have sexual intercourse. She had learnt from other visitors that this was not uncommon on such occasions. Each time the respondent refused and seemed more interested in trying to persuade the petitioner to bring him various material goods from outside—some of which were illegal. The petitioner refused and was told by the respondent that he no longer desired her visits. When asked his future plans on his release from custody the respondent showed no interest in living with the petitioner. The petitioner ceased visiting in about March 1986 as she could see no future in the marriage. In July 1986 the respondent was granted a home visit on the condition that he reside for the period in question with the petitioner. The petitioner duly met him from prison. The respondent was extremely unpleasant to her and at his insistence the petitioner drove the respondent to the home of his former girl-friend. The petitioner independently decided that she did not want to live with him and did not see him thereafter.

Judge Goodman decided that as there was no official provision for conjugal visits in prisons in this country, refusal to have sexual intercourse during a visit would not in itself constitute a wilful refusal to consummate. However, despite the lack of reasonable opportunity for consummation, the respondent's conduct by December 1985 showing, as it did, an unswerving determination not to consummate the marriage or to live with the petitioner as man and wife at any time in the future, amounted to a wilful refusal to consummate. (See also *Ponticelli* v *Ponticelli* [1958] P 204.) Accordingly, a decree of nullity was pronounced.

Note on Ford v Ford

This decision seems to go further than other cases on wilful refusal, because the judge accepted that there had been no reasonable opportunity to consummate the marriage, whereas, in earlier cases, it has been the respondent's failure to create such an opportunity which has grounded the finding of a wilful refusal to consummate (see, e.g. *Kaur* v *Singh* [1972] 1 WLR 105). None the less, the judge found that the respondent's obviously cold and unpleasant behaviour towards his wife amounted to such a refusal, since it revealed a determination not to consummate in the future.

KAUR v *SINGH* [1972] 1 WLR 105 (CA)

DAVIES LJ: The facts are in a very short compass indeed. The husband had been living in this country for some seven to ten years prior to the events in question. He was a Sikh too. He was a student at Surrey University, where he met one of the brothers of the wife. The wife up to then had lived all her life in the Punjab in India where she had been born. Eventually, it was arranged between the brothers and the father of the wife, on the one hand, and the husband, on the other hand, that he should marry the wife.

It is beyond question that in order fully to marry according to Sikh religion and practice it is necessary to have not only a civil ceremony in a register office but also a Sikh religious ceremony in a Sikh temple. It was the belief of all these parties, the wife and the brothers, and no doubt the husband as well, that they should in due course go through such a Sikh ceremony. Indeed, one of the brothers did at some time make tentative arrangements with the committee of the Sikh temple for a religious ceremony to take place. No sign of any step by the husband in that behalf was forthcoming, and so the brother or brothers on a number of occasions approached him and asked him what he was proposing to do about the religious ceremony. He gave various excuses. On one occasion, he said that he had tonsillitis and was ill for a fortnight or so. On another occasion, he said that he could not really deal with the matter at that particular time because he was engaged in writing a thesis for a degree of Doctor of Philosophy and that he could not consider the matter while that was in hand. He failed, he apparently told one of the brothers, in his examination to obtain his degree. To put it quite shortly. on every occasion when one of the brothers spoke to him he gave one excuse or another. Finally, he told them that he had no intention of arranging for the religious ceremony at all.

There was no evidence here of any approach by the husband to the wife and no evidence that the wife was refusing, on a sincere religious belief or at all, to have intercourse with him before a religious ceremony was performed. The facts were that he never went near her again, and never tried to persuade her to live with him and have intercourse with him. It may very well be true that, if he had made any such approach, she, according to her religious beliefs, might have said that she was unwilling to allow it before the ceremony. But that never happened.

The facts of the present case, are as clear as they could be. The husband from the time of the register office ceremony entirely failed and refused to arrange a religious ceremony of marriage, and so failed to implement the marriage. I think that it is clear that in failing to implement the marriage he wilfully refused to consummate it. I would allow this appeal and grant the wife a decree.

Borkowski, A, Wilful Refusal to Consummate: 'Just Excuse', [1994] Family Law 684

Wilful refusal to consummate is a ground for annulment of marriage under s. 12(b) of the Matrimonial Causes Act 1973. Although there is no statutory definition of 'wilful refusal' it appears to be established that a nullity petition on that ground must fail if the respondent has 'just excuse' for refusing to consummate the marriage. In *Horton* v *Horton* [1947] 2 All ER 871, HL, Lord Jowitt LC described 'wilful refusal' as follows at p. 874:

The words connote, I think, a settled and definite decision come to without just excuse, and, in determining whether there has been such a refusal, the judge should have regard to the whole history of the marriage.

This dictum is often cited as laying down an authoritative principle (see, for example, *Halsbury's Laws of England* (Butterworths, 4th edn) 13, p. 550) but the matter is not free from doubt. In particular, two issues arise. How established is the requirement that the refusal should have been without 'just excuse'?; and what is meant by 'just excuse'?

REFUSAL WITHOUT 'JUST EXCUSE': THE AUTHORITY

Wilful refusal to consummate was not a nullity ground until 1937, but provided a defence to a petition for restitution of conjugal rights, and could be regarded in certain circumstances as evidence of incapacity. The author has not been able to trace any pre-1937 case which insisted that refusal should be without just excuse. When wilful refusal became a nullity ground under the Matrimonial Causes Act 1937 there was no requirement included that the refusal had to be without 'just excuse'. Section 7(1)(a) provided that a marriage was voidable if it had not been consummated 'owing to the wilful refusal of the respondent to consummate the marriage'. That legislative formula has been repeated in the several re-enactments of the provision since 1937.

What of *Horton* v *Horton* (above) itself? In that case there was a conflict of evidence as to which spouse had refused to consummate. The House of Lords held that on the evidence adduced the petitioner had failed to prove wilful refusal by his wife. Only one opinion was delivered and the brief report does not refer to any authorities. It seems, however, that whether the wife had refused to consummate without 'just excuse' was not an issue. Thus Lord Jowitt's inclusion of 'just excuse' in his description of wilful refusal was obiter; his Lordship introduced a principle that was neither supported by previous authority nor readily justifiable as a matter of statutory interpretation. In fairness to Lord Jowitt, he made it clear that he was not attempting to define wilful refusal and, indeed, that it was undesirable to do so. He was intending a description rather than a definition, and expressed it somewhat tentatively: 'the words connote, I think . . .'. Such language is hardly appropriate for establishing an important principle. So Lord Jowitt's dictum has acquired a status well beyond that intended by his Lordship.

How has the dictum fared in subsequent cases? The answer is, erratically. In some cases it is hardly mentioned even though the facts suggest that the existence of a just excuse might have been a relevant issue (for example, *A* v *J (Nullity Proceedings)* [1989] 1 FLR 110 and *Ford* v *Ford* [1987] Fam Law 232). In contrast, in cases such as *Jodla* v *Jodla* [1960] 1 All ER 625 and *Potter* v *Potter* (1975) Fam Law 161, the dictum is clearly applied. However, the judge in *Jodla* v *Jodla* (above), Hewson J, cannot resist adding his own gloss. In that case two Polish Roman Catholics married in a register office, intending a church ceremony later. It was understood that they would not consummate the marriage until after the ceremony. The wife obtained a nullity decree because the husband's refusal to arrange the ceremony was held to amount to wilful refusal to consummate. The judge stated (at p. 626) that the husband's behaviour provided the wife with 'a reasonable and just cause' for her refusal to consummate. But it is not clear whether the addition of 'reasonable' is intended to add anything of substance. The confusion is compounded later in the judgment when the judge appears to treat 'reasonable' and 'just' as alternatives. Referring to the wife's requests that a ceremony should be arranged, Hewson J states (at p. 626): 'as I have said, these requests were refused without any reasonable *or* just cause on his part' (emphasis added).

Jodla v *Jodla* (above) was applied by the Court of Appeal in *Kaur* v *Singh* [1972] 1 All ER 292 in which two Sikhs married in a register office on the understanding that a religious ceremony would follow, and that until then the parties would not regard themselves as married. The husband's refusal to arrange the ceremony was held to amount to wilful refusal. Little is said in the judgments about the question of just excuse on the facts of the case. However, Davies LJ does refer to the judgment in *Jodla* v *Jodla* (above) but his summary of the comments on just excuse by Hewson J is not precise, and uses phrases which the latter did not employ. Referring to the wife's refusal in *Jodla* v *Jodla* (above) to live with the husband until he had arranged a church ceremony, Davies LJ states (at p. 294):

Hewson J took the view that that did not amount to wilful refusal by the wife, because she had a *legitimate and proper excuse* in the circumstances. (emphasis added)

It thus appears that the requirements that wilful refusal must be without just excuse is based on dubious authority, and is one that has been applied in an erratic fashion, sometimes couched in language different from that to be found in Lord Jowitt's dictum.

WHAT DOES 'JUST EXCUSE' MEAN?

It is surprising that there appears to be no clear answer—or any answer—to the question posed. I have been unable to trace any case which contains an analysis or explanation of the meaning of just excuse. This state of affairs is made worse by the inconsistency of the judges—'reasonable', 'legitimate', 'proper' have been used to qualify 'excuse' or 'cause' (see above), and yet there are obvious questions to be asked about the meaning of just excuse. For example, is the matter to be viewed objectively or subjectively? Suppose that a wife discovers after the marriage ceremony that her husband is suffering from AIDS. Would she have just cause in refusing to consummate the marriage? The answer is, most probably. But what if she mistakenly thought that the husband had AIDS? Would it also make a difference whether her belief was reasonable? One would expect that a subjective test would be applied: a judge might be reluctant to find that refusal was 'wilful' if the wife genuinely believed that she was justified in her behaviour, however unreasonable her belief. But would the answer be the same if the excuse had to be 'reasonable' or 'legitimate and proper'?

The cases on wilful refusal fail to pose such questions, let alone answer them. The courts have been content to declare whether a just excuse existed on the facts without any analysis or explanation of the meaning of the concept. Indeed, there are very few reported cases in which a decree has been refused on the ground that there has been a just excuse for wilful refusal.

I have tried to argue that the proposition that wilful refusal must be without just excuse is based on dubious authority, that it has not received sufficient judicial analysis, that it has been expressed in alternative (and confusing) terms, and that its actual application has been rare. It could even be argued that the just excuse defence should have no place in the law in any case. What is the point of preserving a marriage where one of the parties takes as radical a step—given the sensitivity of the matter and the attendant embarrassment—as bringing a petition to end it on the grounds of wilful refusal to consummate? But I would not wish to go that far. In my view, it is desirable that there should be some qualification on the bringing of petitions for wilful refusal along the lines 'described' by Lord Jowitt in *Horton* v *Horton* (above). However, it is also desirable that such a qualification should be based on clear legal authority and that it should be given some meaningful content.

3.2.2 CONSENT

SZECHTER (ORSE. KARSOV) v *SZECHTER* [1971] 2 WLR 170

The parties went through a ceremony of marriage in February 1968 in a Polish prison, where the wife was serving a three-year prison sentence passed upon her in October 1967 for 'anti-state activities.' At the time of the ceremony both parties were domiciled in Poland and the wife, who had endured severe privation and hardship over many years and whose health was seriously impaired and deteriorating, believed that she would be unable to survive her prison sentence. The ceremony was gone through with the object of extricating the wife from prison. The plan succeeded and both parties came to reside in England where they had acquired a domicile of choice. On a petition by the wife for a decree declaring that the marriage was void for duress.

SIR JOCELYN SIMON P: So far as English law is concerned, private reservations or motives are not in general matters cognisable to vitiate an ostensibly valid marriage. As was said by Sir William, Scott in *Dalrymple* v *Dalrymple* (1811) 2 Hag Con 54, 105, 106:

It is in the intention of the parties that the substance of every species of contract subsists, and what is beyond or adverse to their intent does not belong to the contract. But then that intention is to be collected (primarily at least) from the words in which it is expressed; and in some systems of law, as in our own, it is pretty exclusively so to be collected, You are not to travel out of the intention expressed by the words, to substitute an intention totally different and possibly inconsistent with the words.

But it will be noted that Sir William Scott is, even in his general statement, recognising that there may be exceptions. He stated at p. 104:

It is said that the marriage contract must *not be extorted by force or fraud*. Is it not the general law of contracts, that they are vitiated by proof of either?

Although I do not think that in modern law the rules relating to duress as vitiating the reality of consent to an ostensibly valid contract of marriage differ from those relating to other species of contract, in the law of marriage the concept derives from the dirimentary defect of metus in the cation law (this should, I suppose, be translated as 'fear,' though Esmein in *Le Mariage en Droit Canonique* (1929) vol. 1, pp. 342 to 344 uses the word 'violence' in describing the impediment). As the American writer Bishop states in his *Commentaries on the Law of Marriage and Divorce*, 6th ed., (1881) vol. 1, para. 210, p. 177:

Where a formal consent is brought about by force, menace, or duress—a yielding of the lips, not of the mind—it is of no legal effect. This rule, applicable to all contracts, finds no exception in marriage.

In the nature of things the source of the fear and the agent of duress will generally be the other party to the marriage. But this is not necessarily so. Thus, in *H v H* [1954] P 258, the source of fear was the political and social danger to the life, liberty and virtue of the petitioner in her native country of Hungary. In order to obtain a foreign passport she went through a ceremony of marriage with a French citizen, and by agreement separated from him immediately thereafter. She was able thereby to escape to England, and in due course she presented here a petition for nullity on the ground of alleged duress. No allegation was made against the respondent or his agents. Karminski J heard argument not only on behalf of the petitioner but also by the Attorney-General on behalf of the Queen's Proctor. In a reserved judgment he held that the petitioner's fears were reasonably entertained, and were of such a kind as to negative her consent to the marriage, which was accordingly void.

It is, in my view, insufficient to invalidate an otherwise good marriage that a party has entered into it in order to escape from a disagreeable situation, such as penury or social degradation. In order for the impediment of duress to vitiate an otherwise valid marriage, it must, in my judgment, be proved that the will of one of the parties thereto has been overborne by genuine and reasonably held fear caused by threat of immediate danger (for which the party is not himself responsible), to life, limb or liberty, so that the constraint destroys the reality of consent to ordinary wedlock. I think that in the instant case that test is satisfied. In my view, English law returns the same answer to the juridical situation as the Polish law as deposed to by Mr Jaxa.

In those circumstances I made a decree nisi of nullity at the conclusion of the argument, reserving my reasons, which I have now delivered.

HIRANI v *HIRANI* [1982] 4 FLR 232 (CA)

ORMROD LJ: The brief facts are these. At the time the wife was 19 years of age, living with her parents in England. They are Indian Hindus. She made the acquaintance of a young Indian, Mr Hussain, who is a Muslim. Her parents were very upset when they discovered this and naturally objected to her association with this man. According to Mrs Hirani's evidence, which the judge accepted, her parents immediately made arrangements for her to marry Mr Hirani. That was in early January 1981. Her evidence went on to say that she had never seen Mr Hirani, nor indeed had her parents ever seen Mr

Hirani, but, within a fortnight of that first conversation, they had arranged for her to marry Mr Hirani at a registry office on 17 January. They put great pressure on her to go through with this ceremony, the threat being:

> You want to marry somebody who is strictly against our religion; he is a Muslim, you are a Hindu; you had better marry somebody we want you to, otherwise pack up your belongings and go. If you do not want to marry Mr Hirani and you want to marry Mr Hussain, go.

Of course she had no place to go and no means of supporting herself at that age if she did leave the family home, and so, in those circumstances, in spite of her opposition, she was forced to go through with the civil ceremony and after that she returned to her parents. She did not go to live with her husband until after the subsequent religious ceremony which took place on 27 February. She said that she was crying all the way through it and was utterly miserable, but after that ceremony she did live with Mr Hirani for 6 weeks. After that she left and went to Mr Hussain. She has never been back and there was no sexual intercourse between her and Mr Hirani during that 6 weeks.

On that evidence Mr Fox invited the judge to pronounce a decree on the ground of duress, but the judge asked in the course of argument whether that evidence '. . . was anything like enough to say that her mind was overborne by this threat?' Mr Fox referred the judge to two cases: *Parojcic v Parojcic* [1959] 1 All ER 1 and *Scott v Sebright* (1886) 12 PD 31 and the well-known passage in the judgment of Butt J, but the judge had *Rayden on Divorce* before him and it is clear from his judgment that he was greatly influenced by an extract from a judgment of Sir Jocelyn Simon P which appears in the current edition of *Rayden* at p. 179 at the end of note (b). It is an extract which comes right at the end of the judge's judgment in a case called *Szechter v Szechter* [1971] P 286. The passage cited in *Rayden* reads thus:

> . . . while it 'is insufficient to invalidate an otherwise good marriage that a party has entered into it in order to escape from a disagreeable situation, such as penury or degradation', this was a case where 'the will of one of the parties hereto has been overborne by genuine and reasonably held fear by the threat of immediate danger, for which the party is not responsible to life, limb or liberty, so that the constraint destroys the reality of consent to ordinary wedlock'. . . .

Reading that passage—and one can understand what the judge had in mind—he felt that he had to find threat to life, limb or liberty in order to find duress. With respect I do not for one moment think that the President intended that result. He was merely contrasting a disagreeable situation with one which constituted a real threat. But the matter can be dealt with quite shortly by referring to a recent case in the Privy Council dealing with duress and its effect on a contract. It is a case called *Pao On v Lau Yiu Long* [1980] AC 614. Lord Scarman, giving the opinion of the Privy Council and dealing with the duress question, at p. 635 said this:

> Duress, whatever form it takes, is a coercion of the will so as to vitiate consent.

He then quoted a dictum of Kerr J in another case (*The Siboen and The Sibotre* [1976] 1 Lloyd's Rep 293 at p. 336):

> There must be present some factor 'which could in law be regarded as a coercion of his will so as to vitiate his consent'.

The crucial question in these cases, particularly where a marriage is involved, is whether the threats, pressure, or whatever it is, is such as to destroy the reality of consent and overbears the will of the individual. It seems to me that this case, on the facts, is a classic case of a young girl, wholly dependent on her parents, being forced into a marriage with a man she has never seen and whom her parents have never seen in order to prevent her (reasonably, from her parents' point of view) continuing in an association with a Muslim which they would regard with abhorrence. But it is as clear a case as one could want of the overbearing of the will of the petitioner and thus invalidating or vitiating her consent.

In those circumstances I would allow the appeal and pronounce the decree nisi.

3.3   Bars to the Annulment

MATRIMONIAL CAUSES ACT 1973

13.   Bars to relief where marriage is voidable

(1)   The court shall not, in proceedings instituted after 31st July 1971, grant a decree of nullity on the ground that a marriage is voidable if the respondent satisfies the court—

(a)   that the petitioner, with knowledge that it was open to him to have the marriage avoided, so conducted himself in relation to the respondent as to lead the respondent reasonably to believe that he would not seek to do so; and

(b)   that it would be unjust to the respondent to grant the decree.

(2)   Without prejudice to subsection (1) above, the court shall not grant a decree of nullity by virtue of section 12 above on the grounds mentioned in paragraph (c), (d), (e) or (f) of that section unless—

(a)   it is satisfied that proceedings were instituted within the period of three years from the date of the marriage, or

(b)   leave for the institution of proceedings after the expiration of that period has been granted under subsection (4) below.

(3)   Without prejudice to subsections (1) and (2) above, the court shall not grant a decree of nullity by virtue of section 12 above on the grounds mentioned in paragraph (e) or (f) of that section unless it is satisfied that the petitioner was at the time of the marriage ignorant of the facts alleged.

(4)   In the case of proceedings for the grant of a decree of nullity by virtue of section 12 above on the grounds mentioned in paragraph (c), (d), (e) or (f) of that section, a judge of the court may, on an application made to him, grant leave for the institution of proceedings after the expiration of the period of three years from the date of the marriage if—

(a)   he is satisfied that the petitioner has at some time during that period suffered from mental disorder within the meaning of the Mental Health Act 1983, and

(b)   he considers that in all the circumstances of the case it would be just to grant leave for the institution of proceedings.

(5)   An application for leave under subsection (4) above may be made after the expiration of the period of three years from the date of the marriage.

3.4   Who can Apply for the Marriage to be Annulled?

Section 12, MCA, 1973

Incapacity to consummate	Can be relied upon by either party – including the person with the incapacity
Wilful refusal to consummate	Can only be relied upon by the non-refusing party
Duress, mistake or unsoundness of mind	Can be relied upon by either party – although in practice most applicants will rely on their own faults
Mental illness	Can be relied upon by either party
Venereal disease	Can only be relied upon by the party without VD
Pregnancy	Can be relied upon by the husband

3.5 Consequences of Nullity

3.5.1 PARTIES' RIGHTS: VOID MARRIAGES

J v S-T (FORMERLY J) (TRANSSEXUAL) **[1997] 1 FLR 402**

WARD LJ: As the provisions are now set out, s. 23 of the Matrimonial Causes Act 1973 provides:

> (1) On granting a decree of divorce, a decree of nullity of marriage . . ., the court may make any one or more of the following orders, that is to say—
>
> (a) . . . periodical payments . . .;
> . . .
> (c) . . . lump sum . . .

Section 24 confers the power to make transfer of property orders and other property adjustment orders. Section 25 provides for the matters to which the court is to have regard in deciding how to exercise those powers:

> (1) It shall be the duty of the court in deciding whether to exercise its powers . . . and, if so, in what manner, to have regard to all the circumstances of the case, first consideration being given to the welfare which a minor of any child . . .
> (2) . . . the court shall in particular have regard to . . .
> (a) the income [etc];
> (b) the financial needs [etc];
> (c) the standard of living . . .;.
> (d) the age of each party . . . and the duration of the marriage;
> (e) any . . . disability . . .;
> (f) the contributions . . . made . . . to the welfare of the family . . .;
> (g) the conduct of each . . . if that conduct is such that it would . . . be inequitable to disregard it;
> (h) [loss of] any benefit (for example, a pension) . . .

It is, however, neither necessary nor appropriate in this case to rule or even to speculate whether *Corbett* [1971] P 83 remains good law. Consequently, the essential facts upon which this judgment must rest are:

(1) The purported 'marriage' between the plaintiff and the defendant has been declared null and void. The defendant submitted to that decree and does not challenge it in this court.

(2) Accordingly, this court must proceed on the basis that in law there never was a marriage between the plaintiff and the defendant. Such a 'marriage' was and is a legal impossibility, and it was and it is a meretricious not a matrimonial union.

(III) Was the crime of perjury committed by the defendant?
The offence under s. 3 of the Perjury Act 1911 is that of knowingly and wilfully making a false declaration for the purpose of procuring a marriage. In *R v Ryan* (1914) 10 Cr App R 4, 7 it was held that:

> 'Wilfully' means 'intentionally', and 'intentionally' means that he knew at the time of the making of these certificates that he was making false statements in relation to documents which purported to be made under the Act . . .

The false declaration which concerns us in this appeal is the defendant's declaration of his belief that there was no lawful hindrance to the marriage. The issue is whether the plaintiff established that the defendant did not believe there was such hindrance, or putting it another way, whether he did believe that he could validly marry a woman.

Consequently, I accept the judge's finding that the defendant knew there was an impediment to his marrying. He was guilty of perjury in making a false declaration that there was no lawful hindrance to his marriage to the plaintiff.

(c)   Does this rule that no one shall be allowed to profit from his crime apply to this perjury?
I do not as instinctively answer in the affirmative as I did in *Whiston* v *Whiston* [1995] 2
FLR 268. Two matters concern me:

(1)   In that case there was a direct link between the crime and the claim. The act of
bigamy was the celebration of the marriage, the annulment of which gave rise to the
claim, just as, leaving the Forfeiture Act 1982 aside, murder causes the death from which
the Inheritance Act claim proceeds. Here the perjury is not as directly connected. The
perjury is committed by the making of the false declaration and whilst that is a
prerequisite to the marriage taking place, it still needs the subsequent ceremony to be
performed. Unlike bigamy here the marriage is at one remove. It is, therefore, not
without some hesitation that I come to the conclusion that the perjury is sufficiently
proximate to be able to say that the defendant is seeking to profit from his crime. My
reasons are:

(i)   The offence is linked to marriage by its definition: the false declaration must
be made 'for the purpose of procuring a marriage'.

(ii)   Although it is a decision of the Divisional Court and so not binding on us,
nevertheless the judgment in *R* v *Secretary of State for the Home Department, ex parte Puttick*
[1981] QB 767 is very persuasive and it is not easy to see why this case should be
distinguished from it. Donaldson LJ said at 775G:

> . . . bearing in mind additionally that citizenship is not only a matter of private right
> but also of public status and concern, in my judgment, Parliament can never have
> intended that a woman should be entitled to claim registration as a citizen of the
> United Kingdom and Colonies on the basis of a marriage achieved only by the
> commission of serious crime. In this case Mrs Puttick's impersonation of Frau
> Sauerbier and the commission of the crime of perjury and forgery formed the
> foundation of her marriage to Robin Puttick and, in my judgment, disentitled her to
> rely upon the right which she would otherwise have had to claim registration as a
> citizen of the United Kingdom and Colonies.

The case was cited with approval by this court in *R* v *Registrar General ex parte Smith*
[1991] 2 QB 393, [1991] 1 FLR 255. Consequently, I am persuaded to accept that the claim
is not too remote from the crime because 'the commission of the crime of perjury' also
'formed the foundation' of the defendant's marriage and has 'disentitled [him] to rely on
the right which [he] would otherwise have to claim' ancillary relief.

(2)   I have another hesitation. Bigamy is a discrete offence but perjury may cover a
wide range of false statements, some more serious than others. As already explained, I
would be very disinclined to find that a false declaration of bachelorhood was so heinous
as to debar a subsequent claim. Thus I accept that perjury per se does not necessarily
invoke the rule and each case may have to be judged on its own facts to establish the
requisite degree of seriousness. I appreciate there is, therefore, always some uncertainty
as to the application of the rule, but it seems to me to present the court with no more
difficult a task than has been accepted in deciding whether or not individual cases of
manslaughter meet the necessary criterion of culpability. I therefore see no reason to
make perjury an exception to the rule.

(d)   Conclusion
Being satisfied of the defendant's moral culpability and of the proximity of the crime and
the claim, I see no escape from the conclusion that the rule of public policy does apply.
Hollis J was right to hold that it did. Whilst those conclusions might be sufficient to
dismiss this appeal, I none the less prefer to explore whether the case can be viewed on
an alternative and perhaps a wider basis. I do this partly to save the defendant the
ignominy of being branded a criminal and partly to escape any remaining discomfort in
relying on perjury as the crime which invokes the ruling. This leads to the next question.

*(VII)   Should the claim be dismissed in the exercise of the court's wide statutory discretion under
s. 25 of the Matrimonial Causes Act 1973?*
I agree with my Lords that:

(1)   The language of s. 25 is wide enough to embrace the conduct we all agree is
thoroughly reprehensible.

(2)   Were the case to be decided as an exercise of the discretion, then, notwithstanding:

(i)   the huge disparity in their respective means;

(ii)   his needs for a roof over his head and some supplement to his income commensurate with the standard of living enjoyed during the 'marriage'; and

(iii)   the contribution he undoubtedly made to the welfare of the family in that he did all that was expected of him during their 17 years together,

nevertheless, no court could in the proper exercise of the wider discretion conferred by s. 25 conclude that any ancillary relief should be granted having regard to all the circumstances of the case, in particular to the sustained deception of the plaintiff.

Where I differ from my Lords is in my judgment that we do not get to the stage where discretion begins to be exercised. The benefit, the enjoyment of which the defendant is to be deprived, is, in my opinion, the right to apply for ancillary relief, the right, in other words, to invite the court to exercise the s. 25 discretion in his favour. For reasons I have already given above, the Act must be construed as being subject to the public policy principle.

POTTER LJ: Thus, while ss. 11(c), 23 and 24 of the 1973 Act now set out explicitly within a single Act the statutory jurisdiction of the court in respect of the grant of decrees of nullity, the power to grant some measure of ancillary relief in association with a decree in respect of a single-sex marriage was not introduced by the 1973 Act; nor, on the face of it, as between the various heads of nullity set out in s. 11(a)–(d), does it appear from the terms or context of the relevant provisions that different principles of law are intended to apply as to the availability of the right in either party to the marriage to apply for such ancillary relief.

In those circumstances, if there is any fetter upon the court's power to entertain an application for ancillary relief as provided in the 1973 Act, it must come from the application of some wider principle dehors the Act to which its terms, as a matter of interpretation, must be intended to be subject.

It was by reference to such wider principle that this court in *Whiston* held that, in the case of a bigamous marriage knowingly contracted by one of the parties, that party was precluded from making application for ancillary relief, on the public policy ground that the claim was necessarily founded upon a serious criminal offence.

The matter seems to have been principally argued, and the public policy argument upheld by Hollis J, not on the general basis of a deception practised on the plaintiff, but on the basis that, the appellant having committed perjury by his declaration to the registrar, the outcome was necessarily determined by the decision in *Whiston* since, in seeking ancillary relief, the appellant was seeking to profit from his own serious crime.

I do not think Hollis J was bound to apply *Whiston*. Further, it seems to me undesirable that the decision in *Whiston* should be applied beyond the confines of what I have indicated appears to be its ratio decidendi. My reasons are as follows.

It seems to me that the broad scope and interest of the 1973 Act in relation to nullity is to set out the multiplicity of grounds upon which a nullity decree might previously be obtained (see the Nullity of Marriage Act 1971 as now consolidated in the 1973 Act, s. 11 (void marriages) and s. 12 (voidable marriages)), and to provide that in respect of all, without distinction, the court should have power on grant of decree, to entertain an application for ancillary relief of all or any of the various types set out in Part II of the Act, if and insofar as the granting of such relief may appear appropriate. I underline those last words, because, apart from the enabling words 'may make', which govern the exercise of the various powers in Part II, the court has a duty to have regard to all the circumstances of the case including, but not limited to, the number of considerations specifically set out in s. 25.

Furthermore it seems to me plain that Parliament must be taken to have given this power to the court in the knowledge that, so far as nullity suits are concerned, the conduct of one party may well have involved some form of fraud, deceit or immorality, whether in the form of representations made to, or matters withheld from, the other party to the marriage, or in the form of a false declaration to the registrar of marriages. So far as the parties are concerned, Ward LJ has listed a number of matters which might be instrumental in persuading an innocent or ignorant party into a ceremony of marriage to which otherwise he or she would have refused to be party. So far is concerns false declarations to the registrar, as Ward LJ has also indicated, such declarations may be of a type which are more or less serious in effect.

Thus, in broad terms, it seems to me, first, that the court should approach the question of the impact of public policy as a disqualifying factor in a very restrictive manner, on the basis that the court, when considering 'all the circumstances of the case' under s. 25(1) of the 1973 Act, has, and was intended to have, the power to refuse an order for ancillary relief in any case where it seems appropriate by reason of the conduct of the parties and/or the effect of the order if made. Secondly, that however inappropriate, bizarre, or even impudent an application by one party who has deceived another may appear, the 1973 Act intends and anticipates that the applicant should be considered as at least a candidate for the exercise of all, any, or none of the forms of relief which it is within the power of the court to grant following decree. The fact that such application may be made following a meretricious marriage, whereby the applicant is seeking to obtain a form of relief which would never have been open to him/her had they merely cohabited together as single parties, rather than abusing the institution of marriage as it is legally defined and recognised, seems to me a circumstance which the court can and should take into account when deciding whether and, if so, in what manner to exercise its discretion in the applicant's favour.

In *Whiston*, the conduct of the appellant in 'marrying' (ie knowingly going through a form of bigamous marriage with) the plaintiff was itself a criminal offence. Thus, the crime concerned not only went 'to the very heart of the institution of marriage' but was itself the 'marriage' founding the claim. In this case, the crime of perjury complained of was a collateral matter which, albeit it enabled the 'marriage' to proceed, was not itself the crime complained of. So far as the deception practised by the appellant upon the plaintiff was concerned, sad and reprehensible as it was, the profound betrayal of trust involved did not in itself constitute a crime. As I have already indicated, short (as decided in *Whiston*) of reliance by the applicant upon a marriage which was itself a crime, I consider that the 1973 Act intends that all matters of conduct as between the parties should be brought into a discretionary post-decree balancing exercise so far as ancillary relief is concerned. In doing so, the court may and should take account of principles of public policy in exercising its discretion. I would therefore hold that, if and insofar as the judge's decision was to strike out the application of the appellant for ancillary relief in limine on the basis that the claim in *Whiston* obliged him to do so, it was in error.

That said, however, I have no doubt that the right result was achieved. Section 25(1) of the 1973 Act provides that:

It shall be duty of the court in deciding whether to exercise its powers under section 23, 24 or 24A above and, if so, in what manner, to have regard to all the circumstances of the case . . .

before going on to provide that:

. . . first consideration should be given to the welfare while a minor of any child of the family . . .

It then enumerates in s. 25(2) the particular matters to which the court shall have regard in relation to the exercise of its powers under those sections. Having carefully considered those specific matters, the overwhelming circumstances of this case seem to me to be, first, the fact that the appellant deceived the plaintiff into a marriage which would not have taken place had she known the truth as to his sexual position; secondly, that, by doing so, he has placed himself in a position where he has the opportunity to apply for a wide range of relief which would never have been open to him had he been frank with the plaintiff and simply lived in a state of cohabitation with her (if she were so content) during the period of the 'marriage'. He has thereby artificially enjoyed a standard of living throughout the 'marriage' far higher by reason of the plaintiffs means than would otherwise have been the case, for reasons which reflect no credit upon him and which in my view do not call for any favourable consideration of his claims on equitable grounds as a 'spouse', as opposed to a cohabitee. That view is based upon a careful consideration of all the material before the court as to the relative means and contributions of the parties and making all assumptions in the appellant's favour where issues appear.

I would only add that it is the plaintiff who has the care of the children, for whom she provides, and it does not seem to me that the welfare of either child requires the payment of any sum to the appellant.

I would therefore dismiss the appeal.

WHISTON v WHISTON [1995] 2 FLR 268 (CA)

WARD LJ: The respondent to this appeal, Mrs Whiston, is a bigamist. That is not a fact she has always been ready to admit. In wardship proceedings, and in a defended suit when her bigamy was in issue, she denied it; indeed she swore affidavits which were untruthful. Eventually she admitted her bigamy and a decree of nullity was granted to the appellant, Mr Whiston, on that ground.

The respondent then claimed to be entitled to orders for ancillary relief.

The stark point in the appeal is, therefore, whether or not that doctrine of public policy which ordains that one should not benefit from one's own crime is available to the appellant and whether or not the respondent should be debarred from pursuing her claim because ex turpi causa non oritur actio.

Thorpe J held that the respondent was entitled to pursue her claim and he rejected Mr Scott's submissions, which have been repeated to us today. His Lordship gave these reasons for his conclusion:

First, bigamy towards the close of the twentieth century does not carry the gravity that it did when the statutory offence was created in 1861. Nowadays when marriages can be so readily dissolved some of the gravity of the offence is reduced. Secondly, it has always been regarded as a crime necessary to protect the innocent woman from the male bigamist. There does not seem to be much sentencing policy surviving in respect of the female bigamist. Thirdly, I would deplore any conclusion that curtailed or removed the judicial discretion in making financial provision for adults of children post marital breakdown. Part of the ground that Mr Scott was able to develop derived from the fact that unusually the care and control of the children had been committed to the husband and not to the wife. It would be very serious if a woman who had a responsibility to bring up young children could not assert claims for ancillary relief for herself simply because she was guilty of bigamy. Finally, I find I difficult to see how Mr Scott's principle would apply in the more usual case where the bigamist was the respondent husband.

As to the seriousness of the offence, which on the facts before us has quite clearly been committed by this appellant, even though she has not been charged with it, I would agree that the crime of bigamy is treated less seriously today than it was, and it is of course now hardly the most serious in the criminal calendar. It was made a statutory felony in 1603 when the maximum penalty for the crime was death. Under s. 57 of the Offences Against the Person Act 1861 the penalty is now 7 years' imprisonment, though recent sentencing policy set out in Thomas *Current Sentencing Practice* (Sweet & Maxwell, loose-leaf) would indeed suggest that the bracket of 4 to 6 months for male defendants may be more appropriate. That a bigamous lady may be more leniently treated—to assume she will be—is her good fortune, but it does not in my judgment reduce her culpability. It remains an offence committed by either a man or a woman, and it is an offence which is capable of causing keen distress, as indeed Thorpe J found it had in this case. He took account of the appellant's evidence that he was devastated by the certain knowledge of his 'wife's' previous marriage, that he regarded himself as a victim and a man who had been wronged and, although the district judge did not find that to be genuine, but grossly exaggerated, it was the view of Thorpe J that this was a serious matter for this particular man.

This man would not have gone through a ceremony of marriage to this lady but for the deception that she practised upon him.

I am not certain that I agree with the judge, who expressed the opinion that the purpose of the offence is to protect the innocent woman from the male bigamist. That may indeed have been an important purpose, and is an important purpose, but for my part I see no good reason to treat the female bigamist in any sense differently from the male bigamist. I remind myself of the judgment of Scarman LJ in *Calderbank* v *Calderbank* [1976] Fam 93 at p. 103, where he said:

> Speaking for myself, I rejoice that it should be made abundantly plain that husbands and wives come to the judgment seat in matters of money and property upon a basis of complete equality.

It seems to me that a female bigamist should therefore be treated no differently from the male bigamist.

The judge was reluctant to remove or curtail judicial discretion in making financial provision for adults and children after marital breakdown. It formed the major plank of the respondent's argument to us. Miss Seddon submitted that because s. 25(2)(g) of the Matrimonial Causes Act 1973 expressly placed the court under a duty to have regard to the conduct of each of the parties, if that conduct was such that it would in the opinion of the court be inequitable to disregard it, Parliament intended thereby that the principle of public policy that no one should profit from his crime should be dealt with and only dealt with under that particular heading, and that there was no room otherwise for the application of this well-established principle of public policy.

I do not agree.

The judge found it unacceptable that a woman who had responsibility to bring up young children would not be able to assert claims for ancillary relief for herself simply because she was guilty of bigamy. I regret that I take a different view. If the judge is right, a bigamist would be entitled to assert a claim for ancillary relief which she would not be entitled to make had she not practised her deception and had remained a mere cohabitee of the man with whom she was living. To my mind that distinction would be unacceptable. It seems to me that it gives scant effect to the seriousness of this offence, which is one which strikes at the heart of marriage. It strikes at the institution of marriage because, to quote Professor Kenny's words as set out in J.W.C. Turner (ed), *Outlines of Criminal Law* (Cambridge University Press, 19th edn, 1966), para. 170, the reason for punishing bigamy is the broad ground of its 'involving an outrage upon public decency by the profanation of a solemn ceremony'. Where the criminal act undermines our fundamental notions of monogamous marriage I would be slow to allow a bigamist then to assert a claim, an entitlement at which she only arrives by reason of her offending. It is obviously proper that the 1973 Act should afford the innocent party to a bigamous marriage relief. Where an applicant entered into another 'marriage' genuinely and reasonably believing he or she was free to do, and who was therefore innocent of the crime of bigamy, that person too may have an entitlement, though that is not the matter for us to consider today.

Today we have this respondent seeking to profit from the crime. Her claim derives from the crime. Without her having entered into this bigamous ceremony she would not have got to the judgment seat at all. She should now in my judgment be prevented from going any further. I would therefore allow the appeal. I would accordingly dismiss her application for a lump sum and make no award to her whatever.

3.6   End of Chapter Assessment Questions

1.   Alfred has been undergoing medical treatment for clinical depression. The drug regime has made him intermittently 'hazy' and he has difficulty in understanding or making sense of things. Last week Alfred went through a Register Office wedding with Bernadette. After the ceremony, they booked in to an hotel nearby, and the marriage was consummated. They have not lived together beyond that first night. Alfred has now sought your advice on bringing the marriage to an end.

2.   To what extent can an individual marry whomsoever they wish, wherever they wish?

3.   Andre is married to Steffi and the marriage took place eight months ago. Shortly after the marriage Andre confessed he was bisexual. Due to this, Steffi insisted Andre have an HIV test. This has been returned with a positive result. No sexual intercourse has taken place. Advise Andre who wishes to set up home with Phillip and to relinquish all his marriage ties.

4.   Four years ago Paramjit and Ravi married in their local temple, the marriage having been arranged by their respective families. The couple had not met prior to the ceremony. Ravi was not keen on the prospect of marrying, but due to her age at the time (28) her parents were constantly telling her of the shame she was bringing onto the family. The marriage has never been a happy one – Ravi has never felt able to have physical contact with Pararmjit, and sexual intercourse has never taken place. Again, due to the family concerns she agreed to be artificially inseminated and has borne one child, Amandeep, now eight months old. Advise Ravi on her chances of bringing the marriage to an end.

3.7   End of Chapter Assessment Outline Answers

1.   The issues within this answer will revolve around whether the marriage is void or voidable. You must always be aware of who you are advising since not all the grounds for voidable marriages are available to both parties. Here you are advising Alfred.

Looking initially at void marriages, reflect upon s. 11 of the Matrimonial Causes Act 1973. You would not be expected to list all the grounds upon which a marriage can be avoided under this provision, but to consider if any of them are relevant. The advantage for Alfred of falling within s. 11 would be that the marriage has never existed and hence he would not need to do anything to 'end' the marriage. A decree of nullity would be proof that the marriage was in fact invalid from the start. Does Alfred fall within the section?

Unfortunately there are no grounds for declaring the marriage void that can be identified from the facts given. Whilst the facts are not very detailed, there is no indication of the couple being within the prohibited degrees, they appear to be of the requisite ages, have complied with the formalities (they may of course have lied to obtain the necessary licence to marry), and there is no reference to a previous marriage that is still existing.

Consequently, you would need to turn your attention to the provisions in s. 12 of the 1973 Act. This concerns voidable marriages. These are marriages that are valid, unless and until they are avoided by one of the parties to the marriage. The grounds that are given in s. 12 refer generally to some pre-existing defect which affects the basis of marriage. Again, pick out the most appropriate grounds suitable to Alfred's case, and indicate why others may not be relevant.

Section 12(a) and (b) are not applicable in this scenario, since the facts given show that the marriage has been consummated. You may find more mileage in the next ground in s. 12(c). It is unlikely that the marriage can be avoided by Alfred on the basis of mistake or duress, but there may be a way to avoid the marriage on the basis of Alfred's 'unsoundness of mind'. You are told that Alfred has been undergoing treatment for clinical depression, and in particular that the drug regime has affected his ability to make sense of things. It could be argued that this haziness resulted in Alfred not understanding what he was doing when he went through the ceremony. In other words, he was not mentally capable of consenting to the marriage. Remember that under this ground in s. 12 you are looking at the ability to consent. Also remember that marriage is a simple contract (*Re Park*), and so Alfred's incapacity must be quite severe. Alfred would be able to utilise this ground since it states that 'either party' may rely on unsoundness of mind.

The next ground under s. 12(d) may also be applicable to Alfred. Again, this provision reflects the mental capacity and mental health of one of the parties. The distinctions between this ground and the one in s. 12(c) are that under s. 12(d), there must be a recognisable mental illness as defined by the Mental Health Act 1983. Clinical depression, whilst only a minor mental illness, would fall within the Act's provisions. The issue will be whether or not this mental illness makes Alfred 'unfitted for marriage'. This does not relate to an impediment at the time of the marriage but one which is discovered later. It can be relied on by Alfred, even though it is his own mental state, since the provision states that 'either party' could suffer from a mental incapacity.

The other provisions of s. 12 (VD and pregnancy) would not seem to be applicable to Alfred's situation.

Finally, you would need to mention whether or not Alfred's application to annul the marriage would be prevented under s. 13 of the 1973 Act. From the facts given it would not seem that Alfred has acted in such a way as to lead Bernadette to believe that he would not seek to annul the marriage. Also, the marriage has not existed for more than three years, and hence s. 13(2) is not applicable.

To gain extra marks, a brief consideration of the consequences of a voidable marriage would be necessary. For example, you could discuss the fact that ancillary relief can be obtained and that any children born of the marriage will be legitimate.

2.   This again reflects void and voidable marriages. The question looks at two issues — the marriage to whomsoever an individual chooses, and where the marriage can be conducted.

Dealing with the first issue, you should have looked at s. 11 of the Matrimonial Causes Act 1973, and in particular discussed the following categories:

(a)   Section 11(a)(i) — that the parties are within the prohibited degrees of relationship. Explain what is meant by this, and who is caught by the provision. Refer to the loosening up of the restrictions in the degrees of affinity by the Marriage (Prohibited Degrees of Relationship) Act 1986. Clearly this provision does restrict the freedom of an individual to marry whomsoever they choose. The provisions do not, however, prohibit the cohabitation between individuals within these categories.

(b)   Section 11(a)(ii) — the age of the parties and being below the age of 16. This again is restrictive in the sense that if one of the parties is below the age of 16 no marriage can take place. This can be justified on social grounds, and also if a marriage does take place, the question of unlawful sexual intercourse may arise. You could suggest that this provision is less restrictive than the former, since it is open to the couple to wait until they both become of age.

(c)   Section 11(b) — one of the parties is already married. This provision, whilst again restricting the freedom to marry is linked to criminal law, and the notion that marriage is the union of one man and one woman, forsaking all others. On public policy, the restriction is not unwarranted, and can be resolved by the married party obtaining a divorce.

(d)   Section 11(c) — that the parties are not male and female. This links in to the concept mentioned above, that marriage is the union of one man and one woman. The restriction on same sex marriages does deny homosexuals and lesbians the ability to obtain the same rights and status as married heterosexual couples. It is a restriction, but one which would be justified on public policy grounds.

Moving now to the restriction as to where a marriage can be conducted, this relates to the formalities of marriage. Note that marriages can only be carried out in specified, and registered premises. Failure to comply with this requirement when done wilfully and knowingly may invalidate the marriage. The nature of the restriction, you may suggest, is not that draconian. Since the Marriage Act 1994 authorised the granting of licences to premises other than church and registry offices, the ability to marry where an individual wants is quite wide.

3.   Steffi and Andre's situation falls within the provisions of s. 12 of the Matrimonial Causes Act 1973. Section 11 is not relevant since none of the grounds are applicable. As with question 1, concentrate on the grounds which may be utilised rather than simply discuss all of them.

The marriage has not been consummated, and so your attention should be drawn to s. 12(a) and (b). Andre is the person seeking advice, and under s. 12(a) either party can be incapable. Andre could therefore rely on his own incapacity. The issue would be whether he is in fact incapable of consummating the marriage. The facts are not clear on this, so you would have to explain the meaning and interpretation of this ground.

With regard to wilful refusal to consummate, Andre would have to show that it is Steffi who is refusing to consummate the marriage. From the facts this would appear to be a more likely scenario since she was the one who requested the HIV test. You may also explore the issue of whether the refusal to consummate is refusal per se, or whether Steffi refuses intercourse unless Andre uses a condom. The latter would not amount to wilful refusal and hence Andre would not be able to utilise this ground.

Finally, the issue of HIV needs to be discussed. As you should have mentioned, if a party to the marriage is suffering from VD in a communicable form, then the marriage can be annulled. There are two problems with reference to this scenario. First, Andre has HIV, and so would be unable to rely on s. 12(e) since he is the petitioner, and the provision refers to the respondent having VD. Secondly, there is a question mark over the meaning of VD and whether this in fact includes HIV. Whilst the AIDS virus is normally passed on through sexual contact, this is not the only means whereby the disease will be transmitted. Also, is HIV a disease in its true sense? Medical opinion is not clear, but it can be suggested that HIV is merely the precursor to the disease of AIDS.

4.   This question should have been relatively easy to answer, given the work you have done in the previous three questions.

The main issue is whether the marriage is voidable for lack of consent on the part of Ravi under s. 12(c), or whether it is void for the lack of consummation under s. 12(a) or (b). Unlike the earlier questions, you should have focused on s. 13 more closely here.

Dealing firstly with duress under s. 12(c), mention the reason why duress can invalidate a marriage. The duress should go to the heart of consent to the marriage. The cases of *Szechter* and *Hirani* are relevant authority to quote. Ravi's difficulty would be the influence of s. 13(2), since the marriage has been in existence for more than three years. In addition, under s. 13(1) it may be argued that the fact that Ravi agreed to artificial insemination indicates that she has conducted herself in such a way as to lead the respondent to believe that the marriage would not be anulled.

The fact that Ravi has been artificially inseminated would not prejudice an application under s. 12(a) or (b) since artificial insemination is not within the definition of 'consummation'. She would not be able to rely on wilful refusal since she is the one who is refusing intercourse. To succeed on incapacity she would have to prove that she is psychologically repugnant to the idea of intercourse. This would be difficult since it is harder to show mental difficulties compared to physical difficulties.

CHAPTER FOUR

THE LAW ON DIVORCE — THE MATRIMONIAL CAUSES ACT 1973

4.1 A Historical Perspective

The Law Commission, Facing the Future – A Discussion Paper on the Ground for Divorce (Law Com No. 170)

The relevance of divorce rates

2.14   It is tempting to blame the large increase in the number of divorces upon the reform of the divorce law by the 1969 Act and to suggest that it has fundamentally weakened the institutions of marriage and the family. For several reasons such suggestions are unlikely to be well-founded. First, it is important always to bear in mind the distinction between marital separation and divorce. An increase in the number of divorces does not necessarily indicate a proportionate increase in marriage breakdown. Secondly, research findings indicate that the increase in marital breakdown must largely be explained by factors other than the liberalisation of divorce law. Thirdly, the increase in the divorce rate has not been matched by a wholesale abandonment of marriage and does not necessarily indicate any diminution in the respect in which marriage and the family are held, but rather reflects changed attitudes and expectations. Each of these points will be considered in turn.

2.15   Although it is clear that both the numbers and proportions of marriages breaking down during the parties' lifetimes have increased, it is equally clear that the increase has taken place over a long period and cannot be measured in such a way as to give an obvious explanation of its causes. There are a number of factors which would support the view that the increase in the divorce rate after the implementation of the 1969 Act does not indicate a similar increase in the rate of marriage breakdown. First, there has been a reduction in the use of the magistrates' domestic jurisidiction. Previously, many cases of marital breakdown were dealt with by the magistrates without ever being legally ended by divorce, although they were in fact permanently broken. Today, those same marriages would end in divorce. This is as much due to procedural changes and legal aid, which have brought divorce within the financial reach of all sections of society, as it is to changes in the substantive law. Secondly, as was recognised in The Field of Choice, many cases of marital breakdown did not come before the courts at all, perhaps because no matrimonial offence had been established or because the potential petitioner could not face the ordeal of proving one. The new law allowed many such marriages to be dissolved. Thus, apart from the phenomenon of satisfying pent-up demand for divorce in the early years after the implementation of the new law, divorce figures since 1971 are bound to include cases which would not previously have appeared in any judicial statistics, although the marriages had in fact irretrievably broken down. One obvious effect, and indeed object, of the new law was to make it much more likely that all cases of marriage breakdown would eventually end in divorce. Nonetheless, there is little doubt that there has been an increase in marital breakdown, even if this increase is not as dramatic as the divorce figures would suggest. What are the possible reasons for this?

2.16   Divorce laws as such are incapable of preventing couples from separating by consent, or a spouse who has the means to do so from leaving without consent. It is therefore difficult to ascribe an increase in separation to any liberalisation of the divorce law. The upward trend in the divorce rate started before the implementation of a new law and has been paralleled by similar increases in divorce rates throughout Europe. Even in Ireland, where there is no divorce, the incidence of marital breakdown has increased. There is also empirical evidence from abroad which shows that liberal divorce laws do not necessarily result in a higher rate of marital breakdown. In particular, the adoption of no-fault divorce in many of the States of the U.S.A. does not appear to have had a significant effect on the divorce rate.

2.17   This is not to say that divorce law has no influence on the rate of marital breakdown. Indeed it seems likely that divorce law does have some bearing on the social climate. It may be that less restrictive divorce laws contribute to 'an increasing disposition to regard divorce, not as the last resort, but as the obvious way out when things begin to go wrong'. If so, they may have contributed to some extent to the increased rate of marital breakdown. Nevertheless, since it is quite clear that the phenomenon of increased marital breakdown has been widespread and independent of changes in divorce laws, it must largely be explained by reference to other factors, principally the demographic, socio-economic and attitudinal changes which have taken place throughout Western society during this century. As we examine these, it will be apparent that although some may be matters of regret, many of them are not. It is equally apparent that none of them can be affected by the substance of the divorce law as such.

4.2   The Basic Presumptions of the Modern Divorce

The Law Commission, Reform of the Grounds of Divorce: The Field of Choice
(Law Com No. 6)

REPORT ON A REFERENCE UNDER SECTION 3(1)(e)
OF THE LAW COMMISSIONS ACT 1965

The Objectives of a Divorce Law
13.   Before describing the present basis of English divorce law and the various alternatives, it may be well to set out what, as we see it, the objectives of a good divorce law should be. As a start we cannot do better than quote the words of the Morton Commission:

The Western world has recognised that it is in the best interests of all concerned—the community, the parties to a marriage and their children—that marriage should be monogamous and that it should last for life. It has also always recognised that, owing to human frailty, some marriages will not endure for life and that in certain circumstances it is right that a spouse should be released from the obligations of marriage.

14.   The Archbishop's Group expressed very similar views. They made it clear that Church of England doctrine fully recognises that it is right and proper for the State 'to make provision for divorce and re-marriage', that 'there is nothing to forbid the Church's recognising fully the validity of a secular divorce law within the secular sphere', and that the Church is not committed to defend 'the matrimonial offence as the only admissible basis for dissolving legal marriage'. 'By reason of its legal establishment the Church of England has both a special interest in what happens to the secular matrimonial law and

a special duty to concern itself with that law's improvement', but in so doing 'the only Christian interests that need to be declared are the protection of the weak and the preservation and strengthening of those elements in the law which favour lasting marriage and stable family life. . . .

15.   Accordingly, as it seems to us, a good divorce law should seek to achieve the following objectives:

(i)   To buttress, rather than to undermine, the stability of marriage; and

(ii)   When, regrettably, a marriage has irretrievably broken down to enable the empty legal shell to be destroyed with the maximum fairness, and the minimum bitterness, distress and humiliation.

16.   At first sight it may appear that a divorce law, which is directed essentially towards dissolving the marriage bond, can do nothing towards achieving the first objective. This, however, is not necessarily the case. It can and should ensure that divorce is not so easy that the parties are under no inducement to make a success of their marriage and, in particular, to overcome temporary difficulties. It can also ensure that every encouragement is afforded to a reconciliation and that the procedure is not such as to inhibit or discourage approaches to that end.

17.   The second objective has two facets. First, the law should make it possible to dissolve the legal tie once that has become irretrievably broken in fact. If the marriage is dead, the object of the law should be to afford it a decent burial. Secondly, it should achieve this in a way that is just to all concerned, including the children as well as the spouses, and which causes them the minimum of embarrassment and humiliation. Above all, it should seek to take the heat out of the disputes between husband and wife and certainly not further embitter the relationships between them or between them and their children. It should not merely bury the marriage, but do so with decency and dignity and in a way which will encourage harmonious relationships between the parties and their children in the future.

18.   In addition to these two main objectives, another important requirement is that the divorce law should be understandable and respected. It is pre-eminently a branch of the law that is liable to affect everyone, if not directly at any rate indirectly. Unless its principles are such as can be understood and respected, it cannot achieve its main objectives. If it is thought to be hypocritical or otherwise unworthy of respect, it will not only fail to achieve those objectives but may bring the whole of the administration of justice into disrespect.

Putting Asunder: A Divorce Law for Contemporary Society, Archbishop of Canterbury's Committee, 1966

22   It will make for clarity if, having dealt at some length with the relation between the Church and the matrimonial law of the State, we now give a survey of the course our discussions took and the main conclusions we reached, leaving the reasons for our conclusions, and the implications of what we recommend, to be developed more adequately later.

23   We very soon decided that it would not be an improvement, but the reverse, to introduce the principle of breakdown of marriage into the existing law in the shape of an additional ground for divorce; and our objections to any such compromise multiplied and hardened as the time went on. In our opinion it is a very good thing indeed that the Bills which proposed a 'ground of separation' failed to reach the statute book.

24   Having rejected the addition of new grounds to the existing law, we saw we should have to face a choice of principle. It seemed to us that Lord Hodson had been undeniably right when he said in the debate already mentioned:

There are only two theories alive on this problem—namely, are we going to act on the matrimonial offence, or are we going to act on the breakdown of marriage theory? That is the fight.

Lord Walker had posed the same alternatives, we noted, at the time of the Morton Commission. He said in his minority statement that either the matrimonial offence ought to be abandoned and the principle of breakdown be substituted, or else the principle of the matrimonial offence ought to be maintained as strictly as possible, without the addition of grounds inconsistent with it. We agreed that this was the choice that had to be made.

25   The next step was to look at the existing law more closely and try to answer another question of Lord Hodson's:

Are we going to accept the finding of the Royal Commission, which sat and laboured for about four years and at the end of it all came to the conclusion that if we are to have divorce the basis upon which divorce should be granted should be the matrimonial offence?

Although some of our witnesses still had faith in the matrimonial—offence system, our study of it elicited little to its credit and nothing at all to make us want its perpetuation. What interested us most was the discovery that in practice the courts have already gone a considerable way towards transforming judgements theoretically founded on the matrimonial offence into what are virtually judgements on the state of the marriages in question. We came to the conclusion that, whatever the legal theory might be, legal practice was moving, in company with the mind of society, towards the concept of breakdown of marriage.

26   We had then to decide whether this movement was salutary or the reverse. Various questions called for answer. Was it a movement towards 'divorce by consent'? Did it imply a deterioration in the popular estimate of marriage? Was it a sign that understanding of the marriage covenant as lifelong was weakening? Would it, if it continued, undermine the stability of the family? And so on. We shall have something to say about these and kindred questions later. Here it must suffice to record two conclusions: first, that we found no reason to suppose that the doctrine of breakdown of marriage would favour 'divorce by consent' in the objectionable sense of those words; second, that the conception of marriage underlying the doctrine of breakdown seemed to us to be neither unworthy nor incompatible with a covenant of lifelong intention. Indeed we were persuaded that a divorce law founded on the doctrine of breakdown would not only accord better with social realities than the present law does, but would have the merit of showing up divorce for what in essence it is—not a reward for marital virtue on the one side and a penalty for marital delinquency on the other; not a victory for one spouse and a reverse for the other; but a defeat for both, a failure of the marital 'two-in-oneship' in which both its members, however unequal their responsibility, are inevitably involved together. So we arrived at our primary and fundamental recommendation: that the doctrine of the breakdown of marriage should be comprehensively substituted for the doctrine of the matrimonial offence as the basis of all divorce.

27   The rest of our work consisted in trying to make sure that the substitution was practicable and in considering what consequential changes in law and practice it would entail if made. Again only the briefest account of the questions we encountered will be given at this point.

28   First of all, is breakdown a triable issue? One or two of those who were good enough to give us the benefit of their knowledge and experience had their doubts; but for the most part we were advised that a judge would not find it unduly difficult to decide, after hearing the evidence, whether or not there was reasonable probability, in all the circumstances, of cohabitation being revived. Actions and conduct which under the present law constitute matrimonial offences, though no longer in themselves and by themselves grounds for a decree, would still be available as evidence for breakdown: in addition the court would be at present enabled to take other facts into account which are treated as irrelevant. At this point, however, it was borne in on us that it would not do to change the basis of the law without changing court procedure as well; for if procedure remained as it is, the change of basis, instead of making the grant of decrees more reasonable, equitable, and discriminating, could simply make divorce easier to get. Procedural change is therefore one of the necessary conditions of refounding the substantive law. The court could not be expected to reach true conclusions about the state of matrimonial relationships unless the existing accusatorial procedure were abandoned and something like procedure by inquest substituted for it. It would need, moreover, the means to ensure that all relevant facts and considerations were brought to its notice and,

to that end, more officers to assist it. Could these things be achieved without increasing cost? Obviously not. But later on, when we came to discuss the unification of divorce and ancillary proceedings into a single trial with a single set of pleadings (which is what we recommend) we found reason to think that increased expenditure in one direction would be appreciably offset by economics in another. However that may be, we maintain that society, since it cannot do without divorce, should be prepared to pay for making the administration of it as good as can be contrived.

29   In the second place, the doctrine of breakdown necessarily permits either party to petition. As those who opposed Mrs White and Mr Abse saw very clearly, it could therefore happen in some cases that a spouse who had committed what the present law would treat as a matrimonial offence might take advantage of his or her own wrongdoing to get the marriage dissolved against the will of the other spouse who had committed no such offence. Ought this to be tolerated?

One thing at least was clear to us: that it would be unjust to allow the principle of breakdown to operate freely in such cases unless the legislature had first taken steps to ensure that unoffending respondents, and children, would not be penalized economically and socially by the grant of decrees. This we regard as another necessary condition of reforming the divorce law. Indeed we think that the economic position of wives after divorce calls for increased protection quite apart from any question of introducing the principle of breakdown. We recommend that the court should have power to award a share in pension and insurance benefits, whenever appropriate, in addition to maintenance, and the duty to withhold a decree unless and until satisfied with the provision made for the dependent spouse and any children of the marriage. We further suggest that the possibility of introducing some form of community of property should be explored.

But all that would meet only part of the difficulty, as we recognized. Supposing the economic problems were solved, would not having one's marriage dissolved against one's will on the petition of a partner who had behaved badly be in itself an injury that the law ought not to permit? This question cost us much anxious thought and discussion frequently renewed. New Zealand had experimented, we found, with prohibiting decrees on certain 'grounds of separation' if the initial separation had been due to the conduct of the petitioner and the respondent did not want divorce. This seemed to us inconsistent with the doctrine of breakdown and with the public interest in dissolving 'empty' legal ties which the doctrine presupposes. We agreed rather with the Australian view that the respondent's unwillingness should not suffice by itself to prohibit dissolving a marriage that had clearly broken down. Nevertheless we saw possibilities of injustice here which could not simply be shrugged off.

The conclusion we came to in the end was this. Divorce is a drastic piece of surgery, the unnatural severing of what should be one and indivisible. As such it is bound to cause pain and loss and leave lasting scars. To demand that a divorce law shall let no one be hurt is therefore to ask the impossible. The law and the courts are faced with trying to uphold distributive justice in situations which by their very nature exclude wholly just solutions. If then, as is widely held among responsible people to-day, the public interest requires as a general rule that 'empty' legal ties should be dissolved and that *de facto* unions and their issue should be legitimized, that has to be put in the scales against the injury an unoffending respondent may suffer through the loss of married status. Further, in considering this injury, we found reason to think that, though undoubtedly grave, it would not perhaps be quite as grave as has been alleged, nor indeed quite of the kind that is commonly supposed. On the other hand, we saw that there could be cases in which outrageous conduct on the petitioner's part aggravated the injury beyond the limits of toleration, causing the weight of public interest to shift from one side of the balance to the other. As a necessary safeguard, therefore, we recommend that the court should have a duty to dismiss the petition, even though satisfied that the marriage in question had broken down, if it considered that on balance a decree would be against the public interest because of the conduct of the petitioner.

30   A third question that faced us was this: if divorce proceedings ceased to turn on matrimonial offences, how would maintenance and costs be assigned? We recognized that for these purposes the court would still need to have regard to the conduct of the spouses and to make a comparative estimate of their responsibility for the breakdown of the marriage. That estimate would be distinct, however, from judgement on the state of the marriage. In fact there would be a series of judgements to make. Whether the

marriage had broken down would be the first. After that, in cases where breakdown had been proved to the court's satisfaction there would be the conduct of the parties to be considered, and an estimate to be made of comparative responsibility for the breakdown. Then would come the application of the estimate to maintenance and so forth, the question whether, in spite of the proof of breakdown, a decree ought yet to be refused as being against the public interest, either because of the petitioner's conduct because provision for the dependent spouse and any children was unsatisfactory.

31   Beside considering the principle on which divorce should founded and questions ancillary to that, we turned our attention at an early stage to the matter of reconciliation; it seemed to us to be a merit in the doctrine of breakdown that it implicitly required the court to be satisfied, before treating breakdown as proved, that nothing more could be hoped from attempts to reconcile the parties. In other words, the judgement that a marriage has irreparably broken down necessarily presupposes either genuine, though in the event unsuccessful, attempts at reconciliation, or else a conclusion of the court that in the circumstances no such attempts could have been expected. We would therefore add our voice to those which are already insisting that more financial backing should be given to reconciliation agencies, particularly for the purpose of continuing to improve the training and equipment of personnel. As for rôle of the courts in reconciliation, those with experience of the work who were good enough to help us in this matter advised us, without exception, that any attempt to use compulsion is self-frustrating. We therefore do not recommend that reconciliation procedures should be incorporated into the judicial system, but that the courts should have power, and indeed the duty, to adjourn hearings if not satisfied that the resources of reconciliation had been exhausted.

The Law Commission, The Field of Choice (Law Com No. 6)

Summary and Conclusions

120.   The main conclusions already reached can be summarised as follows:—

(1)   The objectives of a good divorce law should include (a) the support of marriages which have a chance of survival, and (b) the decent burial with the minimum of embarrassment, humiliation and bitterness of those that are indubitably dead (paragraphs 13–18).

(2)   The provision of the present law whereby a divorce cannot normally be obtained within three years of the celebration of the marriage may help to achieve the first objective (paragraph 19). But the principle of matrimonial offence on which the present law is based does not wholly achieve either objective (paragraphs 25–28).

(3)   Four of the major problems requiring solution are:—

(a)   The need to encourage reconciliation. Something more might be achieved here; though little is to be expected from conciliation procedures after divorce proceedings have been instituted (paragraphs 29–32).

(b)   The prevalence of stable illicit unions. As the law stands, many of these cannot be regularised nor the children legitimated (paragraphs 33–37).

(c)   Injustice to the economically weaker partner—normally the wife (paragraphs 38–46).

(d)   The need adequately to protect the children of failed marriages (paragraphs 47–51).

(4)   The field of choice for reform is circumscribed by a number of practical considerations and public attitudes, which cannot be ignored if acceptable and practicable reforms are to be undertaken (paragraph 52).

(5)   The proposals of the Archbishop's Group on Divorce made in *Putting Asunder*, though they are to be welcomed for their rejection of exclusive reliance on matrimonial offence, are proccdurally impracticable. They propose that there should be but one comprehensive ground for divorce—breakdown of the marriage—the court being required to satisfy itself by means of a thorough inquest into the marriage that it has failed irretrievably. It would not be feasible, even if it were desirable, to undertake such an inquest in every divorce case because of the time this would take and the costs involved (paragraphs 56–70).

(6)   However, the following alternative proposals, if any of them were thought desirable, would be practicable in the sense that they could be implemented without insuperable legal difficulty and without necessarily conflicting with the critical factors referred to in (4):—

(a) *Breakdown without Inquest*—a modification of the breakdown principal advocated in *Putting Asunder*, but dispensing in most cases with the elaborate inquest there suggested. The court would, on proof of a period of separation and in the absence of evidence to the contrary, assume that the marriage had broken down. If, however. this were to be the sole comprehensive ground of divorce, it would not be feasible to make the period of separation much more than six months. If, as seems likely, so short a period is not acceptable. breakdown cannot become the sole ground, but might still be introduced as an additional ground on the lines of proposal (c) below (paragraphs 71–76).

(b) *Divorce by Consent*—This would be practicable only as an additional, and not a sole comprehensive, ground. It would not be more than a palliative and would probably be unacceptable except in the case of marriages in which there are no dependent children. Even in the case of childless marriages, if consent were the sole criterion, it might lead to the dissolution of marriages that had not broken down irretrievably (paragraphs 77–84).

(c) *The Separation Ground*—This would involve introducing as a ground for divorce a period of separation irrespective of which party was at fault, thereby affording a place in the law for the application of the breakdown principle. But since the period would be substantially longer than six months, it would be practicable only as an addition to the existing grounds based on matrimonial offence. The most comprehensive form of this proposal would provide for two different periods of separation. After the expiration of the shorter period (two years is suggested either party, subject to safeguards, could obtain a divorce if the other consented, or, perhaps, did not object. After the expiration of the longer period (five or seven years) either party, subject to further safeguards, could obtain a divorce even if the other party objected (paragraphs 85–105).

(7) If any of these proposals were adopted, the following safeguards would appear to be necessary:—

(a) The three year waiting period (see (2) above) should be retained (paragraphs 19 and 106).

(b) The court should have power to adjourn for a limited period to enable the possibilities of reconciliation to be explored (paragraphs 32 and 107).

(c) The court should have a discretion to refuse a decree if attempts had been made by the petitioner wilfully to deceive it; but the present absolute and discretionary bars would be inapplicable to petitions on these new grounds (paragraphs 108 and 109).

(d) Additional safeguards would be needed to protect the respondent spouse and the children. These should include:—

(i) A procedure to ensure that the respondent's decision to consent to or not oppose a divorce, had been taken freely and with a full appreciation of the consequences (paragraphs 83, 97 and 112).

(ii) Retention, and possible improvement, of the provisions of the present law designed to ensure that satisfactory arrangements are made for the future of the children (paragraphs 47 and 110).

(iii) Provisions protecting an innocent party from being divorced against his or her will unless equitable financial arrangements are made for him or her (paragraphs 40 and 113).

(e) It is for consideration whether there should be a further discretionary bar based on protection of interests wider than those of the parties alone. If such a bar were introduced, it should be defined as precisely as possible so as to promote consistency in its exercise and to enable legal advisers to give firm advice to their clients (paragraphs 41 and 114–119).

4.3 The Grounds for Divorce

MATRIMONIAL CAUSES ACT 1973

1. Divorce on breakdown of marriage

(1) Subject to section 3 below, a petition for divorce may be presented to the court by either party to a marriage on the ground that the marriage has broken down irretrievably.

(2)   The court hearing a petition for divorce shall not hold the marriage to have broken down irretrievably unless the petitioner satisfies the court of one or more of the following facts, that is to say—

(a)   that the respondent has committed adultery and the petitioner finds it intolerable to live with the respondent;

(b)   that the respondent has behaved in such a way that the petitioner cannot reasonably be expected to live with the respondent;

(c)   that the respondent has deserted the petitioner for a continuous period of at least two years immediately preceding the presentation of the petition;

(d)   that the parties to the marriage have lived apart for a continuous period of at least two years immediately preceding the presentation of the petition (hereafter in this Act referred to as 'two years' separation') and the respondent consents to a decree being granted;

(e)   that the parties to the marriage have lived apart for a continuous period of at least five years immediately preceding the presentation of the petition (hereafter in this Act referred to as 'five years' separation').

(3)   On a petition for divorce it shall be the duty of the court to enquire, so far as it reasonably can, into the facts alleged by the petitioner and into any facts alleged by the respondent.

(4)   If the court is satisfied on the evidence of any such fact as is mentioned in subsection (2) above, then, unless it is satisfied on all the evidence that the marriage has not broken down irretrievably, it shall, subject to section 5 below, grant a decree of divorce.

(5)   Every decree of divorce shall in the first instance be a decree nisi and shall not be made absolute before the expiration of six months from its grant unless the High Court by general order from time to time fixes a shorter period, or unless in any particular case the court in which the proceedings are for the time being pending from time to time by special order fixes a shorter period than the period otherwise applicable for the time being by virtue of this subsection.

3.   Bar on petitions for divorce within one year of marriage

(1)   No petition for divorce shall be presented to the court before the expiration of the period of one year from the date of the marriage.

(2)   Nothing in this section shall prohibit the presentation of a petition based on matters which occurred before the expiration of that period.

4.3.1   THE FIVE FACTS

4.3.1.1   The respondent has committed adultery and the petitioner finds it intolerable to live with the respondent

The Law Commission, Facing the Future: A Discussion Paper on the Ground for Divorce (Law Com No. 170)

3.8   As to the first point, it was argued that the introduction of the breakdown principle would do more to buttress the stability of marriage than the previous law had done. The requirement of 'intolerability' was added to the adultery fact with the intention of excluding reliance on a single isolated act of adultery which did not affect the marriage relationship. The provision that no divorce could be granted where the marriage had not broken down irretrievably was thus seen as a method of preventing abuse. However, it is clear that the 1969 Act has been no more successful in preventing immediate consensual divorce than its predecessor. Undefended divorces based on adultery or behaviour can be obtained relatively quickly and apparently easily.

3.17   The unfairness caused by this often unjustified stigmatisation of the respondent is exacerbated by several factors. First, the adultery and behaviour facts as formulated in the legislation and interpreted by the courts do not necessarily involve the absolute fault that is suggested by these labels. . . . Similarly, the adultery fact involves not only a finding that the respondent has committed adultery, but also that the petitioner finds it intolerable to live with the respondent. Again, this requires some finding of incompatibility, although in this case the test is entirely subjective. However, it has been held that there need be no causal link between the two requirements. Thus, the petitioner may find it intolerable to live with the respondent for any reason, not necessarily because he has committed adultery. The court or the registrar is in no position to gainsay the petitioner . . .

CLEARY v CLEARY AND ANOTHER [1974] 1 All ER 498 (CA)

LORD DENNING MR: This case raises a short but important point under the Divorce Reform Act 1969. The husband and wife were married on 14th November 1964. They had two children, now aged seven and five. From 1968 there were serious quarrels between them. In November 1971 she went to live in Wales with another man named Hutton and committed adultery with him. After a few weeks she came back to her husband and they lived together for some five or six weeks. In January 1972 she left him finally. But she did not go back to the other man. She went to her mother's with the children. In February 1972 the wife took proceedings in the magistrates' court against her husband complaining that he had treated her with persistent cruelty and had wilfully neglected to maintain her. Her complaint was dismissed. But the husband was ordered to contribute to the maintenance of the children. On 22nd May 1972 the wife petitioned for divorce on the ground that the marriage had broken down irretrievably and that the husband had behaved in such a way that she could not reasonably be expected to live with him. In his answer the husband charged her with adultery with Hutton, the man with whom she had gone away to Wales, and he said that he found it intolerable to live with her. The case was however never contested. The wife withdrew her petition. The case proceeded on his answer. When it came for hearing she did not defend it. So on his cross-prayer it was an undefended case.

An enquiry agent gave evidence of admissions by her as to adultery in Wales in November 1971. The husband told how he had taken her back for the five or six weeks. He said that he had found correspondence between her and the other man during those weeks. But there was no evidence of any further adultery by her. She afterwards left but did nor go back to the other man. She went to her mother's.

Now there is an appeal to this court. It depends on the wording of the Divorce Reform Act 1969. Section 1 says that the sole ground on which it petition for divorce may, be presented to the court shall be that the marriage has broken down irretrievably. Section 2(1) says:

> The court hearing a petition for divorce shall not hold the marriage to have broken down irretrievably unless the petitioner satisfies the court of one or more of the following facts, that is to say—(a) that the respondent has committed adultery and the petitioner finds it intolerable to live with the respondent . . .

On those words a point of law arises on which there is it difference of opinion between the judges. The question is whether the two facts required by s. 2(1)(a) are severable and independent, or whether they are interconnected. In other words is it sufficient for the husband to prove (a) that the wife has committed adultery, and (b) that he finds it intolerable to live with her? Or has he to prove that (a) the wife has committed adultery, and (b) that *in consequence thereof* he finds it intolerable to live with her? Are the words 'in consequence thereof' to be read into s. 2(1)(a).

As a matter of interpretation, I think the two facts in s. 2(1)(a) are independent and should be so treated. Take this very case. The husband proves that the wife committed adultery and that he forgave her and took her back. That is one fact. He then proves that, after she comes back, she behaves in a way that makes it quite intolerable to live with her. She corresponds the other man and goes out at night and finally leaves her husband, taking the children with her. That is another fact. It is in consequence of that second fact that he finds it intolerable—not in consequence of the previous adultery. On that evidence, it is quite plain that the marriage has broken down irretrievably. He complies with s. (2)(1)(a) by proving (a) her adultery which was forgiven; and (b) her subsequent conduct (not adultery), which makes it intolerable to live with her.

I would say one word more. In Rayden on Divorce it is suggested (referring to an extra-judicial lecture by Sir Jocelyn Simon) '. . . it may even be his own adultery which leads him to find it intolerable to live with the respondent'. I cannot accept that suggestion. Suppose a wife committed adultery five years ago. The husband forgives her and takes her back. He then falls in love with another woman and commits adultery with her. He may say that he finds it intolerable to live with his wife, but that is palpably untrue. It was quite tolerable for five years: and it is not rendered intolerable by his love for another woman. That illustration shows that the judges in such cases as these should not accept the man's bare assertion that he finds it intolerable. In particular, what conduct on the part of the wife has made it intolerable? It may be her previous adultery. It may be something else. But whatever it is, the judge must be satisfied that the husband finds it intolerable to live with her.

On the facts of this case I think the judge could and should have found on the evidence the two elements required, (1) the adultery of the wife, and (2) the husband found it intolerable to live with her. I would accordingly allow the appeal and pronouce a decree nisi, on the ground that the marriage has irretrievably broken down. The arrangements, so far as one can see, for the children have been satisfactorily made. I would allow the appeal accordingly.

SCARMAN LJ: I agree. I would only add one comment on the point of construction. Sections 1 and 2 of the Divorce Reform Act 1969 are concerned with matrimonial situations. Section 1 provides that the sole ground of divorce shall be that the marriage has broken down irretrievably, that is to say, the section directs the attention of the court to a state of irretrievable breakdown at the presentation of the petition. When one comes to s. 2(1), one finds set out five different matrimonial situations or states of affairs: (a), (b), (c), (d), (e)—five paragraphs referring to five different situations. The situation with which this case is concerned is situation (a); that is a situation in which there has been the event of adultery and there is a state of affairs in which the petitioner finds it intolerable to live with the respondent. I will not analyse (c), (d), (e); but in each case it is one situation, though it may embrace several events. When, therefore, s. 2(1) speaks of 'the petitioner [satisfying] the court of one or more of the following facts', the word 'fact' is not a reference to an event: it is merely a draftsman's shorthand for 'factual situation'.

A situation of irretrievable breakdown can, and often exist when the petitioner truly finds life with the respondent intolerable, though for reasons other than her adultery. I agree therefore that s. 2(1)(a) does not require to be construed so as to introduce the words 'in consequence' after the word 'and'.

4.3.1.2 The respondent has behaved in such a way that the petitioner cannot reasonably be expected to live with the respondent

ASH v *ASH* [1972] 2 WLR 347 (FamD)

On April 28, 1971 the wife filed a petition for divorce on the ground that the marriage had irretrievably broken down under s. 2(1)(b) of the Divorce Reform Act 1969. By her petition the wife alleged that the husband had behaved in such a way that she could not reasonably be expected to live with him and gave particulars of specific acts of violence and of his intoxication. The husband by his answer admitted some of the acts of violence and also his bouts of drunkenness but declared that the marriage had not broken down irretrievably and did not cross pray for a decree. The petitioner, in evidence, asserted that the marriage had irretrievably broken down.

BAGNALL J: The respondent puts his defence to the petition in two ways. First, he says that notwithstanding the facts that he has admitted and that I have found, nevertheless it should not be held that he has behaved in such a way that the petitioner cannot reasonably be expected to live with him. Secondly, if that be wrong, he says that under s. 2(3) of the Divorce Reform Act 1969 I should conclude that I am satisfied on all the evidence that the marriage has not broken down irretrievably. If he satisfies me upon either of those two submissions, the prayer for dissolution in the petition must be rejected.

I must therefore first consider the true construction of paragraph (b) of s. 2(1) of the Divorce Reform Act 1969. That paragraph, which sets out one of the facts which have to be proved if a petitioner is to satisfy the court that the marriage has broken down irretrievably, reads as follows: 'that the respondent has behaved in such a way that the petitioner cannot reasonably be expected to live with the respondent.' The phrase 'cannot reasonably be expected to live with the respondent' necessarily poses an objective test, in contradistinction to the phrase 'the petitioner finds it intolerable to live with the respondent' in paragraph (a) of the subsection. So much is common ground. The question upon which I heard considerable argument was: what is the meaning of the word 'the petitioner' in paragraph (b)? Two possible constructions were canvassed: one which Mr Craig, who appeared for the petitioner and for whose assistance I am indebted, first submitted was that 'the petitioner' means the ordinary, reasonable spouse, looked at as a petitioner, the alternative which Mr Craig adopted after he had resiled from his first submission was that 'the petitioner' means the particular petitioner in the case under consideration. Faced with a choice between those two meanings, I have no hesitation in adopting the latter; that is the sense in which the words 'the petitioner' are used, so it seems to me, throughout the section and that is the sense which, apart from that, I think the words naturally bear.

In order, therefore, to answer the question whether the petitioner can or cannot reasonably be expected to live with the respondent, in my judgment, I have to consider not only the behaviour of the respondent as alleged and established in evidence, but the character, personality, disposition and behaviour of the petitioner. The general question may be expanded thus: can this petitioner, with his or her character and personality, with his or her faults and other attributes, good and bad, and having regard to his or her behaviour during the marriage, reasonably be expected to live with this respondent? It follows that if a respondent is seeking to resist a petition on the first ground upon which Mr Ash relies, he must in his answer plead and in his evidence establish the characteristics, faults, attributes, personality and behaviour on the part of the petitioner upon which he relies. Then, if I may give a few examples, it seems to me that a violent petitioner can reasonably be expected to live with a violent respondent; a petitioner who is addicted to drink can reasonably be expected to live with a respondent similarly addicted; a taciturn and morose spouse can reasonably be expected to live with a taciturn and morose partner, a flirtatious husband can reasonably be expected to live with a wife who is equally susceptible to the attractions of the other sex; and if each is equally bad, at any rate in similar respects, each can reasonably be expected to live with the other. This conclusion seems to me to be consonant with what have been said to be the objects of the 1969 legislation, which are not, in my view, simply to make divorce easier but, to quote from the Law Commission's Reform of the Grounds of Divorce (Cmnd. No. 3123) November 1966, p. 10, para. 15:

. . . (i) To buttress, rather than to undermine, the stability of marriage; and (ii) When, regrettably, a marriage has irretrievably broken down, to enable the empty legal shell to be destroyed with the maximum fairness, and the minimum bitterness, distress and humiliation.

I must therefore seek to apply that construction of the Act to the facts of this case. As I have indicated, it can be said of this petitioner that she was prepared to take advantage of the good and to enjoy prosperity, but has not been able to tolerate the disadvantages of the bad and of adversity. In general it seems to me that this also is a consideration to be taken into account when answering the question whether a petitioner can reasonably be expected to live with a respondent. However, apart from my clear impression that the petitioner showed a lack of understanding of the problems of the respondent, I have reached the conclusion that she has not shown herself to be of such a character and personality and her behaviour has not been such that I can conclude that she can reasonably be expected to live with the respondent. I therefore hold that the petitioner has satisfied the court of the fact in relation to this marriage set out in paragraph (b) of s. 2(1) of the Act.

I turn therefore to the respondent's second submission and ask myself the question: am I satisfied on all the evidence that the marriage has not broken down irretrievably?

The respondent says, and undoubtedly believes, that what is involved is a temporary difficulty attributable partly to his health and partly to his unemployment, and that if the marriage has broken down, nevertheless it has not broken down irretrievably. The petitioner is adamant that the marriage is at an end and states with force and conviction, both through her counsel and in the witness-box, that there is no possibility of her contemplating living with the respondent as his wife. As a matter of law, I do not think that this is sufficient, because if both parties are agreed that the marriage has not broken down irretrievably, then the question cannot arise for determination. The only circumstances in which the court will have to decide, under s. 2(3) of the Divorce Reform Act 1969, whether the marriage has broken down irretrievably must be when one of the spouses is asserting the affirmative of that proposition and the other is asserting the negative. Simple assertion either way, it seems to me, cannot suffice. What I have to do is to examine the whole of the evidence placed before me, including and giving not inconsiderable weight to the assertions of the parties, and make up my mind, quite generally, whether it can be said that in spite of the behaviour of the respondent, and the reaction to that behaviour of the petitioner, the marriage has not broken down irretrievably. In my opinion, in performing that general exercise on a survey of the evidence, only a general answer is appropriate and no useful purpose would be served by seeking to place quantitative weight on one consideration or another. Performing the best survey that I can of the evidence, and having regard to the personalities of the parties as displayed in the witness-box, I have concluded that I cannot be satisfied on all the evidence that the marriage has not broken down irretrievably and accordingly I must pronounce a decree nisi.

4.3.1.3 The parties have lived apart for a continuous period of two years preceding the presentation of the petition and the respondent consents

MOUNCER v *MOUNCER* [1972] 1 WLR 321 (FamD)

WRANGHAM J: In this case, a petition presented by leave of the court and transferred to this court to be consolidated with the existing proceedings, the husband prays for a divorce upon the ground that the marriage has broken down irretrievably, and relies on the allegations that the parties have lived apart for a continuous period of at least two years immediately preceding the presentation of the petition, and that the respondent wife agrees to a decree being granted.

The facts are not in, dispute. The parties were married on June 17, 1966, and there are two children in the family, a boy of five and a girl of four. By August 1969 the parties were on very bad terms, though they still shared a bedroom at a house at 49 Belmont Road, Sutton in Surrey. On August 13, 1969, the wife presented a petition for divorce on the ground of cruelty. Sometime towards the end of that month it was served upon the husband. He thereupon left 49 Belmont Road and for five weeks lived with his mother. An attempt at reconciliation was then made. On September 25, 1969, the parties went on holiday to Majorca for three weeks and at the end of the holiday they returned together to 49 Belmont Road. However, the reconciliation was not a success, and after three weeks, that is to say sometime in November 1969, the wife left the matrimonial bedroom. Thereafter she slept with the girl in one bedroom and the husband slept with the boy in the other. From then until May 12, 1971, when the husband left 49 Belmont Road, and went to live with his mother once more, the position remained unchanged. The wife and husband, though sleeping in separate rooms, usually took their meals together, cooked by the wife, often but not always in the company of one or both of the children. The cleaning of the house continued to be done by the wife, except upon Fridays and Saturdays when she went out to work all day, and on those occasions it was done by the husband. 49 Belmont Road has a dining room, a living room, two bedrooms, a kitchen and a bathroom. The evidence does not suggest that any of these rooms was particularly allocated to either husband or wife except to the extent that the husband and the boy slept in one room and the wife and the girl in the other; and husband and wife, when they respectively cleaned the house, made no distinction between one part of the house and the other. In his evidence the husband referred to one of the rooms (not his bedroom) As 'the room we lived in.' The wife, however, did no washing for the husband. He made his own arrangements for that to be done elsewhere. The only reason why the husband continued to live in this way at 49 Belmont Road was his wish to continue to live with and help to look after the children. Upon these facts it seems to me to be beyond dispute that husband, wife and children were all living in the same household.

The truth, in my opinion, is that s. 2(5) does not lay down two separate requirements at all. A clue to the true meaning of the subsection can be discovered from comparison with s. 3(6) which reads: 'References in this section to the parties living with each other shall be construed as references to their living with each other in the same household.' It is plain that in that subsection the words 'in the same household' are words of limitation. Not all living with each other is sufficient for the purposes of s. 3(6), only living with each other in the same household. And in my view the same applies to s. 2(5). What it means is that the husband and wife can be treated as living apart, even if they are living with each other, unless that living with each other is in the same household. It follows that in my judgment the draftsman of s. 2(5) was not providing for a case where parties live in the same household but do not live with each other. Indeed I do not think that there is such a case. In my view, the test to be applied to determine whether parties are living apart or not is unaltered by s. 2(5) or s. 3(6) which are really declaratory of the existing law upon this question. For these reasons I have come to the conclusion that it is not proved that these spouses were living apart between November 1969 and May 1971. On the contrary I think that during that period they were living with each other in the same household. The fact that they did this from the wholly admirable motive of caring properly for their children cannot change the result of what they did.

FULLER v FULLER [1973] 1 WLR 730 (CA)

LORD DENNING MR: This case raises the meaning of the words 'living apart' in the new Divorce Reform Act 1969. Section 2(1)(e) says that a marriage is to be held to have broken down irretrievably if 'the parties to the marriage have lived apart for a continuous period of at least five years immediately preceding the presentation of the petition.' Section 2(5) says:

> For the purposes of this Act a husband and wife shall be treated as living apart unless they are living with each other in the same household.

Husband and wife were married on May 25, 1942, more than 30 years ago. He was 28 and she was 18. They have two daughters, born in 1943 and 1951. They lived at 388 King Henry's Drive, New Addington, Croydon. They separated in 1964. The wife left the husband, taking with her the two daughters. She went to live with another man, a Mr Penfold, at 164 South Norwood Hill, South Norwood. The husband remained in the matrimonial home. His wife lived with Mr Penfold as his wife. She slept with him and became known as Mrs Penfold.

Four years later, in 1968, the husband fell ill. He had a coronary thrombosis and was in hospital. He went back for a little while to what had been the matrimonial home, living on his own. He was taken ill again and again he went to hospital. The doctor explained to the wife, who was now living as Mrs Penfold, that the husband could not live on his own again; the main valve of his heart had collapsed; he would only be able to do light office work if ever he worked again; he had only about a year to live.

So in October 1968 the husband was discharged from hospital. Then events took place which raise the problem. The husband went to live at 164 South Norwood Hill, where Mr Penfold was, with the wife now living as Mrs Penfold, and a daughter. The husband, if I may still use that word, went and became a lodger in the house. Mr Penfold and the wife still continued to live together in one bedroom. The husband just slept in the back bedroom. He got his own cup of tea in the morning himself. In the evening he came back to have a meal with the family. On Saturday he was out all day. The wife gave him food and he ate his meals with some of the others in the house. She did the washing. He paid like a lodger at first £5 a week, and later £7 a week. In spite of the doctor's gloomy forecast, he is still alive.

Four years passed in this way. Then in April 1972 the wife petitioned for a divorce on the ground of living apart for five years. The husband was only too willing to recognise this. He signed a form of consent. But at the hearing the judge held that he had no jurisdiction to grant a divorce because he thought that when the husband came back to the house, he and his wife were not living apart.

In this case we have to consider the physical relationship of the parties. From 1964 to 1968 the parties were undoubtedly living apart. The wife was living with the other man as the other man's wife in that household, and the husband was separate in his household. From 1968 to 1972 the husband came back to live in the same house but not as a husband. He was to all intents and purposes a lodger in the house. Subsection (5) says they are to be treated as living apart 'unless they are living with each other in the same household.' I think the words 'with each other' mean 'living with each other as husband and wife.' In this case the parties were not living with each other in that sense. The wife was living with Mr Penfold as his wife. The husband was living in the house. as a lodger. It is impossible to say that husband and wife were or are living with each other in the same household. It is very different from *Mouncer* v *Mouncer* [1972] 1 WLR 321 where the husband and wife were living with the children in the same household—as husband and wife normally do—but were not having sexual intercourse together. That is not sufficient to constitute 'living apart.' I do not doubt the correctness of that decision. But the present case is very different. I think the judge put too narrow and limited a construction on the Act. I would allow the appeal and pronounce the decree nisi of divorce.

4.4   Relationship Between the Ground for Divorce and the Facts

BUFFERY v BUFFERY [1988] 2 FLR 365 (CA)

MAY LJ: This was a suit based upon the provisions of s. 1(2)(b) of the Matrimonial Causes Act 1973. The judge found, and there is no dispute, that the marriage had irretrievably broken down. The wife, however, contends that in considering whether the court was satisfied of the requirement in subs. (2)(b) the judge below applied the wrong test. It was submitted that had he applied the right test he ought to have granted a decree, or alternatively that the matter should go back to be reheard.

The parties were married in July 1964. They are now respectively 51 and 62 years of age. There are three children, all of them girls. They are now grown up and employed; two live at home. Although, when the matter came before the recorder, the husband and wife were still living under the same roof, we understand that recently the situation has altered to the extent that, at any rate temporarily, the wife has moved out of the matrimonial home and is living elsewhere. The two girls apparently still remain at home . . . it is convenient to deal with a preliminary question which arose in the course of argument. In his judgment the recorder referred to the cause of the irretrievable breakdown and held that this could not be blamed on the husband. It was submitted on behalf of the wife, and not contended otherwise on behalf of the husband, that the requirements in s. 1(1) and (2) of the 1973 Act are to be read disjunctively; that is to say that there is no requirement, on a proper construction of the relevant statutory provision, that the behaviour of the husband complained of must be a cause of the irretrievable breakdown before the statutory requirements are satisfied. I agree that they are separate requirements. First, that the marriage has irretrievably broken down and, secondly, that the court is satisfied of one or more of the facts set out in the paragraphs in subs. (2). I do not think that point needs further elaboration.

In asking himself whether or not the wife had made out her case for a decree of dissolution, in my opinion the recorder applied considerations and tests which might have been apposite if he had been considering a case of constructive desertion or cruelty in the old days. But on the authorities this is not the correct test in law under the new statutory provisions. In the course of his judgment the recorder said:

> . . . I have to bear in mind that the conduct alleged against the [husband] must be grave and weighty and that conduct must be such that the [wife] cannot reasonably be expected to continue to live with the [husband].

Later, he said:

> . . . I cannot find that his conduct in respect of those matters should be regarded as gross or grave and weighty.

The same theme was repeated five lines down the page, where the recorder concluded:

> . . . the cause of the breakdown cannot really be levelled at the [husband] in the sense that he has been guilty of misbehaviour of a grave and weighty nature.

It may be that particular conduct can be stigmatized as so grave that it is behaviour after which the petitioner cannot reasonably be expected to live with the respondent. But for my part, with Dunn J in that case, on a proper reading of the statute and an assessment of the facts of a given case, the gravity or otherwise of the conduct complained of is of itself immaterial. What has to be asked, as will appear from the judgment in *O'Neill* [1975] 1 WLR 1118, is whether the behaviour is such that the petitioner cannot reasonably be expected to live with the respondent. If it is grave, the answer is probably no.

Thus one looks to this husband and this wife, or vice versa, but one also looks at what is reasonable. That is the point referred to by Roskill LJ in his judgment in the same case, at p. 1125, where he adopted as correct the test which Dunn J had applied in the *Livingstone-Stallard* [1974] Fam 47 case in a part of his judgment which I have not quoted. Roskill LJ said:

> I would respectfully adopt as correct what Dunn J said in *Livingstone-Stallard*, at p. 54:
>
> > 'Coming back to my analogy of a direction to a jury, I ask myself the question: Would any right-thinking person come to the conclusion that this husband has behaved in such a way that this wife cannot reasonably be expected to live with him, taking into account the whole of the circumstances and the characters and personalities of the parties.'

Then, towards the end of his judgment, the recorder said:

> Although the [wife] has established that the marriage has irretrievably broken down, the cause of the breakdown cannot really be levelled at the [husband] in the sense that he has been guilty of misbehaviour of a grave and weighty nature. The [wife] has been quite candid about this; when asked she said the marriage has broken down; we cannot communicate; we have nothing in common—and there lies, in my view, the crux of the matter. The situation is that neither is really at fault.

Reading the judgment of the recorder in full, I conclude that in so far as any dissension over money matters was concerned, although the husband had been somewhat insensitive, nevertheless this did not constitute sufficient behaviour within the relevant statutory provision. In truth, what has happened in this marriage is the fault of neither party; they have just grown apart. They cannot communicate. They have nothing in common and there lies, as the recorder said, the crux of the matter.

It was submitted that if the matter went back to the recorder he could make various findings on the evidence about the sensitivity, for instance, of the wife in relation to these matters and various further findings of fact about the nature and extent of the husband's behaviour complained of. I, for my part, do not think he could. He heard all the evidence and the conclusion to which he came was that nobody was really at fault here, except that both had grown apart. In those circumstances, in my judgment, clearly the wife failed to make out her case under s. 1(2)(b), although she satisfied the recorder that the marriage had broken down irretrievably. I do not think any advantage would be gained by sending this matter back for a retrial. The matter was fully investigated and the recorder made the findings to which I have referred. In those circumstances, I would reach the same conclusion as did the recorder, namely that the petition should be dismissed, but for reasons different from those relied on by him, having regard to the authorities to which I have referred.

4.5   Which Facts are most Commonly Used?

Divorce Statistics, 1994

Fig 3   Divorces by fact proven, 1994, England and Wales

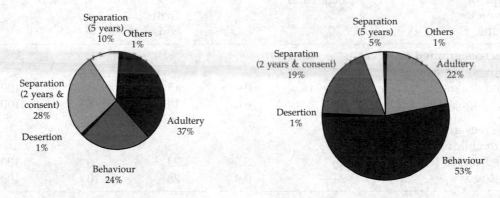

Divorces granted to husbands (44,914)   Divorces granted to wives (112, 407)

71 per cent of divorces were granted to wives where the most frequent grounds given were behaviour (53 per cent) and adultery (22 per cent). Of those granted to the husband adultery (37 per cent) and separation (2 years and consent) (28 per cent) were the most frequently given.

OPCS Updates, November 1995 and February 1996

Table 1   Divorces by party to whom granted and presence of children in family

Thousands

Type of divorcing couple	Party to whom granted			
	Wife	Husband	Both parties	Total
with children aged under 16	68	21	0.3	88
with no children aged under 16	45	24	0.1	69
All divorcing couples	112	45	0.4	158

Note: Table excludes annulments. Components may not sum to totals because of rounding.

71 per cent of all divorces awarded to a single party were granted to wives (Table 1). 56 per cent of all divorces were to couples with children aged under 16 (at the time of petition in their family).

Table 2   Divorces* by fact proven, party to whom granted, and presence of children in family

Percentages

Type of divorcing couple	Fact proven					
	Adultery	Unreasonable behaviour	Desertion	2 years separation (with consent)	5 years' separation	Total
Decrees granted to wives						
with children						
aged under 16	22	60	0.4	15	3	100
all couples	22	54	0.6	19	5	100
Decrees granted to husbands						
with children						
aged under 16	46	26	0.5	22	6	100
all couples	37	24	0.9	28	10	100

* Single fact divorces granted to a single party.

A slightly higher proportion of divorces were granted for either adultery or unreasonable behaviour amongst divorcing couples with children in their family compared with all couples. This finding applies irrespective of whether the husband or the wife was granted the divorce (Table 2).

The Law Commission, Facing the Future: A Discussion Paper on the Ground for Divorce (Law Com No. 170)

Use of the five facts

2.10   Since the beginning of 1971, when the 1969 Act came into force, the number of divorces each year has more than doubled. In the early years after the reform, this was largely accounted for by reliance on the new separation provisions, which enabled marriages which had broken down many years earlier to be dissolved. However, by 1986 74 per cent of all decrees were based on adultery or behaviour. Studies by Gwynn Davis and Mervyn Murch, of the Socio-Legal Centre for Family Studies at the University of Bristol, and by John Haskey, of the Office of Population Censuses and Surveys, into the use of these facts have provided important evidence about the operation of divorce law in practice.

2.11   Perhaps the most marked trend discernible from the statistics is the increased use of the behaviour fact. Although this trend is apparent among both men and women petitioners, behaviour is predominantly used by women. In 1986, 89 per cent of behaviour decrees were granted to wives, compared to 72 per cent of all decrees; almost half the divorces granted to women were based on behaviour, compared to approximately a quarter on adultery and a quarter on separation. Haskey's study has shown that the behaviour fact is more likely to be used by those in lower socio-economic classes whereas adultery and separation are more frequently used among the middle classes. A correlation has also been found between the age at divorce and fact used. Thus, those using five years' separation tend to be the oldest and those using two years' separation the youngest. However, among those with dependent children behaviour is dominant among 'young' divorces. Generally, those with dependent children are more likely to use the behaviour and adultery facts.

2.12   Those researchers who have interviewed parties or looked at solicitors' files have concluded that these phenomena do not necessarily indicate that particular types of marital misconduct are more prevalent among particular groups. Rather, the evidence suggests that behaviour and adultery are frequently used because of the need to obtain a quick divorce. In particular, it is noteworthy that the separation grounds are least used by those petitioners who are least able to effect a separation—women, in lower social classes, and particularly those with dependent children. Davis and Murch found that 28 per cent of those petitioning on the basis of behaviour and 7 per cent of those petitioning on the basis of adultery were still living together when the petition was filed. These same groups are also most likely to need to have ancillary issues relating to custody, maintenance and housing determined quickly. This is most likely to occur once the petition has been filed.

2.13   The choice between adultery and behaviour seems to depend on social mores and on the state of the relations between the parties, as much as upon their marital history. Thus, adultery would seem to carry less stigma particularly among the middle classes and is more likely to be employed than behaviour where the parting was consensual or at least amicable. Behaviour petitions seem much less likely to have been discussed between the parties or their solicitors in advance and sometimes take respondents completely by surprise.

4.6   Bars to Divorce and Stopping the Clock

MATRIMONIAL CAUSES ACT 1973

2.   Supplemental provision as to facts raising presumption of breakdown

(1)   One party to a marriage shall not be entitled to rely for the purposes of section 1(2)(a) above on adultery committed by the other if, after it became known to him that the other had committed that adultery, the parties have lived with each other for a period exceeding, or periods together exceeding, six months.

(2)   Where the parties to a marriage have lived with each other after it became known to one party that the other had committed adultery, but subsection (1) above does not apply, in any proceedings for divorce in which the petitioner relies on that adultery the fact that the parties have lived with each other after that time shall be disregarded in determining for the purposes of section 1(2)(a) above whether the petitioner finds it intolerable to live with the respondent.

(3)   Where in any proceedings for divorce the petitioner alleges that the respondent has behaved in such a way that the petitioner cannot reasonably be expected to live with him, but the parties to the marriage have lived with each other for a period or periods after the date of the occurrence of the final incident relied on by the petitioner and held by the court to support his allegation, that fact shall be disregarded in determining for the purposes of section 1(2)(b) above whether the petitioner cannot reasonably be expected to live with the respondent if the length of that period or of those periods together was six months or less.

(4)   For the purposes of section 1(2)(c) above the court may treat a period of desertion as having continued at a time when the deserting party was incapable of continuing the necessary intention if the evidence before the court is such that, had that party not been so incapable, the court would have inferred that his desertion continued at that time.

(5)   In considering for the purposes of section 1(2) above whether the period for which the respondent has deserted the petitioner or the period for which the parties to a marriage have lived apart has been continuous, no account shall be taken of any one period (not exceeding six months) or of any two or more periods (not exceeding six months in all) during which the parties resumed living with each other, but no period during which the parties lived with each other shall count as part of the period of desertion, or of the period for which the parties to the marriage lived apart, as the case may be.

(6)   For the purposes of section 1(2)(d) and (e) above and this section a husband and wife shall be treated as living apart unless they are living with each other in the same household, and references in this section to the parties to a marriage living with each other shall be construed as references to their living with each other in the same household.

(7)   Provision shall be made by rules of court for the purpose of ensuring that where in pursuance of section 1(2)(d) above the petitioner alleges that the respondent consents to a decree being granted the respondent has been given such information as will enable him to understand the consequences to him of his consenting to a decree being granted and the steps which he must take to indicate that he consents to the grant of a decree.

MATRIMONIAL CAUSES ACT 1973

5. Refusal of decree in five year separation cases on ground of grave hardship to respondent

(1)   The respondent to a petition for divorce in which the petitioner alleges five years' separation may oppose the grant of a decree on the ground that the dissolution of the marriage will result in grave financial or other hardship to him and that it would in all the circumstances be wrong to dissolve the marriage.

(2)   Where the grant of a decree is opposed by virtue of this section, then—

(a)   if the court finds that the petitioner is entitled to rely in support of his petition on the fact of five years' separation and makes no such finding as to any other fact mentioned in section 1(2) above, and

(b)   if apart from this section the court would grant a decree on the petition, the court shall consider all the circumstances, including the conduct of the parties to the marriage and the interests of those parties and of any children or other persons concerned, and if of opinion that the dissolution of the marriage will result in grave financial or other hardship to the respondent and that it would in all the circumstances be wrong to dissolve the marriage it shall dismiss the petition.

(3)   For the purposes of this section hardship shall include the loss of the chance of acquiring any benefit which the respondent might acquire if the marriage were not dissolved.

10. Proceedings after decree nisi: special protection for respondent in separation cases

(1)   Where in any case the court has granted a decree of divorce on the basis of a finding that the petitioner was entitled to rely in support of his petition on the fact of two years' separation coupled with the respondent's consent to a decree being granted and has made no such finding as to any other fact mentioned in section 1(2) above, the court may, on an application made by the respondent at any time before the decree is made absolute, rescind the decree if it is satisfied that the petitioner misled the respondent (whether intentionally or unintentionally) about any matter which the respondent took into account in deciding to give his consent.

(2)   The following provisions of this section apply where—

(a)   the respondent to a petition for divorce in which the petitioner alleged two years' or five years' separation coupled, in the former case, with the respondent's consent to a decree being granted, has applied to the court for consideration under subsection (3) below of his financial position after the divorce; and

(b)   the court has granted a decree on the petition on the basis of a finding that the petitioner was entitled to rely in support of his petition on the fact of two years' or five years' separation (as the case may be) and has made no such finding as to any other fact mentioned in section 1(2) above.

(3)   The court hearing an application by the respondent under subsection (2) above shall consider all the circumstances including the age, health, conduct, earning capacity, financial resources, and financial obligations of each of the parties, and the financial position of the respondent as, having regard to the divorce, it is likely to be after the death of the petitioner should the petitioner die first; and, subject to subsection (4) below, the court shall not make the decree absolute unless it is satisfied—

(a)   that the petitioner should not be required to make any financial provision for the respondent, or

(b)   that the financial provision made by the petitioner for the respondent is reasonable and fair or the best that can be made in the circumstances.

(4)   The court may if it thinks fit make the decree absolute notwithstanding the requirements of subsection (3) above if—

(a)   it appears that there are circumstances making it desirable that the decree should be made absolute without delay, and

(b)   the court has obtained a satisfactory undertaking from the petitioner that he will make such financial provision for the respondent as the court may approve.

LE MARCHANT v LE MARCHANT [1977] 1 WLR 559

ORMROD LJ: This is an appeal from the granting by Purchas J of decree nisi to the husband under the provisions of s. 1(2)(e) of the Matrimonial Causes Act 1973. Purchas J dealt with the case in Winchester on circuit on March 26, 1976.

The case has followed I think a course which can only be described as unsatisfactory in almost all possible respects. The husband's petition originally alleged separation for five years from 1968. At the hearing there seemed to be some doubt as to whether the actual separation could be dated back as early as 1968, but there was no doubt that the separation had certainly begun by 1970, so as the matter was before the judge in March 1976 he gave leave to file a second petition to make sure that there was no problem about the five-year separation.

Much the most important paragraph in her answer is paragraph 9, which reads: 'That if a dissolution is granted the respondent will lose her pension rights under the Post Office employees' pension scheme.' She said in effect that that would cause her, within the meaning of section 5 of the Act of 1973, grave financial hardship. Prima facie, one would suppose there could be no doubt as to that particularly when it emerges, as it does, that this is what we can now call an 'index-linked pension,' or for the moment it is, so that she has a high degree of protection against inflation, and it is therefore a very valuable asset to her. So when the case came before the judge, he had nothing before him except the evidence that she would lose this pension and the details of the pension position were gone into by him. I think it can be shortly stated that a document was put before him which sets out what was then known as to the pension position. It showed that, assuming the husband retired on the date of the letter, which was shortly before the hearing, he would under scheme A get a pension of £2,016 a year and a lump sum of £6,050, off which £2,653 had to be taken in respect of the widows' and children's pension scheme, leaving him with a lump sum payment of £3,397. The alternative scheme B offered him a slightly higher pension and a slightly higher lump sum but it also transpired that the widow's pension, at that stage, would have been about £1,300 a year, index-linked. That was before the judge. No precise offer was made by the husband in the proceedings before the judge. In my judgment the right approach to this sort of problem is that adopted by Cumming-Bruce J in *Parker* v *Parker* [1972] Fam 116, 119 et seq. The right way to approach these cases is as set out there, namely, that the pleadings should allege by way of answer—because the onus is, in the first place, on the respondent to show grave financial or other hardship—the grave financial or other hardship relied upon. The reply should meet that allegation, if it is possible to meet it, with sufficient detail. If the pleadings are in order, it is then quite simple to ask for and obtain discovery in the ordinary way which will reveal and produce all the relevant financial information which the court will require. That was not done in this case because, as I have already said, not even the letters referring to the offers were produced, and so the judge was faced with a lot of bits and pieces of information about pensions, and the wife, I suppose, was in the position of not knowing at all clearly at the hearing below where she stood, but her case before the judge, I think, appears quite clearly from his judgment. She was saying that what she was concerned about was that she should be adequately protected from the loss of her pension rights by reason of a divorce.

It would be quite wrong to approach this kind of case on the footing that the wife is entitled to be compensated pound for pound for what she will lose in consequence of the divorce. She has to show, not that she will lose something by being divorced, but that she will suffer grave financial hardship, which is quite another matter altogether. It is quite plain that, prima facie, the loss of the pension, which is an index-linked pension in the order of £1,300 a year at the moment, is quite obviously grave financial hardship in the circumstances of a case like this unless it can be in some way mitigated. The judge, however, did not approach the case in this way. He said that s. 5 of the Act of 1973 had to be read with s. 10. Section 10 is the section which provides that before a decree nisi is made absolute in cases such as the present, the court is required at the request of the wife to investigate the financial position, and not to make the decree absolute until it is satisfied either that the petitioning husband should not be required to make any financial provision for the wife, or that the financial provision made by him is reasonable and fair or (and these are the words which cause the trouble) 'the best that can be made in the circumstances.' So, as Mr Jackson says, s. 10 offers an elusive or, perhaps better, an unreliable protection to a wife placed in the position in which this wife is placed. The marriage would have been dissolved by the decree nisi, there would have been therefore a finding of fact that she has not suffered grave financial hardship in consequence of the decree and she would then have to do the best she could under s. 10.

It is also right to point out that there are many cases, and this is one, in which the powers of the court, extensive as they are under ss. 23 and 24 as well as s. 10, are not wide enough to enable the court to carry out by order various things which a petitioner husband can do voluntarily, even if compelled to do it voluntarily, so s. 10 is not an adequate substitute. The judge, in a sentence, took the view that if he could see from the husband's financial position that he would be able one way or the other to alleviate sufficiently the financial hardship falling on the wife as a result of the loss of her pension, that was good enough. In the view of this court, that is not right. The right way to approach this problem is Cumming-Bruce J's approach in *Parker* v *Parker* [1972] Fam 116 that is, that the answer should set up a prima facie case of financial hardship, that the petition should be dismissed unless the petitioner can meet that answer in his reply by putting forward a proposal which is acceptable to the court as reasonable in all the circumstances, which is sufficient to remove the element of grave financial hardship which otherwise would lead to the dismissal of the petition.

One of the extraordinary features in this case is that the husband never, as far as I can make out, actually put forward until the last possible minute—that is a few moments ago in this court—any reasonable proposal to mitigate the financial hardship.

In my judgment the true analysis of the case is this: at the conclusion of the hearing before the judge the wife had plainly established a prima facie case of grave financial hardship. The husband had not started, before the judge, to rebut that defence and consequently the judge ought, in my judgment, to have dismissed this petition or, at any rate, to be practical, he should have adjourned the case and told the husband that he would dismiss the petition unless some sensible offer was forthcoming to relieve the financial hardship on the wife which would flow from the granting of a divorce. I find it very difficult to understand why the judge took the view he did, because it would be difficult to see how any court could order this husband to make the necessary provision although he can do it, as it is now clear, voluntarily. Secondly, the judge for some reason which I am bound to say I do not understand, ordered the wife to pay the costs of the proceedings below; although she was legally aided, such costs were not to be taxed until further order, which left her vulnerable to being ordered to pay the costs out of any capital provision which might be made for her hereafter.

RUKAT v *RUKAT* [1975] 2 WLR 201 (CA)

MEGAW LJ: This is an appeal from an order of Hollings J made on February 22, 1974, by which he granted a decree nisi of divorce to the petitioner husband. The respondent wife in those proceedings appeals against that decree nisi of divorce and asks that this court should set it aside. The issue which arises on the appeal stems from provisions of the Divorce Reform Act 1969, now included in the Matrimonial Causes Act 1973. It is desirable that I should at the outset read the two provisions of the Divorce Reform Act 1969 which are relevant to the appeal. Section 1 provides:

After the commencement of this Act the sole ground on which a petition for divorce may be presented to the court by either party to a marriage shall be that the marriage has broken down irretrievably.

Section 2(1) provides:

The court hearing a petition for divorce shall not hold the marriage to have broken down irretrievably unless the petitioner satisfies the court of one or more of the following facts, that is to say . . .

Then there are set out paragraphs (a) to (e); and paragraph (e), which is the relevant paragraph here, reads:

. . . that the parties to the marriage have lived apart for a continuous period of at least five years immediately preceding the presentation of the petition.

Then comes s. 4 (now s. 5 of the Matrimonial Causes Act 1973) . . .

I shall deal immediately with the only question of construction of the Act which has been raised. I can deal with it independently of the facts, to which I shall refer in a moment. Mr Seufrert, for the wife, with the leave of this court, has amended the grounds set out in his notice of appeal to include the ground that, on the true construction of s. 4(1) and (2) of the Act of 1969. the adjective 'grave' in the phrase 'grave financial or other hardship' applies only to *financial* and not to *other* hardship. That submission was not put forward in the court below. Hollings J was invited to deal and did deal with the matter on the basis that, on the true construction of s. 4, the adjective 'grave' applied to 'other' hardship as well as to 'financial' hardship. For myself, I am satisfied that there is no doubt whatever, on the true construction of the section, that the adjective 'grave' should be treated as applying, not merely to financial but also to other hardship.

Hollings J, in dealing with the wife's evidence, accepted fully and entirely her honesty and sincerity as a witness. He paid high tribute more than once to the wife. It is sufficient for that purpose, I think, if I read a passage which appears in the transcript of the judgment:

Substantially in every case where there is a conflict between the evidence of the petitioner and the respondent I prefer the evidence of the respondent, Mrs Rukat. While I am dealing with this aspect let me say this. I have found her throughout this case a most sincere woman who has quite evidently not only been seeking to tell me the truth about the facts but also seeking to tell the truth about her emotions and the effect of various matters on her and her friends and relations.

On the basis of that evidence, which I have tried to summarise in that way and which the judge summarised much more fully, what conclusions did the judge come to that are relevant on the question of 'grave other hardship'? As I understand his judgment, the conclusion to which he came was, in effect, 'I fully accept the sincerity of the wife. I fully accept that at the moment she feels that if this decree of divorce were made absolute she would not feel it right or possible to go back to Sicily because of the attitude that would be adopted towards her there.' The judge had accepted, as I understand it, that that is an honest statement of her attitude, reflected in the answer I have read that she would die in England. On the other hand, the judge has held that the evidence as to the reality of those fears or apprehensions is, if I may put it this way, hopelessly weak. There is really in the evidence no basis or substance for the suggestion, either that anybody in Palermo or Sicily would be likely to know about the decree of divorce or that, if they did know, after she had explained that this was a decree which involved no fault on her part whatever, these fears or apprehensions that she had as to the social conditions that would apply in Palermo could really have any substance. Moreover, the judge has taken the view that there is no reason why there should be substantially any greater hardship or inconvenience or social distress to the wife in respect of the decree of divorce, if it be made, than there has been over all the years in relation to what must have been known to anybody in Palermo who had any interest in the wife: that is, that she has in fact for many many years been living apart from her husband: he in England, she in Sicily. The judge, I think, was entitled on the evidence, such as it was, to come to the conclusion that there would be no substantial increase in any social distress by reason of the one as compared with the other, and that is even on the assumption that the fact that the wife had been divorced became known in Italy. But why should it become known? We have here no evidence whatever as to whether or not this English decree would, as a matter of Italian law, be given effect to in Italian law and, therefore, whether there would be any legal consequences of any sort on the status of one who was living in Italy. Moreover, as appears from the evidence which I have read, the wife, according to her own evidence, which the judge has accepted as entirely truthful, has sought to conceal from her parents over all these 25 years the fact that something had gone wrong with the marriage. There is no reason offered in the evidence why that concealment, which has been with some degree of success applied to the fact of separation, should not equally be applied to the fact of the divorce. The wife's evidence (I need not read the passage again) as to what she would feel obliged to do, if a decree of divorce were pronounced, in relation to telling her parents, is indeed very weak and, if I may say so, unconvincing. By that I do not mean that she was being untruthful; but no reason was offered why she would really feel it necessary to distress her parents—if it was going to distress them—by telling them of the divorce, or why she should make it known to other persons, when she had not felt it necessary to disclose to them, over all the 25 years, that the marriage had factually broken down by separation.

I regard the conclusions expressed by the judge as being conclusions to which he was most clearly entitled to come upon the evidence, and on the basis of those conclusions he was entitled as a matter of law to express the result which he ultimately did express: first, that there is here no 'grave other hardship' established; and, second, that, even if there were, it would not be right, in the circumstances of the case to refuse a decree. Accordingly, I would dismiss the appeal.

4.7   The Divorce Process

The Law Commission, Facing the Future: A Discussion Paper on the Ground for Divorce (Law Com No. 170)

2.8   The introduction of the special procedure has undoubtedly had an effect upon the way in which the substantive law operates. The Booth Committee found that:

> . . . the ability of the court to carry out its statutory duty to inquire into the facts alleged is greatly circumscribed. In the great majority of cases the court is quite simply in no position to make findings of fact or, in a case based on behaviour, to evaluate the effect of the respondent's behaviour on the petitioner. In reality, the registrar can do no more than read the few documents before him.

This conclusion would seem to support the view that registrars act as little more than 'rubber stamps'. However, there is a dearth of statistical or other information about the progress of cases through the special procedure; the number of cases in which the registrar refuses his certificate on the basis that he is not satisfied that the petitioner has sufficiently proved the contents of the petition and is entitled to a decree; the number of cases in which the registrar asks for further particulars and which then go before him more than once; or the number of cases which the registrar adjourns to be heard by a judge in open court. A recent small-scale study of solicitors' files suggests that there may be more double handling of cases by registrars than the 'rubber stamp' image might suggest, but that the registrars' queries are more concerned with technical than substantive matters and thus only operate to delay decrees. If this is the case, then such queries and hearings would seem to serve little purpose and their expense difficult to justify. Hence the Booth Committee has recommended that the special duty of inquiry on a divorce court should be removed and the court should merely be required to be satisfied on the evidence, as in other civil cases.

2.9   In the view of some commentators, the procedural changes of the 1970s were 'more radical departures than was the introduction of irretrievable breakdown as the sole ground of divorce'. In practice, the ability of the court to conduct a proper inquiry in the course of an oral hearing in an undefended case has always been strictly limited. The close interrelationship between substance and procedure in divorce law was stressed in the Booth Report. The Committee clearly felt that the present law, by retaining the fault element, made it more difficult for them to make procedural proposals which would mitigate the intensity of disputes and encourage settlements (as they had been asked to do) and that early review of the ground for divorce would be welcome. Nonetheless, many of their recommendations, if implemented, would have a profound effect on the operation of the substantive law. These will be referred to in this paper as they arise.

4.8   End of Chapter Assessment Questions

1.   Joyce and Ralph married ten years ago and approached their relationship on an 'open marriage' basis. Consequently both partners have had casual relationships outside the marriage. Last year Ralph began to have a change of heart, and decided that he would not participate in any such casual relationships. Joyce did not concur with this decision and has continued to act in the same way, much to Ralph's disgust. Recently he learnt that for the last seven months Joyce has been having an affair with Anne-Marie.

Advise him on his rights to divorce. Is there any way that Joyce could prevent it?

2.   Peggy and Tony married 15 months ago and cohabited for two months before Tony left the matrimonial home. He has recently contacted Peggy and asked to give the marriage a second chance. Advise Peggy how this would affect her potential rights to seek a divorce.

3.   Evaluate the effectiveness of the divorce provisions in the Matrimonial Causes Act 1973.

4.9   End of Chapter Assessment Outline Answers

1.   As with the answers to the questions in **Chapter 3**, you should always remember who you are advising. Ralph is your client in this scenario. He is seeking a divorce and for the purposes of this question you need to consider the divorce legislation under the Matrimonial Causes Act 1973.

To commence, you would have to advise him that there is only one ground for divorce under s. 1(1) — that the marriage has broken down irretrievably. From the facts in the question, it would appear that as far as Ralph is concerned the marriage has broken down.

However, you would need to advise him that to prove irretrievable breakdown, one or more of five facts will need to be proven too. It would be unnecessary to recite all the facts under s. 1(2), you should focus on the relevant ones. In this case, s. 1(2)(a) or (b) would seem to be the most appropriate to discuss.

Section 1(2)(a) deals with the respondent's adultery and the fact that the petitioner finds it intolerable to live with the respondent. Ralph and Joyce have previously enjoyed an open marriage. Whilst this constitutes adultery, it would be questionable whether Ralph found it intolerable to live with Joyce. As you should have commented, the fact of intolerability is not related to the adultery.

Also mention that it would not be possible for Ralph to cite Joyce's current relationship with Anne-Marie as being adulterous. For adultery to take place the intercourse must be between a male and female one of whom is not a party to the marriage. Clearly therefore a lesbian relationship will not count as adultery. The date when Joyce last had intercourse with a male partner would need to be identified, and also whether or not Ralph knew about it. This refers to the content of s. 2(1). Under this section a party to a marriage cannot rely on the other's adultery if, knowing that the adultery has occurred, they have lived together for a period of six months after the last act of adultery.

Given that the success of a petition under s. 1(2)(a) seems in doubt, the fact in s. 1(2)(b) may be more applicable. Under this fact the breakdown can be shown by proving that the respondent has behaved in such a way that the petitioner cannot reasonably be expected to live with them. The fact that Ralph has now changed his opinions as to open marriages may be sufficient, together with the continued actions of Joyce with her lesbian partner. The question you may like to pose is whether it is unreasonable to expect Ralph to live with Joyce, using the authority of *Ash*, since he too has had relationships outside the marriage. Would it make a difference that Joyce's new partner is female if Ralph has always had heterosexual relationships in the past? The fact of continued 'living together' could detract from the reasonableness of cohabitation, but as Ralph is seeking to take action shortly after discovering the facts of the relationship, this is unlikely.

If Joyce wished to prevent the divorce, she would have to rely on s. 5 or s. 10 of the 1973 Act. The former acts as a power to refuse a decree of divorce, and s. 10 acts as a delaying tactic. Joyce unfortunately will be unable to avail herself of these provisions, since they relate purely to the separation facts in s. 1(2)(d) and (e).

2.   In this situation you are focussing on the separation facts, and also the reconciliation provisions of s. 2(5). If Peggy is contemplating a divorce, there are two facts which she could be advised to apply under in future. The first would be desertion under s. 1(2)(c) for a period of two years. To be successful there must be no just cause for Tony's leaving the matrimonial home, and Peggy must have been willing for the marriage to continue. If at this stage she refuses to accept Tony's return, he could argue that it is Peggy that is now deserting rather than himself! A better option would be two years' separation with consent. The difficulty would be, not in proving that the couple have lived apart, but in getting consent, if Tony continues to request a reconciliation. If consent is not forthcoming, then the only option would be to wait for a total of five years.

Insofar as the wish to reconcile, the MCA does attempt to promote the saving of marriages by permitting trial reconciliations, without necessarily affecting the fact that is to be relied upon. Under s. 2(5) where desertion or separation is to be relied upon 'no account shall be taken of any one period (not exceeding six months) or of any two or more periods (not exceeding six months in total) during which the parties resumed living with each other, but no period . . . shall count as part of the period for which the parties to the marriage lived apart'. Therefore, if the reconciliation is not successful, Peggy will still be able to rely on s. 1(2)(d) but will not be able to count the period of reconciliation as part of the two year separation.

CHAPTER FIVE

THE FAMILY LAW ACT 1996 AND DIVORCE

5.1 Why the Change?

The Law Commission, Family Law: The Ground for Divorce (Law Com No. 192)

Criticisms of the present law and practice

2.7 The criticisms of the present law, and in particular its failure to live up to its original objectives, were set out at length in Facing the Future. There is no need for us to repeat them here, but we should like to draw attention to the features which seem to us most objectionable. These, not only in our view but also in that of our respondents, add up to a formidable case for reform.

(i) It is confusing and misleading

2.8 There is a considerable gap between theory and practice, which can on lead to confusion and lack of respect for the law. Indeed, some would call it downright dishonest. There are several aspects to this. First, the law tells couples that the only ground for divorce is irretrievable breakdown, which apparently does not involve fault. But next it provides that this can only be shown by one of five 'facts', three of which apparently do involve fault. There are several recent examples of divorces being refused despite the fact that it was clear to all concerned that the marriage had indeed irretrievably broken down. The hardship and pain involved for both parties can be very great.

2.9 Secondly, the fact which is alleged in order to prove the breakdown need not have any connection with the real reason why the marriage broke down. The parties may, for example, have separated because they have both formed different associations, but agree to present a petition based on the behaviour of one of them, because neither wishes their new partner to be publicly named. The sex, class and other differences in the use of the facts make it quite clear that these are chosen for a variety of reasons which need have nothing to do with the reality of the case. This is a major source of confusion, especially for respondents who do not agree with the fact alleged. As has long been said, 'whatever the client's reason for wanting divorce, the lawyer's function is to discover grounds'.

2.10 The behaviour fact is particularly confusing. It is often referred to as 'unreasonable behaviour', which suggests blameworthiness or outright cruelty on the part of the respondent; but this has been called a 'linguistic trap', because the behaviour itself need be neither unreasonable nor blameworthy: rather, its effect on the petitioner must be such that it is unreasonable to expect him or her to go on living with the respondent, a significantly different and more flexible concept which is obviously capable of varying from case to case and court to court. Although the test is to be applied by an objective reasonable outsider, the character and personality of the petitioner are particularly relevant in deciding what conduct he or she should be expected to bear.

2.11 Finally, and above all, the present law pretends that the court is conducting an inquiry into the facts of the matter, when in the vast majority of cases it can do no such thing. This is not the fault of the court, nor is it probably any more of a problem under the present law and procedure than it was under the old. It may be more difficult to evaluate the effect of the respondent's behaviour from the papers than from the petitioner's account in the witness box, but it has always been difficult to get at the truth in an undefended case. Moreover, the system still allows, even encourages, the parties to lie, or at least to exaggerate, in order to get what they want. The bogus adultery cases of the past may have all but disappeared, but their modern equivalents are the 'flimsy' behaviour petition or the pretence that the parties have been living apart for a full two years. In that 'wider field which includes considerations of truth, the sacredness\of oaths, and the integrity of professional practice', the present law is just as objectionable as the old.

(ii)   It is discriminatory and unjust

2.12   83% of respondents to our public opinion survey thought it a good feature of the present law that couples who do not want to put the blame on either of them do not have to do so, but these couples have to have lived apart for at least two years. This can be extremely difficult to achieve without either substantial resources of one's own, or the co-operation of the other spouse at the outset, or an ouster order from the court. A secure council house tenancy, for example, cannot be re-allocated between them without a court order which is only obtainable on divorce or judicial separation. The law does recognise that it is possible to live apart by conducting two separate households under the same roof. In practice, this is impossible in most ordinary houses or flats, especially where there are children: it inevitably requires the couple to co-operate in a most unnatural and artificial lifestyle. It is unjust and discriminatory of the law to provide for a civilised 'no-fault' ground for divorce which, in practice, is denied to a large section of the population. A young mother with children living in a council house is obliged to rely upon fault whether or not she wants to do so and irrespective of the damage it may do.

2.13   The fault-based facts can also be intrinsically unjust. 'Justice' in this context has traditionally been taken to mean the accurate allocation of blameworthiness for the breakdown of the marriage. Desertion is the only fact which still attempts to do this: it requires that one party has brought about their separation without just cause or consent. Desertion, however, is hardly ever used, because its place has been taken by the two year separation fact. A finding of adultery or behaviour certainly need not mean that the respondent is any more to blame than the petitioner for the breakdown of the marriage. If one has committed adultery or behaved intolerably there is usually nothing to stop the other obtaining a divorce based upon it, even though that other may have committed far more adulteries or behaved much more intolerably himself or herself. Nor does the behaviour fact always involve blame: it may well be unreasonable to expect a petitioner to live with a spouse who is mentally ill or disabled or has totally incompatible values or lifestyle. Even when the catalogue of complaints contained in the petition includes violence or other obviously blameworthy behaviour, this might look different if weighed against the behaviour of the other. In a defended case, the petitioner's own character and conduct may be relevant in determining the effect of the respondent's conduct upon her, but if his conduct is sufficient, it is irrelevant that she may have behaved equally badly in some other way. In an undefended case, of course, the matter will appear even more one-sided.

2.14   This inherent potential for injustice is compounded by the practical problems of defending or bringing a cross-petition of one's own. It is extremely difficult to resist or counter allegations of behaviour. Defending them requires time, money and emotional energy far beyond the resources of most respondents. Even if the parties are prepared to go through this, what would be the point? If the marriage is capable of being saved, a long-fought defended divorce, in which every incident or characteristic that might amount to behaviour is dragged up and examined in detail, is not going to do this. It can only serve to make matters worse and to consume resources which are often desperately needed elsewhere, particularly if there are children. Legal aid will only be granted if the case cannot be disposed of as an undefended suit without detriment to the interests of either party. As the basis on which the divorce is granted is usually irrelevant to ancillary issues, the parties' *legal* positions are unlikely to be affected whatever their personal views. Small wonder, then, that lawyers advise their clients not to defend and that their clients feel unjustly treated.

(iii)   It distorts the parties' bargaining positions

2.15   Not only can the law be unjust in itself, it can also lead to unfair distortions in the relative bargaining positions of the parties. When a marriage breaks down there are a great many practical questions to be decided: with whom are the children to live, how much are they going to see of the other parent, who is to have the house, and what are they all going to live on? Respondents to Facing the Future told us that the battles which used to be fought through the ground for divorce are now more likely to be fought through the so-called ancillary issues which in practice matter so much more to many people. The policy of the law is to encourage the parties to try and resolve these by agreement if they can, whether through negotiation between solicitors or with the help of a mediation or conciliation service. Questions of the future care of children, distribution of family assets, and financial provision are all governed by their own legal criteria. It is not unjust for negotiations to be affected by the relative merits of the parties' cases on these matters. Yet negotiations may also be distorted by whichever of the parties is in a stronger position in relation to the divorce itself. The strength of that position will depend upon a combination of how anxious or reluctant that party is to be divorced and how easy or difficult he or she will find it to prove or disprove one of the five facts. That might not matter if these represented a coherent set of principles, reflecting the real reasons why the marriage broke down; but as we have already seen, they do not. The potentially arbitrary results can put one party at an unfair disadvantage.

(iv)   It provokes unnecessary hostility and bitterness

2.16   A law which is arbitrary or unjust can exacerbate the feelings of bitterness, distress and humiliation so often experienced at the time of separation and divorce. Even if the couple have agreed that their marriage cannot be saved, it must make matters between them worse if the system encourages one to make allegations against the other. The incidents relied on have to be set out in the petition. Sometimes they are exaggerated, one-sided or even untrue. Allegations of behaviour or adultery can provoke resentment and hostility in a respondent who is unable to put his own side of the story on the record. We are not so naive as to believe that bitterness and hostility could ever be banished from the divorce process. It is not concerned with cold commercial bargains but with the most intimate of human relations. The more we expect of marriage the greater the anger and grief when marriage ends. But there is every reason to believe that the present law adds needlessly to the human misery involved. Our respondents confirmed this.

(v)   It does nothing to save the marriage

2.17   None of this is any help with the law's other objective, of supporting those marriages which have a chance of survival. The law cannot prevent people from separating or forming new relationships, although it may make it difficult for people to get a divorce. The law can also make it difficult for estranged couples to become reconciled. The present law does make it difficult for some couples—in practice a very small proportion—to be divorced, but does so in an arbitrary way depending upon which facts may be proved. It also makes it extremely difficult for couples to become reconciled. A spouse who wishes to be divorced is obliged either to make allegations against the other or to live apart for a lengthy period. If the petitioner brings proceedings based on behaviour, possibly without prior warning, and sometimes while they are still living together, the antagonism caused may destroy any lingering chance of saving the marriage. The alternative of two or five years' separation may encourage them to part in order to be able to obtain a divorce, when their difficulties might have been resolved if they had stayed together. From the very beginning, attention has to be focussed on how to prove the ground for divorce. The reality of what it will be like to live apart, to break up the common home, to finance two households where before there was only one, and to have or to lose that day-to-day responsibility for the children which was previously shared, at least to some extent: none of this has to be contemplated in any detail until the decree nisi is obtained. If it had, there might be some petitioners who would think again.

2.18   It is a mistake to think that, because so few divorces are defended, the rest are largely consensual. There are many, especially behaviour cases, in which the respondent indicates an intention to defend, but does not file a formal answer, or files an answer which is later withdrawn. Some of these are a reaction to the unfairness of the allegations made against them, but some reveal a genuine desire to preserve the marriage. A defended suit is not going to do this, and if a case is, or becomes, undefended, there is little opportunity to explore the possibility of saving the marriage. An undefended decree can be obtained in a matter of weeks. If both parties are contemplating divorce, the system gives them every incentive to obtain a 'quickie' based on behaviour or separation, and to think out the practical consequences later.

(vi)   It can make things worse for the children

2.19   The present system can also make things worse for the children. The children themselves would usually prefer their parents to stay together. But the law cannot force parents to live amicably or prevent them from separating. It is not known whether children suffer more from their parents' separation or from living in a household in conflict where they may be blamed for the couple's inability to part. It is probably impossible to generalise, as there are so many variables which may affect the outcome, including the age and personality of the particular child. But it is known that the children who suffer least from their parents' break-up are usually those who are able to retain a good relationship with them both. Children who suffer most are those whose parents remain in conflict.

2.20   These issues have to be faced by the parents themselves, as they agonise over what to do for the best. However regrettably, there is nothing the law can do to ensure that they stay together, even supposing that this would indeed be better for their children. On the other hand, the present law can, for all the reasons given earlier, make the conflict worse. It encourages couples to find fault with one another and disputes about children seem to be more common in divorces based on intolerable behaviour than in others. The alternative is a long period of separation during which children can suffer from the uncertainty before things can be finally sorted out or from the artificiality of their parents living in separate households under the same roof. This is scarcely an effective way of encouraging the parents to work out different ways of continuing to discharge their shared parental responsibilities. It is often said that couples undergoing marital breakdown are too wrapped up in their own problems to understand their children's needs. There are also couples who, while recognising that their own relationship is at an end, are anxious to do their best for their children. The present system does little to help them to do so.

5.1.1   OPTIONS FOR REFORM AND BASIC PRINCIPLES

The Law Commission, Family Law: The Ground for Divorce (Law Com No. 192)

The aims of the law

3.1   In reviewing possible models for reform we have in mind the following broad objectives for the law which we believe to be generally agreed:

(i)   It should try to support those marriages which are capable of being saved.

(ii)   It should enable those which cannot be saved to be dissolved with the minimum of avoidable distress, bitterness and hostility.

(iii)   It should encourage, so far as possible, the amicable resolution of practical issues relating to the couple's home, finances and children and the proper discharge of their responsibilities to one another and to their children.

(iv)   It should seek to minimise the harm that the children of the family may suffer, both at the time and in the future, and to promote so far as possible the continued sharing of parental responsibility for them.

3.2   These aims are similar to those expressed in The Field of Choice but with important differences in emphasis. There is now a much greater understanding of the needs of children whose parents divorce. It is important for their sake that the law should seek to minimise bitterness and hostility and to promote amicable settlements. There is also a sound public interest in doing so. It does no good to anyone if resources are wasted away in costly legal battles. The family's claims on the public purse may also increase, if parents are not obliged at the outset of their marital difficulties to consider how their financial responsibilities, principally towards their children but also to one another, should be met.

3.3   There is also a sound public interest in helping to preserve those marriages which can be saved. It is generally accepted that the law neither can nor should force people to live together or keep alive the empty shell of a marriage which is undoubtedly dead. There are also some marriages which cannot or should not be saved. It is important, both for their sake and for the sake of their children, that people whose marriages have failed are not burdened with an even greater sense of guilt or personal failure. But it is legitimate to try to avoid the damage done by decisions taken in haste and without full consideration of the consequences. As our predecessors put it, 'a divorce law . . . can and should ensure that divorce is not so easy that the parties are under no inducement to make a success of their marriage and, in particular, to overcome temporary difficulties'.

3.4   The aim of supporting those marriages which can be saved can be distinguished from the aim of upholding the institution of marriage itself. For some of our respondents, as for our predecessors, it was important that divorce law should send the right messages, to the married and the marrying, about the seriousness and permanence of the commitment involved. We agree. Despite a rapid recent growth in cohabitation outside marriage, marriage remains an extremely popular institution. Couples see it as offering, not only an 'important signifier' of their commitment to one another, but also a home of their own, financial and emotional security, and an 'accepted context' for having children. Marriage involves mutual legal obligations of support and sharing which other relationships do not. The law should certainly do its utmost to recognise and enforce these. It must also be realistic and practical. If people who are unhappily married are denied a means of reordering their lives in a sensible fashion, many of them will simply walk away. Others may be deterred from marrying in the first place, but will live together instead. Support for the institution of marriage cannot be achieved by turning it into an institution which no-one any longer wishes to enter. But the recognition that a marriage has broken down does not mean that the obligations resulting from it should be ignored.

FAMILY LAW ACT 1996

1.   The general principles underlying Parts II and III
The court and any person, in exercising functions under or in consequence of Parts II and III, shall have regard to the following general principles—
   (a)   that the institution of marriage is to be supported;
   (b)   that the parties to a marriage which may have broken down are to be encouraged to take all practicable steps, whether by marriage counselling or otherwise, to save the marriage;
   (c)   that a marriage which has irretrievably broken down and is being brought to an end should be brought to an end—
      (i)   with minimum distress to the parties and to the children affected;
      (ii)   with questions dealt with in a manner designed to promote as good a continuing relationship between the parties and any children affected as is possible in the circumstances; and
      (iii)   without costs being unreasonably incurred in connection with the procedures to be followed in bringing the marriage to an end; and
   (d)   that any risk to one of the parties to a marriage, and to any children, of violence from the other party should, so far as reasonably practicable, be removed or diminished.

5.2   The Divorce Process

5.2.1   THE ORDERS AVAILABLE

FAMILY LAW ACT 1996

2.   Divorce and separation
   (1)   The court may—
      (a)   by making an order (to be known as a divorce order), dissolve a marriage; or

(b) by making an order (to be known as a separation order), provide for the separation of the parties to a marriage.

(2) Any such order comes into force on being made.

(3) A separation order remains in force—

(a) while the marriage continues; or

(b) until cancelled by the court on the joint application of the parties.

5.2.2 WHEN WILL THE ORDERS BE GRANTED?

FAMILY LAW ACT 1996

3. Circumstances in which orders are made

(1) If an application for a divorce order or for a separation order is made to the court under this section by one or both of the parties to a marriage, the court shall make the order applied for if (but only if)—

(a) the marriage has broken down irretrievably;

(b) the requirements of section 8 about information meetings are satisfied;

(c) the requirements of section 9 about the parties' arrangements for the future are satisfied; and

(d) the application has not been withdrawn.

(2) A divorce order may not be made if an order preventing divorce is in force under section 10.

(3) If the court is considering an application for a divorce order and an application for a separation order in respect of the same marriage it shall proceed as if it were considering only the application for a divorce order unless—

(a) an order preventing divorce is in force with respect to the marriage;

(b) the court makes an order preventing divorce; or

(c) section 7(6) or (13) applies.

7. Period for reflection and consideration

(1) Where a statement has been made, a period for the parties—

(a) to reflect on whether the marriage can be saved and to have an opportunity to effect a reconciliation, and

(b) to consider what arrangements should be made for the future,

must pass before an application for a divorce order or for a separation order may be made by reference to that statement.

(2) That period is to be known as the period for reflection and consideration.

(3) The period for reflection and consideration is nine months beginning with the fourteenth day after the day on which the statement is received by the court.

(4) Where—

(a) the statement has been made by one party,

(b) rules made under section 12 require the court to serve a copy of the statement on the other party, and

(c) failure to comply with the rules causes inordinate delay in service,

the court may, on the application of that other party, extend the period for reflection and consideration.

(5) An extension under subsection (4) may be for any period not exceeding the time between—

(a) the beginning of the period for reflection and consideration; and

(b) the time when service is effected.

. . .

(7) Subsection (8) applies if, at any time during the period for reflection and consideration, the parties jointly give notice to the court that they are attempting a reconciliation but require additional time.

(8) The period for reflection and consideration—

(a) stops running on the day on which the notice is received by the court; but

(b) resumes running on the day on which either of the parties gives notice to the court that the attempted reconciliation has been unsuccessful.

(9)   If the period for reflection and consideration is interrupted under subsection (8) by a continuous period of more than 18 months, any application by either of the parties for a divorce order or for a separation order must be by reference to a new statement received by the court at any time after the end of the 18 months.

(10)   Where an application for a divorce order is made by one party, subsection (13) applies if—

(a)   the other party applies to the court, within the prescribed period, for time for further reflection; and

(b)   the requirements of section 9 (except any imposed under section 9(3)) are satisfied.

(11)   Where any application for a divorce order is made, subsection (13) also applies if there is a child of the family who is under the age of sixteen when the application is made.

(12)   Subsection (13) does not apply if—

(a)   at the time when the application for a divorce order is made, there is an occupation order or a non-molestation order in force in favour of the applicant, or of a child of the family, made against the other party; or

(b)   the court is satisfied that delaying the making of a divorce order would be significantly detrimental to the welfare of any child of the family.

(13)   If this subsection applies, the period for reflection and consideration is extended by a period of six months, but—

(a)   only in relation to the application for a divorce order in respect of which the application under subsection (10) was made; and

(b)   without invalidating that application for a divorce order.

(14)   A period for reflection and consideration which is extended under subsection (13), and which has not otherwise come to an end, comes to an end on there ceasing to be any children of the family to whom subsection (11) applied.

5.2.3   IRRETRIEVABLE BREAKDOWN

Law Commission, Family Law: Ground for Divorce (Law Com No. 192)

(iii)   Consideration and Reflection

3.26   The final model discussed in Facing the Future treated the grant of a divorce, not as a separate event, but as part of a process of facing up to and resolving its practical, social and emotional consequences over a period of time. A divorce would be granted only after a fixed period, not necessarily of separation, but for consideration, both of the alternatives and of the practical consequences involved. This model shares many of the advantages of divorce after a fixed period of separation. It avoids the injustices and other problems associated with the retention of fault. The lapse of a substantial period of time provides solid evidence of a permanent breakdown in the marital relationship. It restrains hasty or rash applications and ensures that the couple have given some consideration to what the future will hold before finally committing themselves to a divorce. It provides an opportunity to reflect upon the children's best interests and to explore the possibility of reconciliation.

3.27   It also avoids two of the major pitfalls associated with insisting on a period of separation. First, the period of consideration could be initiated by a formal statement, which would be officially recorded, that one or both of the parties believed that the marital relationship had broken down. There would then be no scope for pretending that it had begun when in fact it had not. Secondly, the court could have power to deal with the practical questions, the arrangements to be made for the children, the home, and financial support, as well as protection from violence and other forms of molestation, at any time during the period, rather than after it had elapsed. This would avoid the discrimination against the more needy and deserving petitioners involved in requiring them to separate. In practice, of course, few couples would remain together throughout the period but those who wished to do so in the hope of saving their marriage would not be prevented. Only at the end of the period could an application for a divorce be made.

3.35   However, there was understandable concern among some of our respondents about the details of how it would work in practice. We shall discuss those details further in Part V; but we should point out here the central features which were implicit, or in some cases explicit, in the support which it received. First, a substantial period of time should be required to elapse, in order to demonstrate quite clearly that the marriage has irretrievably broken down. There can be no better proof of this than that one or both parties to the marriage have stated their belief that their marital relationship has broken down and that either or both of them persist in that belief after the lapse of a considerable period. This must be longer than the present interval between petition and decree, which is six months or less in a substantial proportion of cases. It must also give the parties a realistic time-scale within which, in the great majority of cases, the practical questions about the children, the home and the finances can be properly resolved. It must avoid rushing them towards a resolution of those issues, so that they can go at their own pace and draw back if they wish. It must discourage hasty and ill-thought-out applications. In our view, an overall period of one year would be required to achieve all these objectives.

5.2.4   THE INFORMATION SESSION

FAMILY LAW ACT 1996

8.   Attendance at information meetings

(1)   The requirements about information meetings are as follows.

(2)   A party making a statement must (except in prescribed circumstances) have attended an information meeting not less than three months before making the statement.

(3)   Different information meetings must be arranged with respect to different marriages.

(4)   In the case of a statement made by both parties, the parties may attend separate meetings or the same meeting.

(5)   Where one party has made a statement, the other party must (except in prescribed circumstances) attend an information meeting before

   (a)   making any application to the court—
      (i)   with respect to a child of the family; or
      (ii)   of a prescribed description relating to property or financial matters; or
   (b)   contesting any such application.

(6)   In this section 'information meeting' means a meeting organised, in accordance with prescribed provisions for the purpose—

   (a)   of providing, in accordance with prescribed provisions, relevant information to the party or parties attending about matters which may arise in connection with the provisions of, or made under, this Part or Part III; and

   (b)   of giving the party or parties attending the information meeting the opportunity of having a meeting with a marriage counsellor and of encouraging that party or those parties to attend that meeting.

(7)   An information meeting must be conducted by a person who—

   (a)   is qualified and appointed in accordance with prescribed provisions; and

   (b)   will have no financial or other interest in any marital proceedings between the parties.

(8)   Regulations made under this section may, in particular, make provision—

   (a)   about the places and times at which information meetings are to be held;

   (b)   for written information to be given to persons attending them;

   (c)   for the giving of information to parties (otherwise than at information meetings) in cases in which the requirement to attend such meetings does not apply;

   (d)   for information of a prescribed kind to be given only with the approval of the Lord Chancellor or only by a person or by persons approved by him; and

   (e)   for information to be given, in prescribed circumstances, only with the approval of the Lord Chancellor or only by a person, or by persons, approved by him.

(9)   Regulations made under subsection (6) must, in particular, make provision with respect to the giving of information about—

(a) marriage counselling and other marriage support services;

(b) the importance to be attached to the welfare, wishes and feelings of children;

(c) how the parties may acquire a better understanding of the ways in which children can be helped to cope with the breakdown of a marriage;

(d) the nature of the financial questions that may arise on divorce or separation, and services which are available to help the parties;

(e) protection available against violence, and how to obtain support and assistance;

(f) mediation;

(g) the availability to each of the parties of independent legal advice and representation;

(h) the principles of legal aid and where the parties can get advice about obtaining legal aid;

(i) the divorce and separation process.

(10) Before making any regulations under subsection (6), the Lord Chancellor must consult such persons concerned with the provision of relevant information as he considers appropriate.

(11) A meeting with a marriage counsellor arranged under this section—

(a) must be held in accordance with prescribed provisions; and

(b) must be with a person qualified and appointed in accordance with prescribed provisions.

(12) A person who would not be required to make any contribution towards mediation provided for him under Part IIIA of the Legal Aid Act 1988 shall not be required to make any contribution towards the cost of a meeting with a marriage counsellor arranged for him under this section.

(13) In this section 'prescribed' means prescribed by regulations made by the Lord Chancellor.

Lloyd, H., 'Family Law Act 1996: pilot projects', Law Society Gazette, 21 May 1997

In March 1997 the Lord Chancellor announced the first five locations selected for pilots of divorce information meetings to begin in June 1997. Those areas are Birmingham and Coventry, East Anglia, Cardiff and Swansea, Leicestershire and South Yorkshire.

As solicitors are aware, attendance at information meetings will become compulsory, pursuant to s. 8 of the Family Law Act 1996, prior to filing a statement of marital breakdown, once the Act has been implemented. The provision of information is to be tested during the pilot project when attendance at meetings will be voluntary.

In December 1996, the Lord Chancellor's Department (LCD) approached local branches of four voluntary agencies to submit bids to provide divorce information, only two of which, National Family Mediation (NFM) and Relate submitted bids. Voluntary agencies were approached to form the first phase of the pilot project since they qualify for grant in aid.

In targeting areas the LCD looked for areas with a through-put of approximately 6,000 divorce petitions per annum. It aims to achieve attendance at the voluntary meetings of up to ten per cent of that number over a period of up to nine months. If this number is achieved, the LCD believes its research into the project will be statistically valid.

Whilst the project in any of the five areas will be led by Relate or NFM, the information presenters (ten in each area) will be recruited from a variety of backgrounds, comprising two solicitors, two counsellors, two mediators, two court welfare officers and two from other professional backgrounds, e.g. nurses. Recruitment was carried out by the lead agency in each area during April 1997, following local advertising. Training of presenters began during May in readiness for commencement of the pilot in June.

The National Council for Family Proceedings (NCFP) will act as project manager for the pilots and will co-ordinate the training of presenters and production of written and oral material. NCFP has invited a number of organisations, including the Law Society, to draft leaflets to form part of the information pack to be handed to the public at the meetings. These organisations have also been given the task of providing background information for the presenter's script to be used at the meetings. A video is also being produced for use at the group meeting (see below) and its effectiveness will be tested during the pilot project.

Whilst s. 8(9) of the Act details what information is to be included at the meeting, the Act does not specify where meetings are to be held, how long the meeting is to last or who will conduct the meeting. To some extent therefore, the meeting can be developed in any way.

During the pilot project, the LCD is to test different types of meeting with interested parties being allocated to meetings at random:

- an individual meeting of up to one hour
- an individual meeting of up to one half hour and the opportunity to attend at a group meeting lasting up to one hour
- a group meeting aimed at those who have children but who are either unmarried or not intending to divorce.

The group meetings will be conducted by two presenters comprising either a lawyer, a mediator or a court welfare officer and there is some suggestion that the LCD wishes to involve judges as presenters at the group meetings. A variety of venues are also to be tested: meetings can be held in existing business premises, although a nameplate must be displayed outside the premises and lead agencies have been asked by the LCD to specify at least one neutral venue at which the group meeting may be held. It appears that, at least during the first phase of the pilot, dedicated premises will be used for both the individual and group meetings. A second phase of pilot projects is due to begin in September 1997 and it is anticipated that this will involve the commercial sector (to include solicitors) under a contractual relationship with the LCD.

Specific areas have not yet been identified, although it is known that pilots will not run in competition with each other and the South coast appears to be a likely target. Again, the areas covered are likely to be wide, for example, Bournemouth would also cover Winchester, Andover, Newport, Southampton and Basingstoke and the same criteria for presenters and venues are likely to be applied to the commercial sector.

The Law Society is very keen to ensure that good quality information is provided in a cost-effective manner. The LCD has recently announced that it will pay presenters £15 an hour for an individual meeting and £22.50 an hour for a group meeting.

Although the Law Society's family law committee has been most anxious to encourage solicitors to be involved in the second stage of the pilot, the committee recognises that the remuneration will be unattractive to the majority of the profession.

The Law Society is unable to bid for a divorce information contract, but there would appear to be no reason why local law societies, consortia of firms, or individual firms could not submit bids. Once the Act is implemented, solicitors who become divorce information providers will not subsequently be able to act for parties to whom they have given divorce information.

5.2.5   THE STATEMENT OF MARITAL BREAKDOWN

FAMILY LAW ACT 1996

5.   Marital breakdown

(1)   A marriage is to be taken to have broken down irretrievably if (but only if)—

(a)   a statement has been made by one (or both) of the parties that the maker of the statement (or each of them) believes that the marriage has broken down;

(b)   the statement complies with the requirements of section 6;

(c)   the period for reflection and consideration fixed by section 7 has ended; and

(d)   the application under section 3 is accompanied by a declaration by the party making the application that—

(i)   having reflected on the breakdown, and

(ii)   having considered the requirements of this Part as to the parties' arrangements for the future,

the applicant believes that the marriage cannot be saved.

6.   Statement of marital breakdown

(1)   A statement under section 5(1)(a) is to be known as a statement of marital breakdown; but in this Part it is generally referred to as 'a statement'.

(2) If a statement is made by one party it must also state that that party—

(a) is aware of the purpose of the period for reflection and consideration as described in section 7; and

(b) wishes to make arrangements for the future.

(3) If a statement is made by both parties it must also state that each of them—

(a) is aware of the purpose of the period for reflection and consideration as described in section 7; and

(b) wishes to make arrangements for the future.

(4) A statement must be given to the court in accordance with the requirements of rules made under section 12.

(5) A statement must also satisfy any other requirements imposed by rules made under that section.

(6) A statement made at a time when the circumstances of the case include any of those mentioned in subsection (7) is ineffective for the purposes of this Part.

(7) The circumstances are—

(a) that a statement has previously been made with respect to the marriage and it is, or will become, possible—

(i) for an application for a divorce order, or

(ii) for an application for a separation order,

to be made by reference to the previous statement;

(b) that such an application has been made in relation to the marriage and has not been withdrawn;

(c) that a separation order is in force.

7. Period for reflection and consideration

. . .

(6) A statement which is made before the first anniversary of the marriage to which it relates is ineffective for the purposes of any application for a divorce order.

The Law Commission, Family Law: The Ground for Divorce (Law Com No. 192)

Initiation of the period of consideration and reflection

5.8 Initiation of this period should be regarded as a serious step and we therefore *recommend* that it should involve the making and lodging of a formal statement.

The statement of marital breakdown

5.9 We *recommend* that the statement take the form of a document stating that the maker, or makers, believe that the marital relationship has broken down. This form of wording places a greater personal responsibility on initiators by requiring them to express a view about the state of their relationship rather than merely recite a statutory ground which may bear no resemblance to what they are thinking or feeling. They should not, however, be required at this stage to state that the breakdown is irreparable. One of the purposes of the period itself is to test this out and the parties should not be encouraged to reach a final conclusion at the outset.

Joint and sole statements

5.10 We also *recommend* that it should be possible for the parties to make such a statement jointly. This reflects the recommendations of the Booth Committee, who were anxious to move away from the adversarial and pejorative connotations of the law's present insistence that there be one 'petitioner' and one 'respondent'. This is difficult to avoid if fault-based facts are retained, but if they are not it should present no problem. Where both spouses are agreed that their relationship has broken down, their joint acknowledgement of this should help considerably towards the amicable resolution of the practical matters involved and to avoid unnecessary bitterness between them. It will also reflect the widespread view revealed in our public opinion survey that couples should be able to dissolve their marriages by agreement.

5.11 If the spouses are not agreed, then one should make the statement which would then be sent to the other. Once the period has been initiated in this way, however, it should be open to either spouse to apply for a separation or divorce at the end of it. This again would avoid the adversarial connotations of one spouse proceeding *against* the other and allow both to participate as equals in the processes of negotiation and consideration of the eventual arrangements. Considerable injustice might otherwise be done to the spouse who did not make the initial statement, but who came to terms with the other's decision and co-operated fully in making the necessary arrangements, only to find that the other withdrew at the last moment. It would also emphasise to the sole initiator the importance of the step being taken, in that matters would no longer be wholly within his or her control. This is a considerable source of grievance in the present law, which allows so much power to the spouse who happens to be petitioner. Both parties would be in exactly the same position and entitled to the same remedies and also to the same protection.

Formalities

5.15   The precise formalities to be observed in the making and lodging of statements of marital breakdown are matters for subordinate rather than primary legislation. Nevertheless, we consider it important that these are framed with two main objects in mind: first to emphasise the seriousness of the step being taken; and secondly to ensure so far as possible that both spouses understand the nature, purpose and requirements of the period upon which they are embarking, and are fully acquainted with the various types of professional help which may be required and how to obtain it.

5.16   Furthermore, although many people will be legally represented at this stage, the procedure should be designed to cater just as satisfactorily for those who are not. Even under the present procedure, this is a not insignificant proportion. In particular, there are couples who are able to agree upon their own arrangements and who may prefer not to take what may be seen as the hostile step of instructing a lawyer who, of necessity— may act for only one of them. Also, although we have recommended that statements be lodged at a court, they should, so far as possible, be differentiated from the bringing of ordinary civil proceedings by one person against another.

5.17   Accordingly, to meet the first objective in paragraph 5.15 above, we *recommend* that statements of marital breakdown be made on a prescribed form and sworn (or affirmed) in the usual manner before a Commissioner for Oaths or court official. The prescribed form should be so drafted as to emphasise the seriousness of the step being taken and to outline its legal consequences. These are, first, that it sets in motion a period during which steps will be taken to consider the arrangements to be made should the breakdown prove irreparable; and secondly, that at the end of the period either party may, should he or she then be of the view that the breakdown is irreparable, apply for a divorce or separation order to be issued. Only in exceptional circumstances can the period be extended or a hardship bar imposed.

5.18   However, making the statement should not be seen merely as the formal initiation of a predominantly legal process. There is as yet no formal application, either for divorce or separation, or for any ancillary relief, before the court. If the period is to be put to good and effective use, it is important that both parties are made aware of the various sources of help available to them and their children during this difficult time. They need to know the differences between marriage guidance, counselling and reconciliation, conciliation and mediation, and divorce counselling. They need to know what services for all of these purposes are available locally and how they may be contacted. In many ways, it would be ideal if statements were to be made in person during an interview with a senior official who could give such explanations in person. It would, however, be quite impracticable to require this in every case. For one thing, it would be impossible to insist on the attendance of both parties in all cases. Further, there are some couples whose marriages have clearly broken down and who have no need of such information or services. There are also circumstances in which they are quite inappropriate. It would be equally inappropriate for such an official to proffer advice or counselling of any sort or to conduct an inquiry into the reasons for the breakdown in the relationship. To do so would be to reintroduce the inquiry into the past which is the major objection to the present law and to confuse the distinct functions of the various professions and services involved. There would also be the risk of deterring the very people who are most in need of the protection of the law.

5.2.6 THE PERIOD OF REFLECTION AND CONSIDERATION

The Law Commission, Facing the Future: The Ground for Divorce (Law Com No. 192)

The period of consideration and reflection
Objectives
5.25 As we explained earlier, the period is primarily designed to provide convincing proof that the breakdown in the marital relationship is indeed irreparable. It should also give the parties a realistic time within which to resolve the practical questions and to decide whether or not they wish to be reconciled. Unlike the current system, the parties will have to consider the consequences of a separation or divorce order before it actually happens. This will entail the often painful exercise of deciding whether or not their home should be sold, with whom the children are to live, how much contact the other parent is to have with the children, and how their furniture and other possessions should be divided. This will be in addition to learning to adjust emotionally, socially and psychologically to the dramatic change of circumstances in their lives. In some cases, the period may become a more potent encouragement to remain together than the present system, which provides an almost automatic passport to divorce, with every encouragement to dwell on the past and ignore the future.

5.26 It should therefore be distinguished from a purely passive period, during which parties merely wait out the legally required time without any clear objectives and without any real attempt to focus upon the dramatic changes which will occur if and when divorce does actually happen. Where the marriage has obviously and irreparably broken down before the period begins, consideration of the practical consequences will be a much more constructive use of the inevitable delay before a divorce can be obtained. Where there remains any doubt at the outset, a more active preparation for life apart will provide far more cogent evidence that the parties have no future together—why else would the person or persons concerned wish to put themselves through such an experience? When faced with the problems of dealing with the practical consequences some couples may come to realize that they need to re-consider their position and, perhaps with the help of counselling, find some way of re-negotiating their relationship so that they and their children can have a future together.

Length
5.27 There was overwhelming agreement amongst respondents to Facing the Future that these objectives could not be achieved in less than nine months. The great majority favoured a period of nine or twelve months, with only a few suggesting longer. It was pointed out that a twelve month period would make divorce a significantly more lengthy process for a substantial number of people. Respondents to our public opinion survey chose periods ranging from six months to over two years, with the highest number (35%) choosing one year. We *recommend* an overall period of twelve months. This should give sufficient time to enable all but the most difficult and complex matters to be decided and to establish that the breakdown is indeed irreparable. It should also allow sufficient time for the benefits of conciliation or mediation to be explored. We also *recommend* that the actual application for a separation or divorce order should not be made until at least eleven months of the period have elapsed. However, there would be no compulsion to apply for an order upon expiration of this time. Parties could take longer if they wished, as an order should not be made unless it is actually applied for. Once applied for, it would not be granted for a further month, making a minimum total of one year overall.

5.28 A few respondents to Facing the Future suggested that the period should be longer if there were children. Most, however, did not support this. A child's sense of time is quite different from an adult's and considerable harm can be done by prolonged uncertainty. Harm may also be done by the additional bitterness which can be caused by having to wait longer on their account. The general view, both on this and on previous occasions, has been that to make divorce inevitably more difficult for those who have children will not benefit the children themselves and could make matters worse. Thus, 'it would amount to a denial that childless marriage is real marriage . . . Unhappy motives would be introduced for having, or not having, children; and a child once there could become a focus of bitterness for the parent who wanted to be free'. We *recommend*, therefore, that the period should not automatically be longer where there are children. The parties and the court will, however, have to consider what arrangements should be made for them and, if it is desirable to prolong the period in their interests, this should be done.

5.2.6.1   Financial arrangements

FAMILY LAW ACT 1996

9.   Arrangements for the future

(1)   The requirements as to the parties' arrangements for the future are as follows.

(2)   One of the following must be produced to the court—

(a)   a court order (made by consent or otherwise) dealing with their financial arrangements;

(b)   a negotiated agreement as to their financial arrangements;

(c)   a declaration by both parties that they have made their financial arrangements;

(d)   a declaration by one of the parties (to which no objection has been notified to the court by the other party) that—

(i)   he has no significant assets and does not intend to make an application for financial provision;

(ii)   he believes that the other party has no significant assets and does not intend to make an application for financial provision; and

(iii)   there are therefore no financial arrangements to be made.

(3)   If the parties—

(a)   were married to each other in accordance with usages of a kind mentioned in section 26(1) of the Marriage Act 1949 (marriages which may be solemnized on authority of superintendent registrar's certificate), and

(b)   are required to co-operate if the marriage is to be dissolved in accordance with those usages,

the court may, on the application of either party, direct that there must also be produced to the court a declaration by both parties that they have taken such steps as are required to dissolve the marriage in accordance with those usages.

(4)   A direction under subsection (3)—

(a)   may be given only if the court is satisfied that in all the circumstances of the case it is just and reasonable to give it; and

(b)   may be revoked by the court at any time.

(5)   The requirements of section 11 must have been satisfied.

(6)   Schedule 1 supplements the provisions of this section.

(7)   If the court is satisfied, on an application made by one of the parties after the end of the period for reflection and consideration, that the circumstances of the case are—

(a)   those set out in paragraph 1 of Schedule 1,

(b)   those set out in paragraph 2 of that Schedule,

(c)   those set out in paragraph 3 of that Schedule, or

(d)   those set out in paragraph 4 of that Schedule, it may make a divorce order or a separation order even though the requirements of subsection (2) have not been satisfied.

(8)   If the parties' arrangements for the future include a division of pension assets or rights under section 25B of the 1973 Act or section 10 of the Family Law (Scotland) Act 1985, any declaration under subsection (2) must be a statutory declaration.

Section 9(6)   **Schedule 1**
                                           Arrangements for the future

Court orders and agreements

5.—(1)   Section 9 is not to be read as requiring any order or agreement to have been carried into effect at the time when the court is considering whether arrangements for the future have been made by the parties.

(2)   The fact that an appeal is pending against an order of the kind mentioned in section 9(2)(a) is to be disregarded.

Financial arrangements

6.   In section 9 and this Schedule 'financial arrangements' has the same meaning as in section 34(2) of the 1973 Act.

Negotiated agreements

7.   In section 9(2)(b) 'negotiated agreement' means a written agreement between the parties as to future arrangements—
   (a)   which has been reached as the result of mediation or any other form of negotiation involving a third party; and
   (b)   which satisfies such requirements as may be imposed by rules of court.

Declarations

8.—(1)   Any declaration of a kind mentioned in section 9—
   (a)   must be in a prescribed form;
   (b)   must, in prescribed cases, be accompanied by such documents as may be prescribed; and
   (c)   must, in prescribed cases, satisfy such other requirements as may be prescribed.
   (2)   The validity of a divorce order or separation order made by reference to such a declaration is not to be affected by any inaccuracy in the declaration.

Schedule 1   Section 9 exemptions

The first exemption

1.   The circumstances referred to in section 9(7)(a) are that—
   (a)   the requirements of section 11 have been satisfied;
   (b)   the applicant has, during the period for reflection and consideration, taken such steps as are reasonably practicable to try to reach agreement about the parties' financial arrangements; and
   (c)   the applicant has made an application to the court for financial relief and has complied with all requirements of the court in relation to proceedings for financial relief but—
      (i)   the other party has delayed in complying with requirements of the court or has otherwise been obstructive; or
      (ii)   for reasons which are beyond the control of the applicant, or of the other party, the court has been prevented from obtaining the information which it requires to determine the financial position of the parties.

The second exemption

2.   The circumstances referred to in section 9(7)(b) are that—
   (a)   the requirements of section 11 have been satisfied;
   (b)   the applicant has, during the period for reflection and consideration, taken such steps as are reasonably practicable to try to reach agreement about the parties' financial arrangements;
   (c)   because of—
      (i)   the ill health or disability of the applicant, the other party or a child of the family (whether physical or mental), or
      (ii)   an injury suffered by the applicant, the other party or a child of the family, the applicant has not been able to reach agreement with the other party about those arrangements and is unlikely to be able to do so in the foreseeable future; and
   (d)   a delay in making the order applied for under section 3—
      (i)   would be significantly detrimental to the welfare of any child of the family; or
      (ii)   would be seriously prejudicial to the applicant.

The third exemption

3.   The circumstances referred to in section 9(7)(c) are that—
   (a)   the requirements of section 11 have been satisfied;
   (b)   the applicant has found it impossible to contact the other party; and
   (c)   as a result, it has been impossible for the applicant to reach agreement with the other party about their financial arrangements.

The fourth exemption

4.   The circumstances referred to in section 9(7)(d) are that—
   (a)   the requirements of section 11 have been satisfied;
   (b)   an occupation order or a non-molestation order is in force in favour of the applicant or a child of the family, made against the other party;
   (c)   the applicant has, during the period for reflection and consideration, taken such steps as are reasonably practicable to try to reach agreement about the parties' financial arrangements;
   (d)   the applicant has not been able to reach agreement with the other party about those arrangements and is unlikely to be able to do so in the foreseeable future; and
   (e)   a delay in making the order applied for under section 3—
      (i)   would be significantly detrimental to the welfare of any child of the family; or
      (ii)   would be seriously prejudicial to the applicant.

5.2.6.2   Arrangements for children

FAMILY LAW ACT 1996

11.   Welfare of children

   (1)   In any proceedings for a divorce order or a separation order, the court shall consider—
   (a)   whether there are any children of the family to whom this section applies; and
   (b)   where there are any such children, whether (in the light of the arrangements which have been, or are proposed to be, made for their upbringing and welfare) it should exercise any of its powers under the Children Act 1989 with respect to any of them.
   (2)   Where, in any case to which this section applies, it appears to the court that—
   (a)   the circumstances of the case require it, or are likely to require it, to exercise any of its powers under the Children Act 1989 with respect to any such child,
   (b)   it is not in a position to exercise the power, or (as the case may be) those powers, without giving further consideration to the case, and
   (c)   there are exceptional circumstances which make it desirable in the interests of the child that the court should give a direction under this section,
it may direct that the divorce order or separation order is not to be made until the court orders otherwise.
   (3)   In deciding whether the circumstances are as mentioned in subsection (2)(a), the court shall treat the welfare of the child as paramount.
   (4)   In making that decision, the court shall also have particular regard, on the evidence before it, to—
   (a)   the wishes and feelings of the child considered in the light of his age and understanding and the circumstances in which those wishes were expressed;
   (b)   the conduct of the parties in relation to the upbringing of the child;
   (c)   the general principle that, in the absence of evidence to the contrary, the welfare of the child will be best served by—
      (i)   his having regular contact with those who have parental responsibility for him and with other members of his family; and
      (ii)   the maintenance of as good a continuing relationship with his parents as is possible; and
   (d)   any risk to the child attributable to—
      (i)   where the person with whom the child will reside is living or proposes to live;

(ii)   any person with whom that person is living or with whom he proposes to live; or

(iii)   any other arrangements for his care and upbringing.

(5)   This section applies to—

(a)   any child of the family who has not reached the age of sixteen at the date when the court considers the case in accordance with the requirements of this section; and

(b)   any child of the family who has reached that age at that date and in relation to whom the court directs that this section shall apply.

5.2.7   PREVENTING THE ORDER

FAMILY LAW ACT 1996

10.   Hardship: orders preventing divorce

(1)   If an application for a divorce order has been made by one of the parties to a marriage, the court may, on the application of the other party, order that the marriage is not to be dissolved.

(2)   Such an order (an 'order preventing divorce') may be made only if the court is satisfied—

(a)   that dissolution of the marriage would result in substantial financial or other hardship to the other party or to a child of the family; and

(b)   that it would be wrong, in all the circumstances (including the conduct of the parties and the interests of any child of the family), for the marriage to be dissolved.

(3)   If an application for the cancellation of an order preventing divorce is made by one or both of the parties, the court shall cancel the order unless it is still satisfied—

(a)   that dissolution of the marriage would result in substantial financial or other hardship to the party in whose favour the order was made or to a child of the family; and

(b)   that it would be wrong, in all the circumstances (including the conduct of the parties and the interests of any child of the family), for the marriage to be dissolved.

(4)   If an order preventing a divorce is cancelled, the court may make a divorce order in respect of the marriage only if an application is made under section 3 or 4(3) after the cancellation.

(5)   An order preventing divorce may include conditions which must be satisfied before an application for cancellation may be made under subsection (3).

(6)   In this section 'hardship' includes the loss of a chance to obtain a future benefit (as well as the loss of an existing benefit).

The Law Commission, Family Law: The Ground for Divorce (Law Com No. 192)

Grave financial or other hardship

5.72   Section 5 of the Matrimonial Causes Act provides a safeguard for respondents to petitions based on five years' separation, in that the court can refuse a decree if this would result in grave financial or other hardship to the respondent and it would in all the circumstances be wrong to dissolve the marriage. This was designed to meet the small number of cases in which the divorce itself will cause more hardship than the marital breakdown has already done. Generally, it is the separation, and the problems of running two households rather than one, which causes financial hardship, often to both of the parties. In practice, the only significant hardship which may flow from the divorce itself is the potential loss of an occupational widow's pension for which the husband is unable to provide sufficient compensation by way of periodical payments, lump sum or property adjustment. The bar is therefore rarely invoked and even more rarely successful. It is possible to think of other grave hardships which might flow from the divorce, where for example divorce will result in severe stigma in the community where the respondent lives, with possible exclusion from religious and social life, and perhaps no prospect of remarriage within that community, but as yet no divorce has been refused on this basis.

5.73   In Facing the Future we pointed out that the rationale of this provision was to safeguard the position of the innocent spouse who did not wish to be divorced. In a no-fault system there is clearly a case for extending the protection of a hardship bar to all who wish to invoke it. There is still a substantial economic imbalance between the spouses in most marriages which have lasted for more than a few years, especially if there are children. The fact that the bar is rarely invoked does not mean that it is ineffective. In combination with the present five year delay in such cases, it may well have an effect upon the couple's bargaining positions whichever of the five facts is eventually relied upon. Furthermore, no means has yet been discovered of dividing occupational pensions on divorce so as to mitigate the potential hardship involved. To remove the bar would therefore be to remove what may be a substantial protection for the economically weaker spouse.

5.74   Against this, of course, it must be acknowledged, as does the present bar, that there are some spouses who do not deserve such protection, however great the hardship will be. Considerations of fault, or at least of relative hardship to the other spouse of denying the divorce, would have to be taken into account. There is the further difficulty that to retain such a bar would raise the possibility, however remote, of a contentious hearing in every case. If successful, it would leave intact the empty shell of a marriage which on all objective criteria was undoubtedly dead.

5.75   Despite these disadvantages, those respondents to Facing the Future who discussed this issue were all in favour of retaining the bar. It provides an important protection for a small group of people who may still face serious hardship which the law is unable at present to redress in other ways. If it retains substantially the same form as the present bar, it is unlikely to be invoked, and even less likely to succeed, in any but a tiny minority of cases. On balance, therefore, we *recommend* that it should be possible to resist the grant of a divorce, on the ground that the dissolution of the marriage would result in grave financial or other grave hardship to the person concerned, and that it would be wrong, in all the circumstances, for the marriage to be dissolved.

5.3 Mediation

5.3.1   WHO WILL NEED TO USE MEDIATION?

FAMILY LAW ACT 1996

26.   Legal aid for mediation in family matters
   (1)   In the Legal Aid Act 1988 insert, after section 13—

'PART IIIA
MEDIATION

13A.   Scope of this Part
   (1)   This Part applies to mediation in disputes relating to family matters.
   (2)   "Family matters" means matters which are governed by English law and in relation to which any question has arisen, or may arise—
      (a)   under any provision of—
         (i)   the 1973 Act;
         (ii)   the Domestic Proceedings and Magistrates' Courts Act 1978;
         (iii)   Parts I to V of the Children Act 1989;
         (iv)   Parts II and IV of the Family Law Act 1996; or
         (v)   any other enactment prescribed;
      (b)   under any prescribed jurisdiction of a prescribed court or tribunal; or
      (c)   under any prescribed rule of law.
   (3)   Regulations may restrict this Part to mediation in disputes of any prescribed description.
   (4)   The power to—
      (a)   make regulations under subsection (2), or
      (b)   revoke any regulations made under subsection (3), is exercisable only with the consent of the Treasury.'

(2)   In section 2 of the 1988 Act, after subsection (3), insert—

'(3A) ''Mediation'' means mediation to which Part IIIA of this Act applies; and includes steps taken by a mediator in any case—
    (a) in determining whether to embark on mediation;
    (b) in preparing for mediation; and
    (c) in making any assessment under that Part.'
(3)   In section 43 of the 1988 Act, after the definition of 'legal representative' insert—
'''mediator'' means a person with whom the Board contracts for the provision of mediation by any person.'

27.   Provision and availability of mediation
After section 13A of the 1988 Act, insert—

'13B.   Provision and availability of mediation
(1)   The Board may secure the provision of mediation under this Part.
(2)   If mediation is provided under this Part, it is to be available to any person whose financial resources are such as, under regulations, make him eligible for mediation.
(3)   A person is not to be granted mediation in relation to any dispute unless mediation appears to the mediator suitable to the dispute and the parties and all the circumstances.
(4)   A grant of mediation under this Part may be amended, withdrawn or revoked.
. . .
(6)   Any contract entered into by the Board for the provision of mediation under this Part must require the mediator to comply with a code of practice.
(7)   The code must require the mediator to have arrangements designed to ensure—
    (a)   that parties participate in mediation only if willing and not influenced by fear of violence or other harm;
    (b)   that cases where either party may be influenced by fear of violence or other harm are identified as soon as possible;
    (c)   that the possibility of reconciliation is kept under review throughout mediation; and
    (d)   that each party is informed about the availability of independent legal advice.
(8)   Where there are one or more children of the family, the code must also require the mediator to have arrangements designed to ensure that the parties are encouraged to consider—
    (a)   the welfare, wishes and feelings of each child; and
    (b)   whether and to what extent each child should be given the opportunity to express his or her wishes and feelings in the mediation.'

28.   Payment for mediation
(1)   After section 13B of the 1988 Act, insert—

'13C.   Payment for mediation under this Part
(1)   Except as provided by this section, the legally assisted person is not to be required to pay for mediation provided under this Part.
(2)   Subsection (3) applies if the financial resources of a legally assisted person are such as, under regulations, make him liable to make a contribution.
(3)   The legally assisted person is to pay to the Board in respect of the costs of providing the mediation, a contribution of such amount as is determined or fixed by or under the regulations.'

29.   Mediation and civil legal aid
In section 15 of the 1988 Act, after subsection (3E) insert—

'(3F)   A person shall not be granted representation for the purposes of proceedings relating to family matters, unless he has attended a meeting with a mediator—
    (a)   to determine—

(i)   whether mediation appears suitable to the dispute and the parties and all the circumstances, and

(ii)   in particular, whether mediation could take place without either party being influenced by fear of violence or other harm; and

(b)   if mediation does appear suitable, to help the person applying for representation to decide whether instead to apply for mediation.

(3G)   Subsection (3F) does not apply—

(a)   in relation to proceedings under—

(i)   Part IV of the Family Law Act 1996;

(ii)   section 37 of the Matrimonial Causes Act 1973;

(iii)   Part IV or V of the Children Act 1989;

(b)   in relation to proceedings of any other description that may be prescribed; or

(c)   in such circumstances as may be prescribed.

(3H)   So far as proceedings relate to family matters, the Board, in determining under subsection (3)(a) whether, in relation to the proceedings, it is reasonable that a person should be granted representation under this Part—

(a)   must have regard to whether and to what extent recourse to mediation would be a suitable alternative to taking the proceedings; and

(b)   must for that purpose have regard to the outcome of the meeting held under subsection (3F) and to any assessment made for the purposes of section 13B(3).'

5.3.2   THE ROLE FOR LAWYERS

Shepherd, N, The Family Law Bill — Key Concerns [1996] Fam Law 118

MEDIATION

For mediation to work it must be entered into voluntarily and independent legal advice must be available before, during and after mediation as well as when it is inappropriate or breaks down. The Government has made a fundamental mistake in maintaining that mediation is suitable for the majority of couples going through divorce and in anchoring its reform proposals to this misconception. Although mediation of children disputes is now fairly well established, financial mediation is still largely untested. The research to date has been limited and evaluative rather than comparative. The Government relied heavily on research undertaken by the Joseph Rowntree Association into five pilot projects run by National Family Mediation, but this was based on questionnaires returned by only 54 users of all-issues mediation. The group was by definition self-selecting and nearly all had access to their own solicitors during mediation. Even then, 20% failed to reach agreement on any issues and only 39% agreed everything. The SFLA wanted to inform its response to the divorce reform proposals by seeking the views of our clients and in the summer of 1995 members were asked to send questionnaires to the ten clients to whom they next happened to write. The responses went to a central point and the results were analysed. Forty-eight per cent said they would not feel comfortable mediating and less than one-third thought that the issues could be resolved amicably through a mediator. Thirteen per cent cited domestic violence as a concern. Seventy-seven per cent said that if they were to mediate they would want access to their own solicitor throughout the process. These views were not expressed out of ignorance about mediation. Eighty per cent correctly defined mediation when given a range of options, before being given a proper definition for the purposes of the rest of the survey. The findings support the view that mediation is probably suitable for at best 30/40% of the divorcing population.

The Government says, of course, that it has no intention of making mediation compulsory, but one only has to look at clause 24 of the Bill to put that statement into context. This provides for an amendment to the Legal Aid Act 1988 to the effect that there should be a presumption, when considering the granting of legal aid for representation for proceedings, that mediation will be more appropriate 'except to prescribed . . . proceedings or in prescribed circumstances' — one law for the poorer on State funding and another for the better off. Combine this with the fact that the Bill leaves open the possibility that those who mediate may not be subject to the statutory charge, whereas those who negotiate or litigate through solicitors will, and there is a definite sense of coercion, if not actual compulsion. Independent legal advice must be available to everyone, whatever their means and at all stages, if the new system is to be fair and just.

Cretney, S, Lawyers under the Family Law Act, text of a lecture given in Middle Temple Hall on 26 March 1997 [1997] Fam Law 405

ON THE WAY OUT?

About one thing there can be no doubt. The Government believes that the use of lawyers in the divorce process should be diminished. There is (said the 1995 White Paper) a tendency for couples whose marriage is in difficulties 'to use a solicitor's office as the automatic first port of call'. Couples contemplating divorce might 'need to obtain some specific legal advice about their own legal rights and obligations'; they might even need 'some assistance with the preparation of the necessary divorce papers', and perhaps some 'legal assistance in translating the agreements', which the new legislation expects them to have reached, into either an enforceable agreement or a draft consent order 'correctly phrased and within the powers of the court'; but the public purse is no longer to fund 'uncontrolled access to lawyer representation' nor the employment of solicitors at the public expense 'to go over the ground already covered' in the negotiation process unnecessarily.

THE REASON WHY

One reason for this approach is cost—the community cannot afford the escalating burden of funding family litigation. However, there are other strands in the critical approach to the involvement of lawyers in the divorce process. At the level of ideology, there is a questioning of the whole notion of professional status. Lawyers may think that professional status involves acceptance of some form of control exercised by fellow professionals on the basis of their own knowledge and experience over such matters as qualifications, standards, and conduct, and enforced by effective disciplinary sanctions—not least the power to deprive offenders of that professional status and thereby (because the law restricts certain activities to members of the profession) of the right to offer professional services such a representation in court. However, this benevolent view of the role of the professions has long been under attack. Claims to professional status (it is said) involve the imposition of artificial and irrelevant tests—such as the ability to eat dinners—intended to restrict entry and thereby to stifle competition. The professions seek to complicate and mystify procedures (such as writing wills or defining the issues which need to be resolved in a dispute), which, so it is said, are in reality quite straightforward. In this view, far from serving the public interest, the professions are primarily concerned to further the interests of their members at the expense of the community; and the restrictive practices they employ are no more entitled to respect and recognition than the restrictive practices associated, for example, with trade unions in the printing industry or in the docks.

At a more specific level there is suspicion of the adversarial process—with its two teams of expensive gladiators, each seeking to demolish the other. How can that be consistent with the objectives, boldly asserted in s. 1 of the Family Law Act 1996, that the institution of marriage is to be supported; that couples whose marriage is in trouble should be encouraged to take all practicable steps (whether by marriage counselling or otherwise) to save the marriage; and that broken marriages should be brought to an end 'with minimum distress to the parties and children affected, with questions dealt with in a manner designed to promote as good a continuing relationship between the parties and any children affected as is possible in the circumstances and without costs being unreasonably incurred in connection with the procedures to be followed in bringing the marriage to an end'? Surely these laudable ends could be better achieved by a process—let us call it mediation—in which (I quote from the Lord Chancellor's Department's recently published 'Explanation' of the new legislation) an impartial third party helps couples considering divorce to 'meet together to deal with the arrangements to be made for the future'.

I suspect that many in this audience would sympathise with these critical approaches. Few people today would wish to defend the situation prevailing within the memories of some of us in which a person wishing to practise in the Bow County Court might be required to demonstrate a comprehensive mastery of the rule in *Alhusen* v *Whittel* (1867) LR 4 Eq 295 in all its branches, of the procedures for barring entails, and of the rules governing the emancipation of slaves in classical Roman law. The professions today have come to accept that they must be prepared to compete on level terms with others who have the necessary skills, whether to transfer the legal estate in real property or to negotiate the financial and other consequences of relationship breakdown. Again, many practising lawyers enthusiastically supported marriage guidance—let us not forget that State funding for marriage guidance was first provided on the recommendation of a committee composed largely of lawyers and chaired by a judge of what has become the Family Division. The 'preservation of the marriage tie' (proclaimed the Denning Committee in 1947) 'is of the highest importance in the interests of society' as well as the parties and their children. 'Reconciliation should be attempted in every case where there is a prospect of success; and help and guidance should be available both in preparation for marriage and also in difficulties after marriage'. Above all, the legal profession can hardly be accused of being unaware of the benefits of mediation in suitable cases—indeed, lawyers took the lead in founding and supporting by their own involvement many if not most out-of-court mediation services; whilst in-court conciliation would never have been heard of had it not been for the initiatives and encouragement of the judiciary and of practising lawyers. However, it does not follow from this that we should have unrealistic expectations about the effectiveness of counselling; and it certainly does not follow that we should assume that everything done in the name of mediation is to be supported. Still less does it follow that lawyers should be hesitant in asserting the importance and value of their own distinctive role. Part of that role is to understand and expound the law as it is found in legislation and elsewhere; and we should not make the assumption that everyone else shares the skills in which lawyers are trained.

INFORMATION GIVING AND MEDIATION
Let me give an example of what I mean. The structure of the Family Law Act 1996 seems to me to draw a very clear distinction between the functions of information giving and those of mediation. Thus attendance at an information meeting is an essential legal prerequisite to filing the statement of marital breakdown on the basis of which alone the court can hold that the marriage has irretrievably broken down and the legal status of marriage terminated by a divorce order. In contrast, although there are various provisions in the Act intended to ensure that the parties are aware of the availability of mediation, there is no provision which requires anyone to engage in mediation rather than employing the most adversarial of adversarial lawyers to look after his interests. You will understand that the question whether he is to receive public funding for this purpose is a different matter and you will understand that court rules may provide machinery—such as the financial dispute resolution (FDR) procedure—whereby a settlement oriented approach is encouraged. But, that apart, it is up to the parties to decide how they go about making their arrangements for the future. The obligation to inform the court about arrangements for the children and to provide prescribed information about financial matters if, but only if, a financial order is sought remain; that apart, it is up to the parties whether simply to decide matters for themselves, whether to seek the help of the impartial mediator in agreeing those matters, or whether—and again, I use the language of the Official Guide to the legislation—to 'negotiate at arm's length through two separate lawyers and [litigate] through the courts'.

Information Meetings to be available Nationwide before Implementation
The fact that attendance at an information meeting is, whereas participation in mediation is not, an essential procedural step in the divorce process has important consequences. First—as the Lord Chancellor stated in the parliamentary debates (*Hansard*, HL Deb, cols 1407–10, 30 January 1996)—it is 'vitally important that the information sessions should be in place and working' before the substantive changes in the divorce law are brought into force, still intended (according to the LCD Press Release of 11 March 1997) to be 'early in 1999'. Provision for mediation is a different matter. To deny access to the information meeting is to deny access to the courts; to deny access to mediation would merely be to deny the opportunity of using one particular method of dispute resolution.

The Mediation Dimension

The Government's explanatory leaflet about the Family Law Act 1996 states that the Act encourages greater use of mediation by allowing the Legal Aid Board to cover the cost of mediation for those eligible for legal aid. As the Legal Aid Board points out in *Franchising Family Mediation Services* (LAB, February 1997)—the detailed, fully worked out, and to me realistic and credible, account of its approach to securing the provision of family mediation services for clients eligible for legal aid—the provision of out-of-court family mediation services is 'very limited with less than 100 suppliers currently providing any significant volume of mediation work throughout England and Wales'. The Board also points out that, although an increasing number of services are training mediators to deal with all issues mediation (finance and property as well as children) the majority of mediators are still trained only to deal with arrangements for children. The Board draws attention to the contribution, conspicuously ignored in much of the discussion of mediation, that in reality a considerable amount of 'mediation'—over 19,000 cases per year, it seems—is provided by the Divorce Court Welfare Service, and it is clear that the place of court-based mediation needs consideration.

The Legal Aid Board envisages a four-phase operation intended to enable it to ensure the availability of publicly funded mediation services for clients eligible for legal aid; but there is one rather surprising feature about the timetable the Board envisages. The ongoing arrangements are not expected to be settled until early in 2000—more than a year after the date on which the Lord Chancellor's officials envisage that the new divorce provisions will have been brought into force. Moreover, the Legal Aid Board has explained that it regards the timetable set as a 'challenging' one, and the 'shortest possible . . . for effectively piloting and introducing contracting arrangements'. The Board warns that, as the pilot progresses, it may become apparent that a longer timescale is required. It seems, therefore, that the Lord Chancellor's Department is content to see the Act brought into force before—perhaps substantially before—the Legal Aid Board's funded schemes are fully in place.

I have said that the Legal Aid Board's proposals are fully worked out; but it seems likely that the relationship between legal aid funded and privately funded mediation will be problematic. Certainly, existing private sector services may find some parts of the Board's paper—for example, the statement (paras 1.57–1.58) that it is unlikely the Board will contract with not-for-profit mediation services 'unless they can demonstrate that there is ongoing funding from other organisations', and that such services will be expected to 'build up a substantial private client income in order to be financially viable'—worrying. Perhaps some ongoing funding will be provided to the private sector by the Probation Service; but there must be more than one mediation service (desperately seeking to keep its operation going by repeated appeals to those the Board's paper describes as 'existing funders') who had expected legal aid to provide the necessary core financial support, and who will wish that someone could explain to the charities and individuals concerned that the Board expects 'existing funders' to continue this role. Will those who have struggled for so long share the confidence expressed by the Board's Director of Resources and Supplier Development (*New Law Journal*, 21 February 1997, p. 265) that the extension of legal aid franchising on these terms will 'facilitate the expansion of mediation to meet the demand created by the Family Law Act 1996'?

The UK College of Family Mediators

There has been another important recent development in relation to mediation—the foundation in January 1996 of the UK College of Family Mediators, which is committed to building on the best mediation practice and the development of standards—by, amongst other things, establishing a register of those who meet prescribed standards, and a code of professional practice and conduct for family mediators. The eminence of those who serve the College is well known. The aims of the College in seeking to minimise the sometimes fissiparous tendency observable in mediation as in other idealistically motivated vocations are widely supported; and the College's commitment—as befits its logo motto: 'Creating the firm foundation for a growing profession'—to protection of the public against the incompetent, the exploitative, and it may even be the dishonest is universally welcomed. The publication in January 1997 of the College's 'Standards for Mediators' and the 'Guidelines thereto' is, on any basis, a noteworthy event; but I am afraid I must make two rather negative comments.

First, how realistic are the 'standards' which it is hoped to establish? There are 7 pages of 'guidelines', each closely printed. Two lines on those pages prescribe an 'appropriate knowledge of family law and legal processes' as one of the 'training requirements'; but an appendix supplies the missing detail. Not just 'the current legislation concerning families, family breakdown, and financial support', not just the Family Law Act 1996 and its changes to divorce legislation, and legal aid legislation, the range of orders relating to children, issues regarding domestic violence, but also the legislation relating to pensions and divorce and how it works in practice, the Child Support Act 1991 and, in particular, how clean break settlements are dealt with and the law relating to mainten- ance and capital settlements.

I have serious doubts about how realistic this is, and I repeat the question: who is going to inform those contemplating divorce just what options are open to them? This is not the stuff of millionaires' defences, it is the ordinary lower middle class case where there is one heavily mortgaged home and, perhaps, an occupational pension. The information meeting is not going to advise 'attendees' that, for example, a husband might want to limit the wife's occupation of the family home so that it would terminate if she were to install a partner there. Would this be one of the options that the mediator would put to the couple at their joint meeting? Lawyers can do this because under our maligned adversarial system loyalties are not divided—you tell your client what he may seek if he wishes to do so, and then it is up to him to instruct you. So, what is to be the status of the negotiated agreement which emerges from a successful mediation if the husband subsequently complains that no one told him? Perhaps this kind of explanation will be part of the 'legal assistance in translating the agreements' into legal form which you are still to be expected to provide? If so, it is surely not excessively pessimistic to see an awful lot of successful mediations being re-opened. If not, there may be a significant increase in the number of applications to set aside apparently concluded agreements.

What about the objective of protecting the public? It is all very well to have standards, but how are they to be enforced? This audience knows the consequences of being struck off the roll or being disbarred. A doctor knows the consequence of having his name removed from the medical register. Practitioners may still be able to use the skills they acquired to practise their profession—they may draft wills, peddle pharmaceutical products, if all else fails they may even become law teachers, but they cannot hold themselves out as members of the profession concerned, nor can they perform any of the functions (admittedly now limited) of which their profession has a monopoly. The UK College of Family Mediators is to have a Complaints Committee and, indeed, a Disciplinary Committee which no doubt—the documents I have seen are not very explicit—will have the ultimate sanction of expulsion available to it. However, as far as the law of England is concerned, that will not stop you practising as a 'mediator'. The sad reality is that the UK College has, in this context, no powers whatsoever—the emperor is almost completely naked.

Why only 'almost'? Because that is how the Society of Gentlemen Practitioners in the Courts of Law and Equity (now better known as The Law Society) began. No doubt there will be advantages to membership of the College—for example, perhaps practitioners will find it difficult to get a legal aid franchise to practise mediation unless they are accredited by the College. It may be that in time the well informed will know that they are taking a risk if they entrust their affairs to someone not in the College's directory. It may even be that a government less hostile to the professions than that in office for the last 18 years will consider enacting legislation for the regulation of the emerging profession—after all, even the Society of Gentlemen Practitioners began with a limited monopoly in relation to certain kinds of litigation. All these things may be . . . but they are not so now; and we delude ourselves if we pretend otherwise.

THE LAWYER'S ROLE?

What of the lawyer in practice? I return to the original subtitle of this lecture 'Hired Gun or Nanny?' The 'hired gun' I have no doubt will flourish, perhaps as never before. In particular, we can confidently anticipate a decade of prosperity for the Family Law Bar Association, perhaps comparable to that experienced in the decade following the massive judicialisation of child care brought about by the Children Act 1989. Not only all that new (and, in parts, hurriedly drafted) legislation waiting to be construed, but as I have said all those agreements hurriedly arrived at as the price of getting a divorce and now so vulnerable to the cry 'if only we had known'.

What about the nanny role—'comprehensive client care' I suppose is how we should describe it? Of course 'nanny' is a term with socio-economic overtones. We are not talking about those hard-pressed parents whose finances are such that they have no choice other than to entrust their child care arrangements to a child-minder. They—financially eligible for legal aid—are not to be forced into mediation against their will; and the legal profession—not to say their clients—should properly be grateful to Sir James Lester MP who was responsible for persuading the Government to remove from the Bill the provision which would have required the Legal Aid Board to assume mediation to be preferable to legal representation. However, whether such couples are likely to be able to find a solicitor able to explain what the presenter at the Information meeting meant by the statement (found in the LCUs explanatory pamphlet about the Act) that the 'new law makes clear [sic] that . . . conduct will be assessed by the court in making a financial settlement on divorce in those cases where it would be inequitable not to do so' remains to be seen. Perhaps there will be a role for the legal aid solicitor as mediation 'supervisors'. Perhaps, even, it will prove impracticable to find adequate mediation services in small towns and the process will go on in such places much as it does at the moment—clients being better informed, of course, by the obligatory information meeting. Things may also be different if clients seek and obtain a 'domestic violence' order under Part IV of the Act, for which representation will still be available and which would surely satisfy those concerned that mediation could not take place without the client being influenced by fear of violence or other harm (s. 29). But this possibility apart—and would it not be paradoxical if the main effect of the reforms were a dramatic increase in the number of ouster applications, particularly if the courts come to accept the widely publicised researchers' conclusions that any incident of violence should lead to a termination of child contact—I cannot pretend that the outlook in terms of legal practice—of course, some will make up the gap by qualifying as mediators—is other than bleak.

At the other extreme, the seriously rich are still no doubt going to want and expect the one-stop service they have traditionally enjoyed from specialist practitioners who will no doubt welcome the encouragement for clients to resolve the arrangements for the children face to face and perhaps with the help of a mediator. As always, it is those betwixt and between who are going to constitute the problem. If I were a practising solicitor I would dread the prospect of being assailed by a certain kind of client who, fired with a little of the knowledge traditionally acquired at dinner parties but now to be officially disseminated at the information session, would demand to know why I did not advise her to apply for an order preventing divorce, why I do not think her husband's no doubt appalling behaviour should be taken into account (after all, the new law makes it clear, so the presenter said), and so on. . . .

So far as some, perhaps many, solicitors are concerned it may be that the Act will make little real difference to everyday practice—the end of the need to settle petitions alleging one of the facts specified in the 1973 Act will be a positive advantage not only to clients but also to solicitors; and mediation as and when it is available will be as advantageous as it always has been. There is a downside, of course—in particular, although the obligation to submit to an information meeting may do some good in some cases, it seems bound to add to the expense of divorce, likely to seem patronising and demeaning to some, and to serve no useful purpose to many. We had—we still have—many excellent providers of information about the divorce process: they are called solicitors.

However, I fear I reveal my own prejudices—I am a divorce sceptic. I suspect that it is easy to exaggerate the extent to which bitterness, distress, and humiliation can by institutional means be removed from the divorce process, and that no amount of skilled counselling will remove altogether the evils attributable (as the Lord Chancellor once reminded us) to the hardness of men's hearts, or if you prefer, to human nature. Even so, I am sure mediation has a valuable role— what a pity it is that the Government, by refusing minimal funding for so many years, missed the opportunity to encourage natural evolution, and growth in this field. However, as it is, mediators and solicitors are going to have to demonstrate what they have to offer; and it is to be for the consumer to opt for mediation if he wants it and can afford it, and negotiation between solicitors if he wants it and can afford it. That, I believe, is what the Act provides. But is it how the choice is to be presented?

STACKED CARDS AND A PACKED JURY?

It is implicit in the Government's commitment to the dissemination of information that this process can be value free, and I have told you that I have doubts about this; but at least those who are responsible for informing the public ought to be scrupulous in their concern for accuracy. I am sorry to say that I think the Lord Chancellor's Department's explanatory leaflet on the Act is defective in this respect. The leaflet states that information meetings are intended to ensure that people thinking about divorce have information about the *advantages of* mediation. The same document tells the reader that the Act 'gives the court the power to direct the parties to attend a meeting with a mediator for an explanation of the availability *and benefits* of mediation'. Neither of these statements is wholly accurate. The Act, in fact, provides that the court may direct such a meeting to enable 'an explanation to be given of the facilities available to the parties for mediation . . . and of providing an opportunity for each party to agree to take advantage of those facilities'; it also provides that Regulations are to make provision with respect to the giving of information about 'mediation'—a process which certainly has advantages and benefits in some cases, but equally has a downside. Just a matter of emphasis, you may think. But perhaps some people will share my concern that these repeated misrepresentations are symptomatic; and that the cards are—of course, with the best of motives—going to be stacked, and the information meeting little more than a thinly disguised sales pitch for the benefits of mediation, little emphasis being given to any possible disadvantage. Again, I have drawn attention to the prominence of particular professional backgrounds amongst those so far nominated both as lead agencies for the pilot information projects and amongst those who are to evaluate its outcome. Of course, I do not cast any doubt on the integrity and objectivity of those concerned, but if the Lord Chancellor's Department can be guilty of what I believe to be a significant misinterpretation of the legislation, can we be confident that all those appointed will understand the criteria in fact laid down by law? I am afraid I think that a lawyer, confronted with a jury so overwhelmingly dominated by those with a counselling/ mediation background, might feel his client would want to exercise the right to challenge.

5.4   End of Chapter Assessment Question

Evaluate the effect of the Family Law Act 1996 on divorce.

5.5   End of Chapter Assessment Outline Answer

Clearly this question does not just require a description of the provisions of the Family Law Act 1996, you must question and evaluate the changes that are to be introduced. Will the Act solve the perceived problems with the 'old' divorce law? Will the changes work? What are the problems with the changes, etc?

Initially, you should have introduced the new Act, and made clear that the provisions are not yet in force, and that no date has been set to bring the provisions into force. You may have commented on the fact that the changes were hotly debated, and were accused of making the divorce process too easy — this could be reflected in your analysis of the changes later on. You should also have made it clear in your introduction that in order to evaluate the changes, you have to discuss, to some extent, what was wrong with the old law, and the grounds under which a divorce could be sought.

I would suggest that a quick review of the Matrimonial Causes Act 1973 would probably be the best start. Refer to the fact that the 1973 Act was designed to introduce the concept of 'no-fault' divorce and that this was achieved by the ground of 'irretrievable breakdown' of the marriage. However, you can easily introduce one of the major criticisms of the Act, in that it required irretrievable breakdown to be proved by reference to one or more of the 'facts', and in particular, that three of those facts are indeed based on fault (adultery, behaviour and desertion). Use statistics to illustrate that the fault facts are the most commonly used facts on which to base a divorce petition.

Other criticisms that have been levelled at the 1973 Act include the adherence to an adversarial system (although many would in fact dispute the validity of the criticism). It is true that the process maintains its links with the adversarial justice system, and this may lead to an entrenchment of attitudes. It certainly will assist in the increase of costs to both the parties and the legal aid fund. This too was criticised, since most of the 'expensive' litigation takes place after the divorce, e.g. the ancillary matters. The lack of opportunity to discuss the divorce, face to face, has also been seen to make a divorce harder on any children of the relationship, and the lack of consideration of the impact of divorce on children is also a major criticism.

You may also have mentioned the concerns as to the ease with which couples can get a divorce. This would require some mention of the special procedure, and the fact that the divorce is dealt with 'on paper'. Little investigation is made into the circumstances of the situation — again you may link this into the proposals for change — do they address this concern?

Having made mention of the problems with the Matrimonial Causes Act 1973, look at the main substance of the question — the changes in the Family Law Act 1996 and their effectiveness.

The changes are numerous — the need to support and promote marriage as an institution is made far more apparent, with all involved with divorce being required to keep reconciliation and marriage guidance in mind for the couple. The 1996 Act works on a basis that divorce is to be a process rather than an event — hence much of the post-divorce proceedings will need to be dealt with prior to the court being able to make the divorce order. This is intended to make the parties more responsible for the future, and these matters are supposed to be dealt with by discussion between the separating couple. You may feel that this is beneficial, harmonious break-ups are always better, especially if children are involved. But, the 1996 Act emphasises mediation throughout, and yet it is recognised that many couples would not find mediation helpful, that it is certainly not suitable for all couples, that any resolutions may not meet legal requirements, and that there is not yet a recognised national governing body or standards for mediators. Also, and this is my own unsubstantiated opinion, it may be that during this period of negotiation, couples may realise they simply cannot afford to divorce — is it better to have an unhappy married couple, just to improve our divorce statistics?

The process of filing a statement of breakdown, information meetings, the period of reflection all need to be mentioned. The latter is especially important, since it will mean that marriages must exist for at least one year nine months, or even longer if children are involved. This will clearly have an impact on the couple, and may lead to more applications in nullity, since the same restrictions do not apply.

Another issue that would usefully be mentioned is the change to the legal aid scheme, in that civil legal aid may be refused if the matter is considered suitable for mediation and yet the parties refuse to go to sessions. You may feel it highlights a conflict of interest since it seems to be the mediator who will assess the suitability of the case for mediation. The inability to get state funding for legal advice may also be highlighted as a potential area of concern with the changes.

You would not be expected to go into great detail of the changes to the financial orders, and the changes that have been made here. However, it is true to say that a similar question arises in respect of assessment of financial settlements negotiated between the parties and the special procedure. As yet it is unclear to what extent the judiciary will go behind the settlement to assess its suitability.

Your conclusion would obviously draw together the threads — are the changes going to be effective? It certainly depends on how the judiciary, the legal profession and the parties themselves adapt — there are clearly some benefits but my own view (again personal) is that some sections of the 1996 Act operate under a very misguided view as to human nature and the attitudes of couples undergoing divorce, and finally that the Act is ultimately a cost saving device to the public legal aid bill. You may choose to agree or dispute my views!

CHAPTER SIX

PROPERTY AND FINANCE ON DIVORCE

6.1 Financial Orders: Section 23

MATRIMONIAL CAUSES ACT 1973

23. Financial provision orders in connection with divorce proceedings, etc.

(1) On granting a decree of divorce, a decree of nullity of marriage or a decree of judicial separation or at any time thereafter (whether, in the case of a decree of divorce or of nullity of marriage, before or after the decree is made absolute), the court may make any one or more of the following orders, that is to say—

(a) an order that either party to the marriage shall make to the other such periodical payments, for such term, as may be specified in the order;

(b) an order that either party to the marriage shall secure to the other to the satisfaction of the court such periodical payments, for such term, as may be so specified;

(c) an order that either party to the marriage shall pay to the other such lump sum or sums as may be so specified;

(d) an order that a party to the marriage shall make to such person as may be specified in the order for the benefit of a child of the family, or to such a child, such periodical payments, for such term, as may be so specified;

(e) an order that a party to the marriage shall secure to such person as may be so specified for the benefit of such a child, or to such a child, to the satisfaction of the court, such periodical payments, for such term, as may be so specified;

(f) an order that a party to the marriage shall pay to such person as may be so specified for the benefit of such a child, or to such a child, such lump sum as may be so specified;

subject however, in the case of an order under paragraph (d), (e) or (f) above, to the restrictions imposed by section 29(1) and (3) below on the making of financial provision orders in favour of children who have attained the age of eighteen.

(2) The court may also, subject to those restrictions, make any one or more of the orders mentioned in subsection (1)(d), (e) and (f) above—

(a) in any proceedings for divorce, nullity of marriage or judicial separation, before granting a decree, and

(b) where any such proceedings are dismissed after the beginning of the trial, either forthwith or within a reasonable period after the dismissal.

(3) Without prejudice to the generality of subsection (1)(c) or (f) above—

(a) an order under this section that a party to a marriage shall pay a lump sum to the other party may be made for the purpose of enabling that other party to meet any liabilities or expenses reasonably incurred by him or her in maintaining himself or herself or any child of the family before making an application for an order under this section in his or her favour;

. . .

(c) an order under this section for the payment of a lump sum may provide for the payment of that sum by instalments of such amount as may be specified in the order and may require the payment of the instalments to be secured to the satisfaction of the court.

. . .

(5)   Without prejudice to the power to give a direction under section 30 below for the settlement of an instrument by conveyancing counsel, where an order is made under subsection (1)(a), (b) or (c) above on or after granting a decree of divorce or nullity of marriage, neither the order nor any settlement made in pursuance of the order shall take effect unless the decree has been made absolute.

(6)   Where the court—

(a)   makes an order under this section for the payment of a lump sum; and

(b)   directs—

(i)   that payment of that sum or any part of it shall be deferred; or

(ii)   that that sum or any part of it shall be paid by instalments,

the court may order that the amount deferred or the instalments shall carry interest at such rate as may be specified by the order from such date, not earlier than the date of the order, as may be so specified, until the date when payment of it is due.

6.1.1   PERIODICAL PAYMENTS

MATRIMONIAL CAUSES ACT 1973

28.   Duration of continuing financial provision orders in favour of party to marriage, and effect of remarriage

(1)   Subject in the case of an order made on or after the grant of a decree of divorce or nullity of marriage to the provisions of sections 25A(2) above and 31(7) below, the term to be specified in a periodical payments or secured periodical payments order in favour of a party to a marriage shall be such term as the court thinks fit, except that the term shall not begin before or extend beyond the following limits, that is to say—

(a)   in the case of a periodical payments order, the term shall begin not earlier than the date of the making of an application for the order, and shall be so defined as not to extend beyond the death of either of the parties to the marriage or, where the order is made on or after the grant of a decree of divorce or nullity of marriage, the remarriage of the party in whose favour the order is made; and

(b)   in the case of a secured periodical payments order, the term shall begin not earlier than the date of the making of an application for the order, and shall be so defined as not to extend beyond the death or, where the order is made on or after the grant of such a decree, the remarriage of the party in whose favour the order is made.

(1A)   Where a periodical payments or secured periodical payments order in favour of a party to a marriage is made on or after the grant of a decree of divorce or nullity of marriage, the court may direct that that party shall not be entitled to apply under section 31 below for the extension of the term specified in the order.

(2)   Where a periodical payments or secured periodical payments order in favour of a party to a marriage is made otherwise than on or after a grant of a decree of divorce or nullity of marriage, and the marriage in question is subsequently dissolved or annulled but the order continues in force, the order shall, notwithstanding anything in it, cease to have effect on the remarriage of that party, except in relation to any arrears due under or on the date of the remarriage.

(3)   If after the grant of a decree dissolving or annulling a marriage either party to that marriage remarries, whether at any time before or after the commencement of this Act, that party shall not be entitled to apply, by reference to the grant of that decree, for a financial provision order in his or her favour, or for a property adjustment order, against the other party to that marriage.

6.1.2   MAINTENANCE PENDING SUIT

MATRIMONIAL CAUSES ACT 1973

22.   Maintenance pending suit

On a petition for divorce, nullity of marriage or judicial separation, the court may make an order for maintenance pending suit, that is to say, an order requiring either party to the marriage to make to the other such periodical payments for his or her maintenance and for such term, being a term beginning not earlier than the date of the presentation of the petition and ending with the date of the determination of the suit, as the court thinks reasonable.

6.2 Property Orders: Section 24

MATRIMONIAL CAUSES ACT 1973

24. Property adjustment orders in connection with divorce proceedings, etc.

(1) On granting a decree of divorce, a decree of nullity of marriage or a decree of judicial separation or at any time thereafter (whether, in the case of a decree of divorce, or of nullity of marriage, before or after the decree is made absolute), the court may make any one or more of the following orders, that is to say—

(a) an order that a party to the marriage shall transfer to the other party, to any child of the family or to such person as may be specified in the order for the benefit of such a child such property as may be so specified, being property to which the first-mentioned party is entitled, either in possession or reversion;

(b) an order that a settlement of such property as may be so specified, being property to which a party to the marriage is so entitled, be made to the satisfaction of the court for the benefit of the other party to the marriage and of the children of the family or either or any of them;

(c) an order varying for the benefit of the parties to the marriage and of the children of the family or either or any of them any ante-nuptial or post-nuptial settlement (including such a settlement made by will or codicil) made on the parties to the marriage.

(d) an order extinguishing or reducing the interest of either of the parties to the marriage under any such settlement;

subject, however, in the case of an order under paragraph (a) above, to the restrictions imposed by section 29(1) and (3) below on the making of orders for a transfer of property in favour of children who have attained the age of eighteen.

(2) The court may make an order under subsection (1)(c) above notwithstanding that there are no children of the family.

(3) Without prejudice to the power to give a direction under section 30 below for the settlement of an instrument by conveyancing counsel, where an order is made under this section on or after granting a decree of divorce or nullity of marriage, neither the order nor any settlement made in pursuance of the order shall take effect unless the decree has been made absolute.

24A. Orders for sale of property

(1) Where the court makes under section 23 or 24 of this Act a secured periodical payments order, an order for the payment of a lump sum or a property adjustment order, then, on making that order or at any time thereafter, the court may make a further order for the sale of such property as may be specified in the order, being property in which or in the proceeds of sale of which either or both of the parties to the marriage has or have a beneficial interest, either in possession or reversion.

(2) Any order made under subsection (1) above may contain such consequential or supplementary provisions as the court thinks fit and, without prejudice to the generality of the foregoing provision, may include—

(a) provision requiring the making of a payment out of the proceeds of sale of the property to which the order relates, and

(b) provision requiring any such property to be offered for sale to a person, or class of persons, specified in the order.

(3) Where an order is made under subsection (1) above on or after the grant of a decree of divorce or nullity of marriage, the order shall not take effect unless the decree has been made absolute.

(4) Where an order is made under subsection (1) above, the court may direct that the order, or such provision thereof as the court may specify, shall not take effect until the occurrence of an event specified by the court or the expiration of a period so specified.

(5)   Where an order under subsection (1) above contains a provision requiring the proceeds of sale of the property to which the order relates to be used to secure periodical payments to a party to the marriage, the order shall cease to have effect on the death or re-marriage of that person.

(6)   Where a party to a marriage has a beneficial interest in any property, or in the proceeds of sale thereof, and some other person who is not a party to the marriage also has a beneficial interest in that property or in the proceeds of sale thereof, then, before deciding whether to make an order under this section in relation to that property, it shall be the duty of the court to give that other person an opportunity to make representations with respect to the order; and any representations made by that other person shall be included among the circumstances to which the court is required to have regard under section 25(1) below.

6.2.1   TRANSFERS AND SETTLEMENT OF PROPERTY

6.2.1.1   Types of property adjustment orders

HANLON v HANLON [1978] 1 WLR 592 (CA)

ORMROD LJ: The marriage was ultimately dissolved after two years' separation on May 15, 1974. The parties had lived at no. 106, Trinity Lane, Waltham Cross, which is an ordinary three-bedroom/two sitting room type of house. The marriage, at the time when it broke up, had lasted 14 years. There are four children, all of whom are still living with the wife at 106, Trinity Lane. The family consists of two boys, now both over 18 and both in apprenticeship; a girl called Katherine, who is 14 and a girl called Clare who is 12. The house itself was bought in 1963 in the sole name of the husband for £4,200, with a mortgage of £3,900, the balance being found, we are told, from the husband's bank. The current value of the property is said to be about £14,000; the mortgage outstanding is £3,639, and for all practical purposes it has been treated in this litigation as having an equity value of roughly £10,000. There are at the moment arrears under the mortgage amounting to something slightly over £400; those arrears have arisen since the wife became responsible for making the mortgage repayments and she recognises, without any question, that the liability to pay those arrears is hers. The husband had been paying the mortgage instalments up to 1976.

In the result, the registrar decided that the best way of dealing with the matter in the interests of both parties was, in effect, to order an immediate sale of the property, but recognising that this would have the effect of destroying the family home for the wife and her four children, he suggested, and eventually ordered, that the wife should buy the husband out, buying him out on the footing that their beneficial interests in this house were equal; that meant in practice that the wife had to raise £5,000 to buy out the husband's interest. This suggestion apparently was put forward at a comparatively late stage, and the wife's advisers had not had an opportunity of going into it in detail particularly as to whether the wife could finance such an arrangement.

After the registrar's order, investigations were made and it became at once apparent, as everyone agrees now, that she could not possibly finance it. The reasons for that were—and it was oven more obvious then than it might have been today—that in order to raise the further £5,000 she would have to pay off the existing mortgage of £3,600, making a total of something over £8,000 that she would have to raise, on terms which, of course, were more onerous relatively, pound for pound, than the old mortgage; and also she had to carry out repairs. There was a controversy about the cost of the repairs; she put it at some £900, but it may well be that that was an overstatement. The husband's advisers put it at about £200, but that was probably based on inadequate information. No finding as to the precise figure was made by the judge, or indeed could have been made; it is sufficient to say that the wife, in order to get any further mortgage on this property, would have to carry out the minimum repairs required by the building society, which presumably would have cost her something between those two figures. Taking into account her income position, it was apparent that she could not possibly finance any such mortgage, so it became impossible to comply with the registrar's order.

So the wife applied for leave to appeal against this order out of time. Faulks J rejected her application and refused her leave; she came to this court; this court gave her leave to appeal and the matter went back to Rees J and hence back again to this court.

In the end—and I think it is not unfair to say, almost in despair of solving the problem—the judge reverted to what he called 'the normal order.' By 'the normal order' he meant a *Mesher* v *Mesher* [1980] 1 All ER 126 type of order; that is to say, the sale of the house to be postponed until the youngest child reached the age of 17 and the proceeds of sale divided equally. He had *Martin (B.H.)* v *Martin (D.)* [1977] 3 WLR 101 cited to him, and no doubt he took account of it. There have been other cases in this court, in which the court has drawn attention to the fact that *Mesher* v *Mesher* was not, in any sense of the word, a typical case. So the judge, in despair, made the *Mesher* v *Mesher* type of order.

It is agreed by both sides that the result of making such order in this particular case will really be almost disastrous.

In my judgment it is as well in this case to have another look at the history. Up to now everybody has been approaching the case on the footing that the interests of these two parties in this property were equal. That seems to me to be a doubtfully accurate assumption, or premise. Putting them as shortly as I can, the facts are these. Over 14 years of cohabitation these two parties no doubt contributed broadly equally to this family in terms of money, in terms of work and so on. From 1971 onwards—that is now for over 5 years—the wife has had the upbringing of these four children and has been working full time as a community nurse. She has maintained the house as well as she could during those years, and on any view she has taken a considerable load off the shoulders of the husband over a period of five years, and she will continue to take a large load off his shoulders from now until the youngest child leaves home—which of course will not necessarily by any manner of means be in five years' time. A family like this will not simply dissolve completely on the 17th birthday of the youngest child. In fact, of course, she will be, as the mother of this family, maintaining the nucleus of the home effectively for a considerable number of years, until the girls are married and settled on their own, and the boys are similarly married and settled on their own; that is what it really means in real life. So in my view she has made a very large contribution to this family. She has much less good prospects than the husband's so far as her future is concerned, because he will be able to retire when he is 58 and, like many police officers, will be able to take other employment, certainly for another seven years or maybe longer if he wishes. He is a completely free agent so far as his life is concerned; he is living to all intents and purposes a bachelor existence, at the moment contributing £7 per week under the judge's order, for each of these two children. As I have said before, on any view £7 a week for girls, one of 14 and one of 12, is manifestly inadequate to cover the cost of feeding and clothing and all the other expenses which are unavoidable.

So the view I take of the case is that, as the cards have fallen, apart no doubt from his being unhappy at being on his own, in financial terms he has done a lot better than his wife and is likely to go on doing a lot better.

If any other type of order were made, which involves postponing the sale of the house, it is plain that she will be contributing all the time to the upkeep of the house, and paying off substantial amounts of the loan. In my judgment it would be a quite wrong exercise of the discretion in accordance with the principles of section 25 to make any order which had the result of forcing her to leave that property in the foreseeable future. It was suggested that this might be the kind of case which could be met by postponing the sale indefinitely until further order, and then distributing the proceeds of sale, not necessarily on a 50–50 basis; but I do not think that that in this case would be in the least satisfactory; it would leave the wife in a state of perpetual uncertainty and neither party would know where ultimately they were going to be. It seems to me far better that the parties' interests should be crystallised now, once and for all, so that the wife can know what she is going to do about the property and the husband can make up his mind about what he is going to do about rehousing.

I would only add this, that if this property is to be sold in accordance with the judge's order the result would probably have been to put the responsibility of housing the wife on the local authority in subsidised accommodation. If Mr Johnson's gloomy prognosis of the husband's future turns out to be right, he too would be joining the queue for council accommodation when his right to occupy the police flat comes to an end. Each of them would then have £2,500 in cash which would not be required for their housing. In my judgment that is not a fair or satisfactory result.

So in my view the fair way of dealing with this case, taking into account contributions, income, liabilities now and in the future and lump sums in the future and needs particularly, is to transfer this house to the wife absolutely and to reduce the order for periodical payments for the children to a nominal sum; if there are arrears they can be remitted; I do not know whether there are any.

I would therefore allow the appeal and substitute that order.

MORTIMER v *MORTIMER-GRIFFIN* [1986] 2 FLR 315 (CA)

SIR JOHN DONALDSON MR: This appeal concerns a property adjustment order made in matrimonial proceedings. The husband and wife were married in 1967. The husband is now aged about 46, and his ex-wife is aged about 43. I will refer to them as husband and wife, notwithstanding that their divorce has become final. A daughter, C, was born, who is now aged 14.

Until 1976 the husband was out at work and so was the wife until C was born. So if matters are viewed as at 1976, both parties had contributed to the marriage more or less on equal terms, because it would be quite wrong to suggest that if a husband earns money and a wife looks after a child, that means that the two cannot be equated, one with the other, even if it is easier to put a figure on the husband's activities than on the wife's activities.

After 1976, when the marriage came to an end, the wife retrained as a teacher. Thereafter, and until this day, she has been solely responsible for looking after C, and, subject to the receipt of £78 a month by way of child maintenance between 1976 and 1984, she has been solely responsible for all the expenses involving her own maintenance and that of C, which includes education at a private school in the London area.

So far as the mortgage on the house was concerned, that was paid by the husband until 1977, when he ceased paying. He was at that time still in employment, but no doubt he took the view that as he was no longer living in the house, there was no reason why he should continue to pay the mortgage. I do not necessarily criticize him for that very natural reaction. But it is a fact that the whole cost of the mortgage fell on the wife as from 1977.

. . . He is therefore in a position to say that his liabilities, both in relation to his ex-wife and his daughter, are at an end.

Unfortunately, neither party can say the same regarding the legal aid fund because each has a potential liability to that fund of some £7,000.

The mortgage on this house is supported by a with-profits insurance policy, but it is accepted that that policy was taken out by the wife and has been wholly maintained by her. It is not a very significant sum—being worth only some £700 at the present time, although it will become worth a great deal more in the course of time—subject, of course, to the wife continuing to pay the premiums. In the orders made by the registrar, attempts were made to bring that policy into account, but in my judgment it is very much easier to ignore it and to treat it as only being worth some £700; and to treat the house as being subject to a mortgage.

So far as the house is concerned, Mr Registrar Angel thought that the appropriate way to deal with the matter was to declare that the husband should have a 20% interest in it, and the wife an 80% interest, and to postpone sale until a large number of events, which can basically be summarized by saying until C reaches the age of 25, or completes her full-time education.

On appeal to Bush J, the judge varied the apportionment figure as to 40% to the husband and 60% to the wife, and included rather more elaborate (and probably better) *termini ad quem*, for the sale of the property.

The wife appeals to this court, and basically the submission made by counsel on her behalf is that we should either restore the order of the registrar; or, alternatively—and this is naturally his main submission—that we should give the husband a lump sum at the present time, there being no point, so far as he is concerned, in giving him anything between £2,500 and, say, £9,500 to £10,000, as the balance would merely find its way back to the legal aid fund. So the wife submits the figure of £2,500 would be the correct figure to adopt.

In my view in the latter years since this marriage broke down the wife has been shouldering a wholly disproportionate burden as compared with the husband. I do not criticize him for that; but it is a fact. Against that, the husband is entitled to point out her earning capacity.

However, looking to the future—and it may be quite a long future—there is a suggestion that C may go on to higher education and there is talk that she may even decide to go into the medical profession, which again suggests an almost open-ended commitment for the wife.

Bearing those factors in mind, it seems to me that even 20% to the husband could not be justified. In those circumstances, I would be minded to accept counsel for the wife's first submission, namely, that the husband should receive a sum of £2,500 now, as being a proper method of applying the test which we are required to apply by s. 25 of the Matrimonial Causes Act 1973.

I appreciate and pay tribute to the experience, both of the registrar and of the judge, but I am heartened (and perhaps supported) in my temerity in interfering with both by the fact that neither agreed with the other. It does seem to me that both orders suffer from the defects to which Ormrod LJ drew attention, that 'chickens come home to roost' at an unpredictable time and in unpredictable circumstances; and that while an adjustment based on percentages seems attractive at the time, experience shows that it is subject to all kinds of difficulties and objections when it is worked out in the event.

Accordingly, I would allow this appeal and, subject to any detailed consideration of the order, in essence make an order that the wife pay the husband £2,500.

KNIBB v KNIBB [1987] 2 FLR 396 (CA)

SHELDON J: The property was originally in the parties' joint names. It was common ground that, following the breakdown of the marriage, the wife should continue to live there with her children, and indeed that upon suitable terms, the sole title to the property should be vested in her. Such a vesting order was made on 5 August 1985.

On the same day and reciting that fact, and upon undertakings being given by the wife to obtain her husband's release from the then existing mortgage, and to indemnify him against any further liability under it, a further order was made by Mr Registrar Simons, containing the following terms:

(1)   That the petitioner [the wife] do within 14 days of being so required execute a charge in favour of the respondent to secure to him 40% of the net value of the property as hereinafter defined.

(2)   That the charge shall provide:

(i)   that the statutory power of sale thereunder shall be deemed to arise on the happening of the first of the following events: (a) the petitioner's death; (b) the petitioner's remarriage; (c) the petitioner's cohabitation with a man for a period of 3 months; (d) the petitioner's voluntary removal from the property; and

(ii)   that the charge may be redeemed within 4 months of 5 August 1985 by the payment by the petitioner to the respondent of the sum of £3,500.

(3)   That the petitioner's claim for all types of ancillary relief are upon the making of the said vesting order dismissed' [with a further prohibition on any further claims].

HANLON v HANLON [1978] 1 WLR 592 (CA)

ORMROD LJ: The youngest child is 12, so we are talking about a postponement of sale for five years. In five years' time each of these parties will, we assume, receive £5,000, plus such inflationary increase as takes place in those five years. The Law Society, under the present regime, which was not in force at the time of the registrar's order, will have a charge on each of those sums of £5,000 for the costs incurred by the respective parties. It is common ground, having regard to the scale of costs in this case, that inevitably neither of them can possibly in fact receive a sum in excess of the maximum fixed by the regulation, namely, £2,500. That is the amount which is at present exempt from the Law Society's charge.

So the result of the judge's order is that in five years' time each of them will get £2,500, increased by whatever the inflationary increase is by then. (One hopes that if inflation is severe, sooner rather than later the exemption figure will be raised.) But dealing with it in 1977 prices, they will each get £2,500 only.

It is common ground that that figure is inadequate to provide either of them with a home. Obviously the wife cannot provide a home for herself on that sum, let alone for any children who are still at home in five years' time. It is said that the husband equally. on his income, cannot possibly raise enough money to buy himself a flat if he is minded to.

So the effect of the order will be, in the short term, to make the wife and such of the children who are still with her, homeless in five years' time—that is, in 1982—while the husband, assuming that he is still in the police force, will have a perfectly safe house or flat, until he chooses to leave the force or has to leave the force. That is a situation which one cannot contemplate as being satisfactory in any sense of the word at all, and so we have to look at the matter again,

In looking at the matter again there is one other factor to be brought into account; that is that when each of these parties reaches retiring age they will receive lump sums. There is a very considerable disparity between the lump sums that each will get. The husband can retire at any time between 1980 and 1985. At the earliest retirement he will get a lump sum of just over £4,000 at present rates; if he stays on until 1985 he will receive a lump sum of just under £7,000. The wife, on the contrary, cannot retire until 1988 when she will get a lump sum of £3,000, which she can increase by another five years' work by the not very substantial sum of £600, giving her £3,600, So the husband, on retirement, will quite obviously be substantially better off than the wife.

I think it is right to say once again that the *Mesher* v *Mesher* type of order is not, in a great many cases. a satisfactory way of solving these cases. The facts in *Mesher* v *Mesher* were very different; in that case both parties were intending to remarry when the case came before the court, and the primary concern in the case was to preserve the home for the children.

6.3 How Will the Court Reach its Decision?

6.3.1 THE CRITERIA TO BE TAKEN INTO ACCOUNT

MATRIMONIAL CAUSES ACT 1973

25. Matters to which court is to have regard in deciding how to exercise its powers under sections 23, 24 and 24A

(1) It shall be the duty of the court in deciding whether to exercise its powers under section 23, 24 or 24A above and, if so, in what manner, to have regard to all the circumstances of the case, first consideration being given to the welfare while a minor of any child of the family who has not attained the age of eighteen.

(2) As regards the exercise of the powers of the court under section 23(1)(a), (b) or (c), 24 or 24A above in relation to a party to the marriage, the court shall in particular have regard to the following matters—

(a) the income, earning capacity, property and other financial resources which each of the parties to the marriage has or is likely to have in the foreseeable future, including in the case of earning capacity any increase in that capacity which it would in the opinion of the court be reasonable to expect a party to the marriage to take steps to acquire;

(b) the financial needs, obligations and responsibilities which each of the parties to the marriage has or is likely to have in the foreseeable future.,

(c) the standard of living enjoyed by the family before the breakdown of the marriage;

(d) the age of each party to the marriage and the duration of the marriage;

(e) any physical or mental disability of either of the parties to the marriage;

(f) the contributions which each of the parties has made or is likely in the foreseeable future to make to the welfare of the family, including any contribution by looking after the home or caring for the family;

(g)   the conduct of each of the parties, if that conduct is such that it would in the opinion of the court be inequitable to disregard it.

(h)   in the case of proceedings for divorce or nullity of marriage, the value to each of the parties to the marriage of any benefit (for example, a pension) which, by reason of the dissolution or annulment of the marriage, that party will lose the chance of acquiring.

6.3.2   SECTION 25(1): AN OVERVIEW

SUTER v SUTER AND ANOTHER [1987] 2 FLR 232 (CA)

SIR ROUALEYN CUMMING-BRUCE: This appeal raises questions about the meaning and application of s. 25(1) of the Matrimonial Causes Act 1973 as amended by the Matrimonial and Family Proceedings Act 1984, and the correct exercise of the powers and duties conferred on the court by s. 25A.

The second submission made on behalf of the appellant is that the judge, following the approach of the registrar, misdirected himself upon the proper construction and effect of s. 25 of the 1973 Act, as amended by s. 3 of the 1984 Act. By s. 25(1):

> It shall be the duty of the court in deciding whether to exercise its powers under section 23, 24 or 24A above and, if so, in what manner, to have regard to all the circumstances of the case, first consideration being given to the welfare while a minor of any child of the family who has not attained the age of eighteen.

This subsection is new, and in effect replaces the words formerly enacted in s. 25 at the end of the list of matters from (a) to (g) to which the court had to have regard amongst all the circumstances of the case. The previous words, which have disappeared from the section as now amended, were:

> . . . and so to exercise these powers as to place the parties, as far as practicable and, having regard to their conduct, just to do so, in the financial position in which they would have been if the marriage had not broken down and each had properly discharged his or her financial obligations and responsibilities towards the other.

The husband submits that both the judge and the registrar treated the welfare of the children as first and paramount, in the sense in which that phrase was interpreted by Lord MacDermott in the context of s. 1 of the Guardianship of Infants Act 1925 (see J v C [1970] AC 668, 710). There Lord MacDermott considered the two adjectives in the phrase, and said:

> That is the first consideration because it is of first importance and the paramount consideration because it rules upon or determines the course to be followed.

I agree with the submission that counsel culled from a commentary by a distinguished commentator that the phrase 'first and paramount' means simply 'overriding', and that if the draftsman had omitted the adjective 'first' the meaning and effect of the single adjective 'paramount' would have been the same. We are faced with the problem of discovering the intention of Parliament when it used the phrase 'the first consideration' without the conjunction of the adjective 'and paramount' which gave the phrase in s. 1 of the Guardianship of Infants Act 1925 its dominant force and effect.

The duty of the court under s. 25(1) as amended is to have regard to all the circumstances, first consideration being given to the welfare while a minor of any child of the family under the age of 18. As regards the exercise of the powers in relation to a party to the marriage, the court shall in particular have regard to the matters set out in s. 25(2)(a) to (h). Section 25(2)(g) introduces a matter not previously included:

> (g)   the conduct of each of the parties, if that conduct is such that it would in the opinion of the court be inequitable to disregard it. . . .

Having regard to the prominence which the consideration of the welfare of children is given in s. 25(1), being selected as the first consideration among all the circumstances of the case, I collect an intention that this consideration is to be regarded as of first importance, to be borne in mind throughout consideration of all the circumstances, including the particular circumstances specified in s. 25(2). But if it had been intended to be paramount, overriding all other considerations pointing to a just result, Parliament would have said so. It has not. So I construe the section as requiring the court to consider all the circumstances, including those set out in s. 25(2), always bearing in mind the important consideration of the welfare of the children, and then try to attain a financial result which is just as between husband and wife.

Consideration of the judge's judgment, taken in conjunction with paras 15 and 16, of the judgment of the registrar which he clearly approved, shows that the judge treated the consideration of the children's welfare as paramount, and controlling the effect of the interplay of all other matters. Though the registrar and the judge gave some effect by way of reduction of the periodical payments to the financial contribution of Mr J to the wife's finances, which the judge held would be substantial, the order was calculated in such a way as to provide the wife with a periodical payments order which would enable her to make all the mortgage payments. And the reasoning thus proceeded because it was considered that the children's welfare required that solution, although the registrar for the reasons that he gave thought that ordinary people would regard the result as unjust. In my view, the judge fell into error in treating s. 25(1) as requiring him to give effect to a consideration of the children's welfare as the overriding or paramount consideration. This was a misdirection, and this court is entitled to review the facts, apply the statute on its proper construction, and decide how to determine the wife's financial claim for periodical payments.

6.3.3 RESOURCES AND EARNINGS

LIVESEY (FORMERLY JENKINS) v *JENKINS* [1985] FLR 813 (HL)

LORD BRANDON OF OAKBROOK: My Lords, this appeal arises in the field of family law and concerns the making by the court of consent orders for financial provision and property adjustment following a divorce.

Before the husband left both he and the wife had consulted different firms of solicitors about their marital troubles. As a result an exchange of letters between these two firms, relating to the affairs of the husband and the wife and the two children, had begun on 9 September 1981 and continued for a long time afterwards. In the course of that correspondence the two firms of solicitors succeeded in reaching agreement on a number of matters on behalf of their respective clients.

The first agreement was that, since the marriage had broken down irretrievably, the wife should divorce the husband on the basis of a written confession of adultery to be provided by him. The second agreement was that the wife should have custody of the two children, with reasonable access for the husband. The third agreement was that, following the proposed divorce, there should be a consent order of the court in respect of financial provision and property adjustment, which would dispose finally of all claims by both the husband and the wife in respect of such matters.

In accordance with these agreements the wife presented a petition for divorce in the Plymouth county court, and on 1 March 1982 was granted a decree nisi in an undefended suit. That decree was made absolute on 14 April 1982. Meanwhile negotiations with regard to the proposed consent order for financial provision and property adjustment were continuing, and on or about 12 August 1982 the solicitors on either side reached final agreement about the form and terms of such order.

The proposed consent order so agreed contained two essential provisions material to this appeal. The first such provision was that the husband should transfer to the wife his half share in the matrimonial home, subject to the mortgage on it, for which the wife would, after such transfer, have sole responsibility. The expressed purpose of this transfer was to provide the wife with a home entirely of her own, in which she could live with the two children. The second essential provision was that, with the wife's consent, all her claims for financial provision for herself should be finally dismissed.

Section 25(1) of the Act of 1973, as originally enacted, provided as follows:

It shall be the duty of the court in deciding whether to exercise its powers under s. 23(1)(a), (b) or (c) or s. 24 above in relation to a party to the marriage and, if so, in what manner, to have regard to all the circumstances of the case including the following matters, that is to say—

(a)   the income, earning capacity, property and other financial resources which each of the parties to the marriage has or is likely to have in the foreseeable future.

(b)   the financial needs, obligations and responsibilities which each of the parties to the marriage has or is likely to have in the foreseeable future. . . .

. . .

I stated earlier that, unless a court is provided with correct, complete and up-to-date information on the matters to which, under s. 25(1), it is required to have regard, it cannot lawfully or properly exercise its discretion in the manner ordained by that subsection. It follows necessarily from this that each party concerned in claims for financial provision and property adjustment (or other forms of ancillary relief not material in the present case) owes a duty to the court to make full and frank disclosure of all material facts to the other party and the court. This principle of full and frank disclosure in proceedings of this kind has long been recognized and enforced as a matter of practice. The legal basis of that principle, and the justification for it, are to be found in the statutory provisions to which I have referred.

My Lords, once it is accepted that this principle of full and frank disclosure exists, it is obvious that it must apply not only to contested proceedings heard with full evidence adduced before the court, but also to exchanges of information between parties and their solicitors leading to the making of consent orders without further inquiry by the court. If that were not so, it would be impossible for a court to have any assurance that the requirements of s. 25(1) were complied with before it made such consent orders.

Applying this principle to the facts of the present case, there can be no doubt whatever that the fact that the wife had, on 18 August 1982, become engaged to be remarried shortly to Thomas Livesey was a matter which she was under a duty to disclose before the agreement with regard to financial provision and property adjustment previously reached between the solicitors on either side was put into effect, as it was on 2 September 1982, by the making of a consent order in the form and terms so agreed. This is because the fact of the wife's engagement was one of the circumstances of the case referred to in line 4 of s. 25(1), and was further of direct relevance to the particular matters specified in paras. (a) and (b) of that subsection. Such disclosure should have been made by the wife to her own solicitors, and through them to the husband's solicitors. and the husband himself, as soon as the engagement to remarry took place. Since it was not made, the consent order was invalid, and the husband should be entitled, in order to prevent injustice, to have it set aside.

LEADBEATER v LEADBEATER [1985] FLR 789 (FamD)

BALCOMBE J: In September of this year the wife secured a part-time job as a receptionist at an optician at an hourly rate of £1.60 an hour, which has since been increased to £1.70 an hour and her annual earnings are now, in round figures, £1,680 a year.

. . . I put the wife's reasonable income requirements at £8,000 a year net which again, in very round terms because it is obvious that one cannot be precise in this sort of case, I round up to £10,000 a year gross. From that, one deducts her earning capacity which I put at £2,500 a year. At the moment, as I have said, she is earning £1,680. She has no particular skills. At the time of her marriage to her former husband she was a secretary. She rightly says that she has not adapted to the new methods which are now used in offices—word processors, and so on. At her age of 47 I think it is wholly unreasonable to expect her to do so. But equally she has shown initiative. She has got a part-time job with an optician and I expect the hours that she works there, or in some similar job, could be increased and so I have taken her earning capacity at £2,500 a year. That leaves, on the £10,000 a year gross that I put as her reasonable income requirements, a shortfall of £7,500, from which in turn falls to be deducted her estimated income from her investments of £3,000; so that I put her net shortfall for the foreseeable future at a figure of £4,500 a year. If one were giving a capital sum to buy an annuity to cover that shortfall it would be of the order (and I stress of the order only) of £50,000.

M v M (FINANCIAL PROVISION) [1987] 2 FLR 1 (FamD)

HEILBRON J: The main issues at the outset of this matter were said to be:

(1)   whether the wife's needs as put forward by her were reasonable, excessive or, indeed, as to some, inflated;

(2)   her job prospects and her potential earning capacity, and whether or not she had since the marriage break-up genuinely attempted to obtain work;

(3)   the duration for payment of periodical payments—whether there should be a cut-off point or whether they should be for joint lives; and

(4)   whether the wife should be paid a lump sum in addition to periodical payments.

The wife worked in a secretarial capacity prior to the marriage. It was varied typing and secretarial work and included some basic book-keeping and setting-out and typing trust accounts. That was a very long time ago and, although after marriage she continued to work for 2 years (between 1965 and 1967), when the daughter was born in 1968 she devoted her full time to bringing her up, to the home and to her husband's and child's welfare. It was not until 1975 that she worked outside the home again when she was engaged for a few months in some simple market research and, after a gap of another 3 years, she worked for a marketing company, between 1978 and 1980, and, either before or after that period—she could not remember exactly which—she worked for a few months at a firm for 2 or 3 days a week. She worked during this period in order to help the family out financially at a time when an extra income was welcome. The wife seems to have given satisfaction in those positions and could have continued working, probably part-time only, which is what she wanted to do if she worked at all, but it was never her intention, and not her husband's either, that she should be a working wife in the sense of a wife who worked outside the home nor, in my view, that she should do this, or any other work, for any length of time. So, save for a few months between March to May 1984, when she worked at a job where she did nothing more skilful than typing envelopes and such like, she did no more work until her situation changed on the breakdown of the marriage. Her total working life after her marriage spanning a period of 20 years was, therefore, no more than some $4\frac{1}{2}$ to 5 years.

The net result is that at the age of 46 or 47 she now has to face the prospect of working again, starting virtually from scratch, after a somewhat shattering marriage breakdown, with such secretarial experience as she has had, in the main copy, and audio typing, although she has used a word processor and she acquired some elementary computer skills and basic trust accounts experience. She might improve her rusty skills somewhat with a 6-weeks refresher course, which was put to her on the suggestion of her husband, although she is unlikely, in my view, to achieve more than a fairly humble job in the secretarial field at her age and with her job experience.

The wife, however, tried, I believe valiantly and persistently, to seek employment. She applied to several agencies and obtained some temporary work. She answered many advertisements unsuccessfully. She also approached a number of well-known organizations, rather over-optimistically I am afraid, for at 47, with her sort of background and lack of suitable experience, such organizations were unlikely to offer her a position. But no one could really blame her for trying and, if she had been fortunate enough to find an opening there, that would have been very nice.

I have heard evidence about the numerous applications she made, the work she managed to get, the interviews she had and about the jobs she did not get. I have listened to a long, skilful and penetrating cross-examination by Mr Hayward-Smith on behalf of the husband. At the end of it all I am completely satisfied that the wife made serious, genuine and strenuous efforts to obtain employment; that her attempts to obtain congenial employment, though out of her reach, were perfectly understandable. Indeed, her husband said he had considered 60 positions himself before he took his present one, because he desired job satisfaction.

It is not surprising that these constant applications for jobs were painful and I fully understand her distress when applying for a type of work which is in the main the sort of position sought after by much younger woman and, although not elderly, she is a mature lady and not in the age group of those who would normally be considered for this sort of employment, although there are exceptions.

All in all, it is quite obvious that she has considerable disadvantages in such a competitive field and I accept that she has lost a good deal of confidence in this somewhat, to her, demoralizing pursuit of employment. She suffers from a long-standing condition of asthma, albeit in a mild form. She has had problems with her nerves for quite a long time, ante-dating the divorce, and has a somewhat vulnerable personality. Having seen her in the witness-box, I am satisfied that that is the situation, although, of course, I have also had a medical report to consider.

All that is not to say she is totally unemployable in one sort of position or another. Recently, she has developed a taste for buying and selling antiques. Indeed, she has already started to do so, although on a small scale, and she is fortunate in this regard in having advice and assistance from her friend, Mr G, and from another friend, Mrs L. She would like to attend an art course which would cost some £3,500 but which would interest her greatly and might, indeed, help her in the antique world.

I believe her future may lie in this direction, with possibly some part-time typing to help her along with the provision of some income.

After a great deal of careful probing, it transpired in the end that there was very little difference between the parties as to the wife's probable potential earning capacity. The husband tentatively put the figure forward of £7,000. The wife's counsel suggested £5,000 to £6,000, and, indeed, her solicitor had written some time ago with the suggested figure of £6,000. It is a little speculative and one does the best one can, but, in my view, taking everything into account, the earning potential of the wife is £6,000 p.a.

HARDY v HARDY [1981] 2 FLR 321 (CA)

ORMROD LJ: The husband is the son of an extremely well-known bookmaker, who is also a racehorse trainer on a large scale. He is the second son and he has been working as, and is called, an assistant trainer, for his father. It is quite apparent that the father is an extremely rich man. He has two businesses—a bookmaking business and a racehorse training business—both of which clearly are on a very large scale. The husband, working for his father as assistant trainer, receives at the present time the minimum salary payable under union arrangements for assistant trainers, of £70 a week, and it is upon that basis that the court is expected to deal with the financial provision for the wife. . . .

Where the court is dealing with a case like this, where it is not unreasonable to assume, looking at the background and all the circumstances, that the husband's salary is quite artifically low and that he and his father have an arrangement which suits them admirably, it is not unreasonable for the court, to protect the wife.

So far as the husband's cross appeal is concerned, the judge raised the amount of the periodical payments very substantially. Under his order the wife's periodical payments are raised to £20 a week and the children's to £15 per week for each child, those sums being fixed on the basis that the education of the children is already provided for. The mother's parents are paying for one child and the father's parents are paying for the other. But it was on the basis that the education was provided for that the order was made in those sums. It is said that those are very high sums. They amount to £50 a week and take the greater part of the husband's income of £70 a week. But it is elementary that in these cases, and particularly in this type of case, that the court does not look at the paper figures. The court looks, first at the realities and the standard of living adopted by the husband and, secondly, at his potential earning capacity. The judge, very rightly, in this part of the judgment said that the earning potential of the husband can be considerably in excess of that which he acknowledged. He went on to say that the husband must be able to command a higher wage than he now earns. That is not a means of putting pressure on the father to pay a proper rate of pay to his son, it is simply a recognition of a fact of life, that this man, with his capacity and experience, is in a position to command in the market a very much higher wage than £70 a week. There is no doubt about that. If it suits him and is to his long-term financial advantage to accept so low a payment, so be it, but it does not follow that his wife and children have similarly to be depressed. In my judgment the judge, on that part of the case, was perfectly right.

WAGSTAFF v *WAGSTAFF* [1992] 1 All ER 275 (CA)

BUTLER-SLOSS LJ: This appeal raises a difficult question as to the way in which a large sum of damages awarded to the husband in respect of serious personal injuries suffered by him should be treated in the application for financial relief made by the wife after a decree of judicial separation. The resolution of the problem turns very much on the special facts of this unusual case. It is a good illustration of the point made time and time again by this court in ancillary relief appeals, that, in applying the criteria set out in ss. 25 and 25A of the Matrimonial Causes Act 1973 as amended, each case has to be looked at on its own facts.

On 12 June 1981 the husband suffered very serious injuries from a road accident rendering him paraplegic, with head and other injuries. He is confined to a wheelchair. Over the period immediately after the accident the wife, according to the report of a consultant psychiatrist, was extremely supportive to him and looked after him in a 'really devoted fashion'. The marriage did not, however, endure and in November 1983 they parted, and the wife retained the former matrimonial home, a rented council house. In 1984 the wife petitioned for judicial separation and on 2 May 1985 obtained a decree. In 1985 the wife was offered the opportunity of buying the former matrimonial home for £10,500 at a time when it was worth £24,500.

In 1988 the husband's claim for damages for personal injuries was settled at £418,000 and he was paid £325,000; the balance had already been received by way of interim payments. The wife received a small sum, partly to compensate her for loss of earnings and partly for expenses she had incurred.

Prior to the decision of this court in *Daubney* v *Daubney* [1976] 2 All ER 453 there was a difference of judicial opinion as to whether damages could form part of the 'family assets' for consideration in ancillary relief applications. This issue was resolved in *Daubney's* case, in which both spouses received damages for injuries received in a car accident. The wife subsequently left the husband and bought a flat with her award of damages and a mortgage. The judge held that the value of the flat should be excluded since it was not a family asset. This court unanimously held that the award of damages was not to be left out of account in considering s. 25 (as it then was). In coming to that conclusion Cairns LJ deprecated the concept of family assets in the sense of that which came to the parties as spouses. Scarman LJ said ([1976] 2 All ER 453 at 459):

> I think that the Act is capable of no other interpretation than that damages of this class fall to be considered as part of the resources or property, as the case may be, of one of the parties to the marriage. It is the duty, of course, of the court to have regard to all the circumstances and to conduct.

O'Connor LJ in *Pritchard* v *J H Cobden Ltd* [1987] 1 All ER 300 at 310 said:

> It is common ground that damages for personal injuries recovered by a spouse shall be included in the 'pot' which is to be shared: see *Daubney* v *Daubney*.

There is consequently no argument but that damages fall to be considered as part of a spouse's financial resources under s. 25(2)(a) of the 1973 Act.

However, Scarman LJ went on to say in *Daubney's* case [1976] 2 All ER 453 at 459:

> I accept the submission made by counsel for the wife that it is relevant to note that such compensation is given for pain and suffering and loss of amenity. Although it is not this case, it would not be a correct exercise of the discretion under s. 25 to make an order which in effect would deprive the spouse of all the benefit by way of compensation for loss of amenity and pain and suffering intended to be conveyed by the award of damages.

Mr Sylvester for the husband sought to rely on Scarman LJ's observation above in support of the proposition that, since damages are awarded under various heads, the purpose for which they have been made should not be invalidated by paying to the wife part of sums allocated for a specific purpose. In my view, this proposition is incorrect. I do not understand Scarman LJ as saying that no part of damages awarded under the head of pain, suffering and loss of amenity should be charged by the other spouse but, if he did, then I respectfully disagree. The reasons for the availability of the capital in the hands of one spouse, together with the size of the award, are relevant factors in all the circumstances of s. 25. But the capital sum awarded is not sacrosanct nor any part of it secured against the application of the other spouse. There may be instances where the sum awarded was small and was specifically for pain and suffering in which it would be unsuitable to order any of it to be paid to the other spouse. In some cases the needs of the disabled spouse may absorb all the available capital, such as the requirement of residential accommodation. Mr Eccles conceded that any calculations made in respect of the capital of the parties should reflect a substantial discount for the fact that the money was received as damages. In general, the reasons for the availability of the capital by way of damages must temper the extent of, and in some instances may exclude the sharing of, such capital with the other spouse. It is important to stress yet again that each case must be considered on its own facts. The specific concern raised by Scarman LJ is most unlikely to arise other than in most exceptional circumstances, which do not arise in this appeal.

Consequently, the circumstances in which the capital came into the hands of the husband are highly relevant to the exercise of the discretion carried out by the deputy registrar and the judge, but do not fetter that discretion.

SCHULLER v SCHULLER [1990] 2 FLR 193 (CA)

BUTLER-SLOSS LJ: The parties were married on 31 May 1956 and there were two children of the family, both of whom are in their thirties and now married. The wife left the matrimonial home in March 1977 after 21 years of marriage. The husband presented a petition on the grounds of 5 years' separation, that is to say under s. 1(2)(e) of the Matrimonial Causes Act 1973, in 1986 and the decree absolute of that divorce was on 4 March 1987. The wife considers that she has not been awarded adequate provision from the assets which have been built up over the years of their marriage. . . .

After the separation the husband remained in the matrimonial home, whereas the wife went to work as a housekeeper for an elderly friend in Dorset. He bought a flat in their joint names and on his death she inherited the whole of the flat in which she now lives, and she also was the residuary beneficiary of his estate which was worth something over £4000.

Mr Webster, counsel for the wife, in his very careful skeleton argument and his argument to this court today makes three main points: first, that after-acquired assets—that is to say, those which the wife has inherited subsequent to the parting, not technically after-acquired assets but certainly those which had nothing whatever to do with, as counsel puts it, the endeavours of the spouses during the marriage—should be treated in a different way from the money which has been acquired during the continuance of the cohabitation. He accepts, however, that they cannot be disregarded.

Turning to the first point (the after-acquired assets) Mr Webster very helpfully provided us with photostats of what I believe he is right in saying are the only two decisions on how the courts should deal with after-acquired assets. The first of them is *Lombardi* v *Lombardi* [1973] 3 All ER 625 and *Pearce* v *Pearce* (1980) 2 FLR 261, both decisions of this court. I will refer to a brief passage from each. At p. 629 Cairns LJ in *Lombardi* said:

Another way in which the judgment is criticised is that it is said that the judge was wrong to take into account that the husband's fortune had accrued to him since the parting. Again, I think that that is a proper circumstance to pay regard to. It was never suggested in this case, as it was in *Jones* v *Jones* [1971] 3 All ER 1201, that the position crystallised at the time of the parting and that thereafter any change in the husband's means was irrelevant. The increase in the husband's means is plainly relevant; but it is also, in my view, relevant to remember that it is something which has happened since the parting.

It is of some importance to say that the judge had both aspects of that well in mind, both were taken into account, and secondly to remember that they were assets which were acquired later.

The second passage is from the judgment of Ormrod LJ in *Pearce* at p. 267:

Then the last point taken in the notice of appeal is the point that the money and the source of the fund was acquired by gift or inheritance 9 years after the dissolution had been made. Again, that is clearly a matter which the court must take into account in exercising its discretion in these matters. It may be again a very important consideration. In some cases such as *Lombardi* v *Lombardi* [1973] 1 WLR 1276, for example, the fact that the husband's position had greatly improved through the efforts of himself and his mistress long after the parting of the husband and wife was a very relevant consideration, very relevant to the justice of the case, but there is no justification in my judgment for trying to create, as it were, reserved funds, or reserved sources of money to which the court should not, in proper cases, have resort. It has been argued that damages for personal injuries should be excluded from the figure of the resources for the purposes of s. 25. That is not so. The word 'resources' in s. 25 is entirely unqualified, there are no words of limitation upon it, and so the court should approach the matter realistically, taking into account all the available resources and doing justice in all the circumstances of the case between the spouses in a realistic fashion, dealing with real figures and not with artificially produced figures.

I respectfully endorse and adopt every word of Ormrod LJ's observations in *Pearce*, and for my part I take the view that these after-acquired assets were properly taken into account in this case and they were extremely relevant. Indeed, counsel for the wife accepts that if, for instance, the wife had, subsequent to the parting, won the football pools in a sum of a million pounds she would not be justified in returning to the court and saying 'nevertheless I want my half share of the matrimonial home and the assets which have been built up over the years'. Mr Webster recognises that that would be unjust, and he says, as is undoubtedly the case, it is a question of degree. In this case, as is pointed out by Mr Cusworth, counsel for the husband, the position of the parties is somewhat similar. Each has accommodation one a house and the other a flat. As it happens the wife's accommodation is worth somewhat more than the husband's in that his is worth £127,500 and hers is worth £130,000. However, he has an endowment policy which she does not have. He has, without taking it into account, the incidence of costs in this case, which has now wended its way through the registrar, the judge, and to this court, so I have no doubt that the figures to which I refer are in fact artificial. The figures show that his current savings at the date before the judge were twice hers, so that he was somewhat better off than her and that was adjusted by the registrar to give her the lump sum of £8,500, and as I have already said the judge points out that that is perhaps £700 or so less than a strict accounting figure.

But where there are no special circumstances in the way in which the money which is the after-acquired property has been achieved and where the resources of the parties are not particularly great, each living in quite an expensive house but if they were to sell it and buy anywhere else they would not achieve very much money unless they went very much downmarket, and each of them has small amounts of savings, there is a considerable degree of parity and what has been criticised as a somewhat crude or indeed unsophisticated approach of the registrar in adding all the assets together and then dividing them does not appear to me in any way to be outside the contemplation of the observations of Ormrod LJ when he said in particular that one should look realistically at the figures.

I, for my part, do not see that the judge in accepting the approach of the registrar, having very carefully considered the case and having himself, as was his duty, independently considered each relevant factor under s. 25, was plainly wrong or that in coming to this conclusion he erred in the exercise of his discretion.

6.3.3.1 New partners

FRARY v FRARY AND ANOTHER [1993] 2 FLR 696 (CA)

RALPH GIBSON LJ: The parties separated some time before September 1991. The petitioner remained at the matrimonial home. She applied for financial relief, including maintenance and capital transfer.

The petitioner submitted a questionnaire to the respondent on 6 February 1992, which was answered in April of that year. The answers ran to some thirteen pages and gave much information about his means. The detailed information does not matter. As to Mrs R, he had made no financial disposition of any kind to her save for his contributions to the housekeeping costs. In reply to the question as to the means and other relevant circumstances of Mrs R, the respondent answered:

On advice the respondent has never discussed any aspect of [Mrs R's] financial affairs with her. The respondent has no more information than that [Mrs R] comes from a well-known family who used to trade as newsagents. The respondent's occupation of [the house] is regulated by an agreement between himself and [Mrs R] dated 2 December 1991, a copy of which the respondent produces at pp. 222–224.

The respondent gave answers to other questions relating to his assets.

The agreement between the respondent and Mrs R, which was produced by the respondent under that answer, is dated 2 December 1991 and recited the facts that Mrs R owns the house in which she lives and that she and the respondent have been living together there. It listed the agreed terms as follows, namely that the respondent occupied the property as licensee without beneficial interest in it; that each would contribute to the outgoings of the property in such proportions as they should from time to time agree, but without thereby any acquisition by the respondent of the interest in it; that the parties should not be classed as dependents of each other for the purposes of the Inheritance (Provision for Family and Dependants) Act 1975; that neither party should be entitled to make any claim against the estate of the other for support or provision, and that the agreement should not be revoked or varied by any subsequent marriage of the parties to each other.

There followed certain correspondence after the receipt of that answer to the questionnaire in which contentions were made with reference to the assets of Mrs R. The petitioner had been informed by a letter of 24 January 1992, if she did not know before, that the respondent had set up house with Mrs R. After receipt of his replies to the questionnaire, the petitioner's solicitors observed that Mrs R's circumstances would clearly be relevant within the ancillary proceedings. Information as to the financial position of Mrs R was, they said, being deliberately withheld. A request was made for Mrs R to produce outline details of her property, capital and income position. If that was not done, the petitioner would be compelled to require Mrs R to attend the hearing of the application to be examined in further detail as to her means.

The reply from the respondent's solicitors, dated 8 May 1992, was that, except that Mrs R will pay her share of the expenses relating to any accommodation she shares with the respondent, her means were not relevant to the issues between the petitioner and the respondent. Mrs R was not willing to provide any details of her financial position to the petitioner or to the respondent.

The petitioner's solicitors, by letter of 21 May 1992, stated their intention to subpoena Mrs R to attend the hearing of the ancillary application. On 26 May 1992 the respondent's solicitors gave warning that objection would be taken to the incurring of costs by such procedure. On 16 July 1992 the petitioner replied in the divorce proceedings by summons addressed to the respondent and to Mrs R for hearing on 18 August 1992 for an order that Mrs R attend the Harlow County Court on a day to be fixed and there produce the documents specified in the schedule.

On 18 August 1992 District Judge Pearson at Harlow County Court dismissed the petitioner's application and ordered that the petitioner pay Mrs R costs on an indemnity basis.

There followed the appeal to the judge. The appeal was heard by his Honour Judge O'Brien on 28 September 1992.

The decision of Judge O'Brien, in summary, proceeded by the following steps:

(1) The application was too wide . . .

(2) Otherwise the information sought was relevant to the financial needs of the respondent and also to the resources which the respondent was likely to have in the foreseeable future. Because the respondent had been cohabiting with Mrs R for a year

and the respondent said that the relationship was developing well and strongly, the means of Mrs R were relevant to the consideration to which the court is to have regard in deciding the matter.

(3)   Since there was no provision in the rules for an order by Mrs R to provide an outline statement of assets, the petitioner had been constrained to make the application in its present form.

(4)   Mrs R had not discharged her duty by providing her affidavit. It said in essence no more than that she and the respondent had kept their finances separate and that she refused to provide for him.

(5)   There was force in the contention that if this application was rejected it is difficult to see how anyone would succeed under r. 2.62(7). This was not a common or garden case as Mrs R had very, very considerable resources indeed. That was not a necessary ingredient to his decision, but it was all the more important in such a case for there to be maximum disclosure to enable the court to apply the statutory criterion.

In my judgment this appeal should be allowed and the judge's order set aside.

The petitioner, however, had no intention of calling Mrs R. Mere production of the documents would be of little, if any, use without evidence as to what the documents were. If the petitioner had intended to call Mrs R to prove in full detail all her assets etc and if on the facts it was right to order the attendance at the hearing for production at the production appointments, it might be made out that it was right so to do, but it seems to me to be most unlikely that such a course would appear right or convenient save in very rare cases. Before the application has been opened, it is difficult for the court to be satisfied of the need for such information. In *Wynne v Wynne* [1981] 1 WLR 69, Bridge LJ, with whose judgment Eveleigh LJ agreed, said at p. 74H:

The third, and perhaps most significant pointer, in my judgment, to the proper construction of this rule lies in this consideration, that it will only be in the rarest cases that it will be possible to say that a person who is a stranger to the lis involved in a party's claim to ancillary financial relief ought, in the words which are used in r. 73, as the spouses are required to do, to make an affidavit containing full particulars of his or her property and income. It will only be in the rarest cases where it will be possible to say that full information about the property and income of the third party, whether the third party is a new spouse, a new mistress, a new lover, a rich uncle or a mother or any other friend or relation from whom one of the spouses has expectations, will be relevant to the issue which the court has to consider under s. 25 of the Matrimonial Causes Act 1973. Indeed, at the end of the day, I do not think Mr Jackson in this case was contending that, if the court had jurisdiction, the order which it would be appropriate to make against this co-respondent would be an order that she gave full particulars of her property and income. In his reply he formulated the order which he was suggesting would define the scope of the affidavit which she should be required to make, namely, that she should be required to state from February 1978—the date when she and the husband began cohabiting—what contributions she had made, in what form and from what source, to the support of the husband. But once it is recognised that if this power is a power to order strangers to the lis to make affidavits, it will, in 99 cases out of 100, be necessary carefully to define the scope of the affidavit they are required to make, one is really driven to recognise that so construed this is an order which empowers the court to interrogate, in advance of the hearing, a witness who is not a party to the lis. That is such an exceptional proceeding that I would need the clearest possible statutory language to drive me to the conclusion that that is what the legislature had intended.

. . . There was in my judgment nothing in the case which could make it a proper exercise of the court's discretion to order Mrs R to attend to be examined at the trial and produce the documents listed or merely to produce those documents. The question whether Mrs R was providing support and benefits to the respondent was plainly relevant. Both the respondent and Mrs R acknowledged that she was. If there was a dispute as to what she was providing and what that was worth, it might well be right to order her to attend and to produce documents in order to demonstrate what she was providing. That, however, was not the point, nor is it now, and there was no attempt to get nor any need to seek for such information.

Next, nothing in the case suggests that Mrs R had given assets to the respondent or that the respondent had given assets to her, and it was not suggested that they had. As the decision of Balcombe J in *W* v *W* (1981) FLR 291 demonstrates, when a case is made that the respondent's assets have not been fully or properly described, a non-party may be required to provide relevant information even if in so doing that person's private documents must be disclosed. All there is in this case, in my judgment, is the fact that Mrs R has 'very, very considerable resources indeed', as the judge said, and as, I think, was plain from the evidence and general circumstances. Again, as Balcombe J indicated in *W* v *W* at p. 293, if the respondent chooses not to arrange for Mrs R to provide information as to the precise limits of her means or cannot persuade her to do so, the remedy of the petitioner is to comment that Mrs R clearly has the ability, for example, to increase her contribution to the costs of the shared property if she is minded so to do. In the circumstances of this case I can see no sufficient relevance in the precise limits of Mrs R's very considerable resources to justify the order. The task of the court in the exercise of its discretion is to balance the interests of the petitioner in obtaining the information against the interests and wishes of the third party not to divulge it.

6.3.4   THE FINANCIAL NEEDS, OBLIGATIONS AND RESPONSIBILITIES

6.3.4.1   What is the test of 'need'?

LEADBEATER v LEADBEATER [1985] FLR 789 (FamD)

BALCOMBE J: I now turn to her housing requirements, and again this was subject to a lot of contested evidence. Putting it bluntly, she says she needs a three-bedroomed house, one bedroom for herself, one for her son and one for her daughter, in an area which she knows and considers a suitable, attractive residential area. She puts the price of such a house at a figure of £65,000 and she says she needs a further £20,000 to furnish it. On the other hand the husband says she does not need a house of that size and does not need to go to such an up-market area. I find that, so far as the husband's liability to provide for the wife's housing requirements is concerned, or, putting it the other way round, how far the wife's requirements are reasonable, *vis-à-vis* her claim against the husband, a two-bedroomed house should be sufficient. There is no realistic prospect, it seems to me, of the wife's daughter returning and, in any event, it is not the husband's responsibility to house the children of his wife's former marriage. On the other hand, a two-bedroomed house would be appropriate (she must have a spare bedroom either for her son or for guests) and the evidence satisfies me that in an area which would be appropriate for her, such a house could be bought for £40,000. Again, there was argument as to how much she should have for furnishing it. She put forward a figure of £20,000, based on insurance calculations. The husband put forward a figure of something just around £6,000, based on estimates made from a Habitat catalogue but omitting carpets. I propose to take a round figure of £10,000, giving a total of £50,000 for the wife's housing requirements. As I have just said, she has existing net assets of £80,000; take away £50,000 from that for the cost of buying herself a house and that would leave her with £30,000 to generate some income. Taking a round figure of 10% per annum, which is not unreasonable in present conditions, a £30,000 free capital could generate some £3,000 a year income.

I turn to the wife's income requirements, or those of her requirements which in my judgment are reasonable to be taken into account for the purposes of this application. I use, as my standard, an adequate recognition of the lifestyle she enjoyed both before and after her marriage to the husband, because it was common ground that during the fairly short period of her marriage to the husband she enjoyed a much enhanced lifestyle — considerable expensive travel which it is accepted she had not previously enjoyed. Again, I do not think it would be particularly helpful for me to go into great detail as to how I reach these figures. I have before me a financial statement prepared by Mr Robinson, the wife's accountant, which goes into considerable detail in estimating her requirements. But it is sufficient if I break the figures down in the same way as Mr Robinson, without going into precise details. For housing costs, which include rates, both general and water, electricity, gas, insurance, telephone, repairs and maintenance. I take an overall sum of £2,500 a year. For her motor car, because it is conceded that the wife needs and is reasonably entitled to run the small Fiesta motor car which she at present owns, to include a figure for depreciation spread over the reasonable life of that car, I take a figure of £1,450. For household and private, which covers virtually everything else including food, household requisites, cigarettes, hairdressing, newspapers, clothes, holidays, television rental and license, sundry cash allowance and optician's costs, I take an overall figure of £4,000.

It seems to me that the major factors that I have to take into account are, the wife's reasonable needs (which, as I have said, I put at a maximum of £50,000), and, secondly, the length of marriage, namely, 4 years. In all the circumstances of the case I do take into account the fact that, during that marriage, the husband paid a number of payments which were primarily the wife's liabilities. He paid, for example, the tax on that part of the money she received from her former husband, which represented the interest earned by the moneys from the sale of the wife's former matrimonial home which had been put on deposit in the bank. He paid some £4,000 towards the litigation involving the wife and her former husband and he paid some part of the wife's children's school fees, which were not recovered from the former husband. Although he puts the figures much higher in his affidavit, I am prepared to consider that he paid some £10,000 in all which, had he not paid them, the wife would have paid and would have depreciated her capital by that amount. She is prepared to give an undertaking in regard to one particular sum of £3,427, which represents income tax refunds which are still clue on payments made by the husband towards the school fees of her children, and when those are eventually received from her former husband she will account to the husband for that sum. So I put the wife's reasonable needs at £50,000. It seems to me proper to make a discount from that, both for the short length of the marriage and for those payments which I have just referred to, though the short length of the marriage seems to me the primary factor. I propose, and like all these things it is a somewhat arbitrary test, to make a discount of 25%, which leaves a figure of £37,500, which is the lump sum I order and, although I will hear argument on the question, it seems to me, in view of the extent of the free assets which the husband has, there is no reason why that should not be paid by the end of January, and 31 January would be the date that I would suggest.

DART v DART [1996] 2 FLR 286 (CA)

The parties, who were US nationals, married in October 1980 when both had just turned 20 years old. The husband had a wealthy background as his father ran an extremely lucrative manufacturing business. Two children were born of the union. The matrimonial home was established in Michigan where the family enjoyed a lavish lifestyle. In August 1993, in furtherance of a scheme to vest a substantial part of the family fortune in the husband, the parties and the children came to London with the intention of taking up permanent residence. The husband renounced his US citizenship. By 1995 the marriage was beginning to break down. The husband presented a petition for dissolution of the marriage in 1995. A decree nisi pronounced in September 1995 was made absolute in October 1995. In ancillary relief proceedings the wife, seeking an order of £122m and the house in Michigan, served on the husband a detailed questionnaire and sought disclosure relating to the extent of the husband's wealth. The husband responded that he was willing and able to comply with any order that the court might make. The wife's solicitors refused to accept that defence. The husband then served his answer which comprised 19 pages of schedules and 7,000 supporting documents contained in 35 ringbinders. The judge made an order, inter alia, requiring the husband to transfer the Michigan house to the wife together with a lump sum of £9m. The wife was ordered to pay the husband's costs of the ancillary relief proceedings. The wife appealed.

Held (dismissing the appeal): . . .

(3) The court, when considering financial provision for a wife who had made no direct contribution to the husband's wealth, had to declare the boundary between the wife's reasonable and unreasonable requirements. There was no justification for applying

a mathematical solution—one-third or one half as suggested in *Wachtel* v *Wachtel* [1973] 1 All ER 829—and to do so would be inconsistent with the guidance consistently given by the Court of Appeal in cases dating back to 1976. The correct test was to calculate what a spouse reasonably requires, whilst having regard to the other criteria mentioned in Matrimonial Causes Act 1973, s. 25(2).

(4) There is no justification for making an award going beyond the spouse's need founded upon homes, children and lifestyle. Redistribution of capital outside that requirement is not within the statutory provisions: *Preston* v *Preston* [1982] Fam 17. Although the expression 'a Besterman cushion' is sometimes used there is no justification for making an award which does more than satisfy the needs as set out above: *O'Neill* v *O'Neill* [1975] 1 WLR 1118. In any event, in the present case the judge had allowed the wife some £3m to enable her to meet some occasional expenditure, even luxury. The fact that, in the event, the wife had wasted this sum in legal costs did not entitle her to have a further payment.

THORPE LJ: The judge must direct himself by reference to the s. 25 criteria and not use fractions other than within the context of an broad analysis of outcome.

The greatest professional uncertainty was as to outcome in big money cases. The larger the figures the wider the band of possible discretionary conclusion. *O'D* v *O'D* [1976] Fam 83 was the first of the substantial cases to reach the Court of Appeal and it initiated a judicial evolution that culminated in the case of *Preston* v *Preston* [1982] Fam 17. Between *O'D* and *Preston* two other substantial cases had reached this court, namely *Sharpe* v *Sharpe* (unreported) 16 July 1980 and *Page* v *Page* (1981) 2 FLR 198. Ormrod LJ delivered the telling judgments in all four cases. In *Preston* v *Preston* he reviewed the evolution over which he had presided in these terms:

> It is only in the rare case where the assets are very large and there is no serious liquidity problem, that it becomes necessary to consider the ultimate limits of the court's discretionary powers under this section. Hitherto, only three cases involving very large sums have reached this court. (He then reviewed *O'D*, *Sharpe* and *Page*.)
>
> Although the decision in each of these cases depended largely on its individual circumstances, some general propositions can be extracted from them. In the first place the court should approach the problem by following the directions set out (in s. 25(1)), i.e. by considering all the circumstances of the case and, in particular, the factors set out, seriatim in paras (a) to (g) . . .
>
> It is, therefore, wrong In principle to adopt a purely arithmetical approach by considering what proportion of the total assets should be allocated to the wife. The judgments in all three of the cases are agreed on this point. The suggestion in *Wachtel* v *Wachtel* of one half or one-third of the total assets is, therefore, no more than a guide-line, though it may be a useful check on the tentative figure which emerges from working through the considerations set out in the section.

Mr Munby's alternative submission was that if the statutory criteria offer the only guide then the courts have fallen into error in big money cases in treating the applicant's need as the paramount or determinative consideration when it should have no greater weight than the first consideration, namely the extent of the assets which each has or is likely to have in the foreseeable future. There is obviously more force in this alternative submission. It may have its origin in an elegant paper presented to the Family Law Bar Association by Mr Peter Singer QC (before his elevation to the bench) in May 1992 and it deserves careful consideration on the authorities. Again the all-important judicial guidance is to be found in the judgments of Ormrod LJ in the cases already cited. In *O'D* v *O'D* he said this:

> The next stage is to consider the wife's position, not from the narrow point of 'need', but to ascertain her reasonable requirements, bearing in mind that she will have to provide an appropriate home and background for herself and the children.

Then in *Preston* v *Preston* he said:

> Secondly, the word 'needs' in paragraph (b) of s. 25(1) in relation to the other provisions in the subsection is equivalent to 'reasonable requirements', having regard to the other factors and the objective set by the concluding words of the subsection . . .

From those passages it is implicit that reasonable requirements are more extensive than needs. As a matter of ordinary language what a person requires is likely to be greater than what that person needs. So the check on what the applicant subjectively requires is the word 'reasonable'. There must be an objective appraisal of what the applicant subjectively requires to ensure that it is not unreasonable. But the objective appraisal must have regard to the other criteria of the section, obviously including what is available, the standard of living to which the parties are accustomed, their age and state of health and, perhaps less obviously, the duration of the marriage, contributions, and pension rights both as affected by the marriage and as accrued or likely to accrue. Used thus the consideration of needs ceases to be paramount or determinative but an elastic consideration that does not exclude the influence of any of the others. As Mr Singleton rightly submitted, in a big money case where the wife has played an equal part in creating the family fortune it would not be unreasonable for her to require what might be even an equal share. Therefore in my judgment the essential function of the judge in the big money case is to declare the boundary between the applicant's reasonable and unreasonable requirements applying all the statutory criteria to the myriad relevant facts of the individual case.

The next point that must be considered in this area is whether the court has power to make provision for a need that cannot be founded upon homes, children and lifestyle. Mr Munby by further alternative submission contends that there is no limitation to the purpose for which capital can be provided whilst Mr Singleton supports the limited jurisdiction. Again I conclude that authority is on Mr Singleton's side.

BUTLER-SLOSS LJ: Mr Munby suggested that the wording of s. 25 implied a starting-point of one half. Not only is it clear from the decided cases that such is not the case, but interestingly it is clear from proposed legislation to which we have been referred in Hansard that in Parliamentary debate, at least, such a starting-point was not even contemplated by those arguing from whichever point of view of the existing legislation.

In the process of applying the s. 25(2) criteria to the facts of this case, the needs of the wife are a highly relevant factor. 'Needs' has been defined by Ormrod LJ in *Page* v *Page* (1981) 2 FLR 198, 201 as the 'reasonable requirements' of the spouse seeking an order. Where the resources are great Ormrod LJ in *Preston* v *Preston* [1982] Fam 17 said at 28 respectively that there had to be a levelling off or a ceiling on the amounts to be taken into account.

Although Mr Munby does not accept the principle of a ceiling as such, he does recognise that the starting-point is far below the 50/50. He suggested £100m as the starting-point, well below half of the figure found by the judge to comprise the assets, and he recognised that in the Michigan court the wife might be awarded substantially less. I have no doubt, however, that we are bound by the line of decisions in which Ormrod LJ gave the leading judgments and that we have to recognise a levelling off in a case with capital of this size.

The court is not bound by any percentage but must have regard to all the relevant criteria in s. 25(2). The judge considered the wife's reasonable requirements together with all the other relevant factors in coming to his decision. In doing so he also took into account that the wealth has been generated by the husband's family and the wife has made no direct contribution to that family business which is another highly relevant factor both in our jurisdiction and, we understand, in the Michigan legislation. Within the principles enunciated in the line of cases set out in the judgment of Thorpe LJ there is no ground upon which this appellate court might interfere with his exercise of discretion or substitute a higher figure than the award made by the judge in his excellent judgment.

I agree with Thorpe LJ, for the reasons which he has given, that we should not interfere with the effect of costs upon the lump sum awarded.

6.3.4.2   How are needs calculated: what is the starting point?

WACHTEL v *WACHTEL* [1973] 1 All ER 829 (CA)

LORD DENNING MR: Mr and Mrs Wachtel were married on 9th January 1954. They were both then 28 years of age. They have two children, a son now aged 14 and a girl of 11. The husband is a dentist in good practice. On 31st March 1972 the wife left the home. On 21st July 1972 there was a divorce on the ground that the marriage had irretrievably broken down. In consequence many things have to be settled. The parties have made arrangements for the children. The son is with the father. He is a boarder at Epsom College, where his fees are paid by his grandfather. The daughter is with the mother. She goes to day-school. There remain the financial consequences. The parties have not agreed on them. So they have to be settled by the courts.

On 3rd October 1972 Ormrod J ordered the husband to pay to his wife (i) a lump sum of £10,000, or half the value of the former matrimonial home in Norwood, South London, whichever be the less; (ii) a periodical payment of £1,500 per annum, less tax; and (iii) a further payment of £500 per annum, less tax, in respect of the 11 year old daughter. The husband appeals to this court.

The appeal raises issues of wide importance. This court is asked to determine, for the first time, after full argument, the principles which should be applied in the Family Division when granting ancillary relief pursuant to the powers conferred by the Matrimonial Proceedings and Property Act 1970 (in this judgment called 'the 1970 Act') following dissolution of marriage pursuant to the Divorce Reform Act 1969 (in this judgment called 'the 1969 Act'). We were told by counsel both for the husband and for the wife that it was hoped that this court might feel able, to quote the phrase used in the argument, 'to lay down some guide lines' which would be of help in the future. There are divergences of view and of practice between judge and registrars. Furthermore, counsel and solicitors are unable to advise their clients with a reasonable degree of certainty as to the likely outcome of any contested proceedings. It is very desirable to remove that uncertainty and to assist parties to come to agreement.

The one-third rule

In awarding maintenance the divorce courts followed the practice of the ecclesiastical courts. They awarded an innocent wife a sum equal to one-third of their joint incomes. Out of it she had to provide for her own accommodation, her food and clothes, and other expenses. If she had any rights in the matrimonial home, or was allowed to be in occupation of it, that went in reduction of maintenance.

That one-third rule has been much criticised. In *Kershaw* v *Kershaw* [1964] 3 All ER 635 Sir Jocelyn Simon P spoke of it as 'the discredited "one-third rule"'. But it has retained its attraction for a very simple reason: those who have to assess maintenance must have some starting point. They cannot operate in a void. No better starting point has yet been suggested that the one-third rule. In *Ackerman* v *Ackerman* [1972] 2 All ER 420 at 426 Phillimore LJ said: '. . . the proper course is to start again. I would begin with the 'one-third rule'—bearing in mind that it is not a rule.'

There was, we think, much good sense in taking one-third as a starting point. When a marriage breaks up, there will thenceforward be two households instead of one. The husband will have to go out to work all day and must get some woman to look after the house—either a wife, if he remarries, or a housekeeper, if he does not. He will also have to provide maintenance for the children. The wife will not usually have so much expense. She may go out to work herself, but she will not usually employ a housekeeper. She will do most of the housework herself, perhaps with some help. Or she may remarry, in which case her new husband will provide for her. In any case, there are two households, the greater expense will, in most cases, fall on the husband than the wife. As a start has to be made somewhere, it seems to us that in the past it was quite fair to start with one-third. Counsel for the wife criticised the application of the so-called 'one-third rule' on the ground that it no longer is applicable to present-day conditions, notwithstanding what was said in *Ackerman* v *Ackerman*. But this so-called rule is not a rule and must never be so regarded. In any calculation the court has to have a starting point. If it is not to be one-third, should it be one-half? or one-quarter? A starting point at one-third of the combined resources of the parties is as good and rational a starting point as any other, remembering that the essence of the legislation is to secure flexibility to meet the justice of particular cases, and not rigidity, forcing particular cases to be fitted into some so-called principle within which they do not easily lie. There may be cases where more than one-third is right. There are likely to be many others where less than one-third is the only practicable solution. But one third as a flexible starting point is in general more likely to lead to the correct final result than a starting point of equality, or a quarter.

There is this, however, to be noted. Under the old dispensation, the wife, out of her one-third, had to provide her own accommodation. If she was given the right to occupy the matrimonial home, that went to reduce the one-third. Under the new dispensation, she will get a share of the capital assets; and, with that share, she will be able to provide accommodation for herself, or, at any rate, the money to go some way towards it.

If we were only concerned with the capital assets of the family, and particularly with the matrimonial home, it would be tempting to divide them half and half, as the judge did. That would be fair enough if the wife afterwards went her own way, making no further demands on the husband. It would be simply a division of the assets of the partnership. That may come in the future. But at present few wives are content with a share of the capital assets. Most wives want their former husband to make periodical payments as well to support them; because, after the divorce, he will be earning far more than she; and she can only keep up her standard of living with his help. He also has to make payments for the children out of his earnings, even if they are with her. In view of these calls on his future earnings, we do not think she can have both—half the capital assets, and half the earnings.

Under the new dispensation, she will usually get a share of each. In these days of rising house prices, she should certainly have a share in the capital assets which she has helped to create. The windfall should not all go to the husband. But we do not think it should be as much as one-half, if she is also to get periodical payments for her maintenance and support. Giving it the best consideration we can, we think that the fairest way is to start with one-third of each. If she has one-third of the family assets as her own—and one-third of the joint earnings—her past contributions are adequately recognised, and her future living standard assured so far as may be. She will certainly in this way be as well off as if the capital assets were divided equally—which is all that a partner is entitled to.

We would emphasise that this proposal is not a rule. It is only a starting point. It will serve in cases where the marriage has lasted for many years and the wife has been in the home bringing up the children. It may not be applicable when the marriage has lasted only a short time, or where there are no children and she can go out to work.

Looking at it broadly

In all these cases it is necessary at the end to view the situation broadly and see if the proposals meet the justice of the case. On our proposals here the wife gets £6,000 (nearly one-third of the value of the matrimonial home). She gets it without any conditions at all. This seems to represent a fair assessment of her past contributions, when regard is had to the fact that she will get periodical payments as well. She also gets £1,500 a year by way of periodical payments, which is about one-third of their joint incomes. She will also have the management of £300 a year for the daughter who is at a good school, and aged 11. These provisions are as much as the husband can reasonably be expected to make. It will mean that each will have to cut down their standard of living: but it is as much as can be done in the circumstances.

The appeal should be allowed to the extent indicated. The wife's cross-appeal will be dismissed.

BURGESS v *BURGESS* [1996] 2 FLR 34 (CA)

WAITE LJ: This appeal has an unfortunate background in the failure of the marriage of two professional people who were together for many years, and by their joint efforts achieved both prosperity for themselves and a successful launching in life for the children who are now being trained to follow them in their respective callings. The husband is a solicitor now aged 51 and the wife a doctor now aged 52. From the time of their marriage in 1969 (when he was an assistant solicitor and she a senior house officer) they were both in full-time work, apart from a period when their three children (two daughters and a son) were very young and the wife worked only part-time.

The breakdown of the marriage was accompanied by much bitterness. Conduct was in issue at first, in both the divorce and the financial proceedings, but in the end it ceased to play any part in either. It was common ground by the date of the financial hearing that this was a case for a 'clean break' order extinguishing all future claims by either spouse against the other, or against his or her estate. The husband's earlier prosecution of the financial proceedings had, however, been vigorous . . .

When the financial proceedings came on for final hearing before Hale J on 20 May 1995, she directed that the joint assets of the parties (effectively the home and its contents) should be divided between them 50/50—and on that footing made the usual clean break order.

From those orders the husband now, by leave of this court, appeals. He accepts that the joint assets should be divided, but contends that the division should have been 2 to 1 in his own favour.

In the course of her judgment the judge had said, in justification of the decision to divide the joint assets equally:

It seems to me in a case like this where there has been a long partnership marriage, and both have careers of their own, the court should in principle seek to divide their current assets equally and let each go their separate ways into the future.

Mr Horowitz QC, the husband's counsel, acknowledges—and indeed relies upon—the fact that the powers conferred on the family jurisdiction by ss. 23 to 25A of the Matrimonial Causes Act 1973 embody a judicial discretion of the widest import. He contends, however, that it is not a discretion to be constrained by the application of any a priori rule or principle. In authorities extending from *Wachtel* v *Wachtel* [1973] Fam 72 and *Page* v *Page* (1981) 2 FLR 198 in the earlier days of the jurisdiction to *W* v *W (Judicial Separation: Ancillary Relief)* [1995] 2 FLR 259 in our own time, it has been repeatedly emphasised that although there can be no objection to the court proceeding from some convenient and familiar starting-point (such as the two-thirds proportion when assessing income provision or a 50/50 division when dealing with the interests in a matrimonial home) they remain starting-points only, and must never be allowed the status of a rule or principle governing (as opposed to initiating) the judicial process involved in exercising the discretion. When the judge's words are read in conjunction with the striking financial disparity in which, after division of their joint assets on the basis she directed, her order now leaves the parties, the conclusion becomes inescapable, so Mr Horowitz submits, that the judge had lost sight of this long-standing principle of family law and misdirected herself by introducing a rule or precept that working spouses are entitled to share joint assets representing the fruits of their combined labour in equal shares, unless the circumstances of the case include unusual features compelling the court to adopt some other proportion.

The judge's approach
The judge turned first to the specific matters to which the court is required by s. 25(2) to have regard. She dealt in detail with the earnings, earning potential, contributions to the marriage, and general resources of both spouses—analysing in particular detail their respective existing and future financial needs. After that survey, she prefaced her decision by the statement I have already quoted.

There are three principal respects in which the judge's approach to the circumstances of the case are relied on by Mr Horowitz as betraying what he would describe as a misguided allegiance to some supposed overriding principal of equality of interest of working spouses in their joint property.

First she made light, he says, of the disparity between their incomes—content to accept fatalistically that it was an inevitable result of the different rewards of their respective callings, and making no effort to use her own powers of capital disposition to redress the imbalance. I would reject that submission. Once the judge had found, as she did during her examination of the parties' needs and resources, that the husband would be capable of supporting himself, probably for a number of years still to come, from his solicitor's practice, no departure from the approach enjoined by s. 25 was involved in leaving undisturbed a state of affairs in which their earnings, though in neither case negligible, would continue to be different. There is nothing in Part II of the 1973 Act to justify an inference of parliamentary policy that the s. 25 discretion should be exercised in such a way as to achieve broad equality between spouses.

Secondly, Mr Horowitz relies on the disparate treatment by the judge of the parties' respective housing needs. The judge's approach (in the findings I have already described) was so favourable to the wife and unfavourable to the husband that so extreme a result can only be explained by blind adherence, he submits, to equal division as an imperative formula. Again, I am for my part unable to agree. The whole tenor of the judge's findings in this respect was directed to taking due account of the demands on the wife's side of proximity to her patients as well as her need to provide a base for student children who are unfortunately estranged from their father; and was directed also to achieving a balance between those requirements and those of the husband's future accommodation. It was a classic exercise of the s. 25 jurisdiction in its broadest aspects, and I can find no hint in the judge's reasoning of an automatic response to the alleged, or any, preconceived formula.

Mr Horowitz relies finally upon the position in which the parties are left by the judge's order at the end of the day. It can only be explained, he submits, by a dismissive attitude adopted by the judge to the striking disparity between the husband's indebtedness on his firm's capital account and the value of the wife's corresponding account with her own partnership; to the disparity between her investments and his; and to the difference in scale between her undoubted (although still reversionary) interests and his inheritance prospects from his own elderly parents (which it was agreed at the trial should be treated as negligible). For my part I do not find it at all surprising that the judge decided to leave those differences undisturbed. She had every justification for the view that the deficit on the husband's capital account reflected the result of decisions of his own—the purchase of furniture for example in the name of his partnership; the continuance of his policy of overdrawing against profits after his family maintenance obligations (apart from his half-share of the mortgage payments on the matrimonial home) had been ended at his own insistence; and the fact that since the separation he had arranged for an £18,000 motor car to be purchased by the firm on hire purchase for his own use.

For these reasons I find nothing in the judge's treatment of the case which could fairly be regarded as attributable to any misdirection on her part.

With that in mind, one turns to consider again the passage in the judgment on which Mr Horowitz relies. I would accept that, as a matter of grammatical interpretation, the judge's remarks—read in isolation—would be capable of being construed as applying a precept that the interests of working spouses in joint assets acquired through their combined efforts are to be treated equally. If that is the correct interpretation, then the judge would certainly be in error; and the risk, vividly portrayed by Mr Horowitz, of her remarks being acclaimed by zealous commentators as introducing into family law a new charter for the rights of the working spouse, would become a real one. But in my view, when her words are read in the context of a judgment which demonstrably seeks to apply s. 25 of the Act to the letter, and which produced nothing in its result which betrays the least sign of error or misplaced emphasis, it becomes clear that the judge was really intending to say no more than this. When the court is dealing with the joint assets of working spouses, common sense and equity require that equality of interest should be adopted as a starting-point. It is, however, only a starting-point, and will yield to the requirements of all the circumstances of the case including the specific factors to which s. 25(2) requires regard. That is an unexceptionable approach, adopted by a very experienced judge, and for my part I would wholly support it.

In summary, it appears to me that the judge's decision cannot be criticised for any error of approach, and that it is impossible to say that her decision was wrong—still less plainly wrong. I would therefore dismiss the appeal from the judge's main order.

6.3.5 THE CONDUCT OF THE PARTIES

WACHTEL v *WACHTEL* [1973] 1 All ER 829 (CA)

LORD DENNING MR:

The conduct of the parties

When Parliament in 1857 introduced divorce by the courts of law, it based it on the doctrine of the matrimonial offence. This affected all that followed. If a person was the guilty party in a divorce suit, it went hard with him or her. It affected so many things.

The custody of the children depended on it. So did the award of maintenance. To say nothing of the standing in society. So serious were the consequences that divorce suits were contested at great length and at much cost.

All that is altered. Parliament has decreed: 'If the marriage has broken down irretrievably, let there be a divorce'. It carries no stigma, but only sympathy. It is a misfortune which befalls both. No longer is one guilty and the other innocent. No longer are there long contested divorce suits. Nearly every case goes uncontested. The parties come to an agreement, if they can, on the things that matter so much to them. They divide up the furniture. They arrange the custody of the children, the financial provision for the wife, and the future of the matrimonial home. If they cannot agree, the matters are referred to a judge in chambers.

When the judge comes to decide these questions, what place has conduct in it? Parliament still says that the court has to have 'regard to their conduct': see s. 5(1) of the 1970 Act. Does this mean that the judge in chambers is to hear their mutual recriminations and go into their petty squabbles for days on end, as he used to do in the old days? Does it mean that, after a marriage has been dissolved, there is to be a post mortem to find out what killed it? We do not think so. In most cases both parties are to blame—or, as we would prefer to say—both parties have contributed to the breakdown.

It has been suggested that there should be a 'discount' or 'reduction' in what the wife is to receive because of her supposed misconduct, guilt or blame (whatever word is used). We cannot accept this argument. In the vast majority of cases it is repugnant to the principles underlying the new legislation, and in particular the 1969 Act. There will be many cases in which a wife (although once considered guilty or blameworthy) will have cared for the home and looked after the family for very many years. Is she to be deprived of the benefit otherwise to be accorded to her by s. 5(1)(f) because she may share responsibility for the breakdown with her husband? There will no doubt be a residue of cases where the conduct of one of the parties is in the judge's words 'both obvious and gross', so much so that to order one party to support another whose conduct falls into this category is repugnant to anyone's sense of justice. In such a case the court remains free to decline to afford financial support or to reduce the support which it would otherwise have ordered. But, short of cases falling into this category, the court should not reduce its order for financial provision merely because of what was formerly regarded as guilt or blame. To do so would be to impose a fine for supposed misbehaviour in the course of an unhappy married life. Counsel for the husband disputed this and claimed that it was but justice that a wife should suffer for her supposed misbehaviour. We do not agree. Criminal justice often requires the imposition of financial and indeed custodial penalties. But in the financial adjustments consequent on the dissolution of a marriage which has irretrievably broken down, the imposition of financial penalties ought seldom to find a place.

BEACH v *BEACH* [1995] 2 FLR 160 (FamD)

The parties were married in 1980. The applicant husband, who had been married previously, acquired a dairy farm in 1969. His first wife had acquired a proprietary interest in the farm, in consideration for which it was agreed that she should receive a £100,000 share. The respondent wife assumed the first wife's proprietary role by providing the £100,000 necessary to discharge the applicant's liability to his former wife from the proceeds of the sale of her former home. In the 1980s the farm did not prosper. In 1983 the respondent assented to the refinancing of the farm and in 1989 the respondent, in consideration for the applicant's agreement actively to market the property for sale, agreed to the execution of a legal charge over the farm in favour of a creditor, the Milk Marketing Board. The applicant, however, did not proceed with the marketing of the farm and the respondent gave notice to the bank preventing any further increase in borrowings. That freeze on further borrowings was lifted by the wife following a meeting with the applicant in February 1990, intended to lead to the early sale of the farm. It was agreed between the parties that the wife should receive £450,000 net from the proceeds of the sale of the farm in full and final settlement of any claims by either party under the Matrimonial Causes Act 1973. None the less, the applicant again failed to market the farm. In December 1990 he was declared bankrupt, and in

March 1992 the farm was sold for £1.1m. The wife received £360,000 from the proceeds of sale together with a bungalow agreed to be worth approximately £55,000. The applicant, whose bankruptcy was discharged in 1993, made an application for a lump sum payment. At the time, he was living with his parents and was in receipt of income support.

THORPE J: The present position of the parties is that the husband resides with his parents. He is on income support. For some time he has been seeking to develop entrepreneurial opportunities in the Ukraine. Nothing has yet resulted, although he declares high hopes and expectations. His claim for a lump sum is advanced on the basis that he needs capital to buy himself a home, he needs capital to set up an export business to the Ukraine and he would like to pay off some of the unsecured creditors.

The wife's position contrasts strongly. With the money received from the sale of the commercial property, together with the money received from the trustee, she has assets of about £820,000. She has bought a home for herself in Somerset at a cost of £217,000. She has roughly £400,000 invested for yield in the Channel Islands and the bungalow transferred to her by the trustee, which is let out to produce rent. She therefore has an income from the Channel Island trust, from the bungalow and from the residue of her investment capital, which is worth in the order of £140,000. So it would appear that she has, or could have, an income of approximately £30,000 a year to enable her to live comfortably in her new home.

The case for the husband is opened boldly by Mr Moor, who says that all the history is irrelevant to the decision that I have to take.

He says that I should simply do the s. 25 exercise upon the parties' positions as they now are, and that a fair, discretionary decision would give his client a lump sum of £270,000, being a third of the wife's capital.

Inevitably Miss Ralphs for the wife places the greatest stress on the history. She emphasises the agreement of 20 February 1990, freely entered into on independent advice. It is not asserted that that advice was bad or unsatisfactory, and the agreement protects the wife from any claim since she has not yet received her entitlement under its terms.

Alternatively, if this is a case to be assessed on the s. 25 criteria, it is a case of manifest financial misconduct and in the exercise of discretion the application for lump sum should be dismissed: the husband has nobody but himself to blame for his present circumstances.

Obviously, in reaching a conclusion between two such differing presentations, of primary importance is my conclusion on the reliability of the parties as witnesses and upon the reality of their subjective accounts of the history.

The husband I find to be an unreliable witness. He has very little capacity for detachment or objectivity. He sees every issue through his own eyes. I have no doubt at all that this is the consequence of the emotional trauma suffered through public failure and public eviction from his land and from his stock. It must be very difficult to maintain self-esteem after such a public failure. It must be very difficult to maintain self-esteem, having talked other people into lending money and then having let them down. The unsecured creditors include not only members of his own family but even past employees.

It must be very difficult emotionally to accept responsibility for failure and for having misled other people into contributing to the cost of failure. In such circumstances many people find it necessary to blame disaster either on others or on fate. So through the husband's evidence there are many themes that seek to cast blame and responsibility upon others or upon chance.

By contrast, the wife was a very contained witness, seemingly dispassionate. Despite all her experiences she seemed to me to be careful, accurate and reliable. So wherever there is a conflict I unhesitatingly accept the evidence of the wife in preference to the evidence of the husband. I unhesitatingly prefer her presentation of the history.

The history is a financial tragedy, and one of the ingredients of that tragedy is the wife's forbearance. Time and time again, she was talked round. Had the farm been sold in 1983, there would have been money. Had the farm been sold in 1989, there would have been substantial money. Even had the farm been sold in early 1990, there would have been substantial money.

The agreement of February 1990 should have provided for a market launch on 1 May 1990. I accept the wife's evidence that although the market had fallen back, it was still a relatively easy market in which to sell in the spring of 1990. The forbearance which she gave orally on 10 February 1990 I am in no doubt did not go beyond an acceptance that if the money came from another source by 1 May 1990 that would supplant the term for agreed.

It seems to me sad from everybody's point of view that the wife did not insist upon a launch on 1 May 1990, but I can understand how difficult it must have been in the face of the husband's resistance, since he is obviously a powerful man.

The reality is that over the whole years of the marriage the farming trade was loss-making and the extent of the burden of debt was steadily increasing.

Looking to the s. 25 criteria, I must have regard to the income and assets of the parties, as they are, or as they are likely to be in the foreseeable future. As they are at present is not open to dispute and is already recorded in this judgment. As they may be in the foreseeable future is much harder to determine. Each has expectations or hope of inheritance on the death of surviving parents. It does not seem to me that this is a factor of much significance. The older generation on both sides have already been generous. Probably the husband will share his parents' estate with his brother; probably the wife will share her mother's estate with her sisters.

What is much more difficult to assess is the husband's potential to develop income in the future. He has proved over the course of the last 20 years to have been a bad, even a disastrous, businessman. He had considerable talent as a stockman but could not harness that talent to financial controls. The market in which he now seeks to trade is completely removed from his known skills and sufficiently distant to make proof or disproof of his assertions all the more difficult. Is it reality or is it the sort of hope that he desperately needs in order to survive his adversities? Only time will tell. I would be extremely loath to rest any capital award on the basis that it was prudently invested in the set-up costs of the intended export business. One of the realities of speculative trade is that there is greater freedom to risk your own money than to risk the money of others, even family members.

Needs? The wife's needs are well met. Mr Moor obviously emphasises the husband's need for a home of his own. I have been shown a range of particulars, the husband illustrating what he would like, the wife illustrating the bare minimum that buys a basic home in the Hampshire area. I would not be inclined to include start-up costs of a business within properly assessed needs. After all that has happened, it seems to me that any new trade must be self-financed out of achieved profits. The first 2 years of exploration have yet to achieve any income.

So the crux of the case is really the responsibility for the present near-destitution of the husband. How has this come about? Who is responsible for this state of affairs? Is it the product of the husband's misconduct?

I have already recorded the developments and find the history as the wife presents it. I utterly reject Mr Moor's submission that this history is irrelevant to the outcome of this case. I think Miss Ralphs is fully entitled to suggest that the husband's conduct amounted to conduct which it would be inequitable to disregard.

He obstinately, unrealistically and selfishly trailed on to eventual disaster, dissipating in the process not only his money but his family's money, his friends' money, the money of commercial creditors unsecured and eventually his wife's money, insofar as the disaster that eventually developed did not even pay for her specified agreed sum. It would have been in her interest, it would have been in his interest, had she forced him into accepting a properly marketed sale in the 1980s. She cannot be blamed for having failed to achieve that result. She secured formal agreement, she obtained orders in Chancery. But I can understand how difficult it must have been for her, living under the same roof with somebody so deluded. The responsibility is, in my judgment, not shared, not hers, but his.

So, on one view, why should he have anything when she has not even had what should have been her due under the freely negotiated contract? My first impression was to dismiss this claim as Miss Ralphs invited me to do. However, on further reflection I have concluded that the disparity between the present position of the husband and the wife is so great that that would not be a fair application of the s. 25 criteria.

The relationship between the wife's financial contribution of £240,000 and her negotiated share of £450,000 fairly reflected the fact that £100,000 was a realty disposal and reinvestment at 1980 values. The additional £140,000 was contributed over a decade, but quite substantial sums early on to meet school fees for the children of the husband's first marriage. I do not think a conversion of her £240,000 into 1990 money would have been overstated at £450,000.

But that is a speculative judgment, and I have reached the conclusion that to reduce her receipts by a sum that would provide basic accommodation for the husband would leave her with her financial contribution intact and only its inflation accretion invaded.

I have considered the suggestion from Miss Ralphs that any provision for the husband should be by way of life tenancy or life interest but I accept Mr Moor's submission that any capital provided to the husband must be on an absolute basis and that the break between them must be complete. Obviously, provision in that form gives him the opportunity to use the money not to provide himself with the home, as I intend, but to finance some risky trade. Over that I have no control.

I have reached the conclusion that the sum that would enable him to obtain some basic accommodation without at the same time removing from the wife the return of her basic financial contribution is £60,000, and I order the wife to pay the husband a lump sum in that amount within 28 days.

KOKOSINSKI v KOKOSINSKI [1980] 3 WLR 55 (FamD)

WOOD J: The issues in this case arise on claims by each party against the other for financial relief and ancillary matters following a divorce. In his final submissions Mr Price did not pursue the husband's claim for ancillary relief and I therefore consider only the petitioner's claims against the husband. In the main her claim is for a lump sum.

The petitioner, to whom I shall refer as 'the wife,' was born on December 4, 1922, in the United Kingdom. Her present age is, therefore, nearly 57. She is living in Berkshire, occupying a small single bedroom in a three-bedroom bungalow where also live her mother, aged 91, and her sister. The respondent, to whom I shall refer as 'the husband,' was born on December 16, 1910, in Poland and is now aged nearly 69. He lives in Kilburn at a house which was the former matrimonial home.

The marriage took place on September 1, 1971, and cohabitation effectively ceased in January or February 1972. A petition was filed on July 6, 1977, and a decree nisi was granted on the basis of the husband's desertion on November 11, 1977. The wife's application for ancillary relief is dated January 13, 1978, and the husband's cross-application May 24, 1979. No decree absolute has been granted.

The facts thus baldly stated indicate a very short marriage and Mr Price for the husband relies upon this fact more than any other in his submission that this is not a case where any lump sum should be awarded. However, when the whole picture of the relationship between this man and this woman is examined, a very different picture presents itself.

The husband was first married in Poland on June 26, 1933. He is Polish by origin, coming from a humble home. His first wife was some four years his senior. A son was born of that marriage on April 7, 1939, W, who is now aged 40.

The husband was by occupation an engineer, an expert in hydraulics of landing gear for aircraft. When the invasion of Poland by Germany occurred he escaped and made his way to this country. Thereafter he joined the Polish forces and trained in Scotland. Whilst in Scotland he suffered some injury as the result of which he spent a number of months in hospital. After a period of time he came to a hospital in Surrey for a period of convalescence and left there in 1943.

He was unfit to return to the forces and it was then that he met the wife for the first time. She was helping to produce aircraft parts and her sister was also working in this small factory. The husband also started to make small engineering parts and for the remainder of the war, and until about 1946 or 1947, he and his wife were working together and with others in engineering production.

Sometime early in 1946 a small engineering company, EBS Engineering Ltd, was formed by the husband, together with some of his friends. The factory was in Kilburn, London, NW2.

During 1947 the husband and the wife started to live together. From about this time until 1950, when C, their son was born, she worked as a bus conductress. This occupation ceased shortly before his birth on July 22, 1950, and she did not return to it after her confinement.

It was in September 1950 that the matrimonial home, in Kilburn, London, NW6, was purchased in the sole name of the husband. In that same month the wife started work at EBS Engineering Ltd. and took C with her to work. She was working to some extent part-time and during the ensuing summers she took C to the coast for a month or more by arrangement with the husband. However, when C was able to go to play-school she was able to work virtually full-time in the company. It was during 1955 that the wife changed her name to Kokosinski by deed poll.

Pausing at this juncture in the recital of historical fact, I would turn to the relationship over the years between the husband and the wife. It was well known to them both that it would be impossible for the husband to obtain a divorce in Poland unless his wife divorced him. The wife in these proceedings, had spoken to W about this matter on a number of occasions. The husband had always promised and made it clear that as soon as he could he would be prepared and willing to marry the wife. From 1947 until 1950 the wife had always used her wages towards the maintenance of the home which she and the husband had set up together. He had undoubtedly contributed by buying specific items, but her wages had consistently been used towards the household maintenance. From 1950 onwards, indeed thereafter, the wife has been in full-time employment with the company—save for the limitation when C was young—and her income has been used, virtually in its entirety, towards the maintenance of the household. Until 1972 the husband benefited directly, and thereafter indirectly in that he has been relieved of his liability to maintain.

The wife looked after the home and gave birth to and brought up C. C was educated at a public school and, as I have said, at university where he obtained a degree in engineering. He is a son of whom his parents can be proud.

As far as I understand the case for the husband, there is no criticism of the wife in her faithful devotion and support of her husband, in her devotion to her home and her child, and to her hard work in maintaining the home and bringing up this child, In addition she worked in a most responsible and important position in the business . . .

It had been clear since 1976 that divorce proceedings would be inevitable and indeed the husband had asked for a divorce during that year. The wife told me that while she was involved in the company proceedings, in the course of which she was required to go back through the company accounts and documentation for about 20 years, she was in no position to deal with her immediate matrimonial problems. I accept this. Once, however, the sum of £40,000 had been paid it was clear her position had to be protected. Her petition was filed on July 6, 1977.

The wife's case is quite simple. She now lives in a small bedroom of the bungalow. She has to travel daily to London. She needs a flat somewhere near the factory in Kilburn. For this she needs a lump sum. She also says that a lump sum is justified because she has looked after the home, brought up C and over the years helped to build up the prosperity of Microfinish Ltd; and although C was and is under some moral obligation to provide a roof for his parents, it is wrong to suggest that he should be obliged to house each parent separately. She is prepared to have her claim for periodical payments dismissed and also asks that the court should make an order under s. 15 of the Inheritance (Provision for Family and Dependants) Act 1975.

I find that a reasonable sum required by her for a flat is about £25,000. Having regard to the figures which ultimately became clear, the wife moderated her original claim for a lump sum of £20,000 to one of £13,500.

Mr Wilson for the wife submits that in reaching my decision I should look in particular at s. 25(1)(f) of the Matrimonial Causes Act 1973 and bear in mind the general provisions towards the start of that section, namely a duty of the court '. . . to have regard to all the circumstances of the case. . . .'

For the husband, Mr Price submits that no lump sum at all should be paid for the following reasons. First, he submits that the whole purpose of ss. 21 to 25 of the Matrimonial Causes Act 1973 is to ensure justice in the widest sense between a husband and a wife—not between a man and his mistress—commonly but erroneously referred to as a 'common law husband' and a 'common law wife.' He draws attention to

s. 25(1)(d) and says that in effect this present marriage only lasted a few months, namely, from September 1971 to early 1972. He also submits that s. 25(1)(f) (contribution to the family) relates to the same period; secondly, he points to the fact that C agreed that his father's generosity to him in earlier years was not based solely on fiscal reasons, but also in part as recompense to C's mother for the years when she lived with him as his wife, and that therefore she should look to C, not only for a gift, but also for her future maintenance; thirdly, that had the marriage continued, the husband and wife would have been living in a house owned by C, and that by giving her any capital now the court would be putting her in a better position than she would have been had the marriage continued; fourthly, he submits that the husband needs every penny of capital which he now has in order to provide some security for the future, whether invested in shares or in some future business. There is, therefore, no capital properly available from which the husband could be expected to make any payment of a lump sum. He further re-emphasised his client's previous generosity to C.

In approaching problems under ss. 21 to 25 of the Matrimonial Causes Act 1973, a number of propositions are clearly established by authority. The function and duty of the court is to reach a physical and financial resolution of the problems of that family which is fair, just and reasonable as between the parties. The court must look to the statutory guidance now provided by s. 25 of the Act of 1973.

Secondly, in exercising this wide discretionary jurisdiction it is important that the court should be careful not to limit its discretion by a narrow construction, of the statutory guidelines. . . .

Section 25 of the Act of 1973 further requires me to have regard to the conduct of the parties, and also to all the circumstances of the case. The latter phrase is very wide, but the word 'conduct' has received judicial attention.

It is argued, and indeed it is true, that the factor of 'conduct' has for the most part been used in order to cut down the amount of financial relief which the court might otherwise have awarded to a party, and not for the purpose of increasing that amount. In my judgment there is nothing in the language of the section itself which supports this restricted view. My initial approach, therefore, is that any such restriction is unwarranted.

Behaviour which has occurred outside the span of the marriage itself has been taken into account by a court when exercising its discretion under s. 25 of the Act of 1973, at least in cases where such conduct has affected the finance of the other spouse: see *W* v *W* [1976] Fam 107, 110.

I find nothing therefore in the authorities to suggest that a broad and general approach to the words 'conduct' and 'in all the circumstances of the case' is undesirable or wrong.

In this case, the wife has given the best years of her life to the husband. She has been faithful, loving and hard-working. She has helped him to build what is in every sense a family business. She has managed his home and been a mother to and helped him bring up a son of whom they are both justly proud. I believe that she has earned for herself some part of the value of the family business.

Having set out those matters prior to the ceremony of marriage itself, which seem to me to be relevant, I ask myself whether I can do justice—that which is fair, just and reasonable between these parties—if I ignore the earlier history and the wife's behaviour during those earlier years. To put the question in a different form: would it really offend a reasonable person's sense of justice to ignore those events and that behaviour? I have no doubt that the answer from the reasonable man would be that they must be taken into account and, in my judgment, not only can I take these matters into account—whether under the phrase 'conduct' or 'in all the circumstances of the case' in s. 25 of the Act of 1973—but that same section casts a duty upon me to do so.

6.3.6   THE FAMILY LAW ACT 1996

FAMILY LAW ACT 1996

Schedule 8

9.   —. . .

   (3)   In subsection (2)—

(a)   for 'section 23(1)(a), (b) or (c)' substitute 'section 22A or 23 above to make a financial provision order in favour of a party to a marriage or the exercise of its powers under section 23A,';

(b)   in paragraph (g), after 'parties' insert ',whatever the nature of the conduct and whether it occurred during the marriage or after the separation of the parties or (as the case may be) dissolution or annulment of the marriage,'; . . .

6.3.7   THE LOSS OF FUTURE BENEFITS, ESPECIALLY PENSIONS

6.3.7.1   The Pensions Act 1995

BROOKS v *BROOKS* [1995] 2 FLR 13 (HL)

The parties, both previously married, married one another in 1977. In that year the husband's firm was incorporated and the wife was paid a salary for nominal services. The husband's retirement benefits scheme was a non-contributory exempt approved scheme set up in 1980 by his company to provide for him benefits in accordance with certain rules. Rule 1(e) of the scheme provided that at his retirement the husband was to be entitled to elect to give up a portion of his pension to provide, from the date of his death, a deferred pension for life for his spouse or any other person financially dependent on him. A lump sum benefit was payable to dependants and any person nominated by the husband if he should die while still employed by the company or within 5 years of beginning to draw the pension and rule 2(c) provided that those death benefits were payable at the discretion of the company. The benefits were non-commutable and non-assignable. Rule 7 provided that if a benefit payable under the policy were to exceed the maximum amount of benefit permissible under an exempt approved scheme, the company was entitled to use the excess to augment other existing benefits or to provide additional benefits to those under the policy, subject to Inland Revenue limits. The marriage broke down in 1989. The wife, now aged 56, claimed successfully in financial proceedings against the husband, now aged 64, that his pension scheme had the character of a postnuptial settlement. The district judge, inter alia, varied the terms so as to provide:

(1)   an immediate index-linked pension for the wife, with the right for her to commute that provision, within the limits imposed by the Inland Revenue, for a lump sum, and

(2)   a contingent dependant's pension for her payable on the husband's death.

The husband appealed against the orders, both generally on the ground that the general provision made for the wife was excessive and specifically on the ground that there was no jurisdiction to vary the pension scheme. In the Family Division of the High Court, Ewbank J reduced the wife's share of the proceeds of sale of the matrimonial home and the amount of costs the husband had been ordered to pay, but refused to disturb the order varying the trusts of the pension fund scheme. The wife appealed against the reduction in the amount of her financial provision and the husband cross-appealed against the variation of the pension fund policy. The Court of Appeal dismissed both appeal and cross-appeal saying that it was the husband who was entitled to the benefits of the pension fund policy and it was he alone who within those limits had the power at the time of his retirement to surrender part of his pension entitlement for the benefit of a spouse and/or other financial dependant. It was that power which gave the scheme the character of a settlement and it was the inclusion of a spouse within its objects which gave the settlement its nuptial element. The scheme amounted to a post-nuptial settlement. The husband appealed, the issue being whether the court had jurisdiction to make the order varying the terms of the pension scheme.

Held (dismissing the appeal):

(1)   'Settlement' in the present context meant, broadly, that the disposition must be one which made some form of continuing provision for both or either of the parties to

a marriage, with or without a provision for children. In order to promote the best interests of the parties and their children on divorce it was desirable that the court should have the power to alter the terms of the settlement. The purpose of s. 24(1)(c) of the Matrimonial Causes Act 1973 was to give the court that power.

(2)   The husband's purpose when entering the scheme was to provide for the retirement of himself and his wife by the highly tax-efficient means afforded by the scheme. If his wife were still alive when he retired, he could then direct that that part of his pension benefit should be used to make separate provision for her after his death. Should he die prematurely, the death benefits would be available to her. In the circumstances, a disposition of that character fell within the wide meaning given to marriage settlement in the matrimonial legislation. The feature which placed the scheme on the marriage settlement side of the line was the presence of rules 1(e) and 2(c). The court had power to vary the present scheme so far as it constituted a settlement made by the husband.

(3)   The pension and death benefits provided by the scheme had to be distinguished from the rule 7 surplus money. It was only in respect of the settled property that the court had power to vary. The surplus money belonged to the company but the settler was the husband, so the surplus did not form part of the settled money. In this case the scheme would be varied by directing that the two pensions for the wife should be provided in priority to, and if necessary in diminution of, the pension payable to the husband who had allowed the company to be struck off the register. The company was insolvent and owed money to the bank and to the Inland Revenue which would claim tax in respect of any unused surplus money in the pension scheme. The burden would be placed on the husband to sort out the mess brought about by his letting the company be struck off. He would have to take the necessary steps to enable the surplus to be used to maintain his pension at the maximum permissible level if part of the fund was used for making pension provision for the wife.

Per curiam: not every pension scheme constituted a marriage settlement and, even when a scheme did fall within the court's jurisdiction to vary a marriage settlement, it would not be right for the court to vary one scheme member's rights to the prejudice of other scheme members. Directing a variation which did not meet with Inland Revenue approval would normally be prejudicial to the rights of the other scheme members. A feature of the instant case was that there was only one scheme member and, moreover, the wife had earnings of her own from the same employer which would sustain provision of an immediate pension for her. If the court were to be able to split pension rights on divorce in the more usual case of a multi-member scheme where the wife had no earnings of her own from the same employer, or to direct the taking out of life insurance, legislation would still be needed.

Decision of the Court of Appeal ([1994] 2 FLR 10) upheld.

PENSIONS ACT 1995

166.   Pensions on divorce etc

(1)   In the Matrimonial Causes Act 1973, after section 25A there is inserted—

'25B.   Pensions

(1)   The matters to which the court is to have regard under section 25(2) above include—

(a)   in the case of paragraph (a), any benefits under a pension scheme which a party to the marriage has or is likely to have, and

(b)   in the case of paragraph (h), any benefits under a pension scheme which, by reason of the dissolution or annulment of the marriage, a party to the marriage will lose the chance of acquiring,

and, accordingly, in relation to benefits under a pension scheme, section 25(2)(a) above shall have effect as if 'in the foreseeable future' were omitted.

(2)   In any proceedings for a financial provision order under section 23 above in a case where a party to the marriage has, or is likely to have, any benefit under a pension scheme, the court shall, in addition to considering any other matter which it is required to consider apart from this subsection, consider—

(a)   whether, having regard to any matter to which it is required to have regard in the proceedings by virtue of subsection (1) above, such an order (whether deferred or not) should be made, and

(b)   where the court determines to make such an order, how the terms of the order should be affected, having regard to any such matter.

(3)   The following provisions apply where, having regard to any benefits under a pension scheme, the court determines to make an order under section 23 above.

(4)   To the extent to which the order is made having regard to any benefits under a pension scheme, the order may require the trustees or managers of the pension scheme in question, if at any time any payment in respect of any benefits under the scheme becomes due to the party with pension rights, to make a payment for the benefit of the other party.

(5)   The amount of any payment which, by virtue of subsection (4) above, the trustees or managers are required to make under the order at any time shall not exceed the amount of the payment which is due at that time to the party with pension rights.

(6)   Any such payment by the trustees or managers—

(a)   shall discharge so much of the trustees or managers liability to the party with pension rights as corresponds to the amount of the payment, and

(b)   shall be treated for all purposes as a payment made by the party with pension rights in or towards the discharge of his liability under the order.

(7)   Where the party with pension rights may require any benefits which he has or is likely to have under the scheme to be commuted, the order may require him to commute the whole or part of those benefits; and this section applies to the payment of any amount commuted in pursuance of the order as it applies to other payments in respect of benefits under the scheme.

25C.   Pension: lump sums

(1)   The power of the court under section 23 above to order a party to a marriage to pay a lump sum to the other party includes, where the benefits which the party with pension rights has or is likely to have under a pension scheme include any lump sum payable in respect of his death, power to make any of the following provision by the order.

(2)   The court may—

(a)   if the trustees or managers of the pension scheme in question have power to determine the person to whom the sum, or any part of it, is to be paid, require them to pay the whole or part of that sum, when it becomes due, to the other party,

(b)   if the party with pension rights has power to nominate the person to whom the sum, or any part of it, is to be paid, require the party with pension rights to nominate the other party in respect of the whole or part of that sum,

(c)   in any other case, require the trustees or managers of the pension scheme in question to pay the whole or part of that sum, when it becomes due, for the benefit of the other party instead of to the person to whom, apart from the order, it would be paid.

(3)   Any payment by the trustees or managers under an order made under section 23 above by virtue of this section shall discharge so much of the trustees, or managers, liability in respect of the party with pension rights as corresponds to the amount of the payment.'

6.3.7.2   Pensions and the Family Law Act 1996

FAMILY LAW ACT 1996

16.   Division of pension rights: England and Wales

(1)   The Matrimonial Causes Act 1973 is amended as follows.

(2)   In section 25B (benefits under a pension scheme on divorce, etc.), in subsection (2), after paragraph (b), insert—

'(c)   in particular, where the court determines to make such an order, whether the order should provide for the accrued rights of the party with pension rights (''the pension rights'') to be divided between that party and the other party in such a way as to reduce the pension rights of the party with those rights and to create pension rights for the other party.'.

(3)   After subsection (7) of that section, add—

'(8) If a pensions adjustment order under subsection (2)(c) above is made, the pension rights shall be reduced and pension rights of the other party shall be created in the prescribed manner with benefits payable on prescribed conditions, except that the court shall not have the power—

    (a) to require the trustees or managers of the scheme to provide benefits under their own scheme if they are able and willing to create the rights for the other party by making a transfer payment to another scheme and the trustees and managers of that other scheme are able and willing to accept such a payment and to create those rights; or

    (b) to require the trustees or managers of the scheme to make a transfer to another scheme—

        (i)   if the scheme is an unfunded scheme (unless the trustees or managers are able and willing to make such a transfer payment); or

        (ii)   in prescribed circumstances.

(9) No pensions adjustment order maybe made under subsection (2)(c) above—

    (a) if the scheme is a scheme of a prescribed type, or

    (b) in prescribed circumstances, or

    (c) insofar as it would affect benefits of a prescribed type.'

Ellison, R, Pensions Reform — The new Section 25B [1995] Fam Law 504

The political pressure in the last 12 months for the reform of the law relating to the division or allocation of pension rights and expectations on divorce has been immense, and rather oddly, in these circumstances, there has also been a great deal of consensus on what should be done. The Pensions Management Institute/Law Society Working Party Report in 1993 seemed, perhaps because the working party included most of the interest groups (including the Bar, academic circles, actuaries, and others), to achieve a degree of acceptance almost unique amongst such reports. The report recommended what has come to be known as 'pensions-splitting'— that on divorce, a spouse's pension should be available to be divided as the parties or the court thought fit, and the court should have the power to direct pension providers and trust to split the pension rights accordingly. Even the pensions industry itself, notoriously suspicious of such moves, accepted the proposals. Professor Goode's committee, later in 1993, looking mostly at pensions law, rather than divorce law, took a sideways glance and pronounced that the Pensions Management Institute (PMI) proposals seemed fine, even though further research was needed into their application. The Government, however; was more doubtful, and pleaded for further time for reflection and review. It decided not to include divorce reform in the Pensions Act 1995. It was, however, eventually outflanked by the pressure groups and forced to accept reforms, albeit not involving splitting.

The Government had had a point. While the advantages of splitting are clear (they include certainty at divorce, compliance with the clean break principle, and the treatment of pensions like any other community asset) the process possesses significant though less obvious problems. Many of them reflect the issues of policy and definition. While pension rights can be valued, such valuation (often using the statutory cash equivalent method) is usually inappropriate. It involves dividing the indivisible, because a pension right is not a conventional asset; it is a risk protection system.

WHAT IS A PENSION—ASSET OR INCOME?

Trying to treat a pension as an asset may be immediately attractive, but it leads to anomalies and injustices. For example, in a final salary scheme, if a scheme member dies before decree absolute, there would be a widow's pension; if he dies one day later, there is none. For a member on a salary of £25,000 and a survivor's pension of around £12,000. the value of the survivor's pension would be around £200,000. But that £200,000 is not there one day and gone the next; it is not the equivalent of a building society account. Yet the splitting option tries to achieve the objective of converting the chalk of a risk system into the cheese of a bank account, and it does it in a crude fashion, at the expense of future third parties, with significant administrative overheads and with complex tax and social security consequences, many of which are unintended.

The new Matrimonial Causes Act 1973, s. 25B (introduced by the Pensions Act 1995 (the Act)) takes the alternative approach, that of deferred income. This approach was dismissed by the PMI report on the grounds that it breaches the clean break principle, and that it provides only a share of the member's pension on his retirement (and stops when it does), and does not provide a benefit for the spouse in her own right. The new section attempts two main reforms. First, that it is now a duty of the court (rather than an option) to examine the pensions position and, secondly, that it grants power to the court to impose an attachment order on the paying trustees or insurers once the pension comes into payment. Such an order must be limited to the amount of the pension payable to the member or policyholder, although it could be up to 100% of it. The provisions in principle look clean and simple, and not much more than is in fact presently available to the courts if only they thought about it.

There are some problems, however, with the wording of the section which may produce as many, if not more, problems than it solves. It is difficult at the time of writing to be too practical in the critique, because the regulations have yet to be produced which will set out the technical implementation, including the provision of information by the trustees to the parties, and the effect of any subsequent change of circumstances (an issue which has caused concern to the adherents of clean break).

Just before the Act received the Royal Assent the Brooks decision (*Brooks* v *Brooks* [1995] 2 FLR 13 emerged from the House of Lords. This is a deeply flawed judgment, based on a misunderstanding or the nature of pension schemes (well-understood however and expressed with great lucidity by Lord Hoffmann in the Court of Appeal decision ([1994] 2 FLR 10). Fortunately, its effect is limited and the decision applies in exceedingly rare cases (where each of the following circumstances concurrently apply spouse has been employed by the same employer and in the same scheme as the member, the scheme is in surplus, and no third parties are affected), and is limited to awarding a pension based on service and remuneration even though not a scheme member. It did not require pension splitting, ie the diminution of one party's pension rights to enhance the other's. Since it is based on the strained assumption that the jurisdiction of the court extends to pension schemes established under trust because they are settlements as referred to in the MCA 1973, it is highly improbable that it applies to personal pensions which are invariably established under contract.

Personal Pensions

The section applies not only to rights under occupational schemes (which is what the Pensions Act 1995 is devoted to) but also rights under personal pensions, as well as rights transferred between such schemes. The valuation of interests under personal pensions is, however, a contentious issue; some personal arrangements involve spouse's benefits; others do not, and the value can vary widely between surrender values (often minimal) and fund values (often unreal).

Unfunded Pensions

The section is also extended to unfunded private sector pensions, in a wide-ranging reference to 'benefits under a pension scheme include any benefits by way of pension, whether under a pension scheme or not'. These arrangements are increasingly common for higher earners (currently over £78,600).

THE NEW SECTION 25B

The drafting of the new section clearly leaves something to be desired. It was introduced hurriedly, under pressure, and in the wrong place and by the wrong department. Matrimonial law is normally dealt with in a Matrimonial Causes Act or an Administration of Justice Act (sponsored by the Lord Chancellor's Department) rather than the Department of Social Security. Its implementation also requires additional regulations, to be produced, yet to be issued, plus a commencement order. Both may be some time, perhaps not until early to mid-1996. There will also need to be deep changes to the Inland Revenue rules. Section 25B, introduced by the Pensions Act 1995, s. 166 takes the non-splitting approach to the pensions problem. It provides, in a very complex form, for the very simple concept of an attachment order on pensions when they fall into payment. It does so by inserting a new section, s. 25B, into the Matrimonial Causes Act 1973.

For practitioners it makes little practical change to the existing system under which advisers (following *Griffiths* v *Dawson & Co* [1993] 2 FLR 315) have to give advice on pensions. Although previously the court had no obligation, but it had the power to consider pensions, *Griffiths* made it professional negligence for advisers to fail properly to review pensions in giving divorce advice. The new section brings English courts into line with Scottish law by imposing an obligation on the court, rather than a permission, to consider pensions. The drafting, however, is going to give long-term employment to the House of Lords in cases involving interpretation of the provisions.

WHAT NEXT?

Other more fertile and analytic minds will in due course find further anomalies, ambiguities, and inconsistencies in the drafting. The section will be discussed at conferences and in papers for some time, and the courts will be bored to tears with the references to *Pepper* v *Hart* [1991] 2 All ER 824 in the months and years to come.

The pensions industry, although highly critical or the new system, may in time come to love it. It should be relatively simple to administer (provided the regulations meet the industry's needs), and cause little day-to-day disruption. There will need to be some form of tracing service, perhaps requiring spouses to register their interests as a form of Class F land charge, to enable paying trustees and others to ensure that one or their members has no order against him before paying. This is especially critical where members have the right to move their pension arrangements about from provider to provider. The courts (and the legal aid fund) will devote huge resources to working out what kinds of changed circumstances would enable an order to be changed in the future; remarriage of either or both of the parties for example, or changes in the benefit levels which have nothing to do with the period of marriage. The nature of orders against unfunded schemes will pose considerable difficulties, especially where employers merge or reconstruct or dissolve and acquire or discharge pre-existing liabilities. We have also to consider what effect the Child Support Agency syndrome on retrospective agreements may have.

There is no doubt that the previous arrangements caused serious unease, and a sense of unfairness, especially in cases where spouses had modest assets but one party had a good pension built up over the years of the marriage. In many cases the existing powers for maintenance orders (with the option of attachment for bad payers) might have been sufficient, if the courts felt it appropriate, which clearly they usually did not. As time passes we may come to appreciate that doing nothing, as the Government intended all along, might have been the wisest move of all, and have achieved the least injustice at the lowest possible cost.

Salter, D, Pensions and Divorce — Where Now? [1996] Fam Law 574

PENSION-SPLITTING

Family Law Act, s. 16 provides a vehicle for pension-splitting, which is widely regarded as defective. In essence, the Government has accepted the principle of pension-splitting, whilst wishing to work through its full consequences for pension schemes, the taxpayer, parties involved in marriage breakdown, and third parties. That is the principal aim of the green paper, to which responses are invited by 29 November 1996. A White Paper is envisaged in the spring of 1997 with a view to further legislation whether by way of amendment to Family Law Act 1996, s. 16 or otherwise.

In 1994, the Department of Social Security commissioned independent research by the Social & Community Planning Research. The full findings of this research programme were recently published in two volumes of the Department of Social Security Research Report series *Women and Pensions* (Report No. 49) and *Pensions and Divorce* (Report No. 50). Solicitors involved in the research indicated that account was taken of pension assets in 70% of divorce cases, although this figure rose to 84% where the pension rights were substantial. The research did, however, record a very different perception on the part of recently divorced women. It is interesting to note that the most common reason (43%) given by solicitors for not taking pensions into account was that they were not relevant in terms of the foreseeable future. The green paper expresses the Government's view that pension-splitting should only apply where a marriage is terminated, which ignores the fact that potential rights may be lost on a separation (whether informal or judicial). It is intended that the new pension-splitting jurisdiction should not be retrospective. Much of the initial press coverage on the publication of the green paper surrounded the fact that because of 'technical and operational difficulties' implementation was not likely to take place until April 2000. The green paper suggests that it is not necessary for pension-splitting to apply to the State basic pension because of the right to substitution referred to above. However, the issue is raised as to whether SERPS should be included within the scope of the pension-splitting powers and alongside it contracted-out rights, which are affected from April 1997 by major changes in the Pensions Act 1995. It is recognised by the green paper that, in order to maintain equity between pre- and post-retirement divorcees, it may be appropriate for pension-splitting to embrace pensions in payment. The green paper also canvasses the issues of a specific de minimis limit having particular regard to the cost of splitting small pensions. The green paper addresses the thorny issue of valuation and makes it clear that the Government does not consider that pension-splitting justifies a different valuation methodology from that already put in place by the Pensions Act 1995 in the earmarking context. It is, however, envisaged that only accrued pension rights will be valued rather than the anticipation of pension rights relating to periods of future employment until retirement. This in part meets the thinking behind the decisions in *H v H (Financial Provision: Capital Assets)* [1993] 2 FLR 335.

The green paper reviews the two basic approaches to pension-splitting, the one being scheme membership involving the internal transfer of rights within the pension arrangement and the other being an external transfer involving the transfer of rights out of the pension arrrangement to another occupational or personal pension scheme or to some other type of approved arrangement. The Government's current thinking is, surprisingly, that, whilst the court should have the power to order a split of pension rights, it should not be able to decide by which of the two approaches this should be achieved. It is thought that this is a matter for the pension provider. The green paper goes on to review the status of the former spouse following the pension split in terms of the entitlement and rights of the individual and the duties of the pension provider. A new category of membership within occupational pension schemes specifically for former spouses is considered. Further complications which are also addressed include the issue of whether a former spouse should have the entitlement to a future transfer from a pension scheme where the scheme membership approach has been adopted, the issues which arise where both partners are members of the same scheme and what might be the appropriate vehicle to be used to accept a transfer of funds for a non-employed former spouse acquiring pension rights as a result of a pension split. It is assumed that pension-splitting will apply to pensions in payment. There follows a review of the benefits available to a former spouse following a pension split and the consequences for the scheme member. For example, under current legislation, an occupational pension scheme may normally pay a member's pension of up to two-thirds of that person's final salary. The issue therefore arises as to whether a former spouse's split pension rights should be counted against her or the scheme member's benefit limit.

The green paper is, on any view, useful background reading for the family lawyer as, quite apart from the discussion of the proposals for pension-splitting, it contains brief annexes on contracting-out of SERPS, an overview on the tax treatment of provision for retirement and valuation as well as a glossary of pensions terminology. In his foreword to the green paper, Peter Lilley indicates that '[pension-splitting] is far more complex than at first appears. It raises many thorny problems which need to be resolved before legislation can be introduced'. The green paper therefore presents an opportunity to deal with pension-splitting in a more considered way than has been possible with the passage of the Pensions Act 1995 and the Family Law Act 1996 through Parliament. That opportunity must be seized.

6.3.8 THE CLEAN BREAK

MATRIMONIAL CAUSES ACT 1973

25A. Exercise of court's powers in favour of party to marriage on decree of divorce or nullity of marriage

(1)   Where on or after the grant of a decree of divorce or nullity of marriage the court decides to exercise its powers under section 23(1)(a), (b) or (c), 24 or 24A above in favour of a party to the marriage, it shall be the duty of the court to consider whether it would be appropriate so to exercise those powers that the financial obligations of each party towards the other will be terminated as soon after the grant of the decree as the court considers just and reasonable.

(2)   Where the court decides in such a case to make a periodical payments or secured periodical payments order in favour of a party to the marriage, the court shall in particular consider whether it would be appropriate to require those payments to be made or secured only for such term as would in the opinion of the court be sufficient to enable the party in whose favour the order is made to adjust without undue hardship to the termination of his or her financial dependence on the other party.

6.4   When Will the Orders be Made?

FAMILY LAW ACT 1996

Schedule 2

3.—. . .

22B. Restrictions affecting section 22A

(1)   No financial provision order, other than an interim order, may be made under section 22A above so as to take effect before the making of a divorce order or separation order in relation to the marriage, unless the court is satisfied—

(a)   that the circumstances of the case are exceptional; and

(b)   that it would be just and reasonable for the order to be so made.

(2)   Except in the case of an interim periodical payments order, the court may not make a financial provision order under section 22A above at any time while the period for reflection and consideration is interrupted under section 7(8) of the 1996 Act.

(3)   No financial provision order may be made under section 22A above by reference to the making of a statement of marital breakdown if, by virtue of section 5(3) or 7(9) of the 1996 Act (lapse of divorce or separation process), it has ceased to be possible—

(a)   for an application to be made by reference to that statement; or

(b)   for an order to be made on such an application.

(4)   No financial provision order may be made under section 22A after a divorce order has been made, or while a separation order is in force, except—

(a)   in response to an application made before the divorce order or separation order was made; or

(b)   on a subsequent application made with the leave of the court.

(5)   In this section, 'period for reflection and consideration' means the period fixed by section 7 of the 1996 Act.

6.5   Preventing or Delaying the Divorce

6.5.1 PREVENTING THE DIVORCE

FAMILY LAW ACT 1996

10. Hardship: orders preventing divorce

(1)   If an application for a divorce order has been made by one of the parties to a marriage, the court may, on the application of the other party, order that the marriage is not to be dissolved.

(2) Such an order (an 'order preventing divorce') maybe made only if the court is satisfied—

(a) that dissolution of the marriage would result in substantial financial or other hardship to the other party or to a child of the family; and

(b) that it would be wrong, in all the circumstances (including the conduct of the parties and the interests of any child of the family), for the marriage to be dissolved.

(3) If an application for the cancellation of an order preventing divorce is made by one or both of the parties, the court shall cancel the order unless it is still satisfied—

(a) that dissolution of the marriage would result in substantial financial or other hardship to the party in whose favour the order was made or to a child of the family; and

(b) that it would be wrong, in all the circumstances (including the conduct of the parties and the interests of any child of the family), for the marriage to be dissolved.

(4) If an order preventing a divorce is cancelled, the court may make a divorce order in respect of the marriage only if an application is made under section 3 or 4(3) after the cancellation.

(5) An order preventing divorce may include conditions which must be satisfied before an application for cancellation may be made under subsection (3).

(6) In this section 'hardship' includes the loss of a chance to obtain a future benefit (as well as the loss of an existing benefit).

K v K (FINANCIAL RELIEF: WIDOW'S PENSION) [1997] 1 FLR 35 (FamD)

COLLINS J: This case provides a graphic illustration of inadequacy of the law and practice relating to pensions in the context of matrimonial breakdown.

I have before me a husband's petition for divorce presented on 19 September 1994 asserting irretrievable breakdown of the marriage and that the parties have lived separate and apart for at least 5 years prior to the presentation of the petition. The answer, relying on s. 5 of the Matrimonial Causes Act 1973, resists the grant of a decree on the ground that grave financial hardship would be caused to the wife in that she would lose the substantial widow's pension she would enjoy if the husband were to pre-decease her. The reply denies grave financial hardship and in the alternative makes proposals to relieve it, if the court were to take a different view.

The husband is likely to carry on working until 2003, 55 being the compulsory retirement age. But on the basis of the agreed figures, he could retire in 1998 when he is 50 with an index-linked pension of £15,674 a year. If he took the maximum possible lump sum, his pension would fall to £11,755 a year. The capital sum would be £57,877. The widow's pension would be one half of the husband's gross pension. The wife is likely to retire at 60 but, even if she works to 65, her pension will only be £3,388 a year or £2,727 and a lump sum of £7,460. She would receive a state pension.

I have no hesitation in concluding that the wife has made out the clearest case in support of her answer. Although the position might be different for a much younger woman, the wife is exactly the kind of person for whom the protection of the statute was devised . . .

In my judgment, the husband's proposals do not being to offer the wife anything which compensates reasonably for the loss of the right to a substantial pension for the whole of her life in the event of his death.

I do not propose to dismiss the petition today. This marriage should be brought to an end, if possible, and I shall take the advice of Ormrod LJ in Le Marchant [1977] 3 All ER 610 and adjourn it to a date to be fixed. I do not accept Miss Harrington's suggestion that I should grant a decree and leave the wife to the protection of s. 10 of the 1973 Act. . . .

Reverting to the opening sentence of this judgment, the court has only limited power to make orders against the husband in this case which would have the effect of protecting the wife because of the lack of capital and income resources which could be the subject of an order. In particular, the court has no power to order the husband to make an allocation or take out insurance policies. It is, therefore, possible for him to obtain a decree absolute under s. 10 while leaving the wife in grave financial hardship.

What can the husband do to satisfy the court? Under the terms of his pension scheme (to which I have only been provided with a guide, although perusal of the regulations would seem to be essential) he is able to allocate a sum towards a pension after his death for someone who would not otherwise be entitled. The husband was not in a position to tell me what proportion of his fund would need to be allocated to provide a decent pension for the wife. Since it would depend on an actuarial assessment of both their life expectancies, it might not be as intimidating as he thinks. Since the maximum proportion for commutation and allocation combined is one-third, it is likely that both husband and wife would receive a significantly smaller lump sum.

Critically for the husband, the allocation is irrecoverable in the event of the wife predeceasing him. He has not sought a quotation for insurance against this possibility. The only sure way for the husband, given his limited means and resources, to protect the wife against the grave financial hardship I have held she would suffer in the event of his predeceasing her after divorce, is to make an allocation which will provide her not necessarily with half his pension entitlement but with a proportion of it similar to that which would be appropriate on an application for ancillary relief. This would carry with it the disadvantage to the wife of reducing the lump sum which she would like to have. She is perfectly free to bargain with the husband for reduction in the allocation for an increase in the lump sum over and above what she would be likely to receive in any event in an application for one on his retirement. But it does not seem to me that the court has a role to play in this bargaining process.

Allocation is the obvious way of protecting the wife. The pension scheme provides it presumably for just this sort of case. Insurance is another, although the husband's abilities seem disablingly limited in this area. I have already drawn attention to the absence of evidence as to the cost of funding a limited widow's pension, although I am aware that there is discussion of the question in the Family Law Bar Association publication *At a Glance*. He may choose to offer some other combination of jam today and margarine tomorrow in an attempt to persuade the wife that it would be in her interest to give up her pension rights and abandon her opposition to the divorce. He is not precluded from any other proposals. But, if they are unacceptable to the wife, they will only be acceptable to the court if they precisely and reasonably address the risk to his wife of being financially unprotected for decades of life in the event of his early death.

6.6   Variation and Appealing of Orders

6.6.1   APPEALS

BARDER v *BARDER* [1987] 1 FLR 18 (HL)

LORD BRANDON OF OAKBROOK: My Lords, the appellant David Barder ('the husband') and Christina Barder ('the wife') were married in 1973. There were two children of the family: . . .

In February 1984 the wife presented in the Basingstoke County Court a petition for divorce founded on the husband's adultery. The suit was undefended and in July 1984 the wife was granted a decree nisi and care and control of the children with reasonable access to the husband. In September 1984 the decree was made absolute and the husband remarried.

Proceedings for ancillary relief ensued and came before Mr Registrar Fuller in the Basingstoke County Court on 20 February 1985. Negotiations took place at the court and agreement was reached on the terms of a consent order on a clean break basis. The registrar gave his approval and made a consent order in the terms agreed. The order was expressed to be made in full and final settlement of all claims made or capable of being made by the wife or the husband against each other or their respective estates. It provided that the husband should within 28 days transfer to the wife all his legal and equitable interest in Hollybourn and its contents, the wife undertaking that on such transfer being made she would redeem the existing mortgages on the house. There were also undertakings by the husband to effect the re-assignment to the wife of three policies of life assurance held by one of the mortgagees, and by the wife to effect the re-assignment to the husband of two other policies of life assurance held by the other mortgagees. The husband was further ordered to make substantial periodical payments to the children.

On 25 March 1985 an appalling tragedy supervened when the wife unlawfully killed the two children and then committed suicide.

At the time of the wife's death the registrar's order dated 20 February 1985 was still executory, the various instruments necessary to give effect to it not yet having been completed. The time for appealing against the order, fixed at five days by r. 124(1) of the Matrimonial Causes Rules 1977 (SI 1977 No. 344), had expired about a month earlier.

On 23 April 1985 the husband issued a notice in the Basingstoke County Court asking for leave to appeal out of time against the registrar's order. . . .

In paragraph 5 he set out the grounds of the husband's application as follows:

The basis upon which the order was made has been fundamentally and unforeseeably altered by the circumstances of the death of the petitioner and of the two children. The net effect of the order if it were to stand would be to confer a wholly unexpected benefit upon the petitioner's mother who is not a member of the family unit for whom the Matrimonial Causes Act is intended to make provision, and who it is understood is a woman of substantial means in her own right.

. . . The purpose of the statutory right of appeal is to enable decisions of a county court which are unjust to be set aside or varied by the Court of Appeal. The fulfilment of that purpose is not made any the less necessary or desirable by the death of one of the parties to the cause in which the decision was made. In a case other than a matrimonial cause I do not think that it would even be suggested that the statutory right of appeal would lapse because of the death of one of the parties to it. I cannot see why a matrimonial cause should be different in this respect. Where an appeal is brought or continued after the death of one of the parties to a cause, procedural steps have to be taken to substitute another party for the party who has died. Provision for the taking of such steps is made by rules of court. In the present case the deceased wife's mother was given leave to intervene in the suit as her personal representative, although it may be that the procedure prescribed by Ord. 5, r. 11 of the County Court Rules 1981 (SI 1981 No. 1687) should have been followed. However, the point was not argued before your Lordships and I therefore express no opinion upon it.

The question of merits

There can, in my opinion, be no doubt that the consent order dated 20 February 1985 was agreed between the husband and the wife through their respective solicitors, and approved by the registrar, upon a fundamental, though tacit, assumption. The assumption was that for an indefinite period, to be measured in years rather than months or weeks, the wife and the two children of the family would require a suitable home in which to reside. That assumption was totally invalidated by the deaths of the children and the wife within five weeks of the order being made.

The merits of an appeal by the husband against the order fall necessarily to be considered on the hypothesis that leave to appeal out of time has rightly been given, for without such leave no appeal could be brought. On the hearing of the appeal the judge would be bound to take the factual situation as it then existed, and not as it was when the order appealed from was made: in other words he would be bound to recognise that the fundamental assumption on which the order had been agreed and made had in the meantime become totally invalidated. The circumstance that the order was a consent order would, moreover, be of little significance in a matrimonial proceeding of this kind. This is because the property and financial arrangements agreed between the parties in such a proceeding derive their effect from the order itself, and not from the agreement: *de Lasala* v *de Lasala* [1980] AC 546; *Thwaite* v *Thwaite* [1982] Fam 1; *Jenkins* v *Livesey (formerly Jenkins)* [1985] AC 424.

On behalf of the intervener it was strenuously contended that where, as in the present case, an order relating to financial provision and property transfer was made on a clean break basis, the parties took their chances with regard to the occurrence of any future events that might invalidate any assumption on which the order was made. The whole object of such an order was to achieve finality and that object would be defeated if an appeal were to be allowed because of the occurrence of such events. In support of this contention reference was made to *Minton* v *Minton* [1979] AC 593 and to the observations of Lord Scarman in *Jenkins* v *Livesey (formerly Jenkins)* [1985] AC 424, 430. I recognise the importance, in general, of according to clean break orders the finality which they are intended to achieve. But if, by reason of supervening events occurring within a relatively short time, the fundamental assumption on the basis of which such an order was made has become totally invalidated, I cannot see why the circumstance that a clean break was intended should make any difference. The intention to produce a clean break on the terms of the order will itself have been founded on the subsequently invalidated assumption.

Having regard to the matters which I have discussed above I am clearly of the opinion that, on the hypothesis that leave to appeal out of time has rightly been given, the merits of the appeal are all one way: the appeal should be allowed and the order of Judge Smithies restored.

VICARY v *VICARY* [1992] 2 FLR 271 (CA)

PURCHAS LJ: At the time of the marriage the parties lived in comparatively modest circumstances. During the marriage there were a number of matrimonial homes. The first at 1 Kirkdale Road, Langho, near Blackburn, was a gift to the husband from his mother before the marriage. There then followed a second matrimonial home which was in the husband's sole name. After the birth of A in July 1973 a third matrimonial home was bought in the joint names of the parties at Hillside Cottage, Nant Road, Coedpoth, near Wrexham. The fourth matrimonial home at 63 Acton Gate, Wrexham, was purchased in joint names in July 1981, and the fifth and final matrimonial home at Bronwylfa Hall, Bronwylfa, near Wrexham, was purchased in July 1985, again in the joint names of the parties. By this time the husband's business had prospered and the standard of living enjoyed by the parties had substantially increased.

The marriage broke down in 1987. On 25 April 1987 the wife left Bronwylfa Hall taking with her the youngest daughter, D. The husband remained with A and G in the matrimonial home. On 11 June 1987 the wife petitioned for the dissolution of the marriage on the grounds of the husband's adultery with the lady who has since become his second wife. The decree nisi was pronounced on 23 March 1988 and this was made absolute on 12 May 1988.

On 28 March 1988 a consent order was made in the proceedings for ancillary relief on the wife's claim for financial provision. The central provision of the order was that the husband should pay to the wife a lump sum payment of £250,000 as follows:

(a) Credit to be given in respect of two payments, made by the husband, on 6 and 20 July 1987, representing monies expended by the husband on the purchase of the wife's present home. These totalled £76,184.23.

(b) £123,815.77 on or before 15 April 1988, or forthwith after the, decree absolute whichever was the later and if not duly paid to carry interest at 15 per cent pa from 15 April 1988 until payment.

(c) £50,000 by annual instalments of £10,000 plus accrued interest of 15 per cent pa on the outstanding balance calculated from 18 March 1988, such payments to be made from 15 April in each year commencing 1989.

(d) On the payment of £123,815.77 the wife should transfer to the husband all her interest in the former matrimonial home at Bronwylfa Hall.

The order also provided for periodical payments to be paid by the husband for the benefit of D; that the husband should pay the wife's costs on an indemnity basis and finally provided that the order should be in full and final settlement of any claim that either party might have against the other and that neither should be at liberty to make a claim under the Inheritance (Provision for Family Dependants) Act 1975. This order was agreed to by the wife on the basis of evidence from the husband to the effect that the husband's holding in a company known as the Balderton Company Ltd was worth some £347,000 and that his net assets amounted to about £430,000.

The husband had not disclosed that negotiations were taking place for the sale of his shares in the Balderton Company Ltd of which he must have been aware. These were completed shortly after the making of the consent order for a consideration worth £2.8m.

When the wife discovered the true state of affairs, she successfully initiated proceedings which resulted in the consent order being set aside by order of his Honour Judge Roberts QC on 22 March 1989. In his judgment the judge held that the husband had by knowing non-disclosure of the true position about the value of his assets led the wife to agree to the terms of the consent order. He rejected the defence of acquiescence upon which the husband attempted to rely. It was in these circumstances that Rattee J had to consider what order should be made under s. 23(1)(c) of the Act on the position as it was established before him.

Before the proceedings to set the consent order aside the husband lost no time in moving under the consent order, and within 8 days had already paid the sum of £123,815.77 to the wife and had received the transfer from her of all her interest in Bronwylfa Hall. Before Rattee J it was agreed between the parties that the wife's claim should be settled by an order for a lump sum on a clean break basis. The sum claimed by the wife was of the order of £470,000, whereas the husband contended that she should have no more than £250,000. The husband accepted before Rattee J, however, that in view of his liquidity he could, if it were necessary, meet an order for the payment for £470,000. He obviously could do this since he had investments which on his own figures could be realised for £798,000 net, quite apart from his holdings in Anglo United itself which were worth some further £898,000 but which, according to the husband, were not readily realisable because of his employment within that Group.

6.7 End of Chapter Assessment Questions

1. To what extent will s. 25(2) of the Matrimonial Causes Act 1973 become irrelevant after the coming into force of the Family Law Act 1996?

2. In June 1996 Jayne (32) walked out on her husband, Trevor (45), taking their daughters, Abigail (8) and Lucie (6) with her. She moved back into her parents' home. The cause of the split was Trevor's increasingly violent behaviour and his chronic alcohol dependence. Jayne did not seek any maintenance since at that stage she was in full-time employment. She filed a statement of marital breakdown at the local county court in September 1996. She has now been made redundant but due to having been with the company for less than two years has received no redundancy pay.

Advise her on her rights to maintenance for herself and the children.

6.8 End of Chapter Assessment Outline Answers

1. This could be quite a long and involved question, especially if you do not know much about s. 25(2) Matrimonial Causes Act 1973! The best way to tackle it is probably to start with explaining what s. 25(2) is all about, and then to go on to discuss reasons why it may become irrelevant post Family Law Act 1996.

Section 25(2) of the 1973 Act is the list of guidelines or criteria to which the court is to have regard when deciding how to exercise its powers under ss. 23 and 24. So, s. 25 is applicable to financial and property orders following divorce. You would not need to discuss and explain the meaning of each of the criteria in depth, an overview would suffice, since this question is not directed simply at the interpretation of the section.

In divorce cases under the 1973 Act, the court will deal with all ancillary claims, either by dealing with a contested application, or by ratifying a consent order that has been negotiated between the parties themselves. In the event that the ancillary relief has been negotiated by the parties the court will still check that the order is appropriate — or rather that it does not appear to be outside the parameters of the court's jurisdiction. The considerations in s. 25(2) will therefore still play a role.

By contrast, when the Family Law Act 1996 comes into force, the regime to deal with ancillary matters will alter. Refer to the provisions of s. 9 and the emphasis on non-court imposed decisions. The thrust of s. 9 being that the parties should agree themselves, either with or without the assistance of a third party negotiator who will normally be a mediator. If agreement has been reached, this must be put before the court, but as yet it is unclear to what extent, and how, the court will investigate these agreements.

Insofar as s. 25(2) is concerned, if the parties take it upon themselves to reach an agreement, without input from a legally qualified person, they are unlikely to have any regard to the various factors at all. If the agreement is negotiated with the assistance of a third party mediator, again, it can be questioned to what extent the existence of these criteria will be raised. If the mediator is not legally qualified, the potential is still there for the criteria to be ignored. You may like to reflect upon the extent to which legally qualified persons will be involved with divorce and ancillary settlements if legal aid will primarily be directed at mediation if deemed suitable by the mediator. A lack of legal advice will lead, potentially, to s. 25(2)'s irrelevance.

Whilst there is the possibility that s. 25 will lose its place in the actual negotiation of settlements, it is fair to say that this will not happen with regard to appeals. Reflect upon the fact that with agreements *not* being overseen to the same extent by lawyers, there is a greater chance of one party being hard done by. This may be due to lack of disclosure, inequality of bargaining power, or simply lack of knowledge of potential rights. Consequently the number of appeals against 'unfair' bargains will increase, and arguably the courts, when dealing with such appeals will approach the matter on the basis of s. 25(2) factors.

2. This essay falls into two neat sections for discussion purposes: the consideration of the rules for claiming maintenance as a spouse, or ex-spouse; and the rules in relation to children. However, the two elements are inter-dependent, since the issue of maintenance for Jayne, will affect the impact of the legislation for the children. It is not really that important which one you choose to consider first as long as you *do* deal with both!

Starting with Jayne, as a spouse, there is a duty to support which may be enforced against Trevor. It is irrelevant that it was Jayne who walked out of the relationship, when she is considering claiming financial orders. Her conduct may become relevant, but this will be mentioned later. If Trevor is unwilling to pay maintenance voluntarily, which should always be discussed with clients, Jayne will need to think about court action. You will also need to be aware of the fact that Jayne has filed a statement of marital breakdown, which will affect the ability of the court to order any financial provision, since the Family Law Act 1996 has made some changes to the Matrimonial Causes Act 1973. During Jayne's period for reflection (which you will recall is 15 months and 14 days since there are minor children), she should try to settle the arrangements for the future. Part of this includes making financial arrangements. Jayne should try to reach an agreement with Trevor and the use of a mediator may assist. Before a divorce order is granted she will need to supply to the court a statement that financial arrangements have been made. This may be by producing a court order (whether by consent or otherwise), a negotiated agreement, or a statement that they have made their arrangements or that there are no arrangements to be made. You may also refer to the emphasis the 1996 Act seems to place on non-court based decisions and the parties' own ability to settle matters (s. 9).

If the negotiated/own decision process is not successful then court action may be needed. The 1973 Act will need to be considered as this will allow Jayne to apply for maintenance.

Under s. 22A of the 1973 Act (inserted by the 1996 Act) the court is able to make an order at the appropriate time, which is:

- any time after a statement of marital breakdown has been received by the court and before an application is made to the court for a divorce or separation order;
- any time after a divorce order has been applied for and not been withdrawn; or
- any time after a divorce order has been made.

Clearly Jayne falls within these criteria. However, any order made by the court before the divorce order is granted will be nothing more than interim (s. 22B). Upon the granting of the divorce order, a final order may be made although it should be noted that in making an application for an interim order, Jayne may in fact prejudice any attempts to seek a negotiated settlement prior to the divorce. If Jayne has to use this Act, she may seek a periodical payment order, or lump sum order.

When a court is considering making an order under s. 22A, it is required to have regard to the criteria in s. 25 of the 1973 Act. Insofar as Jayne is concerned, her situation as carer of the children, her lack of employment, and possible lack of future employment chances will all go in her favour. Given the lack of substantive detail in the question you would not be able to go into too much detail with regard to these factors.

If Jayne is successful in getting maintenance for herself, then it may be that the question of the maintenance for the children can be dealt with without recourse to the Child Support Agency. You should state that the Agency has jurisdiction over all new cases of child maintenance, unless within one of the exceptions.

If Jayne will be receiving welfare benefits (e.g. Income Support) then the Agency has no option but to get involved. Explain the basis upon which the Agency works. The notion of person with care and absent parent needs to be mentioned, as does the strict formula approach. You are not required to do detailed calculations, a brief synopsis will suffice — i.e. that the Agency use Income Support levels to assess a maintenance requirement for the children, they then establish the levels of income of both parties, and calculate the level of income that is available to meet the maintenance requirement. Subject only to the provisions of departure, the absent parent will be required to pay up to 50% of available income for child support. Note that there are other limits as to the maximum payable in relation to exempt income.

Jayne may be able to avoid the application of the CSA 1991 if not on benefit, although it is always open to her to make use of this agency. The Act can be avoided by the parents reaching a voluntary maintenance agreement and having that embodied into a consent order by the court. So, part of her negotiations should include the requirements of the children. If the agreement is not embodied into an order, the Agency may intervene at any stage.

Additionally, Jayne may use the courts if the Agency does not have jurisdiction, although this is unlikely. She may use the courts to obtain top up maintenance, over and above the level obtained by the Agency. Again, unless Trevor is exceptionally wealthy, or the children attend private fee paying schools, this is an unlikely option.

Your advice should, if Jayne is not on benefit, be to reach an agreement and obtain a consent order from the court, advising her that only a consent order can be made, and that the courts do not have jurisdiction on contested maintenance orders. If the Agency do not have jurisdiction on a case, and no agreement can be reached between the parents, this creates a potential loophole, with no means of resolution for Jayne.

Conclude briefly as to the nature of your advice to Jayne.

CHAPTER SEVEN

PROPERTY AND FINANCE WITHOUT DIVORCE

7.1 Maintenance without Divorce

7.1.1 CLAIMING MAINTENANCE

7.1.1.1 The MCA 1973

MATRIMONIAL CAUSES ACT 1973

27. Financial provision orders, etc., in case of neglect by party to marriage to maintain other party or child of the family

(1)   Either party to a marriage may apply to the court for an order under this section on the ground that the other party to the marriage (in this section referred to as the respondent)—

(a)   has failed to provide reasonable maintenance for the applicant, or

(b)   has failed to provide, or to make a proper contribution towards, reasonable maintenance for any child of the family.

(2)   The court shall not entertain an application under this section unless—

(a)   the applicant or the respondent is domiciled in England and Wales on the date of the application; or

(b)   the applicant has been habitually resident there throughout the period of one year ending with that date; or

(c)   the respondent is resident there on that date.

(3)   Where an application under this section is made on the ground mentioned in subsection (1)(a) above, then, in deciding—

(a)   whether the respondent has failed to provide reasonable maintenance for the applicant, and

(b)   what order, if any, to make under this section in favour of the applicant,

the court shall have regard to all the circumstances of the case including the matters mentioned in section 25(2) above, and where an application is also made under this section in respect of a child of the family who has not attained the age of eighteen, first consideration shall be given to the welfare of the child while a minor.

(6)   Where on an application under this section the applicant satisfies the court of any ground mentioned in subsection (1) above, the court may make any one or more of the following orders, that is to say—

(a)   an order that the respondent shall make to the applicant such periodical payments, for such term, as may be specified in the order;

(b)   an order that the respondent shall secure to the applicant, to the satisfaction of the court, such periodical payments, for such term, as may be so specified;

(c)   an order that the respondent shall pay to the applicant such lump sum as may be so specified;

(d)   an order that the respondent shall make to such person as may be specified in the order for the benefit of the child to whom the application relates, or to that child, such periodical payments, for such term, as may be so specified;

(e)   an order that the respondent shall secure to such person as may be so specified for the benefit of that child, or to that child, to the satisfaction of the court, such periodical payments, for such term, as may be so specified.

(f)   an order that the respondent shall pay to such person as may be so specified for the benefit of that child, or to that child, such lump sum as may be so specified; subject, however, in the case of an order under paragraph (d), (e) or (f) above, to the restrictions imposed by section 29(1) and (3) below on the making of financial provision orders in favour of children who have attained the age of eighteen.

(6A)   An application for the variation under section 31 of this Act of a periodical payments order or secured periodical payments order made under this section in favour of a child may, if the child has attained the age of sixteen, be made by the child himself.

(7)   Without prejudice to the generality of subsection (6)(c) or (f) above, an order under this section for the payment of a lump sum—

(a)   may be made for the purpose of enabling any liabilities or expenses reasonably incurred in maintaining the applicant or any child of the family to whom the application relates before the making of the application to be met,

(b)   may provide for the payment of that sum by instalments of such amount as may be specified in the order and may require the payment of the instalments to be secured to the satisfaction of the court.

28.   Duration of continuing financial provision orders in favour of party to marriage, and effect of remarriage

(2)   Where a periodical payments or secured periodical payments order in favour of a party to a marriage is made otherwise than on or after a grant of a decree of divorce or nullity of marriage, and the marriage in question is subsequently dissolved or annulled but the order continues in force, the order shall, notwithstanding anything in it, cease to have effect on the remarriage of that party, except in relation to any arrears due under or on the date of the remarriage.

7.1.1.2   The DPMCA 1978

DOMESTIC PROCEEDINGS AND MAGISTRATES' COURTS ACT 1978

1.   Grounds of application for financial provision

Either party to a marriage may apply to a magistrates' court for an order under section 2 of this Act on the ground that the other party to the marriage—

(a)   has failed to provide reasonable maintenance for the applicant; or

(b)   has failed to provide, or to make a proper contribution towards, reasonable maintenance for any child of the family; or

(c)   has behaved in such a way that the applicant cannot reasonably be expected to live with the respondent; or

(d)   has deserted the applicant.

2.   Powers of court to make orders for financial provision

(1)   Where on an application for an order under this section the applicant satisfies the court of any ground mentioned in section 1 of this Act, the court may, subject to the provisions of this Part of this Act, make any one or more of the following orders, that is to say—

(a)   an order that the respondent shall make to the applicant such periodical payments, and for such term, as may be specified in the order;

(b)   an order that the respondent shall pay to the applicant such lump sum as may be so specified;

(2)   Without prejudice to the generality of subsection (1)(b) or (d) above, an order under this section for the payment of a lump sum may be made for the purpose of enabling any liability or expenses reasonably incurred in maintaining the applicant, or any child of the family to whom the application relates, before the making of the order to be met.

(3)   The amount of any lump sum required to be paid by such an order under this section shall not exceed [£1,000] or such larger amount as the Lord Chancellor may from time to time by order fix for the purposes of this subsection.

Any order made by the Secretary of State under this subsection shall be made by statutory instrument and shall be subject to annulment in pursuance of a resolution of either House of Parliament.

3. Matters to which court is to have regard in exercising its powers under s. 2

(1)   Where an application is made for an order under section 2 of this Act, it shall be the duty of the court, in deciding whether to exercise its powers under that section and, if so, in what manner, to have regard to all the circumstances of the case, first consideration being given to the welfare while a minor of any child of the family who has not attained the age of eighteen.

(2)   As regards the exercise of its powers under subsection (1)(a) or (b) of section 2, the court shall in particular have regard to the following matters—

(a)   the income, earning capacity, property and other financial resources which each of the parties to the marriage has or is likely to have in the foreseeable future, including in the case of earning capacity any increase in that capacity which it would in the opinion of the court be reasonable to expect a party to the marriage to take steps to acquire;

(b)   the financial needs, obligations and responsibilities which each of the parties to the marriage has or is likely to have in the foreseeable future;

(c)   the standard of living enjoyed by the parties to the marriage before the occurrence of the conduct which is alleged as the ground of the application;

(d)   the age of each party to the marriage and the duration of the marriage;

(e)   any physical or mental disability of either of the parties to the marriage.

(f)   the contributions which each of the parties has made or is likely in the foreseeable future to make to the welfare of the family, including any contribution by looking after the home or caring for the family;

(g)   the conduct of each of the parties, if that conduct is such that it would in the opinion of the court be inequitable to disregard it.

4. Duration of orders for financial provision for a party to a marriage

(1)   The terms to be specified in any order made under section 2(1)(a) of this Act shall be such terms as the court thinks fit except that the term shall not begin earlier than the date of the making of the application for the order and shall not extend beyond the death of either of the parties to the marriage.

(2)   Where an order is made under the said section 2(1)(a) and the marriage of the parties affected by the order is subsequently dissolved or annulled but the order continues in force, the order shall, notwithstanding anything in it, cease to have effect on the remarriage of the party in whose favour it was made, except in relation to any arrears due under the order on the date of the remarriage.

25. Effect on certain orders of parties living together

(1)   Where—

(a)   periodical payments are required to be made to one of the parties to a marriage (whether for his own benefit or for the benefit of a child of the family) by an order made under section 2 or 6 of this Act or by an interim maintenance order made under section 19 of this Act (otherwise than on an application under section 7 of this Act),

the order shall be enforceable notwithstanding that the parties to the marriage are living with each other at the date of the making of the order or that, although they are not living with each other at that date, they subsequently resume living with each other; but the order shall cease to have effect if after that date the parties continue to live with each other, or resume living with each other, for a continuous period exceeding six months.

7.1.1.3   Other orders in the magistrates' courts

DOMESTIC PROCEEDINGS AND MAGISTRATES' COURTS ACT 1978

6. Orders for payments which have been agreed by the parties

(1)   Either party to a marriage may apply to a magistrates' court for an order under this section on the ground that either the party making the application or the other party to the marriage has agreed to make such financial provision as may be specified in the

application and, subject to subsection (3) below, the court on such an application may, if—

(a) it is satisfied that the applicant or the respondent, as the case may be, has agreed to make that provision, and

(b) it has no reason to think that it would be contrary to the interests of justice to exercise its powers hereunder,

order that the applicant or the respondent, as the case may be, shall make the financial provision specified in the application.

(2) In this section 'financial provision' means the provision mentioned in any one or more of the following paragraphs, that is to say—

(a) the making of periodical payments by one party to the other,

(b) the payment of a lump sum by one party to the other,

(c) the making of periodical payments by one party to a child of the family or to the other party for the benefit of such a child,

(d) the payment by one party of a lump sum to a child of the family or to the other party for the benefit of such a child,

and any reference in this section to the financial provision specified in an application made under subsection (1) above or specified by the court under subsection (5) below is a reference to the type of provision specified in the application or by the court, as the case may be, to the amount so specified as the amount of any payment to be made thereunder and in the case of periodical payments, to the term so specified as the term for which the payments are to be made.

7. Powers of court where parties are living apart by agreement

(1) Where the parties to a marriage have been living apart for a continuous period exceeding three months, neither party having deserted the other, and one of the parties has been making periodical payments for the benefit of the other party or of a child of the family, that other party may apply to a magistrates' court for an order under this section, and any application made under this subsection shall specify the aggregate amount of the payments so made during the period of three months immediately preceding the date of the making of the application.

(2) Where on an application for an order under this section the court is satisfied that the respondent has made the payments specified in the application, the court may, subject to the provisions of this Part of this Act, make one or both of the following orders, that is to say—

(a) an order that the respondent shall make to the applicant such periodical payments, and for such term, as may be specified in the order;

(b) an order that the respondent shall make to the applicant for the benefit of a child of the family to whom the application relates, or to such a child, such periodical payments, and for such term, as may be so specified.

(3) The court in the exercise of its powers under this section—

(a) shall not require the respondent to make payments which exceed in aggregate during any period of three months the aggregate amount paid by him for the benefit of the applicant or a child of the family during the period of three months immediately preceding the date of the making of the application;

(b) shall not require the respondent to make payments to or for the benefit of any person which exceed in amount the payments which the court considers that it would have required the respondent to make to or for the benefit of that person on an application under section 1 of this Act;

(c) shall not require payments to be made to or for the benefit of a child of the family who is not a child of the respondent unless the court considers that it would have made an order in favour of that child on an application under section 1 of this Act.

(4) Where on an application under this section the court considers that the orders which it has the power to make under this section—

(a) would not provide reasonable maintenance for the applicant, or

(b) if the application relates to a child of the family, would not provide, or make a proper contribution towards reasonable maintenance for that child,

the court shall refuse to make an order under this section, but the court may treat the application as if it were an application for an order under section 2 of this Act.

(5) The provisions of section 3 of this Act shall apply in relation to an application for an order under this section as they apply in relation to an application for an order under section 2 of this Act subject to the modification that for the reference in subsection 2(c) of the said section 3 to the occurrence of the conduct which is alleged as the ground of the application there shall be substituted a reference to the living apart of the parties to the marriage.

(6) The provisions of section 4 of this Act shall apply in relation to an order under this section which requires periodical payments to be made to the applicant for his own benefit as they apply in relation to an order made under section 2(1)(a) of this Act.

7.2 Occupation Rights and the Matrimonial Home

7.2.1 THE MATRIMONIAL HOMES ACT 1983

MATRIMONIAL HOMES ACT 1983

1. Rights concerning matrimonial home where one spouse has no estate, etc.
(1) Where one spouse is entitled to occupy a dwelling house by virtue of a beneficial estate or interest or contract or by virtue of any enactment giving him or her the right to remain in occupation, and the other spouse is not so entitled, then, subject to the provisions of this Act, the spouse not so entitled shall have the following rights (in this Act referred to as 'rights of occupation')
(a) if in occupation, a right not to be evicted or excluded from the dwelling house or any part thereof by the other spouse except with the leave of the court given by an order under this section;
(b) if not in occupation, a right with the leave of the court so given to enter into and occupy the dwelling house.
(2) So long as one spouse has rights of occupation, either of the spouses may apply to the court for an order—
(a) declaring, enforcing, restricting or terminating those rights, or
(b) prohibiting, suspending or restricting the exercise by either spouse of the right to occupy the dwelling house, or
(c) requiring either spouse to permit the exercise by the other of that right.
. . .

FAMILY LAW ACT 1996

30. Rights concerning matrimonial home where one spouse has no estate, etc.
(1) This section applies if—
(a) one spouse is entitled to occupy a dwelling-house by virtue of—
(i) a beneficial estate or interest or contract; or
(ii) any enactment giving that spouse the right to remain in occupation; and
(b) the other spouse is not so entitled.
(2) Subject to the provisions of this Part, the spouse not so entitled has the following rights ('matrimonial home rights')—
(a) if in occupation, a right not to be evicted or excluded from the dwelling-house or any part of it by the other spouse except with the leave of the court given by an order under section 33;
(b) if not in occupation, a right with the leave of the court so given to enter into and occupy the dwelling-house.

7.2.1.1 Criteria for the court

MATRIMONIAL HOMES ACT 1983

1. Rights concerning matrimonial home where one spouse has no estate, etc.
. . .
(3) On an application for an order under this section, the court may make such order as it thinks just and reasonable having regard to the conduct of the spouses in relation

to each other and otherwise, to their respective needs and financial resources, to the needs of any children and to all the circumstances of the case, and, without prejudice to the generality of the foregoing provision—

(a)   may except part of the dwelling house from a spouse's rights of occupation (and in particular a part used wholly or mainly for or in connection with the trade, business or profession of the other spouse),

(b)   may order a spouse occupying the dwelling house or any part thereof by virtue of this section to make periodical payments to the other in respect of the occupation,

(c)   may impose on either spouse obligations as to the repair and maintenance of the dwelling house or the discharge of any liabilities in respect of the dwelling house.

FAMILY LAW ACT 1996

33.   Occupation orders where applicant has estate or interest etc. or has matrimonial home rights

. . .

(3)   An order under this section may—

(a)   enforce the applicant's entitlement to remain in occupation as against the other person ('the respondent');

(b)   require the respondent to permit the applicant to enter and remain in the dwelling-house or part of the dwelling-house;

(c)   regulate the occupation of the dwelling-house by either or both parties;

(d)   if the respondent is entitled as mentioned in subsection (1)(a)(i), prohibit, suspend or restrict the exercise by him of his right to occupy the dwellinghouse;

(e)   if the respondent has matrimonial home rights in relation to the dwelling-house and the applicant is the other spouse, restrict or terminate those rights;

(f)   require the respondent to leave the dwelling-house or part of the dwelling-house; or

(g)   exclude the respondent from a defined area in which the dwelling-house is included.

. . .

(6)   in deciding whether to exercise its powers under subsection (3) and (if so) in what manner, the court shall have regard to all the circumstances including—

(a)   the housing needs and housing resources of each of the parties and of any relevant child;

(b)   the financial resources of each of the parties;

(c)   the likely effect of any order, or of any decision by the court not to exercise its powers under subsection (3), on the health, safety or well-being of the parties and of any relevant child; and

(d)   the conduct of the parties in relation to each other and otherwise.

7.2.2   PROTECTION OF RIGHTS

BARNETT v *HASSETT* [1981] 1 WLR 1385 (FamD)

WOOD J: The question which I have to decide is whether the use of a Class F charge under the provision of the Matrimonial Homes Act 1967 is proper where its sole purpose is to freeze the assets of a spouse.

This application is made as one of urgency, and I am deciding it upon affidavit evidence alone. In essence the relief sought is to set aside the charge and to permit the sale of a house owned by the applicant wife at 2, Spaniards Close, London, NW11. It was her matrimonial home during a previous marriage.

Some of the facts are not in dispute and can be summarised. The parties first met in 1976. The marriage took place on February 25, 1980. Each party had been married previously. As a result of the financial provision ordered in October 1979 at the end of her first marriage the wife now owns 2, Spaniards Close. She was also awarded a lump sum of £130,000. She has two children by her former marriage a boy 14 and a girl 15. They live with her. The respondent husband also has two children by his former marriage. His previous home was in Barnet and it was sold for £100,000 on March 22, 1980. He is now living with his two children in rented accommodation. The rent is £375 per week and he pays £75 per week for a housekeeper.

On November 8, 1979, contracts were exchanged between the husband and the owners of Hadley Hurst, Monken Hadley, Barnet, of that property to him for the sum of £410,000. The deposit of £41,000 was paid by him.

On March 7, 1980, the husband moved into 2, Spaniards Close with his two children. On July 28, 1980, they left. His belongings were all finally removed during October 1980, Each side claims that he or she has a case upon which to pray for a judicial separation on the grounds of unreasonable behaviour. No petition has yet been filed.

At the beginning of May 1980 the husband through his solicitors informed the vendors of Hadley Hurst that he could not complete. In September 1980 that house was sold for £342,000. He has forfeited the deposit of £41,000, and he has spent other sums on surveys and legal fees; they are said to total £80,000—a total loss of about £120,000. I was told that he had been served with a writ by the vendors but I do not know the date. On June 12, he received a bill from solicitors acting in the purchase for £2,557.

On July 17, 1980, the wife exchanged contracts with a South American gentleman for the sale of 2, Spaniards Close for the price of £395,000. A deposit of £35,000 was paid on exchange of contracts and two further interim payments of £35,000 have been made on September 30 and November 30, 1980, respectively, a total of £105,000. The balance is payable on completion. The value of the house today is some £145,000 less than the contract price.

Before exchanging contracts solicitors for the purchaser required a letter from the husband so as to ensure that no Class F charge would be placed on the property before completion, and on July 17, 1980, he signed a letter in the following terms. The letter is addressed from the address 2, Spaniards Close, London, NW11, and dated July 17, 1980: it is addressed to the purchaser. It says:

Dear Sir,
Re 2 Spaniards Close, London NW11
In consideration of you today entering into a contract to puchase the above freehold property from my wife Carole Hassett I hereby confirm that I have not and will not register any charge against the said property under the Matrimonial Homes Act and that I will vacate the said properly on or before the agreed completion date of January 31, 1981.

Yours faithfully,

and he signs it.

In November 1980 the husband instructed his present solicitors, although it would seen from a letter dated February 2, 1981, that his former solicitors were still acting in connection with Hadley Hurst, I have no affidavit from either of them. On December 15, 1980, these new solicitors applied to register a Class F charge on 2, Spaniards Close. It was registered on December 17, 1980, and they were notified of the registration on December 23, 1980. It is not entirely clear to me whether these solicitors were at the time aware of the contents of the letter of July 17, 1980, signed by the husband. The partner dealing with the matter was on holiday from before Christmas until January 20, 1981, and by letter dated January 22, 1981, he wrote in the following terms. There is obviously no reference for the wife's solicitors, and the husband's solicitors' reference is RMP/PS/ and then a number, and it is dated January 22, 1981.

Dear Sir,
Re Mr and Mrs Hassett
We act on behalf of Mr H E Hassett and understand that you act on behalf of his wife Mrs C. A. Hassett (formerly Barnett). We are instructed by our client that unhappily the marriage has broken down. We would also notify you that our client has registered a matrimonial homes caution in respect of his right of occupation in the home 2, Spaniards Close, London NW11,

and it is signed 'Yours faithfully' with the signature of the firm of solicitors.

That letter was the first indication to the wife or her advisers that a Class F charge had been registered on behalf of the husband and it was the first communication between solicitors on this topic. This present application dated February 3, 1981, was a reaction to that letter which must have been anticipated.

On reading the affidavits it was clear to me that whatever the issues between the parties and however they were decided the husband's position would be amply protected if I were to keep control of the purchase moneys. On being pressed by me, Mr Price for the husband agreed that this was so, but he indicated that the loss had either been agreed or could only be proved to the amount of £60,000 and that this was the amount of the proceeds of sale which he now submitted should be frozen. I have therefore allowed completion to take place on February 27, 1981, that is last Friday, and give my judgment now as soon as possible thereafter with the knowledge that this wife would not have parted with £60,000 prior to my judgment.

Mr Scott Baker for the wife submits that it would be an abuse of process for me to make an order freezing any part of the purchase moneys.

Before turning to the law I analyse the husband's case as follows: (i) he has rights under s. 1(1)(b) of the Matrimonial Homes Act 1967 as a spouse not in occupation of the matrimonial home; (ii) he does not wish to occupy that home or any part of it; (iii) he does not now wish to prevent its sale (although I doubt whether that was his attitude until very recently); (iv) he wants to freeze part of the proceeds of sale— £60,000; (v) he therefore registered a Class F charge to force his wife to apply to this court to set it aside.

I turn to the Act of 1967 itself. It is unnecessary for me to review the history of the rights between husband and wife prior to the passing of this Act; suffice it to say that the provisions of the Act introduce new rights.

By s. 1 the Act protects a spouse who has no rights to remain in the matrimonial home. It does not protect a spouse who has proprietary, contractual or statutory rights of occupation: see *Gurasz* v *Gurasz* [1970] P 11. If not in occupation the right of a spouse is 'with the leave of the court so given to enter into and occupy the dwelling house': s. 1(1)(b). The whole emphasis of the Act is to create and protect the right to occupation of a spouse not in occupation or a spouse already in occupation. This is made clear throughout the Act. The right to occupation must relate to a matrimonial home, and only continues during the existence of the marriage. A Class F charge is intended to protect that right.

One thing is abundantly clear, namely that this husband does not seek 'to enter into and occupy' the whole or any part of the matrimonial home. Is he entitled to ask the court to freeze any part of the proceeds of sale? I do not think so. Mr Price did not draw my attention to any specific parts of the Act itself, but quite apart from the points to which I have already referred, s. 3 of the Act seems to me to emphasise that any interest other than a right to occupy is to be excluded or disregarded. By that section a charge can only be registered on one matrimonial home at a time. If the intention of the Act had been to allow a spouse to place his or her hands upon proceeds of sale or to allow the prevention of such a sale then I would have thought that a charge on a matrimonial home not in occupation and when a sale was likely would be an obvious source for funds.

7.3 Rights of Ownership

Gray, K, Elements of Land Law, 2nd edn, Butterworths, 1993

JOINT TENANCY

The essence of joint tenancy consists in the theory that each joint tenant is 'wholly entitled to the whole' of the estate or interest which is the subject of co-ownership. No joint tenant holds any specific share in the property himself, but each is (together with the other joint tenant or tenants) invested with the total interest in the land. The whole is not so much the sum of the parts, for each and every part is itself co-extensive with the whole. In Bracton's expressive language, each joint tenant *totum tenet et nihil tenet*; each holds everything and yet holds nothing.

(1) An undifferentiated form of co-ownership

Joint tenancy is thus an undifferentiated kind of co-ownership in which an entire estate or interest in property—rather than any defined proportion or aliquot share—is vested simultaneously in all the co-owners. The co-owned property is a single estate held by joint owners who are bound together in a 'thorough and intimate union of interest and possession' and who together comprise but one composite person in the eyes of the law.

(2) Absence of shareholding

Any reference to ownership in specific 'shares' (e.g. A owns a one-quarter interest and B a three-quarters interest) is normally sufficient to establish that A and B co-own not as joint tenants, but rather as tenants in common. Even to say that A and B hold property in equal shares is, in strict terms and in the absence of any other evidence, to indicate that A and B are tenants in common.

TENANCY IN COMMON

Tenancy in common is firmly to be distinguished from joint tenancy. It is frequently said that, unlike joint tenants, tenants in common hold land in 'undivided shares'. The phrase 'undivided shares' may seem confusing at first, since it appears to conjure up a picture of the amorphous undifferentiated co-ownership which characterises joint tenancy. However, the key to the distinction between joint tenancy and tenancy in common lies in the reference to the word 'shares'. It is only in the tenancy in common that the co-owners hold distinct shares at all. It is only of tenants in common that it can be meaningful to say, for instance, that A has a one-quarter interest and B a three-quarters interest, or even that A and B, are each entitled to a one-half share. The allocation of shares or proportions is not possible as between joint tenants, who are of course wholly entitled to the whole. Tenants in common are however owners of distinct shares, albeit in property which has not yet been divided up physically. It is not possible to point to one parcel or area of the co-owned land rather than any other. as belonging to a particular tenant in common: tenants in common own specific, but undivided, shares in the land.

7.4 Resulting Trusts

7.4.1 VOLUNTARY TRANSFERS OF PROPERTY

LAW OF PROPERTY ACT 1925

60. Abolition of technicalities in regard to conveyances and deeds

. . .

(3) In a voluntary conveyance a resulting trust for the grantor shall not be implied merely by reason that the property is not expressed to be conveyed for the use or benefit of the grantee.

7.4.2 THE PRESUMPTION OF AN ADVANCEMENT

7.4.2.1 Transfers to a wife

PETTITT v PETTITT [1969] 2 All ER 385 (HL)

LORD DIPLOCK: the intention with which an act is done affects its legal consequences and the evidence does not disclose what was the actual intention with which he did it. This situation commonly occurs when the actor is deceased. When the act is of a kind to which this technique has frequently to be applied by the courts the imputed intention may acquire the description of a 'presumption'—but presumptions of this type are not immutable. A presumption of fact is no more than a consensus of judicial opinion disclosed by reported cases as to the most likely inference of fact to be drawn in the absence of any evidence to the contrary—for example, presumptions of legitimacy, of death, of survival and the like. But the most likely inference as to a person's intention in the transactions of his everyday life depends on the social environment in which he lives and the common habits of thought of those who live in it. The consensus of judicial opinion which gave rise to the presumptions of 'advancement' and 'resulting trust' in transactions between husband and wife is to found in cases relating to the propertied classes of the nineteenth century and the first quarter of the twentieth century among whom marriage settlements were common, and it was unusual for the wife to contribute by her earnings to the family income. It was not until after World War II that the courts were required to consider the proprietary rights in family assets of a different social class. The advent of legal aid, the wider employment of married women in industry, commerce and the professions and the emergence of a property-owning, particularly a real-property-mortgaged-to-a-building-society-owning, democracy has compelled the courts to direct their attention to this during the last 20 years. It would, in my view, be an abuse of the legal technique for ascertaining or imputing intention to apply to transactions between the post-war generation of married couples 'presumptions' which are based on inferences of fact which an earlier generation of judges drew as to the most likely intentions of earlier generations of spouses belonging to the propertied classes of a different social era.

7.4.3 OWNERSHIP OF THE MATRIMONIAL HOME

GISSING v GISSING [1970] 2 All ER 780

The parties were married in 1935. In 1951, the matrimonial home was purchased for £2,695 and conveyed into the sole name of the appellant. The purchase price was raised as to £2,150 on mortgage repayable by instalments, as to £500 by a loan to the appellant by his employers, and the balance of £45 and the legal charges were paid by the appellant from his own money. At no time was there any express agreement as to how the beneficial interest in the matrimonial home should be held. The respondent (who was earning £500 per annum) made no direct contribution to the initial deposit or legal charges, nor to the repayment of the loan of £500 nor to the mortgage instalments. The respondent provided some furniture and equipment for the house and for improving the lawn and in an spent £220 on this. The respondent also paid for her and her son's clothes and some extras. It was not suggested that either the respondent's efforts or earnings made it possible for the appellant to raise the £500 loan or the mortgage. Nor was it suggested that the purchase of the respondent's clothes, or her son's was undertaken to assist the appellant in meeting the repayment of the loan or the payment of the mortgage instalments which he undertook. The appellant also paid the outgoings on the house and gave to the respondent a housekeeping allowance, and he paid for the holidays. In 1961, the marriage broke down and, in 1966, the respondent obtained a decree absolute. On the question whether the respondent had any beneficial interest in the former matrimonial home.

HELD: On the facts it was not possible to draw an inference that there was any common intention that the respondent should have any beneficial interest in the matrimonial home.

LORD DIPLOCK: . . . In all the previous cases about the beneficial interests of spouses in the matrimonial home the arguments and judgments have been directed to the question whether or not an agreement between the parties as to their respective interests can be established on the available evidence. This approach to the legal problem involved is in most cases adequate, but it passes over the first stage in the analysis of the problem, viz the role of the agreement itself in the creation of an equitable estate in real property. In the instant appeal, I think it is desirable to start at the first stage.

Any claim to a beneficial interest in land by a person, whether spouse or stranger, in whom the legal estate in the land is not vested must be based on the proposition that the person in whom the legal estate is vested holds it as trustee on trust to give effect to the beneficial interest of the claimant as cestui que trust. The legal principles applicable to the claim are those of the English law of trusts and in particular, in the kind of dispute between spouses that comes before the courts, the law relating to the creation and operation of 'resulting, implied or constructive trusts'. Where the trust is expressly declared in the instrument by which the legal estate is transferred to the trustee or by written declaration of trust by the trustee, the court must give effect to it. But to constitute a valid declaration of trust by way of gift of a beneficial interest in land to a cestui que trust the declaration is required by s. 53(1) of the Law of Property Act 1925, to be in writing. If it is not in writing it can only take effect as a resulting, implied or constructive trust to which that section has no application.

A resulting, implied or constructive trust—and it is unnecessary for present purposes to distinguish between these three classes of trust—is created by a transaction between the trustee and cestui que trust in connection with the acquisition by the trustee of a legal estate in land, whenever the trustee has so conducted himself that it would be inequitable to allow him to deny to the cestui que trust a beneficial interest in the land acquired. And he will be held so to have conducted himself if by his words or conduct he has induced the cestui que trust to act to his own detriment in the reasonable belief that by so acting he was acquiring a beneficial interest in the land.

This is why it has been repeatedly said in the context of disputes between spouses as to their respective beneficial interests in the matrimonial home, that if at the time of its acquisition and transfer of the legal estate into the name of one or other of them an express agreement has been made between them as to why in which the beneficial interests shall be held, the court will give effect to it—notwithstanding the absence of any written declaration of trust. Strictly speaking this states the principle too widely, for if the agreement did not provide for anything to be done by spouse in whom the legal estate was not vested, it would be a merely voluntary declaration of trust and unenforceable for want of writing. But in the express oral agreements contemplated by these dicta it has been assumed sub silentio that they provide for the spouse in whom the legal estate in the matrimonial home is not vested to do something to facilitate its acquisition, by contributing to the purchase price or to the deposit or the mortgage instalments when it is purchased on mortgage or to make some other material sacrifice by way of contribution to or economy in the general family expenditure. What the court gives effect to is the trust resulting or implied from the common intention expressed in the oral agreement between the spouses that if each acts in the manner provided for in the agreement the beneficial interests in the matrimonial home shall be held as they have agreed.

An express agreement between spouses as to their respective beneficial interests in land conveyed into the name of one of them obviates the need for showing that the conduct of the spouse into whose name the land was conveyed was intended to induce the other spouse to act to his or her detriment on the faith of the promise of a specified beneficial interest in the land and that the other spouse so acted with the intention of acquiring that beneficial interest. The agreement itself discloses the common intention required to create a resulting, implied or constructive trust. But parties to a transaction in connection with the acquisition of land may well have formed a common intention that the beneficial interest in the land shall be vested in them jointly without having used express words to communicate this intention to one another, or their recollections of the words used may be imperfect or conflicting by the time any dispute arises. In such a case—a common one where the parties are spouses whose marriage has broken down—it may be possible to infer their common intention from their conduct.

As in so many branches of English law in which legal rights and obligations depend on the intentions of the parties to a transaction, the relevant intention of each party is the intention which was reasonably understood by the other party to be manifested by that party's words or conduct notwithstanding that he did not consciously formulate that intention in his own mind or even acted with some different intention which he did not communicate to the other party. On the other hand, he is not bound by any inference which the other party draws as to his intention unless that inference is one which can reasonably be drawn from his words or conduct. It is in this sense that in the branch of English law relating to constructive, implied or resulting trusts effect is given to the inferences as to the intentions of parties to a transaction which a reasonable man would draw from their words or conduct and not to any subjective intention or absence of intention which was not made manifest at the time of the transaction itself. It is for the court to determine what those inferences are.

In drawing such an inference, what spouses said and did which led up to the acquisition of a matrimonial home and what they said and did while the acquisition was being carried through is on a different footing from what they said and did after the acquisition was completed. Unless it is alleged that there was some subsequent fresh agreement, acted on by the parties, to vary the original beneficial interests created when the matrimonial home was acquired, what they said and did after the acquisition was completed is relevant if it is explicable only on the basis of their having manifested to one another at the time of the acquisition some particular common intention as to how the beneficial interests should be held. But it would in my view be unreasonably legalistic to treat the relevant transaction involved in the acquisition of a matrimonial home as restricted to the actual conveyance of the fee simple into the name of one or other spouse. Their common intention is more likely to have been concerned with the economic realities of the transaction than with the unfamiliar technicalities of the English law of legal and equitable interests in land. The economic reality which lies behind the conveyance of the fee simple to a purchaser in return for a purchase price the greater part of which is advanced to the purchaser on a mortgage repayable by instalments over a number of years, is that the new freeholder is purchasing the matrimonial home on credit and that the purchase price is represented by the instalments by which the mortgage is repaid in addition to the initial payment in cash. The conduct of the spouses in relation to the payment of the mortgage instalments may be no less relevant to their common intention as to the beneficial interests in a matrimonial home acquired in this way than their conduct in relation to the payment of the cash deposit.

It is this feature of the transaction by means of which most matrimonial homes have been acquired in recent years that makes difficult the task of the court in inferring from the conduct of the spouses a common intention as to how the beneficial interest in it should be held. Each case must depend on its own facts but there are a number of factual situations which often recur in the cases. Where a matrimonial home has been purchased outright without the aid of an advance on mortgage it is not difficult to ascertain what part, if any, of the purchase price has been provided by each spouse. If the land is conveyed into the name of a spouse who has not provided the whole of the purchase price, the sum contributed by the other spouse may be explicable as having been intended by both of them either as a gift or as a loan of money to the spouse to whom the land is conveyed or as consideration for a share in the beneficial interest in the land. In a dispute between living spouses the evidence will probably point to one of these explanations as being more probable than the others, but if the rest of the evidence is neutral the prima facie inference is that their common intention was that the contributing spouse should acquire a share in the beneficial interest in the land in the same proportion as the sum contributed bears to the total purchase price. This prima facie inference is more easily rebutted in favour of a gift where the land is conveyed into the name of the wife; but as I understand the speeches in *Pettitt v Pettitt* [1969] 2 All ER 385 four of the members of your Lordships' House who were parties to that decision took the view that even if the 'presumption of advancement' as between husband and wife still survived today, it could seldom have any decisive part to play in disputes between living spouses in which some evidence would be available in addition to the mere fact that the husband had provided part of the purchase price of property conveyed into the name of the wife.

Similarly when a matrimonial home is not purchased outright but partly out of moneys advanced on mortgage repayable by instalments, and the land is conveyed into the name of the husband alone, the fact that the wife made a cash contribution to the deposit and legal charges not borrowed on mortgage gives rise, in the absence of evidence which makes some other explanation more probable, to the inference that their common intention was that she should share in the beneficial interest in the land conveyed. But it would not be reasonable to infer a common intention as to what her share should be without taking account also of the sources from which the mortgage instalments were provided. If the wife also makes a substantial direct contribution to the mortgage instalments out of her own earnings or unearned income this would be prima facie inconsistent with a common intention that her share in the beneficial interest should be determined by the proportion which her original cash contribution bore either to the total amount of the deposit and legal charges or to the full purchase price. The more likely inference is that her contributions to the mortgage instalments were intended by the spouses to have some effect on her share.

Where there has been an initial contribution by the wife to the cash deposit and legal charges which points to a common intention at the time of the conveyance that she should have a beneficial interest in the land conveyed to her husband, it would however be unrealistic to attach significance to the wife's subsequent contributions to the mortgage instalments only where she pays them directly herself. It may be no more than a matter of convenience which spouse pays particular household accounts, particularly when both are earning, and if the wife goes out to work and devotes part of her earnings or uses her private income to meet joint expenses of the household which would otherwise be met by the husband, so as to enable him to pay the mortgage instalments out of his moneys, this would be consistent with and might be corroborative of an original common intention that she should share in the beneficial interest in the matrimonial home and that her payments of other household expenses were intended by both spouses to be treated as including a contribution by the wife to the purchase price of the matrimonial home.

Even where there has been no initial contribution by the wife to the cash deposit and legal charges but she makes a regular and substantial direct contribution to the mortgage instalments it may be reasonable to infer a common intention of the spouses from the outset that she should share in the beneficial interest or to infer a fresh agreement reached after the original conveyance that she should acquire a share. But it is unlikely that the mere fact that the wife made direct contributions to the mortgage instalments would be the only evidence available to assist the court in ascertaining the common intention of the spouses.

Where in any of the circumstances described above contributions, direct or indirect, have been made to the mortgage instalments by the spouse into whose name the matrimonial home has not been conveyed, and the court can infer from their conduct a common intention that the contributing spouse should be entitled to *some* beneficial interest in the matrimonial home, what effect is to be given to that intention if there is no evidence that they in fact reached any express agreement as to what the respective share of each spouse should be?

I take it to be clear that if the court is satisfied that it was the common intention of both spouses that the contributing wife should have a share in the beneficial interest and that her contributions were made on this understanding, the court in the exercise of its equitable jurisdiction would not permit the husband in whom the legal estate was vested and who had accepted the benefit of the contributions to take the whole beneficial interest merely because at the time the wife made her contributions there had been no express agreement as to how her share in it was to be quantified. In such a case the court must first do its best to discover from the conduct of the spouses whether any inference can reasonably be drawn as to the probable common understanding about the amount of the share of the contributing spouse on which each must have acted in doing what each did, even though that understanding was never expressly stated by one spouse to the other or even consciously formulated in words by either of them independently. It is only if no such inference can be drawn that the court is driven to apply as a rule of law, and not as an inference of fact, the maxim 'equality is equity', and to hold that the beneficial interest belongs to the spouses in equal shares.

The same result however may often be reached as an inference of fact. The instalments of a mortgage to a building society are generally repayable over a period of many years. During that period, as both must be aware, the ability of each spouse to contribute to the instalments out of their separate earnings is likely to alter, particularly in the case of the wife if any children are born of the marriage. If the contribution of the wife in the early part of the period of repayment is substantial but is not an identifiable and uniform proportion of each instalment, because her contributions are indirect or, if direct, are made irregularly, it may well be a reasonable inference that their common intention at the time of acquisition of the matrimonial home was that the beneficial interest should be held by them in equal shares and that each should contribute to the cost of its acquisition whatever amounts each could afford in the varying exigencies of family life to be expected during the period of repayment. In the social conditions of today this would be a natural enough common intention of a young couple who were both earning when the house was acquired but who contemplated having children whose birth and rearing in their infancy would necessarily affect the future earning capacity of the wife.

The relative size of their respective contributions to the instalments in the early part of the period of repayment, or later if a subsequent reduction in the wife's contribution is not to be accounted for by a reduction in her earnings due to motherhood or some other cause from which the husband benefits as well, may make it a more probable inference that the wife's share in the beneficial interest was intended to be in some proportion other than one-half. And there is nothing inherently improbable in their acting on the understanding that the wife should be entitled to a share which was not to be quantified immediately on the acquisition of the home but should be left to be determined when the mortgage was repaid or the property disposed of, on the basis of what would be fair having regard to the total contributions, direct or indirect, which each spouse had made by that date. Where this was the most likely inference from their conduct it would be for the court to give effect to that common intention of the parties by determining what in all circumstances was a fair share.

Difficult as they are to solve, however, these problems as to the amount of the share of a spouse in the beneficial interest in a matrimonial home where the legal estate is vested solely in the other spouse, only arise in cases where the court is satisfied by the words or conduct of the parties that it was their common intention that the beneficial interest was not to belong solely to the spouse in whom the legal estate was vested but was to be shared between them in some proportion or other.

Where the wife has made no initial contribution to the cash deposit and legal charges and no direct contribution to the mortgage instalments nor any adjustment to her contribution to other expenses of the household which it can be inferred was referable to the acquisition of the house, there is in the absence of evidence of an express agreement between the parties, no material to justify the court in inferring that it was the common intention of the parties that she should have any beneficial interest in a matrimonial home conveyed into the sole name of the husband, merely because she continued to contribute out of her own earnings or private income to other expenses of the household. For such conduct is no less consistent with a common intention to share the day-to-day expenses of the household, while each spouse retains a separate interest in capital assets acquired with their own money or obtained by inheritance or gift. There is nothing here to rebut the prima facie inference that a purchaser of land who pays the purchase price and takes a conveyance and grants a mortgage in his own name intends to acquire the sole beneficial interest as well as the legal estate; *and the difficult question of the quantum of the wife's share does not arise.*

HUSSEY v *PALMER* [1972] 3 All ER 744

In 1967, when the plaintiff sold her condemned house, she was invited by her daughter and her son-in-law, the defendant, to live with them in their house which was owned by the son-in-law. As the house was too small for them all the son-in-law arranged to have a bedroom built on to it as an extension for the plaintiff's use, it being assumed that she would live in the house, using the bedroom, for the rest of her life. The extension was built between April and September 1967. It cost £607 and was paid for by the plaintiff direct to the builder, in June and September 1967. The son-in-law said nothing to the plaintiff about repaying the £607 to her. When the extension was completed the plaintiff moved into it. She lived in the house until March 1968 when, because of differences between her and the daughter and son-in-law she left and went to live elsewhere. She became hard up but the son-in-law refused her request for financial help. In April 1970 the plaintiff brought proceedings against the son-in-law claiming from him, as money lent, the £607 which she had paid for the extension. At the hearing of the claim the registrar intimated his view that the £607 was not a loan but was paid by the plaintiff under a family arrangement, accordingly the plaintiff submitted to a non-suit and in July 1971 brought fresh proceedings against the son-in-law claiming the £607 on a resulting trust. In these proceedings the plaintiff gave evidence that she had lent the £607 to the son-in-law, he elected to call no evidence. On that evidence the county court judge held that the £607 was a loan and that there was no case for a resulting trust, and he dismissed the plaintiff's claim. He did not think it right to insist on amendment of the particulars of claim to add a claim for money lent since the plaintiff had twice elected not to pursue such a claim. On the plaintiff's appeal.

HELD (Cairns LJ dissenting): The case came within the principle that where it was inequitable on the grounds of justice and good conscience that the legal owner of property should take the property for himself and exclude another from it, the law would impute or impose a trust for the other's benefit. A person who paid for an extension to be added to the legal owner's property acquired an equitable interest in the property because justice and good conscience so required; the court would look at the circumstances of each case to decide in what way the equity could be satisfied. In the circumstances of the present case the court should impose or impute a resulting trust for the plaintiff by which the son-in-law held the house on terms which gave the plaintiff an interest in the house proportionate to the £607 she had put into it in paying for the extension, even if (*per* Phillimore LJ) the transaction was a loan for that would not be inconsistent with it also involving a resulting trust. The appeal would therefore be allowed . . .

LORD DENNING MR: . . . If there was no loan, was there a resulting trust? and, if so, what were the terms of the trust? Although the plaintiff alleged that there was no resulting trust, I should have thought that the trust in this case, if there was one, was more in the nature of a constructive trust; but this is more a matter of words than anything else. The two run together. By whatever name it is described, it is a trust imposed by law whenever justice and good conscience require it. It is a liberal process, founded in large principles of equity, to be applied in cases where the defendant cannot conscientiously keep the property for himself alone, but ought to allow another to have the property or a share in it. The trust may arise at the outset when the property is acquired, or later on, as the circumstances may require. It is an equitable remedy by which the court can enable an aggrieved party to obtain restitution. It is comparable to the legal remedy of money had and received which, as Lord Mansfield said, is very beneficial and, therefore, much encouraged. Thus we have repeatedly held that, when one person contributes towards the purchase price of a house, the owner holds it on a constructive trust for him, proportionate to his contribution even though there is no agreement between them, and no declaration of trust to be found, and no evidence of any intention to create a trust. Instances are numerous where a wife has contributed money to the initial purchase of a house or property; or later on to the payment of mortgage instalments; or has helped in a business: see *Falconer* v *Falconer* [1970] 1 WLR 1333, *Heseltine* v *Heseltine* [1971] 1 All ER 952 and *Re Cummins (decd) Cummins* v *Thompson* [1972] Ch 62. Similarly, when a mistress has contributed money, or money's worth, to the building of a house: *Cooke* v *Head*. Very recently a purchaser has been held to hold on trust for an occupier: *Binions* v *Evans* [1972] Ch 359. In all those cases it would have been quite inequitable for the legal owner to take the property for himself and exclude the other from it. So the law imputed or imposed a trust for his or her benefit.

The present case is well within the principles of those cases. Just as a person, who pays part of the purchase price, acquires an equitable interest in the house, so also he does when he pays for an extension to be added to it. . . .

It seems to me to be entirely against conscience that he should retain the whole house and not allow Mrs Hussey any interest in it, or any charge on it. The court should, and will, impose or impute a trust by which Mr Palmer is to hold the property on terms under which, in the circumstances that have happened, she has an interest in the property proportionate to the £607 which she put into it. She is quite content if he repays her the £607. If he does not repay the £607, she can apply for an order for sale, so that the sum can be paid to her. But, the simplest way for him would be to raise the £607 on mortgage and pay it to her. But, on the legal point raised, I have no doubt there was a resulting trust, or, more accurately, a constructive trust, for her, and I would so declare. I would allow the appeal accordingly.

PHILLIMORE LJ: I agree. It is common ground that Mrs Hussey paid £607 to enable her son-in-law to have an extension made to his house in which she was going to live. It is quite clear that she did not intend to make him a gift of the money. She herself said she regarded it as a loan. It is true that the son-in-law in his defence said that he assumed the money was paid by her as a gift to him; but in a later amended defence he said that she was to be repaid if the house was sold at an early date. That clearly does not fit with a gift: it goes a long way to confirm her case that it was not a gift. Here is an example of what so often happens. This mother-in-law advanced money to improve the property of her son-in-law. She did not intend to make a gift of the money. She could not afford to do that. No terms of repayment were agreed except perhaps in the event of the house being sold at an early date. She has described it as a loan, and that might be true. I do not for myself think that it would be inconsistent with the transaction also being or involving a resulting trust. In all the circumstances here, in the absence of clear arrangements for repayment and in circumstances where repayment on demand might be very difficult for the son-in-law, I should have thought it was more appropriate to regard it as an example of a resulting trust; and I would accordingly entirely agree with Lord Denning MR that she has an interest in this house proportionate to the £607 which she paid. It follows that this appeal should be allowed.

CAIRNS LJ: I am afraid I differ from Lord Denning MR and Phillimore LJ in this case; and, but for the fact that they have both taken the view that the plaintiff was entitled to succeed, I should have regarded this as a plain case where she had failed to establish the cause of action which she set up. . . .

In my view it is going a very long way to say that, all that evidence having been given by this lady, there was some misunderstanding by her of the legal position and that she was describing as a loan something which was not a loan at all. It is to my mind nothing to the point that in all probability no express terms as to repayment were ever agreed. It must be a common thing indeed for a parent or a parent-in-law to make a loan of money to a son or daughter or a son-in-law which both of them know is a loan, as to which it is obvious that there is no immediate prospect of repayment, but which in law is a loan repayable on demand. In my view that is the position here. As it was a loan, I think it is quite inconsistent with that to say that it could create a resulting trust at the same time. I accept as a correct statement of law the short passage in Underhill's *Law of Trusts and Trustees*, in these words:

> Where the purchase money is provided by a third party at the request of and by way of loan to the person to whom the property is conveyed there is no resulting trust in favour of the third party, for the lender did not advance the purchase-money as purchaser, but merely as lender.

And it seems to me that that proposition is equally applicable where it is not a matter of the property being purchased, but a matter of a builder being paid for an extension to a property which already belongs to the borrower of the money. For these reasons I consider that the plaintiff was certainly not entitled to succeed on the evidence which she had given.

GRANT v EDWARDS AND ANOTHER [1986] 2 All ER 426

Between 1967 and 1969 the plaintiff, a married woman with two young children, had a casual relationship with the defendant. In 1969 the plaintiff gave birth to the defendant's son and the couple decided to live together on a more permanent basis. A house was purchased and transferred into the name of the defendant and his brother, who was a purely nominal party with no beneficial interest in the property. The defendant told the plaintiff that her name would not go onto the title because it would cause some prejudice in the matrimonial proceedings pending between the plaintiff and her husband. The purchase price was £5,576 which together with legal costs was provided by a cash payment of £1,049 made by the defendant and by two mortgages totalling £4,533. Prior to 1969 the plaintiff worked but between 1969 and 1972 she was on supplementary benefit. However, she contributed £6 a week towards general expenses for a time after they moved into the house. In 1971 a second child was born. From August 1972 onwards the plaintiff made very substantial indirect contributions to the mortgage repayments by applying her earnings to the joint household expenses, and by housekeeping and bringing up the children. In February 1975, after a fire at the property, the family moved into council accommodation. The defendant received £4,000 from a fire insurance policy, the bulk of which was spent on making repairs to the property, which was then let, the rent being used to pay the instalments on the first mortgage. The second mortgage was paid off in October 1974. In September 1975 the sum of £1,037 left over from the moneys from the fire insurance policy was paid into a joint account at a building society which was shared equally between the plaintiff and the defendant. In 1980 the couple separated. There was then £3,800 outstanding on the first mortgage. The plaintiff claimed a share in the beneficial interest in the property on the grounds, inter alia, that she had contributed very substantially to the repayment of both mortgages by means of her contribution to the joint household expenses, and by housekeeping, feeding and bringing up the children. The judge found, inter alia, (i) that, the defendant had never had any real intention of replacing his brother with the plaintiff on the title deed, and (ii) that, except for instalments under the second mortgage paid by the plaintiff as part of the general household expenses, all instalments under both mortgages had been paid by the defendant. The judge dismissed the plaintiff's claim and she appealed.

NOURSE LJ: . . . In order to decide whether the plaintiff has a beneficial interest in 96 Hewitt Road we must climb again the familiar ground which slopes down from the twin peaks of *Pettitt* v *Pettitt* [1969] 2 All ER 385 and *Gissing* v *Gissing* [1970] 2 All ER 780. In a case such as the present, where there has been no written declaration or agreement, nor any direct provision by the plaintiff of part of the purchase price so as to give rise to a resulting trust in her favour, she must establish a common intention between her and the defendant, acted on by her, that she should have a beneficial interest in the property. If she can do that, equity will not allow the defendant to deny that interest and will construct a trust to give effect to it.

In most of these cases the fundamental, and invariably the most difficult, question is to decide whether there was the necessary common intention, being something which can only be inferred from the conduct of the parties, almost always from the expenditure incurred by them respectively. In this regard the court has to look for expenditure which is referable to the acquisition of the house: see *Burns* v *Burns* [1984] 1 All ER 244 at 252–253, *per* Fox LJ. If it is found to have been incurred, such expenditure will perform the twofold function of establishing the common intention and showing that the claimant has acted on it.

There is another and rarer class of case, of which the present may be one, where, although there has been no writing, the parties have orally declared themselves in such a way as to make their common intention plain. Here the court does not have to look for conduct from which the intention can be inferred, but only for conduct which amounts to an acting on it by the claimant. And, although that conduct can undoubtedly be the incurring of expenditure which is referable to the acquisition of the house, it need not necessarily be so.

The clearest example of this rarer class is *Eves* v *Eves* [1975] 3 All ER 768. That was a case of an unmarried couple where the conveyance of the house was taken in the name of the man alone. At the time of the purchase he told the woman that, if she had been 21 years of age, he would have put the house into their joint names, because it was to be their joint home. He admitted in evidence that that was an excuse for not putting the house into their joint names, and this court inferred that there was an understanding between them, or a common intention, that the woman was to have some sort of proprietary interest in it; otherwise no excuse would have been needed. After they had moved in, the woman did extensive decorative work to the downstairs rooms and generally cleaned the whole house. She painted the brickwork of the front of the house. She also broke up with a 14-lb sledge hammer the concrete surface which covered the whole of the front garden and disposed of the rubble into a skip, worked in the back garden and, together with the man, demolished a shed there and put up a new shed. She also prepared the front garden for turfing. Pennycuick V-C at first instance, being unable to find any link between the common intention and the woman's activities after the purchase, held that she had not acquired a beneficial interest in the house. On an appeal to this court the decision was unanimously reversed, by Lord Denning MR on a ground which I respectfully think was at variance with the principles stated in *Gissing* v *Gissing* and by Browne LJ and Brightman J on a ground which was stated by Brightman J as follows ([1975] 3 All ER 768 at 774):

> The defendant clearly led the plaintiff to believe that she was to have some undefined interest in the property, and that her name was only omitted from the conveyance because of her age. This, of course, is not enough by itself to create a beneficial interest in her favour; there would at best be a mere voluntary declaration of trust which would be unenforceable for want of writing: *Gissing* v *Gissing*. If however, it was part of the bargain between the parties, expressed or to be implied. that the plaintiff should contribute her labour towards the reparation of a house in which she was to have some beneficial interest, then I think that the arrangement becomes one to which the law can give effect. This seems to be consistent with the reasoning of the speeches in *Gissing* v *Gissing* [1970] 2 All ER 780 at 790.

He added that he did not find much in inferring the link which Pennycuick V-C had been unable to find, observing in the process that he found it difficult to suppose that the woman would have been wielding the 14-lb sledge hammer and so forth except in pursuance of some expressed or implied arrangement and on the understanding that she was helping to improve a house in which she was to all practical intents and purposes promised that she had an interest. Browne LJ agreed with Brightman J about the basis for the court's decision in favour of the woman and was prepared to draw the inference that the link was there (see [1975] 3 All ER 768 at 772–773).

About that case the following observations may be made. First, as Brightman J himself observed. if the work had not been done the common intention would not have been enough. Second, if the common intention had not been orally made plain, the work would not have been conduct from which it could be inferred. That, I think, is the effect of the actual decision in *Pettitt* v *Pettitt*. Third, and on the other hand, the work was conduct which amounted to an acting on the common intention by the woman.

It seems therefore, on the authorities as they stand, that a distinction is to be made between conduct from which the common intention can be inferred on the one hand and conduct which amounts to an acting on it on the other. There remains this difficult question: what is the quality of conduct required for the latter purpose? The difficulty is caused. I think, because, although the common intention has been made plain, everything else remains a matter of inference. Let me illustrate it in this way. It would be possible to take the view that the mere moving into the house by the woman amounted to an acting on the common intention. But that was evidently not the view of the majority in *Eves* v *Eves*. And the reason for that may be that, in the absence of evidence, the law is not so cynical as to infer that a woman will only go to live with a man to whom she is not married if she understands that she is to have an interest in their home. So what sort of conduct is required? In my judgment it must be conduct on which the woman could not reasonably have been expected to embark unless she was to have an interest in the house. If she was not to have such an interest, she could reasonably be expected to go and live with her lover, but not, for example, to wield a 14-lb sledge hammer in the front garden. In adopting the latter kind of conduct she is seen to act to her detriment on the faith of the common intention.

In order to see how the present case stands in the light of the views above expressed, I must summarise the crucial facts as found, expressly or impliedly, by the judge. They are the following.

(1) The defendant told the plaintiff that her name was not going onto the title because it would cause some prejudice in the matrimonial proceedings between her and her husband. The defendant never had any real intention of replacing his brother with the plaintiff when those proceedings were at an end. Just as in *Eves* v *Eves*, these facts appear to me to raise a clear inference that there was an understanding between the plaintiff and the defendant, or a common intention, that the plaintiff was to have some sort of proprietary interest in the house; otherwise no excuse for not putting her name onto the title would have been needed.

(2) Except for any instalments under the second mortgage which may have been paid by the plaintiff as part of the general expenses of the household, all the instalments under both mortgages were paid by the defendant. Between February 1970 and October 1974 the total amount paid in respect of the second mortgage was £812 at a rate of about £162

each year. Between 1972 and 1980 the defendant paid off £4,745 under the first mortgage at an average rate of £527 per year.

(3) The £6 per week which the defendant admitted that the plaintiff paid to him, at least for a time after they moved into the house, was not paid as rent and must therefore have been paid as a contribution to general expenses.

(4) From August 1972 onwards the plaintiff was getting the same sort of wage as the defendant, i.e. an annual wage of about £1,200 in 1973, out of which she made a very substantial contribution to the housekeeping and to the feeding and bringing up of the children. From June 1973 onwards she also received £5 a week from her former husband which went towards the maintenance of her two elder sons.

As stated under (1) above, it is clear that there was a common intention that the plaintiff was to have some sort of proprietary interest in 96 Hewitt Road. The more difficult question is whether there was conduct on her part which amounted to an acting on that intention or, to put it more precisely, conduct on which she could not reasonably have been expected to embark unless she was to have an interest in the house.

From the above facts and figures it is in my view an inevitable inference that the very substantial contribution which the plaintiff made out of her earnings after August 1972 to the housekeeping and to the feeding and to the bringing up of the children enabled the defendant to keep down the instalments payable under both mortgages out of his own income and, moreover, that he could not have done that if he had had to bear the whole of the other expenses as well. For example, in 1973, when he and the plaintiff were earning about £1,200 each, the defendant had to find a total of about £643 between the two mortgages. I do not see how he would have been able to do that had it not been for the plaintiff's very substantial contribution to the other expenses. There is certainly no evidence that there was any money to spare on either side and the natural inference is to the contrary. In this connection, it is interesting to note that when dealing with the moneys in the Leeds Permanent Building Society account the judge said: 'They lived from hand to mouth, as I see it. They put their money in, and, when there was some money to spare, they would share it out in this way.'

In the circumstances, it seems that it may properly be inferred that the plaintiff did make substantial indirect contributions to the instalments payable under both mortgages. This is a point which seems to have escaped the judge, but I think that there is an explanation for that. He was concentrating, as no doubt were counsel, on the plaintiff's claim that she herself had paid all the instalments under the second mortgage. It seems very likely that the indirect consequences of her very substantial contribution to the other expenses were not fully explored.

Was the conduct of the plaintiff in making substantial indirect contributions to the instalments payable under both mortgages conduct on which she could not reasonably have been expected to embark unless she was to have an interest in the house? I answer that question in the affirmative. I cannot see on what other basis she could reasonably have been expected to give the defendant such substantial assistance in paying off mortgages on his house. I therefore conclude that the plaintiff did act to her detriment on the faith of the common intention between her and the defendant that she was to have some sort of proprietary interest in the house.

I should add that, although *Eves* v *Eves* [1975] 3 All ER 768 was cited to the judge, I think it doubtful whether the significance of it was fully brought to his attention. He appears to have assumed that the plaintiff could only establish the necessary common intention if she could point to expenditure from which it could be inferred. I do not find it necessary to decide whether, if the common intention had not been orally made plain, the expenditure in the present case would have been sufficient for that purpose. That raises a difficult and still unresolved question of general importance which depends primarily on a close consideration of the speeches of their Lordships in *Gissing* v *Gissing* [1970] 2 All ER 780 and the judgments of Fox and May LJJ in *Burns* v *Burns* [1984] 1 All ER 244. If it be objected that the views which I have expressed will expose the possibility of further fine distinctions on these intellectual steeps, I must answer that that is something which is inherent in the decision of the majority of this court in *Eves* v *Eves*. Be that as it may, I am in no doubt that that authority is a sure foundation for a just decision of the present case, a justness which was fully demonstrated in the concise and commonsensical argument of counsel on behalf of the plaintiff in this court.

Finally, it is necessary to determine the extent of the plaintiff's beneficial interest in 96 Hewitt Road. Here again reference may be made to *Eves* v *Eves* [1975] 3 All ER 768 at 775, where Brightman J regarded this question as the most difficult part of the case. Although I can understand that difficulties may arise in other cases, there is a particular feature of the present case to which we can turn for guidance. That is the crediting of the £1,037 balance of the fire insurance moneys to what the judge found was intended as a joint account. He would evidently have been more impressed by that if, as I have now held, the plaintiff had made a greater contribution than he thought. In my view it was a very significant step for the defendant be have taken. Although on the judge's findings the plaintiff did not contribute anything towards the £1,043 which had to be found in cash to complete the purchase and did not make any substantial contribution, direct or indirect, to the mortgage payments before August 1972, I nevertheless think that this act of the defendant, when viewed against the background of the initial common intention and the substantial indirect contributions made by the plaintiff to the mortgage repayments from August 1972 onwards, is the best evidence of how the parties intended that the property should be shared. I would therefore hold that the plaintiff is entitled to a half interest in the house.

SIR NICOLAS BROWNE-WILKINSON V-C: I agree. In my judgment, there has been a tendancy over the years to distort the principles as laid down in the speech of Lord Diplock in *Gissing* v *Gissing* [1970] 2 All ER 780 by concentrating on only part of his reasoning. For present purposes, his speech can be treated as falling into three sections: the first deals with the nature of the substantive right; the second with the proof of the existence of that right; the third with the quantification of that right.

(1)   *The nature of the substantive right* (see [1970] 2 All ER 780 at 790). If the legal estate in the joint home is vested in only one of the parties (the legal owner) the other party (the claimant), in order to establish a beneficial interest, has to establish a constructive trust by showing that it would be inequitable for the legal owner to claim sole beneficial ownership. This requires two matters to be demonstrated: (a) that there was a common intention that both should have a beneficial interest; *and* (b) that the claimant has acted to his or her detriment on the basis of that common intention.

(2)   *The proof of the common intention*

   (a)   Direct evidence (see [1970] 2 All ER 780 at 790). It is clear that mere agreement between the parties that both are to have beneficial interests is sufficient to prove the necessary common intention. Other passages in the speech point to the admissability and relevance of other possible forms of direct evidence of such intention (see [1970] 2 All ER 780 at 791–792).

   (b)   Inferred common intention (see [1970] 2 All ER 780 at 790–792). Lord Diplock points out that, even where parties have not used express words to communicate their intention (and therefore there is no direct evidence), the court can infer from their actions an intention that they shall both have an interest in the house. This part of his speech concentrates on the types of evidence from which the courts are most often asked to infer such intention, viz contributions (direct and indirect) to the deposit, the mortgage instalments or general housekeeping expenses. In this section of the speech, he analyses what types of expenditure are capable of constituting evidence of such common intention; he does not say that if the intention is proved in some other way such contributions are essential to establish the trust.

(3)   *The quantification of the right* (see [1970] 2 All ER 780 at 792–793). Once it has been established that the parties had a common intention that both should have a beneficial interest and that the claimant has acted to his detriment, the question may still remain: what is the extent of the claimant's beneficial interest? This last section of Lord Diplock's speech shows that here again the direct and indirect contributions made by the parties to the cost of acquisition may be crucially important.

If this analysis is correct, contributions made by the claimant may be relevant for four different purposes, viz: (1) in the absence of direct evidence of intention, as evidence from which the parties' intentions can be inferred; (2) as corroboration of direct evidence of intention; (3) to show that the claimant has acted to his or her detriment in reliance on the common intention (Lord Diplock's speech does not deal directly with the nature of the detriment to be shown); (4) to quantify the extent of the beneficial interest.

I have sought to analyse Lord Diplock's speech for two reasons. First, it is clear that the necessary common intention can be proved otherwise than by reference to contributions by the claimant to the cost of acquisition. Second, the remarks of Lord Diplock as to the contributions made by the claimant must be read in their context.

In cases of this kind the first question must always be whether there is sufficient direct evidence of a common intention that both parties are to have a beneficial interest. Such direct evidence need have nothing to do with the contributions made to the cost of acquisition. Thus in *Eves* v *Eves* [1975] 3 All ER 768 the common intention was proved by the fact that the claimant was told that her name would have been on the title deeds but for her being under age. Again, in *Midland Bank plc* v *Dobson and Dobson* [1986] 1 FLR 171, this court held that the trial judge was entitled to find the necessary common intention from evidence which he accepted that the parties treated the house as 'our house' and had a 'principle of sharing everything'. Although, as was said in the latter case, the trial judge has to approach such direct evidence with caution, if he does accept such evidence the necessary common intention is proved. One would expect that in a number of cases the court would be able to decide on the direct evidence before it whether there was such a common intention. It is only necessary to have recourse to inferences from other circumstances (such as the way in which the parties contributed, directly or indirectly, to the cost of acquisition) in cases such as *Gissing* v *Gissing* and *Burns* v *Burns* [1984] 1 All ER 244 where there is no direct evidence of intention.

Applying those principles to the present case, the representation made by the defendant to the plaintiff that the house would have been in the joint names but for the plaintiff's matrimonial disputes is clear direct evidence of a common intention that she was to have an interest in the house: see *Eves* v *Eves*. Such evidence was in my judgment sufficient by itself to establish the common intention; but in any event it is wholly consistent with the contributions made by the plaintiff to the joint household expenses and the fact that the surplus fire insurance moneys were put into a joint account.

But as Lord Diplock's speech ([1970] 2 All ER 780 at 790) and the decision in *Midland Bank plc* v *Dobson and Dobson* make clear, mere common intention by itself is not enough: the claimant has also to prove that she has acted to her detriment in the reasonable belief that by so acting she was acquiring a beneficial interest.

There is little guidance in the authorities on constructive trusts as to what is necessary to prove that the claimant so acted to her detriment. What 'link' has to be shown between the common intention and the actions relied on? Does there have to be positive evidence that the claimant did the acts in conscious reliance on the common intention? Does the court have to be satisfied that she would not have done the acts relied on but for the common intention, eg would not the claimant have contributed to household expenses out of affection for the legal owner and as part of their joint life together even if she had no interest in the house? Do the acts relied on as detriment have to be inherently referable to the house, e.g. contribution to the purchase or physical labour on the house?

I do not think it is necessary to express any concluded view on these questions in order to decide this case. *Eves* v *Eves* indicates that there has to be some 'link' between the common intention and the acts relied on as a detriment. In that case the acts relied on did inherently relate to the house (viz the work the claimant did to the house) and from this the Court of Appeal felt able to infer that the acts were done in reliance on the common intention. So, in this case, as the analysis of Nourse LJ makes clear, the plaintiff's contributions to the household expenses were essentially linked to the payment of the mortgage instalments by the defendant: without the plaintiff's contributions, the defendant's means were insufficient to keep up the mortgage payments. In my judgment where the claimant has made payments which, whether directly or indirectly, have been used to discharge the mortgage instalments, this is a sufficient link between the detriment suffered by the claimant and the common intention. The court can infer that she would not have made such payments were it not for her belief that she had an interest in the house. On this ground therefore I find that the plaintiff has acted to her detriment in reliance on the common intention that she had a beneficial interest in the house and accordingly that she has established such beneficial interest.

I suggest that, in other cases of this kind, useful guidance may in the future be obtained from the principles underlying the law of proprietary estoppel which in my judgment are closely akin to those laid down in *Gissing* v *Gissing*. In both, the claimant must to the knowledge of the legal owner have acted in the belief that the claimant has or will obtain an interest in the property. In both, the claimant must have acted to his or her detriment in reliance on such belief. In both, equity acts on the conscience of the legal owner to prevent him from acting in an unconscionable manner by defeating the common intention. The two principles have been developed separately without cross-fertilisation between them; but they rest on the same foundation and have on all other matters reached the same conclusions.

In many cases of the present sort, it is impossible to say whether or not the claimant would have done the acts relied on as a detriment even if she thought she had no interest in the house. Setting up house together, having a baby and making payments to general housekeeping expenses (not strictly necessary to enable the mortgage to be paid) may all be referable to the mutual love and affection of the parties and not specifically referable to the claimant's belief that she has an interest in the house. As at present advised, once it has been shown that there was a common intention that the claimant should have an interest in the house, any act done by her to her detriment relating to the joint lives of the parties is, in my judgment, sufficient detriment to qualify. The acts do not have to be inherently referable to the house: see *Jones v Jones* [1977] 2 All ER 231 and *Pascoe v Turner* [1979] 2 All ER 945. The holding out to the claimant that she had a beneficial interest in the house is an act of such a nature as to be part of the inducement to her to do the acts relied on. Accordingly, in the absence of evidence to the contrary, the right inference is that the claimant acted in reliance on such holding out and the burden lies on the legal owner to show that she did not do so: see *Greasley v Cooke* [1980] 3 All ER 710.

The possible analogy with proprietary estoppel was raised in argument. However, the point was not fully argued and, since the case can be decided without relying on such analogy, it is unsafe for me to rest my judgment on that point. I decide the case on the narrow ground already mentioned.

When then is the extent of the plaintiff's interest? it is clear from *Gissing v Gissing* that, once the common intention and the actions to the claimant's detriment have been proved from direct or other evidence, in fixing the quantum of the claimant's beneficial interest the court can take into account indirect contributions by the plaintiff such as the plaintiff's contributions to joint household expenses: see *Gissing v Gissing* [1970] 2 All ER 780 at 793. In my judgment, the passage in Lord Diplock's speech ([1970] 2 All ER 780 at 793) is dealing with a case where there is no evidence of the common intention other than contributions to joint expenditure; in such a case there is insufficient evidence to prove any beneficial interest and the question of the extent of that interest cannot arise.

Where, as in this case, the existence of some beneficial interest in the claimant has been shown, prima facie the interest of the claimant will be that which the parties intended: see *Gissing v Gissing* [1970] 2 All ER 780 at 792. In *Eves v Eves* [1975] 3 All ER 768 at 775 Brightman LJ plainly felt that a common intention that there should be a joint interest pointed to the beneficial interests being equal. However, he felt able to find a lesser beneficial interest in that case without explaining the legal basis on which he did so. With diffidence, I suggest that the law of proprietary estoppel may again provide useful guidance. If proprietary estoppel is established, the court gives effect to it by giving effect to the common intention so far as may fairly be done between the parties. For that purpose, equity is displayed at its most flexible: see *Crabb v Arun DC* [1975] 3 All ER 865. Identifiable contributions to the purchase of the house will of course be an important factor in many cases. But, in other cases, contributions by way of the labour or other unquantifiable actions of the claimant will also be relevant.

LLOYDS BANK PLC v ROSSET [1990] 1 All ER 1111 (HL)

In 1982 the husband and wife decided to buy a semi-derelict farmhouse for £57,000 using money given to the husband by the trustees of a family trust, who insisted that the house be purchased in the husband's sole name. It was the common intention of the parties that the renovation of the house would be a joint venture, after which it was to be the family home. The vendors permitted the husband and wife to enter on the property prior to completion and the builders engaged by the husband and wife started on the extensive repairs that were necessary to make the house habitable. The wife spent almost every day at the property from the beginning of November 1982 helping the builders. The husband, without the wife's knowledge, obtained a bank overdraft to provide £15,000 towards the purchase price and the cost of repairs to the property. The husband exchanged contracts for the purchase on 23 November. The purchase was completed on 17 December and on the same day the husband executed a charge in favour of the bank. The transfer and the bank's charge were not registered until 7 February 1983. By mid-February the work on the house was substantially complete and the parties moved in. The amount owing on the husband's overdraft continued to rise and in February 1984 the bank demanded repayment of the amount outstanding, which was then nearly £23,000. The husband was unable to repay the amount owing, with the result that the bank started proceedings for possession and sale of the property. The wife resisted the bank's claim on the ground that she had an overriding interest under s. 70(1)(g) of the Land Registration Act 1925 because she had a beneficial interest in the property under a constructive trust and had been in actual occupation of the land on the date when the bank's charge was registered. The judge found that the husband held the property as constructive trustee for himself and his wife but upheld the bank's claim for possession, on the grounds that the proprietor of a legal charge took subject to overriding interests which were subsisting on the date of creation of the charge rather than the date of its registration, that the wife was not in actual occupation of the property on 17 December 1982 when the charge was created and that therefore her equitable interest was not protected as an overriding interest by s. 70(1)(g) so as to prevail against the bank's legal charge. The Court of Appeal affirmed the judge's decision that the relevant date on which the wife had to show that she was in actual occupation in order to establish an overriding interest was the date of the creation of the bank's charge, but allowed the appeal on the ground that she was in actual occupation on that date. The bank appealed to the House of Lords.

LORD BRIDGE OF HARWICH: . . . It is clear from these passages in the judgment that the judge based his inference of a common intention that Mrs Rosset should have a beneficial interest in the property under a constructive trust essentially on what Mrs Rosset did in and about assisting in the renovation of the property between the beginning of November 1982 and the date of completion on 17 December 1982. Yet by itself this activity, it seems to me, could not possibly justify any such inference. It was common ground that Mrs Rosset was extremely anxious that the new matrimonial home should be ready for occupation before Christmas if possible. In these circumstances, it would seem the most natural thing in the world for any wife, in the absence of her husband aboard, to spend all the time she could spare and to employ any skills she might have, such as the ability to decorate a room, in doing all she could to accelerate progress of the work quite irrespective of any expectation she might have of enjoying a beneficial interest in the property. The judge's view that some of this work was work 'on which she could not reasonably have been expected to embark unless she was to have an interest in the house' seems to me, with respect, quite untenable. The impression that the judge may have thought that the share of the equity to which he held Mrs Rosset to be entitled had been 'earned' by her work in connection with the renovation is emphasised by his reference in the concluding sentence of his judgment to the extent to which her 'qualifying contribution' reduced the cost of the renovation.

On any view the monetary value of Mrs Rosset's work expressed as a contribution to a property acquired at a cost exceeding £70,000 must have been so trifling as to be almost de minimis. I should myself have had considerable doubt whether Mrs Rosset's contribution to the work of renovation was sufficient to support a claim to a constructive trust in the absence of writing to satisfy the requirements of s. 51 of the Law of Property Act 1925 even if her husband's intention to make a gift to her of half or any other share in the equity of the property had been clearly established or if he had clearly represented to her that that was what he intended. But here the conversations with her husband on which Mrs Rosset relied, all of which took place before November 1982, were incapable of lending support to the conclusion of a constructive trust in the light of the judge's finding that by that date there had been no decision that she was to have any interest in the property. The finding that the discussions 'did not exclude the possibility' that she should have an interest does not seem to me to add anything of significance.

These considerations lead me to the conclusion that the judge's finding that Mr Rosset held the property as constructive trustee for himself and his wife cannot be supported and it is on this short ground that I would allow the appeal. In the course of the argument your Lordships had the benefit of elaborate submissions as to the test to be applied to determine the circumstances in which the sole legal proprietor of a dwelling house can properly be held to have become a constructive trustee of a share in the beneficial interest in the house for the benefit of the partner with whom he or she has cohabited in the house as their shared home. Having in this case reached a conclusion on the facts which, although at variance with the views of the courts below, does not seem to depend on any nice legal distinction and with which, I understand, all your Lordships agree, I cannot help doubting whether it would contribute anything to the illumination of the law if I were to attempt an elaborate and exhaustive analysis of the relevant law to add to the many already to be found in the authorities to which our attention was directed in the course of the argument. I do, however, draw attention to one critical distinction which any judge required to resolve a dispute between former partners as to the beneficial interest in the home they formerly shared should always have in the forefront of his mind.

The first and fundamental question which must always be resolved is whether, independently of any inference to be drawn from the conduct of the parties in the course of sharing the house as their home and managing their joint affairs, there has at any time prior to acquisition, or exceptionally at some later date, been any agreement, arrangement or understanding reached between them that the property is to be shared beneficially. The finding of an agreement or arrangement to share in this sense can only, I think, be based on evidence of express discussions between the partners, however imperfectly remembered and however imprecise their terms may have been. Once a finding to this effect is made it will only be necessary for the partner asserting a claim to a beneficial interest against the partner entitled to the legal estate to show that he or she has acted to his or her detriment or significantly altered his or her position in reliance on the agreement in order to give rise to a constructive trust or proprietary estoppel.

In sharp contrast with this situation is the very different one where there is no evidence to support a finding of an agreement or arrangement to share, however reasonable it might have been for the parties to each such an arrangement if they had applied their minds to the question, and where the court must rely entirely on the conduct of the parties both as the basis from which to infer a common intention to share the property beneficially and as the conduct relied on to give rise to a constructive trust. In this situation direct contributions to the purchase price by the partner who is not the legal owner, whether initially or by payment of mortgage instalments, will readily justify the inference necessary to the creation of a constructive trust. But, as I read the authorities, it is at least extremely doubtful whether anything less will do.

The leading cases in your Lordships' House are *Pettitt* v *Pettitt* [1969] 2 All ER 385 and *Gissing* v *Gissing* [1970] 2 All ER 780. Both demonstrate situations in the second category to which I have referred and their Lordships discuss at great length the difficulties to which these situations give rise. The effect of these two decisions is very helpfully analysed in the judgment of Lord MacDermott LCJ in *McFarlane* v *McFarlane* [1972] NI 59.

Outstanding examples on the other hand of cases giving rise to situations in the first category are *Eves* v *Eves* [1975] 3 All ER 768 and *Grant* v *Edwards* [1986] 2 All ER 426. In both these cases, where the parties who had cohabited were unmarried, the female partner had been clearly led by the male partner to believe, when they set up home together, that the property would belong to them jointly. In *Eves* v *Eves* the male partner had told the female partner that the only reason why the property was to be acquired in his name alone was because she was under 21 and that, but for her age, he would have had the house put into their joint names. He admitted in evidence that this was simply an 'excuse'. Similarly, in *Grant* v *Edwards* the female partner was told by the male partner that the only reason for not acquiring the property in joint names was because she was involved in divorce proceedings and that, if the property were acquired jointly this might operate to her prejudice in those proceedings. As Nourse LJ put it ([1986] 2 All ER 426 at 433):

Just as in *Eves* v *Eves*, these facts appear to me to raise a clear inference that there was an understanding between the plaintiff and the defendant, or a common intention, that the plaintiff was to have some sort of proprietary interest in the house; otherwise no excuse for not putting her name onto the title would have been needed.

The subsequent conduct of the female partner in each of these cases, which the court rightly held sufficient to give rise to a constructive trust or proprietary estoppel supporting her claim to an interest in the property, fell far short of such conduct as would by itself have supported the claim in the absence of an express representation by the male partner that she was to have such an interest. It is significant to note that the share to which the female partners in *Eves* v *Eves* and *Grant* v *Edwards* were held entitled were one-quarter and one-half respectively. In no sense could these shares have been regarded as proportionate to what the judge in the instant case described as a 'qualifying contribution' in terms of the indirect contributions to the acquisition or enhancement of the value of the houses made by the female partners.

I cannot help thinking that the judge in the instant case would not have fallen into error if he had kept clearly in mind the distinction between the effect of evidence on the one hand which was capable of establishing an express agreement or an express representation that Mrs Rosset was to have an interest in the property and evidence on the other hand of conduct alone as a basis for an inference of the necessary common intention.

MIDLAND BANK v COOKE AND ANOTHER [1995] 2 FLR 215 (CA)

WAITE LJ: This appeal, concern[s] disputed beneficial interests in a matrimonial home . . .

Mr and Mrs Cooke were married on 31 July 1971. After the wedding they moved into their new home in Abbotsley Cambridgeshire (to which I shall refer as 'the property'). On 1 July 1971, shortly before the marriage, Mr Cooke, who is the first defendant in the proceedings but has played no part in the current appeal, had taken a conveyance of the property in his sole name. He was then 19 years of age and his fiancée was a little older. The purchase price was £8500, of which £6540 was provided by way of a mortgage from the Leeds Permanent Building Society. The balance of the purchase price and costs was paid in cash provided as to £1100 by Mr Cooke's parents, and as to the remainder by a contribution in the region of £1000 by Mr Cooke out of his own savings. The mortgage was of the conventional building society type providing for repayment by monthly instalments of capital and interest.

Mrs Cooke, who is the second defendant in the action and appellant in this appeal, was a student teacher at the time of the wedding and qualified soon afterwards. Virtually from the outset husband and wife were both working she as a teacher and he as a self-employed proprietor of a business selling kits for the making of lampshades. Mrs Cooke did not make any direct payments of mortgage instalments but was discharging other household outgoings out of her earnings. She remained in work, although there were brief spells of part-time working when their three children were born in 1972, 1974 and 1984 respectively.

The building society mortgage was replaced from 26 June 1978 by a general mortgage of that date in favour of the Midland Bank ('the bank') who are plaintiffs in the proceedings and respondents to this appeal. This mortgage (which I shall call 'the mortgage') was granted by Mr Cooke in his sole name and charged the property to the bank to secure repayment on demand of the business overdraft of Mr Cooke's company.

From the outset of their occupation the wife devoted much time and energy to the improvement of the house and garden. The judge's finding about that was:

> Quite plainly the wife was engaged in a considerable amount of work on the property, with or without the assistance of contractors, on the interior of the property and in particular the garden. The works she has described in her evidence—and I do not propose to go through it in detail—could be described as falling into the three categories of redecoration, alterations/improvements and repair.

It is common ground that the evidence which the judge was there summarising included undisputed evidence that she had paid a number of contractors' bills out of her own earnings. It will be convenient to refer to Mrs Cooke's efforts in this respect as 'the maintenance and improvement contribution'.

In about 1984 Mrs Cooke brought Married Women's Property Act proceedings against Mr Cooke in the county court in which an order was made by consent declaring that the property was held by the spouses jointly. That order was recited in a conveyance of 12 March 1985 made between the spouses and transferring the property into their joint names, holding beneficially as tenants in common.

On 15 July 1987 the bank brought these present proceedings against Mr and Mrs Cooke as first and second defendant respectively in the Bedford County Court claiming payment of the sum of £52,491 then claimed to be due under the mortgage and possession in default of payment.

On 4 November 1987 Mrs Cooke served a defence in the action. It contained first a plea that the mortgage was statute-barred, secondly a claim that her signature to the consent form had been procured to the knowledge of the bank by Mr Cooke's undue influence, and thirdly an assertion that she was entitled to a one-half beneficial interest in the property overriding any interests of the bank under the mortgage. She counter-claimed for declarations against the bank that she was the joint legal owner of the property and entitled to one half of the beneficial interest free of any claim or interest of the bank. The bank joined issue by their reply and defence to counter-claim of 25 January 1988.

In his judgment delivered on 10 February 1992 Judge Hamilton dealt as follows with the initial contributions to the purchase price:

That was followed by the finding (already quoted) as to Mrs Cooke's maintenance and improvement contribution. The judge held that it did not amount to a contribution to the purchase price, with the result that her beneficial interest depended upon her monetary contribution (ie her half-share of the joint wedding present from her in-laws) alone. There can be no doubt that this holding was entirely justified by the authorities, ranging from *Pettitt* v *Pettitt* [1970] AC 777 to *Lloyds Bank plc* v *Rosset and Another* [1991] 1 AC 107.

The judge accordingly proceeded to announce his concluded finding in regard to the proportions of beneficial entitlement. He held that Mrs Cooke was entitled to a beneficial interest of 6.47% of the property, that being the proportion born by her half of the wedding present (£550) to the total cost (£8500). It is implicit in that finding (though the judge did not spell it out in so many words) that he did not regard any other aspect of the course of dealing between the parties—whether it be the maintenance and improvement contribution, or the assumption of mortgage liability, or the sharing of household expenses or any other factor—as capable of having any influence at all upon the quantification of the current interests of husband and wife.

The judge's final order accordingly dismissed the bank's claim to possession as against Mrs Cooke, adjourned the bank's claim against Mr Cooke for hearing at a later date, and declared (on Mrs Cooke's counterclaim in the action) that she had a beneficial interest in the property amounting to 6.47%.

From that order Mrs Cooke now appeals to this court, contending that the judge, having correctly found that she had a beneficial interest, adopted the wrong approach to its quantification; and the bank cross-appeals, contending that the judge ought to have held that Mrs Cooke had no beneficial interest at all.

(B)   *Is the proportion of Mrs Cooke's beneficial interest to be fixed solely by reference to the percentage of the purchase price which she contributed directly, so as to make all other conduct irrelevant?*

In contending that it is, Mr Bergin submits that:

(a)   It is now well settled that in determining (in the absence of evidence of express agreement) whether a party unnamed in the deeds has any beneficial interest in the property at all the test is the stringent one stated by Lord Bridge of Harwich in *Lloyds Bank plc* v *Rosset and Another* [1991] 1 AC 107 at p. 133:

In this situation direct contributions to the purchase price by the partner who is not the legal owner, whether initially or by payment of mortgage instalments, will readily justify the inference necessary to the creation of a constructive trust. But, as I read the authorities, it is at least extremely doubtful whether anything less will do.

(b) By parity of reasoning, in cases where a direct contribution has been duly proved by the partner who is not the legal owner (thus establishing a resulting trust in his or her favour of some part of the beneficial interest) the proportion of that share will be fixed at the proportion it bears to the overall price of the property. Although the proportion may be enlarged by subsequent contribution to the purchase price, such contributions must be direct—ie further cash payments or contribution to the capital element in instalment repayments of any mortgage under which the unpaid proportion of the purchase remains secured. Nothing less will do.

Mr Bergin derives support for that submission from *Springette* v *Defoe* [1992] 2 FLR 388. That was a case where cohabitees of mature years bought in their joint names (so there was no dispute that they both had some beneficial interest) a council house of which one of them had been the sitting tenant. After crediting the former tenant with the discount in the purchase price attributable to her rights as a sitting tenant and taking account of the contributions to that price which each partner had made in cash, the proportions of their initial contributions stood at 75:25%. Part of the purchase price was provided by a mortgage, and by express agreement the parties contributed to the mortgage instalments equally. The judge held that the beneficial interests were equal. He was overruled on appeal, where it was held that the parties were beneficially entitled in the proportions of 75:25%. Dillon LJ said (at p. 393) in regard to the common intention to be imputed to the parties, in the absence of express agreement, as to what their precise shares should be:

> The common intention must be founded on evidence such as would support a finding that there is an implied or constructive trust for the parties in proportions to the purchase price. The court does not as yet sit, as under a palm tree, to exercise a general discretion to do what the man in the street, on a general overview of the case, might regard as fair. . . .
>
> Since, therefore, it is clear in the present case that there never was any discussion between the parties about what their respective beneficial interests were to be, they cannot, in my judgment, have had in any relevant sense any common intention as to the beneficial ownership of the property . . . The presumption of resulting trust is not displaced.

That decision has to be compared with *McHardy and Sons (A Firm)* v *Warren and Another* [1994] 2 FLR 338, a case in which (as here) it became necessary to quantify the interests of husband and wife on a strict equitable basis because of third-party claims against the property. The purchase of the first matrimonial home was (again as in this case) partly financed by a contribution from the husband's parents, but with the difference that in that instance the husband's parents paid the whole of the deposit (using that term in the sense of the net purchase price not covered by a mortgage) for the property, which was registered in the husband's sole name. The two subsequent homes successively purchased by the parties out of the net proceeds of sale of the former home were similarly taken in his name alone. The husband then executed a charge on the current home to secure his indebtedness to the plaintiffs who were trade creditors. In proceedings by the plaintiffs against both husband and wife to enforce their charge, the plaintiffs asserted that the wife either had no beneficial interest or at most an interest equivalent to 8.97% representing the proportion that half the initial deposit of £650 bore to the total purchase price of the first home. The judge rejected that claim, holding that the parties were beneficially entitled in equal shares. He was upheld on appeal.

I confess that I find the differences of approach in those two cases mystifying. In the one a strict resulting trust geared to mathematical calculation of the proportion of the purchase price provided by cash contribution is treated as virtually immutable in the absence of express agreement; in the other a displacement of the cash-related trust by inferred agreement is not only permitted but treated as obligatory. Guidance out of this difficulty is to be found, fortunately, in the passage in the speech of Lord Diplock in *Gissing* v *Gissing* [1971] AC 886 where he is dealing (at p. 908) with the approach to be adopted by the court when evaluating the proportionate shares of the parties, once it has been duly established through the direct contributions of the party without legal title, that some beneficial interest was intended for both. He said:

Where in any of the circumstances described above contributions, direct or indirect, have been made to the mortgage instalments by the spouse into whose name the matrimonial home has not been conveyed, and the court can infer from their conduct a common intention that the contributing spouse should be entitled to some beneficial interest in the matrimonial home, what effect is to be given to that intention if there is no evidence that they in fact reached any express agreement as to what the respective share of each spouse should be?

I take it to be clear that if the court is satisfied that it was the common intention of both spouses that the contributing wife should have a share in the beneficial interest and that her contributions were made upon this understanding, the court in the exercise of its equitable jurisdiction would not permit the husband in whom the legal estate was vested and who had accepted the benefit of the contributions to take the whole beneficial interest merely because at the time the wife made her contributions there had been no express agreement as to how her share in it was to be quantified.

In such a case the court must first do its best to discover from the conduct of the spouses whether any inference can reasonably be drawn as to the probable common understanding about the amount of the share of the contributing spouse upon which each must have acted in doing what each did, even though that understanding was never expressly stated by one spouse to the other or even consciously formulated in words by either of them independently. It is only if no such inference can be drawn that the court is driven to apply as a rule of law, and not as an inference of fact, the maxim 'equality is equity', and to hold that the beneficial interest belongs to the spouses in equal shares.

The same result, however, may often be reached as an inference of fact. The instalments of a mortgage to a building society are generally repayable over a period of many years. During that period, as both must be aware, the ability of each spouse to contribute to the instalments out of their separate earnings is likely to alter, particularly in the case of the wife if any children are born of the marriage. If the contribution of the wife in the early part of the period of repayment is substantial but is not an identifiable and uniform proportion of each instalment, because her contributions are indirect or, if direct, are made irregularly, it may well be a reasonable inference that their common intention at the time of acquisition of the matrimonial home was that the beneficial interest should be held by them in equal shares and that each should contribute to the cost of its acquisition whatever amounts each could afford in the varying exigencies of family life to be expected during the period of repayment. In the social conditions of today this would be a natural enough common intention of a young couple who were both earning when the house was acquired but who contemplated having children whose birth and rearing in their infancy would necessarily affect the future earning capacity of the wife.

The relative size of their respective contributions to the instalments in the early part of the period of repayment, or later if a subsequent reduction in the wife's contribution is not to be accounted for by a reduction in her earnings due to motherhood or some other cause from which the husband benefits as well, may make it a more probable inference that the wife's share in the beneficial interest was intended to be in some proportion other than one half. And there is nothing inherently improbable in their acting on the understanding that the wife should be entitled to a share which was not to be quantified immediately upon the acquisition of the home but should be left to be determined when the mortgage was repaid or the property disposed of, on the basis of what would be fair having regard to the total contributions, direct or indirect, which each spouse had made by that date. Where this was the most likely inference from their conduct it would be for the court to give effect to that common intention of the parties by determining what in all the circumstances was a fair share.

Difficult as they are to solve, however, these problems as to the amount of the share of a spouse in the beneficial interest in a matrimonial home where the legal estate is vested solely in the other spouse, only arise in cases where the court is satisfied by the words or conduct of the parties that it was their common intention that the beneficial interest was not to belong solely to the spouse in whom the legal estate was vested but was to be shared between them in some proportion or other.

The decision of this court in *Grant* v *Edwards and Edwards* [1986] 1 Ch 638 also affords helpful guidance. The context was different, in that the court was there dealing with a legal owner who had made representations to the occupier on which the latter had relied to her detriment so as to introduce equities in the nature of estoppel. Once a beneficial interest had been established by that route, however, the court then proceeded—as I read the judgments—to fix the proportions of the beneficial interests on general grounds which were regarded as applying in all cases.

The general principle to be derived from *Gissing* v *Gissing* and *Grant* v *Edwards* can in my judgment be summarised in this way. When the court is proceeding, in cases like the present where the partner without legal title has successfully asserted an equitable interest through direct contribution, to determine (in the absence of express evidence of intention) what proportions the parties must be assumed to have intended for their beneficial ownership, the duty of the judge is to undertake a survey of the whole course of dealing between the parties relevant to their ownership and occupation of the property and their sharing of its burdens and advantages. That scrutiny will not confine itself to the limited range of acts of direct contribution of the sort that are needed to found a beneficial interest in the first place. It will take into consideration all conduct which throws light on the question what shares were intended. Only if that search proves inconclusive does the court fall back on the maxim that 'equality is equity'.

My answer to Question (B) would therefore be 'No'. The court is not bound to deal with the matter on the strict basis of the trust resulting from the cash contribution to the purchase price, and is free to attribute to the parties an intention to share the beneficial interest in some different proportions.

Lawson-Cruttenden, T, and Odutola, A, Constructive Trusts — a Practical Guide [1995] Fam Law 560

The doctrine of constructive trusts has become more important not only because of the current economic recession but because of increasingly complex human relationships. The marriage relationship itself is recognised in law and has been so recognised since the inception of the English legal system. Legal recognition is not afforded to the relationship arising on cohabitation (whether heterosexual or homosexual) which has no legal standing per se (although aspects of such relationships are, of course, governed by both common law and statute). It is in relation to property ownership that such trusts arise and such rights are considered. Most trusts, therefore, arise in the context of a marital or cohabitation relationship, and in most cases the courts are concerned with respective property rights over a 'family home' and its division following the breakdown of that relationship. In some cases, however, the courts are also concerned with the rights of a third party which are normally acquired by virtue of the investment of substantial sums of money into that home. In those cases the investing party will normally be the mortgagee, and the dispute concerned with whether or not a party who does not own the legal estate has priority to, or takes subject to, the rights of the mortgagee who is normally secured under a legal charge. Although these are the principal areas in which the doctrine of constructive trust is applied, there are, of course, many other instances where the doctrine is relevant.

DEFINITION

The classic constructive trust arises when one party owns the legal estate (the owning party) and he faces a claim from a former partner who does not own the legal estate (the claiming party) in relation to a property (the property). The basis of the claim is the making of substantial contributions of money towards the purchase price of the property, its repair or renovation, and/or the undertaking of substantial works to that property. The extent of the equitable interest conferred on the claiming party is normally calculated arithmetically by reference to the proportion of the contributions as to the whole purchase price and cost of repair or renovation.

The issue of constructive trusts does not often arise in the context of marital breakdown—first, because of the legal status of marriage and, secondly, because ss. 23 and 24 of the Matrimonial Causes Act 1973 confer upon the court considerable power to make property transfer orders in favour of the vulnerable or disadvantaged spouse. In the context of a marriage relationship, the issue of a constructive trust often arises when considering the rights of the parties *vis-à-vis* the mortgagee.

It is submitted that the doctrine of constructive trusts is of primary importance when practitioners are concerned with the break-up of a cohabitation relationship, where only the common law can be applied to the property rights of the respective parties (hence the use of the much misunderstood phrase 'common law wife' which could be applied to both genders). The purpose of this article is to explore areas which, in the opinion of the authors, are not yet explored but are clearly areas where the doctrine of constructive trusts ought to be either established, extended or considered because, after all, 'equity is not yet past child bearing' (Lord Denning in *Eves* v *Eves* [1975] 1 WLR 1338).

THE TEST
Gissing v *Gissing* [1971] AC 886 (Lord Diplock) laid down two requisite tests as follows:

(1)   a common intention that the parties should have a beneficial interest in the relevant property (test 1);

(2)   that the claimant has acted to his or her detriment (test 2) (on the basis of, or in reliance upon, such common intention).

The equitable interest is normally calculated by reference to the extent of the detriment suffered by the claiming party in relation to the property which is the subject of the claim.

DIFFICULTIES OF APPLICATION
The real difficulty faced by the court is that most couples who set up home together, whether married or unmarried, do not normally discuss in a formal manner their respective proprietary interests in the property which is or is to be their home. These difficulties are compounded by the common misunderstanding that the cohabitation relationship is a 'legal shadow' of the marriage relationship. Many cohabitees labour under the misapprehension, at least, in relation to property, that they have rights not dissimilar to those under the Matrimonial Causes Act 1973, and that those rights are acquired by virtue of 'common law'. Hence the apparent and erroneous doctrine of 'common law wife'.

It follows that there is undoubtedly a variance between the rights recognised by courts under the constructive trust doctrine on the one hand, and those rights which most ordinary people consider have been acquired by virtue of a cohabitation relationship on the other. The courts draw a distinction between sharing the practical benefits of occupying the home whoever owns it on the one hand (which is no more than a right to reside there by virtue of the relationship and does not establish a constructive trust), and sharing the beneficial interest in the property asset which the home represents on the other hand (which may establish a constructive trust if the tests are satisfied). Furthermore, the courts also draw a distinction (when applying test 2) between detrimental conduct referable to the relationship itself (which may fall short of establishing test 2) and detrimental conduct referable to the property which way be sufficient.

Matters are compounded further by the differing treatment of direct and indirect contributions. Direct contributions to the property itself include money committed to the purchase price, and/or money spent on repairing or renovating the property. Indirect contributions are normally concerned with money committed to joint finances which cannot be identified as a direct investment into the property. Under the classic constructive trust only direct contributions normally suffice. The courts adopt a restrictive approach to indirect contributions. It is, however, clear that if one party spends most of his or her income on food, clothing, holidays, and domestic items thereby enabling the other party to pay the mortgage on the property, such indirect contributions are normally sufficient (at least, in relation to test 2) to prove detriment and an equitable interest to the extent of such detriment will be established if test 1 is satisfied.

Test 1
It seems quite clear that any claimant must surmount the hurdle of test 1. Any claimant who fails to do so will not establish a constructive trust however he or she may have acted to his or her detriment. Common intention is a matter of fact in each particular

case. It is often not obvious and, therefore, has to be established by reference to understandings between the parties (whether evidenced in writing or orally), conduct, and/or inferences, the clear effect of which was that the claiming party was to have had, and should therefore be granted a proprietary interest in the property. Evidence from relatives or friends may have to be called.

The courts may have to consider the entire relationship, and a detailed course of dealing in order to infer evidence or common intention. This is a difficult area and very careful thought and consideration often has to be given to this issue. Practitioners will be particularly keen to surmount the hurdle of test 1 when a long-term cohabitation relationship has broken down, and the claimant faces great prejudice in not being able to rehouse himself or herself. This is particularly important if there are young children and the claiming party is a woman who is engaged in their full-time well-being, or relying upon social security, or living on a low income.

It appears from the authorities that the courts are taking a relatively narrow interpretation of test 1. In *Grant* v *Edwards and Edwards* [1987] 1 FLR 87 Nourse LJ found that the necessary common intention had to be inferred 'almost always from the expenditure incurred by them (the parties) respectively'. He continued '. . . in this regard one has to look for expenditure which is referable to the acquisition of the house'. The apparent doctrine of direct expenditure was developed by Lord Bridge in *Lloyds Bank plc* v *Rosset and Another* [1990] 2 FLR 155 who stated that 'direct contributions to the purchase price by the partner who is not the legal owner, whether initially or by payment of mortgage instalments will readily justify the inference necessary to the creation of a constructive trust but, as I read the authorities, it is at least extremely doubtful whether anything less will do'.

Notwithstanding this dictum, it is clear that indirect contributions to housekeeping expenses which assist the owning party in paying off the mortgage are often regarded as conduct upon which the claiming party can reasonably have been expected to embark on the expectation and implied agreement that the claiming party has an interest in the property.

Test 2

Once the courts are prepared to make a finding under test 1, it is the submission of the author that it is far easier to ground a constructive trust under test 2. Sir Nicolas Browne-Wilkinson V-C made this clear in *Grant* v *Edwards and Edwards* (above) when he stated that 'as at present advised, once it has been shown that there was a common intention that the claimant should have an interest in the house, any acts done by her to her detriment relating to the joint lives of the parties is, in my judgment, sufficient detriment to qualify. The acts do not have to be inherently referable to the house'. This argument was developed further in *Stokes* v *Anderson* [1991] 1 FLR 391 which held that 'all payments made and acts done by the claimant are to be treated as illuminating the common intention as to the extent of the beneficial interest'.

It seems that the apparently narrow approach to test 1 contrasts with the increasingly broad approach to test 2 and that courts are becoming increasingly liberal as to what may be regarded as detrimental conduct. It seems that the liberal approach applies principally to conduct relied on as a detriment (which goes to the issue of the extent of equitable ownership), and assumes that the common intention that the claiming party shall have a beneficial interest has been clearly established.

It is the opinion of the authors that this contrasting approach appears illogical and difficult to consider in practice. Once the courts have to consider the entire conduct of the parties, the course of their relationship, and have to infer and imply understandings in order to make a finding under test 1, it seems to the authors that the courts should adopt a broad-minded and liberal approach in relation to test 1 as well as in relation to test 2. Certainly this is necessary if the courts become embroiled in a detailed analysis of the relationship between the parties in order to infer or conclude that a common intention existed under test 1.

An attempt to illustrate the present state of the law, and the way in which it is developing, is set out in the flowchart below. What the authors understand as the present law is stated in italicised print. The remaining parts of the flowchart illustrate areas where the doctrine could be established (depending upon the facts of the case), extended, or considered. It deals, inter alia, with the very difficult areas of implied agreements, inferred understandings, intellectual contributions, conduct referable to sacrifice of career and care of family and home, and indeed the whole area of what is commonly termed a 'modern relationship' (cohabitation or otherwise).

FLOWCHART — CONSTRUCTIVE TRUSTS (IN RELATION TO 'FAMILY HOMES')

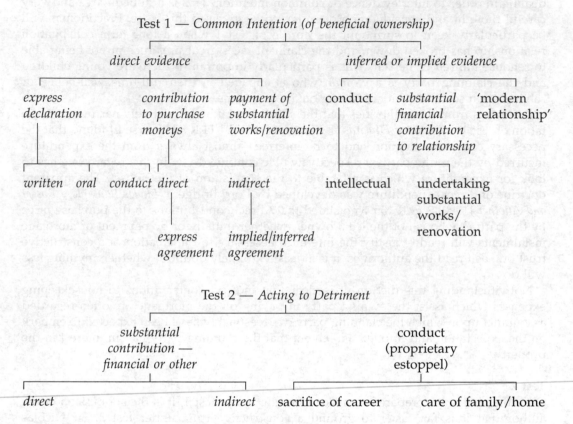

Test 1 — *Common Intention (of beneficial ownership)*

direct evidence   *inferred or implied evidence*

express declaration   *contribution to purchase moneys*   *payment of substantial works/renovation*   *conduct*   *substantial financial contribution to relationship*   'modern relationship'

written   *oral*   *conduct*   *direct*   *indirect*   *intellectual*   undertaking substantial works/ renovation

express agreement   *implied/inferred agreement*

Test 2 — *Acting to Detriment*

substantial contribution — financial or other   *conduct (proprietary estoppel)*

direct   *indirect*   sacrifice of career   care of family/home

Notes
(1)   What the authors understand as the present law is stated in italicised print.
(2)   The remaining parts of the flowchart to some extent represent 'uncharted waters'.

DEVELOPMENTS OF THE DOCTRINE

It seems surprising that a broad approach has not yet been sufficient to include (either as evidence of common intention under test 1, or evidence of acting to detriment under test 2, the contributions of a woman to the care of the family and house and the possible sacrifice of a career for those purposes. This is the obvious area for the doctrine to develop. It is the opinion of the authors (although not yet established law) that it is in the public interest for it to do so in order to protect, inter alia, the whole class of young unmarried mothers engaged in the full-time care of young children.

Such a development would be radical, and would inevitably be based on the premise that a cohabitation relationship which was concerned with rearing children could well satisfy both tests, ie parenthood (common intention—test 1) and acting to detriment (sacrifice of career and/or dependency on either partner in order to care for family or home—test 2). In order to make findings under these heads the court would have to gravitate towards finding a common intention under test 1 where either there has been a long-term relationship, or the parties have engaged in, or are engaged in, raising young children. The courts would therefore have to recognise that in a 'modern relationship' there is usually a pooling of the resources which belong to the parties, and that to varying degrees of extent one of the parties has acted to his or her detriment with the other party's acquiescence. The courts would then need to abandon what the authors consider are artificial distinctions between the financial aspects of the relationship on the one hand and the common ownership of the property on the other hand. It is accepted that this proposition is controversial and that the present doctrine falls far short of such a development.

It also seems to the authors that a liberal approach should be adopted when there has been a breakdown of a long-term cohabitation relationship lasting many years. It is difficult to set a cut-off date on the length of such a relationship, but one of the authors has recently been engaged in representing women making claims after 20 years and 12 years of respective cohabitation when the former woman was reaching retirement age, and the latter in middle life. In both cases the legal estate of the property was vested in the man and there was no formal or direct agreement of common intention for the purposes of test 1. Consequently, a detailed analysis of the relationship had to be undertaken in each case.

It is also surprising that the common law development of intellectual property rights has not so far extended itself to the area of constructive trusts. It is a well known fact that engaging an interior designer or estate agent is expensive, but despite this fact courts seem to give very little credit to a claimant seeking to put forward a claim based on contributions to the property which are of an indirect and intellectual nature. Everyone engaged in the area of conveyancing knows how much time has to be spent finding a property, decorating it, giving it character, and turning it into a marketable and saleable asset.

One of the authors recently represented a woman who was very much the driving force behind the decision to move from a suburban area into a relatively eligible property in a small village. The particular property was purchased in 1985/86 for £85,000 and sold at the height of the market in 1989 for £185,000, representing an increase in price of 118%. The average rise in house prices in this area, according to the building society index of house prices was 91%. It was argued that the additional 29 percentage points which the property realised over the average were entirely attributable to his female client who organised the move and chose the property, and that her skill and creativity in selecting the property constituted a direct contribution in moneys worth to the property and should be recognised as such. The case settled and, consequently, the trial judge did not make a finding on this line of argument.

CONCLUSION

The Matrimonial Causes Act 1973 enables the courts to make property adjustment orders and, consequently, this doctrine does not often have to be considered within the context of a marital relationship. Since the 1973 Act was passed, society's attitude to marriage has altered dramatically. Heterosexual cohabitation is widespread and considered conventional. Homosexual cohabitation is established. Neither enjoy the full protection of statutory law. Both types of relationship must look for redress to the common law, and principles like the doctrine of constructive trusts. The challenge for the courts and for the legal profession is to ensure that such doctrines provide adequate frameworks within which to consider such relationships, whether they be conventional or otherwise.

ADDENDUM

This article was offered prior to the decision of the Court of Appeal in *Midland Bank Plc* v *Cooke, The Times*, 13 July 1995. It is submitted that the decision fully supports the opinions expressed in this article. The dicta of Lord Justice Waite is pertinent and is as follows '. . . the duty of the (trial) judge is to undertake a survey of the whole course of dealing between the parties relevant to their ownership and occupation of the property and their sharing of its burdens and advantages. That scrutiny will . . . take into consideration all conduct which throws light on the question what shares were intended'.

7.5 Proprietary Estoppel

PASCOE v *TURNER* [1979] 1 WLR 431 (CA)

CUMMING-BRUCE LJ: This is an appeal from the orders made on April 21, 1978, by Mr McKintosh, sitting as a deputy circuit judge in the Camborne and Redruth County Court, whereby he dismissed the plaintiff's claim for possession of a house at 2, Tolgarrick Road,

Tuckingmill, Camborne in Cornwall, and granted the defendant declarations upon her counterclaim that the plaintiff held the house an trust for the defendant her heirs and assigns absolutely and that the contents of the house belonged to her. The plaintiff asks for an order of possession, and that the counterclaim be dismissed.

The issues
. . . (a) Did the defendant prove the trust found by the judge? (b) Did she prove such facts as prevented the plaintiff by estoppel from asserting his legal title?

The facts
The plaintiff was a business man in a relatively small way and at all material times was and had been building up some capital assets which he invested in purchases of private and commercial property. In 1961 or 1962 he met the defendant, a widow recovering from the distressing circumstances of her husband's death. She had invested about £4,500 capital and had some income from this and from an invalidity pension.

The plaintiff's business was expanding, and she worked in the business as well as doing the housekeeping. She did all that a wife would have done. He offered marriage, but she declined. In 1965 they moved. He took her to see 2, Tolgarrick Road, asked her if she liked it. He bought it. They moved in and continued living there as man and wife. He paid for the house and contents, He gave her £3 a week housekeeping. She used her own money to buy her clothes. She only bought small things for the house.

In 1973 Cupid aimed his arrow. It struck the plaintiff, who began an affair with a Mrs Pritchard. All unknowing, the defendant went for a few days with her daughter to Capri. In her absence the plaintiff moved in for two days to the house with Mrs Pritchard, but they removed themselves before her return. Immediately the defendant got back, he visited her. There was a conflict of evidence on what was then said. His version was that all he told her was that he would never see her without a roof over her head. The account given by the defendant and the witnesses called on her behalf was that he declared to her and later to them that she had nothing to worry about as the house was hers and everything in it. The judge rejected the plaintiff's evidence and accepted the evidence of the defendant and her witnesses. The plaintiff declared to the defendant not once but on a number of occasions after he had left her 'The house is yours and everything in it.' He told a Mrs Smejhal and a Mrs Green the same thing. To Mrs Smejhal he said that he'd put it in a solicitor's hands. Mrs Green asked him at the end of 1973 if he'd given the defendant the deeds, and he replied that he hadn't yet but was going to see to it. In fact he never did. There was no deed of conveyance, nothing in writing at all. The defendant stayed on in the house. She thought it was hers and everything in it. In reliance upon the plaintiff's declarations that he had given her the house and its contents, she spent money and herself did work on redecoration, improvements and repairs. The judge found that the plaintiff as donor stood by knowingly while she improved the property thinking it was hers.

But the facts did not stop there. On the judge's findings the defendant, having been told that the house was hers, set about improving it within and without. Outside she did not do much: a little work on the roof and an improvement which covered the way from the outside toilet to the rest of the house, putting in a new door there, and Snowcem to protect the toilet. Inside she did a good deal more. She installed gas in the kitchen with a cooker, improved the plumbing in the kitchen and put in a new sink. She got new gas fires, putting a gas fire in the lounge. She redecorated four rooms. The fitted carpets she put in the bedrooms, the stair carpeting, and the curtains and the furniture that she bought are not part of the realty, and it is not clear how much she spent on those items. But they are part of the whole circumstances. There she was, on her own after he left her in 1973. She had £1,000 left of her capital, and a pension of some kind. Having as she thought been given the house, she set about it as described. On the repairs and improvement to the realty and its fixtures she spent about £230. She had £300 of her capital left by the date of the trial, but she did not establish in evidence how much had been expended on refurbishing the house with carpets, curtains and furniture. We would describe the work done in and about the house as substantial in the sense that that adjective is used in the context of estoppel. All the while the plaintiff not only stood by and watched but encouraged and advised, without a word to suggest that she was putting her money and her personal labour into his house. What is the effect in equity?

The cases relied upon by the plaintiff are relevant for the purpose of showing that the judge fell into error in deciding that on the facts a constructive trust could be inferred. They are the cases which deal with the intention of the parties when a house is acquired. But of those cases only *Inwards* v *Baker* [1965] 2 QB 29 is in point here. For this is a case of estoppel arising from the encouragement and acquiescence of the plaintiff between 1973 and 1976 when, in reliance upon his declaration that he was giving and, later, that he had given the house to her, she spent a substantial part of her small capital upon repairs and improvements to the house. . . .

The final question that arises is: to what relief is the defendant entitled . . .

So the principle to be applied is that the court should consider all the circumstances, and the counterclaimant having at law no perfected gift or licence other than a licence revocable at will, the court must decide what is the minimum equity to do justice to her having regard to the way in which she changed her position for the worse by reason of the acquiescence and encouragement of the legal owner. The defendant submits that the only appropriate way in which the equity can here be satisfied is by perfecting the imperfect gift as was done in *Dillwyn* v *Llewelyn*.

We take the view that the equity cannot here be satisfied without granting a remedy which assures to the defendant security of tenure, quiet enjoyment, and freedom of action in respect of repairs and improvements without interference from the plaintiff. The history of the conduct of the plaintiff since April 9, 1976, in relation to these proceedings leads to an irresistible inference that he is determined to pursue his purpose of evicting her from the house by any legal means at his disposal with a ruthless disregard of the obligations binding upon conscience. The court must grant a remedy effective to protect her against the future manifestations of his ruthlessness. It was conceded that if she is granted a licence, such a licence cannot be registered as a land charge, so that she may find herself ousted by a purchaser for value without notice. If she has in the future to do further and more expensive repairs she may only be able to finance them by a loan, but as a licensee she cannot charge the house. The plaintiff as legal owner may well find excuses for entry in order to do what he may plausibly represent as necessary works and so contrive to derogate from her enjoyment of the licence in ways that make it difficult or impossible for the court to give her effective protection.

Weighing such considerations this court concludes that the equity to which the facts in this case give rise can only be satisfied by compelling the plaintiff to give effect to his promise and her expectations. He has so acted that he must now perfect the gift.

COOMBES v SMITH [1986] 1 WLR 808 (ChD)

JONATHAN PARKER QC: The plaintiff in this action, Mrs Eileen Margaret Coombes, seeks relief against the defendant, Mr Robert Anthony Smith, in respect of a freehold property known as 33, Stanway Road, Benfleet, Essex, which is owned by the defendant (subject to a mortgage to the Woolwich Equitable Building Society) but in which the plaintiff has been living since 1977. The plaintiff seeks primarily an order that the defendant convey and transfer the property and its contents to her absolutely; alternatively, she claims a declaration that the defendant is bound to allow her to occupy the property and to use the contents thereof during her life and to discharge the mortgage, and she seeks an injunction to protect that occupation. The property consists of a detached two-bedroomed bungalow, with gardens at front and rear. Its current market value is in the region of £45,000. The claim is based primarily on proprietary estoppel, with an alternative claim that the plaintiff is entitled to a contractual licence to occupy the property for her life.

The plaintiff first met the defendant in about April 1974. The meeting was a casual one and was followed by other meetings of a similarly casual nature. The defendant was married, with a family, with whom he was living. The relationship between the plaintiff and the defendant developed quickly, and in a month to six weeks after their first meeting they became lovers. In June or July 1974 the defendant told the plaintiff that he wanted them to live together. They discussed having a child. The plaintiff was trying to become pregnant, and the defendant knew that. In about August 1974 the defendant started looking for a house for them to live in. He showed the plaintiff a cutting from a newspaper advertising houses in Shoeburyness. In September or October 1974 the defendant bought a house in Shoeburyness, namely 67, Bulwark Road. This was a new house, and the plaintiff chose the colours for the interior decoration. The plaintiff's understanding was that this house would be for them to live in together. This also appears to have been the defendant's understanding, for he said to the plaintiff such things as, 'It'll be nice when we're living together—we'll spend the rest of our lives together.' In October 1974 the plaintiff became pregnant by the defendant. She believes that this occurred during a week's holiday from work which she and the defendant took in October 1974, during which they spent the daytime hours at 67, Bulwark Road, returning to their respective homes at night.

On 5 December 1974, when the plaintiff was some two months pregnant, she moved into 67, Bulwark Road. The defendant helped her move. He did not, however, move in himself. He told her that he would move in after Christmas, so that he would be able to spend Christmas with his children.

In the event, the defendant did not move into 67, Bulwark Road after Christmas 1974 or indeed at all.

On 9 June 1975 the plaintiff gave birth to a daughter, Clare.

In 1977 it was decided that the plaintiff and Clare should move to a house closer to the defendant's work. It seems that the initiative for this move came from the defendant, but the plaintiff accepted it without objection. In August 1977 the defendant bought 33, Stanway Road, Benfleet, the property with which I am concerned in this action.

At some time during the 1970s (the plaintiff could not be more precise than that, nor could she recall whether it was before or after the move to Stanway Road) she asked the defendant if he would have the property in which she was then living put into joint names, but the defendant refused. Sometime during 1980 or 1981 the plaintiff asked the defendant what security she and Clare would have if something happened to him. This was something which by then was worrying her. The defendant replied, 'Don't worry. I have told you I'll always look after you,' or words to that effect. The plaintiff said in evidence, 'I didn't ask that sort of question in the early days. I thought things would be OK. I let things drift along, then as time went on I started to ask him.'

The plaintiff told me she never thought of leaving 33, Stanway Road, as she always hoped that the defendant would come to live with her. The plaintiff's marriage was dissolved in 1978, but I have not been told anything of the terms of the dissolution.

The plaintiff, who is something of a handywoman, redecorated 33, Stanway Road throughout a number of times (redecoration being required more frequently than would otherwise have been the case by reason of problems with rising damp), and she installed decorative wooden beams in the living room and kitchen. She also tidied the garden, which was in a poor state when she moved in. In November 1985 (some nine months after the issue of the writ in this action) she caused central heating to be installed, but she accepted that this was done without the knowledge of the defendant.

The defendant asked if the plaintiff would move into a cheaper property as he was finding it difficult to pay the mortgage instalments. Although she agreed at first, the plaintiff later decided to stay where she was. When he heard of her decision, the defendant said that he would not pay any further mortgage instalments, and would leave the building society to take proceedings for possession. Later, however, he telephoned the plaintiff and they arranged to meet. At that meeting, the defendant said he was sorry, and offered the plaintiff £10,000 to move out of 33, Stanway Road, saying that he would like to part friends. The plaintiff said she would think about it, but in the event she did not take up the offer. The writ in this action was issued on 2 February 1985.

I turn now to the pleadings. As I mentioned at the beginning of this judgment, the plaintiff's claim is based primarily on proprietary estoppel, alternatively on contractual licence. So far as proprietary estoppel is concerned, the plaintiff pleads that she has changed her position on the faith of oral assurances by the defendant,

Thus the issues which I have to decide are whether, on the evidence placed before me, the plaintiff has either (a) an equity in the property entitling her to something greater than a mere right of occupation until Clare attains the age of 17 (that being the extent of the concession in the pleadings), and if so, the extent of that equity; alternatively (b) a contractual right to remain in occupation of the property for the rest of her life. Although it is pleaded as an alternative, I turn first to the claim based on contractual licence.

In my judgment, the evidence before me does not justify the inference of any contract entitling the plaintiff to be accommodated at 33, Stanway Road or, for that matter, at an equivalent house, for the rest of her life. If there was any contract, it must have been concluded when the plaintiff moved into 67, Bulwark Road, and that indeed is how the claim is pleaded.

I turn, therefore, to the claim based on proprietary estoppel or, in other words, estoppel by acquiescence.

For a statement of the relevant principles applicable to the doctrine of estoppel by acquiescence, I refer to the much-cited passage in the judgment of Fry J in *Willmott* v *Barber* (1880) 15 ChD 96, 105–106, quoted by Scarman LJ in *Crabb* v *Arun District Council* [1976] Ch 179, 194–195, where Fry J lists the five elements or requisites necessary to establish the required degree of fraud or unconscionableness: (1) the plaintiff must have made a mistake as to his legal rights; (2) the plaintiff must have expended some money or done some act on the faith of his mistaken belief; (3) the defendant must know of the existence of his own right which is inconsistent with the right claimed by the plaintiff; (4) the defendant must know of the plaintiff's mistaken belief in his right; and (5) the defendant must have encouraged the plaintiff in the expenditure of money, or in the other acts which he has done, either directly or by abstaining from asserting his legal right.

I now turn to consider whether the five elements or requisites listed by Fry J have been established in the instant case.

First, did the plaintiff hold a mistaken belief as to her legal rights? In the context of the facts of the instant case, and applying *Willmott* v *Barber* the mistaken belief would have to be a belief on the part of the plaintiff that she had a legal right to occupy 33, Stanway Road which would entitle her to remain there notwithstanding that her relationship with the defendant had come to an end and that the defendant wished her to leave. In my judgment, no such mistaken belief has been established. I agree with Mr Nield that although she did not say in evidence that the defendant had assured her in terms that she would always have a roof over her head, the plaintiff's evidence as to what the defendant said to her amounted to much the same thing. But a belief that the defendant would always provide her with a roof over her head is, to my mind, something quite different from a belief that she had a legal right to remain there against his wishes. Moreover, all the statements relied upon by the plaintiff were made by the defendant while his relationship with the plaintiff was continuing. There is no evidence before me of any discussion at all between the plaintiff and the defendant as to what should happen in the event of their relationship breaking down and of the defendant choosing to live with another woman. Nor does it appear that this possibility had occurred to the plaintiff. Her state of mind during the first six or seven years of the relationship seems to me to appear very clearly from what she said in evidence in reference to the occasion in 1980 or 1981 when she raised the question of her security with the defendant, a passage I have already quoted. She said, 'I didn't ask that sort of question in the early days. I thought things would be OK. I let things drift along. Then as time went on I started to ask him' (i.e. about her security). And from 1980 or 1981 until their relationship finally came to an end in mid-1984, the plaintiff continued to hope that the defendant would move in with her at 33, Stanway Road. Moreover, I agree with Mr Susman that it is material that on two occasions the plaintiff asked the defendant to, in effect, provide security for her by putting the property in which she was then living in joint names; and on each occasion he refused. In my judgment, therefore, the plaintiff has wholly failed to establish that while her relationship with the defendant was continuing she acted under a mistaken belief that she was legally entitled to security of tenure.

The facts in the instant case are not, in my judgment, comparable with the facts in *Pascoe* v *Turner* [1979] 1 WLR 431.

That conclusion makes it strictly unnecessary for me to consider whether the other four elements or requisites listed by Fry J are established, but it may be convenient if I briefly state my conclusions on those questions also. The second element or requisite is that the plaintiff must have expended money, or otherwise prejudiced himself or acted to his detriment, on the faith of his mistaken belief in his legal rights. In considering this question, therefore, I have to assume, contrary to the conclusion which I have already reached, that the plaintiff at all material times believed that she had a legal right to stay at 33, Stanway Road, or, possibly, an equivalent house, for the rest of her life, whether or not her relationship with the defendant was still on foot.

The first point to make in this connection is that this is not, as Mr Nield acknowledged, a case in which expenditure of money on the property can be relied upon as creating the equity. The only relevant expenditure (on the installation of central heating) was incurred long after the issue of the writ and without the knowledge of the defendant. The acts of detriment relied upon are those which I listed earlier in this judgment. I take them in turn. Two questions have, it seems to me, to be asked in relation to each of them: (1) was it done in reliance on the defendant's assurances or, in other words, on the faith of the plaintiff's mistaken belief, the existence of which I have, for present purposes, to assume? and (2) by doing it, did the plaintiff prejudice herself or otherwise act to her detriment? The first act relied on by the plaintiff is allowing herself to become pregnant by the defendant. In my judgment, it would be wholly unreal, to put it mildly, to find on the evidence adduced before me that the plaintiff allowed herself to become pregnant by the defendant in reliance on some mistaken belief as to her legal rights. She allowed herself to become pregnant because she wished to live with the defendant and to bear his child. The second question accordingly does not arise, but I would in any event have been unable to treat the act of the plaintiff in allowing herself to become pregnant as constituting detriment in the context of the doctrine of proprietary estoppel.

The second act relied on as detriment was the plaintiff's act in leaving her husband and moving to 67, Bulwark Road. As I have already said, I know nothing about the plaintiff's marriage save that it was not a happy one, and that it was never consummated. In his closing speech, Mr Nield suggested that by moving to 67, Bulwark Road the plaintiff was giving up the chance that her marriage might survive. But I cannot conjecture, let alone making any finding about, what the chances may have been of the plaintiff's marriage becoming a happy and successful one. The reality is that the plaintiff decided to move to 67, Bulwark Road because she preferred to have a relationship with, and a child by, the defendant rather than continuing to live with her husband.

I can deal with the remaining elements or requisites in Fry J's list, *Willmott* v *Barber*, 15 ChD 96, 105–106, much more briefly. Elements (3) and (4) both involve knowledge on the part of the defendant. I am certainly prepared to infer that the defendant knew that he had a legal right to recover possession of the property, but I have no evidence from which I could infer that he was aware of any relevant mistaken belief on the part of the plaintiff. As I have already indicated, a statement by the defendant to the effect that he would always provide a roof over the plaintiff's head does not, in my judgment, amount to a representation that the plaintiff had a legal right to remain in the property contrary to his wishes.

Lastly element (5), the defendant must have encouraged the plaintiff to act on her mistaken belief. Such encouragement may either be direct, or it may take the form of acquiescence, by the defendant standing back and allowing the plaintiff to act to her detriment. On the evidence, the most that the defendant did, as I see it, was to lead the plaintiff to believe, at least until towards the end of 1983, that he was intending to join her at 33, Stanway Road. The fact that he did not do so cannot, in my judgment, be sufficient to found a proprietary estoppel.

For the reasons which I have endeavoured to express, therefore, I reach the conclusion that the plaintiff has no right, in law or equity, to remain in occupation of 33, Stanway Road once Clare is no longer under the age of 17, that being in effect the issue which I have to decide, as presented by the pleadings.

In these circumstances, I think that the correct course for me to take is that which was urged upon me by Mr Susman, namely to dismiss the action, on the defendant's undertaking to provide accommodation for the plaintiff at 33, Stanway Road so long as Clare shall be under the age of 17 years, and to keep up the mortgage payments throughout the period of such occupation. I take it also to be implicit in the defendant's concession in his defence that he will undertake to keep the property in good repair, at his own expense, throughout the period of such occupation. I am not clear what is the defendant's position in relation to the rates on 33, Stanway Road, and I will hear counsel on that point.

Subject to that, however, I dismiss the action on those terms.

MATHARU v MATHARU [1994] 2 FLR 597 (CA)

In 1968 the plaintiff bought the property which became the matrimonial home of the defendant and the plaintiff's son, after their marriage in 1971. During the course of the marriage, the defendant's husband made extensive improvements to the property at his own expense. In 1988 the marriage broke down, and in 1990 the defendant obtained an order excluding the husband from the house. The husband died in 1991. Later that year, the plaintiff emigrated to Canada but returned the following year. On his return, the plaintiff demanded that the defendant vacate the property. His application for a possession order was dismissed at first instance on the ground of a proprietary estoppel in the defendant's favour. It was also held that the defendant enjoyed an unquantifiable beneficial interest in the property, which was declared to be held on trust for sale. The plaintiff appealed.

ROCH LJ: . . . the law of equitable estoppel was analysed and spelt out in the judgment of Fry J in *Willmott* v *Barber* (1880) 15 ChD 96. If that is so these are the elements which have to be established by the person claiming the equity:

(1)   that that person has made a mistake as to his or her legal rights;
(2)   that that person has expended some money or done some act on the faith of that mistaken belief;
(3)   the possessor of the legal right must know of the existence of his legal right which is inconsistent with the equity, if it exists;
(4)   the possessor of the legal right must know of the other person's mistaken belief as to his or her rights;
(5)   the possessor of the legal right must have encouraged the other person in his or her expenditure of money or in doing the other acts on which the other person relies, either directly or by abstaining from asserting his legal right.

In my judgment the respondent was able to satisfy each of those requirements and the judge was correct in deciding that this was a case where the respondent had an equity which defeated the appellant's claim for possession. The alterations and improvements to the house and the making of mortgage repayments by Raghbir to the appellant were, in my judgment, money expended and acts done of which the respondent is entitled to take advantage. Although the respondent did not know that her husband was making mortgage repayments to the appellant, she nevertheless knew that Raghbir was paying the mortgage and other outgoings on the house when the improvements were made. The respondent was married to and living with Raghbir at the relevant time, and the expenditure of those sums by Raghbir meant that the amount of his income available to benefit the respondent and their children was less than it otherwise would have been. Although the money would have been earned by Raghbir, it would be wrong in my view to consider that it was money solely, belonging to him.

The requirement of a mistake on the part of the respondent as to her legal rights is also satisfied in my view. There can be little doubt that when she agreed to resume cohabitation with Raghbir in 1981, she did so in the belief that she was going to a house which he owned on the basis that the house would be as much hers as it was his.

The expenditure on the new kitchen which was made by the respondent using money borrowed from her family, being made after the respondent knew that the appellant owned the house cannot be money expended on the faith of the respondent's mistaken belief. Nevertheless, it is, in my opinion, conduct by the respondent which confirms that the respondent had gone to live at 223 Coventry Road under a mistaken belief as to her rights and that the appellant had by his conduct between 1981 and 1990 led the respondent to believe, once she learned that he was the owner, that he would abstain from asserting his legal rights.

The third requirement is satisfied because it was never disputed that the appellant knew at all material times that he was the owner of 223 Coventry Road.

In my judgment it is inconceivable that the appellant did not know the basis on which his son had been successful in persuading the respondent to drop her court proceedings against him and to resume cohabitation with him at 223 Coventry Road, particularly against the background that Raghbir had lived at that address prior to the respondent leaving 90 Henley Road in 1979 or 1980 with his mistress, a fact which on the respondent's affidavit was well known to the appellant, because the appellant's wife had actually taunted the respondent with that information. This is an inference of fact which this court has power to draw under RSC Ord. 59, r. 10(3) and should draw in this case. Thus I would conclude that the fourth requirement is satisfied.

The respondent's affidavit, in my judgment, contains clear evidence that the appellant and his wife created and encouraged the respondent's mistaken understanding of the basis on which she and her husband occupied 223 Coventry Road. Statements to outsiders, family relatives and friends to the effect that the respondent and Raghbir had moved into their own property and that they were living alone were clearly calculated to create or encourage the respondent's belief that site hid a permanent home at that address because it was the property of her husband.

Having found the existence of an equity or a proprietary estoppel, the judge was correct that he had to determine the extent of the equity, see Scarman LJ in *Crabb* v *Arun District Council* [1976] Ch 179 at p. 193A. However, on this aspect of the case I have the misfortune to disagree with the judge's finding that the respondent has a beneficial interest in the property owing to the proprietary estoppel. In my judgment what has been created on the facts of this case is a licence for the respondent to remain in this house for her life or such shorter period as she may decide.

The third and final question is what relief is necessary to give effect to the equity? In my view the relief necessary is to refuse the appellant's claim for possession, on terms, along the following lines, subject to argument and discussion.

(1)   that the first defendant is to be responsible for the outgoings on the house, namely council tax, repayments under the mortgage with the Portman Building Society dated 22 March 1968, insurance premiums, water and electricity and gas;

(2)   that the first defendant is to keep the premises in good decorative repair;

(3)   that the plaintiff is to be responsible for the structural repair of the premises;

(4)   that the first defendant is to repay the plaintiff the sums that the plaintiff has paid to the Portman Building Society in respect of the said mortgage since October 1991 by suitable instalments.

7.6   End of Chapter Assessment Question

Simon and Janice have lived together for seven years. They bought their current house in 1991; each having sold previously owned properties. As Janice was still going through her divorce, the new house was conveyed into Simon's sole name. The relationship between Simon and Janice has now broken down, albeit they are still living in the same property.

The house is worth £120,000 with an endowment mortgage of £50,000. Janice contributed £40,000 towards the purchase price, with Simon contributing £30,000. Janice, despite only working part-time, has paid half the endowment fees.

Explain how the courts will assess her claim to be entitled to a half share in the property.

7.7   End of Chapter Assessment Outline Answer

This is not a difficult question to answer, and hence you may find the outline here somewhat short! The issue for discussion is the application of constructive/resulting trust doctrines to Janice's case. As Janice does not have her name on the title deeds to the property, and there is no evidence on the facts given that a declaration of trust has been executed, it is to be assumed that Simon is the legal and beneficial owner. To claim entitlement therefore, Janice will have to prove that in reality the beneficial entitlement is shared between them. Your answer will consequently consider the way in which the courts approach the doctrine of constructive trusts.

The first thing that the courts will need to establish is whether there was a common intention that the property should be shared (*Gissing* v *Gissing*). In relation to this test, the court may look for direct evidence of intention or implied evidence. The former is naturally easier to establish. The types of direct evidence that the courts will look for are:

- express declarations;
- contribution to the purchase monies;
- payment of substantial works/renovation.

Janice may fall within one of these categories.

There does not seem to be any express declaration on the facts presented to you. Janice has, however, provided a large contribution to the purchase monies, being £40,000 to the purchase price, and subsequent payments to the mortgage. Even if purchase money has been paid by the party claiming a beneficial share, it is still open to the other party to argue that the money was a loan or even a gift. Fortunately for Janice, the presumption of advancement operates in marital relationships only, and anachronistically, only in favour of the wife.

The payment of purchase monies may be sufficient to satisfy the courts that the couple did have a common intention to share the property beneficially, and therefore it may be unnecessary to consider the implied evidence to satisfy the courts. However, it would be useful to mention the nature of that evidence, i.e. conduct, especially undertaking substantial works to the property (bearing in mind *Lloyds Bank* v *Rossett*), or financial contribution to the relationship (again bearing in mind that with cohabitant's payment of bills in the absence of an express declaration may be treated as the equivalent of rent).

There is no evidence that Janice has done any works of improvement, or paid for the same. However, following *Rossett*, the carrying out of works on premises is of a lesser evidential weight. Paying for the works increases the weight of the evidence.

The second element to the test is to establish if the party claiming the beneficial entitlement has acted to their detriment. This test is often subsumed into the first. Here it is arguable that Janice has acted to her detriment since she paid a large sum of money to help purchase the property and has continued to pay the endowment.

Finally, having established that a common intention exists, the court will have to assess the extent of that beneficial ownership. As you will recall, there has been a split in the way that the courts approach this, one line of argument being that a purely financial view is taken — what percentage the claimant put in equals what they will get out. The second line of argument considers what the parties intended the percentage share to be. The latter system includes a degree of crystal ball gazing, and may be deemed inappropriate. However, following *Midland Bank* v *Cooke* this seems to be the line the courts are taking. On the basis of Janice's contributions, she will qualify for a 30% share in the equity of the property. More difficult to assess would be the share she should receive by virtue of her payments towards the mortgage (on the assumption that the court views this as rights bearing rather than occupation rent). The question states that she is paying half the endowment fees, which leaves Simon paying the other half, together with the interest on the capital sum. Without precise figures, you cannot estimate the exact share this would entitle her to. This purely financial calculation would result in less than the half share she is claiming. If the court approach the claim on a *Cooke* basis, she may well get her half share, but it is unlikely that she would get any more.

CHAPTER E

DOMEST

8.1 Civil Rem

KF

The plaintiff, whose f
respect of her complai
against her and peste
that he continued to t
great stress. The judge
violence to, harassing
Held: dismissing the a
threats to commit a t
unwanted telephone
reasonable enjoymen
restrained quia timet
to a threat but causing
also be restrained qui
the judge was justifie
   (2)   That it was de
person restrained cou
exercise of his discr
expressed; and that,

DILLON LJ: Miss I
indicated, that an inj
or threatening to as
granted to restrain th
could be an injunctic
of the plaintiff's ha
sufficiently proved, t
relation to the teleph
or leasehold interes
persistent unwanted
the parental home, a
in reliance on the de
of the tort of private
and therefore the pl
proprietary interest,
and harassing teleph
   To my mind, it i
deliberately harassir
civil courts if the r
proprietary interest

Thomas submits, hovho are living with each
or invasion of privacyhe parties to a marriage
[1964] AC 1129, intimccordingly.
out above, the defend
under the English civ
right to complain. I ge grants an injunction
nuisance, which origig violence against the
protect private property
It is stated in *Clerk &*
essence of nuisance is a child living with the
enjoyment of land.'
   That a legal ownenr from a specified area
nuisance, to restrain p
decided by the Appl actual bodily harm to
Motherwell (1976) 73 onsiders that he is likely
authority, a submissio

                                      riage include references
that the common law household as husband
of privacy as either ome shall be construed
and that it has lost
ills arising in a gr
principle to meet the a person to whom the
the principle as the

                                      f 24 hours beginning at
Consequently, notwith
had also the right to ree direction of the judge;
JA, who delivered the time after the expiry of

Here we have a wifof 24 hours, no account
live there with her l
of the matrimonial rtion, a constable arrests
she is entitled to therthwith seek the direc-

   I respectfully agree,Court, of that court, and
approach. The court h
social conditions; in thiefore a judge.
of this appeal began, w
If the wife of the owne
do not see why that sh

                                      CA)

8.1.1 THE DOMESTI Matrimonial Homes Act
ACT 1976 n for such an order:

   DOMESTIC VIOnable having regard to
                    wise, to their respective

1.   **Matrimonial injun**l to all the circumstances
   (1)   Without prejudi
party to a marriage a nself accordingly, then
containing one or more
   (a)   a provision rection refers. He had of
applicant;   ne husband towards the
   (b)   a provision res before him at the same
applicant;   as 1984 there had been
   (c)   a provision exc getting on well together
matrimonial home or frhildren. They would get
   (d)   a provision r temper, or as the judge
remain in the matrimorand break objects. In the
whether or not any othe gave before the judge

below on these summonses, substantial allegations of actual violence by the husband on the wife were made.

The judge moved on to deal with the husband's evidence on these matters, and found it to be very honest and straightforward. The husband agreed that things had been rocky for some time, and the judge in the end concluded that the wife's evidence had been exaggerated to some extent; indeed in the course of cross-examination she herself admitted that there had been no actual violence by the husband upon her. In relation to one particular incident which the wife had alleged had occurred on 4 May, while they were separated and met either at, or just outside, a public house, the wife's allegation was that, after abuse, the husband had thrown a drink over the back of her coat while she was on her way from one of the public houses. He said that the boot was on the other foot, if I may mix metaphors, and the judge found that it was more likely than not that it was the wife who threw lager over her husband rather than the other way round. That was an incident which was perhaps trivial in itself, but the judge's finding on it and perhaps generally preferring the husband's evidence in effect to that of the wife was, I think, indicative of the way that he approached this particular matter.

Summing the matter up in so far as the conduct of the parties was concerned, the judge expressed himself in this way:

> So far as conduct is concerned it is six of one and half a dozen of the other. I don't think that either was mature enough to cope with the stresses and strains of marriage and three children. I am satisfied that there were repeated loud quarrels.

In relation to those quarrels the judge found that the atmosphere latterly before the parties separated had been quite impossible, and that the children were being frightened and affected by the noise of their parents quarrelling. The judge said:

> As far as the children are concerned, I do not think it is in their best interests that there should be a continuation of these bitter quarrels in the matrimonial home, to which these young children will be witness.

In so far as the respective needs of the parties were concerned, the judge set out the situation in which each was or would be. At the time of the hearing the wife was with her parents. The evidence was that it might be difficult for her to remain there, as extensive works were to be carried out, but the judge was not unduly impressed by that argument. Of course, at that stage the husband for his part was still in the matrimonial home, a three-bedroomed council house which is in the name of the wife.

As far as the situation for the husband was concerned if an ouster order was made, as the judge pointed out, he had never been part of his own mother's family, but had been brought up by his grandmother. At the material time she was an elderly lady who had lost her sight and was not in the best of health. She had a two-bedroomed house and has her son, that is to say the husband's uncle, living in the other bedroom. In those circumstances it was the husband's evidence before the judge that he had nowhere to go were an ouster injunction to be made. It would take 6 months to get a flat, and he would be in that difficulty and would perhaps have to sleep on a settee in the living-room of his grandmother's house. The judge found that he did not accept that the husband would be without a roof if he made an order. As things have turned out, he is not. He has a roof over his head—the roof of his grandmother's house. But as I have just indicated, it does involve him sleeping on a settee in that house.

Having assessed those various aspects of the case in that way, the judge added in respect of the children:

> They should have their own home. It is not right for children to be brought up in their grandparent's home. The family should stand on its own feet if possible.

In this particular instance, however, when the judge came to the point in his judgment where, with respect, I think that he ought to have put all the matters to which I have referred, and which are mentioned in the statute, into the balance to reach a conclusion about what order was just and reasonable, I am not satisfied that he did in fact do just that. In fact the words which he used, which I shall quote in a moment, seem to me to indicate that he really applied criteria which do not find their place in s. 1(3) which I have quoted. Right at the end of his judgment the judge said:

Having regard to these factors' [the children, the conduct, the needs of the parties and so on] 'and all the circumstances of the case, I think that at this time, it might be beneficial for there to be a break for a while. It may be a forlorn hope but might ease a reconciliation. I have come to the conclusion, not without difficulty, that I ought to make an order excluding the respondent from the matrimonial home on balance.

For my part I do not find it easy to be certain what the judge meant by his reference to it being 'beneficial for there to be a break for a while', or indeed that it 'might ease a reconciliation' were he to make an ouster order, but if, as may be the situation, the view that he took and the reason why he made the ouster order was to allow the dust to settle for a time, which might perhaps then lead to a fresh reconciliation as there had been only 2 months earlier, in my opinion this is not the approach which the statute requires the court to take. In addition, it does seem to me that the judge failed to include in the balance of the exercise of his discretion what in this and in many cases is an important consideration, namely the Draconian nature of such an ouster order and the effect that it has upon the party against whom it is made.

In those circumstances therefore, both on the basis that, as I think, the judge approached the exercise of his discretion taking into account at the least matters which he ought not to have taken into account, and I think possibly also, with respect, omitting to take into account an aspect of these cases which he ought to have taken into account, I do not think that the ouster order as made can stand, and I for my part would allow the appeal against that decision.

KERR LJ: I agree. When I first read the note of the judgment and having heard the argument this morning, I was and remain under the clear impression that the judge directed his mind primarily to the non-molestation application and less to the more important ouster application with which he deals at the end of his judgment. His conclusion on this comes as something of a surprise. I agree that one cannot feel satisfied that he carried out the balancing exercise in that regard in a manner which carries conviction and with everything that May LJ has said in that connection. My hesitation has been whether the court ought to allow this appeal and set aside the ouster order, or whether there should be a fresh trial. I bear in mind that this is always undesirable from the point of view of the tension and uncertainty that it creates and the costs involved. However, I do not feel that this court is in a position to substitute its own conclusion on the balancing exercise for that of the judge, who has seen the parties and may only have expressed himself in a way which is open to criticism. Although his findings concerning conduct, needs and children led me to doubt whether this is a case in which a Draconian order ousting the husband was in any event appropriate, I do not feel that we are in a position so to conclude. I am also to some extent influenced by the fact that this matter came back before Judge Williams QC on 31 May 1985 and I see from the order that he heard oral evidence both from the wife and the husband, but nevertheless declined to accede to the application to extend the time when the husband had to leave the matrimonial home by more than 24 hours.

RICHARDS v *RICHARDS* [1983] 2 All ER 807 (HL)

LORD HAILSHAM OF ST MARYLEBONE LC: At the beginning of June 1982, Mrs Richards left home again. She took the children with her. She went to stay with a Mrs Moore at Mrs Moore's house in conditions admittedly overcrowded. Mrs Moore's house is eight miles away in Swanage.

So matters rested until 15 October 1982. On that date the wife issued a summons making an application intituled in the pending suit from which the present appeal ultimately stems. There was no reference in the heading indicating which jurisdiction the wife was seeking to invoke. It was simply an interlocutory application in the suit. In it, the wife claimed an injunction against molestation and another restricting communication. Both of these were rejected and are not now persisted in. She also sought an order that the husband should quit and deliver up possession of the matrimonial home, and not return thereto. There was an affidavit in support. Both the summons and the supporting affidavit were served on 3 November 1982. On 8 November 1982 the husband filed an affidavit in reply. This was the date of the hearing before Judge Pennant. Both parties gave brief evidence to the judge. Mrs Richards said she could not stay at the house of her friend beyond 22 November, and that, although she had tried to get accommodation from the council, the best they could offer, at least at that moment, was a caravan. She added that she would not return to the matrimonial home while her husband was there. In these circumstances, Judge Pennant was called on to make his decision on the wife's application.

The judge found that Mrs Richards 'has no reasonable ground for refusing to return to live in the same house as her husband', but that the existing accommodation where she was then living was 'overcrowded and not a fit home for the children'. Contrasting the case with *Samson* v *Samson* [1982] 1 All ER 780 he said that the wife had told him that she 'could not bear to be in the same house as the husband'. He added: 'The wife is strong-willed and does not wish to be in the same house as her husband and says she cannot bear to be with him. *But it is not true that she cannot*' (my emphasis).

The judge further found: 'I think it is thoroughly unjust to turn out this father, but justice no longer seems to play any part in this branch of the law.' He felt himself constrained to follow *Samson* v *Samson* rather than *Myers* v *Myers* [1982] 1 All ER 776, on the ground that the matrimonial home 'was a house provided by the public as a home for these four people, and that being so, the public interest [sic] is best met by installing the children in that home, which means in practice installing their mother too'. He added:

I find that it is by no means certain that there will be a divorce on the present grounds, and I have come to the conclusion that although it is unjust to the husband, it seems right to grant the order sought in the interests of the children.

In the event the judge made an order, not in the terms asked for by the wife but in the following terms:

That the [husband] do vacate the matrimonial home [at] 13, Stoborough Green, Stoborough, Wareham, Dorset on or before the 22nd November 1982.

As will appear from the above facts and findings, it must now be clear, and I believe that it ought to have been clear all along, that the wife has never made out a case for excluding the husband from the home. If there had been any doubt about this, the matter has now been established by the subsequent events beyond a peradventure. It therefore follows that I entirely accept the reasoning on this point of my noble and learned friend Lord Scarman.

I have now to consider the decision of the Court of Appeal, and the general principles of law involved. The court were quite right in thinking that the previous decisions of the Court of Appeal in this jurisdiction, to mention only *Elsworth* v *Elsworth* (1979) 1 FLR 245, *Myers* v *Myers*, *Samson* v *Samson* and *Bassett* v *Bassett* [1975] 1 All ER 513 appear to conflict. In the event, the court chose to follow *Bassett* v *Bassett* and *Samson* v *Samson* and disapprove *Elsworth* v *Elsworth* and *Myers* v *Myers*. Since I believe all four to have erred to some extent in principle, though not necessarily on the facts before them, I believe it is right to begin at the beginning and trace back the error to its source.

From the start it struck me as strange that in none of the cases cited before us was the statutory basis of the jurisdiction to grant these ouster injunctions properly discussed or investigated, and, as a result, the criteria which should actuate the court in exercising it were never properly considered or formulated. This is the more strange, since the jurisdiction of the Supreme Court to grant or withhold ouster injunctions is, I believe, based on statute and statute alone, and the criteria which should be applied are now, to my mind, adequately formulated in the relevant statutory provisions.

Prior to 1967, the jurisdiction of the High Court to grant or withhold injunctions, final or interlocutory, was contained in what was then s. 45 of the Supreme Court of Judicature (Consolidation) Act 1925. With the omission of the now inappropriate reference to mandamus, the section is now found in s. 37 of the Supreme Court Act 1981, the material words of which read:

> (1) The High Court may by order (whether interlocutory or final) grant an injunction . . . in all cases in which it appears to the court to be just and convenient to do so . . .

I do not think it necessary to proceed to consider whether, apart from the section, the court has any inherent jurisdiction. If it has, I believe it is indistinguishable in its application to the jurisdiction conferred by the section. I prefer to say that any inherent jurisdiction is absorbed by the section.

Being in general terms, the section is silent as to the criteria to be followed, and since the section applies to all divisions, such criteria had before 1967 been the subject of case law jurisprudence of a wide and multifarious kind. The section is still in force, and still applies in principle to all divisions of the High Court. Nevertheless, and while it is still there in reserve in cases where the special legislation to which I will be referring does not apply, in my opinion, where, as here, Parliament has spelt out in considerable detail what must be done in a particular class of case it is not open to litigants to bypass the special Act, nor to the courts to disregard its provisions by resorting to the earlier procedure, and thus choose to apply a different jurisprudence from that which the Act prescribes.

Any other conclusion would, I believe, lead to the most serious confusion. The result of a particular application cannot depend on which of two alternative statutory provisions the applicant invokes, where one is quite general and the other deals in precise detail with the situation involved and was enacted at a time when the general provision already existed.

The rights conferred by s. 37 were however subject to one serious limitation which applies to all equitable remedies of this class, whether statutory or arising from inherent jurisdiction, namely that an injunction could only be used in support of a legal right (and therefore only doubtfully in a number of ouster applications in the matrimonial jurisdiction), and despite statements (mostly obiter) to the effect that the court might apply different principles where the welfare of children was in question (cf *Stewart* v *Stewart* [1973] 1 All ER 31, *Adams* v *Adams* (1965) 109 SJ 899, *Phillips* v *Phillips* [1973] 2 All ER 423) neither the extent of the jurisdiction nor the criteria for its exercise were fully explored. Before the passing of the legislation to which I am about to refer this jurisdiction was also regularly invoked in ouster cases: see eg *Silverstone* v *Silverstone* [1953] 1 All ER 556, *Montgomery* v *Montgomery* [1964] 2 All ER 22, at 24. There was, indeed, no other basis for its exercise, since the section is wide enough to cover applications for ouster, and all-embracing enough to make any inherent jurisdiction superfluous.

Nevertheless, in my opinion, a new era opened with the passage of the Matrimonial Homes Act 1967 . . .

I do not for a moment suggest that the general jurisdiction conferred by s. 37 of the Supreme Court Act 1981 has been abolished or that it cannot be invoked in appropriate cases (eg molestation) for the protection of minors. But in my view the effect of s. 1 of the Matrimonial Homes Act 1967, which was in no way referred to in argument in the Court of Appeal or, so far as I can make out, in any of the reported cases cited, is to codify and spell out, where it is applicable, the jurisdiction of the High Court and county court in ouster injunctions between spouses whether in pending proceedings or by way of originating applications, and the criteria to be applied are those referred to in sub-s. (3) and not any other criteria sometimes treated as paramount by reported decisions of the court. I do not know that they differ very much from those developed by the case law evolved prior to 1967 and 1976 as respects the more limited jurisdiction of the court. But in so far as any decisions of the Court of Appeal whether before or after the passing of the Matrimonial Homes Act 1967 (with its amendments and additions) suggest any other criteria than those set out in sub-s. (3), particularly any which may claim that one set of criteria are to be treated as prior to, or paramount over, any or all of the others, in my opinion they are not to be regarded as sound law, although I wish to say that most if not all the decisions in which such dicta occur are probably to be justified on the particular facts, and even the general observations when taken in the context of their particular facts, but not out of context, may well be justifiable.

LORD BRANDON OF OAKBROOK: Before 1967 the only power which the High Court had to make an ouster order was the general power to grant injunctions conferred on it by s. 45(1) of the Supreme Court of Judicature (Consolidation) Act 1925. That subsection provided, so far as material:

> The High Court may grant . . . an injunction . . . by an interlocutory order in all cases in which it appears to the court to be just and convenient.

The subsection replaced in substantially the same terms s. 25(8) of the Supreme Court of judicature Act 1873, in respect of which it had long been held that, despite the apparently wide words of the subsection, the High Court only had jurisdiction to grant injunctions for the purpose of protecting legal or equitable rights: see *North London Ry Co.* v *Great Northern Ry Co.* (1883) 11 QBD 30 at 40 per Cotton LJ. It follows that s. 45(1) of the 1925 Act, and s. 37(1) of the Supreme Court Act 1981, by which it has now been replaced in substantially the same terms, must be interpreted as subject to the like limitation in their scope.

My Lords, until the radical social changes which have occurred in this country during the last two or three decades, the usual situation with regard to the ownership of a matrimonial home was that the whole estate in it, both legal and equitable, was vested in the husband. It followed from this that most wives could not apply for an ouster order under s. 45(1) of the 1925 Act on the ground that they had any legal or equitable interest in the matrimonial home which such an order could protect. However, a wife against whom no disqualifying matrimonial offence had been proved had a common law right to be provided by her husband with a home in which to live, and the High Court regarded itself as having jurisdiction under s. 45(1) of the 1925 Act to make an ouster order against a husband in order to protect that right pending suit: see *Silverstone* v *Silverstone* [1953] 1 All ER 556; *Gurasz* v *Gurasz* [1969] 3 All ER 822.

Parliament, however, did not regard this limited right of protection under s. 45(1) of the 1925 Act as adequate, as a result of which it passed the Matrimonial Homes Act 1967. Section 1 of the 1967 Act provided, so far as material:

> (1) Where one spouse is entitled to occupy a dwelling house by virtue of any estate or interest or contract or by virtue of any enactment giving him or her the right to remain in occupation, and the other spouse is not so entitled, then, subject to the provisions of this Act, the spouse not so entitled shall have the following rights (in this Act referred to as 'rights of occupation');—(a) if in occupation, a right not to be evicted or excluded from the dwelling house or any part thereof by the other spouse except with the leave of the court given by an order under this section; (b) if not in occupation, a right with the leave of the court so given to enter into and occupy the dwelling house.
>
> (2) So long as one spouse has rights of occupation, either of the spouses may apply to the court for an order declaring, enforcing, restricting or terminating those rights or regulating the exercise by either spouse of the right to occupy the dwelling house.
>
> (3) On an application for an order under this section the court may make such order as it thinks just and reasonable having regard to the conduct of the spouses in relation to each other and otherwise, to their respective needs and financial resources, to the needs of any children and to all the circumstances of the case . . .

In 1976 the legislature enacted the Domestic Violence and Matrimonial Proceedings Act of that year in order to deal with the problem of those persons who are commonly called 'battered wives'. Section 1 of the 1976 Act conferred on county courts, without prejudice to the jurisdiction of the High Court, power to grant, on the application of one party to a marriage, injunctions containing one or more of the following provisions: (a) a provision restraining the other party to the marriage from molesting the applicant; (b) a provision restraining the other party from molesting a child living with the applicant; (c) a provision excluding the other party from the matrimonial home or part of the matrimonial home or from a specified area in which the matrimonial home is included; (d) a provision requiring the other party to permit the applicant to enter and remain in the matrimonial home or a part of the matrimonial home.

Section 2 of the 1976 Act empowered judges, when granting certain kinds of injunctions designed to protect one party to a marriage, or a child living with that party, from violence by the other party to the marriage, in certain specified circumstances to attach a power of arrest to such injunctions.

My Lords, I indicated earlier my view that, in order to determine this appeal and to give guidance for the future, it was necessary for your Lordships to examine, and having examined to pay regard to, the statutory framework within which courts to which applications for ouster orders are made are not only empowered, but also obliged, to operate.

Having performed the first part of that task by setting out, or referring to, what appear to me to be the essential statutory provisions applicable, I conclude that it was the intention of the legislature, in passing and later amending and extending the scope of the 1967 Act, and in passing the 1976 Act, that the power of the High Court to make, during the subsistence of a marriage, orders relating to the occupation of a matrimonial home, including in particular an ouster order, which had previously been derived from s. 45(1) of the 1925 Act, should for the future be derived from, and exercised in accordance with, s. 1 of the 1967 Act. In this connection it is to be observed that, in s. 1(1) of the 1967 Act as originally enacted, it was expressly provided that, where one of the spouses was entitled to occupy the matrimonial home by virtue of any estate, interest or contract, and the other spouse was not so entitled, the latter should have rights of occupation, including a right 'not to be evicted or excluded . . . *except with the leave of the court given by an order under this section*' (my emphasis). If spouse A can only oust spouse B pursuant to an order made under s. 1 of the 1967 Act, it must surely follow that spouse B can only oust spouse A pursuant to a like order.

I reach a similar conclusion with regard to ouster orders made in a county court, namely that it was the intention of the legislature that the power of a county court to make ouster orders, which had been previously derived from the very general provisions of s. 74 of the County Courts Act 1959, should for the future be derived from, and exercised in accordance with, the provisions of the 1967 Act. County courts were given in additional power to make ouster orders by s. 1 of the 1976 Act, but it seems to me to be a necessary inference that the legislature intended such additional power to be exercised in accordance with the principles laid down in the 1967 Act.

The result of the conclusion which I have reached on these matters, when applied to the facts of the present case, is that the application issued by the wife in the Weymouth District Registry on 15 October 1982, in so far as it sought an ouster order against the husband, was in substance, though not in form (a matter to which I shall return later), an application for an order under s. 1 of the 1967 Act. The case was one in which, because the requirements of s. 1(1) of the 1967 Act as amended were fulfilled, the wife had the rights of occupation given by that subsection, and was therefore entitled to apply to the court for whatever order might be appropriate under s. 1(2) and (3).

On the footing that the wife's application was one made under the 1967 Act, the court to which it was made was obliged to follow the principles relating to such applications prescribed by that Act. Those principles are contained in s. 1(3), the essential parts of which I set our earlier. That subsection requires the court to make such order as it thinks just and reasonable having regard to a number of specified matters. The matters so specified are these: (1) the conduct of the spouses to each other and otherwise; (2) the respective needs and financial resources of the spouses; (3) the needs of any children; and (4) all the circumstances of the case. With regard to these matters it is, in my opinion, of the utmost importance to appreciate that none of them is made, by the wording of s. 1(3), necessarily of more weight than any of the others, let alone made paramount over them. All the four matters specified are to be regarded, and the weight to be given to any particular one of them must depend on the facts of each case.

8.1.1.2 Duration of orders

Practice Note [1978] 2 All ER 1056

To secure uniformity of practice, the President has issued the following note with the concurrence of the Lord Chancellor.

1.   Section 1(1)(c) of the Domestic Violence and Matrimonial Proceedings Act 1976 empowers a county court to include in an injunction provisions excluding a party from the matrimonial home or a part of the matrimonial home or from a specified area in which the matrimonial home is included. Where a power of arrest under s. 2 of the 1976 Act is attached to any injunction containing such provisions, the respondent is liable to be arrested if he enters the matrimonial home or part thereof or specified area at any time while the injunction remains in force.

2.   It is within the discretion of the court to decide whether an injunction should be granted and, if so, for how long it should operate. But whenever an injunction is granted excluding one of the parties from the matrimonial home (or a part thereof or specified area), consideration should be given to imposing a time limit on the operation of the injunction. In most cases a period of up to three months is likely to suffice, at least in the first instance. It will be open to the respondent in any event to apply for the discharge of the injunction before the expiry of the period fixed, for instance on the ground of reconciliation, and to the applicant to apply for an extension.

G v G (OUSTER: EX PARTE APPLICATION) [1990] 1 FLR 395 (CA)

LORD DONALDSON OF LYMINGTON MR: This is an appeal by the respondent wife in divorce proceedings, against an ouster order which was made ex parte by his Honour Judge Griffiths sitting in the Portsmouth County Court on 15 November 1989. The matrimonial home to which the ouster order applied is in Portsmouth. The other background matter which I should mention is that there are three children of the marriage, aged 6, 4 and 2.

The order itself was in the following terms:

1.   The respondent do forthwith vacate and shall not return to or enter the property known as [then it gave the address].
2.   The respondent her servants or agents be forthwith restrained from assaulting or molesting the petitioner.
3.   This Order do continue until Tuesday, 2 January 1990 at 10.30 when this matter will be further considered by this court allowing a hearing time of 2 hours.
4.   There be liberty to either party to apply to discharge or vary this order upon giving 48 hours' notice.
5.   A power of arrest be attached to this order.
6.   There be no order as to costs save that there be legal aid taxation of the petitioner's costs.
7.   There be a certificate for counsel for the petitioner.

. . .

Various points arise on this unhappy history, and I think that I can summarise them as follows:

1.   Should an ex parte order have been made?
2.   Should the return date have been 7 weeks later (i.e. 2 January 1990)?
3.   Should the order have required 48 hours' notice for any application to discharge or vary it?

I can take the first three of those points together—namely, whether or not there should have been an ex parte order, what return date it should have had, and what restrictions there should have been on any application to discharge or vary it. This type of case was considered by this court in *Ansah* v *Ansah* [1977] 2 All ER 638, which was a matrimonial case Ormrod LJ said this at p. 642:

Orders made *ex parte* are anomalies in our system of justice which generally demands service or notice of the proposed proceedings on the opposite party (see *Craig* v *Kanseen* [1943] All ER 108 at p. 113). None the less, the power of the court to intervene immediately and without notice in proper cases is essential to the administration of justice. But this power must be used with great caution and only in circumstances in which it is really necessary to act immediately. Such circumstances do undoubtedly tend to occur more frequently in family disputes than in other types of litigation because the parties are often still in close contact with one another and, particularly when a marriage is breaking up, in a state of high emotional tension; but even in such cases the court should only act *ex parte* in an emergency when the interests of justice or the protection of the applicant or a child clearly demands immediate intervention by the court. Such cases should be extremely rare, since any urgent application can be heard *inter partes* on two days' notice to the other side (see *Rayden on Divorce* and the notice in the Daily Cause List headed 'Matrimonial Causes and Matters — Urgent Applications'). Circumstances, of course, may arise when prior notice cannot be given to the other side; for example, cases where one parent has disappeared with the children, or a spouse, usually the wife, is so frightened of the other spouse that some protection must be provided against a violent response to service of proceedings, but the court must be fully satisfied that such protection is necessary.

Leaving out a paragraph which deals with the facts of that case, Ormrod LJ continued:

The order that was made in this case is quite unacceptable for another reason. If an order is to be made *ex parte*, it must be strictly limited in time if the risk of causing serious injustice is to be avoided. The time is to be measured in days, i.e. the shortest period which must elapse before a preliminary hearing *inter partes* can be arranged, and the order must specify the date on which it expires. (If difficulty in serving the other party is anticipated it may, exceptionally, be permissible to fix a longer period and to provide in the order that the other party may apply on 24 hours' notice to discharge the injunction.) The formula used in this case, namely 'until the further hearing of this application which will take place at the Royal Courts of Justice, Strand, London WC2, at the time and place to be notified', is quite unjustifiable and improper. It has resulted in this *ex parte* injunction remaining in force from 13 September until the hearing of this appeal—which was in fact on 13 December—'for the simple reason that no time or place for the hearing in London has ever been "notified" to the wife'.

Of course, in the present case a hearing date was fixed in the order and it was not as long as 3 months, but a hearing date of 7 weeks is completely unjustifiable. . . .

I come back to the question of whether an ex parte order should have been made. Given the fact that the wife was known to be readily available for service and given the fact that there was no reason at all why the judge could not have made a non-molestation order in the widest possible terms ex parte which could have been served on the wife at the same time as notice of an *inter partes* hearing for consideration of an application for an ouster injunction, in my judgment this order should never have been made. If it was made, there could be no possible justification for putting on a 48-hour notice provision. Clearly, if the wife were to apply to discharge the ex parte order, the husband had to be notified. But all that was required in this case where the husband was represented by local solicitors was liberty to either party to apply to discharge or vary the order upon notice and, in the case of the husband, such notice to be given to his solicitors.

8.1.2   THE DOMESTIC PROCEEDINGS AND MAGISTRATES' COURTS ACT 1978

DOMESTIC PROCEEDINGS AND MAGISTRATES' COURTS ACT 1978

16.   Powers of court to make orders for the protection of a party to a marriage or a child of the family

(1)   Either party to a marriage may, whether or not an application is made by that party for an order under section 2 of this Act, apply to a magistrates' court for an order under this section.

(2)   Where on an application for an order under this section the court is satisfied that the respondent has used, or threatened to use, violence against the person of the applicant or a child of the family and that it is necessary for the protection of the applicant or a child of the family that an order should be made under this subsection, the court may make one or both of the following orders, that is to say—

(a)   an order that the respondent shall not use, or threaten to use, violence against the person of the applicant;

(b)   an order that the respondent shall not use, or threaten to use, violence against the person of a child of the family.

(3)   Where on an application for an order under this section the court is satisfied—

(a)   that the respondent has used violence against the person of the applicant or a child of the family, or

(b)   that the respondent has threatened to use violence against the person of the applicant or a child of the family and has used violence against some other person, or

(c)   that the respondent has in contravention of an order made under subsection (2) above threatened to use violence against the person of the applicant or a child of the family,

and that the applicant or a child of the family is in danger of being physically injured by the respondent (or would be in such danger if the applicant or child were to enter the matrimonial home) the court may make one or both of the following orders, that is to say—

(i)   an order requiring the respondent to leave the matrimonial home;

(ii)   an order prohibiting the respondent from entering the matrimonial home.

(4)   Where the court makes an order under subsection (3) above, the court may, if it thinks fit, make a further order requiring the respondent to permit the applicant to enter and remain in the matrimonial home.

(5)   Where on an application for an order under this section the court considers that it is essential that the application should be heard without delay the court may hear the application notwithstanding—

(a)   that the court does not include both a man and a woman,

(b)   that any member of the court is not a member of a family panel, or

(c)   that the proceedings on the application are not separated from the hearing and determination of proceedings which are not family proceedings.

(6)   Where on an application for an order under this section the court is satisfied that there is imminent danger of physical injury to the applicant or a child of the family, the court may make an order under subsection (2) above notwithstanding that the respondent has not been given such notice of the proceedings as may be prescribed by rules and any order made by virtue of this subsection is in this section and in section 17 of this Act referred to as an 'expedited order.'

(7)   . . .

(8)   An expedited order shall not take effect until the date on which notice of the making of the order is served on the respondent in such manner as may be prescribed or, if the court specifies a later date as the date on which the order is to take effect, that later date, and an expedited order shall cease to have effect on whichever of the following dates occurs first, that is to say—

(a)   the date of the expiration of the period of 28 days beginning with the date of the making of the order; or

(b)   the date of the commencement of the hearing, in accordance with the provisions of Part II of the Magistrates' Courts Act 1980, of the application for an order under this section.

(9)   An order under this section may be made subject to such exceptions or conditions as may be specified in the order and, subject in the case of an expedited order to subsection (8) above, may be made for such term as may be so specified.

(10)   The court in making an order under subsection (2)(a) or (b) above may include provision that the respondent shall not incite or assist any other person to use, or threaten to use, violence against the person of the applicant, or, as the case may be, the child of the family.

18.   Powers of arrest for breach of s. 16 order

(1)   Where a magistrates' court makes an order under section 16 of this Act which provides that the respondent—

(a)   shall not use violence against the person of the applicant, or

(b)   shall not use violence against a child of the family, or

(c)   shall not enter the matrimonial home,

the court may, if it is satisfied that the respondent has physically injured the applicant or a child of the family and considers that he is likely to do so again, attach a power of arrest to the order.

(2) Where by virtue of subsection (1) above a power of arrest is attached to an order, a constable may arrest without warrant a person whom he has reasonable cause for suspecting of being in breach of any such provision of the order as is mentioned in paragraph (a), (b), or (c) of subsection (1) above by reason of that person's use of violence or, as the case may be, his entry into the matrimonial home.

(3) Where a power of arrest is attached to an order under subsection (1) above and the respondent is arrested under subsection (2) above—

(a) he shall be brought before a justice of the peace within a period of 24 hours beginning at the time of his arrest, and

(b) the justice of the peace before whom he is brought may remand him.

In reckoning for the purposes of this subsection any period of 24 hours, no account shall be taken of Christmas Day, Good Friday, or any Sunday.

(4) Where a court has made an order under section 16 of this Act but has not attached to the order a power of arrest under subsection (1) above, then, if at any time the applicant for that order considers that the other party to the marriage in question has disobeyed the order, he may apply for the issue of a warrant for the arrest of that other party to a justice of the peace for the commission area in which either party to the marriage ordinarily resides; but a justice of the peace shall not issue a warrant on such an application unless—

(a) the application is substantiated on oath, and

(b) the justice has reasonable grounds for believing that the other party to the marriage has disobeyed that order.

(5) The magistrates' court before whom any person is brought by virtue of a warrant issued under subsection (4) above may remand him.

8.2 The Family Law Act 1996

8.2.1 NON-MOLESTATION ORDERS

FAMILY LAW ACT 1996

42. Non-molestation orders

(1) In this Part a 'non-molestation order' means an order containing either or both of the following provisions—

(a) provision prohibiting a person ('the respondent') from molesting another person who is associated with the respondent;

(b) provision prohibiting the respondent from molesting a relevant child.

(2) The court may make a non-molestation order—

(a) if an application for the order has been made (whether in other family proceedings or without any other family proceedings being instituted) by a person who is associated with the respondent; or

(b) if in any family proceedings to which the respondent is a party the court considers that the order should be made for the benefit of any other party to the proceedings or any relevant child even though no such application has been made.

(3) In subsection (2) 'family proceedings' includes proceedings in which the court has made an emergency protection order under section 44 of the Children Act 1989 which includes an exclusion requirement (as defined in section 44A(3) of that Act).

(4) Where an agreement to marry is terminated, no application under subsection (2)(a) may be made by virtue of section 62(3)(e) by reference to that agreement after the end of the period of three years beginning with the day on which it is terminated.

(5) In deciding whether to exercise its powers under this section and, if so, in what manner, the court shall have regard to all the circumstances including the need to secure the health, safety and well-being—

(a) of the applicant or, in a case falling within subsection (2)(b), the person for whose benefit the order would be made; and

(b) of any relevant child.

(6) A non-molestation order may be expressed so as to refer to molestation in general, to particular acts of molestation, or to both.

(7) A non-molestation order may be made for a specified period or until further order.

(8) A non-molestation order which is made in other family proceedings ceases to have effect if those proceedings are withdrawn or dismissed.

8.2.1.1 The applicant

FAMILY LAW ACT 1996

62. Meaning of 'cohabitants', 'relevant child' and 'associated persons'
  (1) For the purposes of this Part—
  (a) 'cohabitants' are a man and a woman who, although not married to each other, are living together as husband and wife; and
  (b) 'former cohabitants' is to be read accordingly, but does not include cohabitants who have subsequently married each other.
  (2) In this Part, 'relevant child', in relation to any proceedings under this Part, means—
  (a) any child who is living with or might reasonably be expected to live with either party to the proceedings;
  (b) any child in relation to whom an order under the Adoption Act 1976 or the Children Act 1989 is in question in the proceedings; and
  (c) any other child whose interests the court considers relevant.
  (3) For the purposes of this Part, a person is associated with another person if—
  (a) they are or have been married to each other;
  (b) they are cohabitants or former cohabitants;
  (c) they live or have lived in the same household, otherwise than merely by reason of one of them being the other's employee, tenant, lodger or boarder;
  (d) they are relatives;
  (e) they have agreed to marry one another (whether or not that agreement has been terminated);
  (f) in relation to any child, they are both persons falling within subsection (4); or
  (g) they are parties to the same family proceedings (other than proceedings under this Part).
  (4) A person falls within this subsection in relation to a child if—
  (a) he is a parent of the child; or
  (b) he has or has had parental responsibility for the child.
  (5) If a child has been adopted or has been freed for adoption by virtue of any of the enactments mentioned in section 16(1) of the Adoption Act 1976, two persons are also associated with each other for the purposes of this Part if—
  (a) one is a natural parent of the child or a parent of such a natural parent; and
  (b) the other is the child or any person—
     (i) who has become a parent of the child by virtue of an adoption order or has applied for an adoption order, or
     (ii) with whom the child has at any time been placed for adoption.
  (6) A body corporate and another person are not, by virtue of subsection (3)(f) or (g), to be regarded for the purposes of this Part as associated with each other.

8.2.2 OCCUPATION ORDERS

FAMILY LAW ACT 1996

33. Occupation orders where applicant has estate or interest etc. or has matrimonial home rights
  (1) If—
  (a) a person ('the person entitled')—

(i)   is entitled to occupy a dwelling-house by virtue of a beneficial estate or interest or contract or by virtue of any enactment giving him the right to remain in occupation, or

(ii)   has matrimonial home rights in relation to a dwelling-house, and

(b)   the dwelling-house—

(i)   is or at any time has been the home of the person entitled and of another person with whom he is associated, or

(ii)   was at any time intended by the person entitled and any such other person to be their home,

the person entitled may apply to the court for an order containing any of the provisions specified in subsections (3), (4) and (5).

(2)   If an agreement to marry is terminated, no application under this section may be made by virtue of section 62(3)(e) by reference to that agreement after the end of the period of three years beginning with the day on which it is terminated.

(3)   An order under this section may—

(a)   enforce the applicant's entitlement to remain in occupation as against the other person ('the respondent');

(b)   require the respondent to permit the applicant to enter and remain in the dwelling-house or part of the dwelling-house;

(c)   regulate the occupation of the dwelling-house by either or both parties;

(d)   if the respondent is entitled as mentioned in subsection (1)(a)(i), prohibit, suspend or restrict the exercise by him of his right to occupy the dwellinghouse;

(e)   if the respondent has matrimonial home rights in relation to the dwelling-house and the applicant is the other spouse, restrict or terminate those rights;

(f)   require the respondent to leave the dwelling-house or part of the dwelling-house; or

(g)   exclude the respondent from a defined area in which the dwelling-house is included.

(4)   An order under this section may declare that the applicant is entitled as mentioned in subsection (1)(a)(i) or has matrimonial home rights.

(5)   If the applicant has matrimonial home rights and the respondent is the other spouse, an order under this section made during the marriage may provide that those rights are not brought to an end by—

(a)   the death of the other spouse; or

(b)   the termination (otherwise than by death) of the marriage.

(6)   In deciding whether to exercise its powers under subsection (3) and (if so) in what manner, the court shall have regard to all the circumstances including—

(a)   the housing needs and housing resources of each of the parties and of any relevant child;

(b)   the financial resources of each of the parties;

(c)   the likely effect of any order, or of any decision by the court not to exercise its powers under subsection (3), on the health, safety or well-being of the parties and of any relevant child; and

(d)   the conduct of the parties in relation to each other and otherwise.

(7)   If it appears to the court that the applicant or any relevant child is likely to suffer significant harm attributable to conduct of the respondent if an order under this section containing one or more of the provisions mentioned in subsection (3) is not made, the court shall make the order unless it appears to it that—

(a)   the respondent or any relevant child is likely to suffer significant harm if the order is made; and

(b)   the harm likely to be suffered by the respondent or child in that event is as great as, or greater than, the harm attributable to conduct of the respondent which is likely to be suffered by the applicant or child if the order is not made.

(8)   The court may exercise its powers under subsection (5) in any case where it considers that in all the circumstances it is just and reasonable to do so.

(9)   An order under this section—

(a)   may not be made after the death of either of the parties mentioned in subsection (1); and

(b)   except in the case of an order made by virtue of subsection (5)(a), ceases to have effect on the death of either party.

(10)   An order under this section may, in so far as it has continuing effect, be made for a specified period, until the occurrence of a specified event or until further order.

35.   One former spouse with no existing right to occupy

(1)   This section applies if—

(a)   one former spouse is entitled to occupy a dwelling-house by virtue of a beneficial estate or interest or contract, or by virtue of any enactment giving him the right to remain in occupation;

(b)   the other former spouse is not so entitled; and

(c)   the dwelling-house was at any time their matrimonial home or was at any time intended by them to be their matrimonial home.

(2)   The former spouse not so entitled may apply to the court for an order under this section against the other former spouse ('the respondent').

(3)   If the applicant is in occupation, an order under this section must contain provision—(a) giving the applicant the right not to be evicted or excluded from the dwelling-house or any part of it by the respondent for the period specified in the order; and

(b)   prohibiting the respondent from evicting or excluding the applicant during that period.

(4)   If the applicant is not in occupation, an order under this section must contain provision—

(a)   giving the applicant the right to enter into and occupy the dwelling-house for the period specified in the order; and

(b)   requiring the respondent to permit the exercise of that right.

(5)   An order under this section may also—

(a)   regulate the occupation of the dwelling-house by either or both of the parties;

(b)   prohibit, suspend or restrict the exercise by the respondent of his right to occupy the dwelling-house;

(c)   require the respondent to leave the dwelling-house or part of the dwelling-house; or

(d)   exclude the respondent from a defined area in which the dwelling-house is included.

(6)   In deciding whether to make an order under this section containing provision of the kind mentioned in subsection (3) or (4) and (if so) in what manner, the court shall have regard to all the circumstances including—

(a)   the housing needs and housing resources of each of the parties and of any relevant child;

(b)   the financial resources of each of the parties;

(c)   the likely effect of any order, or of any decision by the court not to exercise its powers under subsection (3) or (4), on the health, safety or well-being of the parties and of any relevant child;

(d)   the conduct of the parties in relation to each other and otherwise;

(e)   the length of time that has elapsed since the parties ceased to live together;

(f)   the length of time that has elapsed since the marriage was dissolved or annulled; and

(g)   the existence of any pending proceedings between the parties—

(i)   for an order under section 23A or 24 of the Matrimonial Causes Act 1973 (property adjustment orders in connection with divorce proceedings etc.);

(ii)   for an order under paragraph 1(2)(d) or (e) of Schedule 1 to the Children Act 1989 (orders for financial relief against parents); or

(iii)   relating to the legal or beneficial ownership of the dwelling-house.

(7)   In deciding whether to exercise its power to include one or more of the provisions referred to in subsection (5) ('a subsection (5) provision') and (if so) in what manner, the court shall have regard to all the circumstances including the matters mentioned in subsection (6)(a) to (e).

(8)   If the court decides to make an order under this section and it appears to it that, if the order does not include a subsection (5) provision, the applicant or any relevant child is likely to suffer significant harm attributable to conduct of the respondent, the court shall include the subsection (5) provision in the order unless it appears to the court that—

(a)   the respondent or any relevant child is likely to suffer significant harm if the provision is included in the order; and

(b)   the harm likely to be suffered by the respondent or child in that event is as great as or greater than the harm attributable to conduct of the respondent which is likely to be suffered by the applicant or child if the provision is not included.

(9)   An order under this section—

(a)   may not be made after the death of either of the former spouses; and

(b)   ceases to have effect on the death of either of them.

(10)   An order under this section must be limited so as to have effect for a specified period not exceeding six months, but may be extended on one or more occasions for a further specified period not exceeding six months.

(11)   A former spouse who has an equitable interest in the dwelling-house or in the proceeds of sale of the dwelling-house but in whom there is not vested (whether solely or as joint tenant) a legal estate in fee simple or a legal term of years absolute in the dwelling-house is to be treated (but only for the purpose of determining whether he is eligible to apply under this section) as not being entitled to occupy the dwelling-house by virtue of that interest.

(12)   Subsection (11) does not prejudice any right of such a former spouse to apply for an order under section 33.

(13)   So long as an order under this section remains in force, subsections (3) to (6) of section 30 apply in relation to the applicant—

(a)   as if he were the spouse entitled to occupy the dwelling-house by virtue of that section; and

(b)   as if the respondent were the other spouse.

36.   One cohabitant or former cohabitant with no existing right to occupy

(1)   This section applies if—

(a)   one cohabitant or former cohabitant is entitled to occupy a dwellinghouse by virtue of a beneficial estate or interest or contract or by virtue of any enactment giving him the right to remain in occupation;

(b)   the other cohabitant or former cohabitant is not so entitled; and

(c)   that dwelling-house is the home in which they live together as husband and wife or a home in which they at any time so lived together or intended so to live together.

(2)   The cohabitant or former cohabitant not so entitled may apply to the court for an order under this section against the other cohabitant or former cohabitant ('the respondent').

(3) If the applicant is in occupation, an order under this section must contain provision—

(a)   giving the applicant the right not to be evicted or excluded from the dwelling-house or any part of it by the respondent for the period specified in the order; and

(b)   prohibiting the respondent from evicting or excluding the applicant during that period.

(4)   If the applicant is not in occupation, an order under this section must contain provision—

(a)   giving the applicant the right to enter into and occupy the dwelling-house for the period specified in the order; and

(b)   requiring the respondent to permit the exercise of that right.

(5)   An order under this section may also—

(a)   regulate the occupation of the dwelling-house by either or both of the parties;

(b)   prohibit, suspend or restrict the exercise by the respondent of his right to occupy the dwelling-house;

(c)   require the respondent to leave the dwelling-house or part of the dwelling-house; or

(d)   exclude the respondent from a defined area in which the dwelling-house is included.

(6)   In deciding whether to make an order under this section containing provision of the kind mentioned in subsection (3) or (4) and (if so) in what manner, the court shall have regard to all the circumstances including—

(a)   the housing needs and housing resources of each of the parties and of any relevant child;

(b)   the financial resources of each of the parties;

(c)   the likely effect of any order, or of any decision by the court not to exercise its powers under subsection (3) or (4), on the health, safety or well-being of the parties and of any relevant child;

(d)   the conduct of the parties in relation to each other and otherwise;

(e)   the nature of the parties' relationship;

(f)   the length of time during which they have lived together as husband and wife;

(g)   whether there are or have been any children who are children of both parties or for whom both parties have or have had parental responsibility;

(h)   the length of time that has elapsed since the parties ceased to live together; and

(i)   the existence of any pending proceedings between the parties—

(i)   for an order under paragraph 1(2)(d) or (e) of Schedule 1 to the Children Act 1989 (orders for financial relief against parents); or

(ii)   relating to the legal or beneficial ownership of the dwelling-house.

(7)   In deciding whether to exercise its powers to include one or more of the provisions referred to in subsection (5) ('a subsection (5) provision') and (if so) in what manner, the court shall have regard to all the circumstances including—

(a)   the matters mentioned in subsection (6)(a) to (d); and

(b)   the questions mentioned in subsection (8).

(8)   The questions are—

(a)   whether the applicant or any relevant child is likely to suffer significant harm attributable to conduct of the respondent if the subsection (5) provision is not included in the order; and

(b)   whether the harm likely to be suffered by the respondent or child if the provision is included is as great as or greater than the harm attributable to conduct of the respondent which is likely to be suffered by the applicant or child if the provision is not included.

(9)   An order under this section—

(a)   may not be made after the death of either of the parties; and

(b)   ceases to have effect on the death of either of them.

(10)   An order under this section must be limited so as to have effect for a specified period not exceeding six months, but may be extended on one occasion for a further specified period not exceeding six months.

(11)   A person who has an equitable interest in the dwelling-house or in the proceeds of sale of the dwelling-house but in whom there is not vested (whether solely or as joint tenant) a legal estate in fee simple or a legal term of years absolute in the dwelling-house is to be treated (but only for the purpose of determining whether he is eligible to apply under this section) as not being entitled to occupy the dwelling-house by virtue of that interest.

(12)   Subsection (11) does not prejudice any right of such a person to apply for an order under section 33.

(13)   So long as the order remains in force, subsections (3) to (6) of section 30 apply in relation to the applicant—

(a)   as if he were a spouse entitled to occupy the dwelling-house by virtue of that section; and

(b)   as if the respondent were the other spouse.

37.   Neither spouse entitled to occupy

(1)   This section applies if—

(a)   one spouse or former spouse and the other spouse or former spouse occupy a dwelling-house which is or was the matrimonial home; but

(b)   neither of them is entitled to remain in occupation—

(i)   by virtue of a beneficial estate or interest or contract; or

(ii)   by virtue of any enactment giving him the right to remain in occupation.

(2)   Either of the parties may apply to the court for an order against the other under this section.

(3)   An order under this section may—

(a)   require the respondent to permit the applicant to enter and remain in the dwelling-house or part of the dwelling-house;

(b)   regulate the occupation of the dwelling-house by either or both of the spouses;

(c)   require the respondent to leave the dwelling-house or part of the dwelling-house; or

(d)   exclude the respondent from a defined area in which the dwelling-house is included.

(4)   Subsections (6) and (7) of section 33 apply to the exercise by the court of its powers under this section as they apply to the exercise by the court of its powers under subsection (3) of that section.

(5)   An order under this section must be limited so as to have effect for a specified period not exceeding six months, but may be extended on one or more occasions for a further specified period not exceeding six months.

38.   Neither cohabitant or former cohabitant entitled to occupy

(1)   This section applies if—

(a)   one cohabitant or former cohabitant and the other cohabitant or former cohabitant occupy a dwelling-house which is the home in which they live or lived together as husband and wife; but

(b)   neither of them is entitled to remain in occupation—

(i)   by virtue of a beneficial estate or interest or contract; or

(ii)   by virtue of any enactment giving him the right to remain in occupation.

(2)   Either of the parties may apply to the court for an order against the other under this section.

(3)   An order under this section may—

(a)   require the respondent to permit the applicant to enter and remain in the dwelling-house or part of the dwelling-house;

(b)   regulate the occupation of the dwelling-house by either or both of the parties;

(c)   require the respondent to leave the dwelling-house or part of the dwelling-house; or

(d)   exclude the respondent from a defined area in which the dwelling-house is included.

(4)   In deciding whether to exercise its powers to include one or more of the provisions referred to in subsection (3) ('a subsection (3) provision') and (if so) in what manner, the court shall have regard to all the circumstances including—

(a)   the housing needs and housing resources of each of the parties and of any relevant child;

(b)   the financial resources of each of the parties;

(c)   the likely effect of any order, or of any decision by the court not to exercise its powers under subsection (3), on the health, safety or well-being of the parties and of any relevant child;

(d)   the conduct of the parties in relation to each other and otherwise; and

(e)   the questions mentioned in subsection (5).

(5)   The questions are—

(a)   whether the applicant or any relevant child is likely to suffer significant harm attributable to conduct of the respondent if the subsection (3) provision is not included in the order; and

(b)   whether the harm likely to be suffered by the respondent or child if the provision is included is as great as or greater than the harm attributable to conduct of the respondent which is likely to be suffered by the applicant or child if the provision is not included.

(6)   An order under this section shall be limited so as to have effect for a specified period not exceeding six months, but may be extended on one occasion for a further specified period not exceeding six months.

8.2.3   NATURE OF PROCEEDINGS

FAMILY LAW ACT 1996

45.   Ex parte orders

(1)   The court may, in any case where it considers that it is just and convenient to do so, make an occupation order or a non-molestation order even though the respondent

has not been given such notice of the proceedings as would otherwise be required by rules of court.

(2) In determining whether to exercise its powers under subsection (1), the court shall have regard to all the circumstances including—

(a) any risk of significant harm to the applicant or a relevant child, attributable to conduct of the respondent, if the order is not made immediately;

(b) whether it is likely that the applicant will be deterred or prevented from pursuing the application if an order is not made immediately; and

(c) whether there is reason to believe that the respondent is aware of the proceedings but is deliberately evading service and that the applicant or a relevant child will be seriously prejudiced by the delay involved—

(i) where the court is a magistrates' court, in effecting service of proceedings; or

(ii) in any other case, in effecting substituted service.

(3) If the court makes an order by virtue of subsection (1) it must afford the respondent an opportunity to make representations relating to the order as soon as just and convenient at a full hearing.

(4) If, at a full hearing, the court makes an occupation order ('the full order'), then—

(a) for the purposes of calculating the maximum period for which the full order may be made to have effect, the relevant section is to apply as if the period for which the full order will have effect began on the date on which the initial order first had effect; and

(b) the provisions of section 36(10) or 38(6) as to the extension of orders are to apply as if the full order and the initial order were a single order.

(5) In this section—

'full hearing' means a hearing of which notice has been given to all the parties in accordance with rules of court;

'initial order' means an occupation order made by virtue of subsection (1); and

'relevant section' means section 33(10), 35(10), 36(10), 37(5) or 38(6).

8.2.4 UNDERTAKINGS

FAMILY LAW ACT 1996

46. Undertakings

(1) In any case where the court has power to make an occupation order or non-molestation order, the court may accept an undertaking from any party to the proceedings.

(2) No power of arrest may be attached to any undertaking given under subsection (1).

(3) The court shall not accept an undertaking under subsection (1) in any case where apart from this section a power of arrest would be attached to the order.

(4) An undertaking given to a court under subsection (1) is enforceable as if it were an order of the court.

(5) This section has effect without prejudice to the powers of the High Court and the county court apart from this section.

8.2.5 ENFORCEMENT

FAMILY LAW ACT 1996

47. Arrest for breach of order

(1) In this section 'a relevant order' means an occupation order or a non-molestation order.

(2) If—

(a) the court makes a relevant order; and

(b) it appears to the court that the respondent has used or threatened violence against the applicant or a relevant child,

it shall attach a power of arrest to one or more provisions of the order unless satisfied that in all the circumstances of the case the applicant or child will be adequately protected without such a power of arrest.

(3)   Subsection (2) does not apply in any case where the relevant order is made by virtue of section 45(1), but in such a case the court may attach a power of arrest to one or more provisions of the order if it appears to it—

(a)   that the respondent has used or threatened violence against the applicant or a relevant child; and

(b)   that there is a risk of significant harm to the applicant or child, attributable to conduct of the respondent, if the power of arrest is not attached to those provision immediately.

(4)   If, by virtue of subsection (3), the court attaches a power of arrest to an, provisions of a relevant order, it may provide that the power of arrest is to have effect for a shorter period than the other provisions of the order.

(5)   Any period specified for the purposes of subsection (4) may be extended by the court (on one or more occasions) on an application to vary or discharge the relevant order.

(6)   If, by virtue of subsection (2) or (3), a power of arrest is attached to certain provisions of an order, a constable may arrest without warrant a person whom he has reasonable cause for suspecting to be in breach of any such provision.

(7)   If a power of arrest is attached under subsection (2) or (3) to certain provisions of the order and the respondent is arrested under subsection (6)—

(a)   he must be brought before the relevant judicial authority within the period of 24 hours beginning at the time of his arrest; and

(b)   if the matter is not then disposed of forthwith, the relevant judicial authority before whom he is brought may remand him.

In reckoning for the purposes of this subsection any period of 24 hours, no account is to be taken of Christmas Day, Good Friday or any Sunday.

(8)   If the court has made a relevant order but—

(a)   has not attached a power of arrest under subsection (2) or (3) to any provisions of the order, or

(b)   has attached that power only to certain provisions of the order,

then, if at any time the applicant considers that the respondent has failed to comply with the order, he may apply to the relevant judicial authority for the issue of a warrant for the arrest of the respondent.

(9)   The relevant judicial authority shall not issue a warrant on an application under subsection (8) unless—

(a)   the application is substantiated on oath; and

(b)   the relevant judicial authority has reasonable grounds for believing that the respondent has failed to comply with the order.

(10)   If a person is brought before a court by virtue of a warrant issued under subsection (9) and the court does not dispose of the matter forthwith, the court may remand him.

(11)   Schedule 5 (which makes provision corresponding to that applying in magistrates' courts in civil cases under sections 128 and 129 of the Magistrates' Courts Act 1980) has effect in relation to the powers of the High Court and a county court to remand a person by virtue of this section.

(12)   If a person remanded under this section is granted bail (whether in the High Court or a county court under Schedule 5 or in a magistrates' court under section 128 or 129 of the Magistrates' Courts Act 1980), he may be required by the relevant judicial authority to comply, before release on bail or later, with such requirements as appear to that authority to be necessary to secure that he does not interfere with witnesses or otherwise obstruct the course of justice.

8.3   Stalking

PROTECTION FROM HARASSMENT ACT 1997

1.   Prohibition of harassment

(1)   A person must not pursue a course of conduct—

(a)   which amounts to harassment of another, and

(b)   which he knows or ought to know amounts to harassment of the other.

(2)   For the purposes of this section, the person whose course of conduct is in question ought to know that it amounts to harassment of another if a reasonable person in possession of the same information would think the course of conduct amounted to harassment of the other.

(3)   Subsection (1) does not apply to a course of conduct if the person who pursued it shows—

(a)   that it was pursued for the purpose of preventing or detecting crime,

(b)   that it was pursued under any enactment or rule of law or to comply with any condition or requirement imposed by any person under any enactment, or

(c)   that in the particular circumstances the pursuit of the course of conduct was reasonable.

2.   Offence of harassment

(1)   A person who pursues a course of conduct in breach of section 1 is guilty of an offence.

(2)   A person guilty of an offence under this section is liable on summary conviction to imprisonment for a term not exceeding six months, or a fine not exceeding level 5 on the standard scale, or both.

(3)   In section 24(2) of the Police and Criminal Evidence Act 1984 (arrestable offences), after paragraph (m) there is inserted—

'(n)   an offence under section 2 of the Protection from Harassment Act 1997 (harassment).'.

3.   Civil remedy

(1)   An actual or apprehended breach of section 1 may be the subject of a claim in civil proceedings by the person who is or may be the victim of the course of conduct in question.

(2)   On such a claim, damages may be awarded for (among other things) any anxiety caused by the harassment and any financial loss resulting from the harassment.

(3)   Where—

(a)   in such proceedings the High Court or a county court grants an injunction for the purpose of restraining the defendant from pursuing any conduct which amounts to harassment, and

(b)   the plaintiff considers that the defendant has done anything which he is prohibited from doing by the injunction,

the plaintiff may apply for the issue of a warrant for the arrest of the defendant.

(4)   An application under subsection (3) may be made—

(a)   where the injunction was granted by the High Court, to a judge of that court, and

(b)   where the injunction was granted by a county court, to a judge or district judge of that or any other county court.

(5)   The judge or district judge to whom an application under subsection (3) is made may only issue a warrant if—

(a)   the application is substantiated on oath, and

(b)   the judge or district judge has reasonable grounds for believing that the defendant has done anything which he is prohibited from doing by the injunction.

(6)   Where—

(a)   the High Court or a county court grants an injunction for the purpose mentioned in subsection (3)(a), and

(b)   without reasonable excuse the defendant does anything which he is prohibited from doing by the injunction,

he is guilty of an offence.

(7)   Where a person is convicted of an offence under subsection (6) in respect of any conduct, that conduct is not punishable as a contempt of court.

(8)   A person cannot be convicted of an offence under subsection (6) in respect of any conduct which has been punished as a contempt of court.

(9)   A person guilty of an offence under subsection (6) is liable—

(a)   on conviction on indictment, to imprisonment for a term not exceeding five years, or a fine, or both, or

(b)   on summary conviction, to imprisonment for a term not exceeding six months, or a fine not exceeding the statutory maximum, or both.

4. Putting people in fear of violence

(1) A person whose course of conduct causes another to fear, on at least two occasions, that violence will be used against him is guilty of an offence if he knows or ought to know that his course of conduct will cause the other so to fear on each of those occasions.

(2) For the purposes of this section, the person whose course of conduct is in question ought to know that it will cause another to fear that violence will be used against him on any occasion if a reasonable person in possession of the same information would think the course of conduct would cause the other so to fear on that occasion.

(4) A person guilty of an offence under this section is liable—

(a) on conviction on indictment, to imprisonment for a term not exceeding five years, or a fine, or both, or

(b) on summary conviction, to imprisonment for a term not exceeding six months, or a fine not exceeding the statutory maximum, or both.

(5) If on the trial on indictment of a person charged with an offence under this section the jury find him not guilty of the offence charged, they may find him guilty of an offence under section 2.

(6) The Crown Court has the same powers and duties in relation to a person who is by virtue of subsection (5) convicted before it of an offence under section 2 as a magistrates' court would have on convicting him of the offence.

5. Restraining orders

(1) A court sentencing or otherwise dealing with a person ('the defendant') convicted of an offence under section 2 or 4 may (as well as sentencing him or dealing with him in any other way) make an order under this section.

(2) The order may, for the purpose of protecting the victim of the offence, or any other person mentioned in the order, from further conduct which—

(a) amounts to harassment, or

(b) will cause a fear of violence,

prohibit the defendant from doing anything described in the order.

(3) The order may have effect for a specified period or until further order.

(4) The prosecutor, the defendant or any other person mentioned in the order may apply to the court which made the order for it to be varied or discharged by a further order.

(5) If without reasonable excuse the defendant does anything which he is prohibited from doing by an order under this section, he is guilty of an offence.

(6) A person guilty of an offence under this section is liable—

(a) on conviction on indictment, to imprisonment for a term not exceeding five years, or a fine, or both, or

(b) on summary conviction, to imprisonment for a term not exceeding six months, or a fine not exceeding the statutory maximum, or both.

Lawson-Cruttenden, T, The Government's Proposed Stalking Law — a Discussion Paper [1996] Fam Law 755

THE GOVERNMENT'S PROPOSALS

These are still relatively vague and are not presently supported by draft legislation. In the paper which Home Office Minister David Maclean presented to the Suzy Lamplugh Trust conference the proposals were specifically qualified by the following words: 'I cannot yet tell you how the Parliamentary Draftsman would suggest putting it'. However, in essence it seems that what the Government seeks to deal with is, essentially, the following:

The use of words or behaviour, on more than one occasion, which causes a person (either A) to fear that violence would be used against him (high level criminal offence) (or B) to be harassed, alarmed or distressed (lower level criminal offence) where this is either intentional or occurs in circumstances where a reasonable person would have realised that this would be the effect.

Consequently, there are to be two new criminal offences, described respectively as high level and low level offences, and a new statutory (civil) tort of molestation in exactly the same terms as the lower level offence. The high level offence is to carry a maximum penalty of 5 years' imprisonment and an unlimited fine, and the low level offence carries a maximum penalty of 6 months' imprisonment and/or a £5000 fine. Breach of a civil injunction under the new tort of molestation is to constitute a high level offence, and is automatically an arrestable offence. Whilst the criminal courts would not have powers to award the equivalent of interlocutory civil injunctions, on conviction they are to have powers to impose 'restraint orders' ordering the convicted defendant not to contact or come near the victim. The police are to have powers to search a suspected stalker's property, without a warrant, for evidence such as letters, videotapes and photographs. A defence is proposed to the lower level offence of acting 'reasonably and necessarily in the pursuit of a business, trade, profession or other lawful activities'. It is not proposed to define further the apparent offence of stalking.

PROBLEMS WITH THE EXISTING CIVIL LAW
It is submitted that the civil law presently offers a reasonably effective remedy against stalkers. However, it suffers four difficulties as follows.

(1)   The civil courts are still relatively expensive. Legal aid is limited. Many plaintiffs are reluctant to compound the difficulties of dealing with stalkers with the need to resource what could be an expensive action.

(2)   The police are often reluctant to interfere in civil matters, and as a result police assistance can be limited.

(3)   There is no power of arrest at common law.

(4)   The contempt procedure is not streamlined and is very bureaucratic.

It is submitted that there is no need for a new civil tort of molestation as proposed by the Government, and neither is there any need for a specially designed injunction under that tort. The civil courts have wide powers to deal with stalkers following *Burris* v *Azadani* [1996] 1 FLR 266, and it is submitted that these powers are sufficient. The Government proposes to deal with the problems outlined above in points (2)–(4) by making it a criminal offence to breach a civil injunction. Consequently, it is proposed that the police would immediately arrest an alleged contemnor and charge him with a criminal offence. The author would prefer to see the introduction (by statute) of a discretionary common law power of arrest, and for a much more streamlined contempt procedure. Such a reform would mean that 'stalkers' who breach injunctions could be arrested and dealt with under the civil contempt procedure.

PROBLEMS WITH THE EXISTING CRIMINAL LAW
It is submitted that the criminal law has three major problems, particularly when dealing with stalkers, as follows.

(1)   The criminal burden of proof which places (quite properly) high evidential hurdles in the way of prosecution.

(2)   Criminal courts only have power on conviction. Consequently, it is conviction or nothing.

(3)   Criminal courts do not have power to order, at interlocutory level, the equivalent of civil injunctions, compulsory medical treatment or counselling (bail restrictions are inadequate).

The problems in points (2) and (3) above have been emphasised by the acquittal of Chambers in September 1996 of the relatively new offence of psychological assault. Notwithstanding that he had clearly perpetrated a long and concerted campaign against his victim, his acquittal meant that the courts could neither impose an injunction nor force him to undergo medical or counselling treatment.

THE GOVERNMENT'S PROPOSALS REGARDING THE CRIMINAL BURDEN OF PROOF
The Government's proposals in relation to the criminal burden of proof appear to be twofold, namely:

(1) the complete absence of a definition of the words or behaviour which it seeks to criminalise and;

(2) an extremely low offence threshold, namely words or behaviour used on 'more than one occasion'.

Consequently, the offence is apparently going to be drafted entirely by reference to the impact that such words or behaviour have on the alleged victim. Such impact is not to be subjective to the victim, but is to be measured by reference to an objective test as to whether 'a reasonable person would have realised that this behaviour would cause the alleged victim to fear the use of violence or to be harassed, alarmed or distressed'. In adopting this wide definition the Government is choosing to ignore the anti-stalking laws passed in the other common law jurisdictions, as well as a legal definition of stalking which was approved in committee stage in the House of Lords, and which is set out in Table 2 (below). It is submitted that very careful thought needs to be given to a definition of the words and behaviour which it is sought to criminalise. Whilst it is accepted that stalkers are often skilled at evading the law, it is doubtful whether juries will be happy to convict vast numbers of stalkers whose words and behaviour are mostly not legally defined.

The Government is not proposing to give the criminal courts powers equivalent to the interlocutory civil injunctions used so effectively in the civil courts. It is submitted that the most effective way of dealing with stalkers will be to arrest them for a properly defined offence, bring them before the summary courts, and make common sense orders against them without the necessity of making a criminal finding of guilt. Consequently, it is submitted that the restraint orders proposed by the Government on conviction, should bite not on conviction but should follow precisely the tests laid down in *Burris* v *Azadani*. This would convert restraint orders into the equivalent of interlocutory civil injunctions, although it is submitted that they should provide for compulsory medical treatment or counselling when appropriate. By enabling the criminal courts to make restraint orders in this way, it is submitted that much of the task of combating stalkers can be left to the police (who have the resources and the powers of arrest) and the magistrates' courts. Those courts will be able to use the civil law which is reasonably effective in this area, and orders would be made on the civil burden of proof, on a balance of probabilities, without the need to ruin previous good character.

Table 2: Definition of 'Stalking'

SECTION 1, JANET ANDERSON MP's BILL — MAY 1996
(as approved by the House of Lords in Committee Stage)

1(1) . . . 'stalking' shall mean engaging in a course of conduct whereby a person:
  (a) follows, loiters near, watches or approaches another person;
  (b) telephones (which for the avoidance of doubt shall include telephoning a person but remaining silent during the call), contacts by other electronic means, or otherwise contacts another person;
  (c) loiters near, watches, approaches or enters a place where another person lives, works or repeatedly visits;
  (d) interferes with property which does not belong to him and is in the possession of another person;
  (e) leaves offensive, unwarranted or unsolicited material at a place where another person lives, works or regularly visits;
  (f) gives offensive, unwarranted or unsolicited material to another person; or
  (g) does any other act or acts in connection with another person

so as to be reasonably likely to cause that other person to feel harassed, alarmed, distressed or to fear for his safety . . . (objective test); or for that of one or more third persons to whom he has a duty of protection or with whom he is associated.

CONCLUSION

The leading article in *The Times* on 19 October 1996 ('it's bad to stalk—but the law needs very careful drafting') describes the spectrum of behaviour displayed by stalkers as 'at one end . . . is the besotted adolescent, in the middle is a slightly creepy obsessive, and at the far end is the determined stalker'. Enabling the magistrates' courts to make restraint orders on the civil burden of proof will, it is submitted, deal with the 'besotted adolescent' and the 'slightly creepy obsessive', neither of whom the courts will be keen to give a criminal record. This will, it is hoped, deal with over 90% of the stalking problem and would leave the full weight of the criminal law to be applied to only the most determined stalkers. Juries are likely to convict determined stalkers only when an offence of stalking is properly defined, and only when the burden of proof is discharged.

The criminal burden of proof is always going to impose a difficult hurdle for the victims of stalkers. This is why, it is submitted, the civil law will always remain the most effective way of dealing with these problems. The way ahead must lie in the introduction of the civil law into the criminal jurisdiction. In this way, victims of stalkers can turn to the police immediately for help, and the police can mount prosecutions in the magistrates' courts knowing that those courts have powers to make common sense orders which, in most cases, would provide a legal solution to the problem. Breach of a common sense order would itself constitute a criminal offence and would enable the courts to bring the correct sanctions to bear. It is hoped that the Government's proposals will refine themselves into an emphasis on the criminal jurisdiction and that this jurisdiction will have the effective powers which it needs to deal with this very difficult problem.

This item represents the general position as at 1 November 1996. Rapid changes could occur between then and publication.

8.4   End of Chapter Assessment Question

Four years ago Ingrid began to cohabit with Max, in his three bedroomed house. Ingrid has no rights of ownership.

Max has always been temperamental with frequent bouts of depression. In the last 18 months these have become far more common, and Max has started to exhibit violent tendencies. Ingrid, in the last two months, has visited the local hospital's accident and emergency department twice with broken ribs, bruising, and a dislocated shoulder after being attacked by Max.

Max is always apologetic when he realises what he has done and always swears never to do anything like that again.

Advise Ingrid:

(a)   what rights she has to obtain protection under the law in force before October 1997;

(b)   whether those rights will change under the Family Law Act 1996.

8.5   End of Chapter Assessment Outline Answer

Given the fact that the Family Law Act 1996 is now in force with regard to domestic violence, you may have wondered why you were asked to consider the preceding legislation. By applying the two schemes to a problem-type scenario, you should hopefully have learnt enough about the legislative regimes to enable you to identify the similarity between the provisions, and also to highlight the ways in which the new legislation is different. This will also assist you in the event that you have a discursive-type essay requiring you to compare the two systems. The outline answer here will only consider 'pure' domestic violence legislation — the criminal law and the Protection from Harassment Act 1997 will not be considered (this is not to say this would be inappropriate in an examination).

So, starting with (a), what are Ingrid's rights to protection under the law in force prior to September 1997? Clearly here you are being required to discuss the remedies under the Domestic Violence and Matrimonial Proceedings Act 1976 and/or the Domestic Proceedings and Magistrates' Courts Act 1978. You should have noticed from the beginning that you are dealing with a cohabitant, and not a spouse, and this will have an impact on the legislative remedies available. Therefore, the latter legislation will not be relevant to the scenario, since the DPMCA 1978 only provides protection to spouses (see, for example, s. 16(1) of the Act for verification of this). Consequently, Ingrid would have to be advised to apply for any remedy under the DVMPA 1976.

Under DVMPA 1976 Ingrid may be able to apply for two protective orders — a non-molestation order or an ouster order (both under s. 1). The former is an injunctive order designed to prevent the respondent from molesting the applicant (and can also cover a child living with the applicant). The latter enables the court to exclude the respondent from the matrimonial home, or specified area of the matrimonial home (s. 1(1)(c)). If Ingrid is not in the home she could ask the court to grant her an order to enable her to return (s. 1(1)(d)). The fact that the DVMPA 1976 speaks in terms of the 'matrimonial home' is not that significant since the Act applies 'to a man and a woman who are living with each other in the same household as husband and wife as it applies to the parties to a marriage' (s. 1(2)).

In dealing with a non-molestation order there are no criteria for the court to apply set out in the Act itself. Molestaton does not require violence to occur before the court can make an order. Indeed in *Horner* (1982) the molestation was proven (*inter alia*) by the husband hanging 'scurrilous posters' outside the wife's place of work. However, in Ingrid's situation due to the violence that has occurred there will be sufficient evidence to satisfy the need for some form of protection. It is useful to note that medical evidence from the hospital and Ingrid's General Practitioner will be needed to prove the consequences of Max's behaviour. In addition to advising Ingrid that action could be taken to obtain a non-molestation order, you would also have to advise her that the court has the ability to attach a power of arrest to the order which is intended to provide an extra level of protection. Under the DVMPA 1976, s. 2 the court's powers arise when the judge 'is satisfied that the other party had caused actual bodily harm to the applicant — this has happened here and the court may exercise its discretion, since attaching a power of arrest is not obligatory on the judge. Another factor to be considered in the non-molestation order is whether the court would accept an undertaking from Max. An undertaking is not an order as such (although there is the scope for the court to treat it as such if breached), but is merely a promise made by the respondent not to act in a harassing or violent manner towards the applicant in future. Undertakings can be accepted even though there would appear to be a high level of violence involved in the situation. Finally you would have to advise Ingrid that a non-molestation order, if granted, will not always last indefinitely. The normal perception is that these domestic violence orders are short term, to enable the parties to sort things out. Ingrid may therefore find she only has a limited duration for her protection (usually three months).

In addition to advising Ingrid on the nature of the order, you would also have to advise on the process to obtain the orders. Ingrid could seek a non-molestation order on an *ex parte* basis, if the matter is deemed serious. It is possible to apply on notice, and for domestic violence applications only a short notice period is established. If an *ex parte* application is made, any order that results will be for a very short duration to cover the period before an *inter partes* hearing can take place.

With regard to the ouster situation, it is perfectly permissible for Ingrid to try to oust Max from the 'matrimonial home' under the DVMPA 1976, although she would have to be advised that the courts are not keen to do so due to the Draconian nature of the order. An ouster order under the Act is, on the face of it, subject to the discretion of the court with regard to the factors that will encourage the court to make the order. However, you should be advising Ingrid that the court is required to apply certain criteria to the case before they make the ouster. These criteria are to be found in the Matrimonial Homes Act 1983 (which has been repealed by the Family Law Act 1996). The reason for the importation of the criteria is the House of Lords' decision in *Richards* v *Richards*. Hence the court will look at the parties' conduct, their respective needs and financial resources, the needs of children (if any) and the circumstances of the case. In Ingrid's situation due to the fact that she has no ownership rights in the property, the court will need to consider carefully whether it will be equitable to oust Max from his home and if they do decide to grant an order it is likely to be for a short period of time.

An ouster order *may* be sought on an *ex parte* basis, however it will be the minority of cases that are actually granted an order without the owning party/respondent being present in court.

Turning now to (b), will Ingrid's rights and remedies be different under the Family Law Act 1996 provisions? In the main, they will not, as the 1996 Act's regime is remarkably similar to the DVMPA 1976. There are greater differences between the FLA 1996 and the DPMCA 1978.

Starting with the physical violence, Ingrid can still seek a non-molestation order under s. 42 of the Act as she will be an associated person (the definition of associated person is found in s. 62). The acts that will provide evidence for an order are not specified, hence the meaning of molestation will be the same as under the case law for the DVMPA 1976. The violence inflicted upon Ingrid by Max will clearly be caught by the FLA 1996. Unlike the DVMPA 1976 the court has to consider certain criteria before it can make the order. These are set out in s. 42(5) as being 'all the circumstances including the need to secure the health, safety and well-being [of the applicant]'. In reality the application of the criteria will not make that much difference, albeit that the health, safety and well-being factors promote a more victim-centred approach to the order. The FLA 1996 does not set a minimum or maximum duration for the order, and hence it is still open to the court to make short duration orders in the expectation that the parties will sort the matter out by themselves (presumably by reconciling or by divorce etc.). The court still retains the ability to attach a power of arrest to the non-molestation order although it is important to note that there seems to be a greater emphasis in the FLA 1996 in the court so doing. Powers of arrest are covered in s. 47 and are expressed thus:

(2)   If—
(a)   the court makes a [non-molestation] order; and
(b)   it appears to the court that the respondent has used or threatened violence to the applicant
it shall attach a power of arrest . . . unless satisfied that in all the circumstances of the case the applicant . . . will be adequately protected without such a power of arrest.

Hence the indication within the Act is that a power of arrest should be made unless it is unnecessary. It would seem that it is for the respondent to show this rather than the previous scheme where the applicant had to show the need for a power of arrest to be attached. Equally, the respondent does not have to have used violence, the mere threat will be sufficient to trigger s. 47. There still remains the possibility for the court to accept an undertaking from Max rather than to impose a non-molestation order. Undertakings are dealt with in s. 46, and are little changed. However it should be noted that if the court attaches a power of arrest to an order, then it cannot accept an undertaking from the respondent.

On the procedural side the court can still be approached to make the order on an *ex parte* basis. The ability of the court to make orders *ex parte* is dealt with in s. 45, which lays down factors for the court to consider before making the order requested. These factors include (*inter alia*) the risk of harm to the applicant if the order is not made immediately or the respondent is deliberately avoiding service of proceedings. It should also be noted that the courts empowered to make orders for non-molestation (and orders dealing with occupation of the home) have been widened — it may be possible to obtain the orders from magistrates sitting as the Family Proceedings Court.

With regard to occupation of the 'matrimonial home', the FLA 1996 lays down a series of different regimes and factors for the court to apply when deciding to 'oust' one party from the home. The FLA 1996 therefore tries to avoid the complexity of the previous mixture of statute and case law. The key to advising Ingrid is to establish the status of the two parties and fit this to the legislation. As Ingrid and Max are not spouses or former spouses ss. 33 and 35 will not be relevant. Max has a right to occupy the home due to his ownership — Ingrid has no such rights. Therefore you will be advising Ingrid under s. 36, FLA 1996 which applies to cohabitants or former cohabitants with no existing rights to occupy. Under s. 36 Ingrid can seek to remove Max from the home and for her to remain there, or to re-enter the property if she has been excluded by Max. Before the court will make an occupation order under s. 36 there are several factors to be considered. These are set out in s. 36(6) and (8). In addition to the factors within the section itself, the court is also required to have regard to the fact that the couple have not shown the commitment involved in marriage (s. 41). In addition to the FLA 1996 establishing clear criteria/factors for making the order, it also establishes clear periods of duration for the order. As Ingrid is a cohabitant, she will be entitled on the first application under s. 36 to an order of a maximim period of six months' duration. She will be permitted to apply for an extension to the order and the court can make one such extension. This too will last for a maximum of six months. Thereafter she will have no rights under the FLA 1996 to the property. The court can attach a power of arrest to the occupation order (using the same criteria as for the non-molestation order) and can also consider making the order *ex parte* (again using the same criteria as for the non-molestation order).

As you can hopefully see, there is a lot of information that can be included within this answer — as indicated at the start, knowing the previous legislative code will inform and guide your knowledge on the newly implemented FLA 1996.

CHAPTER NINE

CHILD SUPPORT

9.1 The Child Support Act 1991

9.1.1 THE CHILD SUPPORT AGENCY

CPAG, *Child Support Handbook*, 1996/1997

CSA PERFORMANCE TARGETS

Targets for 1995/96

Performance to date

£300 million of maintenance to be collected either by the CSA or paid direct by absent parents to parents with care (£140 million and £160 million respectively)

£177 million collected in first 9 months of 1995/96 (£87 million via the CSA and £90 millon direct between parents)

90% of parents with care to receive payments within 10 working days of receipt by the CSA from the absent parent

97% of payments made within 10 working days

to achieve a continuing improvement in accuracy so that in at least 75% of cases checked during March 1996, the assessment will be correct

72% of assessments checked in November 1995 were correct

60% of new applications to be cleared within 26 weeks, and no more than 10% of all applications to be over 52 weeks old at 31 March 1996

39% of applications cleared within 26 weeks and 14% of applications awaiting assessments were over 52 weeks old at the end of November 1995

50% of second-tier reviews to be cleared within 13 weeks, 80% within 26 weeks, and no more than 20% to be taking longer than 26 weeks at 31 March 1996

52% of second-tier reviews cleared within 13 weeks, 68% cleared within 26 weeks, and 23% outstanding for more than 26 weeks at end of November 1995

to achieve a 65% client satisfaction score determined by an independent national survey

44% client satisfaction score in 1994/95 (down from 61% in 1993/94)

to manage resources so as to deliver the business plan within the gross budget allocation of £183 million

forecast in line with actual expenditure

CPAG, *Child Support Handbook*, 1997/1998

CSA PERFORMANCE TARGETS

Targets for 1996/97	*Performance at 1966/97 mid-year*	*Targets for 1997/98*
£380-400 million of maintenance to be collected either by the CSA or paid direct by absent parents to parents with care	£183 million collected £112 million via the CSA and £71 million direct between parents)	£500 million to be collected or arranged for direct payment
95% of parents with care to receive payments within 10 working days of receipt by the CSA	98% of payments made within 10 working days	97% of payments to be made within 10 working days
To achieve a continuing improvement in accuracy so that, in at least 85% of cases checked during March 1997, the assessment will be correct	80% of assessments checked in September 1996 were correct	Cash value of 85% of assessments checked in the year to be correct
60% of new applications to be cleared within 26 weeks, and no more than 10% of all applications to be over 52 weeks old at 31 March 1997	51% of applications cleared within 26 weeks and 15% of outstanding applications were over 52 weeks old at the end of September 1996	60% of new applications to be cleared within 26 weeks, and no more than 5% of all applications to be over 52 weeks old on 31 March 1998
—	—	At least 525,000 maintenance application to be cleared
55% of second-tier reviews to be cleared within 13 weeks, 80% within 26 weeks, and no more than 15% to be older than 26 weeks at 31 March 1997	56% of second-tier reviews cleared within 13 weeks, 77% cleared within 26 weeks, and 41% outstanding for more than 26 weeks at end of September 1996	60% of second-tier reviews to be cleared within 13 weeks and 95% within 26 weeks.

9.1.2   TO WHOM DOES THE ACT APPLY?

CHILD SUPPORT ACT 1991

3.   Meaning of certain terms used in this Act
   (1)   A child is a 'qualifying child' if—
      (a)   one of his parents is, in relation to him, an absent parent; or
      (b)   both of his parents are, in relation to him, absent parents.
   (2)   The parent of any child is an 'absent parent', in relation to him, if—
      (a)   that parent is not living in the same household with the child; and
      (b)   the child has his home with a person who is, in relation to him, a person with care.
   (3)   A person is a 'person with care', in relation to any child, if he is a person—
      (a)   with whom the child has his home;
      (b)   who usually provides day to day care for the child (whether exclusively or in conjunction with any other person); and
      (c)   who does not fall within a prescribed category of person.
   (4)   The Secretary of State shall not, under subsection (3)(c), prescribe as a category—

(a)   parents;

(b)   guardians;

(c)   persons in whose favour residence orders under section 8 of the Children Act 1989 are in force;

(d)   in Scotland, persons having the right to custody of a child.

(5)   For the purposes of this Act there may be more than one person with care in relation to the same qualifying child.

(6)   Periodical payments which are required to be paid in accordance with a maintenance assessment are referred to in this Act as 'child support maintenance'.

(7)   Expressions are defined in this section only for the purposes of this Act.

55.   Meaning of 'child'

(1)   For the purposes of this Act a person is a child if—

(a)   he is under the age of 16;

(b)   he is under the age of 19 and receiving full-time education (which is not advanced education)—

(i)   by attendance at a recognised educational establishment; or

(ii)   elsewhere, if the education is recognised by the Secretary of Stare; or

(c)   he does not fall within paragraph (a) or (b) but—

(i)   he is under the age of 18, and

(ii)   prescribed conditions are satisfied with respect to him.

(2)   A person is not a child for the purposes of this Act if he—

(a)   is or has been married;

(b)   has celebrated a marriage which is void; or

(c)   has celebrated a marriage in respect of which a decree of nullity has been granted.

(3)   In this section—

'advanced education' means education of a prescribed description; and

'recognised educational establishment' means an establishment recognised by the Secretary of State for the purposes of this section as being, or as comparable to, a university, college or school.

(4)   Where a person has reached the age of 16, the Secretary of State may recognise education provided for him otherwise than at a recognised educational establishment only if the Secretary of State is satisfied that education was being so provided for him immediately before he reached the age of 16.

(5)   The Secretary of State may provide that in prescribed circumstances education is or is not to be treated for the purposes of this section as being full-time.

(6)   In determining whether a person falls within subsection (1)(b), no account shall be taken of such interruptions in his education as may be prescribed.

(7)   The Secretary of State may by regulations provide that a person who ceases to fall within subsection (1) shall be treated as continuing to fall within that subsection for a prescribed period.

(8)   No person shall be treated as continuing to fall within subsection (1) by virtue of regulations made under subsection (7) after the end of the week in which he reaches the age of 19.

54.   Interpretation

'parent', in relation to any child, means any person who is in law the mother or father of the child;

'parent with care' means a person who is, in relation to a child, both a parent and a person with care.

'parental responsibility' has the same meaning as in the Children Act 1989;

'person with care' has the meaning given in section 3(3); . . .

9.1.3   WHEN WILL THE CSA 1991 BE USED?

CHILD SUPPORT ACT 1991

4.   Child support maintenance

(1)   A person who is, in relation to any qualifying child or any qualifying children, either the person with care or the absent parent may apply to the Secretary of State for

a maintenance assessment to be made under this Act with respect to that child, or any of those children.

(2)   Where a maintenance assessment has been made in response to an application under this section the Secretary of State may, if the person with care or absent parent with respect to whom the assessment was made applies to him under this subsection, arrange for—

(a)   the collection of the child support maintenance payable in accordance with the assessment;

(b)   the enforcement of the obligation to pay child support maintenance in accordance with the assessment.

(3)   Where an application under subsection (2) for the enforcement of the obligation mentioned in subsection (2)(b) authorises the Secretary of State to take steps to enforce that obligation whenever he considers it necessary to do so, the Secretary of State may act accordingly.

(4)   A person who applies to the Secretary of State under this section shall, so far as that person reasonably can, comply with such regulations as may be made by the Secretary of State with a view to the Secretary of State or the child support officer being provided with the information which is required to enable—

(a)   the absent parent to be traced (where that is necessary);

(b)   the amount of child support maintenance payable by the absent parent to be assessed; and

(c)   that amount to be recovered from the absent parent.

(5)   Any person who has applied to the Secretary of State under this section may at any time request him to cease acting under this section.

(6)   It shall be the duty of the Secretary of State to comply with any request made under subsection (5) (but subject to any regulations made under subsection (8)).

(7)   The obligation to provide information which is imposed by subsection (4)—

(a)   shall not apply in such circumstances as may be prescribed; and

(b)   may, in such circumstances as may be prescribed, be waived by the Secretary of State.

(8)   The Secretary of State may by regulations make such incidental, supplemental or transitional provision as he thinks appropriate with respect to cases in which he is requested to cease to act under this section.

(9)   No application may be made under this section if there is in force with respect to the person with care and absent parent in question a maintenance assessment made in response to an application under section 6.

(10)   No application may be made at any time under this section with respect to a qualifying child or any qualifying children if—

(a)   there is in force a written maintenance agreement made before 5th April 1993, or a maintenance order, in respect of that child or those children and the person who is, at that time, the absent parent; or

(b)   benefit is being paid to, or in respect of, a parent with care of that child or those children.

(11)   In subsection (10) 'benefit' means any benefit which is mentioned in, or prescribed by regulations under, section 6(1).

6.   Applications by those receiving benefit

(1)   Where income support, family credit or any other benefit of a prescribed kind is claimed by or in respect of, or paid to or in respect of, the parent of a qualifying child she shall, if—

(a)   she is a person with care of the child; and

(b)   she is required to do so by the Secretary of State,

authorise the Secretary of State to take action under this Act to recover child support maintenance from the absent parent.

(2)   The Secretary of State shall not require a person ('the parent') to give him the authorisation mentioned in subsection (1) if he considers that there are reasonable grounds for believing that—

(a)   if the parent were to be required to give that authorisation; or

(b)   if she were to give it,

there would be a risk of her, or of any child living with her, suffering harm or undue distress as a result.

(3)   Subsection (2) shall not apply if the parent requests the Secretary of State to disregard it.

(4)   The authorisation mentioned in subsection (1) shall extend to all children of the absent parent in relation to whom the parent first mentioned in subsection (1) is a person with care.

(5)   That authorisation shall be given, without unreasonable delay, by completing and returning to the Secretary of State an application—

(a)   for the making of a maintenance assessment with respect to the qualifying child or qualifying children; and

(b)   for the Secretary of State to take action under this Act to recover, on her behalf, the amount of child support maintenance so assessed.

(6)   Such an application shall be made on a form ('a maintenance application form') provided by the Secretary of State.

(7)   A maintenance application form shall indicate in general terms the effect of completing and returning it.

(8)   Subsection (1) has effect regardless of whether any of the benefits mentioned there is payable with respect to any qualifying child.

(9)   A person who is under the duty imposed by subsection (1) shall, so far as she reasonably can, comply with such regulations as may be made by the Secretary of State with a view to the Secretary of State or the child support officer being provided with the information which is required to enable—

(a)   the absent parent to be traced;

(b)   the amount of child support maintenance payable by the absent parent to be assessed; and

(c)   that amount to be recovered from the absent parent.

(10)   The obligation to provide information which is imposed by subsection (9)—

(a)   shall not apply in such circumstances as may be prescribed: and

(b)   may, in such circumstances as may be prescribed, be waived by the Secretary of State.

(11)   A person with care who has authorised the Secretary of State under subsection (1) but who subsequently ceases to fall within that subsection may request the Secretary of State to cease acting under this section.

(12)   It shall be the duty of the Secretary of State to comply with any request made under subsection (11) (but subject to any regulations made under subsection (13)).

(13)   The Secretary of State may by regulations make such incidental or transitional provision as he thinks appropriate with respect to cases in which he is requested under subsection (11) to cease to act under this section.

(14)   The fact that a maintenance assessment is in force with respect to a person with care shall not prevent the making of a new maintenance assessment with respect to her in response to an application under this section.

9.1.3.1   Must be used

CHILD SUPPORT ACT 1991

46.   Failure to comply with obligations imposed by section 6

(1)   This section applies where any person ('the parent')—

(a)   fails to comply with a requirement imposed on her by the Secretary of State under section 6(1); or

(b)   fails to comply with any regulation made under section 6(9).

(2)   A child support officer may serve written notice on the parent requiring her, before the end of the specified period, either to comply or to give him her reasons for failing to do so.

(3)   When the specified period has expired, the child support officer shall consider whether, having regard to any reasons given by the parent, there are reasonable grounds for believing that, if she were to be required to comply, there would be a risk of her or of any children living with her suffering harm or undue distress as a result of complying.

(4)   If the child support officer considers that there are such reasonable grounds, he shall—

(a)   take no further action under this section in relation to the failure in question; and

(b)   notify the parent, in writing, accordingly.

(5)   If the child support officer considers that there are no such reasonable grounds, he may, except in prescribed circumstances, give a reduced benefit direction with respect to the parent.

(6)   Where the child support officer gives a reduced benefit direction he shall send a copy of it to the parent.

(7)   Any person who is aggrieved by a decision of a child support officer to give a reduced benefit direction may appeal to a child support appeal tribunal against that decision.

(8)   Sections 20(2) to (4) and 21 shall apply in relation to appeals under subsection (7) as they apply in relation to appeals under section 20.

(9)   A reduced benefit direction shall take effect on such date as may be specified in the direction.

(10)   Reasons given in response to a notice under subsection (2) may be given either in writing or orally.

(11)   In this section—

'comply' means to comply with the requirement or with the regulation in question; and 'complied' and 'complying' shall be construed accordingly;

'reduced benefit direction' means a direction, binding on the adjudication officer, that the amount payable by way of any relevant benefit to, or in respect of, the parent concerned be reduced by such amount, and for such period, as may be prescribed;

'relevant benefit' means income support, family credit or any other benefit of a kind prescribed for the purposes of section 6; and

'specified', in relation to any notice served under this section, means specified in the notice; and the period to be specified shall be determined in accordance with regulations made by the Secretary of State.

2.   Welfare of children: the general principle

Where, in any case which falls to be dealt with under this Act, the Secretary of State or any child support officer is considering the exercise of any discretionary power conferred by this Act, he shall have regard to the welfare of any child likely to be affected by his decision.

9.1.3.2   May be used

CHILD SUPPORT ACT 1991

8.   Role of the courts with respect to maintenance for children

(1)   This subsection applies in any case where a child support officer would have jurisdiction to make a maintenance assessment with respect to a qualifying child and an absent parent of his on an application duly made by a person entitled to apply for such an assessment with respect to that child.

(2)   Subsection (1) applies even though the circumstances of the case are such that a child support officer would not make an assessment if it were applied for.

(3)   In any case where subsection (1) applies, no court shall exercise any power which it would otherwise have to make, vary or revive any maintenance order in relation to the child and absent parent concerned.

9.1.4   AVOIDING THE CSA 1991

CHILD SUPPORT ACT 1991

Section 8

. . .

(5)   The Lord Chancellor or in relation to Scotland the Lord Advocate may by order provide that, in such circumstances as may be specified by the order, this section shall

not prevent a court from exercising any power which it has to make a maintenance order in relation to a child if—

(a)   a written agreement (whether or not enforceable) provides for the making, or securing, by an absent parent of the child of periodical payments to or for the benefit of the child; and

(b)   the maintenance order which the court makes is, in all material respects, in the same terms as that agreement.

9.2   The Formula

9.2.1   STAGE ONE: THE MAINTENANCE REQUIREMENT

CHILD SUPPORT ACT 1991

Schedule

(1)—(1)   In this Schedule 'the maintenance requirement' means the amount, calculated in accordance with the formula set out in sub-paragraph (2), which is to be taken as the minimum amount necessary for the maintenance of the qualifying child or, where there is more than one qualifying child, all of them.

9.2.2   STAGE TWO: EXEMPT INCOME

9.2.2.1   The basics

CPAG, *Child Support Handbook*, 1997/1998

Eligible housing costs are costs which have to be incurred in order to buy, rent or otherwise secure possession of the parent's home or to carry out repairs and improvements as defined below. Eligible costs are:

- rent (net of housing benefit);
- mortgage interest payments;
- capital repayments under a mortgage;
- premiums paid under an endowment or other insurance policy, a personal equity plan (PEP) or personal pension plan to the extent that the policy was taken out to cover the cost of the mortgage;
- interest payments on any loans for repairs and improvements to the home taken out before the maintenance application or enquiry form is sent to the parent;
- interest payments on loans for major repairs necessary to maintain the fabric of the home and for measures which improve its fitness for occupation, such as the installation of a bath, shower, wash basin or lavatory; the provision of heating, electric lighting and sockets, drainage facilities, or storage facilities for fuel and refuse; improvement to ventilation, natural lighting, insulation or structural condition; or any other improvements considered reasonable by the Child Support Officer (the previous 'unfitness' which necessitated the improvement needs to be demonstrated);
- interest payments under a hire purchase agreement to buy a home;
- payments in respect of a licence or permission to occupy the home;
- payments in respect of or as a result of the occupation of the home (this is intended to cover payments made by a former licensee who occupies premises unlawfully—e.g., after a notice to quit has expired. However, the extent of this provision is unclear but it does not include property and contents insurance, payments in respect of the purchase of a home, nor council tax);
- payments of ground rent or feu duty;
- payments under co-ownership schemes;
- payments of service charges if such payments are a condition for occupying the home;

- mooring charges for a houseboat;
- site rent for a caravan or mobile home;
- payments for a tent and its site;
- payments under a rental purchase scheme;
- payments in respect of croft land;
- payments in respect of a home made to an employer who provides the home;
- payments for Crown tenancy or licence;
- payments in respect of a loan taken out to pay off another loan that covered eligible housing costs;
- the fees (net of any housing benefit), where a parent or a partner lives in a nursing home, residential care home, local authority residential accommodation (part III) or accommodation provided under the NHS Act 1977.

Repayments of an advance of salary used to purchase a home cannot be housing costs.

9.2.2.2 Property settlements pre-1993

CROZIER v CROZIER [1994] 2 WLR 444 (FamD)

BOOTH J: On 8 February 1989 Mr Registrar (now District Judge) Holloway, sitting in the Carlisle County Court, made an ancillary relief order in the divorce proceedings between the husband, Mr Gary John Crozier, and the wife, Mrs Jacqueline Crozier. It was an order made with the consent of both parties. It provided that the husband should transfer to the wife absolutely his share in the matrimonial home in full and final settlement of all her financial claims against him. The order was also made on the agreed basis that there should be a nominal order only for the maintenance of the one child of the family, a boy then aged five years who lived with the wife. It was specifically stated in the order that she would have the full responsibility of maintaining the child in the future.

The wife, however, was unable to earn sufficient to maintain herself and her son and she received income support. Early in 1993 the Secretary of State for Social Security made a complaint in the Carlisle Magistrates' Court under the Social Security Administration Act 1992 for an order requiring the husband to contribute towards the boy's mainten-ance, and on 10 March 1993 an order was made that he should pay £4 per week. The husband has now received documents from the Child Support Agency. It is anticipated that on the application of the formula introduced under the Child Support Act 1991 his liability for his son will be increased to approximately £29 per week. It is in those circumstances that he now asks the court to set aside or vary the consent order so that he may recover his share of the former matrimonial home. The wife objects to this.

The wife is living with another man whom she is shortly to marry. The child of the family lives with them together with the baby of their union, aged six months. It is fortuitous from the husband's point of view that, in view of the wife's forthcoming marriage, the former matrimonial home has recently been sold and the proceeds of approximately £20,000 are being held on deposit pending the outcome of this appeal.

The husband asks that the consent order should now be set aside to enable him to recover his half share of the proceeds of sale of the property. That sum of £10,000 or thereabouts could be invested and from the interest the husband could pay any maintenance now and in the future required of him for the child of the family. It has been calculated that the interest that he could reasonably expect to receive would enable him to meet the sum which it is anticipated that he will in due course be required to pay under the child support formula. The husband does not dispute his obligation to maintain his son. It is his case that he has already fulfilled this obligation by way of the capital payment to the wife represented by his half share of the home. The wife accepts that the property transfer was intended for the benefit of the child and was given and accepted in lieu of periodical payments. By reason of the intervention of the state the husband contends that he is being required to pay twice over, no account being taken of the sum he has already paid.

Although she concedes the basis upon which she and the husband reached agreement in 1989, the wife nevertheless contests the appeal. She intends that half the proceeds of the sale, in effect the husband's half, should be invested for the benefit of their child and that the income therefrom will go towards his maintenance. On her remarriage and with the additional income that she will have she will no longer be entitled to income support. The result will be that the husband may not then be subject either to the present maintenance order or, perhaps more importantly, to any demands made under the Child Support Act 1991.

The initial factual premise of this judgment must be that the parties would never have reached the agreement that they did had they thought that the husband would be required to make periodical payments for the child of the family, certainly of the magnitude of the sum calculated by formula under the Child Support Act 1991, or, probably, at all. His half share of the home represented the entirety of his capital assets. The marriage was not of long duration, having subsisted for seven years at the most. There were no circumstances to suggest that a court would have been reasonably likely to have made an order giving the wife all the available capital for herself even in full and final satisfaction of her claims. Had the parties contemplated a continuing liability for periodical payments either for the wife or the child it is reasonable to suppose that the husband's half share in the property would have been preserved for the use of the wife, qua mother, for as long as she needed it as a home for herself and the child, and thereafter would have reverted to the husband. With the sale of the house and the wife's remarriage that position would now have been reached. It is common ground between the parties that the absolute transfer of the husband's half share to the wife was intended to benefit the child and it is her continuing intention that it should do so. In accordance with s. 25 of the Matrimonial Causes Act 1973, as substituted by s. 3 of the Matrimonial and Family Proceedings Act 1984, the court when making the order was bound to have as its first consideration the welfare of the child, and it is clear from the note written to this court by the registrar that such agreements were at the time regarded as appropriate and beneficial for a child in circumstances such as these where the husband's income was not such that he could afford to make a periodical payment. . . .

As between spouses the clean break principle now forms part of the statutory code governing the court's approach to ancillary relief applications. The court itself is required to consider the exercise of its powers in such a way as will terminate the financial obligations of each party towards the other: see s. 25A of the Matrimonial Causes Act 1973.

Different considerations, however, have applied in relation to child maintenance where the on-going responsibility of the parents has remained a basic factor to which the clean break principle has never applied. In *Preston* v *Preston* [1982] Fam 17, 36–37, Brandon LJ expressed the view that it was neither possible nor desirable to bring about a clean break between father and son. That principle has been consistently applied and was clearly acknowledged by the registrar in this case when he inserted in the order the words, 'save for child maintenance,' thus emphasising the continuing right of the child to be maintained and, therefore, the continuing duty on the parents to do so. While the parties were free to achieve a clean break as between themselves, it was outside their powers to do so in respect of their child. That position could not be changed by reason of the statement of intent which appears upon the face of the order that the wife would assume responsibility for his maintenance. In fact, at the time the order was made the wife was not maintaining the child since she did not have adequate means to do so. Accordingly she was in receipt of income support and so, in effect, the state was assuming that liability on her behalf. In reality the husband could only be relieved of his obligation at the expense of the state.

What was not anticipated by the parties was that the state would intervene to relieve itself, if not rid itself, of that financial burden. Nevertheless, at the time they concluded the agreement and the order was made the state was empowered to seek the recovery of its expenditure on benefit from a person who was liable for maintenance. As to this the relevant statutory provision in force in February 1989 was s. 24 of the Social Security Act 1986, which enabled the Secretary of State to make a complaint to a magistrates' court for an order against a person liable to maintain another who was in receipt of income support. That was by no means a new statutory provision. Its precursor was contained in the Supplementary Benefits Act 1976. That same provision is now to be found in ss. 106 to 107 of the Social Security Administration Act 1992, under the provisions of which the existing periodical payments order of March 1993 was made against the husband.

Mr Goldrein seeks to draw a distinction between the power vested in the Secretary of State to obtain an order in the magistrates' court under the long-standing legislation and an order made in accordance with the new Child Support Act 1991. In the former case, on an application to the court the bench will exercise a judicial discretion, being required by statute to have regard to all the circumstances of the case. No such wide discretion exists under the Act of 1991, which came fully into force on 5 April 1993. The purpose of that Act, as stated in the preamble, is to make provision for the assessment, collection and enforcement of periodical maintenance payable by certain parents with respect to children of theirs who are not in care. To this end the Child Support Act 1991 introduces a machinery, outside the jurisdiction of the courts, whereby liability for child mainten-ance is assessed in accordance with a formula which is based upon income support rates and upon prescribed information as to the financial means of both parents. This calculation does not admit of variation. It is a straight mathematical computation. The result in monetary terms may be very different from the quantum of a court order, as in the present case where the husband's current liability has been determined at £4 per week as against his anticipated liability of £29 per week. Mr Goldrein submits that it is that method of assessment, imposed by Parliament since the making of the consent order, that constitutes a new event which has undermined the basis of the order to the extent that it should be set aside.

I am unable to accept that submission. The fact that Parliament has chosen a new administrative method by which the state may intervene to compel a parent to contribute towards the maintenance of a child, bypassing the jurisdiction of the courts, does not fundamentally alter the position as it was in law in February 1989. The parties were then unable to achieve a clean financial break in respect of their son. The legal liability to maintain him remained on them both as his parents. While the wife was prepared to assume that responsibility as between herself and the husband, she could not in fact fulfil that obligation without the assistance of state moneys. The state was never bound by the agreement or the order. At any time it could have intervened, through the Secretary of State, to seek an order through the courts and the parties were not entitled to assume for the purposes of their agreement that it would not do so. I consider that it is immaterial for this purpose that that same parental liability will now be enforced through an agency outside the courts. That is a difference only in the means by which the state may proceed to relieve itself of the obligation which it is the duty of the parents to discharge. The fact that the sum required of a parent may be greater under the new procedure than under the old is a consequence of the procedural change and not of any new and unforeseen power vested in the state. In my judgment, neither the existing order made in March 1993 under the statutory machinery which existed in February 1989 nor any anticipated liability which may be levied under the new machinery introduced by the Act of 1991 constitutes a new event, in fact or in law, sufficient to invalidate the basis of the consent order.

9.2.3   STAGE THREE: ASSESSABLE INCOME

PHILLIPS v *PEACE* [1996] 2 FLR 230 (FamD)

JOHNSON J: Most people would think that a mother should have no difficulty in obtaining financial support for her child from a father who lives in a house worth £2.6m and whose standard of living is illustrated by his three motor cars worth respectively £36,000, £54,000 and £100,000.

In this case the Child Support Agency thought otherwise. In responding to the mother's application it said, 'The child support officer has calculated that the weekly amount payable by the father is nought pounds'.

In the circumstances of this case that will seem startling to the point of absurdity. However, it is no fault of the agency. If blame is to be borne by anyone, perhaps it should be borne by the architects of the child support scheme whose appreciation of the realities of people's differing financial arrangements has been described by one learned author as naive. As to that I make no comment. My duty as a judge is to seek to construe the Child Support Act 1991, to determine its effect on other legislation, principally the Children Act

1989, and apply the law to the facts of the case as I find them to be. This father carries on business dealing in shares. He does so through a company which he owns and controls. At the time of the mother's application for child support the company was paying him no salary or other remuneration. It is of the essence of the policy underlying the Child Support Act 1991 that child support is to be assessed according to a mathematical formula which is to be applied rigorously, seemingly without any significant element of discretion to cater for the needs of a child in the circumstances of the child with whom I am concerned. The Act focuses attention on income that can be described as actual. No account is taken under the 1991 Act of income that is only potential.

This is quite contrary to the practice of the court which for generations, in seeking to assess entitlements to financial support for former spouses or children, has sought to achieve a result which is fair, just and reasonable, based on the realities and the practicalities. Of course for many citizens their annual tax return and notice of PAYE coding are matters of crucial importance to them and their families. But there are some for whom, for one reason or another, such matters are of little interest as they have been able to shelter their financial arrangements from the depredations of the Revenue. In cases involving such people, lawyers and judges will seek to assess the reality of the situation.

Mr Singleton accepts of course that the jurisdiction remains for the court to order a lump sum but, he submits, the court should not exercise the jurisdiction in such a manner as to make a provision that would be so obviously intended to avoid the terms of s. 8(3). Such a use of the lump sum jurisdiction would be, submits Mr Singleton, no more than a device to avoid the clear intention of Parliament in the Child Support Act 1991. He points out that if the court embarks upon the course proposed by Mr Posnansky, then any mother who is dissatisfied with the assessment made by the Child Support Agency—either because the stated income of the paying parent, the father, is not enough, or on the basis that the agency has been misled—will be able to come before the court and seek a lump sum to augment the periodic provision made by the agency.

There is a limited provision in the Child Support Act for what is called topping up. Such an application may be made to the court in the circumstances set out in s. 8(6). That is not possible in this case. The power to top up an assessment arises, putting the matter in simple terms, only where the agency's assessment has reached the permissible ceiling and the court is asked to make a provision over and above that ceiling. Both counsel agreed before me that that was not possible in this case.

I need to refer to a further statutory provision. The Child Support Act 1995 clearly seeks to meet some of the criticisms made of the earlier Act. In particular it is possible for applications to be made to the agency for what are called departures. Paragraph 5 of sch. 2 to the 1995 Act gives authority to the Secretary of State to make regulations to deal with particular cases. So far as I am aware those regulations have not been made but para. 5 clearly envisages that the regulations could make provision for cases such as the present, where there are assets capable of producing an income but which presently do not, or where a person's lifestyle is inconsistent with the level of his income. The father in the present case told me that he is presently minded to arrange for his company to pay him a salary of perhaps £50,000 a year but that has not yet occurred and, like the regulations under the 1995 Act, it remains a matter of speculation whether there will be circumstances enabling the agency to make a more realistic assessment of the father's income and a more realistic provision for the child.

Despite the assistance which I have received from counsel, I have not found this an easy matter. I have made no secret of my anxiety to make a realistic provision for this child but on reflection I have concluded that Mr Singleton's submission is well founded; that is to say that the undoubted power which I have to make a lump sum award should not be exercised in such a way as to provide for the regular support of the child, which would ordinarily have been provided by an order for periodic payments.

I hold that in a case to which the Child Support Act 1991, and in particular s. 8(1), applies, then in exercising its remaining jurisdictions under sch. 1 to the Children Act 1989, here to award a lump sum, a court should do so only in order to meet the need of a child in respect of a particular item of capital expenditure. By way of example there might be a case in which a child, suffering from physical handicap, needed a capital sum for the modification of the house in which it was to live. Similarly in the present case I propose to exercise the power to make provision for the furnishing of the home in which the child is to live.

For the reasons of law, which I dealt with earlier in this judgment, I make no provision for C's regular support. I reach that conclusion with considerable regret because it seems to me, as I said at the outset, to be absurd that the law binding upon the Child Support Agency should have resulted in the father's liability to support his child being assessed at zero. I express the hope that if and when the father decides that his company shall pay him a salary or other renumeration, and/or that if and when the Secretary of State makes the regulations foreshadowed in the Child Support Act 1995, some arrangement will be forthcoming.

I have throughout my consideration of the case sought to bear in mind the impact upon the mother and upon C of any order that I might make and in particular the effect upon the mother's income support. It would seem that for the time being the mother and C will be dependent upon that benefit and that does not seem to me to be right. I would wish that it had been otherwise. Had I felt able to make a lump sum provision for C's continuing support, then for the next year or so I would have awarded a lump sum based on a figure of £90 per week. I recognise that I will need to adjourn further consideration to enable solicitors and counsel to consider in particular the details of the settled provision.

9.2.4 STAGE FOUR: HOW MUCH WILL BE PAYABLE?

9.2.4.1 Assessable income and calculation of maintenance payable — Stage 4 of the CSA formula

Anne and Bill are unmarried and live apart. They have one child Christopher aged six years. Anne is on benefits and therefore is required to co-operate with the CSA or risk a reduction in that benefit. Bill is employed as a warehouse operator.

The maintenance requirement would be assessed by looking at Christopher's age and IS benefits minus child benefit.

This would comprise:

Carers allowance	£49.15 (adult premium in full)
Income Support child allowance	£16.90
Family premium	£15.75
Sub total	£81.80
Less	
Child benefit	£11.05
Total maintenance requirement	**£70.75**

The exempt income for Bill is calculated again looking at IS levels. Assuming he lives alone and pays rent of £50 pw and he has no costs for travelling to work:

Income Support premium	£49.15
Housing	£50.00
Exempt income	**£95.15**

Assessable income takes into account the amount earned by Bill. His salary is paid weekly and amounts to £156.00 after tax, National Insurance and half his pension contributions have been deducted.

To establish how much of this is potentially available to pay child support the Agency will deduct the exempt income:

Net income	£156.00
Less exempt income	£ 95.15
Assessable income	**£ 60.85**

The income available to pay child support will be no more than 50% of this figure, so Bill may be required to pay £30.43 towards maintaining Christopher.

As the sum of £30.43 is less that the amount in Stage 1, Anne will only receive the available amount from Bill.

If Bill had a weekly salary of £356.00 (after necessary deductions) the calculation would be thus:

Net income	£356.00
Less exempt income	£ 95.15
Assessable income	**£260.85**

The amount available to meet the maintenance requirement is 50% of this, which is £130.43. As this exceeds the maintenance requirement in Stage 1, Bill will be required to pay the total figure calculated as the maintenance requirement being £70.75.

Naturally these figures are simplistic and are based on 1997/98 IS figures, and do not consider the position of the parent with care, and their ability to pay or share the cost of maintaining the child. The additional amount of child support if the absent parent is a high earner has not been included, nor has stage 5—protected income.

9.2.5 STAGE FIVE: PROTECTED INCOME

Using the first set of calculations for Anne and Bill, you will recall that Bill's total possible child support payment was £30.43. In stage 5, this must be assessed as a % of his total net income, since he cannot be made to pay more than 30% of net income in child support.

Bill's total net income is £156.00 per week. 30% of this is £46.80. As this figure is greater than the amount of maintenance assessed (£30.43) Bill does not benefit from the protected income calculation.

9.3   Departure from the Formula

**Deas, S, Discretion, but not as We Know it — Departures from the CSA Formula
[1996] Fam Law 759**

Conceived as a result of pressure from absent parents who considered that the Child Support Act formula did not take into account their personal circumstances, and from parents with care who considered the formula did not properly reflect their former partner's income, the Child Support Act departures scheme was due to come into effect on 2 December 1996 after a 6-month pilot scheme. Twenty thousand Child Support Agency (CSA) 'clients' were approached. Only 6% (1500) actually applied. It is thought that the low response rate arose in part from the realisation that this was only a pilot scheme and therefore there was no real or immediate gain. Applicants relied on all available grounds (see further below) but 'inconsistent lifestyle' was the commonest complaint (18%). Applications came from both absent parents and parents with care (47% and 53% respectively).

The use of the words 'departures' and 'discretion' has probably lulled many CSA clients and even solicitors into believing that this system will enable a more 'realistic' figure for maintenance to be substituted for the formula calculation. This is not correct. What a successful appeal will achieve is the inclusion of a further figure in the exempt income calculation. Special expenses of, for example, £25 will result in a reduction in the absent parent's assessment of only £10 (approximately). Ironically, the pilot scheme was not able to evaluate the very category of case which is probably the most contentious, ie the ground of 'inconsistent lifestyle'. Worryingly, '90% of these applications were eliminated at an early stage as being unsubstantiated by evidence provided' (*Departure Directions Pilot Evaluation Report*, September 1996). Even those who did get over the hurdle could not be evaluated properly because they were likely to be sent straight to the Independent Tribunal Service for a decision. Clearly, the onus is on the parent with care to provide (presumably documentary) evidence. She may not have the time, energy, knowledge, or financial resources (no legal aid is available) to tackle this. The tribunals' investigative powers are very limited and, consequently, there must be a very real worry that the financially astute absent parent will continue to avoid his liabilities. It is predicted that it will take 10 weeks to carry out a departure assessment, but this can be delayed if there are reviews of the original assessment outstanding—of which, 50% take longer than 6 months to complete in the first place.

THE SCHEME IN OUTLINE
There are three groups of grounds—special expenses, property or capital transfers, and 'additional cases'.

Special Expenses
This ground has six categories which are—costs incurred in travelling to work; contact costs; expenses arising from illness or disability (of applicant or dependant); debts incurred before the absent parent became an absent parent; pre-1993 financial commitments, and costs incurred in supporting step-children (where the responsibility was taken on before 5 April 1993). In all these cases the first £15 is disallowed and the child support officer can substitute a lower figure if he considers the figure claimed is unreasonably high. The allowed amount will be included in the exempt income calculation (therefore it does not produce a pound for pound reduction in the assessment).

Pre-1993 Property or Capital Transfers
This ground applies where a court order or other written agreement was in force before 5 April 1993 between the absent parent and parent with care or children, and the amount of child maintenance payable was reduced as a trade-off and was not properly reflected in the CSA assessment (which currently deals with such claims on a broad brush basis). Conversely, a parent with care can claim if the broad brush result is too favourable to the absent parent.

Additional Cases
This ground also has six categories—assets capable of producing (higher) income; 'diverted' income (ie where the absent parent is diverting income to a new partner or third party); inconsistent lifestyle of the absent parent; unreasonably high housing costs of the absent parent; the absent parent claiming for housing costs he does not actually have (because they are paid by his new partner, for example), and the absent parent claiming unreasonably high travel costs (under the existing 'straight line' formula). In all cases the child support officer must decide whether it is 'just and equitable' to give a departure direction and must take into account (inter alia) whether making a direction would be likely to result in the absent parent or parent with care ceasing work. There is also a list of factors which the officer cannot take into account, which includes the circumstances of conception.

PROCEDURE
(1) Appellant applies on a prescribed form.
(2) Further information can be requested (14-day time-limit). The child support officer makes a preliminary finding to weed out hopeless cases.
(3) The other side is invited to make representations.
(4) The child support officer makes decision.
(5) That decision is communicated to both parties.

The effective date will be either the effective date of the original assessment (if the appeal is made within 28 days), or later if the appeal relates to events which occurred later. Since this is a discretionary exercise, s. 2 of the Child Support Act 1991 should be applied.

The SFLA's position has always been that there should be provision within the Act to depart from the formula in special cases, but that those appeals should be to the courts.

I predict that when this departures system comes into operation it will be a great disappointment. Parents with care will find it impossible to provide sufficient evidence in many cases to get their assessments looked at. Absent parents will be disgruntled when the real costs of their, for example, maintaining contact with a child are not reflected in the revised figure. Solicitors and mediators will be unhappy with the uncertainty and further delay that this will introduce into settling ancillary relief claims.

CHILD SUPPORT ACT 1995

Section 6(2)   SCHEDULE 2
                          DEPARTURE DIRECTIONS: THE CASES AND CONTROLS

The following Schedule is inserted in the 1991 Act, after Schedule 4A—

SCHEDULE 4B
DEPARTURE DIRECTIONS: THE CASES AND CONTROLS

PART I   THE CASES

General

1.—(1)   The cases in which a departure direction may be given are those set out in this Part of this Schedule or in regulations made under this Part.

(2)   In this Schedule 'applicant' means the person whose application for a departure direction is being considered.

Special expenses

2.—(1)   A departure direction may be given with respect to special expenses of the applicant which were not, and could not have been, taken into account in determining the current assessment in accordance with the provisions of, or made under, Part I of Schedule 1.

(2)   In this paragraph 'special expenses' means the whole, or any prescribed part, of expenses which fall within a prescribed description of expenses.

(3)   In prescribing descriptions of expenses for the purposes of this paragraph, the Secretary of State may, in particular, make provision with respect to—

(a)   costs incurred in travelling to work;

(b)   costs incurred by an absent parent in maintaining contact with the child, or with any of the children, with respect to whom he is liable to pay child support maintenance under the current assessment;

(c)   costs attributable to a long-term illness or disability of the applicant or of a dependant of the applicant;

(d)   debts incurred, before the absent parent became an absent parent in relation to a child with respect to whom the current assessment was made—

(i)   for the joint benefit of both parents;

(ii)   for the benefit of any child with respect to whom the current assessment was made; or

(iii)   for the benefit of any other child falling within a prescribed category;

(e)   pre-1993 financial commitments from which it is impossible for the parent concerned to withdraw or from which it would be unreasonable to expect that parent to have to withdraw;

(f)   costs incurred by a parent in supporting a child who is not his child but who is part of his family.

(4)   For the purposes of sub-paragraph (3)(c)—

(a)   the question whether one person is a dependant of another shall be determined in accordance with regulations made by the Secretary of State;

(b)   'disability' and 'illness' have such meaning as may be prescribed; and

(c)   the question whether an illness or disability is long-term shall be determined in accordance with regulations made by the Secretary of State.

(5) For the purposes of sub-paragraph (3)(e), 'pre-1993 financial commitments' financial commitments of a prescribed kind entered into before 5th April 1993 in any case where—

(a) a court order of a prescribed kind was in force with respect to the absent parent and the person with care concerned at the time when they were entered into; or

(b) an agreement between them of a prescribed kind was in force at that time.

(6) For the purposes of sub-paragraph (3)(f), a child who is not the child of a particular person is a part of that person's family in such circumstances as may be prescribed.

Property or capital transfers

3.—(1) A departure direction may be given if—

(a) before 5th April 1993—

(i) a court order of a prescribed kind was in force with respect to the absent parent and either the person with care with respect to whom the current assessment was made or the child, or any of the children, with respect to whom that assessment was made, or

(ii) an agreement of a prescribed kind between the absent parent and any of those persons was in force;

(b) in consequence of one or more transfers of property of a prescribed kind—

(i) the amount payable by the absent parent by way of maintenance was less than would have been the case had that transfer or those transfers not been made; or

(ii) no amount was payable by the absent parent by way of maintenance; and

(c) the effect of that transfer, or those transfers, is not properly reflected in the current assessment.

(2) For the purposes of sub-paragraph (1)(b), 'maintenance' means periodical payments of maintenance made (otherwise than under this Act) with respect to the child, or any of the children, with respect to whom the current assessment was made.

(3) For the purposes of sub-paragraph (1)(c), the question whether the effect of one or more transfers of property is properly reflected in the current assessment shall be determined in accordance with regulations made by the Secretary of State.

4.—(1) A departure direction may be given if—

(a) before 5th April 1993—

(i) a court order of a prescribed kind was in force with respect to the absent parent and either the person with care with respect to whom the current assessment was made or the child, or any of the children, with respect to whom that assessment was made, or

(ii) an agreement of a prescribed kind between the absent parent and any of those persons was in force;

(b) in pursuance of the court order or agreement, the absent parent has made one or more transfers of property of a prescribed kind;

(c) the amount payable by the absent parent by way of maintenance was not reduced as a result of that transfer or those transfers;

(d) the amount payable by the absent parent by way of child support maintenance under the current assessment has been reduced as a result of that transfer or those transfers, in accordance with provisions of or made under this Act; and

(e) it is nevertheless inappropriate, having regard to the purposes for which the transfer or transfers was or were made, for that reduction to have been made.

(2) For the purposes of sub-paragraph (1)(c), 'maintenance' means periodical payments of maintenance made (otherwise than under this Act) with respect to the child, or any of the children, with respect to whom the current assessment was made.

Additional cases

5.—(1) The Secretary of State may by regulations prescribe other cases in which a departure direction may be given.

(2) Regulations under this paragraph may, for example, make provision with respect to cases where—

(a)   assets which do not produce income are capable of producing income;

(b)   a person's life-style is inconsistent with the level of his income;

(c)   housing costs are unreasonably high;

(d)   housing costs are in part attributable to housing persons whose circumstances are such as to justify disregarding a part of those costs;

(e)   travel costs are unreasonably high; or

(f)   travel costs should be disregarded.

9.4   When is the CSA 1991 not Applicable?

9.4.1   CSA 1991 NOT AVAILABLE

CHILD SUPPORT ACT 1991

8.   Role of the courts with respect to maintenance for children

. . .

(6)   This section shall not prevent a court from exercising any power which it has to make a maintenance order in relation to a child if—

(a)   a maintenance assessment is in force with respect to the child;

(b)   the amount of the child support maintenance payable in accordance with the assessment was determined by reference to the alternative formula mentioned in paragraph 4(3) of Schedule 1; and

(c)   the court is satisfied that the circumstances of the case make it appropriate for the absent parent to make or secure the making of periodical payments under a maintenance order in addition to the child support maintenance payable by him in accordance with the maintenance assessment.

(7)   This section shall not prevent a court from exercising any power which it has to make a maintenance order in relation to a child if—

(a)   the child is, will be or (if the order were to be made) would be receiving instruction at an educational establishment or undergoing training for a trade, profession or vocation (whether or not while in gainful employment); and

(b)   the order is made solely for the purposes of requiring the person making or securing the making of periodical payments fixed by the order to meet some or all of the expenses incurred in connection with the provision of the instruction or training.

(8)   This section shall not prevent a court from exercising any power which it has to make a maintenance order in relation to a child if—

(a)   a disability living allowance is paid to or in respect of him; or

(b)   no such allowance is paid but he is disabled,

and the order is made solely for the purpose of requiring the person making or securing the making of periodical payments fixed by the order to meet some or all of any expenses attributable to the child's disability.

(9)   For the purposes of subsection (8), a child is disabled if he is blind, deaf or dumb or is substantially and permanently handicapped by illness, injury, mental disorder or congenital deformity or such other disability as may be prescribed.

9.4.2   OTHER LEGISLATION

9.4.2.1   Status

MATRIMONIAL CAUSES ACT 1973

21.   Financial provision and property adjustment orders

(1)   The financial provision orders for the purposes of this Act are the orders for periodical or lump sum provision available (subject to the provisions of this Act) under section 23 below for the purpose of adjusting the financial position of the parties to a marriage and any children of the family in connection with proceedings for divorce, nullity of marriage or judicial separation and under section 27(6) below on proof of neglect by one party to a marriage to provide, or to make a proper contribution towards, reasonable maintenance for the other or a child of the family, that is to say—

(a) any order for periodical payments in favour of a party to a marriage under section 23(1)(a) or 27(6)(a) or in favour of a child of the family under section 23(1)(d), (2) or (4) or 27(6)(d));

(b) any order for secured periodical payments in favour of a party to a marriage under section 23(1)(b) or 27(6)(b) or in favour of a child of the family under section 23(1)(e), (2) or (4) or 27(6)(e); and

(c) any order for lump sum provision in favour of a party to a marriage under section 23(1)(c) or 27(6)(c) or in favour of a child of the family under section 23(1)(f), (2) or (4) or 27(6)(f);

and references in this Act (except in paragraphs 17(1) and 23 of Schedule 1 below) to periodical payments orders, secured periodical payments orders, and orders for the payment of a lump sum are references to all or some of the financial provision orders requiring the sort of financial provision in question according as the context of each reference may require.

23. Financial provision orders in connection with divorce proceedings, etc.

(1) On granting a decree of divorce, a decree of nullity of marriage or a decree of judicial separation or at any time thereafter (whether, in the case of a decree of divorce or of nullity of marriage, before or after the decree is made absolute), the court may make any one or more of the following orders, that is to say—

. . .

(d) an order that a party to the marriage shall make to such person as may be specified in the order for the benefit of a child of the family, or to such a child, such periodical payments, for such term, as may be so specified;

(e) an order that a party to the marriage shall secure to such person as may be so specified for the benefit of such a child, or to such a child, to the satisfaction of the court, such periodical payments, for such term, as may be so specified;

(f) an order that a party to the marriage shall pay to such person as may be so specified for the benefit of such a child, or to such a child, such lump sum as may be so specified;

subject however, in the case of an order under paragraph (d), (e) or (f) above, to the restrictions imposed by section 29(1) and (3) below on the making of financial provision orders in favour of children who have attained the age of eighteen.

(2) The court may also, subject to those restrictions, make any one or more of the orders mentioned in subsection (1)(d), (e) and (f) above—

(a) in any proceedings for divorce, nullity of marriage or judicial separation, before granting a decree; and

(b) where any such proceedings are dismissed after the beginning of the trial, either forthwith or within a reasonable period after the dismissal.

(3) Without prejudice to the generality of subsection (1)(c) or (f) above—

(a) an order under this section that a party to a marriage shall pay a lump sum to the other party may be made for the purpose of enabling that other party to meet any liabilities or expenses reasonably incurred by him or her in maintaining himself or herself or any child of the family before making an application for an order under this section in his or her favour;

(b) an order under this section for the payment of a lump sum to or for the benefit of a child of the family may be made for the purpose of enabling any liabilities or expenses reasonably incurred by or for the benefit of that child before the making of an application for an order under this section in his favour to be met; and

(c) an order under this section for the payment of a lump sum may provide for the payment of that sum by instalments of such amount as may be specified in the order and may require the payment of the instalments to be secured to the satisfaction of the court.

(4) The power of the court under subsection (1) or (2)(a) above to make an order in favour of a child of the family shall be exercisable from time to time; and where the court makes an order in favour of a child under subsection (2)(b) above, it may from time to time, subject to the restrictions mentioned in subsection (1) above, make a further order in his favour of any of the kinds mentioned in subsection (1)(d), (e) or (f) above.

24. Property adjustment orders in connection with divorce proceedings, etc.

(1) On granting a decree of divorce, a decree of nullity of marriage or a decree of judicial separation or at any time thereafter (whether, in the case of a decree of divorce, or of nullity of marriage, before or after the decree is made absolute), the court may make any one or more of the following orders, that is to say—

(a) an order that a party to the marriage shall transfer to the other party, to any child of the family or to such person as may be specified in the order for the benefit of such a child such property as may be so specified, being property to which the first-mentioned party is entitled, either in possession or reversion;

(b) an order that a settlement of such property as may be so specified, being property to which a party to the marriage is so entitled, be made to the satisfaction of the court for the benefit of the other party to the marriage and of the children of the family or either or any of them;

(c) an order varying for the benefit of the parties to the marriage and of the children of the family or either or any of them any ante-nuptial or post-nuptial settlement (including such a settlement made by will or codicil) made on the parties to the marriage;

(d) an order extinguishing or reducing the interest of either of the parties to the marriage under any such settlement;

subject, however, in the case of an order under paragraph (a) above, to the restrictions imposed by section 29(1) and (3) below on the making of orders for a transfer of property in favour of children who have attained the age of eighteen.

25. Matters to which court is to have regard in deciding how to exercise its powers under sections 23, 24 and 24A

(1) It shall be the duty of the court in deciding whether to exercise its powers under section 23, 24 or 24A above and, if so, in what manner, to have regard to all the circumstances of the case, first consideration being given to the welfare while a minor of any child of the family who has not attained the age of eighteen.

. . .

(3) As regards the exercise of the powers of the court under section 23(1)(d), (e) or (f), (2) or (4), 24 or 24A above in relation to a child of the family, the court shall in particular have regard to the following matters—

(a) the financial needs of the child;

(b) the income, earning capacity (if any), property and other financial resources of the child;

(c) any physical or mental disability of the child;

(d) the manner in which he was being and in which the parties to the marriage expected him to be educated or trained;

(e) the considerations mentioned in relation to the parties to the marriage in paragraphs (a), (b), (c) and (c) of subsection (2) above.

(4) As regards the exercise of the powers of the court under section 23(1)(d), (c) or (f), (2) or (4), 24 or 24A above against a party to a marriage in favour of a child of the family who is not the child of that party, the court shall also have regard—

(a) to whether that party assumed any responsibility for the child's maintenance, and, if so, to the extent to which, and the basis upon which, that party assumed such responsibility and to the length of time for which that party discharged such responsibility;

(b) to whether in assuming and discharging such responsibility that party did so knowing that the child was not his or her own;

(c) to the liability of any other person to maintain the child.

27. Financial provision orders, etc., in case of neglect by party to marriage to maintain other party or child of the family

(1) Either party to a marriage may apply to the court for an order under this section on the ground that the other party to the marriage (in this section referred to as the respondent)—

(a) has failed to provide reasonable maintenance for the applicant, or

(b) has failed to provide, or to make a proper contribution towards, reasonable maintenance for any child of the family.

. . .

(3)   Where an application under this section is made on the ground mentioned in subsection (1)(a) above, then, in deciding—

(a)   whether the respondent has failed to provide reasonable maintenance for the applicant, and

(b)   what order, if any, to make under this section in favour of the applicant, the court shall have regard to all the circumstances of the case including the matters mentioned in section 25(2) above, and where an application is also made under this section in respect of a child of the family who has not attained the age of eighteen, first consideration shall be given to the welfare of the child while a minor.

(3A)   Where an application under this section is made on the ground mentioned in subsection (1)(b) above then, in deciding—

(a)   whether the respondent has failed to provide, or to make a proper contribution towards, reasonable maintenance for the child of the family to whom the application relates, and

(b)   what order, if any, to make under this section in favour of the child, the court shall have regard to all the circumstances of the case including the matters mentioned in section 25(3)(a) to (e) above, and where the child of the family to whom the application relates is not the child of the respondent, including also the matters mentioned in section 25(4) above.

. . .

(6)   Where on an application under this section the applicant satisfies the court of any ground mentioned in subsection (1) above, the court may make any one or more of the following orders, that is to say—

. . .

(d)   an order that the respondent shall make to such person as may be specified in the order for the benefit of the child to whom the application relates, or to that child, such periodical payments, for such term, as may be so specified;

(e)   an order that the respondent shall secure to such person as may be so specified for the benefit of that child, or to that child, to the satisfaction of the court, such periodical payments, for such term, as may be so specified;

(f)   an order that the respondent shall pay to such person as may be so specified for the benefit of that child, or to that child, such lump sum as may be so specified; subject, however, in the case of an order under paragraph (d), (e) or (f) above, to the restrictions imposed by section 29(1) and (3) below on the making of financial provision orders in favour of children who have attained the age of eighteen.

(6A)   An application for the variation under section 31 of this Act of a periodical payments order or secured periodical payments order made under this section in favour of a child may, if the child has attained the age of sixteen, be made by the child himself.

(6B)   Where a periodical payments order made in favour of a child under this section ceases to have effect on the date on which the child attains the age of sixteen or at any time after that date but before or on the date on which he attains the age of eighteen, then if, on an application made to the court for an order under this subsection, it appears to the court that—

(a)   the child is, will be or (if an order were made under this subsection) would be receiving instruction at an educational establishment or undergoing training for a trade, profession or vocation, whether or not he also is, will be or would be in gainful employment; or

(b)   there are special circumstances which justify the making of an order under this subsection,

the court shall have power by order to revive the first mentioned order from such date as the court may specify, not being earlier than the date of the making of the application, and to exercise its power under section 31 of this Act in relation to any order so revived.

29.   Duration of continuing financial provision orders in favour of children, and age limit on making certain orders in their favour

(1)   Subject to subsection (3) below, no financial provision order and no order for a transfer of property under section 24(1)(a) above shall be made in favour of a child who has attained the age of eighteen.

(2)   The term to be specified in a periodical payments or secured periodical payments order in favour of a child may begin with the date of the making of an application for the order in question or any later date or a date ascertained in accordance with subsection (5) or (6) below but—

(a)   shall not in the first instance extend beyond the date of the birthday of the child next following his attaining the upper limit of the compulsory school age construed in accordance with section 277 of the Education Act 1993 unless the court considers that in the circumstances of the case the welfare of the child requires that it should extend to a later date, and

(b)   shall not in any event, subject to subsection (3) below, extend beyond the date of the child's eighteenth birthday.

(3)   Subsection (1) above, and paragraph (b) of subsection (2), shall not apply in the case of a child, if it appears to the court that—

(a)   the child is, or will be, or if an order were made without complying with either or both of those provisions would be, receiving instruction at an educational establishment or undergoing training for a trade, profession or vocation, whether or not he is also or will also be, in gainful employment; or

(b)   there are special circumstances which justify the making of an order without complying with either or both of those provisions.

(4)   Any periodical payments order in favour of a child shall, notwithstanding anything in the order, cease to have effect on the death of the person liable to make payments under the order, except in relation to any arrears due under the order on the date of the death.

DOMESTIC PROCEEDINGS AND MAGISTRATES' COURTS ACT 1978

1.   Grounds of application for financial provision

Either party to a marriage may apply to a magistrates' court for an order under section 2 of this Act on the ground that the other party to the marriage—

. . .

(b)   has failed to provide, or to make a proper contribution towards, reasonable maintenance for any child of the family; or

2.   Powers of court to make orders for financial provision

(1)   Where on an application for an order under this section the applicant satisfies the court of any ground mentioned in section 1 of this Act, the court may, subject to the provisions of this Part of this Act, make any one or more of the following orders, that is to say—

. . .

(c)   an order that the respondent shall make to the applicant for the benefit of a child of the family to whom the application relates, or to such a child, such periodical payments, and for such term, as may be so specified;

(d)   an order that the respondent shall pay to the applicant for the benefit of a child of the family to whom the application relates, or to such a child, such lump sum as may be so specified.

. . .

(3)   The amount of any lump sum required to be paid by such an order under this section shall not exceed [£1,000] or such larger amount as the Lord Chancellor may from time to time by order fix for the purposes of this subsection.

3.   Matters to which court is to have regard in exercising its powers under s. 2

(1)   Where an application is made for an order under section 2 of this Act, it shall be the duty of the court, in deciding whether to exercise its powers under that section and, if so, in what manner, to have regard to all the circumstances of the case, first consideration being given to the welfare while a minor of any child of the family who has not attained the age of eighteen.

. . .

(3)   As regards the exercise of its powers under subsection (1)(c) or (d) of section 2, the court shall in particular have regard to the following matters—

(a)   the financial needs of the child;

(b)   the income, earning capacity (if any), property and other financial resources of the child.

(c)   any physical or mental disability of the child,

(d)   the standard of living enjoyed by the family before the occurrence of the conduct which is alleged as the ground of the application;

(e)   the manner in which the child was being and in which the parties to the marriage expected him to be educated or trained;

(f)   the matters mentioned in relation to the parties to the marriage in paragraphs (a) and (b) of subsection (2) above.

(4)   As regards the exercise of its powers under section 2 in favour of a child of the family who is not the child of the respondent, the court shall also have regard—

(a)   to whether the respondent has assumed any responsibility for the child's maintenance and, if he did, to the extent to which, and the basis on which, he assumed that responsibility and to the length of time during which he discharged that responsibility;

(b)   to whether in assuming and discharging that responsibility the respondent did so knowing that the child was not his own child;

(c)   to the liability of any other person to maintain the child.

5.   Age limit on making orders for financial provision for children and duration of such orders

(1)   Subject to subsection (3) below, no order shall be made under section 2(1)(c) or (d) of this Act in favour of a child who has attained the age of eighteen.

(2)   The term to be specified in an order made under section 2(1)(c) of this Act in favour of a child may begin with the date of the making of an application for the order in question or any later date or a date ascertained in accordance with subsection (5) or (6) below but—

(a)   shall not in the first instance extend beyond the date of the birthday of the child next following his attaining the upper limit of the compulsory school age (construed in accordance with section 277 of the Education Act 1993) unless the court considers that in the circumstances of the case the welfare of the child requires that it should extend to a later date; and

(b)   shall not in any event, subject to subsection (3) below, extend beyond the date of the child's eighteenth birthday.

(3)   The court—

(a)   may make an order under section 2(1)(c) or (d) of this Act in favour of a child who has attained the age of eighteen, and

(b)   may include in an order made under section 2(1)(c) of this Act in relation to a child who has not attained that age a provision for extending beyond the date when the child will attain that age the term for which by virtue of the order any payments are to be made to or for the benefit of that child,

if it appears to the court—

(i)   that the child is, or will be, or if such an order or provision were made would be, receiving instruction at an educational establishment or undergoing training for a trade, profession or vocation, whether or not he is also, or will also be, in gainful employment; or

(ii)   that there are special circumstances which justify the making of the order or provision.

(4)   Any order made under section 2(1)(c) of this Act in favour of a child shall, notwithstanding anything in the order, cease to have effect on the death of the person liable to make payments under the order.

CARRON v CARRON [1984] FLR 805 (CA)

ORMROD LJ: This is an appeal from a judgment of Judge Freeman at Ilford county court on 1 May 1981. He had an issue before him as to whether two children, a girl and a boy, were children of the family. They were children of the wife and at all material times the two children lived with the husband and wife as part of their family. So far as the younger child, the boy, is concerned, it is said that the father was not permitted to behave as a father towards the child.

The only question in this case is whether the boy in the words of s. 52(1) of the Matrimonial Causes Act 1973 '. . . has been treated by both these parties as a child of that family'. It is conceded by Mr Gratwicke that, so far as the elder child, the girl, is concerned, it is unarguable but that she was treated as a child of the family, and the fact that the boy was taken into the household by the two of them when they married and formed part of the household for 4 years, the parties having married in 1975 when the boy was 2 and the girl was 8, makes it inevitable, in my judgment, that there should be a finding that both these children were treated by both parties as children of that family. You cannot live with children of this age for 4 years without treating them as children of the family.

The judge, however, based his decision that the children were not children of the family within the definition purely on the ground that there was an existing maintenance order in respect of each of these children against their respective fathers which was being met, in whole or in part, and he said in his judgment:

So far as [the boy] is concerned, the evidence is that his father saw him regularly; so far as his education is concerned, there was a row with the school and he told them not to take instructions from Mr Carron. It is agreed that [the boy] went on holiday with his father, Mr Carron's consent was not asked for.

This is a very difficult question; here is a child with a father. Mr Carron happened to marry his mother. This did not make [the boy] a child of the family simply because he was in the household. Mr Carron was nice to [the boy]. He loved him but I do not think that because one adult marries another it automatically saddles him with maintenance. Therefore [the boy] is not a child of the family.

Then the judge referred to the girl, whose father was paying maintenance of £35 a month and is still paying that sum, and he then continued:

In conclusion this child is not being totally maintained by her real father but I find it impossible to say she is a child of the family. Mr Carron behaved in a kindly, benevolent way towards her but he was not in a position to accept [the girl] as a child of the family. Therefore, I find neither child is a child of the family.

Of course, the acceptance test is wrong. That used to be the test but it is no longer and the judge seems to think there was something inherently impossible about there being two maintenance orders in existence simultaneously in respect of the same child. There is no difficulty that I can see so far as the jurisdiction of the court is concerned.

The whole point of the case is, and the judge's anxiety can be alleviated by applying, the provisions of s. 25(3) of the 1973 Act which reads:

It shall be the duty of the court in deciding whether to exercise its powers under s. 23(1) (d), (e) or (f), (2) or (4) or 24 above against a party to a marriage in favour of a child of the family who is not the child of that party and, if so, in what manner, to have regard (among the circumstances of the case)—
    (a)   to whether that party had assumed any responsibility for the child's main-tenance and, if so, to the extent to which, and the basis upon which, that party assumed such responsibility and to the length of time for which that party discharged such responsibility;
    (b)   to whether in assuming and discharging such responsibility that party did so knowing that the child was not his or her own;
    (c)   to the liability of any other person to maintain the child.

The power is there in the discretion of the court to make any order, or no order as the case may be, which is appropriate in the circumstances of any given case, in respect of the step-father, but it seems to me to be quite impossible to hold that these children are anything other than children of the family. I would allow the appeal.

9.4.2.2 Orders

KIELY v *KIELY* [1988] 1 FLR 248 (CA)

The parties were married in 1970 and had two children born in 1973 and 1975. They separated in 1982 and the marriage was dissolved. The wife remained in the matrimonial home with the children. On the wife's application for ancillary relief a consent order was made, providing that the matrimonial home was to be transferred to the wife subject to the existing mortgage and to a charge in favour of the husband of 50% of the equity, that charge not to be enforced by the husband save on the occurrence of the first of the following events: (a) the agreement of the parties; (b) the death of the wife; (c) the remarriage of the wife; (d) the permanent cohabitation of the wife with another man; or (e) the further order of the court. The husband was ordered to make periodical payments to the wife and to each of the children. The husband ceased to make payments at the end of 1982 and on his application the registrar first reduced the payments to the wife and subsequently the payments to the children to a nominal sum of 5 pence p.a. The wife appealed from the registrar's order and sought a lump sum payment for the children on the basis that the husband had deliberately undertaken financial commitments which would lead to the wife and children becoming dependent on the state while retaining for himself a 50% interest in the matrimonial home. The judge found that the husband did not have the resources to pay more than a nominal sum in periodical payments or to pay a lump sum, but he ordered the husband to pay a lump sum of £4,000 to each child when the younger child reached 18 or on the sale of the matrimonial home, whichever was the sooner. It was specially provided that if the husband could not comply with the order he should be given leave to apply for the charge in respect of the matrimonial home to be enforced. The husband appealed.

BOOTH J: From that order the husband appeals on the broad basis that the judge was wrong to exercise his discretion to make an order for lump sums in favour of the children. Mr Gordon, on his behalf, does not challenge the jurisdiction of the court to grant such relief, but argues that it is contrary to the scheme of the Matrimonial Causes Act 1973, which requires the court to make financial provision for children as children or dependants. He further argues that it is a prerequisite of any lump sum order that the party against whom it is made has, or will have, the financial resources from which to make the payments and that in the circumstances of this case that prerequisite is not fulfilled. The wife seeks to uphold the lump sum order on the basis that the husband has an interest in the house which can be realized, and that in the light of his failure to comply with the periodical payments order it is just that the children, and not the husband, should now benefit from that interest.

Lump sum orders in favour of children, and in particular of children whose parents are of limited means, are rare. The power to make such an order is now derived from s. 23 (1)(f) of the Matrimonial Causes Act 1973, and in deciding whether or not to exercise its discretion to do so the court is required to have regard in particular to the matters contained in s. 25(3) of the Act, as amended by the Matrimonial and Family Proceedings Act 1984. Those matters include the financial needs, income earning capacity and resources of the child and the manner in which he is being educated, as well as the financial resources and needs of the parents, and the standard of living enjoyed by the family before the breakdown of the marriage. In this respect, it is relevant to note that in considering an application for ancillary relief on behalf of a child, the court is not required to have regard to the contributions which each of the parties has made or is likely, in the foreseeable future, to make to the welfare of the family. By the amended provision of s. 25, the court must now also have regard to all the circumstances of the case, first consideration being given to the welfare, while a minor, of any child of the family who has not attained the age of 18. It is further provided by s. 29 of the 1973 Act that no financial provision order and no order for a transfer of property shall be made in favour of a child who has attained the age of 18, save where the child is continuing to receive education, or there are special circumstances which justify the making of such an order. . . .

In this case, so far as the children's financial position was concerned, the judge found that since the husband was unable to make periodical payments for them they would be maintained by the state. There was, however, no evidence before him that the children would suffer hardship or would be materially disadvantaged as a result of this, in comparison with what would have otherwise been their financial situation had the husband complied with the periodical payments order. Nor was there any evidence before the judge as to the children's need for a lump sum, either at the time of the hearing, or in the future. In relation to this the only comment that he was able to make in the course of his judgment was that 'the children at that time [that is when they attained their respective majorities] might find a lump sum very useful indeed, for example setting up a home or a business'. Whether or not that will be the case can only be a matter of speculation. There was, therefore, no evidence before the court to show that those children were placed in special circumstances which made a lump sum payable when the younger child attained the age of 18 either necessary or appropriate.

In considering the resources of the parents, the judge found on the undisputed facts that the husband could not pay a lump sum at the present time, and that it was unknown whether he would be in a position to raise money to do so when the younger child attained the age of 18 other than by the realization of his interest in the matrimonial home. Indeed, the evidence before the court pointed to the fact that it was likely that the only resource available to the husband from which a lump sum payment could be made was his interest in the former matrimonial home. It was upon the basis of the agreed value of that property at the date of the hearing and therefore of the husband's interest in it that the judge assessed the figure of £4,000 as being the appropriate sum for each child to receive. There was no evidence before the court that the husband had any realistic prospect of raising such a sum and certainly no evidence to satisfy the court that even assuming he was in a position to find such monies by some means other than by, the realization of his interest in the home, that it would be just to require him to do so. It is apparent from the judgment that the judge clearly, had it in mind that if the husband was unable otherwise to raise the money, then it would be appropriate for the house to be sold. I have already referred to that passage in his judgment when he observed that the children would be then grown up and it would not be essential for them to have the matrimonial home.

In the likely event that the husband will otherwise be unable to pay the lump sums, the sale of the matrimonial home will be then necessary to enable him to comply with the order and to enable the children to receive the monies then due to them. It is, again, a matter of speculation as to what might be the children's real needs in 6 years' time, when the younger child attains the age of 18, and whether or not they would be better served by retaining a roof over their heads rather than by receiving the capital payments of £4,000 each. . . .

Although it may appear likely that the realization of the husband's charge will produce sufficient resources, this is not a certainty. The precise value of the husband's share in the equity will not be known until the property is sold, and that may take place at any time within the next 6 years. There is presently little, if any, margin between the estimated value of his interest and the financial obligations to which it is subject. It is, therefore, a matter of some speculation as to whether the resources ultimately available on the sale of the property would be sufficient to enable the husband to discharge his liabilities. In those circumstances it seems to me to be an improper exercise of the court's discretion to make a lump sum order against the husband which, if he is unable to discharge, will render him liable to legal sanctions.

In my judgment, the judge wrongly exercised his discretion to make this order. None of the matters to which he was bound to have regard under the provisions of s. 25 of the 1973 Act supported the granting of such relief. There was no evidence of need on the part of the children, or special circumstances which called for capital provision to be made for their benefit, and the husband did not have the means to provide such monies other than by the sale of the property which was, and is, the children's home. The basis for the order was in reality to recompense the wife for the husband's failure to comply with the periodical payments order.

T v S (FINANCIAL PROVISION FOR CHILDREN) [1994] 2 FLR 883 (FamD)

JOHNSON J: The five children concerned are now aged between 15 years and 7. They and their parents lived together in some considerable style, with a house in the country and a flat in London. The father told the district judge that he had been earning and spending at the rate of about £300,000 per year. His occupation was that of a commodity broker.

The relationship between the parents came into difficulties by the beginning of 1989. In May 1989 the mother and the children were living in the house in the country, the children attending private schools there.

The father was living in the flat in London. The police came to his flat. They found in his possession a quantity of cocaine and a sum of £75,000 concealed in a vacuum cleaner. Criminal charges were preferred against him and he was sentenced to 2 years' imprisonment.

Since then the mother and the children have continued to live together, the mother struggling to maintain herself and the children and, in particular, to maintain them at their private schools.

The order of the district judge provided, in the events which have happened, that about £29,000 of the money available should be spent on discharging arrears of school bills, and that a sum of about £36,000 should be used to purchase a small property to house the mother and the children. Under the order of the district judge, that property is to be held by trustees with powers which permit a change in the property, but with a power of sale postponed until the youngest surviving of the five children shall reach the age of 21 years, or cease full-time secondary education, whichever shall be the sooner.

In that event the benefit of the property shall pass to the five children, or such of them as survive, in equal shares.

In this appeal the father has contended that this last provision shall be varied so that, upon the youngest child attaining the age of 21 years or completing full-time secondary education, the benefit of the property, or the property then replacing it, shall be his absolutely. Thus stated it is apparent that by this appeal the father seeks to deprive the children of a benefit conferred upon them by the order of the district judge. . . .

Here it is submitted, on behalf of the father, that the court has no power or alternatively should not exercise a power—to make provision for the children by way of a lump sum or settlement beyond the term which limits the power of the court in relation to orders for periodical payments.

In brief, the limitation referred to the age of the child, or its being in full-time education, or there being special circumstances relating to the child.

The matter is helpfully summarised in *Jackson's Matrimonial Finance and Taxation* (5th edn) where, at p. 171, the authors write:

The approach which has been adopted is that children are entitled to be maintained and educated but that, in the absence of disability or other special circumstances, they have no claim on their parents' resources after seeking to be dependent.

At p. 313:

A father, even the richest father, ought not to be regarded as under 'financial obligations or responsibilities' to provide funds for the purposes of such settlements as are envisaged in this case upon children who are under no disability and whose maintenance and education are secure. The reference to the position in which the child would have been has been removed by the Matrimonial and Family Proceedings Act 1984, so that justification for a settlement beyond the age of 18 and during the whole life of the child is even less likely.

It does seem to me that in the ordinary case . . . the statutory scheme should be construed as enabling the court to:

. . . make proper financial provision for children as children or dependants.

I recognise that there may be circumstances in which it is necessary for the court to make provision for children based upon their having a continuing need after they have attained their majority and, indeed, after they have left full-time education.

Whilst I do not think that the category of 'special circumstances' should be necessarily always so limited, it does seem to me that in its reference to special circumstances in relation to the duration of periodical payments, Parliament was intending the court ordinarily to look at special circumstances related to the children—such, for example, as some physical or other handicap.

There is nothing about these children which seems to me to justify their circumstances being regarded as in any way special or unusual. In my view the jurisdiction of the court should here be exercised so as to make the best possible provision for the children so long as they are, in the words of the order under appeal, '. . . under 21 or in full-time secondary education'. . . .

Moreover, in the particular circumstances of this case I cannot readily see any circumstances in which, judged as a matter of providing for the children during their dependency, a lump sum order would have significant advantages for the children over this order for the capital to be settled.

The reality of the situation is that the father wants to have the return of what he sees as his, rather than as family, capital, once the children's needs have been satisfied on their attaining full age and ceasing to be in full-time education. It is clearly his view that the order of the district judge is almost certain to result in the children together allowing their mother to continue in the house. It is certainly extremely unlikely that these children would insist on their share of the settlement being released to them, as the order provides, with the consequence that their mother would be put out of her home.

9.4.3   THE CHILDREN ACT 1989

CHILDREN ACT 1989

15.   Orders for financial relief with respect to children

(1)   Schedule 1 (which consists primarily of the re-enactment, with consequential amendments and minor modifications, of provisions of section 6 of the Family Law Reform Act 1969, the Guardianship of Minors Acts 1971 and 1973, the Children Act 1975 and of sections 15 and 16 of the Family Law Reform Act 1987) makes provision in relation to financial relief for children.

(2)   The powers of a magistrates' court under section 60 of the Magistrates' Courts Act 1980 to revoke, revive or vary an order for the periodical payment of money and the power of the clerk of a magistrates' court to vary such an order shall not apply in relation to an order made under Schedule 1.

Section 15(1)   SCHEDULE 1
FINANCIAL PROVISION FOR CHILDREN

Orders for financial relief against parents

1.—(1)   On an application made by a parent or guardian of a child, or by any person in whose favour a residence order is in force with respect to a child, the court may—

(a)   in the case of an application to the High Court or a county court, make one or more of the orders mentioned in sub-paragraph (2);

(b)   in the case of an application to a magistrates' court, make one or both of the orders mentioned in paragraphs (a) and (c) of that sub-paragraph.

(2)   The orders referred to in sub-paragraph (1) are—

(a)   an order requiring either or both parents of a child—

(i)   to make to the applicant for the benefit of the child; or

(ii)   to make to the child himself,

such periodical payments, for such term, as may be specified in the order;

(b)   an order requiring either or both parents of a child—

(i)   to secure to the applicant for the benefit of the child; or

(ii)   to secure to the child himself,

such periodical payments, for such term, as may be so specified;

(c)   an order requiring either or both parents of a child—

(i)   to pay to the applicant for the benefit of the child; or

(ii)   to pay to the child himself,

such lump sum as may be so specified;

    (d) an order requiring a settlement to be made for the benefit of the child, and to the satisfaction of the court, of property—

        (i)   to which either parent is entitled (either in possession or in reversion); and

        (ii)   which is specified in the order;

    (e) an order requiring either or both parents of a child—

        (i)   to transfer to the applicant, for the benefit of the child; or

        (ii)   to transfer to the child himself,

such property to which the parent is, or the parents are, entitled (either in possession or in reversion) as may be specified in the order.

    (3) The powers conferred by this paragraph may be exercised at any time.

    (4) An order under sub-paragraph (2)(a) or (b) may be varied or discharged by a subsequent order made on the application of any person by or to whom payments were required to be made under the previous order.

    (5) Where a court makes an order under this paragraph—

    (a) it may at any time make a further such order under sub-paragraph (2)(a), (b) or (c) with respect to the child concerned if he has not reached the age of eighteen;

    (b) it may not make more than one order under sub-paragraph (2)(d) or (e) against the same person in respect of the same child.

    (6) On making, varying or discharging a residence order the court may exercise any of its powers under this Schedule even though no application has been made to it under this Schedule.

    (7) Where a child is a ward of court, the court may exercise any of its powers under this Schedule even though no application has been made to it.

Orders for financial relief for persons over eighteen

    2.—(1) If, on an application by a person who has reached the age of eighteen, it appears to the court—

    (a) that the applicant is, will be or (if an order were made under this paragraph) would be receiving instruction at an educational establishment or undergoing training for a trade, profession or vocation, whether or not while in gainful employment; or

    (b) that there are special circumstances which justify the making of an order under this paragraph,

the court may make one or both of the orders mentioned in sub-paragraph (2).

    (2) The orders are—

    (a) an order requiring either or both of the applicant's parents to pay to the applicant such periodical payments, for such term, as may be specified in the order;

    (b) an order requiring either or both of the applicant's parents to pay to the applicant such lump sum as may be so specified.

    (3) An application may not be made under this paragraph by any person if, immediately before he reached the age of sixteen, a periodical payments order was in force with respect to him.

Duration of orders for financial relief

    3.—(1) The term to be specified in an order for periodical payments made under paragraph 1(2)(a) or (b) in favour of a child may begin with the date of the making of an application for the order in question or any later date or a date ascertained in accordance with sub-paragraph (5) or (6) but—

    (a) shall not in the first instance extend beyond the child's seventeenth birthday unless the court thinks it right in the circumstances of the case to specify a later date; and

    (b) shall not in any event extend beyond the child's eighteenth birthday.

    (2) Paragraph (b) of sub-paragraph (1) shall not apply in the case of a child if it appears to the court that—

    (a) the child is, or will be or (if an order were made without complying with that paragraph) would be receiving instruction at an educational establishment or undergoing training for a trade, profession or vocation, whether or not while in gainful employment; or

(b)   there are special circumstances which justify the making of an order without complying with that paragraph.

(3)   An order for periodical payments made under paragraph 1(2)(a) or 2(2)(a) shall, notwithstanding anything in the order, cease to have effect on the death of the person liable to make payments under the order.

(4)   Where an order is made under paragraph 1(2)(a) or (b) requiring periodical payments to be made or secured to the parent of a child, the order shall cease to have effect if—

(a)   any parent making or securing the payments; and

(b)   any parent to whom the payments are made or secured,

live together for a period of more than six months.

Matters to which court is to have regard in making orders for financial relief

4.—(1)   In deciding whether to exercise its powers under paragraph 1 or 2, and if so in what manner, the court shall have regard to all the circumstances including—

(a)   the income, earning capacity, property and other financial resources which each person mentioned in sub-paragraph (3) has or is likely to have in the foreseeable future;

(b)   the financial needs, obligations and responsibilities which each person mentioned in sub-paragraph (3) has or is likely to have in the foreseeable future;

(c)   the financial needs of the child.

(d)   the income, earning capacity (if any), property and other financial resources of the child;

(e)   any physical or mental disability of the child;

(f)   the manner in which the child was being, or was expected to be, educated or trained.

(2)   In deciding whether to exercise its powers under paragraph 1 against a person who is not the mother or father of the child, and if so in what manner, the court shall in addition have regard to—

(a)   whether that person had assumed responsibility for the maintenance of the child and, if so, the extent to which and basis on which he assumed that responsibility and the length of the period during which he met that responsibility;

(b)   whether he did so knowing that the child was not his child;

(c)   the liability of any other person to maintain the child.

(3)   Where the court makes an order under paragraph 1 against a person who is not the father of the child, it shall record in the order that the order is made on the basis that the person against whom the order is made is not the child's father.

(4)   The persons mentioned in sub-paragraph (1) are—

(a)   in relation to a decision whether to exercise its powers under paragraph 1, any parent of the child;

(b)   in relation to a decision whether to exercise its powers under paragraph 2, the mother and father of the child;

(c)   the applicant for the order;

(d)   any other person in whose favour the court proposes to make the order.

Provisions relating to lump sums

5.—(1)   Without prejudice to the generality of paragraph 1, an order under that paragraph for the payment of a lump sum may be made for the purpose of enabling any liabilities or expenses—

(a)   incurred in connection with the birth of the child or in maintaining the child; and

(b)   reasonably incurred before the making of the order, to be met.

(2)   The amount of any lump sum required to be paid by an order made by a magistrates' court under paragraph 1 or 2 shall not exceed £1000 or such larger amount as the Lord Chancellor may from time to time by order fix for the purposes of this sub-paragraph.

(3)   The power of the court under paragraph 1 or 2 to vary or discharge an order for the making or securing of periodical payments by a parent shall include power to make an order under that provision for the payment of a lump sum by that parent.

(4)   The amount of any lump sum which a parent maybe required to pay by virtue of sub-paragraph (3) shall not, in the case of an order made by a magistrates' court, exceed the maximum amount that may at the time of the making of the order be required to be paid under sub-paragraph (2), but a magistrates' court may make an order for the payment of a lump sum not exceeding that amount even though the parent was required to pay a lump sum by a previous order under this Act.

(5)   An order made under paragraph 1 or 2 for the payment of a lump sum may provide for the payment of that sum by instalments.

(6)   Where the court provides for the payment of a lump sum by instalments the court, on an application made either by the person liable to pay or the person entitled to receive that sum, shall have power to vary that order by varying—

(a)   the number of instalments payable;
(b)   the amount of any instalment payable;
(c)   the date on which any instalment becomes payable.

9.4.3.1   Orders

T v S (FINANCIAL PROVISION FOR CHILDREN) [1994] 2 FLR 883

JOHNSON J: The reality of the situation is that the father wants to have the return of what he sees as his, rather than as family, capital, once the children's needs have been satisfied on their attaining full age and ceasing to be in full-time education. It is clearly his view that the order of the district judge is almost certain to result in the children together allowing their mother to continue in the house. It is certainly extremely unlikely that these children would insist on their share of the settlement being released to them, as the order provides, with the consequence that their mother would be put out of her home.

The sadness here is that, after a long and seemingly happy relationship, this mother of five children, never having been married to their father, has no rights against him of her own. She has no right to be supported by him in the short, still less in the long term; no right in herself to have even a roof over her head.

The father's submission is that the order of the district judge will, in practice if not in legal theory, make a provision for her to which she is not entitled. That submission was accepted by the district judge, who said:

It would be wrong to give the mother a windfall not justified by the benefit to the children.

The district judge concluded:

The balance of capital available must be used to the children's best advantage as a matter of priority. With the sums available any periodical payments would be barely adequate to meet the needs of the family and, by no stretch of the imagination, comparable to the standard of living they are used to.

The district judge thereby rejected the submission of the father.

The district judge recognised the impact that might be made upon the financial situation of both parties by the statutory charge—they both having legal aid for the purpose of these proceedings. I have been told that the costs on the mother's side are of the order of £27,000 and, although some surprise is expressed about that from the father's side, there is no doubt that substantial costs have been incurred in relation to these proceedings.

It was not simply because of the potential impact of the statutory charge but also because of her rejection of a solution which might be seen as giving the mother a windfall that the district judge rejected the solution of a lump sum order to the mother for the benefit of the children.

In fact, however, it seems to me that by making an order for a settlement on the basis that on the trust for sale becoming effective the capital should be divided between the children equally, the district judge arrived at a solution which, in practice, might well lead to the mother having such a windfall.

On this appeal I have to exercise my own discretion in the matter, but I take account of the way that discretion was exercised by the district judge. I, too, would reject the solution of making an order for a lump sum payable to the mother for the benefit of the children.

A v A (A MINOR: FINANCIAL PROVISION) [1994] 1 FLR 657 (FamD)

WARD J: This is a claim by the mother of a girl, A, born on 27 May 1983 in which she seeks orders against A's father for the whole range of financial provision for the child under Sch 1 to the Children Act 1989. She applies for periodical payments, secured periodical payments, a lump sum, a transfer of property and, by late amendment, a settlement of property. . . .

There is, therefore, a distinct trend against making lump sum payments or property adjustment orders in favour of adult children who have ceased their full-time education. That trend is confirmed by the manner in which a child's claim is dealt with under the Inheritance (Provision for Family and Dependants) Act 1975. In *Re Coventry (Deceased); Coventry v Coventry* [1980] Ch 461, Goff LJ held that:

> There must be established some sort of moral claim by the applicant to be maintained by the deceased or at the expense of his estate beyond the mere fact of a blood relationship.

This trend to make financial provision for children 'as children or dependants'—per Booth J in *Kiely* [1988] 1 FLR 248—is reinforced by one particular feature in Sch 1 which does not find its counterpart in the Matrimonial Causes Act. Paragraph 2 provides for orders for financial relief to be made on the application by a person (note 'a person', not 'a child') who has reached the age of 18. If the applicant is receiving instruction or undergoing training or if there are special circumstances which justify the making of the order, then the court can make orders limited to periodical payments or a lump sum. There is no power to make a form of property adjustment. That restriction serves to confirm that property adjustment orders should not ordinarily be made to provide benefits for the child after he has attained his independence.

Mr Focke QC, for the applicant, submits that there are exceptional circumstances which justify the order he seeks which is an outright transfer of the London property either to the applicant for the benefit of the child or to the child herself. He relies on the following matters:

(1)   The circumstances of the purchase of the property. He submits that the property was purchased with the intention that it be and remain the family home. A transfer of the property to A would give effect to that intention. There are difficulties in supporting that submission. At least in the period before her bankruptcy, the applicant mother was in a position of conflict. In order for her to succeed in the application made under the Children Act for a transfer of property, she needs to establish that the property is one to which the respondent father was entitled (either in possession or in reversion). I was at a loss to see how she could advance that proposition and prosecute her counterclaim in which she sought a declaration that the beneficial interest in the property was hers and that the legal and beneficial interest in the property should be transferred to her. I would have expected in those circumstances that a next friend be appointed to represent A. I am not persuaded that where a father buys a property to provide a roof over the head of the unmarried mother and his child, this is such an exceptional circumstance as to justify the transfer of the property to the child absolutely.

(2)   It is then submitted that father is a man not only of immense wealth but also of great power and an outright transfer of the property is necessary to prevent any abuse of that power and to give security to A during her lifetime. I have no evidence to enable me to find that he has abused a power he undoubtedly has and his wealth by itself does not oblige him, nor the court, to make a handsome advance to the child at the start of her independent life.

(3)   It is culturally accepted, even expected, that a man of the father's rank should have many children by many mothers. He regards it as his obligation as pater familias

to provide properly for all children whom he recognises—and he recognises A. He asserts that he will provide for her as he has provided for others. Some attempt has been made to establish how he has provided for others of his children who remain in this country. That evidence falls short of establishing that he has made a provision for any other child by way of an advance of capital or property on the attaining of the child's majority. There is no discernible pattern in the distribution of his largesse and although I bear this possibility in mind when I consider all the circumstances of the case, I do not find this such a special circumstance as to compel the outright transfer.

I turn to consider the matters set out in para. 4 to which I am to have regard in deciding whether to exercise my powers and if so, how. I bear in mind all the circumstances of the case, some of which I shall expand upon in a moment. The father is so rich he could transfer this property and not even be aware that he had done so. His obligations and responsibilities are to provide for the maintenance and education of his child until she has completed that education, including her tertiary education, and reached independence. There is no special circumstance which imposes upon him any moral duty to advance capital or income to her once he has fulfilled that duty. Her financial needs are to he considered and it is noticeable that they are the financial needs of 'the child', which again suggests that adult needs are not ordinarily relevant. The child has no income. She has no physical or mental disability. I must have regard to the manner in which she was being or was expected to be educated or trained and the implication in those words is once more that the obligation to maintain ceases when that education or training cease. I bear in mind the cases to which I have referred above. There is no special circumstance I can find which would require this father to do more than maintain his daughter until she is independent. I therefore reject her claim for the transfer of the property to her absolutely. I reject Mr Blair's invitation to accept the father's undertaking to allow A to continue to occupy. A has a need for financial security and that security comes from knowing that she has a beneficial interest in the property, not just a licence to occupy.

I therefore conclude that the proper order is to require a settlement to be made for the benefit of A and to the satisfaction of the court of the NW3 property which will be further identified in the order.

The terms of the trust, the detail of which can be settled on further argument and if necessary with liberty to apply, should be that the property be conveyed to trustees, preferably, I would have thought, nominees of the mother and father to hold the same for A for a term which shall terminate 6 months after A has attained the age of 18, or 6 months after she has completed her full-time education, which will include her tertiary education, whichever is latest. I give her that period of 6 months to find her feet and arrange her affairs. The trustees shall permit her to enjoy a reasonable gap between completing her school education and embarking upon her further education. I have regard to para. 4(1)(b) which requires me to consider the financial needs, obligation., and responsibilities of each parent and also subpara (c) which requires me to have regard to the financial needs of the child. The mother's obligation is to look after A, and A's financial need is to provide a roof over the head of her caretaker. It is, indeed, father's obligation to provide the accommodation for the living-in help which A needs. Consequently, it must be a term of the settlement that while A is under the control of her mother and thereafter for so long as A does not object, the mother shall have the right to occupy the property to the exclusion of the father and without paying rent therefor for the purpose of providing a home and care and support for A. I deal with questions of the cost of maintaining the property below.

9.5   End of Chapter Assessment Questions

1. In what situations can maintenance be obtained for children without recourse to the Child Support Agency?

2. Steve is 32-years-old and employed as a fireman. He is unmarried. Just over a year ago he split up from his girlfriend, Toni and he has had no contact since. Yesterday he received a letter from the Child Support Agency together with a maintenance enquiry form asking for details of his income etc., with regard to Toni's child, William. Toni is claiming Steve is the father of William.

    Steve seeks your advice. He does not believe that he is the child's father and he wishes to know how the agency will approach this denial. Also he wishes to know how the Agency will assess the claim if he is treated as being the father.

9.6   End of Chapter Assessment Outline Answers

1. In this answer you have to consider all the situations where the Child Support Agency does not have jurisdiction to make an assessment for support, or in the event they have jurisdiction, fail to make an assessment. Consequently you need to mention a variety of different statutes under which maintenance can be ordered as well as the fact that voluntary arrangements may be made.

To start with it may be useful to state briefly when the Agency does have to be approached — those cases where a parent with care is receiving one of the specified state benefits, and there is an absent parent. The existence of a pre-1993 court order or maintenance agreement will not prevent the Agency's involvement if the parent with care is on benefit, and any Agency assessment will override and extinguish the previous arrangements. In this case the compulsory involvement is due to the operation of s. 6 of the Child Support Act 1991.

If a parent with care is not on benefit (or the child is being cared for by someone who is not a parent), then under s. 4 of the 1991 Act an application for assessment by the Agency can be made as the Agency has jurisdiction, but this is not compulsory.

If a pre-1993 written maintenance agreement exists, or there is an existing court order for child support, then a parent with care who is not on benefit cannot seek an assessment by the Agency. If there is a pre-existing agreement or order, the correct approach is to re-negotiate the agreement, or return to court to seek a variation of the order.

If there is no pre-existing agreement/order, then the parent with care may seek maintenance through the Matrimonial Causes Act 1973, the Domestic Proceedings and Magistrates' Court Act 1978 or the Children Act 1989. Factors that would be crucial to mention in your answer are:

*   The inability of the court to make provision other than consent orders in respect of child support. In other words if the parties disagree then the matter will have to go to the Agency.
*   The possibility of making a non-court sanctioned written maintenance agreement, again by consent which would deal with the child support payments but may be harder to enforce if not subsequently embodied in an order.
*   The status of the applicant since the 1973 Act and the 1978 Act are only available to married parents — non-married parents must utilise the Children Act 1989.
*   The factors and criteria to be applied by the courts under these Acts when assessing the appropriateness of the consent order with respect to child support.
*   The ability of the courts to make property adjustment orders under these Acts, which cannot be made by the Agency, although the reluctance of the courts to do so should be mentioned.

If the Child Support Act 1991 does apply the courts may be used to seek a 'top-up' to the maintenance assessment made under the CSA formula. As the formula does not adequately deal with wealthy parents it is permissible to go to court for an additional award of child support to be paid. This is not subject to the same requirement of consent as under s. 4 of the 1991 Act. This 'top-up' may involve additional periodical payments, or may also involve the making of a property adjustment order.

You should also refer to the other situations where the courts have jurisdiction over additional child support, i.e. the situations set out in s. 8 and refer to educational fees and the disability of the child.

Finally, there are certain situations where the Agency has no jurisdiction at all, and where the courts must be used. These situations will arise where the definitions of qualifying child and absent parent/parent with care do not apply. Hopefully, you have mentioned the possible liability of a step-parent who has treated a step child as a child of the family to pay maintenance under the 1971 and 1978 Acts. In addition, if the child is over 16 then they do not class as a qualifying child and support will have to be sought through the courts or a voluntary agreement.

2.   This question concerns other aspects of the Child Support Act 1991 and its operation by the Agency. In this question you are focussing more on the practicalities of the making of the assessment and the formula approach.

To start with advise Steve with regard to the question of paternity. If Steve has been declared the child's father in any other proceedings the Agency are able to presume that he is the father and continue the assessment on that basis. If Steve is adamant that he is not the father and no other presumption of paternity exists, then the Agency are required to stop the assessment until the matter of paternity is concluded.

Paternity will be decided by reference to DNA testing. This can be provided at reduced cost from the Agency, but if Steve is found to be the father then any costs will need to be paid by him. Only if the results of the testing prove him not to be the father will the cost be borne by the Agency. If Toni refuses to co-operate and will not allow blood tests, then adverse inferences can be made to the effect that Steve is not in fact the father.

Assume testing goes ahead and shows that Steve is the father and explain the assessment process and the formula application. Consider the basis upon which the maintenance requirement is calculated (Income Support rates, and including an amount for Toni as carer), the fact that the income of both parents is assessed, the maximum amount of Steve's net income that can be taken for child support and protected income etc. You would also need to mention the consequences of Steve failing to cooperate or return forms quickly, i.e. he would be assessed on an interim basis which invariably is much higher than a full assessment.

The possibility of departure from the formula also has to be covered. It is unlikely that many of the departure grounds will be applicable, Steve will not have a pre-1993 property adjustment to consider nor are his travel to work costs likely to be higher than the requisite mileage. He may have excessive expenditure on property which will entitle Toni to claim under the departure regulations.

CHAPTER TEN

THE LAW RELATING TO CHILDREN

10.1   What is Childhood?

Social Problems and Social Welfare: Inerfering in Peoples Lives,
Open University Press 1988

Postman's argument
Prior to the invention of the printing press in the mid fifteenth century virtually all human communication had been conducted in a direct group way. Information was exchanged by word of mouth, ideas by stories, ballads, fables and wise sayings. Even the reading that was done, was done largely aloud whilst others listened or followed the reader's finger along the characters of the handwritten manuscript. When the printed book became widely available, the reader was able to read for him/herself in privacy and solitude. In reading, 'both the writer and the reader enter into a conspiracy of sorts against social presence and consciousness. Print created a psychological environment in which the claims of individuality became irresistible. The printing press gave us ourselves as unique individuals to think and talk about. Introspections could be shared and reflection about oneself undertaken' (Postman, 1983). The 'individuality', these new opportunities for selfhood, that reading provided did not appear to extend to the child. The child could not read so a whole period—'childhood'—was created in which the child learned to gain access to this adult world by learning to read. Childhood, claims Postman, was the consequence of the new form of adult that arose following the invention of the printing press, the wide dissemination of printed information and the consequences of that for personal growth and self-reflection.

Reading and writing meant, according to Postman's argument, that the individual mind could address not just contemporaries but posterity. Thoughts and deeds need no longer only be communicated by word of mouth to friends, relatives, neighbours, fellow workers, groups. Printed information was also permanent and therefore openly available to anyone who could read and had access to the book. The individual's world of communication had apparently become liberated. There was no longer any need to be tied to the needs of immediate, contemporaneous and local events and happenings. One no longer only learned from one's immediate surroundings and the limited accounts and stories one was told, but increasingly learning came from books. The fixing of ideas in print provided an appropriate environment for the full development of symbolic and abstract thought.

When news was passed on by word of mouth, when discussions took place directly face to face or in a social gathering, there was little possibility of keeping secrets. Print opened up the possibility of a certain sort of privacy. Only people who could read, however, could become party to those secrets, which, of course, excluded children. Written information became the exclusive property of a reader—who could read about sensuality, death, abominations, abuse and so on. The non-reader was excluded from such excitements! Postman goes on to claim that 'print gave us the disembodied mind but left us with a problem of how to control the rest of us. Shame was the mechanism by which such control would be managed.'

In summary, the new form of adult was characterized by:

1. A new concept of an individual, self-reflective self.
2. The development of systematically ordered and symbolic thought.
3. The ability to concentrate, inhibit immediate impulses and exercise self-control.

'Too Young', *Woman*, 7 February 1987

AT WHAT AGE?

At any age
If you are under 18 you cannot enter into a contract (a legally binding agreement) nor will parents be liable for any debts you may incur (unless for necessities which include food and essential clothing). You can be made a ward of court—this means the court will make all the decisions on your upbringing. You can sue anyone in court—but you can only do so through an adult, who acts on your behalf. Certain things can be done if you are old enough or mature enough to understand the consequences of your actions, e.g.,

- choose your own religion
- open a bank account, although until reaching 18 an overdraft won't be available
- apply for access to any personal information held about you on a computer or computer files under the Data Protection Act 1984.

At 5
You will begin compulsory schooling. It is your parents legal responsibility to ensure you receive full time education suitable for your age, aptitude and understanding. If you are not taught in school the LEA will check the standard of your education. You can see a U or PG film. You can drink alcohol in private.

At 10
You can be convicted of a criminal offence. It must be shown that you knew what you were doing was wrong. The police can take your fingerprints, search you and take mug shots. If you are detained or arrested, the police must only question you if you are in the presence of an appropriate adult. You cannot be sent to prison, although you may be placed in secure accommodation or required to attend an attendance centre. You may be placed under the supervision of the local authority. If you have committed an act of homicide, you can be detained indefinitely. If you are a boy, you can be convicted of a sexual offence.

At 12
You can buy a pet. You may be detained in a young persons detention centre.

At 13
You can get a part-time job although the hours you work are limited to a maximum of 2 hours on a school day and Sundays. Your local byelaws may be more restrictive.

At 14
You can be convicted of a criminal offence and your knowledge as to whether you were doing something wrong is irrelevant. You can go into a pub, but can't buy a drink or drink alcohol whilst there. You can possess a shotgun or air-rifle.

At 15
You can see a 15 category film.

At 16
You can leave home, although your parents still have responsibility for you. You can ask a local authority to provide you with accommodation (e.g. foster home or childrens

home) without your parents consent. If you are a girl you can consent to sexual intercourse (if a boy, there is no age at which [heterosexual] intercourse is unlawful per se, however it may be classed as indecent assault even if the minor is consenting).

You can join the Armed Forces. You can get married with your parents consent, or the consent of a court. Failing that you can elope to Scotland. You can consent to medical treatment but probably can't refuse it if your parents consent to the treatment. You can leave school and start full-time work. You can get your NI number. You may qualify for a small number of welfare benefits. You can get a passport in your own name with your parents consent. You can buy cigarettes (although you may smoke at any age). You can drink beer, cider or wine with a meal in a restaurant. You can be made subject to a Probation Order.

At 17

You can be sent to prison. You can drive a car but not a lorry. You can buy or hire any sort of firearm—that hasn't been restricted by legislation. You can hold a pilot's licence. You can become a street trader.

At 18

You reach the age of majority. You can vote, serve on a jury, consent to or refuse medical treatment, own land, enter into legally binding agreements, marry, enter a homosexual relationship, sue people in court, donate your body to science, drink alcohol, buy the stuff, bet, be tattooed and see an 18 category film.

At 21

You can become an MP. You can drive a bus or HGV. You can hold a pub licence and sell alcohol.

10.2   Children's Rights

GILLICK v WEST NORFOLK AND WISBECH AREA HEALTH AUTHORITY
[1986] AC 112 (HL)

In 1980 the DHSS issued a Memorandum Of Guidance which stated

> in any case where a doctor or other professional worker is approached by a person under the age of 16 for advice . . . the doctor or other professional will always seek to persuade the child to involve the parent . . . at the earliest stage of consultation, and will proceed from the assumption that it would be most unusual to provide advice about contraception without parental consent.
>
> It is however, widely accepted that consultations between doctors and patients are confidential. To abandon this principle for children under 16 might cause some not to seek professional advice at all.

Mrs Gillick wrote to the Health Authority purporting to forbid any of its medical staff from giving any of her daughters contraceptive advice without her formal permission. When the Health Authority refused to accede to this request, Mrs Gillick sought a declaration that the notice 'gives advice which is unlawful and wrong and which adversely affects the welfare of the plaintiffs children, and/or the rights of the plaintiff as parent and/or the ability of the plaintiff properly and efficiently to exercise her duties as such a plaintiff.

HELD: The House of Lords did not support Mrs Gillicks contention. Per Lord Fraser:

> . . . there may be circumstances in which a doctor is a better judge that the child's parent. There may well be cases where the doctor feels that because the girl is under the influence of her sexual partner or for some other reason there is no realistic prospect of her abstaining from intercourse. He should of course always seek to persuade her to tell her parents that she is seeking contraceptive advice . . . At least he should persuade her to agree to the doctor's informing the parents. But the doctor

will be justified in proceeding without the parents' consent or even knowledge provided that he is satisfied on the following matters:

1. that the girl (although under 16 years of age) will understand his advice;
2. that he cannot persuade her to inform her patents or to allow him to inform the parents that she is seeking contraceptive advice;
3. that she is very likely to begin or to continue having sexual intercourse with or without contraceptive treatment;
4. that unless she receives contraceptive advice or treatment her physical or mental health are likely to suffer; and,
5. that her best interests require him to give her contraceptive advice, treatment or both without parental consent.

It is contrary to the ordinary experience of mankind to say that a child or young person remains in fact under the complete control of his parents until he attains the definite age of majority, and that on attaining that age he suddenly acquires independence. In practice most wise parents relax their control gradually as the child develops and encourage him or her to become increasingly independent. Moreover, the degree of parental control actually exercised over a particular child does in practice vary considerably according to his understanding and intelligence and it would in my opinion be unrealistic for the courts not to recognise these facts.

LORD SCARMAN: . . . Second, there is the common law's understanding of the nature of parental right. We are not concerned in this appeal to catalogue all that is contained in what Sachs LJ has felicitously described as the 'bundle of rights' which together constitute the rights of custody, care and control (see *Hewer v Bryant* [1969] 3 All ER 578 at 585). It is abundantly plain that the law recognises that there is a right and a duty of parents to determine whether or not to seek medical advice in respect of their child, and, having received advice, to give or withhold consent to medical treatment. The question in the appeal is as to the extent and duration of the right and the circumstances in which outside the two admitted exceptions to which I have earlier referred it can be overridden by the exercise of medical judgment.

As Parker and Fox LJJ noted in the Court of Appeal, the modern statute law recognises the existence of parental right: e.g. ss. 85 and 86 of the Children Act 1975 and ss. 2, 3 and 4 of the Child Care Act 1980. It is derived from parental duty. A most illuminating discussion of parental right is to be found in *Blackstone's Commentaries* (1 Bl Com (17th edn, 1830) vol 1, chs 16 and 17). He analyses the duty of the parent as the 'maintenance . . . protection, and . . . education' of the child (at p. 446). He declares that the power of more effectually to perform his duty, and partly as a recompense for his care and trouble in the faithful discharge of it' (at p. 452). In ch 17 he discusses the relation of guardian and ward. It is, he points out, a relation 'derived out of [the relation of parent and child]: the guardian being only a temporary parent, that is, for so long a time as the ward is an infant, or under age' (at p. 460). A little later in the same chapter he again emphasises that the power and reciprocal duty of a guardian and ward are the same, pro tempore, as that of a father and child and adds that the guardian, when the ward comes of age (as also the father who becomes guardian 'at common law' if an estate be left to his child), must account to the child for all that he has transacted on his behalf (at pp. 462–463). He then embarks on a discussion of the different ages at which for different purposes a child comes of sufficient age to make his own decision; and he cites examples, viz a boy might at 12 years old take the oath of allegiance; at 14 he might consent to marriage or choose his guardian 'and, if his discretion be actually proved, may make his testament of his personal estate'; at 18 he could be an executor: all these rights and responsibilities being capable of his acquiring before reaching the age of majority at 21 (at p. 463).

The two chapters provide a valuable insight into the principle and flexibility of the common law. The principle is that parental right or power of control of the person and property of his child exists primarily to enable the parent to discharge his duty of maintenance, protection and education until he reaches such an age as to be able to look after himself and make his own decisions. Blackstone does suggest that there was a further justification for parental right, viz as a recompense for the faithful discharge of parental duty; but the right of the father to the exclusion of the mother and the reward element as one of the reasons for the existence of the right have been swept away by the guardianship of minors legislation to which I have already referred. He also accepts that by statute and by case law varying ages of discretion have been fixed for various purposes. But it is clear that this was done to achieve certainty where it was considered necessary and in no way limits the principle that parental right endures only so long as it is needed for the protection of the child.

Although statute has intervened in respect of a child's capacity to consent to medical treatment from the age of 16 onwards, neither statute nor the case law has ruled on the extent and duration of parental right in respect of children under the age of 16. More specifically, there is no rule yet applied to contraceptive treatment, which has special problems of its own and is a later comer in medical practice. It is open, therefore, to the House to formulate a rule. The Court of Appeal favoured a fixed age limit of 16, basing itself on a view of the statute law which I do not share and on its view of the effect of the older case law which for the reasons already given I cannot accept. It sought to justify the limit by the public interest in the law being certain. Certainty is always an advantage in the law, and in some branches of the law it is a necessity. But it brings with it an inflexibility and a rigidity which in some branches of the law can obstruct justice, impede the law's development and stamp on the law the mark of obsolescence where what is needed is the capacity for development. The law relating to parent and child is concerned with the problems of the growth and maturity of the human personality. If the law should impose on the process of 'growing up' fixed limits where nature knows only a continuous process, the price would be artificiality and a lack of realism in an area where the law must be sensitive to human development and social change. If certainty be thought desirable, it is better that the rigid demarcations necessary to achieve it should be laid down by legislation after a full consideration of all the relevant factors than by the courts, confined as they are by the forensic process to the evidence adduced by the parties and to whatever may properly fall within the judicial notice of judges. Unless and until Parliament should think fit to intervene, the courts should establish a principle flexible enough to establish justice to be achieved by its application to the particular circumstances proved by the evidence placed before them.

The underlying principle of the law was exposed by Blackstone and can be seen to have been acknowledged in the case law. It is that parental right yields the child's right to make his own decisions when he reaches a sufficient understanding and intelligence to be capable of making up his own mind on the matter requiring decision. . . .

The modern law governing parental right and a child's capacity to make his own decisions was considered in *R v D* [1984] 2 All ER 449. The House must, in my view, be understood as having in that case accepted that save where statute otherwise provides, a minor's capacity to make his or her own decision depends on the minor having sufficient understanding and intelligence to make the decision and is not to be determined by reference to any judicially fixed age limit. The House was faced with a submission that a father, even if he had taken his child away by force or fraud, could nor be guilty of a criminal offence of any kind. Lord Brandon, with whom their other Lordships agreed, commented that this might well have been the view of the legislature and the courts in the nineteenth century, but had this to say about parental right and a child's capacity in our time to give or withhold a valid consent ([1984] 2 All ER 449 at 456):

This is because in those times both the generally accepted conventions of society and the courts by which such conventions were buttressed and enforced, regarded a father as having absolute and paramount authority, as against all the world, over any children of his who were still under the age of majority (then 21), except for a married daughter. The nature of this view of a father's rights appears clearly from various reported cases, including, as a typical example, *Re Agar-Ellis, Agar-Ellis v Lascelles* (1883) 14 ChD 317. The common law, however, while generally immutable in its principles, unless different principles are laid down by statute, is not immutable in the way in which it adapts, develops and applies those principles in a radically changing world and against the background of radically changed social conventions and conditions.

Later he said ([1984] 2 All ER 449 at 457):

> I see no good reason why, in relation to the kidnapping of a child, it should not in all cases be the absence of the child's consent which is material, whatever its age may be. In the case of a very young child, it would not have the understanding or the intelligence to give its consent so that absence of consent would be a necessary inference from its age. In the case of an older child, however, it must, I think, be a question of fact for a jury whether the child concerned has sufficient understanding and intelligence to give its consent; if, but only if, the jury considers that a child has these qualities, it must then go on to consider whether it has been proved that the child did not give its consent. While the matter will always be for the jury alone to decide, I should not expect a jury to find at all frequently that a child under 14 had sufficient understanding and intelligence to give its consent.

In the light of the foregoing I would hold that as a matter of law the parental right to determine whether or nor their minor child below the age of 16 will have medical treatment terminates if and when the child achieves a sufficient understanding and intelligence to enable him or her to understand fully what is proposed. It will be a question of fact whether a child seeking advice has sufficient understanding of what is involved to give a consent valid in law. Until the child achieves the capacity to consent, the parental right to make the decision continues save only in exceptional circumstances. Emergency, parental neglect, abandonment of the child or inability to find the parent are examples of exceptional situations justifying the doctor proceeding to treat the child without parental knowledge and consent; but there will arise, no doubt, other exceptional situations in which it will be reasonable for the doctor to proceed without the parent's consent.

When applying these conclusions to contraceptive advice and treatment it has to be borne in mind that there is much that has to be understood by a girl under the age of 16 if she is to have legal capacity to consent to such treatment. It is not enough that she should understand the nature of the advice which is being given: she must also have a sufficient maturity to understand what is involved. There are moral and family questions, especially her relationship with her parents; long-term problems associated with the emotional impact of pregnancy and its termination; and there are the risks to health of sexual intercourse at her age, risks which contraception may diminish but cannot eliminate. It follows that a doctor will have to satisfy himself that she is able to appraise these factors before he can safety proceed on the basis that she has at law capacity to consent to contraceptive treatment. And it follows that ordinarily the proper course will be for him, as the guidance lays down, first to seek to persuade the girl to bring her parents into consultation, and if she refuses, not to prescribe contraceptive treatment unless he is satisfied that her circumstances are such that he ought to proceed without parental knowledge and consent.

POLOVCHAK v *MEESE* 774 F 2d 731 (US CA, 7th Circuit)

Michael and Anna Polovchak, citizens of the USSR, left that country with their three children and came to the United States in January 1980. They settled in Chicago, but after several months, they decided to return to the Soviet Union. Their two older children, Nataly, then 17 years old, and Walter, then 12, decided that they wished to stay in the United States. Michael and Anna did not agree with Walter's decision. On July 13th 1980, Walter and Nataly left their parents' home and went to live with a cousin, who also lived in Chicago. On July 18th Michael sought the assistance of the Chicago police to bring Walter home. The police took Walter from his cousin's apartment and brought him to the police station, where Walter informed then that he had left home because he did not wish to return to the Soviet Union. Upon the advice of the Immigration Service and the State Department, the police did not take Walter home, but instead instituted custody proceedings in the [County] Court. On July 19th the trial judge temporarily placed Walter in the State's custody as a minor in need of supervision.

Walter later filed for asylum in the US. His parents in the meantime had returned to the Soviet Union. The initial decision was overturned on the basis that the Polovchaks should not have been deprived of their parental rights.

HELD: Whilst the parents interest was indeed strong, the court must also give weight to the wishes of the child, Walter. Hence the Court would not sanction the lifting of the order preventing Walter from leaving the country.

CUDAHY CJ: . . . the parents interest is one of the strongest our society knows . . . The government's interest in its own procedures does not override the weighty interests of Walter's parents, interests that must prevail over all but the strongest countervailing interests.

We do not agree with the District Court that the 'private interest of Walter is by its very nature considerably less than that of his parents.' Even if this were true in 1980 when Walter sought political asylum, Walter's rights have evolved over the past 5 years and the facts and circumstances relevant to such a balancing exercise have changed.

At the age of 12 Walter was presumably near the lower end of an age range in which a minor may be mature enough to assert certain individual rights that equal or override those of this parents; at age 17 (indeed, on the eve of his 18th birthday), Walter is certainly at the high end of such a scale, and the question whether he should have to subordinate his own political commitments to his parents' wishes looks very different. The minors rights grow very compelling with age . . . as a child grows, his parents' influence over him weakens and the time his parents; have to guide him grows shorter . . .

United Nations' Declaration of the Rights of the Child

Preamble
Whereas the peoples of the United Nations have, in the Charter, reaffirmed their faith in fundamental human rights, and in the dignity and worth of the human person, and have determined to promote social progress and better standards of life in larger freedom.

Whereas the United Nations has, in the Universal Declaration of Human Rights, proclaimed that everyone is entitled to all the rights and freedoms set forth therein, without distinction of any kind, such as race, colour, sex, language, religion, political or other opinion, national or social origin, property, birth or other status.

Whereas the child, by reason of his physical and mental immaturity, needs special safeguards and care, including appropriate legal protection, before as well as after birth.

Whereas the need for such special safeguards has been stated in the Geneva Declaration of the Rights of the Child of 1924, and recognized in the Universal Declaration of Human Rights and in the statutes of specialized agencies and international organisations concerned with the welfare of children.

Whereas mankind owes to the child the best it has to give.

Now therefore, the General Assembly proclaims this Declaration of the Rights of the Child to the end that he may have a happy childhood and enjoy for his own good and for the good of society the rights and freedoms herein set forth, and calls upon parents, upon men and women as individuals and upon voluntary organizations, local authorities and national governments to recognize these rights and strive for their observance by legislative and other measures progressively taken in accordance with the following principles.

Principle 1
The child shall enjoy all the rights set forth in the Declaration. All children, without any exception whatsoever, shall be entitled to these rights, without distinction or discrimination on account of race, colour, sex, language, religion, political or other opinion, national or social origin, property, birth or other status, whether of himself or of his family.

Principle 2
The child shall enjoy special protection, and shall be given opportunities and facilities, by law and by other means, to enable him to develop physically, mentally, morally, spiritually and socially in a healthy and normal manner and in conditions of freedom and dignity. In the enactment of laws for this purpose the best interests of the child shall be the paramount consideration.

Principle 3
The child shall be entitled from his birth to a name and a nationality.

Principle 4
The child shall enjoy the benefits of social security. He shall be entitled to grow and develop in health; to this end special care and protection shall be provided both to him and to his mother, including adequate prenatal and postnatal care. The child shall have the right to adequate nutrition, housing, recreation and medical services.

Principle 5
The child who is physically, mentally or socially handicapped shall be given the special treatment, education and care required by his particular condition.

Principle 6
The child, for the full and harmonious development of his personality, needs love and understanding. He shall, wherever possible, grow up in the care and under the responsibility of his parents, and in any case in an atmosphere of affection and of moral and material security; a child of tender years shall not, save in exceptional circumstances, be separated from his mother. Society and the public authorities shall have the duty to extend particular care to children without a family and to those without adequate means of support. Payment of state and other assistance toward the maintenance of children of large families is desirable.

Principle 7
The child is entitled to receive education, which shall be free and compulsory, at least in the elementary stages. He shall be given an education which will promote his general culture, and enable him to develop his abilities, his individual judgement, and his sense of moral and social responsibility, and to become a useful member of society.

The best interests of the child shall be the guiding principle of those responsible for his education and guidance that responsibility lies in the first place with his parents.

The child shall have full opportunity for play and recreation, which should be directed towards the same purposes as education; society and the public authorities shall endeavour to promote the enjoyment of this right.

Principle 8
The child shall in all circumstances be among the first to receive protection and relief.

Principle 9
The child shall be protected against all forms of neglect, cruelty and exploitation. He shall not be the subject of traffic, in any form.

The child shall not be admitted to employment before an appropriate minimum age, he shall in no case be caused or permitted to engage in any occupation or employment which would prejudice his health or education, or interfere with his physical, mental or moral development.

Principle 10
The child shall be protected from practices which may foster racial, religious and any other form of discrimination. He shall be brought up in a spirit of understanding, tolerance, friendship among peoples, peace and universal brotherhood and in full consciousness that his energy and talents should be devoted to the service of his fellow men.

United Nations' Convention on The Rights of The Child

Article 2
1. States Parties shall respect and ensure the rights set forth in the present Convention to each child within their jurisdiction without discrimination of any kind, irrespective of the child's or his or her parent's or legal guardian's race, colour, sex, language, religion, political or other opinion, national, ethnic or social origin, property, disability, birth or other status.

2. States Parties shall take all appropriate measures to ensure that the child is protected against all forms of discrimination or punishment on the basis of the status, activities, expressed opinions, or beliefs of the child's parents, legal guardians, or family members.

Article 3

1. In all actions concerning children, whether undertaken by public or private social welfare institutions, courts of law, administrative authorities or legislative bodies, the best interests of the child shall be a primary consideration.

2. States Parties undertake to ensure the child such protection and care as is necessary for his or her well-being, taking into account the rights and duties of his or her parents, legal guardians, or other individuals legally responsible for him or her, and, to this end, shall take all appropriate legislative and administrative measures.

Article 6

1. States Parties recognize that every child has the inherent right to life.

Article 8

1. States Parties undertake to respect the right of the child to his or her identity, including nationality, name and family relations as recognized by law without unlawful interference.

Article 9

1. States Parties shall ensure that a child shall not be separated from his or her parents against their will, except when competent authorities subject to judicial review determine, in accordance with applicable law and procedures, that such separation is necessary for the best interests of the child. Such determination may be necessary in a particular case such as one involving abuse or neglect of the child by the parents, or one where the parents are living separately and a decision must be made as to the child's place of residence.

Article 12

1. States Parties shall assure to the child who is capable of forming his or her own views the right to express those views freely in all matters affecting the child, the views of the child being given due weight in accordance with the age and maturity of the child.

Article 13

1. The child shall have the right to freedom of expression; this right shall include freedom to seek, receive and impart information and ideas of all kinds, regardless of frontiers, either orally, in writing or in print, in the form of art, or through any other media of the child's choice.

Article 14

1. States Parties shall respect the right of the child to freedom of thought, conscience and religion.

2. States Parties shall respect the rights and duties of the parents and, when applicable, legal guardians, to provide direction to the child in the exercise of his or her right in a manner consistent with the evolving capacities of the child.

3. Freedom to manifest one's religion or beliefs may be subject only to such limitations as are prescribed by law and are necessary to protect public safety, order, health or morals, or the fundamental rights and freedoms of others.

Article 19

1. States Parties shall take all appropriate legislative, administrative, social and educational measures to protect the child from all forms of physical or mental violence, injury or abuse, neglect or negligent treatment, maltreatment or exploitation, including sexual abuse, while in the care of parent(s), legal guardian(s) or any other person who has the care of the child.

Article 23

1.   States Parties recognize that a mentally or physically disabled child should enjoy a full and decent life, in conditions which ensure dignity, promote self-reliance, and facilitate the child's active participation in the community.

2.   States Parties recognize the right of the disabled child to special care and shall encourage and ensure the extension, subject to available resources, to the eligible child and those responsible for his or her care, of assistance for which application is made and which is appropriate to the child's condition and to the circumstances of the parents or others caring for the child.

Article 24

1.   States Parties recognize the right of the child to the enjoyment of the highest attainable standard of health and to facilities for the treatment of illness and rehabilitation of health. States Parties shall strive to ensure that no child is deprived of his or her right of access to such health care services.

Article 28

1.   States Parties recognize the right of the child to education, and with a view to achieving this right progressively and on the basis of equal opportunity, they shall, in particular:
   (a)   make primary education compulsory and available free to all;
   (b)   encourage the development of different forms of secondary education, including general and vocational education, make them available and accessible to every child, and take appropriate measures such as the introduction of free education and offering financial assistance in case of need;
   (c)   make higher education accessible to all on the basis of capacity by every appropriate means;
   (d)   make educational and vocational information and guidance available and accessible to all children;
   (e)   take measures to encourage regular attendance at schools and the reduction of drop-out rates.

Article 32

1.   States Parties recognize the right of the child to be protected from economic exploitation and from performing any work that is likely to be hazardous or to interfere with the child's education, or to be harmful to the child's health or physical, mental, spiritual, moral or social development.

10.3   State Intervention

10.3.1   UP TO THE CHILDREN ACT 1989

Cretney, S, and Masson, J, *Principles of Family Law*, 5th edn, Sweet & Maxwell, 1990

The power to bring care proceedings provides insufficient protection in cases where ill-treatment or risk of harm necessitates the child's immediate removal from home or the prevention of removal from hospital or elsewhere. Under the Children and Young Persons Act 1969 a magistrate could authorise a child's removal to a place of safety for up to 28 days on the application of any person with reasonable cause to suspect that the child was being ill-treated. Place of safety orders were the subject of considerable criticism:—they lasted too long, particularly as they were granted *ex parte* and where not subject to review; the grounds were not sufficiently focussed on emergencies, local authorities sought orders too readily, some apparently used them routinely as a precursor to care proceedings; the applicant had no clear responsibility for the child's welfare, orders were disruptive to children and could result in long periods without contact with the family; local authorities' powers were unclear but probably inadequate to have the child assessed or examined. The police also had the power to detain children on similar grounds for up to eight days without a court order and could obtain a warrant to search for and detain them for up to 28 days.

The Short Committee and the Review of Child Care Law both proposed substantial reform to limit emergency powers to cases where immediate action was required, reduce the duration of orders and allow them to be reviewed. These proposals were accepted by the Government which recognised that the demands of local authority investigations should be kept to a practical minimum. Further proposals were made for a 'child assessment order' under which parents could be required to take the child for a medical examination. These proposals were all incorporated in the Children Act 1989.

10.4   Why the Children Act – Why 1989?

Timmins, N, and Vallely, P, Report blames all services in case, *The Times*, 3 December 1985

Practically every official body involved in the care of Jasmine Beckford aged four, who was battered to death by her stepfather, must bear some responsibility for her death which was predictable and preventable, according to the official report of the panel of inquiry published yesterday.

Magistrates exceeded their jurisdiction when Jasmine and her younger sister Louise were committed into the care of Brent Borough Council.

The primary social worker 'lamentably failed' at the key moment. Her supervisor was grossly negligent'.

The health worker involved partook of the same misconceived approach as the social workers.

The doctor at Jasmine's nursery school failed to carry out basic checks on the child.

Brent councillors involved in the supervising committee were responsible for an 'inordinate delay in responding to Jasmine's death'.

Health, education, and social service authorities, and named individuals are severely criticised in the highly-outspoken report of the committee, chaired by Mr Louis Blom-Cooper QC.

The 450 page report, not confined to the apportioning of blame, makes 68 recommendations. After presenting the report yesterday to Brent council, Mr Blom-Cooper summarized them: 'The time has come to shift the focus of work in the child abuse system from parents to the children. Put the child first and it that means doing something that is disliked by the parents that's what has got to be done.'

Legislation was likely in the near future which would incorporate some of the recommendations. Wrong judgments would occur in the future, he said, but the changes would appreciably reduce the area of risk.

The catalogue of errors which led to the death of the child began in September 1981 at Willesden Juvenile Court. The month before Louise Beckford, aged four months was taken to hospital with a broken arm and damage to her right eye.

Three days later Jasmine was admitted with a broken thigh. The injuries were consistent with physical violence.

At the hearing to place the children in care the magistrates added a rider which the report regards as the crucial mistake.

> Had the magistrates . . . exercised appropriate judicial restraint and refrained from the understandable temptation to pronounce, in the presence of the parents and their legal representatives, their earnest hope that the children would soon be reunited with their parents, it is doubtful whether Jasmine would ever have been returned to her parents' home.

Court officers were remiss in not indicating forcefully to the Bench that such remarks were unhelpful. 'Had the local authority not subsequently structured its handling of the children in a manner likely to fulfil the magistrates expressed hope there was a very real possibility, that the parents would get the care orders revoked', the report says. From this point there was 'a lemming-like movement' towards the girl's death.

'There can be little doubt that by the autumn of 1983 Jasmine and Louise were being exposed daily (even hourly) to physical abuse in the Beckford home' from their educationally subnormal stepfather Morris Beckford, while their mother Beverley Lorrington, described as intellectually sub-normal, looked on.

Throughout that year Miss Gun Wahlstrom and her supervisor, Mrs Diane Dietmann, pursued an approach to the family which concentrated on the parents rather than the children. 'Miss Wahlstrom's approach to her task was fundamentally flawed, Mrs Dietmann's attitude as the supervisor was no less so . . . By her non-intervention she was grossly negligent.'

They failed to see that their prime duty was to the children. 'At no time did the two workers insist on seeing the children nor did they ensure that they were medically examined at the local clinic . . . We fear that their attitude in regarding the parents of children in care as the clients, rather than the children in their own right, may be widespread among social workers.'

Miss Wahlstrom so regarded the children as mere appendages that in a meticulous record of almost 100 pages of detailed notes in her records there was not a single entry devoted exclusively to Jasmine and Louise, the report says. In 78 visits to the house she saw Jasmine once.

'Miss Wahlstrom lamentably failed to see what was crying out to be seen, namely a grossly undernourished, limping child who could not conceivably be described by the most undiscerning of visitors, let alone a trained social worker, as "well and happy".' Yet that was the entry recorded in the official files after the child was seen for the last time.

The social worker also failed to inform Jasmine's nursery school that the child was the subject of a care order. In this way she failed to realise the useful monitoring function of a school in such circumstances. Although, subsequently the school authorities noted erratic attendances which coincide, the report notes, with periods of Jasmine's worst injuries, the teachers were unable to appreciate the absences significance in a child of pre-school age.

But independent checks could have been made and these were inadequate. The report is critical of Dr Peiris, of the Mortimer Road Nursery, who examined the child in a 'development check' but did so without reference to the percentile chart of Jasmine's height and weight available in the clinic files.

The report says that Miss Wahlstrom and the health visitor, Miss Yeng Leong, as the two front-line workers, 'must take some personal responsibility for what happened. But in no sense were either callous or indifferent to Jasmine's welfare. They had little or no training to qualify them to undertake the task of providing a child protection service, and furthermore they were pitchforked by their superiors, into a speciality of case work with very limited if any knowledge and minimal experience in dealing with child abuse'.

The report criticizes their superiors as doing nothing during the winter of 1983–84 'to exercise anything approaching the regular supervision that is expected of senior managers'.

The report emphasizes that a child placed under a care order by a local authority is 'a child in trust' the phrase taken as the report's title.

Routledge, P, Smart, V, Ferriman, A, and Timbs, O, 'Emergency Ward Nine',
The Observer, **28 June 1987**

Outside the gaunt, red-brick building of the Middlesbrough General Hospital, a group of parents keep vigil. Inside, in Ward Nine, their children play games and watch television behind drawn curtains.

The gulf that divides them is filled with anguish, anger and raw emotion. On one side is the local authority who have had the children removed from their parents pending investigations into child abuse; on the other are the indignant parents, egged on by the tabloid Press.

It is a sad state of affairs and a tangled and confused story which has maintained the nation's interest all week. At the core of the dispute in Middlesbrough is a frightening national statistic.

In 1984, the NSPCC reported that 1,500 children had suffered or were at risk from sexual molestation. In 1985, the Society revised their estimate upwards to double the previous year's figure to 3,000 children abused or at risk.

And in figures to be published this week the Society will increase its estimates again to double the 1985 figure. Last year they believe that 6,000 children throughout Britain suffered or were likely to suffer from sexual abuse from adults.

What appears to be happening in the Cleveland area is that two paediatricians, Dr Geoffrey Wyatt and Dr Marietta Higgs, have decided that they will not turn a blind eye to the evidence before them. If they believe that there are signs of sexual abuse of children, they have immediately informed the social services department.

In turn, the social workers are anxious not to found at fault. No doubt aware of the hatred poured on social workers who have ignored warning signs of child abuse—in some recent cases, such as that of Kimberley Carlile, resulting in the deaths of children—the Cleveland Social Services Department is taking no chances. Children have been removed from parents and put into council care.

In the past three months 202 children have been taken into care; so many that Ward Nine of Middlesbrough General Hospital is being used as an emergency overflow, as there are no more spaces in children's homes and no more foster parents to cope with the unprecedented numbers. In the whole of 1986 a total of 76 children were taken by 'place of safety' orders; in the seven weeks between 1 May and today, 202 children have been similarly taken into care.

The scale of numbers has alarmed many, not least the parents of the children taken into care. Is this a case of overzealousness on the part of the two Middlesbrough paediatricians? Is Middlesbrough a proving ground for the theory held by many paediatricians and social workers that one child in 10 throughout Britain is sexually abused?

What exactly are the grounds for removing a child from its parents in a suspected case of sexual abuse? One example is that of a 29-year-old Middlesbrough woman who has two children held in care. Just before 5 p.m. on 19 June she took her seven-year-old son to Middlesbrough General suffering from chronic constipation.

'Dr Wyatt examined my son's back passage and asked me if I had any more children outside,' she said. 'I said yes, a little girl of nine. He asked me if he could examine her. Of course, I said. After a couple of minutes, he went out and came back with Dr Higgs. She took one look at his back passage and they said there were signs of sexual abuse.'

'It all happened so quickly. By 10.30 p. m. they were both taken from me for 28 days under a Place of Safety Order. The children were very distressed. The next morning we went to a solicitor and he said "Join the queue."'

The sort of evidence that doctors look for in sexually abused children is damage to genitals, bruising, swellings and leakages. And there is the 'anal test', in which the buttocks of a child are parted. In most children the anus remains tight closed; in children where anal abuse has occurred, it gapes wide open.

Shy and withdrawn

But just as important to the doctors is the general behaviour of the child. For example, bleeding from a child's anus would not necessarily be sufficient evidence. But if the child was also shy, withdrawn and refused to answer questions about the injury, there would be further investigation. A child with a sore vagina who flirted in a way uncharacteristic for her age might also raise questions in the doctor's mind.

In Cleveland, despite the high numbers of children thought to have suffered sexual or physical abuse, the director of social services, Mr Michael Bishop, is convinced that his department is doing the right thing by the children: 'Other supporting evidence is sufficient for me to be satisfied that a majority of the 200 children taken into care have been abused'.

Isolated from their parents and interviewed by sympathetic social workers who have gained their confidence, many of the children are 'telling us their stories of abuse', according to Sue Richardson, a child-abuse consultant.

One reason social workers are wary of the Cleveland parents' outrage is that, in a crime which can depend on an adult's word against a child's, a guilty adult is very capable of persistent lying. Often the stories they tell are highly plausible. Bruises are attributed to childish horseplay; in the case of one five-year-old suffering from vaginal bleeding, a fall from a bench was blamed.

Sue Richardson claims that the way the Middlesbrough hospital has grasped the child-abuse nettle has been hailed as a breakthrough by those working in the health and social service professions locally. 'Sexual abuse is an uncorroborated crime,' she said, 'and it is just too dangerous to take the word of an adult. As many as one girl in four could be abused.'

What has been criticised, however, is Cleveland's quickness to act in child-abuse cases. On the initial diagnosis of the Middlesbrough General Hospital paediatrician, an application is made through a social worker to a magistrate for a Place of Safety Order under Section 12 of the 1969 Children's Act.

Authority for the order is almost never withheld, even though sometimes it is given an impromptu hearing in the middle of the night 'with the magistrate in his dressing gown'. Neither the social worker nor the magistrate feels sufficiently competent or confident to challenge the view of the hospital consultant. What in some parts of the country can be a protracted business can in Middlesbrough take only a few hours.

This contrasts with Lewisham, for instance, where children are first interviewed without their parents. Then if a medical examination discloses suspected sex abuse, the whole household is interviewed to uncover the 'family dynamics' which usually shows up serious grounds for concern and averts the 'summary judgment' inherent in the Middlesbrough system.

Michael Bishop, however, is unapologetic about Middlesbrough's haste. 'I don't believe we can work with a family until we know who the abuser is. I contend that the child-care law says that we should act immediately. Society would not tolerate leaving them where they are, at risk of further abuse or in danger of being killed.'

An example of insufficient urgency took place in South London three years ago when a hospital failed to recognise a torn hymen in a three-year-old as sexual abuse. Her father had, in fact, raped her and the little girl was back in hospital last week with a vaginal discharge.

But in the face of pressure from hostile parents claiming their innocence, actions tomorrow in the High Court and often hysterical Press attention, Middlesbrough will be making changes to its procedures. Tomorrow Cleveland Council and the Northern Regional Health Authority will start an urgent review of 20 cases of children in care and they will revamp their referral system to include a '72-hour protocol' which will give more safeguards for parents.

Tenfold rise

Social workers are viewing with alarm the effects of the pressure by parents and others which are serving to confuse and confound a system which puts children first. On Friday night, three children—aged five, six and seven—were ordered by a magistrate to be reunited with their parents, a 26-year-old roadsweeper and his wife, 45 days after they were removed on evidence of anal sexual abuse, following a diagnosis by Dr Wyatt at Middlesbrough General. Later this judgment was overruled after an appeal to the High Court.

The court heard rival versions of 'the controversy' over the tenfold rise in sex abuse referrals. Mr Peter Medd, the solicitor acting for the children, said: 'I am very concerned that there is emotionally irresistible pressure on the local authority to return children when perhaps it would be unwise to do so.'

This pressure has included a violent campaign by the local evening paper—summed up by the headline 'Give us back our children'—and a similarly slanted campaign by the *Daily Mail*. Sixteen children in council care have been examined by a Harley Street consultant who claims that all but one of them had not been sexually abused—although his examination took place some time after the events were meant to have taken place.

And parents have banded together around a group called Parents Against Injustice (PAIN) to try to free their children. Their 'free them all' demand has distressed social workers who have knowledge of the cases involved. Some parents are certainly not guilty, they say, although abuse may have been inflicted by close friends of the family or even older brothers and sisters. But the parents' claim for all the children to be released threatens to exonerate some real molesters, they say.

Inevitably the controversy has raged around the arrival in February of Dr Higgs, a new consultant at Middlesbrough General trained in Adelaide, Australia. The rise in the number of child abuse referrals appears to be directly linked to her actions. Although she has been attacked by the parents and the Press—and the Middlesbrough MP, Stuart Bell, has called for her and Dr Wyatt's suspension—she has a good professional reputation.

Dr Nigel Speight, consultant paediatrician at Dryburn Hospital, Durham, in the same health region as Middlesbrough, described her as a 'conscientious, caring paediatrician, trying to do her duty in a difficult area. There is nothing unusual about her. She is a quiet, hard-working person.'

And suggestions that she may be over-zealous or have acquired a crusading zeal which may have led to hasty or inappropriate diagnoses are dismissed with a more mundane explanation. Middlesbrough, according to Dr Speight, 'is a very busy department and up to this year there were only two paediatricians. When you get an additional consultant appointed, who has an interest in child abuse, you are bound to get a considerable increase in referrals. There is a backlog effect.'

And he agreed with Dr Higgs's conclusions. 'I have seen some of the photos of one of the cases involved. I was forcibly impressed by the strength of the evidence.'

Violent coercion

It is not a point of view shared by Dr Alistair Irvine, the senior regional police surgeon. The views of Dr Higgs are, he claims, very controversial:

I examined three of the children some four weeks ago. There was no evidence of abuse. She is making diagnostic mistakes. I think the whole thing is horrendous.

Whatever the outcome of the Middlesbrough child-abuse controversy, starting tomorrow with a High Court hearing over the immediate future of the 16 children examined by the Harley Street doctor, the public awareness of the violent coercion of children into sex with adults will continue to grow.

Dr Speight saw another issue:

The media and the public cannot have it both ways. On the one hand they lambast social workers for not taking children into care, yet when confronted by a conscientious paediatrician acting in good faith, they react with a hysterical backlash.

Faux, R, 'Decision to put children in court care is defended: ritualistic abuse allegations', *The Times*, 12 September 1990

The director of social services for Rochdale has defended the council's action in making 20 children wards of court after allegations that they had been involved in satanic ritualistic abuse.

Gordon Littlemore said that a joint investigation by Rochdale social services and Greater Manchester police was continuing and denied that the action relied on the statements of one boy aged six. He said that comparisons with the Cleveland child abuse affair were inappropriate because that had been concerned solely with sexual abuse.

'Here we are dealing with allegations of emotional abuse, degradation, humiliation, the administration of drugs and exposure to acts of violence, which would not necessarily result in physical injury,' Mr Littlemore said. The view of social services officers and the police was that the abuse that the children described was real and not the product of their imagination, fuelled by watching video horror films.

Several other children involved had independently made statements to the effect that they had been involved in ritualistic abuse, and evidence had been considered on several occasions by High Court judges. The action taken was to protect the children, Mr Littlemore said.

The children had been taken into care and collected from their homes early in the morning without warning, because some of the allegations of abuse implicated members of the children's families. Mr Littlemore said that, had notice been given, there would have been a danger of evidence being destroyed.

The National Society for the Prevention of Cruelty to Children said yesterday that it was convinced that some children are 'ritualistically abused' and that it was investigating a series of cases. The society said that small children generally were unable to invent the type of acts typifying abuse cases.

Faux, R, 'Rochdale workers "ignored rules" on child abuse cases', *The Times*, 10 November 1990

Social workers investigating allegations of 30 cases of child abuse in Rochdale did so in clear breach of government guidelines drawn up in the wake of the Cleveland enquiry, a government investigation has discovered.

Rochdale council said last night, however, that it still felt it had acted properly in taking into care recently another 20 children after allegations of ritual abuse.

Government inspectors have made their conclusion after an investigation into 30 cases of alleged abuse handled by the Rochdale social services team. The department admitted last night that the council's guidelines needed to be updated and a review made of the process of parents' involvement in decision-making.

The council was responding to the report by the Social Services Inspectorate on child care procedures in Rochdale. The inspectors did not investigate the cases in which 20 children have recently been taken into care.

Rochdale borough council said that that decision had never been doubted. 'We took the only proper course of action in protecting those children. That is still the central issue, and must not be lost sight of even though this examination specifically excludes consideration of those cases.'

The council points out that the most up-to-date government guidelines make no reference to organised or ritual abuse. The council said that it understood that the report did not criticise the practice of taking children from home in 'dawn raids'. The authority believed the inspectorate would say there was a fine balance to be maintained between conducting an investigation to provide evidence for possible criminal prosecution and ensuring that the welfare of the children was not subordinated.

The investigation has concluded that social workers ignored parents and children, keeping them ill-informed. Guidelines were said to be out of date and social workers had failed to follow all the recommendations of the Cleveland enquiry.

Inspectors investigated 30 cases of alleged abuse handled by the council, and the report, due for publication on Monday, says there was 'a lack of full involvement of parents and children in the decisions made about them'.

The inspectors found that while some social workers did try to develop a partnership with parents this was not general and not accepted by some other professionals in the field. They concluded that while the council had most of the elements for an efficient professional service, they were not being effectively managed and co-ordinated.

The report makes 41 recommendations, including a call for new procedures to be implemented as a matter of urgency; there should be clarification of which cases should be referred to the police; and more effort taken to involve parents and children.

Sue Emphlett of Parents Against Injustice, the Rochdale-based group campaigning for an enquiry into the conduct of the social services department, said: 'The report confirms all our anxieties. I fear what is happening here could be happening all over the country.'

Clancy, R, 'Care workers "acted irrationally" in Orkney abuse case', *The Times*, 28 October 1992

Child care and social workers failed to keep an open mind when investigating allegations of organised abuse in Orkney, a highly critical report by Lord Clyde, published yesterday, concludes. They acted quickly and irrationally and did not consider an alternative to taking the children into care.

Lord Clyde, who chaired the judicial enquiry into the case, has ordered the Orkney Islands council to improve relations with the 1,000 people on the island of South Ronaldsay. His report recommends changes in the law and improved training for social workers, care officials and police.

The enquiry came after nine children were taken from their homes in February 1991 and returned three months later, after Sheriff David Kelbie said that the investigation by the social work department had been fatally flawed. Lord Clyde agreed that it was right to return the children, but that the move had been carried out too quickly.

'Although by normal standards the return was managed at an undue speed, the decision to achieve an immediate return cannot reasonably be criticised in the circumstances,' he said.

The children were seized after allegations of sex abuse made by three children. Sheriff Kelbie threw out the case in Kirkwall in April last year, saying social workers had coached the children.

They were flown home that day. The strength of the allegations has not been tested. Lord Clyde's remit did not allow him to investigate whether organised abuse was taking place.

Lord Clyde calls for urgent research into all forms of child abuse and a better relationship between agencies involved. The discovery of abuse should not be the monopoly of one organisation.

The report was expected to be hard on the social work department and officials from the Scottish Royal Society for the Prevention of Cruelty to Children, but the extent of the indictment was a surprise. Lord Clyde made 135 criticisms and accused the social work department of not making a detailed enough study of the problem relating to the original family and allowing 'thinking to be coloured by undefined suspicions'.

The list of criticisms included the following findings. The social work department failed to consider the position of the nine children individually or to assess the degree or risk to which they were exposed. Police and social workers failed to distinguish adequately between taking the children's allegations seriously and believing them. Social workers did not give sufficient thought to the question of whether it was necessary to remove the children. They acted too precipitately and failed to take time to pause and think.

The decision to remove the children at dawn was 'beyond serious criticism and the conduct of the workers involved was efficient and supportive. But the children should have been allowed to discuss the allegations during the course of their removal. A ban on them taking personal possessions was inappropriate.

Inadequate consideration was given to the support of the parents, and social workers failed to visit them after the removal of the children. The parents should have been given information about the whereabouts of their children.

The interviewers failed to plan adequately how to deal with a child's denial of allegations and how to introduce explicit information. They over-stressed their belief in the truth of the allegations. The police interviewers were inadequately trained and lack adequate supervision.

Lord Clyde recommended better training for social workers, care workers and police, which should be introduced quickly.

10.5   The Children Act 1989 – Key Principles

CHILDREN ACT 1989

1.   Welfare of the child

(1)   When a court determines any question with respect to—

(a)   the upbringing of a child; or

(b)   the administration of a child's property or the application of any income arising from it, the child's welfare shall be the court's paramount consideration.

(2)   In any proceedings in which any question with respect to the upbringing of a child arises, the court shall have regard to the general principle that any delay in determining the question is likely to prejudice the welfare of the child.

(3)   In the circumstances mentioned in subsection (4), a court shall have regard in particular to—

(a)   the ascertainable wishes and feelings of the child concerned (considered in the light of his age and understanding);

(b)   his physical, emotional and educational needs;

(c) the likely effect on him of any change in his circumstances;

(d) his age, sex, background and any characteristics of his which the court considers relevant;

(e) any harm which he has suffered or is at risk of suffering;

(f) how capable each of his parents, and any other person in relation to whom the court considers the question to be relevant, is of meeting his needs;

(g) the range of powers available to the court under this Act in the proceedings in question.

(4) The circumstances are that—

(a) the court is considering whether to make, vary or discharge a section 8 order, and the making, variation or discharge of the order is opposed by any party to the proceedings; or

(b) the court is considering whether to make, vary or discharge an order under Part IV.

(5) Where a court is considering whether or not to make one or more orders under this Act with respect to a child, it shall not make the order or any of the orders unless it considers that doing so would be better for the child than making no order at all.

17. Provision of services for children in need, their families and others

(1) It shall be the general duty of every local authority (in addition to the other duties imposed on them by this Part)—

(a) to safeguard and promote the welfare of children within their area who are in need; and

(b) so far as is consistent with that duty, to promote the upbringing of such children by their families,
by providing a range and level of services appropriate to those children's needs.

10.5.1 THE CHILD'S WELFARE AND THE WELFARE CHECKLIST

10.5.1.1 Welfare

J v C [1970] AC 668 (HL)

LORD MACDERMOTT: My Lords, the infant respondent is now a boy of ten who has lived in England continuously since July, 1961, with the other respondents, a solicitor and his wife to whom I shall refer as the foster parents. The appellants are the boy's natural parents, a married couple of Spanish nationality who have their home in Madrid. The issue throughout the litigation has been as to the boy's future custody, the rival claimants being, on the one hand, the foster parents with whom the boy has been living and, on the other, the natural parents.

The course of the dispute and certain aspects of the evidence present a story which is involved and at times rather confused; but whether this needs to be traced in detail depends on the answer to be given to a question of law which stands on the threshold of the case and to which I turn at once.

Mr Alexander for the appellants conceded that if the courts below had applied the right principles of law in reaching the decision appealed from he could not succeed in asking your Lordships to disturb that decision. The substance of his main argument may be stated shortly. All parties were agreed that the courts had jurisdiction and a duty to interfere with the natural right of parents to have the care, control and custody of their child if the welfare of the child required and the law permitted that course to be taken. But there agreement ended. For the appellants it was submitted that the courts were in law bound to presume that the welfare of the child was best served by allowing him to live with his parents unless it was shown that it was not for his welfare to do so because of their conduct, character or station in life. Mr Waite for the boy and Mrs Puxon for the foster parents submitted, on the other hand, that there was no such presumption of law, that the paramount and governing consideration was the welfare of the child and that the claim of natural parents, although often of great weight and cogency and often conclusive, had to be regarded in conjunction with all other relevant factors and had to yield if, in the end, the welfare of the child so required.

I have referred to these statutes because, as in the case of the authorities, they record an increasing qualification of common law rights and the growing acceptance of the welfare of the infant as a criterion. In this way, and like the trend of the cases, they serve to introduce the enactment which has been so closely canvassed on the issue of law under discussion. It is s. 1 of the Guardianship of Infants Act 1925, which was passed in the year following the decision in *Ward* v *Laverty* [1925] AC 101. This section follows a preamble which runs thus:

Whereas Parliament by the Sex Disqualification (Removal) Act, 1919, and various other enactments, has sought to establish equality in law between the sexes, and it is expedient that this principle should obtain with respect to the guardianship of infants and the rights and responsibilities conferred thereby:

The section itself reads:

1. Where in any proceeding before any court (whether or not a court within the meaning of the Guardianship of Infants Act, 1886) the custody or upbringing of an infant, or the administration of any property belonging to or held on trust for an infant, or the application of the income thereof, is in question, the court, in deciding that question, shall regard the welfare of the infant as the first and paramount consideration, and shall not take into consideration whether from any other point of view the claim of the father, or any right at common law possessed by the father, in respect of such custody, upbringing, administration or application is superior to that of the mother, or the claim of the mother is superior to that of the father.

The second question of construction is as to the scope and meaning of the words '. . . shall regard the welfare of the infant as the first and paramount consideration.' Reading these words in their ordinary significance, and relating them to the various classes of proceedings which the section has already mentioned, it seems to me that they must mean more than that the child's welfare is to be treated as the top item in a list of items relevant to the matter in question. I think they connote a process whereby, when all the relevant facts, relationships, claims and wishes of parents, risks, choices and other circumstances are taken into account and weighed, the course to be followed will be that which is most in the interests of the child's welfare as that term has now to be understood. That is the first consideration because it is of first importance and the paramount consideration because it rules upon or determines the course to be followed. It remains to see how this 'first view,' as I may call it, stands in the light of authority. . . .

I conclude that my first view construction of section 1 should stand, and that the appellants' proposition of law is ill-founded and must fail. The consequences of this present little difficulty, but before coming to them I would add in summary form certain views and comments on the ground surveyed in the hope that they may serve to restrict misunderstanding in this field. These may be enumerated as follows:

1. Section 1 of the Act of 1925 applies to disputes not only between parents, but between parents and strangers and strangers and strangers.

2. In applying section 1, the rights and wishes of parents, whether unimpeachable or otherwise, must be assessed and weighed in their bearing on the welfare of the child in conjunction with all other factors relevant to that issue.

3. While there is now no rule of law that the rights and wishes of unimpeachable parents must prevail over other considerations, such rights and wishes, recognised as they are by nature and society, can be capable of ministering to the total welfare of the child in a special way, and must therefore preponderate in many cases. The parental rights, however, remain qualified and not absolute for the purposes of the investigation, the broad nature of which is still as described in the fourth of the principles enunciated by FitzGibbon LJ in *In re O'Hara* [1900] 2 IR 232, 240.

4. Some of the authorities convey the impression that the upset caused to a child by a change of custody is transient and a matter of small importance. For all I know that may have been true in the cases containing dicta to that effect. But I think a growing experience has shown, that it is not always so and that serious harm even to young

children may, on occasion, be caused by such a change. I do not suggest that the difficulties of this subject can be resolved by purely theoretical considerations, or that they need to be left entirely to expert opinion. But a child's future happiness and sense of security are always important factors and the effects of a change of custody will often be worthy of the close and anxious attention which they undoubtedly received in this case.

10.5.1.2 The range of orders

CHILDREN ACT 1989

10. Power of court to make section 8 orders

(1) In any family proceedings in which a question arises with respect to the welfare of any child, the court may make a section 8 order with respect to the child if—

    (a) an application for the order has been made by a person who—

        (i) is entitled to apply for a section 8 order with respect to the child; or

        (ii) has obtained the leave of the court to make the application; or

    (b) the court considers that the order should be made even though no such application has been made.

. . .

9. Restrictions on making section 8 orders

(1) No court shall make any section 8 order, other than a residence order, with respect to a child who is in the care of a local authority.

(2) No application may be made by a local authority for a residence order or contact order and no court shall make such an order in favour of a local authority.

. . .

8. Residence, contact and other orders with respect to children

. . .

(3) For the purposes of this Act 'family proceedings' means any proceedings—

    (a) under the inherent jurisdiction of the High Court in relation to children; and

    (b) under the enactments mentioned in subsection (4), but does not include proceedings on an application for leave under section 100(3).

(4) The enactments are—

    (a) Parts I, II and IV of this Act;

    (b) the Matrimonial Causes Act 1973;

    (c) the Domestic Violence and Matrimonial Proceedings Act 1976;

    (d) the Adoption Act 1976;

    (e) the Domestic Proceedings and Magistrates' Courts Act 1978;

    (f) sections 1 and 9 of the Matrimonial Homes Act 1983;

    (g) Part III of the Matrimonial and Family Proceedings Act 1984;

    (h) the Family Law Act 1996.

. . .

10.6   End of Chapter Assessment Questions

1.   The Children Act 1989 is designed to support child rearing with families, and yet to provide the state, through the local authority, with improved powers to protect children.

     Can these principles co-exist?

2.   The welfare checklist in s. 1(3), Children Act 1989 supports the concept of children's rights.

     Discuss.

10.7   End of Chapter Assessment Outline Answers

1.   This is not an easy question to answer, and hence the suggestion that you may wish to return to it as a revision question having completed the rest of the child law chapters.

     At this stage all that you can discuss is the concepts of non-intervention and the principles of working in partnership with parents.

     The notion that the best place for a child to be reared is with its family reflects the existing social structure, that of privacy and reduced state intervention. You may question the basis for this perception. Does the modern way of living, with less support from the extended family, and with many parents both working either full or part time mean that we have moved away from the family structure when it was deemed best for children to be raised within the family at all costs? Or is the support for the family a result of the move away from the traditional family unit? Is it a means to reproduce the concept of father as breadwinner and mother as homemaker? You may also reflect upon the extent to which the state intervenes in any event. Currently the state intervenes by way of health visiting, ante-natal care, public health measures and guidance. This intervention is subtle and far less intrusive than that perceived from the social services but it still exists to reproduce a consistent and focussed direction to parenting and child development.

     The Children Act 1989 through s. 17 and the accompanying schedule promotes the concept of partnership, and directs that a local authority should endeavour to reduce the need to take proceedings. This implies a pro-active role for the authority , but you may raise the question of resources, and the fact that the authority operates more on a reactive basis. In working with a family on a voluntary basis, inevitably there will be a tension between the legal background to the local authority's work and the parent's role. You could highlight the fact that the local authority can always resort to the Children Act 1989 to take proceedings if parents do not comply. Does this therefore mean that parents will comply because of the threat of legal action? If this is so, then is this really a voluntary arrangement?

     The tension that can be identified here is such that the principle of partnership and keeping children within the family cannot always be met within the framework of the existing legislation. Indeed, you may conclude that the mere existence of powers to protect children by removal from the home shows the principles behind the legislation are in torsion from the start.

2.   This question concentrates on a very small part of the Children Act 1989, but one which is central to the whole operation of the legislation. As well as assessing the impact of s. 1(3), you may also find it useful to discuss the concept of children's rights and what is meant by this term.

     There is a difference between promoting a child's rights in a moral sense, to rights that are enforceable in law. You have seen this in the UN Convention of the Rights of the Child, and its preceding declaration. On what basis does the 1989 Act promote children's rights? It can be suggested that the rights included are more legal than moral and in addition, that there are not many rights at all. However, many of these legal rights stem from the ability to seek orders under the Act, which are not apparent from the face of s. 1.

The contents of the welfare checklist are more directed towards the moral rights of the child — the right to be heard. Section 1(3) starts by referring to the 'ascertainable wishes and feelings of the child (in the light of his age and understanding)', which clearly does not introduce any real enforceable right. The list of factors in s. 1(3) is not in order of priority, nor is the list exhaustive. It is also a matter for the court's discretion how much weight is to be placed upon each individual factor. Where a child's wishes and feelings are concerned, the child may be considered unable to express their wishes and feelings if of tender years. Even if an opinion can be given, the court, or any professional involved with the case, may question that opinion on the basis of age and understanding. Children are seen as potentially malleable, and hence their opinions susceptible of disbelief. You may have referred to issues such as a parent influencing the child's voice in divorce and access disputes.

Given this general atmosphere of mistrust the idea of s. 1(3) supporting a child's rights is somewhat misplaced. The welfare checklist may provide the child with a voice, but it is one which can be overborne by adults and professionals who know better than the child. In many cases, the adults will know best, but each case must be decided individually. You should be able to question whether or not lip-service is being paid to the concept of rights, not only in s. 1 but throughout the Children Act 1989.

CHAPTER ELEVEN

THE PRIVATE LAW RELATING TO CHILDREN

11.1 The Concept of Parental Responsibility

11.1.1 A DEFINITION

CHILDREN ACT 1989

3. Meaning of 'parental responsibility'

(1)   In this Act 'parental responsibility' means all the rights, duties, powers, responsibilities and authority which by law a parent of a child has in relation to the child and his property.

11.1.2 SOME INTERPRETATIONS

11.1.2.1 The duty to care and protect

CHILDREN AND YOUNG PERSONS ACT 1933

1.   Cruelty to persons under sixteen

(1)   If any person who has attained the age of sixteen years and [has responsibility for] any child or young person under that age, wilfully assaults, ill-treats, neglects, abandons, or exposes him, or causes or procures him to be assaulted, ill-treated, neglected, abandoned, or exposed, in a manner likely to cause him unnecessary suffering or injury to health (including injury to or loss of sight, or hearing, or limb, or organ of the body, and any mental derangement), that person shall be guilty of a misdemeanour, and shall be liable—

(a)   on conviction on indictment, to a fine . . . , or alternatively, . . . or in addition thereto, to imprisonment for any term not exceeding [ten] years;

(b)   on summary conviction, to a fine not exceeding [the prescribed sum] or alternatively, . . . or in addition thereto, to imprisonment for any term not exceeding six months.

(2)   For the purposes of this section—

(a)   a parent or other person legally liable to maintain a child or young person [, or the legal guardian of a child or young person,] shall be deemed to have neglected him in a manner likely to cause injury to his health if he has failed to provide adequate food, clothing, medical aid or lodging for him, or if, having been unable otherwise to provide such food, clothing, medical aid or lodging, he has failed to take steps to procure it to be provided under [the enactments applicable in that behalf];

(b)   where it is proved that the death of an infant under three years of age was caused by suffocation (not being suffocation caused by disease or the presence of any foreign body in the throat or air passages of the infant) while the infant was in bed with some other person who has attained the age of sixteen years, that other person shall, if he was, when he went to bed, under the influence of drink, be deemed to have neglected the infant in a manner likely to cause injury to its health.

(3)   A person may be convicted of an offence under this section—

(a)   notwithstanding that actual suffering or injury to health, or the likelihood of actual suffering or injury to health, was obviated by the action of another person;

(b)   notwithstanding the death of the child or young person in question.

(4)–(6)   . . .

(7)   Nothing in this section shall be construed as affecting the right of any parent, teacher, or other person having the lawful control or charge of a child or young person to administer punishment to him.

Example of cycle of deprivation

Anne and Bill have a son, Christopher. Bill is a strong believer in corporal punishment, and hence from an early stage in Christopher's life, beats Christopher regularly for misdemeanours. Bill is also somewhat violent, and beats Anne regularly.

Christopher believes this behaviour is normal and when he marries and has children, acts in a similar manner. Christopher's children, raised in this environment believe that it is acceptable to use violence and corporal punishment against wives and children and so they do so when they are adults.

11.1.2.2   The duty to educate

EDUCATION ACT 1944

36.   Duty of parents to secure the education of their children

It shall be the duty of the parent of every child of compulsory school age to cause him to receive efficient full-time education suitable to his age, ability, and aptitude [and to any special educational needs he may have], either by regular attendance at school or otherwise.

CHILDREN ACT 1989

36.   Education supervision orders

(1)   On the application of any local education authority, the court may make an order putting the child with respect to whom the application is made under the supervision of a designated local education authority.

(2)   In this Act 'an education supervision order' means an order under subsection (1).

(3)   A court may only make an education supervision order if it is satisfied that the child concerned is of compulsory school age and is not being properly educated.

(4)   For the purposes of this section, a child is being properly educated only if he is receiving efficient full-time education suitable to his age, ability and aptitude and any special educational needs he may have.

(5)   Where a child is—

(a)   the subject of a school attendance order which is in force under section 37 of the Education Act 1944 and which has not been complied with; or

(b)   a registered pupil at a school which he is not attending regularly within the meaning of section 39 of that Act,

then, unless it is proved that he is being properly educated, it shall be assumed that he is not.

(6)   An education supervision order may not be made with respect to a child who is in the care of a local authority.

(7)   The local education authority designated in an education supervision order must be—

(a)   the authority within whose area the child concerned is living or will live; or

(b)   where—

(i)   the child is a registered pupil at a school; and

(ii)   the authority mentioned in paragraph (a) and the authority within whose area the school is situated agree, the latter authority.

SCHEDULE 3

12.—(1)   Where an education supervision order is in force with respect to a child, it shall be the duty of the supervisor—

(a)   to advise, assist and befriend, and give directions to—

(i)   the supervised child; and

(ii)   his parents,

in such a way as will, in the opinion of the supervisor, secure that he is properly educated;

(b)   where any such directions given to—

(i)   the supervised child; or

(ii)   a parent of his,

have not been complied with, to consider what further steps to take in the exercise of the supervisor's powers under this Act.

(2)   Before giving any directions under sub-paragraph (1) the supervisor shall, so far as is reasonably practicable, ascertain the wishes and feelings of—

(a)   the child; and

(b)   his parents,

including, in particular, their wishes as to the place at which the child should be educated.

(3)   When settling the terms of such directions, the supervisor shall give due consideration—

(a)   having regard to the child's age and understanding, to such wishes and feelings of his as the supervisor has been able to ascertain; and

(b)   to such wishes and feelings of the child's parents as he has been able to ascertain.

(4)   Directions may be given under this paragraph at any time while the education supervision order is in force.

RE O (A MINOR) (CARE ORDER: EDUCATION: PROCEDURE) [1992] 2 FLR 7 (FamD)

EWBANK J: This is an appeal from an order of the Maidenhead Family Proceedings Court made on 23 January 1992. They had before them an application by the local authority for a care order in relation to M, who is now 15 years 4 months old. The case before the magistrates arose because of M's failure to go to school. In the first instance, the local authority took out an application under s. 1 of the Children and Young Persons Act 1969, on the ground she was of school age and was not being educated. That application is dated 19 April 1991.

In October 1991 the Children Act came into force and the local authority decided to drop the application under the old Act and institute proceedings under the new Act, and that application is dated 11 November 1991. Accordingly, it was the proceedings under the new Act that came before the magistrates in January 1992. I am told the case lasted 3 days, which were not consecutive because of the difficulty of having a Bench sitting on consecutive days. At the end of the hearing, the magistrates made a care order on 23 January 1992. They were told that the child and the mother and the father had it in mind to appeal, and they accordingly granted a stay of the care order. Notice of appeal was filed and an application was then made to this court for the stay to be extended, and that was granted and the stay was extended to the hearing of the appeal today.

The magistrates handed down their judgment at the same time as they gave their decision; it is a judgment in writing and it is comparatively short, and it is entirely right it should be comparatively short. It is not a reasoned judgment given by a judge after a hearing; it is a summary of the findings they make and I would not wish it to be thought that it was necessary for them to deal in great detail with the evidence they heard, although, as I say, I think it would be better if they dealt with the specific matters that are set out in the statute.

In the judgment, the magistrates start off by saying:

We are satisfied that M's social and intellectual development is being impaired and that she is suffering and she is likely to suffer significant harm as a result.

These are the first of the threshold conditions in s. 31, justifying a care order. . . .

If a child does not go to school and is missing her education, it is not difficult to draw the conclusion that, if she had gone to school and had not truanted, she would have improved her intellectual and social development.

In relation to whether the harm is significant, on behalf of M it is said that the comparison which has to be made is with a similar child under s. 31(10), and that there is no evidence that she has suffered harm compared with a similar child.

In my judgment, in the context of this type of case, 'similar child' means a child of equivalent intellectual and social development, who has gone to school, and not merely an average child who may or may not be at school. In fact, what one has to ask oneself is whether this child suffered significant harm by not going to school. The answer in my judgment, as in the magistrates' judgment, is obvious.

The second threshold condition is that the harm, or the likelihood of harm, is attributable to the care given to the child not being what it would be reasonable to expect a parent to give him, or the child is beyond parental control. In my judgment, where a child is suffering harm in not going to school and is living at home, it will follow that either the child is beyond her parents' control or that they are not giving the child the care that it would be reasonable to expect a parent to give. . . .

The proposal of the local authority is that M should move to a children's home and should be taken to school from there and, when a pattern of attendance has been achieved, consideration will be given to sending her home. The magistrates took the view, as they say, that the only way of bringing about change is for M to be removed from home, and in those circumstances they decided that a care order ought to be made.

In this appeal, it is necessary for M and her parents to show that the magistrates came to the wrong decision. I have to say that they have wholly failed in that endeavour and, accordingly, this appeal is dismissed.

11.1.2.3 Medical treatment

Murray, I, 'Parents deny killing by insulin ban; Beverley and Dwight Harris', *The Times*, 6 October 1993, p. 3

The parents of a nine-year-old diabetic girl watched her waste away and die in agony because they did not believe it was right to treat her with insulin and instead pursued homoeopathic remedies, a court was told yesterday.

The parents refused to do what was needed to save her, Peter Joyce QC, for the prosecution, told Nottingham Crown Court. They may have cared for her, they may have been misguided. It is sad but true that the death was unnecessary and avoidable.

Dwight Harris, 32, and his wife Beverley, 33, of Radford, Nottingham, pleaded not guilty to the manslaughter of their daughter Nakhira between December 17, 1991, and February 1, 1992, and denied child cruelty over the same period.

Mr Joyce said the girl had been diagnosed as suffering from diabetes by her family doctor in mid-December and was referred to the Queen's Medical Centre in Nottingham where the parents were told that she required immediate treatment with insulin.

It was apparent from conversations between the parents and a doctor that they did not believe in Nakhira receiving insulin, Mr Joyce said. The doctor asked to talk to them away from Nakhira but they would not leave her bedside. The doctor ended up saying in the presence of the child, 'Without insulin your child will die'.

Nakhira received no insulin because she was discharged from the hospital against the advice of the doctors. The next time she went to the medical centre was when she died. In the meantime it is apparent that Mr and Mrs Harris were trying to pursue homoeopathic remedies, Mr Joyce said. 'Whether it is a matter of religious or cultural belief does not matter. The parents had been told that without insulin their child would die.'

Mr Joyce said that, in the six weeks between the visit to the medical centre and her death, Nakhira had lost a third of her weight. When her parents at last brought her back to the centre, she was dehydrated with a very weak pulse and no recordable blood pressure. Three hours later she died.

Nakhira died from diabetes wholly unnecessarily, Mr Joyce said.

Dr Mary Philips, the family doctor, said that after she diagnosed diabetes the father told her that he was going to give his daughter homoeopathic treatment. He was quite distressed at the way Nakhira was seen at hospital and said she was scared of needles, Dr Philips said. 'I told him Nakhira needed insulin for her diabetes and before deciding on an alternative form of treatment he should go back to hospital and discuss it with the experts. I didn't consider homoeopathic medicine as an alternative to insulin.'

The trial continues.

'Insulin ban parents killed their daughter; Nahkira Harris', *The Times*, 29 October 1993, p. 3

A couple who refused to allow their diabetic daughter to receive modern medicine because of their religious beliefs were convicted of her manslaughter yesterday.

Nottingham Crown Court was told that nine-year-old Nahkira Harris wasted away before the eyes of her Rastafarian parents. She went into a diabetic coma and died because Dwight Harris, 32, and Beverley, 33, refused to allow her to be injected with insulin.

The couple, from Radford, Nottingham, were convicted by a 10–2 majority. Mr Justice Tucker, postponing sentencing until next Friday for social enquiry reports, said: 'This is a case of great sensitivity and importance. Do not suppose that I am going to place either of you on probation. Your hopes are not to be raised.'

Last night social workers were deciding whether to take the Harrises' four other children, aged one to 13 years, into care They said the trial had highlighted information about the family not known before.

During the trial, Peter Joyce QC, for the prosecution, said the Harrises were told by doctors at the Queen's Medical Centre, Nottingham, that insulin was the only way to save their daughter, but they took her away and did not return for six weeks, when she was in a coma.

Mr Harris wanted to know from staff if insulin came from animals and said he was not allowed to eat pork and beef. He told nurses that he wanted to take his daughter to Africa to see a faith healer.

The couple did not give evidence. But Nicholas Price QC, for Mr Harris, accused a homoeopathic doctor of gross negligence and said he could have saved the girl's life.

He said the couple took their daughter to see Dr Christopher Hammond at his surgery in Southwell. Dr Hammond spent one and a half hours with the parents before sending them to the Queen's Medical Centre, where their daughter died six hours later.

Colin Hart-Leverton QC, for Mrs Harris, said: 'There is no evidence that they thought they were doing the slightest harm to their daughter or did it on purpose to harm her.'

Berwick, S, 'Judges let parents decide fate of liver boy', *Daily Telegraph*, 25 October 1995

The fate of an 18-month-old boy who faces death without a liver transplant rests with his parents after an Appeal Court decision not to order the operation against their wishes.

Doctors say the child will die within 18 months without a transplant but his parents have refused their consent.

The court ruled yesterday that it was in the boy's interests to leave the decision to his parents, since without his mother's whole-hearted backing and after-care, a transplant might not succeed. Lord Justice Waite said the court had a duty to come to its own conclusion on a child's best interests in such hard cases. But where there was a genuine debate on where those interests lay, and parents were not influenced by mere dogma, the courts would be influenced by their feelings:

> In the last analysis, the best interests of every child include an expectation that difficult decisions affecting the length and quality of its life will be taken by the parent to whom its care has been entrusted by nature.

The parents, who are unmarried and live abroad with their son thousands of miles from Britain, are health care professionals with experience of the care of sick children.

The boy was born in Britain with a congenital liver defect, and had an operation at three and a half weeks that was unsuccessful. That experience, and the pain and distress caused to the child, helped influence his parents against giving consent to a transplant. The boy was placed on a transplant list at a hospital in Britain but his parents then took him abroad, in a country where the operation is not available.

Lady Justice Butler-Sloss said the mother had a deep-seated concern about the effects of surgery, and possible failure, on her son. Evidence had shown her to be devoted and well-informed.

She was focusing, it seems to me, on the present peaceful life of the child who had the chance to spend the rest of his short life without the pain, stress and upset of intrusive surgery against the future with the operation and treatment taking place.

She said she doubted that Mr Justice Connell, who ruled in the High Court that the mother must fly her son to Britain to undergo the operation, was right to say that she was unreasonable. But in any case the child's welfare depended on his mother, and it was necessary to consider whether she could support him through an operation she did not believe was right.

'Once the pressure of this litigation is over it may be the parents will reconsider,' she said. That decision would be up to them, not the court.

Lord Justice Waite said that doctors had unanimously recommended the transplant. But the parents' decision had been made after anxious consideration, and was cogent. Emma Holt, a solicitor representing the parents, said they would be enormously reassured and relieved by the decision, which supported their approach to a difficult case. The boy is well at present. Leave to appeal was refused, but a spokesman for the Official Solicitor, who is the boy's guardian, said afterwards that consideration would be given to petitioning the House of Lords for leave to appeal.

The original case in the High Court was brought by the local authority in which the boy lived in Britain, after doctors at his hospital asked for legal advice. The authorities in the country they now live in have concluded that no action is needed, and there has never been any suggestion that the child be taken into care in either country.

The Appeal Court has ruled that the boy cannot be named.

RE R (A MINOR) (WARDSHIP: MEDICAL TREATMENT) [1992] 1 FLR 190 (CA)

LORD DONALDSON OF LYMINGTON MR: This appeal from an order of Waite J on 9 July 1991 involves a consideration of the power of the court to override a refusal by its ward, a 15-year-old girl, to undergo medical treatment involving the taking of medication. So far as is known, such a question has arisen on only one previous occasion, namely in the case of Re E (decided by Ward J on 21 September 1990), a 15-year-old boy who had religious objections, supported by his parents, to being given a life-saving blood transfusion. Possibly in that case, and certainly in this, the judge accepted that the effect of Gillick v West Norfolk and Wisbech Area Health Authority and Another [1986] AC 112 was that, if a child had achieved a sufficient understanding and intelligence to enable him or her to understand fully what was proposed and to be capable of making up his own mind on the matter, the parental right (and the court's right) to give or refuse consent yielded to the child's right to make his own decisions . . . and that this applied as much to a situation in which the child was refusing consent (this case and Re E) as to the case in which the child was consenting (the assumed position in Gillick). However, in Re E, as in this case, the judge held that the child had not achieved the required degree of understanding. . . .

Mrs Gillick served notice on her local area health authority, formally forbidding any medical staff employed by it from giving contraceptive or abortion advice to her four daughters, whilst they were under the age of 16, without her consent, and invited the authority to advise the doctors employed by it accordingly. The health authority declined so to do and Mrs Gillick sought declarations against the department that the guidance given by it was unlawful and against the authority that no doctor or other professional person employed by it was entitled, as a matter of law, to give contraceptive advice and/or abortion advice and/or treatment to any of her children under the age of 16 without her consent. In a word, she was asserting an absolute right of veto on the part of parents generally, and herself in particular, on medical advice and treatment of the nature specified in relation to their children under the age of 16. . . . She was not challenging the right of a wardship court to exercise its parens patriae jurisdiction. Indeed, she accepted it in her printed case. . . . Nor was she concerned with how that jurisdiction should be exercised.

It is trite law that, in general, a doctor is not entitled to treat a patient without the consent of someone who is authorised to give that consent. If he does so, he will be liable in damages for trespass to the person and may be guilty of a criminal assault. This is subject to the necessary exception that, in cases of emergency, a doctor may treat the patient, notwithstanding the absence of consent, if the patient is unconscious or otherwise incapable of giving or refusing consent and there is no one else sufficiently immediately available with authority to consent on behalf of the patient. However, consent by itself creates no obligation to treat. It is merely a key which unlocks a door. Furthermore, whilst in the case of an adult of full capacity there will usually only be one keyholder, namely the patient, in the ordinary family unit where a young child is the patient there will be two keyholders, namely the parents, with a several as well as a joint right to turn the key and unlock the door. If the parents disagree, one consenting and the other refusing, the doctor will be presented with a professional and ethical, but not with a legal, problem because, if he has the consent of one authorised person, treatment will not without more constitute a trespass or a criminal assault.

If Mrs Gillick was to succeed in her claim to a declaration that the Memorandum of Guidance issued by the department was unlawful, she had to show that no child under the age of 16 could be a keyholder in respect of contraception advice and treatment, or that the parents' key overrode the child's. As Lord Fraser of Tullybelton put it . . . , 'she has to justify the absolute right of veto in a parent'. If she was to succeed in her claim against the area health authority, she had also to show that it was under a duty to inform all medical staff employed by it that Mrs Gillick was exercising that right of veto, but, in the light of the House's finding that there was no such right, this additional factor can be ignored. . . .

Lord Scarman was discussing the parents' right 'to determine whether or not their minor child below the age of 16 will have medical treatment' (my emphasis), and this is the 'parental right' to which he was referring at . . . . A right of determination is wider than a right to consent. The parents can only have a right of determination if either the child has no right to consent, ie is not a keyholder, or the parents hold a master key which could nullify the child's consent. I do not understand Lord Scarman to be saying that, if a child was 'Gillick-competent', to adopt the convenient phrase used in argument, the parents ceased to have an independent right of consent, as contrasted with ceasing to have a right of determination, ie a veto. In a case in which the 'Gillick-competent' child refuses treatment, but the parents consent, that consent enables treatment to be undertaken lawfully, but in no way determines that the child shall be so treated. In a case in which the positions are reversed, it is the child's consent which is the enabling factor, and again the parents' refusal of consent is not determinative. If Lord Scarman intended to go further than this and to say that in the case of a 'Gillick-competent' child, a parent has no right either to consent or to refuse consent, his remarks were obiter, because the only question in issue was Mrs Gillick's alleged right of veto. Furthermore, I consider that they would have been wrong.

IN RE W (A MINOR) (MEDICAL TREATMENT: COURT'S JURISDICTION) [1992] 3 WLR 758 (CA)

W, who was born in 1976, was placed in the care of the local authority following the death of her parents. In 1990, after unsuccessful fostering and further misfortune, she developed symptoms of anorexia nervosa and in 1991 was admitted to an adolescent residential unit tor treatment. When her condition deteriorated the local authority decided, contrary to W's wishes and the opinion of the consultant attending her, to transfer her to unit specialising in the treatment of eating disorders. They accordingly obtained leave to invoke the High Court's inherent jurisdiction and by their summons directed to W, and to her aunt who shared parental responsibility for her, sought the court's leave for such transfer and treatment without her consent.

THE PRIVATE LAW RELATING TO CHILDREN

LORD DONALDSON OF LYMINGTON MR: In *Gillick* v *West Norfolk and Wisbech Area Health Authority* [1986] AC 112 the central issue was *not* whether a child patient under the age of 16 could refuse medical treatment if the parents or the court consented, but whether the parents could effectively impose a veto on treatment by failing or refusing to consent to treatment to which the child might consent.

The House of Lords decisively rejected Mrs Gillick's contentions and held that at common law a child of sufficient intelligence and understanding (the '*Gillick* competent' child) could consent to treatment, notwithstanding the absence of the parents' consent and even an express prohibition by the parents. Only Lord Scarman's speech is couched in terms which might suggest that the refusal of a child below the age of 16 to accept medical treatment was determinative . . . because there could never be concurrent rights to consent:

> the parental right to determine whether or not their minor child below the age of 16 will have medical treatment terminates if and when the child achieves a sufficient understanding and intelligence to enable him or her to understand fully what is proposed.

If the parental right terminates, it would follow that, apart from the court, the only person competent to consent would be the child and a refusal of consent to treatment would indirectly constitute an effective veto on the treatment itself. I say 'indirectly' because the veto would be imposed by the civil and criminal laws, rather than by the refusal of consent.

In the light of the quite different issue which was before the House in *Gillick's* case I venture to doubt whether Lord Scarman meant more than that the *exclusive* right of the parents to consent to treatment terminated, but I may well be wrong. Thorpe J having held that 'there is no doubt at all that J is a child of sufficient understanding to make an informed decision,' I shall assume that, so far as the common law is concerned, Lord Scarman would have decided that neither the local authority nor W's aunt, both of whom had parental responsibilities, could give consent to treatment which would be effective in the face of W's refusal of consent. This is of considerable persuasive authority, but even that is not the issue before this court. That is whether *the court* has such a power. That never arose in *Gillick's* case, the nearest approach to it being the proposition, accepted by all parties, that the court had power to override any minor's consent (*not* refusal) to accept treatment. . . .

On reflection I regret my use in *In re R (A Minor) (Wardship: Consent to Treatment)* [1992] Fam 11, 22, of the keyholder analogy because keys call lock as well as unlock. I now prefer the analogy of the legal 'flak jacket' which protects the doctor from claims by the litigious whether he acquires it from his patient who may be a minor over the age of 16, or a '*Gillick* competent' child under that age or from another person having parental responsibilities which include a right to consent to treatment of the minor. Anyone who gives him a flak jacket (that is, consent) may take it back, but the doctor only needs one and so long as he continues to have one he has the legal right to proceed.

11.1.2.4   Name and religion

CHILDREN ACT 1989

13.   Change of child's name or removal from jurisdiction
   (1)   Where a residence order is in force with respect to a child, no person may—
      (a)   cause the child to be known by a new surname; or
      (b)   remove him from the United Kingdom;
without either the written consent of every person who has parental responsibility for the child or the leave of the court.

W v A (CHILD: SURNAME) [1981] 1 All ER 100 (CA)

DUNN LJ: This is an appeal from an order of his Honour Judge Hutton made on 3rd June 1980 and amended on 20th June whereby in effect he ordered that two children should continue to use their father's surname. The mother appeals against that order. The father has not been represented on the appeal, although it is clear from the letter from his solicitors that he opposes any variation of the order. I say that the effect of the order was that the children's surname should not be changed because, in form, it was an application by the mother to be released from an undertaking to that effect which she gave to the judge as a condition of being allowed to take both children permanently out of the jurisdiction to Australia.

When the question of the change of name came before the judge, he was faced with the dilemma that there are two apparently conflicting lines of authority in this court on the question of changing children's surnames. The first is that the change of a child's surname is an important matter, not to be undertaken lightly. The second is that the change of a child's surname is a comparatively unimportant matter. The judge, faced with the choice between those two lines of authority, opted for the first. The primary grounds of this appeal is that in so doing he erred in law.

It is necessary, accordingly, to look at the various decided cases which have been very helpfully cited to us by counsel for the mother who, if I may say so, has conducted this appeal with great ability and also with great responsibility, having no opponent.

The first case to which he referred was *Re W G* (1976) 6 Fam Law 210. That was a case in which the issue whether or not the child's surname should be changed was the very question which the court had to decide. There was evidence before the trial judge, Faulks J, from the headmistress of the children's school that it was administratively convenient that their names should be changed to the name of their stepfather. Faulks J accepted that view and made an order giving leave for a deed poll to be registered changing their names. The Court of Appeal reversed the judge's order and Cairns LJ is reported as saying (6 Fam Law 210):

It was, of course, important to bear in mind all the way through . . . that it was in the paramount interests of the child with which their Lordships were concerned. It had not been suggested on either side here that the court should approach a decision in the case from any other point of view. But his Lordship thought it important that it should be realised that the mere fact that there had been a divorce, that the mother had remarried and had custody of the child and had a name different from that of the child, was not sufficient reason for changing the child's surname . . . The courts recognise the importance of maintaining a link with the father, unless he had ceased to have an interest in the child or there were some grounds, having regard to his character and behaviour, which made it undesirable for him to have access to the child at all. It must greatly tend to create difficulties in the relations between a father and a child if the child ceased to bear the father's name.

The other two members of the court agreed.

There followed *R (BM)* v *R (DN) (child: surname)* [1978] 2 All ER 33 also in the Court of Appeal. It is I think important to have regard to what the issue which fell to be determined in that case was and what the facts of the matter were. The facts of the matter were that the mother had left the father and four children and had gone to live with a soldier. About two years after she left she obtained a decree nisi and she obtained custody of all the children. The youngest child, C, was unhappy with her and the soldier, and returned to live with the father. The issue in *R* v *R* was whether the custody of C should be granted to the mother who, by that time, had been living for some time with the soldier and the other three children, or whether C should remain with the father. The question of change of name only arose in this way: there was evidence that the three older children living in the army camp with the mother and the soldier, Sergeant W, were known in the camp as W and this was used by those representing the father as an indication that W would try to eliminate the father from the lives of the children and usurp his position. Stamp LJ made this very clear. He said this ([1978] 2 All ER 33 at 37):

I think it is convenient to mention that the point was made by counsel for the father in the course of his submissions in this court that the judge might not have been aware at that point or had it present to his mind at that point in his judgment that the three elder children, now in the camp where they are, are known officially by the surname of W, and it was suggested that this rather tended to counter the judge's findings that Sergeant W would always be ready to remind the children that he was not their real father, and a good deal of play was made by counsel for the father regarding this change in the way the children are known in the camp. I am bound to say I do not think that the fact that the three elder children are known as W now in Bovington camp really signifies anything as regards the characters of Sergeant W and the mother. I think that too much attention is paid to these matters of names of children, the names by which they are known, on some occasions at least, and it must be most convenient that they should be known as W in the camp in which they are being brought up where Sergeant W is the head of the family.

I think it is important to read that last sentence in its context and not to take it out of its context as suggesting the laying down of any general proposition as to changes of name.

Omrod LJ in his judgment, referred to the change of name as a peripheral matter, and no doubt in the facts and circumstances of that case it was a peripheral matter. He went on to make certain general observations as to the question of changing the surnames of children and emphasised the embarrassment for the school authorities if children are not known by the same name as their mother. Those observations were clearly, in my view, obiter. They were not necessary for the decision of the case and they should not be regarded as other than comments on the factual situation which arose in that case. They were in any event inconsistent with *Re W G*.

The second case which was cited by counsel for the mother in support of what he submitted was the proper approach to the question of changing children's names was *D v B (otherwise D) (child: surname)* [1979] 1 All ER 92. That again was a case which was decided by Stamp and Ormrod LJJ. The facts of the matter were somewhat complicated. The child in question was born after the mother had left the father and had gone to live with another man. The mother took the name of the other man. She registered the birth of the child in that man's name, but on the registration form declared that her husband was the father, and she refused him access. The father then issued a summons seeking access and asked for an order that the register of births should be altered so as to show the child's name as being his name, and also asked for a rectification of a deed poll which had been executed by the mother, by which she assumed the other man's surname for herself and any children of hers.

The case came before Lane J who ordered access to the father, ordered that the mother should take all necessary steps to ensure that the deed poll and the register of births should be amended, and also ordered that until the child reached the age of 18, the mother should not let him be known by any other surname than that of the father without the father's consent.

The mother failed to carry out the judge's order, the father applied for directions, and the judge, on that application, directed the mother to execute a statutory declaration and a fresh deed poll and attached a penal notice to the order. It was against that order that the mother appealed.

It appears from the report that, in the course of the appeal, the father consented to the child being known by the mother's name. As it is put in the headnote:

... the father having consented, that part of the order of December 1976 requiring the mother not to allow the child to be known by any other surname than that of the father, would be varied to enable the child to be known by the mother's new surname.

So that, so far as this court was concerned, the question whether or not the child should be known by the father's surname or should he known by the surname which the mother had assumed was not in issue. This is clear from the judgment when Ormrod LJ said ([1979] All ER 92 at 94):

The substantive issue in the case was whether or not the father should have access to a very young boy. The formalistic issues rotate round the question of the name by which this boy is to be known, and it is a great pity that these issues have come to overshadow the real issue of substance, which in fact has been resolved by an earlier decision of the judge.

How then does the law stand with regard to the approach by courts in applications for change of a surname? As in all cases concerning the future of children whether they be custody, access, education or, as in this case, the change of a child's name, s. 1 of the Guardianship of Minors Act 1971 requires that the court shall regard 'the welfare of the [child] as the first and paramount consideration'. Those words were construed by Lord MacDermott in *J v C* [1969] 1 All ER 788 at 820–821 in the following well-known passage:

Reading these words in their ordinary significance, and relating them to the various classes of proceedings which the section has already mentioned, it seems to me that they must mean more than that the child's welfare is to be treated as the top item in a list of items relevant to the matter in question. I think they connote a process whereby, when all the relevant, facts, relationships, claims and wishes of parents, risks, choices and other circumstances are taken into account and weighed, the course to be followed will be that which is most in the interests of the child's welfare as that term has now to be understood. That is the first consideration because it s of first importance and the paramount consideration because it rules on or determines the course to be followed.

That is the first and paramount consideration which must be in the judge's mind. When considering the question of a change of name, that is to be regarded as an important matter (see Cairns LJ in *Re W G*). It is a matter for the discretion of the individual judge hearing the case, seeing the witnesses, seeing the parents, possibly seeing the children, to decide whether or not it is in the interests of the child in the particular circumstances of the case that his surname should or should not be changed; and the judge will take into account all the circumstances of the case, including no doubt where appropriate any embarrassment which may be caused to the child by not changing his name and, on the other hand, the long-term interests of the child, the importance of maintaining the child's links with his paternal family, and the stability or otherwise of the mother's remarriage. I only mention those as typical examples of the kinds of considerations which arise in these cases, but the judge will take into account all the relevant circumstances in the particular case before him. . . .

I have no doubt that the judge had all these matters in mind and there is nothing in his reasons, in his short judgment, which leads me to suppose that he did not. On the contrary, it seems to me that the judge approached this matter entirely rightly. It was a matter for his discretion. I cannot see that this court can possibly interfere with that discretion and, speaking for myself, I should have come to the same conclusion as did the judge.

For these reasons, I would dismiss this appeal.

RE B (CHANGE OF SURNAME) [1996] 1 FLR 791 (CA)

WILSON J: The mother of three children appeals from the refusal of his, Honour Judge Crawford QC, sitting in the Newcastle upon Tyne County Court on 17 May 1995, to give her leave to cause them to by known by a new surname, namely that of her present husband, H.

The three children are K, a boy, who was born on 14 August 1978 and so was aged 16 at the time or the hearing and is now 17, R, a boy, who was born on 12 April 1981 and so is aged 14, and C, a girl, who was born on 7 April 1983 and so is aged 12.

The children live with the mother and her present husband near Whitley Bay. B, the respondent to the appeal, is a bus driver and lives not far away, near Blyth. In 1980 the mother married B. K had already been born to her by another man so B and the mother then formally and jointly adopted him. R and C were natural children of the marriage.

The mother's case before the judge was founded very substantially upon the wishes of all three children that their surname be changed to that of H. She said that since the time of her remarriage her children had become generally known as H, particularly in school, because they had been asked to be known by that name. She said that R had once failed to answer to a new teacher who had addressed him under the name of B and that, when upbraided, he had explained 'That's not my name'. She said, however, that in the formal records of the school, reflected, for example, in the name in which their reports were written, the children continued to bear the name of B and that this was something which irked and embarrassed them and had prompted her to make the application.

She said that, were her application to fail, the two boys were planning themselves to ask the court to permit the change; that the children referred to H as 'Dad'; that she thought it right for them to regard him as their father; that they referred to the father as 'him at Blyth'; and that the cessation of contact had come about by virtue of the children's own wishes. She evaded answering questions about her own wishes in that last respect.

An order had been made for a welfare officer to file a report 'limited to ascertaining the wishes of the three children to the proposed change of surname'. The welfare officer reported as follows:

> All three children refer to themselves as 'H'. They tell me that this is the name by which they are known amongst their friends where they live. In the case of the two younger children, H is the name which they are known by at school.
>
> All three children expressed identical opinions in this matter. They told me that they wished to be known as H and found it embarrassing to be described as anything else. They seemed to have given the matter considerable thought and they expressed their views in a sensible manner.
>
> They told me that they regarded Mr H as their 'dad' and wished to be known by his name. Apparently, they have not seen their natural father for many years.
>
> The children's views are quite clear in this matter. They want to be called H.
>
> Changing their surname officially would simply confirm a situation which has existed for some time and remove a source of embarrassment.

Although in oral evidence the welfare officer denied that he had gone further than his remit, I do read that last sentence as providing some independent professional support for the mother's application. The welfare officer also gave evidence that the children had said that the father 'was of the past and not of the present'.

The basis for the father's opposition to the application was summarised by him in oral evidence as follows:

> With the access not taking place and everything, to me that is just like the final nail in the coffin for them, just to try and cut me off completely, just to get me completely out of their minds.

When it was put to him that, when they became adults, the children could formally after their surname themselves, he said:

> If they get to the age of 18, if that is what they want to do, that is for them to do, because I maintain that she has poisoned them. By the time they get to 18, they have got more chance to get a bit of what I call their own minds back.

But the nature of the prohibition, left untouched by the judge, is different. It does not, because in effect it cannot, proscribe the surname which the children ask teachers, friends and relations to attribute to them. The order represents an inhibition upon the mother not to cause the children to be known by the name of H. Although an oral instruction on her part to a third party to call the children by her husband's name would, if obeyed, be a breach of the prohibition, the much more obvious example of its effect is that the mother cannot sign forms by which the children's surname is identified as that of her husband. Thus, for example, she cannot sign applications for their school registration, for their medical or dental registration, or for the issue of a passport to them, in that name. It is, as the judge pragmatically recognised, a limited prohibition; and it does not purport to oblige adolescent children to do anything which they are refusing to do.

Miss Woolrich resurrects the traditional argument that it is embarrassing for children to be known by a surname other than that of the adults in their household. But the law must not lag behind the times. In these days of such frequent divorce and remarriage, of such frequent cohabitation outside marriage, and indeed increasingly of preservation of different surnames even within marriage, there is, in my view, no opprobrium nowadays upon a child who carries a surname different from that of the adults in his home, That view is supported by a comment of Ralph Gibson LJ in *Re F (Child: Surname), Note*, shortly noted it [1993] 2 FLR 837, 838E. Even if the argument had had any force, it would have borne little reference to the name appropriate to the child for formal purposes.

11.1.2.5 Discipline

SUTTON LONDON BOROUGH COUNCIL v *DAVIS* [1995] 1 All ER 53 (FamD)

WILSON J: This is an appeal against an order made by the Sutton Magistrates' Court on 8 July 1993. Before that court was an appeal brought by Mrs Davis under s. 77(6) of the Children Act 1989. Sutton London Borough Council (the local authority) had concluded that Mrs Davis was not fit to look after children under the age of eight and had exercised the power given to them under s. 71(7)(a) of the Act to refuse to enter the name of Mrs Davis upon their register of child-minders. The magistrates' court allowed the appeal of Mrs Davis against the refusal of the local authority to register her and ordered that she was entitled to be registered. From that order the local authority appeal to this court under s. 94(1)(a) of the Act. The local authority also appeal against an order for costs which the magistrates made against them in favour of Mrs Davis; I am considering that appeal separately.

In the present case the local authority adopted a 'blanket' policy that an applicant who refused to undertake not to smack was unfit. It follows, notwithstanding the submission of Mr Munby, that the local authority was not obliged to adopt that policy. In adopting it they went beyond the guidance of the blue book and therefore went beyond the discharge of their legal duty under s. 7 of the 1970 Act.

Mr Munby relies very strongly upon the fact that the no smacking policy adopted by the local authority was lawful. He says, and I agree, that not only is it legitimate for a local authority to reach individual decisions by reference to a general policy but also that there is no ground for thinking that the policy of his local authority could have been successfully struck down on any application to the High Court for judicial review. He goes on to submit, and again I agree, that, even if the policy had been open to successful challenge upon judicial review, it was no part of the function of the magistrates themselves to query the legality of the policy. Mr Munby relies on *Bugg* v *DPP* [1993] 2 All ER 815 in which it was held that, in criminal proceedings, magistrates could not investigate the validity of the byelaws alleged to have been broken save where they were invalid on their face or patently unreasonable. It was there said that, where byelaws were alleged to be invalid because of non-compliance with procedural requirements referable to their making, magistrates were not properly equipped to carry out the investigation, which was the province solely of the High Court within judicial review.

I think that Mr Munby's argument places much too great a reliance upon the fact that the local authority's policy was lawful and that indeed their decision to refuse to register Mrs Davis was lawful. A decision can be lawful without being correct.

The justices' reasons for allowing the appeal
In their written reasons the justices did not expressly pose or answer the question: are we satisfied that Mrs Davis is not fit to look after children under the age of eight? But it is without doubt implicit in their reasons that they posed the question to themselves and that they answered it in the negative. From their six written pages I distil their reasons as follows.

(1) They addressed s. 7(1) of the 1970 Act and the guidance in the blue book They found that the local authority had given 'too much weight' and 'disproportionate importance' to the guidance about corporal punishment and had accorded to it the status of primary legislation. In the light, in particular, of the evidence of the local authority's past and present assistant directors of Housing and Social Services, they were fully entitled to make that finding. Their phraseology shows however that they correctly accepted that a degree of weight and importance did have to be ascribed to the guidance.

(2) They disagreed, in my view correctly, with the argument of the local authority that the emphasis in the 1993 circular upon flexibility in the implementation of guidance did not apply to the guidance about corporal punishment.

(3)   They found that the inflexibility of the local authority's policy, whereunder an applicant who refused to undertake not to smack was automatically refused registration, made it impossible for a reasonable decision to be reached as to her overall 'fitness'. They went on to conclude, in a sentence which in my view reveals a correct perception of their own function, that the local authority had therefore failed to carry out the correct balancing exercise in determining whether an applicant was fit to be registered.

(4)   They considered parental rights at some length. They (a) correctly held that a parent had a right to chastise his or her child to a reasonable extent; (b) correctly held that a parent could delegate this right to another person; (c) noted that nannies and au pairs did not need to be registered and that therefore there was no inhibition upon the delegation to them of this parental right; (d) noted that in the case of child-minding the contract was between the parent and the child-minder, that the local authority was not a party to it and that the contract would settle all the arrangements for the child's care including, if desired, provision as to the extent if any of the child-minder's right to smack and (e) accepted expert evidence to the effect that it was not in the best interests of a child to be cared for at home by a parent who can and does smack and elsewhere by a child-minder who cannot smack.

Consistently with his submission about the nature of the appeal to the magistrates, Mr Munby argues that these references to parental rights were irrelevant. He goes on to accept that, if a parent permits a registered childminder to smack, the smacking will not be an unlawful assault but says that its consequence will simply be the cancellation of the child-minder's registration in accordance with the local authority's policy.

In my view, the references to parental rights were not irrelevant. I say so for two main reasons.

(1)   The crucial question was the fitness of Mrs Davis and she had at all times been at pains to stress that the ability to smack, which she wished to reserve for herself, was an ability to smack only if and to the extent that the parent wished her to do so.

(2)   In passages to which I have already referred, the blue book had stressed that the policies of local authorities towards child-minders should reflect the importance of parental involvement and had even recommended that the contract between the parent and child-minder should cover 'policy on behaviour and sanctions'. It is important to consider its guidance about corporal punishment in that context.

I also consider that, in weighing the fitness of Mrs Davis for the purposes of s. 71(7) of the Act, it is permissible to have some regard to the emphasis upon parental responsibility which is reflected in so many of the changes in the law wrought by that Act.

The current position in law is therefore as follows. It is a matter for each local authority to decide whether to elevate the guidance in the blue book in relation to corporal punishment into an inflexible policy that those who refuse to undertake not to smack will for that reason alone be declared unfit to look after such children. But, if they decide to adopt such a policy, they must realise that their decision can be appealed to magistrates, who must weigh the issue of fitness for themselves in the light of the guidance. At that hearing the local authority will have full opportunity to seek to persuade the court that the absence of the undertaking does indeed render the applicant unfit. In some cases the magistrates may be persuaded of that fact. But there will be other cases, of which this is an example, where the magistrates will come to a different conclusion, which cannot be disturbed on further appeal. I do not seek to restrict the ambit of such cases when, in relation to this case, I advert in particular to the evidence of the high suitability of Mrs Davis as a child-minder in all other respects, and/or of her wish to be able to smack only if and to the extent that the parent wished her to do so and/or of the fact that she had indeed successfully been minding a child whose parent did wish her to continue to have the facility to smack.

If, as to which my opinion is of no consequence, it is inappropriate for certain child-minders to be registered, notwithstanding their refusal to undertake not to smack, the government should lay regulations before Parliament under s. 72(3)(a) of the Act or propose other legislation which would disentitle them to registration.

11.2   Who has Parental Responsibility

11.2.1   AUTOMATIC PARENTAL RESPONSIBILITY

CHILDREN ACT 1989

2.   Parental responsibility for children

(1)   Where a child's father and mother were married to each other at the time of his birth, they shall each have parental responsibility for the child.

(2)   Where a child's father and mother were not married to each other at the time of his birth—

(a)   the mother shall have parental responsibility for the child;

(b)   the father shall not have parental responsibility for the child, unless he acquires it in accordance with the provisions of this Act.

11.2.2   THE UNMARRIED FATHER

CHILDREN ACT 1989

4.   Acquisition of parental responsibility by father

(1)   Where a child's father and mother were not married to each other at the time of his birth—

(a)   the court may, on the application of the father, order that he shall have parental responsibility for the child; or

(b)   the father and mother may by agreement ('a parental responsibility agreement') provide for the father to have parental responsibility for the child.

(2)   No parental responsibility agreement shall have effect for the purposes of this Act unless—

(a)   it is made in the form prescribed by regulations made by the Lord Chancellor; and

(b)   where regulations are made by the Lord Chancellor prescribing the manner in which such agreements must be recorded, it is recorded in the prescribed manner.

(3)   Subject to section 12(4), an order under subsection (1)(a), or a parental responsibility agreement, may only be brought to an end by an order of the court made on the application—

(a)   of any person who has parental responsibility for the child; or

(b)   with leave of the court, of the child himself.

(4)   The court may only grant leave under subsection (3)(b) if it is satisfied that the child has sufficient understanding to make the proposed application.

11.2.2.1   Parental responsibility orders

RE H (A MINOR) (PARENTAL RESPONSIBILITY) [1993] 1 FLR 484 (CA)

HOLLIS J: This is an appeal by a father from a decision of his Honour Judge Marcus Edwards made in the Brentford County Court on 31 March 1992, whereby he refused the father's application for contact or access to his small child and further refused his application for a parental responsibility order. Insofar as the latter is concerned, the judge obtained an undertaking from the mother that if she and her present husband, Mr S, were minded to apply to adopt the child concerned, the father must be given notice and that no steps to adopt the child should be taken for 10 days after he had been personally served with such notice.

The short facts of this case are as follows. The parties were never married. Apparently they met as long ago as 1981 and started living together in about 1986. The child concerned, A, was born on 15 April 1990 and so he is now approximately 2 years and 3 months old and at the time of the hearing before his Honour Judge Marcus Edwards was just on 2. On 14 July 1990 the mother left the father, taking the small baby with her, and they have never lived together since. In the meantime, in about February 1990, the mother had started to have a relationship with Mr S, who apparently was a friend of the father's.

After the separation, the father had contact with the child quite regularly with the mother's agreement until November 1990. There is little doubt that the mother then refused to allow further contact because of her impending marriage to Mr S and they in fact were married on 15 or possibly 13 December 1990. Immediately thereafter her solicitors were writing to the father, saying that the mother and Mr S wished to adopt A. The father applied for a contact order. The matter came before his Honour judge Tyrer and by consent an order was made giving him fortnightly contact to the child. Such contact continued until the very end of August 1991. In the meantime in August 1991, Mr S had written to the father saying that he was so upset with everything, in particular the father's access, that he, the father, had better have the mother back.

There was no contact after August 1991, and at the end of 1991, or possibly early this year, the mother and Mr S went to live in Scotland where they remain living with A. Then there was the hearing before his Honour Judge Marcus Edwards, which in all covered parts of 3 days in February to 31 March 1992. Later, apparently, the father wrote two cards to the boy. The order that I have recited did not forbid him to do so, but during the course of the judge's judgment he certainly indicated that there should be no such contact between father and son. Furthermore, on two separate occasions he, the father, telephoned the mother, according to him, to talk to her about some motor-car that he had been ordered to return to her, or something of the like. . . .

Then the judge goes on to consider the question of parental responsibility. He says:

> The purpose of a parental responsibility order is the same as the purpose of an order under s. 4 of the Family Law Reform Act 1987 which is that, in appropriate cases, the position of a father of a child born out of wedlock should be equated with that of the father of a legitimate child. It is not necessary that the father should be in a position to exercise rights under that order immediately, for example by access, provided he can show that there is some use or potential use for the order in future. I have been referred, most helpfully, by counsel to . . . cases under the 1987 Act. I take into account the salient factors so far as concern this case, which are: (1) the degree of commitment shown by the father; (2) the degree of attachment between him and A; (3) his reasons for wanting such an order; (4) the fact that A was born not as the result of a casual relationship but as the result of a relationship which had lasted for some 4 years and was like a married relationship save that (a) there was no ceremony, and (b) the father had not shown that extra degree of commitment by marrying the mother, which was a major cause of the breakdown in their relationship; and (5) the circumstances in the future when the father might need to exercise his rights if he had a parental responsibility order. There are two types of possibility here: one is that there might be an application by the mother to adopt, under which he would be heard in regard to giving or not giving consent and would have certain residual rights under ss. 19 and 20 of the Adoption Act 1976, and secondly, in the event of serious misfortunes occurring to the S household, such as serious accidents or breakdowns in the relationship which might occur in any marriage.

Pausing there, I would interpolate that it seems to me that at present, or certainly at the date of the hearing before the judge, Mr S was a most unstable character quite obviously, and therefore, quite apart from any question of access or otherwise, it would certainly not be beyond the bounds of possibility that that marriage might break down. The judgment goes on:

> It is pointed out that an application for a parental responsibility order can be made at any time so it ought to be left until the emergency arises, but that is not of much use to a father if he does not know of any application to adopt or of any serious misfortune.
>
> So far as an application to adopt is concerned, the father's position can be adequately protected by an undertaking, which the mother is prepared to give, in suitable terms to provide prior written notice to the father, served personally on him.

I have already referred to that undertaking given by the mother. On p. 20 he says:

I think it right to put those considerations on one side and consider whether a parental responsibility order ought to be made in regard to the other matters, and if I do the balancing act again and again consider the best interests of A, I see no benefit to him in making the order and some disadvantage, because it will either rouse false hopes in the father, or rouse anxieties in the mother and Mr S that it has aroused false hopes in the father, or both, and it will tend to disrupt relations in the S household, which will be to A's disadvantage in the same way as an access order would. I agree with the court welfare officer in his letter to the court of 25 February 1992 that now is not the time to make a parental responsibility order, though it may come in the future, either if an application for adoption is made or a serious misfortune occurs, or if A comes to know that he has a natural father and wants to get in contact with him.

As to that, we have been referred, first of all, to *Re H (Minors) (Local Authority: Parental Rights) (No. 3)* [1991] Fam 151, sub nom *Re H (Illegitimate Children: Father: Parental Rights) (No. 2)* [1991] 1 FLR 214, a decision of this court. Balcombe LJ said at pp. 217H–218 respectively:

Until the recent changes in the law, the father of a child born out of wedlock had only very limited rights in relation to the child. He was not a parent of the child within the meaning of the Child Care Act 1980 (although he was a relative) . . . he had no parental rights and duties under the Children Act 1975 . . . he was not a parent of the child for the purposes of the Adoption Act 1976 . . . although he might be its guardian if so appointed or if he had custody under the Guardianship of Minors Act 1971 . . . Although as against the mother he could obtain an order for custody of the child under . . . the 1971 Act, he could not obtain such an order if the child was in the care of a local authority . . . Nor was he a parent of the child for the purpose of applying under Part 1A of the 1980 Act for access to the child if in care . . .
    That position has now been changed by the Family Law Reform Act 1987 and, more recently, by the Children Act 1989, although some of the relevant provisions of the latter Act are not yet in force. The method adopted was not to equate the father of a child born out of wedlock with the father of a legitimate child: it was to give the putative (or natural) father the right to apply for an order giving him all the parental rights and duties with respect to the child. (When [sic] s. 24 of the 1989 Act is brought into force he will be able to acquire parental responsibility by agreement with the mother.) The reason why this method was adopted was because the position of the natural father can be infinitely variable; at one end of the spectrum his connection with the child may be only the single act of intercourse (possibly even rape) which led to conception: at the other end of the spectrum he may have played a full part in the child's life from birth onwards, only the formality of marriage to the mother being absent. Considerable social evils might have resulted if the father at the bottom end of the spectrum had been automatically granted full parental rights and duties, and so Parliament adopted the scheme to which we have referred above.
    In considering whether to make an order under s. 4 of the 1987 Act, the court will have to take into account a number of factors, of which the following will undoubtedly be material (although there may well be others, as the list is not intended to be exhaustive):
    (1)   the degree of commitment which the father has shown towards the child;
    (2)   the degree of attachment which exists between the father and the child;
    (3)   the reasons of the father for applying for the order.

Further, we were referred to *Re C (Minors) (Parental Rights)* [1992] 1 FLR 1, again a decision of this court where Waite J, giving the judgment of the court, at p. 3F says:

Given, therefore, that the prospective enforceability of parental rights is a relevant consideration for a judge deciding whether or not to grant them, there is, in our judgment, nothing in the Act to suggest that it should be an overriding consideration. It would be quite wrong, in our view, to assume that just because few or none of the parental rights happen to be enforceable under conditions prevailing at the date of the application, it would necessarily follow as a matter of course that a PRO would be refused. That can be illustrated by looking—as the legislation clearly requires one to look—at the position of a lawful father in analogous circumstances. Conditions may arise (for example in cases of mental illness) where a married father has, regretfully, to be ordered, in effect, to step out of his children's lives altogether. In such a case, his legal status as a parent remains wholly unaffected, and he retains all his rights in law, although none of them may be exercisable in practice. This does not mean that his parental status becomes a dead letter or a mere paper title. It will have real and tangible value, not only as something he can cherish for the sake of his own peace of mind, but also as a status carrying with it rights in waiting, which it may be possible to call into play when circumstances change with the passage of time. It is not difficult to imagine situations in which similar considerations would apply in the case of a natural father. Though existing circumstances may demand that his children see or hear nothing of him, and that he should have no influence upon the course of their lives for the time being, their welfare may require that if circumstances change he should be reintroduced as a presence, or at least as an influence, in their lives. In such a case a PRO, notwithstanding that only a few or even none of the rights under it may currently be exercisable, may be of value to him and also of potential value to the children. Although there may be other factors which weigh against the making of a PRO in such circumstances, it could never be right to refuse such an order out of hand, on the automatic ground that it would be vitiated by the inability to enforce it.

Again at p. 8G Waite J says:

The question which the statute requires us to ask in the present case is, in our judgment, the following: was the association between the parties sufficiently enduring, and has the father by his conduct during and since the application shown sufficient commitment to the children, to justify giving the father a legal status equivalent to that which he would have enjoyed if the parties had been married, due attention being paid to the fact that a number of his parental rights would, if conferred on him by a PRO, be unenforceable under current conditions?

Speaking for myself, I would answer all those questions in the affirmative. It seems to me that this particular father is entirely qualified to be granted the order that he seeks. Indeed if the matter is simply left in the air, suppose, for instance, that the mother and Mr S applied to adopt A in, say, 4 or 5 years' time and the natural father then applied for such an order he would be met by the argument, at any rate, that nothing had happened for the last 4 or 5 years, he had no contact with the child whatsoever by order of the court and there could not really be a weaker case for granting him the order that he sought.

For my part I would find, and do find, that the judge was carried away, I think, with the argument concerning the question of contact and access, but as to the application for parental responsibility his decision was plainly wrong. I would therefore allow that part of the appeal, but that part only, and make such an order.

11.2.3 PARENTAL RESPONSIBILITY FROM OTHER ORDERS

CHILDREN ACT 1989

3.   Meaning of 'parental responsibility'
(5)   A person who—
    (a)   does not have parental responsibility for a particular child; but
    (b)   has care of the child,
may (subject to the provisions of this Act) do what is reasonable in all the circumstances of the case for the purpose of safeguarding or promoting the child's welfare.

12.   Residence orders and parental responsibility
. . .
(2)   Where the court makes a residence order in favour of any person who is not the parent or guardian of the child concerned that person shall have parental responsibility

for the child concerned that person shall have parental responsibility for the child while the residence order remains in force.

11.3   Private Law Orders

CHILDREN ACT 1989

9.   Restrictions on making section 8 orders

(3)   A person who is, or was at any time within the last six months, a local authority foster parent of a child may not apply for leave to apply for a section 8 order with respect to the child unless—

(a)   he has the consent of the authority;

(b)   he is a relative of the child; or

(c)   the child has lived with him for at least three years preceding the application.

(4)   The period of three years mentioned in subsection (3)(c) need not be continuous but must have begun not more than five years before the making of the application.

10.   Power of court to make section 8 orders

(1)   In any family proceedings in which a question arises with respect to the welfare of any child, the court may make a section 8 order with respect to the child if—

(a)   an application for the order has been made by a person who—

(i)   is entitled to apply for a section 8 order with respect to the child; or

(ii)   has obtained the leave of the court to make the application; or

(b)   the court considers that the order should be made even though no such application has been made.

(2)   The court may also make a section 8 order with respect to any child on the application of a person who—

(a)   is entitled to apply for a section 8 order with respect to the child; or

(b)   has obtained the leave of the court to make the application.

(3)   This section is subject to the restrictions imposed by section 9.

(4)   The following persons are entitled to apply to the court for any section 8 order with respect to a child

(a)   any parent or guardian of the child;

(b)   any person in whose favour a residence order is in force with respect to the child.

(5)   The following persons are entitled to apply for a residence or contact order with respect to a child—

(a)   any party to a marriage (whether or not subsisting) in relation to whom the child is a child of the family;

(b)   any person with whom the child has lived for a period of at least three years;

(c)   any person who—

(i)   in any case where a residence order is in force with respect to the child, has the consent of each of the persons in whose favour the order was made;

(ii)   in any case where the child is in the care of a local authority, has the consent of that authority; or

(iii)   in any other case, has the consent of each of those (if any) who have parental responsibility for the child.

. . .

(9)   Where the person applying for leave to make an application for a section 8 order is not the child concerned, the court shall, in deciding whether or not to grant leave, have particular regard to—

(a)   the nature of the proposed application for the section 8 order;

(b)   the applicant's connection with the child;

(c)   any risk there might be of that proposed application disrupting the child's life to such an extent that he should be harmed by it; and

(d)   where the child is being looked after by a local authority—

(i)   the authority's plans for the child's future; and

(ii)   the wishes and feelings of the child's parents.

11.3.1 THE SECTION 8 ORDERS

CHILDREN ACT 1989

8. Residence, contact and other orders with respect to children

(1) In this Act—

'a contact order' means an order requiring the person with whom a child lives, or is to live, to allow the child to visit or stay with the person named in the order, or for that person and the child otherwise to have contact with each other;

'a prohibited steps order' means an order that no step which could be taken by a parent in meeting his parental responsibility for a child, and which is of a kind specified in the order, shall be taken by any person without the consent of the court;

'a residence order' means an order settling the arrangements to be made as to the person with whom a child is to live; and

'a specific issue order' means an order giving directions for the purpose of determining a specific question which has arisen, or which may arise, in connection with any aspect of parental responsibility for a child.

(2) In this Act 'a section 8 order' means any of the orders mentioned in subsection (1) and any order varying or discharging such an order.

(3) For the purposes of this Act 'family proceedings' means any proceedings—

(a) under the inherent jurisdiction of the High Court in relation to children; and

(b) under the enactments mentioned in subsection (4), but does not include proceedings on an application for leave under section 100(3).

(4) The enactments are—

(a) Parts I, II and IV of this Act;

(b) the Matrimonial Causes Act 1973;

(c) the Domestic Violence and Matrimonial Proceedings Act 1976;

(d) the Adoption Act 1976;

(e) the Domestic Proceedings and Magistrates' Courts Act 1978;

(f) sections 1 and 9 of the Matrimonial Homes Act 1983;

(g) Part III of the Matrimonial and Family Proceedings Act 1984.

11.3.2 THE RESIDENCE ORDER

11.3.2.1 Conditions

CHILDREN ACT 1989

11. General principles and supplementary provisions

. . .

(7) A section 8 order may—

(a) contain directions about how it is to be carried into effect;

(b) impose conditions which must be complied with by any person—

(i) in whose favour the order is made;

(ii) who is a parent of the child concerned;

(iii) who is not a parent of his but has parental responsibility for him; or

(iv) with whom the child is living,

and to whom the conditions are expressed to apply;

(c) be made to have effect for a specified period, or contain provisions which are to have effect for a specified period;

(d) make such incidental, supplemental or consequential provision as the court thinks fit.

RE C (A MINOR) (CARE PROCEEDINGS) [1992] 2 FCR 341 (FamD)

The parents had two children, both girls, the elder of whom was born in March 1989 and the younger in July 1991. In March 1990, when the elder child was only 12 months old, the father slapped her across the face sufficiently hard to mark her. The mother told the health visitor and co-operated with the local authority's inquiry into the matter. The local authority regarded it as an exceptional event, noted it but took no further action. In October 1991, when the younger child was only 3 months old, she was found to have a spiral fracture of the right femur. The medical opinions were that this was a serious non-accidental injury to a baby which would have needed considerable force to have inflicted it. The doctors rejected suggestions by the parents that the injury could have been caused by the child shifting in some way in her carrycot, or during a nappy change, or that the elder girl could have caused it. No subsequent explanation was given and the injury remained unexplained.

The local authority commenced care proceedings. An interim care order was made and after a short period with foster parents, a residence order was made in favour of the child's grandparents. At the hearing of the care proceedings in a family proceedings court, the local authority sought a care order and this was recommended by the guardian ad litem. The intention of the local authority was to carry out an assessment of the parents and thereafter consider returning the child to the parents.

The magistrates found that the child had sustained serious non-accidental injury whilst in the care of the parents. They also found that although the father co-operated with the local authority, the mother had a mistrust of social services as a result of having been taken into care when she was 15 following sexual abuse by members of her family. As a result, when the child was taken into care, the mother became unable to co-operate with social services. The magistrates further found that the local authority were inconsistent in expressing no concerns regarding the safety of the elder child who was to remain in the household with the parents whilst contending, as did the guardian ad litem, that there was a need to protect the younger child from risks that were to be identified and assessed following an injury which was the result of an isolated incident.

The magistrates further found that there was no reason why the assessment of the parents should not take place whilst the younger child was with the parents in her home environment, and that there was no suggestion that access to see them or the children would be denied by the parents to social services. The magistrates stated that the younger child was of a tender age and she needed to maintain and increase her bonding with both her parents. It was unclear whether the grandparents would be able to continue as foster parents. The magistrates accepted the opinion of the guardian ad litem that frequent moves would adversely affect the child and that, if the child was removed from the grandparents to foster parents, this would set back the rehabilitation process significantly which would be against the child's best interests.

The magistrates also found that there was no suggestion that the younger child was inadequately cared for as regards nourishment, clothing, or development, and that both children had never gone without.

Having regard to all the circumstances, the magistrates refused to make a care order, but made a supervision order.

The guardian ad litem appealed.

WARD J: I wish in so far as I can not only to deal with this particular case but also to give some guidance to the justices as to how they may exercise new powers under this Act. This was a difficult case of balancing risks. It was made the more difficult by the inadequacy of explanation of the harm which they found. They were, therefore, it seems to me, three ways for them to approach this case. Firstly, to make the order which they did. That is to say, to return the child unconditionally to the parents, but subject to a final supervision order.

Secondly, to make a care order. Or, thirdly, to continue interim orders to await the results of the assessment which was so essential in this case.

In my judgment, it would be wrong for justices to take the risk of returning a battered baby unconditionally to her parents with no more protection than that of a final supervision order, itself not made the subject of any condition. There are much wider powers available to justices than that.

Its principal fault, in my judgment, is that it abdicates the responsibility of care to the parents at a time when the matters are still too uncertain to be confident of their ability properly to exercise that care. To that degree I agree with the submissions of the guardian ad litem and the local authority. But their solution to this case being a care order is equally open, it seems to me, to complaint that it would involve an abdication of the court's responsibility to the local authority at a time when the court is not sufficiently in possession of all the facts to pass responsibility to the local authority.

Those who practised in the High Court enjoyed the wide discretion the High Court had in the exercise of its wardship jurisdiction. That jurisdiction has gone as a remedy available to the local authority, but the range of powers that the High Court had has not gone altogether. They are in very large measure preserved in the Act and are now made available to all courts: county courts and magistrates' courts. The virtues of the flexibility of the wardship jurisdiction must now be recognized by the lower courts and in so far as the same flexibility can be achieved under the Children Act 1989, the options available must be used to their full advantage. That is the message which this judgment seeks to deliver to the justices on this circuit and elsewhere.

I remind them that by s. 11(3) of the Children Act 1989:

Where a court has power to make a section 8 order, it may do so at any time in the course of the proceedings in question even though it is not in a position finally to dispose of those proceedings.

These proceedings being care proceedings do enable residence order, to be made. They can be made by s. 11(7), which is in these terms:

A section 8 order may—
    (a)   contain directions about how it is to be carried into effect;
    (b)   impose conditions which must be complied with by any person—
        (i)   in whose favour the order is made;
        (ii)   who is a parent of the child concerned;
        (iii) who is not a parent of his but who has parental responsibility for him; or
        (iv) with whom the child is living,
and to whom the conditions are conditions are expressed to apply.
    (c)   be made to have effect for a specified period, or contain provisions which are to have effect for a specified period;
    (d)   make such incidental supplemental or consequential provision as the court thinks fit.

When one links that into the power given by s. 38 to make interim orders in care proceedings one has a recipe of wide application. The court there is entitled to make interim orders, whether care orders or supervision orders.

By s. 38(3):

Where, in any proceedings on an application for a care order or supervision order, a court makes a residence order with respect to the child concerned, it shall also make an interim supervision order with respect to him unless satisfied that his welfare will be satisfactorily safeguarded without an interim order being made.

There is no reason, as I understand it, why an interim supervision order cannot be conditional. The power to attach conditions is contained in Schedule 3 to the Act by para. 2:

A supervision order may require the supervised child to comply with any directions given from time to time by the supervisor which require him to do all or any of the following things—
    (a)   to live at a specified place;
    (b)   [which may be relevant here] to present himself to a person or persons specified in the directions at a place or places and on a day so specified;
    (c)   to participate in activities specified in the directions on a day or days so specified.

Thus the supervisor can direct the child to attend at the health visitor or to attend in the case of a child old enough at some form of family therapy.

Then under para. 3 as to the imposition of obligations on a responsible person, such as he who has parental responsibility:

(1)   With the consent of any responsible person, a supervision order may include a requirement—
(a)   that he take all reasonable steps to ensure that the supervised child complies with any direction given by the supervisor under para. 2 . . .

Paragraph 4 enables the supervision order to require the child to submit to medical or psychiatric examinations.

Paragraph 5 enables the court to give direct directions for medical treatment.

There is, therefore, a range of conditions which would be very usefully adapted to this case.

Given (a) the importance of assessment; (b) the uncertainties of the outcome of that assessment; (c) the importance of endeavouring to reunite the family, in my judgment the proper approach for the justices in this case was to deal with this as an interim order, and by way of interim order to direct that the child be returned to the parents, but to make that residence order conditional. It must be conditional upon the parents undertaking a programme of assessment and co-operating with all reasonable requests by the local authority to participate in that programme of assessment; allowing access to the home at any reasonable time, and, if necessary, without notice.

Those conditions are necessary to impress upon the parents that whilst the objective is to keep the child with them, it is still conditional upon their co-operation and their successfully undertaking this programme.

In addition, one must make an interim order in which again the conditions are to be imposed:

(1)   that the supervised child shall present herself to the health visitor as may be specified by the supervising officer;
(2)   that the parents having parental responsibility for this child shall take all reasonable steps to ensure that the child is taken to the health visitor as the supervisor officers may require;
(3)   that the child be submitted for medical examinations from time to time as directed by the supervisor supervisor and undertake such treatment as may be necessary following such examinations.

RE KDT (A MINOR) (CARE ORDER: CONDITIONS) [1994] 2 FCR 721 (CA)

NOURSE LJ: This is an appeal by a local authority from the refusal of His Honour Judge Mott in the Wolverhampton county court on 5 November 1993 to make a care order in respect of a male child KDT born on 31 March 1993 and thus aged just over seven months at the date of the Judge's order. The other parties to the proceedings were KDT's parents and his guardian ad litem, Mrs D.

The judge made a supervision order for 12 months in favour of the local authority and imposed conditions of supervision pursuant to para. 2(1)(b) and (c) and para. 3(1)(a) and (c) of sch. 3 to the Children Act 1989. Those conditions are not specified in his order, but we have been shown a letter dated 23 November 1993 from the principal social worker of the local authority's children and families team dealing with the case addressed to the parents in which the specified conditions are:

(1)   attendance at a local children's day centre on two days a week from 9.30 to 11.30 a.m.
(2)   attendance at clinic appointments as requested by the health visitor and
(3)   notification to the supervision officer of any change in the child's address.

We think that the form of the Judge's order is unsatisfactory. Where, as here, conditions are imposed under a supervision order those conditions ought to be apparent on the face of the order.

He said:

I have no doubt from what I have read and heard that [the parents] are, more than capable of looking after this child, that is to say caring for his everyday needs rearing him as a happy, healthy well stimulated little boy. The clear evidence is that is what has happened and I would have no worries on that score . . .

. . . I cannot say that I have heard anything which convinces me that [the father] is likely to mistreat this boy, certainly not in the way which would justify the intervention of the court. That was my conclusion on this topic on the last occasion and it is still my conclusion. The nub of this case is really the question of sexual abuse and always has been).

The judge then went on to assess the risk of significant harm from sexual abuse in the future. He came to the conclusion on the basis of Dr K's evidence, that the level of risk was relatively low. There was, he found, 'a real, albeit low, risk of sexual abuse in this case'. He also found that the risk could not be described as insignificant and as a consequence the threshold criteria under s. 31 were met. However, the judge concluded that the level of risk was not such as to require the removal of the child from his family, but sufficient to warrant the making of a supervision order.

Mr Anelay for the local authority accepted that he must satisfy this court that the judge was not entitled on the evidence before him to make the findings of fact which we have recited and that his assessment of the level of risk to the child in his home environment was plainly wrong. Mr Anelay also accepted, the s. 31 threshold having been crossed, that the judge had a discretion as to the order which he made and that this court could only interfere to make a care order if on the evidence it could be demonstrated that the judge was plainly wrong. In this context, Mr Anelay accepted that he had to demonstrate that KDT's welfare positively demanded the displacement of the parents from their normal role in his care and upbringing.

Mr Anelay's principal supervision was that the supervision order did not adequately protect the child and that the only order which could adequately protect him and promote his welfare was one which removed him from his family. . . .

These are powerful submissions. Miss Hindley's answer to them was that the judge look into account and duly weighed all the factors listed by Mr Anelay. He considered the nature of the relevant significant harm to the child (the risk of sexual abuse) and evaluated the degree of risk. He considered carefully the merits and demerits of the various courses open to him and exercised a discretion on the evidence available to him. Miss Hindley submitted that it would have been a misapplication of the welfare test to make a care order resulting in the removal of the child when the judge had found that such a removal was contrary to the child's interests and that a supervision order properly operated, as the judge put it 'would be bound at least to reduce the level of risk which in percentage terms is relatively small'.

We think, however, that there is force in Mr Anelay's submission that the judge regarded a supervision order as 'second best', although he may have felt himself in the same difficulty as the guardian ad litem now finds herself. In our view, however, the judge was right to make a supervision order. The threshold criteria for both care and supervision orders are the same, It follows that there will be cases (of which this is one) where the court finds the threshold criteria met, and then has to decide whether the level of risk is such that a care order is necessary to protect the child, or whether the risk of harm can be catered for by a supervision order. The judge plainly took the view that this case fell into the latter category and, given his finding both that the parents were capable of bringing up the child and that it would be inimical to his welfare to be removed from them (both findings that it was open to him to make), it was not then open to him to make a care order.

This case illustrates the difficult and finely balanced decisions which judges have to make in child cases. In our judgment, however, the judge was entitled on the material before him to make a supervision order rather than a care order. It follows that the substantive appeal must be dismissed.

We were, however, concerned to read in the latest report of the guardian ad litem that the father and KDT were both sleeping on a bed settee. The father explained to the social worker that the reason was that they had difficulty in getting the child to sleep, with the result that the parents take it in turns to go to bed with KDT, but that the father is better at getting him to sleep. The father said that once KDT was asleep he leaves him on the settee and gets into bed with the mother on another bed in the same room.

When questioned by the social worker about his practice of sleeping with KDT the father asserted that because he was the father he could of course make whatever arrangements he felt right for his son. He is reported as saying: 'It doesn't matter who he sleeps with. If anything happens you can take action.'

Both the social worker and the guardian ad litem were concerned by this evidence, and we share their concern. Miss Hindley accepted in argument that there was no good reason why the father should share a bed with the child, and that if there was difficulty in getting him to sleep, the mother could get into bed with him. Miss Hindley also accepted that it would be open to us under s. 11(7) of the Children Act 1989 to make it a condition of any residence, order granted to the parents under s. 8 of the Act that the father does not share a bed with the child under any circumstances,

Whilst we are conscious of the practicalities of enforcing any such direction we think it an appropriate one to make. This family is plainly going to be under rigorous scrutiny by the local authority under the supervision order and any renewal by the court of that order: the child will also remain on the at risk register. Given the history of the case and the likely level of supervision we think it also likely that any breach of the condition would come to the attention of the local authority, and whilst the effect of any breach would not normally involve proceedings for contempt, it would at its lowest cast grave doubt over the father's motivation and assist in alerting the local authority to any continuing risk of abuse. We therefore regard such a condition as a useful addition to the child protection measures already in force.

For the reasons we have given, this appeal will be dismissed, but the order of the judge will be varied to make a residence order in favour of the parents with a condition attached that the father will not share a bed with KDT at any stage during his minority.

11.3.2.2   Split orders

CHILDREN ACT 1989

11.   General principles and supplementary provisions

. . .

(4)   Where a residence order is made in favour of two or more persons who do not themselves all live together, the order may specify the periods during which the child is to live in the different households concerned.

A v A (MINORS) (SHARED RESIDENCE ORDER) [1994] 1 FLR 669 (CA)

CONNELL J: This is an appeal from the decision of his Honour Judge MacDonald, sitting in the Newcastle upon Tyne County Court given on 1 October 1993, when he made a shared residence order concerning two young girls. The hearing before the judge had extended over some days, the evidence being heard on 9 July 1993, submissions being made on 15 July 1993 and his judgment being delivered on 1 October 1993.

There were before the judge cross-applications by the mother and the father of two girls, each seeking a residence order in respect of the girls. These were B, born on 20 April 1983, who is 10 years 9 months old, and C, born on 9 October 1986, who is 7 years and 4 months old.

On 20 September 1991, that is approximately 3 months after the parties separated, an order was made granting the interim care and control of the children to the father. The purpose behind the order at that stage was that it was anticipated that the mother would have to go into hospital for surgery, and therefore the interim care and control order in the father's favour was to deal with the period while she was hospitalised. In fact the mother did not go into hospital at that time. Accordingly, on 11 October 1991 the interim care and control of these two young girls was committed to the mother with reasonable access to the father. The access which was ordered at that time was it the discretion of the court welfare officer. In fact, the way that operated was that the father enjoyed access on Saturdays between 10 am and 6 pm. In due course, the father applied for staying access. That matter was resolved by a consent order which was made on 26 February

1992. That order provided for staying access to the father on alternate weekends from Saturday at 10 am to Sunday at 6 pm; the arrangement then being that the children should stay with the father at the home of his mother. On the other weekend, when there was not staying access, the father enjoyed visiting access from 10 am to 6 pm on Saturday. In addition, these orders being made in the context of the dissolution proceedings, there was an interim supervision order relating to that access. A review was directed for May or June of 1992. That review took place on 15 June 1992 when, by consent, District Judge Wilson made further orders relating to what was by then described as, and we know as, contact. The order for contact which was made repeated the previous arrangements for staying contact, but by now it was possible for the children to stay with their father at the former matrimonial home rather than at the grandmother's home. There was also a continuing provision for visiting contact on the other weekend when there was no staying contact, still to be on Saturdays between 10 am and 6 pm. Additionally, and this was a noticeable increase in what had been previously ordered, it was directed that the children should spend half their school holidays with their father and also half their school half-terms. As the judge pointed out in the course of his judgment the effect of this order was to share equally between the mother and the father the time when the children were not at school. Looked at from another angle, it is apparent that the effect of the order was, and is, that the children would spend approximately one-third of the year with their father. Plainly they were spending a significant part of their lives being looked after by him.

In his application for a residence order the father did not seek to change these arrangements relating to contact. By the time that the matter came on for bearing before the judge, the contact arrangements had been in existence for in excess of 12 months. What the father sought was a shared residence order, as envisaged by s. 11(4) of the Children Act 1989. Section 11(4) reads as follows:

Where a residence order is made in favour of two or more persons who do not themselves all live together, the order may specify the period during which the child is to live in the different households concerned.

Accordingly, the father asked the judge to make an order for residence in his favour, providing for the children to live with him in his home when they were having contact to him in accordance with the consent order of 15 June 1992. He did not suggest that there should not also be a residence order in the mother's favour, recognising the fact that the children spent the majority of their time living with their mother.

The mother resisted that application by the father whilst accepting that the previous arrangements relating to contact should continue. Her case was that the appropriate order was that there should be a residence order to her with a contact order, to include extensive staying contact, in favour of the father; in other words, a repetition of the order made on 15 June 1992, together with a residence order in her favour.

Against that background, as the judge observed, the issue before the court was a very narrow one: should the children continue to see their father for the same period of time under the auspices of a contact order or under the auspices of a shared residence order? In the result, the judge made shared residence orders, thereby acceding to the father's application. It is against that decision that the mother now appeals.

The mother, through her counsel, has asked the court to consider delivering what is described in the skeleton argument produced on behalf of mother as a 'declaratory judgment' as to what amounts to exceptional circumstances sufficient to justify such a shared residence order. The mother, through counsel, says that shared orders for residence should rarely be made and then in exceptional circumstances instances. In support of that submission she relies upon the case of Re H (A Minor) (Shared Residence) [1994] 1 FLR 717. She relies in particular upon the judgment of Purchas LJ which begins at p. 726, and in particular on the passage at p. 728 where the Lord Justice said as follows:

It is for those reasons that, in any event, I would not support the making of a joint residence order. That such an order is open to the court, as has been said in the judgment of Cazalet J, is clear from the provisions of s. 11(4) of the Children Act 1989, as was indicated during the debate on the Bill by the Lord Chancellor. But, at the same time, it must be an order which would rarely be made and would depend upon exceptional circumstances. A child, as was emphasised in the case of *Riley* v *Riley* [1986] 2 FLR 429, should have one home, and the other place of spending time, including overnight, is not the home but a place where visits may regularly and frequently be made. The establishment, as it were, of two competing homes only leads to confusion and stress and would be contrary to the paramount concept of the welfare of the child himself.

Counsel relies upon that case, and in particular upon the passage in the judgment of Purchas LJ, when submitting that a shared residence order should only be made in exceptional circumstances. She goes on to say that shared orders can properly be made where they will assist by reducing the differences between mother and father. But she submits it is not so in this case where, on the mother's evidence and on counsel's submission, the evidence was, and is, that the mother and father do not get on. Put in a nutshell, counsel for the appellant says that this is a perfectly normal 'run of the mill' case. There is nothing unusual or exceptional about it. Accordingly a shared order should not have been made. The judge should have made a residence order to the mother with contact to the father.

The court will wish to look to see whether there is something which will be to the positive benefit of the children arising out of such a shared order before finding the circumstances to be so unusual as to justify the making of such in order. Of course, it almost goes without saying that the court must, in considering whether or not to make such all order, be guided by the Children Act 1989 and in particular s. 1(1), treating the child's welfare as the court's paramount consideration, and by matters set out in the welfare checklist in s. 1(3) of the Act.

Against that background, the issue for us to decide in this case, given the need for there to be some such positive benefit to the child and some such unusual circumstances to exist before an order should be made, is: was the judge properly exercising the discretion vested in him, and properly serving the best interests of the children, by making such an order in this case, or alternatively was he plainly wrong to do so?

In my judgment, the exercise which the court has to undertake when considering whether or not to make a shared residence order is what I will describe as the normal s. 1 of the Children Act exercise, bearing in mind the principles set out so clearly and plainly in s. 1(1) and (3). The observation of Cazalet J in *Re H* (above) helpfully indicates matters of importance to be borne in mind when this exercise is carried out, without laying down principles of universal application. In the particular case with which we are dealing, the following features are of particular relevance. First of all, the movements of the children are agreed. There is no issue about the quantum of time which they are to spend, on the one hand, with their mother and, on the other hand, with their father. The only issue is: what is the appropriate order to recognise those movements, and what order will, in the circumstances prevailing, best serve the interests of the children? The father specifically accepts in his application, and in his evidence, that the children's main home is with their mother. . . .

He set that out in his judgment as follows:

However, if it can be shown that a joint residence order would reduce the hostility between the parents it would seem to be in the interests of the child's welfare to make that type of order.

In giving his judgment the judge said this:

Having considered all the facts, the reports and those particular authorities of binding application, this court concludes that there should be two residence orders, an order in favour of each parent.

Thereafter, he gave a number of specific reasons for making the order. First of all, he said that the orders made by the court must reflect the day-to-day reality of the care of these children. I would only differ from the way in which the matter was put by the judge in using the word 'must', by observing that it is usually helpful if an order or orders made by the court do reflect the reality of the situation. The judge went on to say: 'This court finds exceptional circumstances as follows . . .'

He then set out his reasons for so finding which included first that there would be no confusion or stress to the children caused by the making of such an order. Secondly, the father has an exceptional relationship with the children. Thirdly, and in the light of the submissions made this is of particular importance, the court accepted that the communication between the mother and the father, although very poor, was improving. The court looked to the possibility that the making of such an order might assist such improvement.

It is argued that there was no basis on the evidence for the judge to reach that conclusion. In answer to that submission, I would turn to the report of the experienced welfare officer who said in the penultimate paragraph of her last report:

> Communication [between the parent] is still extremely poor. It was because of this difficulty in communicating that in my last report I was unable to recommend residence orders to both parents or the principle of no order to the court. Some time has lapsed since that hearing and regular staying contact is well established. After speaking with both parties I am aware that contact has not been without difficulties . . . I would accept much of the above comment, however it is my belief that both parties have progressed in their ability to accommodate the other and that they both have the ability to improve further . . . perhaps the time is now right for a residence order to he made in favour of both parents.

Fourthly, the judge, in setting out his reasons for finding that these circumstances were exceptional, pointed to the fact that the welfare officer, who had experience of this case over a significant period of time, recommended such an order. He specifically said: 'She [the welfare officer recommends a shared residence order as being in the long-term interests of the girls.'

Of course, it was not the case that the judge was bound to follow the recommendation of an experienced welfare officer. In the course of counsel's submissions the judge made it clear that he realised that that was the case. But equally, it was plainly a matter which he was fully entitled to bear in mind, as he did, and as he said in his judgment.

RE WB (RESIDENCE ORDERS) [1995] 2 FLR 1023 (FamD)

THORPE J: This is an appeal from an order made by the Bath justices on 19 December 1991, in proceedings between N, who is the appellant in this court, and B, who is the respondent.

The notice of appeal was issued on 14 April 1992 and is therefore out of time, but by concession of Mr Rutherford, who represents the respondent, I have extended time. The case is an unusual one and it is important to record its unusual facts.

The appellant and the respondent met in 1979 and they lived together for almost a decade. During that period the mother gave birth to two children, S, who was born on 16 January 1981, and O, born on 30 April 1984.

The parties' cohabitation was largely in the city of Bath, where they started a business in partnership, selling and repairing bicycles. The cohabitation between the parties ended in December 1989, when the respondent left the home which the family unit occupied, and thereafter, for a period of approximately 6 months, the care of these two children was largely shared with the appellant.

In June 1990 the respondent shifted the arrangement to a more conventional one, whereby the appellant had access on alternate weekends. In September 1991, following a disagreement between the parties, the arrangements for contact were terminated.

On 25 November 1991 the justices made an interim order defining two periods of contact pending the substantive hearing, and making a prohibited steps order in relation to the same period. The respondent, although aggrieved at the circumstances in which the blood samples had been taken from the children, was not averse to the principle that there should be scientific investigation, and she herself furnished a sample of blood. The scientific evidence arrived almost on the eve of the final hearing, and the tests established scientifically that the appellant is not the biological father of either child. The hearing took place before the justices over the course of 2 days, 18 and 19 December 1991. . . .

The grounds settled by Mr Wildblood raise two points: (1) that the justices erred in concluding that no order should be made on the appellant's application to restrict the removal of these two children from the jurisdiction; (2) that the justices erred in declining to make a shared residence order pursuant to s. 11(4) of the Children Act 1989. The order which the justices did make provided for a residence order to the respondent and a contact order to the appellant for alternate weekends with a commencement date in January 1992, supported by staying access in the school holidays of one week at Christmas and Easter, and 2 weeks during the summer holidays.

The first point taken by the notice, namely that the justices should have made a shared residence order rather than a residence order to the respondent and a contact order to the appellant, seems to me devoid of any merit. It is advanced by the appellant on the understandable ground that since he was never married to the respondent and since science has established that he is not the biological father, his only route to an order for parental responsibility is via an order of residence; ergo, if he receives only contact, he has not and can never establish parental responsibility.

That, of course, is a perfectly rational submission, but it could lead to the making of an order that would be quite artificial and quite unreflective of the reality. The fact is that the appellant in the court below contended for the restoration of the sort of regime that had existed consensually in the 6 months immediately following separation. The welfare officer had considered how appropriate that arrangement was and how likely it was to promote the welfare of the children. In particular, he sounded the children out as to how they had coped during that period. He received the clear message that they had found it confusing, and he reached the understandable professional conclusion that it would not be good for the children to restore such a regime for the future.

The justices concluded in their reasons that it was very important for the promotion of the welfare of the children that their primary home with their mother should be established and declared. There can, in my judgment, be no challenge to that conclusion. Manifestly, it was the right conclusion on the balance of the evidence.

The sort of order for which the appellant contends, namely a shared residence order, would have been appropriate if and only if the justices had reached the surprising conclusion that a shared regime would most likely promote the interests of the children. Once they had reached the almost inevitable conclusion that a more conventional solution was likely to promote the children's welfare, then, in my judgment, only the order which they made was appropriate to reflect that decision. It would, in my judgment, have been quite wrong had they expressed their conclusion in the shape of a shared residence order for no other reason than to arrive at a finding of parental responsibility in the appellant.

11.3.2.3   Duration of the orders

CHILDREN ACT 1989

9.   Restrictions on making section 8 orders

. . .

(6)   No court shall make any section 8 order which is to have effect for a period which will end after the child has reached the age of 16 unless it is satisfied that the circumstances of the case are exceptional.

(7)   No court shall make any section 8 order, other than one varying or discharging such an order, with respect to a child who has reached the age of 16 unless it is satisfied that the circumstances of the case are exceptional.

11.3.3   CONTACT ORDERS

11.3.3.1   Rights?

M v M (CHILD: ACCESS) [1973] 2 All ER 81 (FamD)

WRANGHAM J: This is an appeal by the mother of a little boy of seven against the decision of the Leicester county justices on 1st June 1972. On that date they had before them a complaint or an application by the mother, the appellant, for a further definition of 'reasonable access', which had been granted under a previous order of that court, and a cross-complaint or application by the father that access should be deleted from the order and that at any rate for a time there should be no access granted to this mother.

The facts of the matter are comparatively short. The parties were married in 1956. On 24th October 1966 they adopted this little boy, now seven, and therefore at that stage a small baby. The fact that this child is adopted and is not the natural child of the parties is in my judgment a fact which is wholly irrelevant to any of the issues to be considered by this court. Indeed there is no indication that it was treated as anything but wholly irrelevant by the Leicester justices. I say no more about that point. . . .

On 4th April 1970 the marriage came to an end. The mother left the home. She left the boy with the father. On 26th June she went to the justices complaining that her husband had treated her with persistent cruelty and asked for the custody of the boy. She was not successful.

. . . custody was awarded to the father, and there was an order for reasonable access to be given to the mother. That was interpreted by the parties as being an order which could be fulfilled by visiting access twice a week. The parties lived at that stage quite close to one another. Subsequently it was reduced by agreement to once a week. . . .

That is a summary of the facts which came before the justices. They heard of course the evidence of the mother and of the father, they had before them the report of the court welfare officer who in addition gave evidence to them, and they also had a report from the boy's schoolmistress, who reported that on the days when access had been taking place the teacher had noticed that after access the little boy was withdrawn and unsettled and that his general development had greatly improved since access came to an end. The natural inference from that is that whether the fault lie with the mother or the father or with both, the fact was that access in the conditions which the parents imposed had exercised a most unhappy effect on the child, and indeed had operated wholly or nearly wholly to his disadvantage. . . .

On the face of it, if one follows the words of Willmer LJ without regard to subsequent cases, there is a very strong argument to be made for the mother. No one has suggested that this mother is a woman who was not a fit and proper person to be brought into contact with the child at all, she has not got a criminal record, and there is not the smallest reason to suppose that she was disposed to act with cruelty towards this child. But since *S v S and P* [1992] 2 All ER 1 was decided there have been other decisions of the Court of Appeal. One is *C v C*, *The Times*, 28 March 1971. The only report before me is the report in the Times newspaper of 28th May 1971. In that case Dunn J had refused access to a mother in the circumstances set out in that report. Again the facts do not bear the smallest resemblance to the facts in this case and are therefore of no importance here. But what is of importance is that Davies LJ in giving his judgment said:

In such cases as the present the welfare of the children was the paramount consideration. Access, custody and care were not to be given as rewards for one parent or taken away as punishment for another.

He adds that he agrees with the learned trial judge and emphasises that the children were living in a happy, secure and serene household. . . .

But Davies LJ comes to deal with the argument based on *S v S and P* and he recites the words of Willmer LJ, that normally it is the basic right of every parent to have access to the child or children. He says: 'That of course is true. But there are exceptions to every rule . . .' The importance of the exception in this case was that on the finding that I had made at first instance there was no real criticism to be made of the father at all, merely a situation had been reached in which, as I then thought, no good could come to the child from companionship with his father, largely no doubt because of the attitude that the mother, who had care and control of the boy, had taken up during the years in which she had been looking after him. The Court of Appeal upheld the order that access should cease on the ground that even though there was no real criticism to be made of the father the paramount consideration was the welfare of the child, and the welfare of the child would not be promoted by access to the father.

It seems to me that the only way which one can really reconcile *S v S and P* with the cases that followed, *C v C* and still more *B v B* [1971] 3 All ER 682, is to say that what

Willmer LJ meant was that the companionship of a parent is in any ordinary circumstances of such immense value to the child that there is a basic right in him to such companionship. I for my part would prefer to call it a basic right in the child rather than a basic right in the parent. That only means this, that no court should deprive a child of access to either parent unless it is wholly satisfied that it is in the interests of that child that access should cease, and that is a conclusion at which a court should be extremely slow to arrive. It is not without significance that Edmund Davies LJ in *B* v *B* said:

> For a court to deprive a good parent completely of access to his child is to make a dreadful order. That is what has been done here, and the impact on both parent and child must have lifelong consequences. Very seldom can the court bring itself to make so Draconian an order, and rarely is it necessary.

RE W (A MINOR) (CONTACT) [1994] 2 FLR 441 (CA)

SIR STEPHEN BROWN P: This is an appeal from a judgment of Judge Vos given at Newcastle upon Tyne County Court, on Monday, 8 February 1993.

The proceedings before Judge Vos concerned a contact application in respect of a boy called R, born on 11 September 1989. Accordingly, he was then almost $3\frac{1}{2}$ years of age, and is now approaching $4\frac{1}{2}$.

The history of the little boy is an unhappy one. His parents were married, but are now divorced. The question of contact with his father has been a source of continual problems.

The decree was made absolute on 29 January 1991. As I have said, the statement of arrangements provided for reasonable access to the father with custody to the mother. In February 1991 the mother met another man, whom she has now married. Both the mother and the other man worked for the same civil service employment branch.

When she met her future second husband, the mother made what appears to have been a quite conscious and deliberate decision to cease allowing the boy to have contact with his father. Indeed, the judge made a specific finding as to that.

In March 1991 the mother terminated all contact by the boy with his father. The father has had no contact with the little boy since that time.

The father consulted solicitors and requested contact. There were delays. He sought legal aid. That was not immediately forthcoming.

On 17 January 1992, time having passed, he applied for contact to be defined because the order which still obtained was simply that he should have 'reasonable contact'. The mother opposed his application. She took the view that the father was incapable of caring for the child, that he had not seen him for a year and, she asserted, he would not retain interest in the child.

She has been obdurate about the matter of contact ever since then. . . .

There was in force an order for reasonable contact which had been made by consent. There has been no application with mother for it to be revoked or varied in any way. This was a situation where despite the order the child had been denied contact with his father for a period of some 2 years, due entirely to the obduracy of the mother and perhaps the stepfather.

It was also the case—and this is important in my judgment—that the little boy was being brought up to believe that the stepfather was his real father and therefore was being deprived of knowledge of his father. It is quite clear that contact with a parent is a fundamental right of a child, save in wholly exceptional circumstances.

In *Re S (Minors) (Access)* [1990] 2 FLR 166, a case which was different on its facts but in which similar principles were involved, it was held by the Court of Appeal (Balcombe and Glidewell LJJ) that the principle was well-established not merely that the welfare of the children was the first and paramount consideration, but that access was the right of a child not of the parents. The child had a right, even though his parents were separated, to know the non-custodial parent. That principle is not challenged.

It appears clear to me that in this case the judge had a positive duty to make some order despite the obduracy of the mother. It was not good enough simply to say: 'The mother insists that she will not allow contact. There is in force an order for reasonable contact. That has not been implemented but I do not propose to make any order'. In my judgment the judge was manifestly wrong in seeking to apply the terms of s. 1(5) of the Children Act to this situation.

I have to say that having carefully recounted in his judgment the development of events since the parties had separated, when it came to the climax of making a decision the judge avoided making one simply on the basis that the mother would not obey an order of the court. That amounted to an abdication of his responsibility.

The problem now is that the emotional impasse has intensified. It is going to be more difficult for R to be reintroduced to the father who loves him and who is his father, but somehow this has to be attempted.

RE M (A MINOR) (CONTACT: CONDITIONS) [1994] 1 FLR 272 (FamD)

WALL J: This appeal, from an order made by the Horsham Family Proceedings Court on 10 May 1993, under ss. 8 and 11(7) of the Children Act 1989, raises a number of interesting questions relating to contact orders to young children.

The order under appeal reads as follows:

Contact shall be by post. In accordance with s. 11(7) of the Children Act 1989 the court imposes the following conditions:

(a) [the mother] shall read to M the contents of any letters addressed to him, received from [the father], and shall give to M any present or card which the father may send.

(b) At least every 3 months the mother shall write to the father giving an account of M's progress.

(c) The court further orders that the father shall write to M at least every 3 months.

(d) Both parties to keep each other informed of their respective addresses.

M was born on 19 October 1990. He is now just 3.

The questions raised by the case are:

(1) Were the justices correct on the facts of the case to order contact by post to a child aged 2 years and 7 months at the time of the hearing before them?

(2) Did the justices have jurisdiction to impose the conditions set out in subparas (a) to (d) of the order?

(3) If they did, does the order constitute a proper exercise of their discretion to make or refuse contact orders, and impose conditions under ss. 8 and 11(7)?

(4) Was this a case in which either 'no order' for contact was appropriate or, alternatively, should the justices have dismissed the father's application for contact and directed that there be no contact for the foreseeable future?

Although the mother and the father lived together until M was aged 13 months, it is the fact that between the date of the separation in November 1991 and his imprisonment in January 1993, the father saw M on only five occasions, the last of which was shortly before he was imprisoned. He has, thus, not seen him now for 9 months, and will not see him again—assuming the court directs no further contact—until after his release from prison.

The mother's attitude to contact appears to have hardened during the course of the proceedings. When she spoke to the welfare officer in the spring of 1992 she accepted that in principle M was entitled to some contact with his father. She was at that stage opposed to staying contact, but was agreeable to limited visiting contact between M and his father in Brighton. However, the mother's evidence to the justices was that she did not want the father to have any contact with M at all. She said he had not proved to her to be a worthy father. She described him as a criminal, and is recorded as saying:

That man is no good for my son, and never will be. I would not agree to contact, and I will only agree to it by order of this court. I left because I didn't want to have any more contact with him.

Looking at the order made by the justices in this case, however, this court is left to infer the justices' intentions. They are not, in my judgment, clearly stated. What I infer is that the justices took the view that whilst the father was in prison, face-to-face contact between him and M was either undesirable or impracticable, but that some form of contact needed to be maintained in order to facilitate the reintroduction to his father after the latter's release from prison.

Logically, since face-to-face contact was not ordered, contact had to be indirect. Accordingly, contact by post was ordered.

I do not know what the justices particularly had in mind when they said that 'M's long-term needs are uncertain', or on what findings of fact they based that assertion. They do not specify what research they had in mind when they said: 'Research indicates that the emotional needs of a child are better satisfied if he knows both parents', although as a general proposition the sentiment behind such a statement is well-established in the case-law and unexceptionable.

It is also not clear to me what they meant when they said: 'Some contact should continue to avoid a sudden change in the future', given that in his short life M had seen his father only on some five occasions since November 1991, and was not to see him again on any view until after June 1994.

I am, moreover, particularly concerned about the phrase: '. . . the child's reaction to father's alleged violence to the mother'. The justices heard evidence from both parties about the father's alleged violence. They should have made a finding about it. Whom did they believe? Did they accept the mother's evidence about the child's reaction? In particular, in my judgment, if they were going to seek to impose on the mother the task of reading the father's letters out loud to the child, they had a duty to assess the weight of the burden they were imposing on her in the light, amongst other factors, of the truth or falsity of the allegations she made against him.

I have to say, however, in the instant case, irrespective of the question of jurisdiction, and whilst I think I understand what the justices were trying to achieve, their reasons and findings of fact are inadequate.

Furthermore, I do not think that they addressed their minds fully to the range of options open to them which plainly included making no order on the basis that the father would reapply on his release from prison; or adjourning the father's application for contact generally, on the basis that he would reapply in June 1994.

These considerations, however, beg the questions:

(1)   whether or not they were right to make an order for contact by post.
(2)   whether they had jurisdiction to impose the conditions they imposed; and, if so,
(3)   as to the suitability of the conditions they in fact imposed.

I was referred by counsel to a number of the many authorities on the question of contact. Miss Edwards, for the mother, submitted there was a divergence of approach in the authorities on the question of the proper approach for the reinstating of contact. One line which asks the question: 'Will starting contact be of any positive benefit to the child?' is *Starling* v *Starling* (1983) FLR 135 and *Re F (A Minor) (Access)* [1992] Fam Law 484. Miss Edwards submits that the second line which asks: 'Are there any cogent reasons why the child should be denied the opportunity of contact with his natural father?' . . .

In my judgment, the overwhelming weight of current authority is in favour of the propositions which Mr Hershman, for the father, advances in his skeleton argument, namely:

(1)   Wherever possible a child should get to know his estranged parent, and cogent reasons should be given for denying contact (*Re R (A Minor) (Contact)* (above)).

(2)   No court should deprive a child of access to a natural parent unless wholly satisfied that it is in the interest of the child that contact should cease and that is a conclusion at which a court should be extremely slow to arrive (*Re KD (A Minor) (Access: Principles)* [1988] AC 806 and *Re H (Minors) (Access)* [1992] 1 FLR 148 at p. 150C, following *M* v *M (Child: Access)* [1973] 2 All ER 81).

(3)   It is the normal assumption that a child would benefit from continued contact with a natural parent (*Re B (Minors) (Access)* [1992] 1 FLR 140 at p. 142A). Moreover, as the Court of Appeal made clear in the case of *Re H* (above), the same principles apply whether one is deciding whether or not contact between a child and his absent parent should cease, or whether it should be reintroduced.

The question on this part of the appeal, therefore, becomes: were the justices correct in making an order for contact by post because to have made no order would have meant no contact which would be against the long-term interests of the child? . . .

On this point I prefer Mr Hershman's submissions, and agree with him that it would be premature at this stage to dismiss the father's application for contact, or direct that there be no contact.

In my judgment, the matters prayed in aid by Miss Edwards do not amount to cogent reasons for denying all future contact. Whether or not a realistic relationship between M and his father can be established, however, is not something which can be ascertained until the father has been discharged from prison.

Accordingly, insofar as the justices' aim was to maintain a link between M and his father, with a view to facilitating a reintroduction on his father's release from prison, I think they were correct. On the principles of making an order against making no order, therefore, I think they were right to make an order; and right not to dismiss the father's application or direct that there be no further contact between M and his father.

That, however, is by no means an end of the matter since I take the view that Miss Edwards' criticisms of the form of the order made by the justices have substantial force. I take the jurisdiction first.

Counsel were agreed that the only jurisdiction to impose conditions on a s. 8 contact order arises from s. 11(7) of the Children Act 1989 . . .

The purpose of a contact order is for the child to have contact with the person named in the order. It does not seem to me to be properly within the jurisdiction of the court in making an order for contact to a child under s. 8 to order the parents to have contact with each other. In my judgment, the definition of a contact order in s. 8 of the Act in the context of indirect contact can only at its widest be construed as meaning an order for the person named in the order to have contact with the child otherwise than by visiting that person or staying with that person. It does not seem to me that either the definition section or s. 11(7), or both when read in combination, can properly embrace an order directing the mother to write to the father about the child's progress. In my judgment, therefore, para. 2(b) of the order, however desirable it may be in certain cases, was made without jurisdiction and must be set aside.

Similarly it seems to me that para. 2(d) is too widely drawn. The proper limit to the jurisdiction seems to me to impose an obligation on the mother to keep the father informed of the whereabouts of the child. Knowledge of the child's whereabouts seems to me properly to be a necessarily incidental provision to a contact order, and can be distinguished from a direction to communicate with the other parent about the child's welfare generally.

Paragraph 2(c) of the order which directs the father to write to M at least every 3 months is likewise, at best, infelicitously expressed, and at worst outside the court's powers. In my judgment, contact orders which provide for indirect contact are permissive, not mandatory. Whilst a father may be permitted by the court to write to a child at specified intervals, or permitted to telephone at specified times, or send presents or cards on specified occasions, an order which directs him to write 'at least every 3 months' is in my judgment wrong in law. Under the order as drawn, prison regulations permitting, the father can write to M every day, and the mother under para. 2(a) will be obliged to read every word to him. In my judgment, therefore, para. 2(c) as phrased, is also bad in law and must be set aside.

In practical terms I am clearly of the view that the court can restrain a parent with whom the child lives from preventing telephone calls or the receipt of letters, cards and presents from the absent parent. I am, however, profoundly unhappy about orders which go beyond this and require the parent to be pro-active in facilitating contact by means of reading communications to the child.

At the end of the day, however, I take the view that this is not a matter of jurisdiction. I am somewhat reluctantly of the view that para. 2(a) of the order was within the jurisdiction of the justices. However, whilst I appreciate what they were trying to achieve, I regard it as wrong in principle and very unwise on the facts of the case. The suggestion that the mother should undertake the task does not appear to have been canvassed with her in evidence. The evidence which she in fact gave shows that she was hostile to any form of contact. The task the justices imposed on her, therefore, was highly uncongenial to her, to put the matter at its lowest. Moreover, how is such an order to be policed, or enforced? In my judgment, contact is by its nature artificial. Any order for contact should seek to reduce the artificiality, not increase it. Paragraph 2(a) of the order is, in my judgment on the facts of this case, artificial in the extreme, even if interpreted with the proviso conceded by Mr Hershman.

In my judgment, therefore, even if the justices had jurisdiction to make the order, they should not have done so unless the mother consented to it and was willing to undertake the task. In this context it seems to me an analogy can properly be drawn with the adoption cases, in which as a matter of practice the court only imposes conditions of the type maintained in the present order by consent (see, for example, *Re D (A Minor) (Adoption Order: Conditions)* [1992] 1 FCR 461).

It follows that the conditions imposed by the justices must be set aside, and since those conditions are an integral part, indeed they define the order for contact by post, it also follows that it is open to this court to exercise its discretion afresh.

11.3.3.2 What is contact?

RE O (CONTACT: IMPOSITION OF CONDITIONS) [1995] 2 FLR 124 (CA)

SIR THOMAS BINGHAM MR: This is an appeal against an order of his Honour Judge Fox, sitting in the Hartlepool County Court on 28 November 1994. The order was made in the course of proceedings under the Children Act 1989. On that date Judge Fox refused an application to discharge part of an earlier order made on 23 August 1994, although he did amend another paragraph of that order.

The case came before his Honour Judge Fox on 23 August 1994. An order was made to which the mother did not consent but which she indicated some reluctant willingness to accept. The order contained these terms:

2. The court orders that there be reasonable contact to [the father] to include the following conditions:

    (1) The respondent mother to send the applicant father photographs of the child J every 3 months commencing 23 November 1994.
    (2) If, and when, the said child commences nursery or playgroup the [mother] shall inform the [father] and send copies of all reports pertaining to the child's progress.
    (3) Should the child stiffer any significant illness, the [mother] shall inform the [father] and supply copies of all medical reports.
    (4) The [mother] shall accept delivery of cards and presents for the said child from the [father] via the public postal service.

The judge also directed that the matter should be reviewed after 6 months with a report from the court welfare officer and that the matter be reserved to him.

On 15 September 1994 the mother issued an application to discharge para. 2 of the order that I have just read—that is the paragraph requiring sending of reports pertaining to the child's progress. It is instructive to look at para. 3(b) of her application in which she says (in the form which is now provided for proceedings of this kind):

I am making this application because, [and there is added to represent her reasons] I am not prepared to have any form of contact with the [father] direct or indirect.

The hearing before the judge then took place on 28 November 1994. He amended para. 4 of the August 1994 order, which was the paragraph dealing with delivery of cards and presents, to the effect that the mother should accept delivery of cards and presents for the child from the father via the public postal service or the family court welfare service and upon acceptance of the same should read and show the child any such communication and deliver any such present to the child. So far as para. 2 of the August 1994 order is concerned—the giving of information and sending copies or reports—the judge refused to amend the order. He refused a stay of execution but on 19 December 1994 granted the mother leave to appeal against his order. That is how the matter comes before us.

The judge referred to s. 8(1) of the Children Act 1989 and also s. 11(7) and concluded that on his reading of s. 8(1) it was in mandatory terms, mandatory, that is to say, as against the residential parent, requiring that parent to do something. He did not accede to a submission of counsel that the language of the section was to be read permissively. He pointed out that with a 2-year-old child there could be no contact with the absent parent without the co-operation of the caring parent, and referred to the desirability of keeping a relationship between father and son alive and nourishing it until such time as there could be face-to-face contact between the two. He concluded that there was nothing wrong in principle with indirect contact, including indirect contact of the type which he had ordered. In his judgment he said:

> Whilst I think that it would be too upsetting for the child to be taken by a distraught mother any longer to supervised contact or to handover points, I do not think she will be so distraught as to have a knock-on effect to the child when she has settled into this routine which I have provided for the time being. At least I do not think that such knock-on effect as there may be will be of such effect that it outweighs the advantages of investing for the future relationship between father and son in order to make that a living, worthwhile relationship.

On the next page of his judgment he referred to an offer made by the court welfare officer to act as an intermediary in the matter of communications and presents, and acknowledged the great amount of work that the court welfare officer had put into this particular case. He expressed the opinion, however, that there comes a time when the family court welfare service is used to the point of exhaustion with some people, and felt that at the end of the day the aim must be for father and son to know each other and to have a living growing relationship and for the mother to accept that, even if she could not promote it. 'There,' he said, 'lies the best interests of this child.' . . .

It may perhaps be worth stating in a reasonably compendious way some very familiar but none the less fundamental principles. First of all, and overriding all else as provided in s. 1(1) of the 1989 Act, the welfare of the child is the paramount consideration of any court concerned to make an order relating to the upbringing of a child. It cannot be emphasised too strongly that the court is concerned with the interests of the mother and the father only insofar as they bear on the welfare of the child.

Secondly, where parents of a child are separated and the child is in the day-to-day care of one of them, it is almost always in the interests of the child that he or she should have contact with the other parent. The reason for this scarcely needs spelling out. It is, of course, that the separation of parents involves a loss to the child, and it is desirable that that loss should so far as possible be made good by contact with the non-custodial parent, that is the parent in whose day-to-day care the child is not. This has been said on a very, great number of occasions . . .

I simply draw attention to the judge's reference to a serious risk of major emotional harm. The courts should not at all readily accept that the child's welfare will be injured by direct contact. Judging that question the court should take a medium-term and long-term view of the child's development and not accord excessive weight to what appear likely to be short-term or transient problems. Neither parent should be encouraged or permitted to think that the more intransigent, the more unreasonable, the more obdurate and the more unco-operative they are, the more likely they are to get their own way. Courts should remember that in these cases they are dealing with parents who are adults, who must be treated as rational adults, who must be assumed to have the welfare of the child at heart, and who have once been close enough to each other to have produced the child. It would be as well if parents also were to bear these points in mind.

Fifthly, in cases in which, for whatever reason, direct contact cannot for the time being be ordered, it is ordinarily highly desirable that there should be indirect contact so that the child grows up knowing of the love and interest of the absent parent with whom, in due course, direct contact should be established. This calls for a measure of restraint, common sense and unselfishness on the part of both parents. If the absent parent deluges the child with presents or writes long and obsessive screeds to the child, or if he or she uses his or her right to correspond to criticise or insult the other parent, then inevitably those rights will be curtailed. The object of indirect contact is to build up a relationship between the absent parent and the child, not to enable the absent parent to pursue a feud with the caring parent in a manner not conducive to the welfare of the child.

The caring parent also has reciprocal obligations. If the caring parent puts difficulties in the way of indirect contact by withholding presents or letters or failing to read letters to a child who cannot read, then such parent must understand that the court can compel compliance with its orders; it has sanctions available and no residence order is to be regarded as irrevocable. It is entirely reasonable that the parent with the care of the child should be obliged to report on the progress of the child to the absent parent, for the obvious reason that an absent parent cannot correspond in a meaningful way if unaware of the child's concerns, or of where the child goes to school, or what it does when it gets there, or what games it plays, and so on. Of course judges must not impose duties which parents cannot realistically be expected to perform, and it would accordingly be absurd to expect, in a case where this was the case, a semi-literate parent to write monthly reports. But some means of communication, directly, or indirectly, is essential if indirect contact is to be meaningful, and if the welfare of the child is not to suffer. . . .

The first paragraph of the skeleton argument reads as follows:

The indirect contact which was ordered by the judge for a child born on 5 November 1992 to his father could only be effected with the assistance of the mother. The judge found that throughout the case the mother has maintained an implacable hostility to the concept of contact between father and son. The judge found the mother's hostility to be an irrational repugnance. In these circumstances the normal assumption that a child would benefit from continued contact with a natural parent was displaced when the contact was indirect and was only effected by the assistance of an unwilling parent.

I would observe that that was not the conclusion which the judge reached, having had the occasion to hear the parties and to follow this case very closely over a period of months. The effect of this submission would be to give every intransigent mother a right of veto over contact, and that is a right which no mother has and no mother should be encouraged to think she has.

The second submission reads:

The court had no power to compel the mother to read to the child the father's communications to the child if the mother were unwilling to do so. (*Re M (A Minor) (Contact: Conditions)* [1994] 1 FLR 272.)

As I read the judgment in that case, the submission is not an entirely accurate reflection of what the judge said. The judge did address the question whether the court had power to compel the mother to read the father's communications to the child, and although expressing some doubt about the court's jurisdiction, concluded in the end that the question was not one of jurisdiction but of the exercise of it. He concluded at p. 282H:

In my judgment, therefore, even if the justices had jurisdiction to make the order, they should not have done so unless the mother consented to it and was willing to undertake the task.

I feel bound to express my own disagreement with that statement of principle. It is tantamount to saying that a mother's withholding of consent and expression of unwillingness to do something is enough to defeat the court's power to order that that should be done. That is in my judgment not only all incorrect statement of law but an extremely dangerous one, since it gives mothers who wish to be intransigent a weapon which they should not be given. . . .

Reviewing this matter overall, I find no fault in the judge's direction on the law, nor in any conclusion of fact, nor in any exercise of discretion. it appears to me that he has handled this case with a high degree of sensitivity, understanding and wisdom, and I would dismiss the appeal.

11.3.3.3   Enforcing contact

RE H (A MINOR) (PARENTAL RESPONSIBILITY) [1993] 1 FLR 484 (CA)

HOLLIS J: This is an appeal by a father from a decision of his Honour Judge Marcus Edwards made in the Brentford County Court on 31 March 1992, whereby he refused the father's application for contact or access to his small child and further refused his application for a parental responsibility order. Insofar as the latter is concerned, the judge obtained an undertaking from the mother that if she and her present husband, Mr S, were minded to apply to adopt the child concerned, the father must be given notice and that no steps to adopt the child should be taken for 10 days after he had been personally served with such notice.

After the separation, the father had contact with the child quite regularly with the mother's agreement until November 1990. There is little doubt that the mother then refused to allow further contact because of her impending marriage to Mr S and they in fact were married on 15 or possibly 13 December 1990. Immediately thereafter her solicitors were writing to the father, saying that the mother and Mr S wished to adopt A. The father applied for a contact order. The matter came before his Honour Judge Tyrer and by consent an order was made giving him fortnightly contact to the child. Such contact continued until the very end of August 1991. In the meantime in August 1991, Mr S had written to the father saying that he was so upset with everything, in particular the father's access, that he, the father, had better have the mother back.

There was no contact after August 1991, and at the end of 1991, or possibly early this year, the mother and Mr S went to live in Scotland where they remain living with A. Then there was the hearing before his Honour Judge Marcus Edwards, which in all covered parts of 3 days in February to 31 March 1992. Later, apparently, the father wrote two cards to the boy. The order that I have recited did not forbid him to do so, but during the course of the judge's judgment he certainly indicated that there should be no such contact between father and son. Furthermore, on two separate occasions he, the father, telephoned the mother, according to him, to talk to her about some motor-car that he had been ordered to return to her, or something of the like. . . .

This is a case where, so far as access or contact is concerned, there is no doubt in my mind at least that the judge would have ordered access to take place between this father and this little boy except for the attitude and stand taken by the mother's husband. He was adamant that there should be no access and went so far as to say that if there was access he would leave the mother. Of course, as the little boy was living with his mother, that would go right to the root of the boy's stability, and in those circumstances the judge considered that no order for access or contact should be made.

Picking up the judgment again:

Mr S's relationship with A appears to be good, normal, and as one would expect in all the circumstances. There is no complaint about the way in which he cares for or looks after A, and A is plainly beginning to relate to him as a normal father.

In my judgment, the position which Mr S has taken is less easy to justify than that of the mother. There is a substantial risk that his attitude will cause real problems later for A. But in proceedings of this sort it is important to say nothing which might make it more difficult in the future for all parties concerned to try to understand each other's point of view, all for the good of the child. I am sure that Mr S wants the best for the mother and A and himself, but I hope that with the passage of time and once these proceedings are over he may try to disengage his own personal feelings and consider the future of A. A knows nothing of the past. He has a whole future to look forward to. His natural father loves him and wants to see him and build a relationship with him which, in my judgment, will all be to A's advantage. What is stopping that is the refusal of Mr S to contemplate any such connection, in my view without sufficient justification. Nevertheless, I am satisfied that the position he has taken is a genuine one and tenaciously held.

It seems to me in the end that this court is really bound by the principles set out in *G v G (Minors: Custody Appeal)* [1985] FLR 894. The judge, with great care, has gone through the balancing exercise. He finds that, as it were, the initial assumption that there should be access is displaced in this particular case because of the exceptional, even if unpalatable, circumstances of Mr S's attitude of mind. Speaking for myself, I do not see how the judge can be faulted. Certainly I would not be prepared to say that he was plainly wrong. Therefore, for my part, as to that part of the appeal, I would dismiss it.

Ingman, T, 'Contact and the Obdurate Parent' [1996] Fam Law 615

THE STATUTORY PROVISIONS
A contact order can be made under s. 10 of the Children Act 1989 whenever a question about a child's welfare arises in the course of specified family proceedings—defined for this purpose in s. 8(3) and (4) as including those in the divorce court and the family proceedings court, applications for ouster or non-molestation injunctions, and those in the High Court under its inherent jurisdiction, as well as in proceedings under the Children Act 1989 itself. A contact order is 'an order requiring the person with whom a child lives, or is to live, to allow the child to visit or stay with the person named in the order, or for that person and the child otherwise to have contact with each other' (s. 8(1)). The order is thus addressed to the caring parent and may provide for 'direct' or 'indirect' contact. The court is given the power by s. 11(7) to impose conditions in the order, to include directions about how it is to be implemented, and to 'make such incidental, supplemental or consequential provision as [it] thinks fit'.

FRUSTRATING THE COURT'S FUNCTION
In a number of cases in recent years the Court of Appeal has had to consider the old problem of the extent to which an obdurate parent can frustrate the court's order-making powers. One of the latest and most important (discussed below) is *Re O (Contact: Imposition of Conditions)* [1995] 2 FLR 124, which is significant also for its consideration of the ambit of the court's jurisdiction to impose conditions in indirect contact orders. In some of the cases, first instance judges have been criticised for refusing to order contact in the face of opposition from parents. Thus in *Re W (A Minor) (Contact)* [1994] 2 FLR 441 a judge who justified his decision not to make a defined contact order by relying upon the 'no order' presumption in s. 1(5) of the Children Act 1989 was held to have abdicated his responsibility by basing his decision to do nothing on the mother's determination not to obey any order he might make. The mother and the stepfather, who were seeking to bring up the child in the belief that the stepfather was the real father, had stated that they would rather go to prison than obey a contact order. The Court of Appeal said that, in the circumstances, the judge had been under a positive duty to make some order despite the mother's recalcitrance. He was wrong, moreover, to have relied upon the 'no order' presumption in s. 1(5) since it was not relevant. (It has also been held inappropriate to use s. 91(14)—stipulating that no application for an order may be made without leave of the court—merely as a device to prevent contact (see *Re H (Child Orders: Restricting Applications)* [1991] FCR 896, *Re F (Child Orders: Restricting Applications)* [1992] FCR 433, and *Re F (Contact: Restraint Order)* [1995] 1 FLR 956).)

Similarly, in *Re S (Minors: Access)* [1990] 2 FLR 166, a judge who declined to make an order on the ground that contact could not realistically work for the time being because of the mother's implacable opposition was held to have ignored the principle that contact is the right of the child, not the parent. On the facts, it would have been appropriate to make a contact order even though the judge thought that contact would not work. By declaring that he would not even try to secure what the child's welfare required, he had effectively failed to perform his duty. The Court of Appeal made an order for reasonable contact and warned the mother that she ran the risk of having the child taken away if she did not co-operate.

IMPOSITION OF CONDITIONS
Re O (Contact: Imposition of Conditions) [1995] 2 FLR 124 concerned a contact order made in respect of the child of an unmarried couple. Following difficulties between the couple over contact, an order had been made in the county court in the course of proceedings under the Children Act 1989. The order was for reasonable contact to the father, but subject to conditions which obliged the mother to send the father photographs of the

child every 3 months, to inform the father if the child commenced nursery or playgroup and to send him copies of all reports on the child's progress, to inform the father of any significant illness suffered by the child and to supply copies of all medical reports, and to accept delivery of cards and presents posted by the father for the child. The mother later applied for the discharge of the condition relating to the sending of reports about the child's progress because, inter alia. she was not prepared to have any form of contact with the father. At the hearing of the mother's application, the judge decided that the order he had made was within the jurisdiction conferred by the Children Act 1989, that no part of the order was wrong in principle, and that it was in the child's best interests for the order to be made. He referred to the mother's implacable hostility to contact between the father and the child as an 'irrational repugnance', indicated that he had formed a favourable impression of the father, and acknowledged the short-term and long-term benefits for the child from contact with the father. The judge declined to accede to the mother's request. Indeed, he expanded the condition relating to cards and presents by including those delivered through the family court welfare service and adding an obligation on the mother to 'read and show the child any such communication and deliver any such present to the child'. The mother's appeal against the amended order, brought with leave of the judge, was dismissed by the Court of Appeal.

Delivering the leading judgment, Sir Thomas Bingham MR said that, unambiguously, s. 8 of the Children Act 1989 authorises both direct and indirect contact, while s. 11(7) confers comprehensive powers to ensure the effectiveness of contact orders in the interests of the child's welfare. While stressing the need to avoid imposing duties which parents cannot realistically be expected to perform, his Lordship considered it entirely reasonable that the caring parent should be obliged to report to the absent parent on the child's progress.

In the Court of Appeal, the judge's order had been attacked on grounds based upon the judgment in *Re M (A Minor) (Contact: Conditions)* [1994] 1 FLR 272. In that case, Wall J doubted whether there was any jurisdiction under s. 11(7) to order the caring parent to read to the child the contents of communications from the absent parent, and held that, in any event, there was a right of censorship in the caring parent. It was also decided that there was no jurisdiction to order the writing of progress reports since that was, in effect, ordering the parents to have contact with each other. Orders for indirect contact were, in Wall J's opinion, permissive and not mandatory and should be limited by a 'not more than' formula. It was further held that the court should not order the caring parent, without that parent's consent, to undertake a facilitative act in order to implement indirect contact. The submissions made in the Court of Appeal on behalf of the mother in *Re O* included the following:

(1)   The judge had no power to compel an unwilling mother to read the father's communications to the child.

(2)   The judge was wrong to give the father implied permission to write to the child as often as he wished; his communications should have been limited by a 'not more than' formula.

(3)   It was wrong in principle, and not conducive to the child's welfare, to compel the mother to read the father's communications to the child when the mother was hostile to such contact.

(4)   The mother's obligation to read out the father's communications should be subject to a right of censorship in her.

(5)   The judge had no power to compel an unwilling mother to send photographs, medical reports and school reports to the father.

(6)   It was wrong in principle to order an unwilling mother to send photographs of the child to the father as often as every 3 months.

The Court of Appeal rejected these submissions together with much of Wall J's judgment in *Re M*. Sir Thomas Bingham MR described the first submission as tantamount to saying that a withholding of consent and an expression of unwillingness to cooperate on the part of the caring parent is enough to defeat the court's order. That, he said, is both an incorrect and a dangerous principle of law since it would reward those who wish to be intransigent. Sir Thomas Bingham MR disagreed with the second submission since it would unnecessarily limit the court's discretion. He found no evidence that the father was writing to the child excessively; accordingly, there was no reason why the judge should have imposed any limit on the father's freedom to communicate with the child. The third submission was rejected because it sought to give the caring parent a veto in circumstances where that parent was under a duty to promote contact with the child. Such a veto would be contrary to the principle that the court, not the parent, is the judge of what is conducive to the child's welfare. For much the same reason, the fourth submission was unacceptable. The caring parent had no general right to decide what should and should not be read to the child, and ought not to be encouraged in the belief that there is liberty to select the material to be read.

As to the fifth submission, his Lordship said that the court was clearly empowered by ss. 8 and 11(7) of the Children Act 1989 to compel the sending of photographs, medical reports and school reports to the absent parent as a necessary means of facilitating contact. As he pointed out, the court's order for contact was unlikely to be successful if the absent parent is not given information about the child's progress.

On the sixth submission, Sir Thomas Bingham MR warned the mother that the order meant what it said and should be complied with. He said that, in any event, she was in a weak position to complain since the order had already been in force for 7 months and she had not sent the father any photograph at all despite the fact that he had given her a camera for the purpose. The sending of a photograph at quarterly intervals was justified on the facts because the child was very young and therefore rapidly changing in appearance.

CONCLUSION

Re O confirms some well-established principles and provides authoritative new guidance on the extent of the jurisdiction to make contact orders. Some of the effects of the decision may be stated as follows.

(1)   The paramount consideration in contact cases is the child's welfare as provided for in Children Act 1989, s. 1(1). The interests of the parents come into the reckoning only insofar as they are relevant to the child's welfare.

(2)   Taken together, ss. 8, 10 and 11(7) of the Children Act 1989 provide a comprehensive jurisdiction, enabling the court to attempt the difficult task of securing the child's welfare. It will be appreciated, however, that the jurisdiction is not completely unfettered. The court, for instance, has no power under these provisions to adjust the parties' occupation rights in the family home since, after the Children Act 1989, the granting of ouster orders continues to be governed by *Richards* v *Richards* [1984] FLR 11 and by the exclusive statutory regime laid down in the Matrimonial Homes Act 1983 and the Domestic Violence and Matrimonial Proceedings Act 1976. Thus it was held in *Re D (Prohibited Steps Order)* [1996] 2 FLR 273, and p. 605 (above), following *Gibson* v *Austin* [1992] 2 FLR 437, *Pearson* v *Franklin (Parental Home: Ouster)* [1994] 1 FLR 246, and *Re M (Minors) (Disclosure of Evidence)* [1994] 1 FLR 760, that the court has no jurisdiction, either by way of a prohibited steps order or by the imposition of conditions therein or in a contact order, to prevent a parent staying overnight in the matrimonial home during contact visits. [Author's note: This needs to be read in the light of the changes brought about by Part IV of the Family Act 1996.]

(3)   It is almost always in the interests of a child who suffers a loss by reason of parental separation that there should be contact with the absent parent so that the loss can, as far as possible, be mitigated.

(4)   The court should be wary of allowing the implacable hostility of the caring parent to deter it from making a contact order where the child's welfare requires one.

(5)   The court should not hesitate to exercise its power to enforce contact orders where the child's welfare demands it. A particularly effective sanction might be to threaten the caring parent with removal of the child.

(6)   In those exceptional cases where a parent's implacable hostility to contact creates a risk of damage to the child's welfare the court should not order immediate direct contact. However, if direct contact is refused, indirect contact should normally be ordered. What degree of risk is required to persuade the court to refuse direct contact is uncertain. Waite LJ in *Re D (A Minor) (Contact: Mother's Hostility)* [1993] 2 FLR 1 said that

there needs to be shown 'a serious risk of major emotional harm' to the child. These words were quoted with apparent approval by Sir Thomas Bingham MR in *Re O* and by Wall J sitting in the Court of Appeal in *Re P (Contact: Supervision)* [1996] 2 FLR 314, but according to Beldam LJ in *Re M (A Minor)* (1995) 10 July (unreported), CA, the court can take into account the likely impact of events upon a child in cases falling short of a serious risk of major emotional harm.

(7)   Indirect contact demands restraint, common sense and unselfishness on the part of both parents. If the absent parent abuses the privilege of indirect contact it can be curtailed.

Sir Thomas Bingham's judgment in *Re O* has been described as the 'definitive exposition' of the principles applicable in contact cases (see *Re P* (above), per Wall J). The tough, common sense approach demonstrated in *Re O* is refreshing, and Sir Thomas Bingham reminder that parents should not be allowed to think that they are likely to get their own way by behaving in an intransigent or unco-operative manner is particularly appropriate. It hardly needs stating that the court's function must not be pre-empted by a parent who asserts, 'I shall not obey an order of the court' (*Re W (A Minor) (Contact)* [1994] 2 FLR 441, at p. 449, per Sir Stephen Brown P).

The potential damage to a child from the 'internecine warfare' of obdurate parents is well known (see, for example, Wall J's description in *Re P* (above)). Adherence in the lower courts to the guidance and statement of principle provided by *Re O* should go some way towards countering the selfishness and short-sightedness of many obstructive parents. Contact orders will, however, remain difficult to enforce against those who are resolutely unco-operative, and performance of the sort of conditions imposed in *Re O* will continue to be especially difficult to monitor. It is generally accepted that neither of the two most serious sanctions available for defiance of the court's order—a prison term for contempt and a change in residence arrangements—will usually be in the child's best interests. It may, therefore, be questioned whether in most cases a threat to remove the child from an obdurate caring parent, as advocated in *Re O*, can ever be anything more than an empty gesture.

A v N (COMMITTAL: REFUSAL OF CONTACT) [1997] 1 FLR 533 (CA)

WARD LJ: This is an appeal by a young mother against the order made by his Honour Judge Poulton yesterday when the judge put into effect a suspended order committing her to prison for 42 days for her contempt of court.

The proceedings arise out of a most unhappy dispute about the child of the parties. That child is a little girl called T. She was born on 13 January 1992. So she is only 4½ years old. Her parents never married. They began to live together sometime in about 1991. Although there was a period of separation shortly before the child's birth, the relationship continued together until they finally separated in September 1994. It follows therefore that there was quite a substantial period of time during which this father played an active part in the life of the child.

It is also a fact which is, in my judgment, a fact of significance, that following the breakdown of this relationship there was no objection whatsoever advanced by this mother to deny the father the contact with this little girl. Indeed on the evidence I have seen she appears at times to have asked him, and he had agreed, to look after the child overnight. Secondly, it is also highly significant, in my judgment, that there was at all times, even after the breakdown of the relationship, a very good constructive communication between the mother and the paternal grandmother and nothing adverse to the paternal grandmother was said or, it seems to me, could have been said adverse to her until the heat of this battle had perhaps destroyed reason.

Following the separation of the parents, the father applied to the court for an order that he be granted parental responsibility over his daughter and that he be afforded contact to her. Those applications were hotly disputed. The mother's objections to contact were based on his lack of commitment, and particularly his violence but, it would seem to me, also substantially based upon an allegation which saw the light of day very late indeed that the applicant was not the father of T. She asserted that blood testing would prove that that was so. Blood tests were accordingly arranged and the DNA profiling revealed quite conclusively that the applicant was indeed the father of T. Notwithstanding the certainty of the scientific evidence and notwithstanding the later finding of the court, this mother has persisted in asserting that another man was the child's father. More worryingly, she appears to have persisted in that wholly false assertion so that the children themselves, for she has another young child of a previous relationship, appear to be living under a lie that the applicant is not T's father.

The matter came before the court on 26 September 1995 when the dispute over contact was decided by his Honour Judge Poulton. He had by then ordered that there should be a court welfare officer's report and the court welfare officer did indeed report to the court on two occasions. In her first report the court welfare officer confirmed the mother's rejection of the DNA testing; . . .

In her second report, which was dated August 1995, the court welfare officer informed the court that: '. . . it would seem to be in T's interest that some form of contact be initiated.'

That was the view of the court welfare officer in August 1995, but sensitive to the mother's fear of his violent behaviour she recommended that it would be in the little girl's interest if that contact were to be initiated with the grandmother's help and supervised by the grandmother. That was apparently advice which found favour with the judge and he duly made an order on 26 September 1995 whereby he ordered that the child have contact with her father on alternate Sundays from 2 pm until 5.30 pm and after about a month increasing contact from 10.30 am to 5.30 pm, such contact to be supervised by the paternal grandmother.

He was quite satisfied that the child would be safe in her grandmother's company. The judge directed that the matter be reviewed some time later.

If one pauses to reflect on the position at that stage, there would seem to be very little reason why the mother's fears could not be accommodated in a manner totally satisfactory to her for she had then no axe to grind with the paternal grandmother and the contact was that recommended by an experienced court welfare officer. Unfortunately, however, this young lady had begun to set her mind totally against any contact taking place at all. The result was that on 30 October 1995 the matter was back before the judge and he had to order on this occasion that the mother admit the grandmother to her home in order to allow her to talk to the child with a view to making some attempt for contact to take place.

The case was again adjourned. On 5 November 1995, by which time there were already the seeds of difficulty, the judge imposed a penal notice. On 13 November 1995 he made yet another contact order. On 20 November 1995 the court welfare officer had again become involved and on this occasion she informed the judge that in her interview with the mother the mother repeated her unwillingness to accept the applicant as the father. She stated she would not allow any contact whatsoever to take place between the little girl and the father and that any relationship that she had formerly with the grandmother had been utterly destroyed by the grandmother's attempts to do that which the court order permitted her to do, namely go and visit and endeavour to talk to her grandchild.

The court welfare officer also said this:

[The mother] has now become so entrenched in her attitude over contact she is prepared to go to prison should the committal application be enforced by this court. She has made plans to have the children cared for by her neighbour . . . who will move into her flat to care for the children.

On 30 January 1996 and on his sixth attempt, the judge made yet another order which I should recite. That provided this time for the mother to permit the child to receive cards and presents and it provided that contact take place from 2 pm until 5.30 pm every alternate Sunday, but this time the mother was again directed to deliver the child to the paternal grandmother at her flat at the commencement of the contact visit and the grandmother was to return the child.

By now it will be no surprise for it to be revealed that that order was flouted and another application to commit was made by the father. It was adjourned on 27 March 1996 and the court welfare officer's help was again invited to assist the court. It came back on 16 April 1996 before the same judge. The mother admitted at least two breaches of the direct contact order, though she contested whether or not she had denied indirect contact. At this bearing the judge again had the benefit of the help from the court welfare officer who, as a result of those inquiries, had to repeat to the judge:

[The mother] is adamant that she will go to prison rather than let [T] go to see [the grandmother or father], she informed me that she has now told the children that she could be going to prison and that [the neighbour] would be looking after them.

I think it is only fair to the father and the grandmother to stress that at that hearing they made it perfectly plain that they did not wish the mother to be sent to prison. Their only wish was that the order be obeyed by the mother. The judge on that occasion found the two breaches proved, as indeed they had been admitted, but he adjourned the question of sentence to a later date. He made another, but this time different, attempt to achieve the desired objective of contact. On this occasion he ordered that contact should be effected by invoking the help of the social services department and he provided that the contact was to be supervised by a member of the social services department at a mutual venue in the hope that that would encourage the mother to comply.

The social services department, through the appropriate social worker, reported to the court: 'The mother has remained firm in her decision she will not agree to contact.' She pointed out that the mother showed no hostility to her department, that she had free access to the home, but it had been impossible to persuade her to comply.

In some desperation, no doubt, application was made by father and grandmother to commit for breach of that order. It came before the court on 23 September 1996. The mother admitted one breach and the judge made an order which was to impose upon her sentences of 28 days' imprisonment concurrent for the two earlier breaches and 14 days consecutive for the final breach, but he suspended the operation of that imprisonment.

It is necessary to consider his judgment in dealing with that application. He recited the relevant history and he dealt with the matter in this way:

The mother, through her solicitor, has been quite frank. She has no intention of attending contact. She wants to ensure that the child grows up with no direct or indirect contact and she says that another man is the father. I do not consider the court would be doing its duty to the child if it allows this to continue.

For the welfare of the child, there must be some contact as the child grows up and the sooner the better. It has been urged on me that if I take the extreme step of sending the mother to prison, it will cause distress to the mother [sic]. [I interpolate that I think he was intending to refer to the child.] This is the view of the court welfare officer and social worker.

Against that, it is important to ensure contact. There is a risk of long-term damage to the child if there is not some contact as she grows up and if she is allowed to grow up under a deliberate false impression.

I consider no other course is open to me but to enforce the order and I propose to commit . . .

He suspended the order and the language of the note, which has been agreed and placed before us, is to this effect:

I further direct that this sentence be suspended and it will be suspended until the next contact day pursuant to the order, because even at this stage I intend to give the mother a last chance. If the sentence is put into effect it will be distressing for the child. The mother is not required to come into contact with [the father] but is required to attend the contact centre and that is what she must do. The next contact day will be in 14 days' time.

I would have thought, speaking for myself, that the language of that judgment is plain and beyond any misunderstanding at all. It made perfectly plain that in the judge's view he felt he had no alternative and that no other course was available to him. He felt that the mother should be given a last chance. He indicated that her not accepting that last chance would inevitably lead to her going to prison. He made it plain that he wished to keep control of the matter and he reserved it to himself and gave directions for it to come back to him on 10 October 1996.

The mother failed to give contact on 7 October 1996 as was required and the matter therefore came back to the judge on 10 October 1996. Mr Feehan's submission is that on the face of the order notice should have been given to the mother. It was not. Therefore he submits there is a fatal defect to the proceedings which should compel us to set the committal aside. This court has the power to correct any errors where no unfairness or material irregularity occurs. As to fairness or unfairness Mr Feehan submits that the mother, attending court yesterday, was taken totally by surprise that she might go to prison. It produced the prejudicial consequence that she had taken no opportunity to make arrangements for the children and that that is so substantial a prejudice that we must take account of it. I do not accept that submission and for these reasons: first, she was in court on 23 September 1996. She heard the judge indicate that the matter would be coming back to him and that prison was inevitable if there was a breach. Secondly, her intransigence, so manifest in the past, has continued and I cannot see that it was unfair if what she had been determined to bring about should in fact be brought about. Thirdly, and importantly, both the mother and her solicitors were present in court yesterday. The order made yesterday was not made in her absence. She had ample opportunity to apply for any adjournment, but did not do so. She had ample opportunity to challenge the evidence laid before the judge that she was in further breach of the order, but neither chose to do so nor, as her counsel fairly concedes to us today, could she do so. She made no attempt whatever to apologise for her contempt. I therefore find no unfairness in the proceedings continuing yesterday. Moreover, in view of the language, plainly understandable, by which the judge adjourned the matter to himself yesterday and in view of her and her solicitor's presence in court any irregularity was immaterial. I find therefore nothing procedurally wrong with putting the committal into effect. . . . He submits that the judge failed to have regard to the welfare of the child. He has referred us to a judgment of this court in *Churchard* v *Churchard* [1984] FLR 635 where Ormrod LJ, with whom Brandon LJ agreed, said this (at 638):

> To accede to the father's application for the committal order would not conceivably be in the best interests of the children. It would mean two things: first, if committed, that their mother would be taken away from them for a time and their father would be branded in their eyes as the man who had put their mother in prison. That is a brand from which no parent in my experience can ever hope to recover. It is the most deadly blow a parent can inflict on his children. There is no doubt and it should be clearly understood—I am speaking for myself now—throughout the legal profession that an application to commit for breach of orders relating to access (and I limit my comments to breaches of orders relating to access) are inevitably futile and should not be made. The damage which they cause is appalling. The damage in this case which they have caused is obvious. To apply for a legalistic but futile remedy, because it is the only thing left to do, is, in my judgment, the last hope of the destitute. The court is only concerned with the welfare of the children and ought not to trouble itself too much about its own dignity.

Accordingly, Mr Feehan submits that in deciding whether or not to commit, welfare is the paramount consideration governing that decision. For my own part, I am far from satisfied that is the position or that Ormrod LJ was in fact saying so. The welfare is paramount in any question affecting the upbringing of the child. Hence it is not paramount where, for example, application is made for leave to apply for orders; it is not paramount where blood tests are ordered; it is not always paramount in questions relating to publicity.

Although quite obviously the upbringing of the child is affected by the implementation of this order, it seems to me that the question which is before the court is whether there should be committal for breach of orders of the court and in that inquiry the upbringing of the child is not a paramount consideration. It is obviously a material consideration and every judge who does any family work at all is always alive to the grievous effect the implementation of an order is likely to have on the life of the children whom the mother is unwisely seeking to protect in her own misguided way. I need not express a concluded view because it is, if I am constrained to look to welfare, quite apparent that the judge yesterday made plain that he was dealing with the matter as he had dealt at length with it on the last occasion. On that occasion he was fully mindful of the distressing consequence of imprisonment on the child and indeed the other child of the mother, but he balanced against that the importance of this child knowing her father as she grows up and the long-term damage that she will suffer, especially if she grows up under a deliberate false impression as to whom her father really is. He did, therefore, take proper account of welfare factors and his balance is not one with which I would interfere.

Then Mr Feehan submits, almost as if it is a matter of principle, though I am prepared to treat this as a matter of the exercise of discretion, that a sentence of imprisonment for breach of a contact order cannot or should not be imposed save as a measure of last resort. He submits, therefore, that there were remedies still available through which the court has to plough before giving effect to its contact order. So, he submits, conciliation could have been tried but has not been tried. I reject that submission. The court welfare officer has made endless visits to this mother and there has been ample opportunity for her to seek conciliation, if that was something she wanted. The social services department have made their facilities available to her. She has rejected them insofar as they are offered to procure a father's relationship with his daughter. He submits that the judge was in error in not sending the police to enforce the order. I reject that submission. A grandmother who at that point was on good terms with her was much better able to collect the little girl than a uniformed police officer, but the mother shut the door upon her, metaphorically if not physically. It is suggested that the Official Solicitor should be involved. His services are invariably valuable, but it is a precious resource and I cannot criticise the judge for not at this stage seeking his help.

The stark reality of this case is that this is a mother who has flagrantly set herself upon a course of collision with the court's order. She has been given endless opportunities to comply with sympathetic attempts made by the judge to meet her flimsy objections to contact taking place. She has spurned all of those attempts. For it to be submitted that the hardship to the child is the result of the court imposing the committal order is wholly to misunderstand the position. This little child suffers because the mother chooses to make her suffer. This mother had it within her power to save T that suffering, but she did not avail of that opportunity. She has it in her power to apologise but thus far there has not been a single word of apology or of regret. The judge bent over backwards to accommodate her but eventually even his boundless patience was exhausted. In my judgment, it is time that it is realised that against the wisdom of the observations of Ormrod LJ is to be balanced the consideration that orders of the court are made to be obeyed. They are not made for any other reason. That has the backing of the full Court of Appeal as recently as 13 May 1996 in the case of *Re F* (unreported). Sir Stephen Brown P, giving a judgment with which Kennedy and Phillips LJJ agreed, upheld an order sending a mother to prison for failure to comply with a contact order. He stated, and it is worth the reminder, that Sir Thomas Bingham MR had pointed the way in his judgment in *Re O (Contact: Imposition of Conditions)* [1995] 2 FLR 124 that orders of the court are to be obeyed. The President said:

It seems to me that, after the opportunities which the mother was given, with a very clear explanation by the judge on each of the previous occasions (August 1994 and June 1995) the mother could have been left in no doubt what was expected of her. Where the order of the court is that there should be contact, it must not be disobeyed. This was, in my judgment, a case where the judge was ultimately obliged to make an order for committal. He was able on the facts of the case to provide that it should be suspended. It was not in any sense a harsh order. It was made sensitively in the hope that the mother, even at this stage, would come to her senses and actively promote contact through the agency of the court welfare service.

I entirely agree with those sentiments and it is perhaps appropriate that the message goes out in loud and in clear terms that there does come a limit to the tolerance of the court to see its orders flouted by mothers even if they have to care for their young children. If she goes to prison it is her fault, not the fault of the judge who did no more than his duty to the child which is imposed upon him by Parliament. The Children Act 1989 makes it his duty and in the circumstances no one else's duty to determine what is in her best interests. He, not this mother, has to decide whether contact will promote the child's welfare. He decided it would. His many orders have not been the subject of any appeal. They were therefore all the more to be enforced. He did not commit this young mother to preserve his own dignity. He was concerned to preserve the due administration of justice which depends on orders of the court being obeyed. He was essentially concerned to do what he thought best for the child in the long term which is to give her the chance to know her father. I see nothing wrong in his actions.

11.3.5   SPECIFIC ISSUES AND PROHIBITED STEPS ORDERS

CHILDREN ACT 1989

9.   Restrictions on making section 8 orders

. . .

(2)   No application may be made by a local authority for a residence order or contact order and no court shall make such an order in favour of a local authority.

. . .

(5)   No court shall exercise its powers to make a specific issue order or prohibited steps order—

(a)   with a view to achieving a result which could be achieved by making a residence or contact order; or

(b)   in any way which is denied to the High Court (by section 100(2)) in the exercise of its inherent jurisdiction with respect to children.

NOTTINGHAM COUNTY COUNCIL v *P* [1993] 3 WLR 637 (CA)

M, who was aged 17, was the oldest of three sisters. She complained that she had been sexually abused by her father and alleged that he was also abusing her 16-year-old sister, who denied that she had been abused. The local authority obtained emergency protection orders, but declined to apply for care or supervision orders under Part IV of the Children Act 1989 and sought a prohibited steps order, as defined in section 8 of the Act of 1989, requiring the father to leave the family home and ordering him to have no contact with his daughters other than as agreed and supervised by the local authority. The judge adjourned the application for the prohibited steps order for investigation of the possibility of the family responding to treatment which would enable them to be kept together. The father was assessed by a residential clinic specialising in the treatment of sexual offenders. The assessment report stated that the father accepted that he was a sexual abuser with a repetitive cycle of offending over many years and recommended 12 months' residential treatment. The local authority recognised that the father posed an unacceptable risk to the children while he remained in the home, but were unable to provide the £15,000 needed to fund the treatment and restored their application for a prohibited steps order. On the resumed hearing the judge refused to make the prohibited steps order on the ground that the application fell within s. 9 of the Act of 1989, which barred a local authority from seeking residence or contact orders.

SIR STEPHEN BROWN P: Mr Karsten for the local authority submitted that the primary purpose of s. 9(5) when read with s. 9(2) is to prevent a child from being placed in care on 'welfare' grounds without the 'significant harm' test of s. 31 having to be satisfied. He complained that the effect of the judge's construction of s. 9(5)(a) is to drive local authorities to apply for a care order under s. 31 and that would oblige them to make what might well be in many cases an excessive intervention in the life of a family. He sought to equate a prohibited steps order with an ouster order. He claimed that an application for a prohibited steps order gives much clearer notice to the recipient that it is sought to oust him than does an application for a residence order. He sought support for his submission from pre-Children Act 1989 procedures. He claimed that previously a local authority could always apply for an injunction for the protection of children through the mechanism of applying for leave to intervene in subsisting matrimonial, custodial or wardship proceedings or indeed of instituting wardship proceedings itself. He said that a court had power to make an ouster order on such an application in the exercise of such jurisdiction. In this case he said the local authority had considered the whole position of this family and took the view that what was required was that the father should not live in the house with the children. Mother was weak and unable to prevent him from doing so and that accordingly a prohibited steps order would provide the necessary sanction.

Counsel for the mother, the father and the guardian ad litem all supported the judge's ruling on the application of the local authority for a prohibited steps order. They all submitted that the application was misconceived and that leave to make the application should not have been granted particularly by means of an ex parte application to a single justice of a family proceedings court. Miss Parker for the mother submitted that the structure and scheme of the Children Act 1989 made it clear that applications made by local authorities were governed principally by Part IV of the Act under which local authorities might apply for care or supervision orders which gave them statutory responsibilities. Part II of the Act principally concerned private law remedies and the remedies provided by s. 8 were essentially private law remedies. Furthermore, local authorities were specifically prohibited from applying for residence and contact orders although they were not debarred with leave from seeking specific issue and prohibited steps orders. However, these were subject to the restrictions contained in s. 9(5) of the Act. Miss Parker supported the judge's decision that the application made in this instance by the local authority fell foul of the restrictions contained in s. 9(5). It was an application which patently sought to determine the residence of the children and the degree of contact which the children might have with the father. Miss Parker also submitted that, in any event, a prohibited steps order could not in fact operate as an exclusion order or much less an order requiring a father to leave his home at the instance of a local authority. . . .

In this case it appears that from the time when the application first came before a circuit judge all the parties other than the local authority were willing to submit to the making of a supervision order under s. 31. The court has been told by Miss Scotland, for the father, that he was prepared to consent to a number of requirements being included in a supervision order. Section 9(5) of the Act of 1989 provides:

No court shall exercise its power to make a specific issue order or prohibited steps order—(a) with a view to achieving a result which could be achieved by making a residence or contact order; or (b) in any way which is denied to the High Court [by section 100(2)] in the exercise of its inherent jurisdiction with respect to children.

In the view of this court the application for a prohibited steps order by this local authority was in reality being made with a view to achieving a result which could be achieved by making a residence or contact order. Section 9(2) specifically provides:

No application may be made by a local authority for a residence order or contact order and no court shall make such an order in favour of a local authority.

The court is satisfied that the local authority was indeed seeking to enter by the 'back door' as it were. It agrees with Ward J that he had no power to make a prohibited steps order in this case.

A prohibited steps order would not afford the local authority any authority as to how it might deal with the children. There may be situations, for example where a child is accommodated by a local authority, where it would be appropriate to seek a prohibited steps order for some particular purpose. However, it could not in any circumstances be regarded as providing a substitute for an order under Part IV of the Act of 1989. Furthermore, it is very doubtful indeed whether a prohibited steps order could in any circumstances be used to 'oust' a father from a matrimonial home.

11.4   End of Chapter Assessment Question

Hussein and Jayne married 10 years ago. They have two children, Robina, aged 5, and Joshua, aged 3. The marriage started to deteriorate shortly after Joshua was born, and now the couple have decided to separate. No divorce is planned yet, although Jayne would like to dissolve the marriage in the not too distant future. Jayne is planning to go to live with her parents, who live in Cumbria in a large farmhouse. She would therefore have plenty of space for herself and the children. Hussein is not pleased at this decision, since it would be very difficult for him to travel the 200 miles to see the children. He is also concerned about Jayne's inability to bring up the children in the Muslim faith.

Advise Hussein who wishes to prevent this move, and would prefer Joshua to remain with him so he can be raised in accordance with the Muslim faith.

What advice would you give Hussein if he wished to take the children to Iran to see their paternal grandparents and other relations?

11.5   End of Chapter Assessment Outline Answer

The issue for consideration in this question is the ability to obtain orders with respect to the children which will enable Hussein to care for Joshua and take the children abroad with him.

First, it is always advantageous to clarify the position regarding parental responsibility in any family problem questions. As Jayne and Hussein are married, and the children were born after the marriage took place, under the provisions of s. 2 of the Children Act 1989, both will automatically gain parental responsibility. This can be exercised independently and without the consent of the other. Part of parental responsibility is the duty to provide care for the child, which will naturally include physical care and the provision of a home. In the current situation, there is nothing to prevent Hussein taking the children to live with him — equally, there is nothing to prevent Jayne moving to Cumbria with both children.

It is also important to mention that orders under the 1989 Act can be obtained regardless of the existence of divorce proceedings. Any applications can be made to the family proceedings court, or the county court. It is for the party applying, on the advice of their legal representative, to decide where to commence proceedings.

The application that will be required, in the absence of any agreement, is for a s. 8 residence order. In the circumstances highlighted in the question, agreement between the two parents is unlikely to occur. Explain or discuss in your answer the consequences and meaning of a residence order. Consider the criteria and factors taken into account by the court when deciding whether to make an order or not. These are found in s. 1 of the 1989 Act.

The primary factor is that the welfare of the child is the court's paramount concern. Linked to that is the welfare checklist in s. 1(3) — a list of non-exhaustive considerations to establish what is in the best interests of the child. Discuss the checklist in the light of the children in question. Here you may have to look at the needs of the two children separately since Hussein appears to be more concerned to care for Joshua than for Robina. Look at a few of the issues that will be relevant. You have the ages of the children to consider, both are young, and generally there is a tendency for young children to be placed in the care of the mother. There is also a strong tendency for siblings to be placed together, and here there is the possibility of them being cared for by different parents. This may be contrary to their welfare. The question of religious upbringing is important in this scenario, but the court will be concerned to evaluate whether the need for Joshua to be brought up in the Muslim faith necessitates his possible separation from his mother. It might be perfectly feasible for Jayne to ensure he is brought up as a Muslim. The court would also be careful to consider the actual arrangements for care of the children — to what extent is Hussein able to provide full time care to one or both children? The court may believe that it will be too stressful for the children to be cared for by Hussein and possibly another carer rather than just Jayne and the maternal grandparents.

As well as the welfare checklist, the court must have regard to the possibility of delay, which can be harmful to the children, and is relevant here since Robina is of school age, and it will be important to settle her at a new school quickly. The court must also have regard to the no-order principle — however it is unlikely that the court will find it appropriate to make a no order if the parents are unable to agree or decide issues with respect to the children amicably.

The question of contact is also important here, and it would appear to be somewhat insurmountable. However, in many situations one parent will be the inevitable 'loser' with regard to child care and contact. The court, even if it has only been asked to deal with a question of residence, may make a contact order. The Children Act 1989 enables the court to make orders without the need for an actual application. If Hussein is unsuccessful in obtaining a residence order, he may be more successful in gaining a contact order.

Turning to the question of taking the children to see the paternal grandparents and relatives in Iran, the ease with which this can be done depends on the outcome of any residence order application. If there were no order made, there would be nothing to prevent Hussein taking the children abroad. The only way Jayne could stop this would be by seeking a prohibited steps order under s. 8 of the 1989 Act.

If, however, a residence order is made, then under s. 13 certain limitations are placed on those with parental responsibility regarding the children's names and removal from the jurisdiction. Under s. 13(1)(b) and (2) where a residence order is in force, a child can only be removed from the jurisdiction for periods up to one month. If a period of removal is to be longer than this, or permanent, the consent of all with parental responsibility, or the consent of the court, is required. Only the person with the residence order is permitted to remove the children from the jurisdiction.

In advising Hussein, you would have to explain all this, and the fact that if Jayne is granted the residence order, he will be unable to take the children to visit their relatives unless he has Jayne's permission, or seeks an order permitting the visit from the court. You may also mention that if any such application is made, Jayne may object on the basis of potential abduction by Hussein. If this is deemed to be likely, the court may fail to give consent to the visit taking place.

CHAPTER TWELVE

THE PUBLIC LAW RELATING TO CHILDREN

PART ONE

12.1 Child Abuse

Cobley, C, Child Abuse and The Law, Cavendish Publishing, 1995

The 1960s—the 'battered baby' syndrome
Similar problems had been experienced in America throughout the first half of this century. Once again, it seems that the American experience was influential in highlighting the problem of child abuse in this country for a second time in the 1960s. In 1962, in an article in the journal of the American Medical Association, Dr Henry Kempe, an American paediatrician, and his associates put the unthinkable into words. They asserted that some of the physical injuries of children were not caused by accidents at all, but were in fact the result of physical assaults by adults on children. The 'battered baby' syndrome came into being, the problem was forced out into the open and public opinion began to change. Dr Kempe himself has admitted that he used shock tactics in an effort to increase recognition of the problem of physical abuse. During a lecture to the British Association of Paediatricians in 1970 he said:

> I was so exasperated by my colleagues' lack of attention that I deliberately used the words 'battered baby' syndrome because they were provocative enough to arouse anger. Indeed, for 10 years previously I had spoken of child abuse, non-accidental injury or inflicted wounds, but few people paid any attention. I therefore wanted to provoke the emotional reaction and shock which more moderate and scientifically more satisfactory terms had not provoked . . .

Dr Kempe's shock tactics worked in America. By 1967, all American states had enacted child abuse reporting laws which made the reporting of suspected child abuse mandatory for certain professionals. Although such a system of mandatory reporting has never been enacted in the UK, public awareness of the problem of child abuse has increased tremendously, partly, it seems, as a result of the American experience. By 1974, following the publication of the Inquiry Report into the death of Maria Colwell, Area Review Committees had been set up on the recommendation of the DHSS as an inter-disciplinary management team to supervise the management of non-accidental injury to children.

The 1970s—emotional abuse
During the 1970s attention began to be focused on the emotionally abused child. All abuse inevitably involves some emotional ill-treatment, but it came to be realised that there were various types of behaviour by an adult which were emotionally harmful to a child, even in the absence of physical or sexual abuse or neglect. For example,

humiliation, scapegoating, extreme inconsistency rejection and unrealistic expectations. Although emotional abuse is difficult to define and the scars are less obvious, it is thought to be probably more common than the combined total of physical and sexual abuse.

The 1980s — sexual abuse

However, at this time, there remained a conspiracy of silence over the existence of child sexual abuse. Society was simply M prepared to entertain the possibility that children were being sexually abused to any great extent just as many were reluctant to recognise physical abuse in the UK in the 1960s, many were reluctant to accept the reality of certain aspects of child sexual abuse in the 1980s. One of Britain's leading experts on child sexual abuse is Dr Arnon Bentovim of Great Ormond Street Hospital. Dr Bentovim had been working with families involved in physical child abuse since the early 1970s, yet during the 1970s saw no evidence of sexual abuse—believing that even if a child reported a sexual encounter, then it must surely be fantasy. He admitted that he was jolted out of this comfortable illusion at a London conference in 1979 addressed by Dr Kempe. Listening to Dr Kempe, he realised that, despite having worked with children for some considerable time, he, Dr Bentovim wasn't seeing cases of sexual abuse at all. This prompted him to enquire closely into referrals, carrying out a questionnaire survey of the professionals who referred cases to him at Great Ormond Street. This in turn sparked new referrals and led to an increasing awareness of child sexual abuse. Such awareness continued to increase during the 1980s, culminating in the crisis in Cleveland in 1987. The resulting inquiry and national media coverage of events in Cleveland ensured that the issue of child sexual abuse was pushed to the fore on a nationwide scale.

The 1990s—satanic and ritual abuse?

Having reached stage 5 in the process of recognition, it now seems that an additional stage should be added—the recognition of organised abuse and, arguably, satanic and ritual abuse. If many found the concept of child sexual abuse a difficult one to comprehend, or even believe, events in the early 1990's suggested what many considered to be a more worrying and sinister development—that of satanic or ritual abuse. The term satanic abuse is said to have originated in America after the publication in 1980 of *Michelle Remembers* by Lawrence Pazder, a psychiatrist, which told the story of a girl who recalled being ritually abused by satanists. Influence by American Christian fundamentalists led to allegations of satanic abuse surfacing in the UK in the late 1980s and early 1990s. In Manchester, 23 children were made wards of court after social workers investigating sexual abuse became convinced that the abuse had taken place within a ritual or ceremonial setting. In Rochdale, 20 children from six families were made wards of court due to alleged involvement in satanic or ritual abuse. In the Orkneys, nine children were removed from their homes after allegations that they had suffered ritual abuse—events that resulted in an inquiry being set up to consider the procedures by police and social workers. Following these cases, the Government commissioned an inquiry into ritual and satanic abuse. Three years later, the report of the inquiry, undertaken by Jean La Fontaine a leading social anthropologist, dismissed satanic abuse as an evangelical myth. The report defines satanism as 'sexual and physical abuse of children as part of rites directed to a magical or religious objective' and concludes that there was no evidence of this in each of the 84 cases reported between 1987 and 1991 which were examined by the inquiry. Ritual abuse of mystical powers to enslave children and keep them quiet was substantiated in three of the cases, but this was found to be secondary to sexual abuse and therefore not satanic. However, in almost all cases the families involved were from deprived economic backgrounds and the report concludes:

> A belief in evil cults is convincing because it draws on powerful cultural axioms. People are reluctant to accept that parents, even those classed as social failures, will harm their own children, and even to invite others to do so, but involvement with the devil explains it . . . The notion that unknown, powerful leaders control the cult revives an old myth of dangerous strangers. Demonising the marginal poor and linking them to unknown satanists turns intractable cases of abuse into manifestations of evil.

However, the conclusion of the inquiry has not been unanimously accepted. A survey into organised and ritual sexual abuse undertaken by the University of Manchester identified 62 cases of alleged ritual abuse between 1988 and 1991. Whilst doubts about the existence of ritual abuse remain, the existence of paedophile rings or organised abuse is now accepted.

. . . The research by the University of Manchester estimates that there would have been 967 cases of organised abuse between 1988 and 1991. Although many cases of organised abuse remain hidden from the public eye, those cases which are successfully investigated tend to hit the headlines. In June 1994 five members of a paedophile ring were jailed at Swansea Crown Court for between four and 15 years for conspiracy to sexually abuse children. The eight month trial leading to the convictions received extensive media coverage. Had the horrific catalogue of events occurred 20, or even 10, years ago, society's response would probably have been one of denial and disbelief—indicating that we should be thankful for the progress made through the stages of recognition in recent years.

12.1.1   WHAT DO WE MEAN BY CHILD ABUSE?

Definitions of abuse

The following categories of abuse in which a child is suffering or is likely to suffer significant harm, apply in these procedures. They should be used when considering placing the child's name on the Child Protection Register or subsequent changes of registration category. The categories should be used singly, or in combinations where these specifically apply.

Physical abuse

A physical injury or suffering to a child, or failure to prevent physical injury or suffering to a child (including deliberate poisoning or suffocation) where there is a definite knowledge or a reasonable suspicion that the injury has been or may be inflicted by another person.

Neglect

A severe or persistent lack of attention to a child's basic needs resulting in significant harmful impairment of health or development or the avoidable exposure of a child to serious danger, including cold or starvation. (This includes abandoned babies/children and children who have been medically diagnosed as non-organic failure to thrive.)

Sexual abuse

The involvement of a child in sexual activity which is unlawful, or, although not illegal to which the child is unable to give informed consent. This includes direct sexual exploitation and abuse of a child by adults whether inside the home or outside. The procedures apply to abuse by parents, or carers or other adults singly or acting in an organised way, or children. It includes abuse which is rewarded or apparently attractive to the child. It includes abuse by adults whether known or strangers.

Emotional abuse

Significant harm to the emotional and physical well-being or development of a child caused by the persistent or severe emotional ill-treatment or rejection of parents/carers. Although most abuse involves some emotional ill-treatment, for registration purposes this category should only be used where it is the main or sole form of abuse.

Indications of abuse

This is a guide to help highlight possible concerns/suspicions of abuse and should not be used by itself as a measure for whether abuse exists.

The following statements should be read before looking at a list of indicators:

A number of these indicators apply to all forms of abuse.

Some conditions can give appearances which arouse suspicion of abuse and should be excluded before assuming abuse is taking place. It should however be remembered that child abuse can coexist with these conditions.

Apparent bruising of the skin may be seen with Mongolian blue spot which is a naturally occurring pigmentation of the skin. Bleeding disorders such as Haemophilia may produce abnormal bruising.

Brittle bone disorders can cause unexplained fractures.

Skin infections, such as Impetigo, can look like healing cigarette burns.

It is crucial that whatever the child, parent or carer says is noted and taken seriously.

The development age of the child/young person must be considered in the assessment of the account of how the injuries occurred.

Whether the injury or signs fit the story given is important.

Any *unexplained injury* in a *very young* child must be taken seriously.

Delay or failure to seek appropriate help may be significant.

Recent research suggests that disabled children are more likely to be at risk of abuse and less likely for it to become evident.

The indicators are that there could be a link between domestic violence and subsequent child abuse.

Physical abuse

All physically injured children where the nature of the injury is not consistent with the account of how it occurred, or no explanation as to how it occurred and where there is definite knowledge or reasonable suspicion that the injury was inflicted (or knowingly not prevented) by any person having custody, charge or care of the child (includes deliberate poisoning, suffocations and Munchausen's syndrome by proxy).

Indicators:

1. Torn frenulum
2. Blood in whites of eyes ⎫ May be associated with
3. Small bruises on head   ⎬ shaking injuries which may
4. Bruising on rib cage   ⎭ not be obvious otherwise.
5. Burns and scalds on hands, feet, buttocks and groins.
6. Cigarette burns.
7. Linear marks, weal marks.
8. Multiple bruising and scratches.
9. Finger tip bruising.
10. Grip/slap marks (anywhere including face and limbs).
11. Injuries and/or fractures in children who are not mobile.
12. Bite marks.
13. Injuries found to be of different ages.
14. Unconscious child—(may have been poisoned or is bleeding internally from other injuries).

Sexual abuse

Sexual abuse is the involvement of dependent, developmentally immature children and adolescents in sexual activities which they do not fully comprehend, to which they are unable to give informed consent (or that violate the social taboos of family roles). This includes children who have been the subject of unlawful sexual activity or whose parents/carers have failed to protect them from unlawful sexual activity, and children abused by other children.

Possible indicators:

1. What the child says.
2. Young children with a lot of sexual knowledge.
3. Excessive sexual play and masturbation.
4. Physical injuries in the genital area.
5. Sexually transmitted diseases, including gonorrhoea, HIV/AIDS.

6.   Pregnancy—under 16 years; concealed.
7.   Children who are exposed to/witness intimate sexual acts.
8.   Children exposed to pornographic materials.

Other possible indicators:

1.   Self harm, such as suicide attempts, self mutilation, substance abuse.
2.   Eating disorders.
3.   Nightmares and disturbed sleep patterns.
4.   Wetting, soiling and smearing of excreta.
5.   Significant changes in child's behaviour.
6.   Persistent offending, non school attending, running away.
7.   Access to known sex offenders.

Please note: These behaviours could also be symptomatic of other circumstances, e.g. parental rejection, separation, severance from family/community etc.

Neglect

Children who have been persistently or severely neglected (including exposure to any kind of danger, cold, drugs, starvation or failure to seek medical treatment) which result or could result in significant impairment of the child's health, including non organic failure to thrive.

Indicators:

1.   Slow growth and development.
2.   Chronic nappy rash.
3.   Cold and puffy hands and feet.
4.   Child's basic needs consistently not met—food, warmth, clothing, hygiene, appropriate medical care.
5.   Situations where very young children are left alone with no carer.
6.   Children deliberately exposed to grave risks.

Emotional abuse

Emotional abuse results from a persistent pattern of parental behaviour unrelated to the child's needs and includes children whose behaviour and emotional development have been severely, adversely affected and whose medical and social assessments indicate that this has been caused by persistent or severe neglect or rejection. All forms of child abuse will cause a degree of emotional abuse, and this category should only be used in circumstances where it is the sole or main for of abuse.

Any child who is abused physically or verbally on the basis of race, ability, religion, class, gender or sexual identity is being emotionally abused.

Children who have been neglected, physically or sexually abused will suffer emotional abuse.

Children who witness violence in the home or who are exposed to extremely violent, inappropriate videos are subject to emotional abuse.

Indicators might include:

1.   Lack of self esteem, identity and positive self image.
2.   Withdrawn, aggressive behaviour, self harm, mutilation, substance abuse, suicide attempts.
3.   Eating disorders.
4.   Degrading or humiliating punishments—e.g. cold water etc.
5.   Children who receive no praise, sense of worth or achievement, who are persistently criticised.
6.   Children who are rejected by a parent/carer/sibling.
7.   Peer bullying at school or in the community.
8.   Recent research shows a link between children who are very small and emotional abuse.

12.1.2   THE EXTENT OF ABUSE

Government Statistical Service, Department of Health, 'Children and Young People on Child Protection Registers Year Ending 31 March 1994 — England', HMSO, 1995

There are 13,000 children registered on the Child Protection Register in England under the category of Physical Abuse. This represents a rate of 12 per 10,000 children, or 0.12% of the child population. This compares with a total of 34,900 children on the Register overall, a rate of 31.7 per 10,000 children, or 0.32% of the child population.

There are 9,600 children registered on the Child Protection Register in England under the category of Sexual Abuse. This represents a rate of 9 per 10,000 children, or 0.09% of the child population. This compares with a total of 34,900 children on the Register overall, a rate of 31.7 per 10,000 children, or 0.32% of the child population.

There are 4,400 children registered on Child Protection Registers in England under the category of Emotional Abuse, representing a rate of 4 per 10,000 children. This compares with a total of 34,900 children on the Register overall, a rate of 31.7 per 10,000 children.

There are 10,300 children registered on the Child Protection Register in England under the category of Neglect, representing a rate of 9 per 10,000 children. This compares with a total of 34,900 children on the Register overall, a rate of 31.7 per 10,000 children.

These statistics are based on the annual statistical return a CPR1 provided by the 109 English Local Authorities to the Department of Health. Where Local Authorities were unable to provide all the relevant data, as much as possible of the information given was used to derive national estimates, and the figures rounded to the nearest 100. The given rates per 10,000 population are based on the number of children in the relevant age group in England.

Cobley, C, *Child Abuse and the Law*, Cavendish Publishing, 1995

Further indications of the extent of sexual abuse—the use of surveys
In 1981, Mrazek, Lynch and Bentovim attempted to establish the incidence and prevalence of cases of child sexual abuse in the UK by carrying out a postal survey of 1,599 GPs, paediatricians, child psychiatrists and police surgeons. Based on the responses, the researchers suggested an annual incidence of 1,500 cases, or 1 in 6,000 children. This is now viewed as a very conservative estimate. The estimated prevalence of 0.3% of the population over childhood has subsequently been shown to be much too low, perhaps because of insufficient account being taken of the 'dark figure' of unreported cases. Further research was carried out in the UK during the period 1982–1984 by Nash and West. Two sample groups of young women were questioned on their early childhood experiences. The percentage of women who experienced some degree of sexual contact with an adult was high in both samples, 42% and 54%,—an average rate of 48%. However, the research definition of sexual abuse was very wide, including verbal suggestions, obscene telephone calls and 'flashers'. This would suggest that the figure of 48% is, perhaps, too high to reflect the true prevalence of the problem. A first attempt to establish a national prevalence rate was made by Dr Baker and Dr Duncan who reported their findings in 1986. The authors collaborated with Market and Opinion Research International (MORI) to produce a nationally representative sample of the population. Those interviewed were aged 15 years and over. The definition of child sexual abuse was given as:

> A child (anyone under 16 years) is sexually abused when another person, who is sexually mature, involves the child in activity which the other person expects to lead to their sexual arousal. This might involve intercourse, touching exposure of the sexual organs, showing pornographic material or talking about sexual things in an erotic way.

The response rate was high—87%. Of the 2,019 respondents, 206 (10%) reported sexual abuse as defined. (Interestingly, in 63% of the cases reported there was only a single abusive experience, compared with only 19% of such cases in the Nash and West survey.) The demographic data provided by the research carried out by Baker and Duncan shows that there is no increased risk associated with specific social class categories or area of residence.

The results of these surveys are inconsistent, with estimated prevalence varying between 0.3% and 48%. More extensive research has been carried out in the US. With the exception of the Nash and West survey, American research has consistently suggested higher rates of abuse than that reported in the UK. For example, Russell found a prevalence rate of 38% amongst a random sample of 930 women aged 18 years and over in San Francisco. This survey did not use quite such a comprehensive definition as that used by Nash and West, and therefore the two results are not incompatible. If the age and sex of the respondent are taken into account, the results of the Nash and West survey and those of the Baker and Duncan survey become less incompatible. Nash and West interviewed only women, aged between 20 and 39 years of age, whereas Baker and Duncan interviewed a sample of both males and females with only a lower age limit of 15 years. It was found by Baker and Duncan that 15–24 year olds reported more abuse than their elders, and that females reported more sexual abuse than males (12% of females reported abuse compared to 8% of males). The survey by Nash and West was carried out on a sample of younger females—a sample within which more abuse is expected. This fact could go some way towards accounting for the discrepancies in the results between the two surveys. In addition, the fact that younger adults are more likely to have been abused may lead to speculation that there has been an increase in child sexual abuse over the years. However, this could well be due to the increased openness with which society regards sexual matters and the recent public awareness and acknowledgement of child sexual abuse.

CONCLUSION

It seems that a 10% prevalence of child sexual abuse in the UK is a somewhat conservative estimate. Using this figure of 10%, Baker and Duncan estimate that over 4.5 million adults (15 years and over) in this country will have been sexually abused as children, and a potential 1,117,000 children will be sexually abused before they are 15 years of age; an estimated 143,000 of these will be abused within the family. When these figures are added to the number of children who are physically or emotionally abused, or neglected, the potential scale of the problem of child abuse becomes clear.

12.2   The Local Authority's Role in Child Protection

12.2.1   THE BASIC DUTIES: S. 17, CA 1989

CHILDREN ACT 1989

17.   Provision of services for children in need, their families and others

(1)   It shall be the general duty of every local authority (in addition to the other duties imposed on them by this Part)—

(a)   to safeguard and promote the welfare of children within their area who are in need; and

(b)   so far as is consistent with that duty, to promote the upbringing of such children by their families,

by providing a range and level of services appropriate to those children's needs.

. . .

(10)   For the purposes of this Part a child shall be taken to be in need if—

(a)   he is unlikely to achieve or maintain, or to have the opportunity of achieving or maintaining, a reasonable standard of health or development without the provision for him of services by a local authority under this Part;

(b)   his health or development is likely to be significantly impaired, or further impaired, without the provision for him of such services; or

(c)   he is disabled,

and 'family,' in relation to such a child, includes any person who has parental responsibility for the child and any other person with whom he has been living.

(11)   For the purposes of this Part, a child is disabled if he is blind, deaf or dumb or suffers from mental disorder of any kind or is substantially and permanently handicapped by illness, injury or congenital deformity or such other disability as may be prescribed; and in this Part—

'development' means physical, intellectual, emotional, social or behavioural development; and

'health' means physical or mental health.

Sections 17, 23 and 29   **SCHEDULE 2**
LOCAL AUTHORITY SUPPORT FOR CHILDREN AND FAMILIES

PART 1   PROVISION OF SERVICES FOR FAMILIES

Identification of children in need and provision of information

1.—(1) Every local authority shall take reasonable steps to identify the extent to which there are children in need within their area.

Prevention of neglect and abuse

4.—(1) Every local authority shall take reasonable steps, through the provision of services under Part III of this Act, to prevent children within their area suffering ill-treatment or neglect.

(2) Where a local authority believe that a child who is at any time within their area—

(a) is likely to suffer harm; but

(b) lives or proposes to live in the area of another local authority they shall inform that other local authority.

(3) When informing that other local authority they shall specify—

(a) the harm that they believe he is likely to suffer; and

(b) (if they can) where the child lives or proposes to live.

Provision to reduce need for care proceedings, etc.

7. Every local authority shall take reasonable steps designed—

(a) to reduce the need to bring—

(i) proceedings for care or supervision orders with respect to children within their area;

(ii) criminal proceedings against such children;

(iii) any family or other proceedings with respect to such children which might lead to them being placed in the authority's care; or

(iv) proceedings under the inherent jurisdiction of the High Court with respect to children;

(b) to encourage children within their area not to commit criminal offences; and

(c) to avoid the need for children within their area to be placed in secure accommodation.

Provision for children living with their families

8. Every local authority shall make such provision as they consider appropriate for the following services to be available with respect to children in need within their area while they are living with their families—

(a) advice, guidance and counselling;

(b) occupational, social, cultural or recreational activities;

(c) home help (which may include laundry facilities);

(d) facilities for, or assistance with, travelling to and from home for the purpose of taking advantage of any other service provided under this Act or of any similar service;

(e) assistance to enable the child concerned and his family to have a holiday.

Family centres

9.—(1) Every local authority shall provide such family centres as they consider appropriate in relation to children within their area.

(2) 'Family centre' means a centre at which any of the persons mentioned in sub-paragraph (3) may—

(a)   attend for occupational, social, cultural or recreational activities;

(b)   attend for advice, guidance or counselling; or

(c)   be provided with accommodation while he is receiving advice, guidance or counselling.

(3)   The persons are—

(a)   a child;

(b)   his parents;

(c)   any person who is not a parent of his but who has parental responsibility for him;

(d)   any other person who is looking after him.

12.2.2   OTHER SERVICES

12.2.2.1   Day care for children aged under five and others

CHILDREN ACT 1989

18.   Day care for pre-school and other children

(1)   Every local authority shall provide such day care for children in need within their area who are—

(a)   aged five or under; and

(b)   not yet attending schools,

as is appropriate.

(2)   A local authority may provide day care for children within their area who satisfy the conditions mentioned in subsection (1)(a) and (b) even though they are not in need.

(3)   A local authority may provide facilities (including training, advice, guidance and counselling) for those—

(a)   caring for children in day care; or

(b)   who at any time accompany such children while they are in day care.

(4)   In this section 'day care' means any form of care or supervised activity provided for children during the day (whether or not it is provided on a regular basis).

(5)   Every local authority shall provide for children in need within their area who are attending any school such care or supervised activities as is appropriate—

(a)   outside school hours; or

(b)   during school holidays.

(6)   A local authority may provide such care or supervised activities for children within their area who are attending any school even though those children are not in need.

(7)   In this section 'supervised activity' means an activity supervised by a responsible person.

12.2.2.2   Accommodation

CHILDREN ACT 1989

20.   Provision of accommodation for children: general

(1)   Every local authority shall provide accommodation for any child in need within their area who appears to them to require accommodation as a result of—

(a)   there being no person who has parental responsibility for him;

(b)   his being lost or having been abandoned; or

(c)   the person who has been caring for him being prevented (whether or not permanently, and for whatever reason) from providing him with suitable accommodation or care.

. . .

(4)   A local authority may provide accommodation for any child within their area (even though a person who has parental responsibility for him is able to provide him with accommodation) if they consider that to do so would safeguard or promote the child's welfare.

. . .

(6)   Before providing accommodation under this section, a local authority shall, so far as is reasonably practicable and consistent with the child's welfare—
    (a)   ascertain the child's wishes regarding the provision of accommodation; and
    (b)   give due consideration (having regard to his age and understanding) to such wishes of the child as they have been able to ascertain.

(7)   A local authority may not provide accommodation under this section for any child if any person who—
    (a)   has parental responsibility for him; and
    (b)   is willing and able to—
        (i)   provide accommodation for him; or
        (ii)   arrange for accommodation to be provided for him, objects.

(8)   Any person who has parental responsibility for a child may at any time remove the child from accommodation provided by or on behalf of the local authority under this section.

(9)   Subsections (7) and (8) do not apply while any person—
    (a)   in whose favour a residence order is in force with respect to the child; or
    (b)   who has care of the child by virtue of an order made in the exercise of the High Court's inherent jurisdiction with respect to children,
agrees to the child being looked after in accommodation provided by or on behalf of the local authority.

. . .

(11)   Subsections (7) and (8) do not apply where a child who has reached the age of 16 agrees to being provided with accommodation under this section.

12.3   The Duty to Investigate

12.3.1   SECTION 47

Home Office Department of Health/Department of Education and Science/Welsh Office, 'Working Together under the Children Act 1989', HMSO, 1991

3.10   Arrangements for the protection of children from abuse, and in particular child protection conferences, can only be successful if the professional staff concerned do all they can to work in partnership and share and exchange relevant information, in particular with social services departments (or the NSPCC) and the police. Those in receipt of information from professional colleagues in this context must treat it as having been given in confidence. They must not disclose such information for any other purpose without consulting the person who provided it.

3.11   Ethical and statutory codes concerned with confidentiality and data protection are not intended to prevent the exchange of information between different professional staff who have a responsibility for ensuring the protection of children. These statements were drawn up with general considerations in mind. The field of child protection is an area which is developing and professionals should recognise that they may need to seek clarification from their professional body in particular cases.

Medical

3.12   . . . On the recommendation of the Standards Committee, the Council in November 1987 expressed the view that, if a doctor has reason for believing that a child is being physically or sexually abused, not only is it permissible for the doctor to disclose information to a third party but it is a duty of the doctor to do so. This is still the stance of the General Medical Council.

. . .

Social Work

3.14   . . . They will respect the privacy of clients and others with whom they come into contact and confidential information gained in their relationships with them. They will divulge such information only with the consent of the client (or informant) except where there is clear evidence of serious danger to the client, worker, other persons or the community or in other circumstances judged exceptional, on the basis of professional consideration and consultation.

CHILDREN ACT 1989

47. Local authority's duty to investigate

(1) Where a local authority—

(a) are informed that a child who lives, or is found, in their area—

    (i)   is the subject of an emergency protection order; or

    (ii) is in police protection; or

(b) have reasonable cause to suspect that a child who lives, or is found, in their area is suffering, or is likely to suffer, significant harm,

the authority shall make, or cause to be made, such enquiries as they consider necessary to enable them to decide whether they should take any action to safeguard or promote the child's welfare.

. . .

(3) The enquiries shall, in particular, be directed towards establishing—

(a) whether the authority should make any application to the court, or exercise any of their other powers under this Act, with respect to the child;

(b) whether, in the case of a child—

    (i)   with respect to whom an emergency protection order has been made; and

    (ii) who is not in accommodation provided by or on behalf of the authority,

it would be in the child's best interests (while an emergency protection order remains in force) for him to be in such accommodation; and

(c) whether, in the case of a child who has been taken into police protection, it would be in the child's best interests for the authority to ask for an application to be made under section 46(7).

. . .

(9) Where a local authority are conducting enquiries under this section, it shall be the duty of any person mentioned in subsection (11) to assist them with those enquiries (in particular by providing relevant information and advice) if called upon by the authority to do so.

(10) Subsection (9) does not oblige any person to assist a local authority where doing so would be unreasonable in all the circumstances of the case.

(11) The persons are—

(a) any local authority;

(b) any local education authority;

(c) any local housing authority;

(d) any health authority [or National Health Service Trust]; and

(e) any person authorised by the Secretary of State for the purposes of this section.

12.3.1.1 Police protection

CHILDREN ACT 1989

46. Removal and accommodation of children by police in cases of emergency

(1) Where a constable has reasonable cause to believe that a child would otherwise be likely to suffer significant harm, he may—

(a) remove the child to suitable accommodation and keep him there; or

(b) take such steps as are reasonable to ensure that the child's removal from any hospital, or other place, in which he is then being accommodated is prevented.

(2) For the purposes of this Act, a child with respect to whom a constable has exercised his powers under this section is referred to as having been taken into police protection.

(3) As soon as is reasonably practicable after taking a child into police protection, the constable concerned shall—

(a) inform the local authority within whose area the child was found of the steps that have been, and are proposed to be, taken with respect to the child under this section and the reasons for taking them;

(b)   give details to the authority within whose area the child is ordinarily resident ('the appropriate authority') of the place at which the child is being accommodated;

(c)   inform the child (if he appears capable of understanding)—

(i)   of the steps that have been taken with respect to him under this section and of the reasons for taking them; and

(ii)   of the further steps that may be taken with respect to him under this section;

(d)   take such steps as are reasonably practicable to discover the wishes and feelings of the child;

(e)   secure that the case is inquired into by an officer designated for the purposes of this section by the chief officer of the police area concerned; and

(f)   where the child was taken into police protection by being removed to accommodation which is not provided—

(i)   by or on behalf of a local authority; or

(ii)   as a refuge, in compliance with the requirements of section 51,

secure that he is moved to accommodation which is so provided.

(4)   As soon as is reasonably practicable after taking a child into police protection, the constable concerned shall take such steps as are reasonably practicable to inform—

(a)   the child's parents;

(b)   every person who is not a parent of his but who has parental responsibility for him; and

(c)   any other person with whom the child was living immediately before being taken into police protection,

of the steps that he has taken under this section with respect to the child, the reasons for taking them and the further steps that may be taken with respect to him under this section.

(5)   On completing any inquiry under subsection (3)(e), the officer conducting it shall release the child from police protection unless he considers that there is still reasonable cause for believing that the child would be likely to suffer significant harm if released.

(6)   No child may be kept in police protection for more than 72 hours.

(7)   While a child is being kept in police protection, the designated officer may apply on behalf of the appropriate authority for an emergency protection order to be made under section 44 with respect to the child.

(8)   An application may be made under subsection (7) whether or not the authority know of it or agree to its being made.

12.3.1.2   The focus and means of investigating

CHILDREN ACT 1989

47.   Local authority's duty to investigate

(6)   Where, in the course of enquiries made under this section—

(a)   any officer of the local authority concerned; or

(b)   any person authorised by the authority to act on their behalf in connection with those enquiries—

(i)   is refused access to the child concerned; or

(ii)   is denied information as to his whereabouts,

the authority shall apply for an emergency protection order, a child assessment order, a care order or a supervision order with respect to the child unless they are satisfied that his welfare can be satisfactorily safeguarded without their doing so.

D v D (COUNTY COURT JURISDICTION: INJUNCTIONS) [1993] 2 FLR 802 (CA)

BALCOMBE LJ: These appeals are against orders made by his Honour Judge Brown in the Lancaster County Court on 30 April and 17 May 1993 in the course of proceedings between divorced parents relating to the residence of, and contact with, the children of the marriage.

Unfortunately relations between the parents have not been good. In October 1992 the mother applied for non-molestation and ouster injunctions and on 16 October 1992 the father gave undertakings to the county court not to molest the mother and to vacate the matrimonial home. There was an incident on 24 November 1992 when the police were called because of an allegation that the maternal grandfather had physically abused L, but nothing further happened on this occasion. The mother now alleges that the father has been manipulating the children to a degree which has affected their emotional welfare; the father asserts that he is concerned about the use of violence by the mother and her parents towards the children.

In January 1992 the mother applied to the county court under s. 10 of the Children Act 1989 ('the 1989 Act') for a residence order in her favour and for contact between the children and the father to be strictly defined.

. . . Over the weekend of 24/25 April 1993 the children were staying with the father. The father had previously been alerted by his mother as to an incident between L, the mother and the maternal grandfather on 22 April 1993. On Saturday, 24 April 1993, L told the father that on the Thursday (22 April 1993) he had been smacked, whacked to the floor and kicked by the mother and sworn at by the mother and the maternal grandfather. L showed his father a bruise on the left side of his rib cage. The father then took L to his general practitioner, Dr Nightingale, whose statement, subsequently filed with the court, reads as follows:

This boy was brought to me by his father at 10.30 in the morning as an emergency on 24 April 1993. The history given to me by the father and confirmed verbally by L was that he had been kicked by his mother on the left side of the chest on the previous Thursday night. The injury was painful and due to the pain he was unable to play football.

On examination the child has a 5 × 2 cm bruise over the region of the ninth and tenth ribs laterally below the left armpit.

He had some discomfort on compressing the sternum and an underlying bony injury to the rib was possible, but it is not routine to X-ray ribs because the management of the pain is not affected in any way.

The father asked me what action should be taken regarding the alleged assault, and I suggested that the discussed the matter with the police due to the potential seriousness of the alleged incident.

The father followed Dr Nightingale's suggestion and contacted the North Yorkshire constabulary. The police took a statement from L and in their turn contacted the social services department of the North Yorkshire County Council ('the council'). L's statement was recorded on video.

. . . On Sunday, 25 April 1993 at about 4 pm a police officer and a social worker visited the mother and told her that the girls should be medically examined and that until that had been done she should remain separate from them. She was told that it would be less traumatic for the girls to be examined by their general practitioner the following day (Monday), rather than by a police surgeon that night. The mother says she told the officers of the pending proceedings in the county court and asserted, as she still asserts, that the whole incident was a manipulation by the father to obtain custody of the children and regain occupancy of the former matrimonial home. However, she left the home, leaving the girls and L with the father, and (whether or not she actually consented) appears to have made no objection to the two girls being examined by their general practitioner. Subsequent examination of the girls revealed nothing untoward.

On 29 April 1993 the father issued an application in the county court for a residence order in respect of the three children under s. 10 of the 1989 Act; he also asked that contact between the mother and the children be supervised. The mother also applied for the following directions (inter alia):

(1)   an expedited hearing of her application under the Children Act;

(2)   that the substance of and results of any medical examination carried out upon the child, L, be filed and served forthwith;

(3)   that the text and/or any recordings of any police and social worker interviews or investigations also be filed and served forthwith.

No copy of this, application was served on either the council or the police.

Also on 29 April 1993 North Yorkshire social services wrote to the mother's solicitors as follows:

RE: D—FAMILY: INFORMATION FOR DIRECTIONS HEARING
After interviewing C and I on 27 April 1993, both social services department and the police officer found no evidence to give sufficient concern to deny either parent contact with or residence of C or I.

Given the recent allegations made by L, we would recommend that L stay with his father until the case conference on 5 May 1993.

The mother's application came before his Honour Judge Brown sitting in the Lancaster County Court on Friday, 30 April 1993. The mother was represented by counsel, the father by a solicitor; no one was present from the police or social services. We have a full transcript of the proceedings and it is apparent that the mother's counsel opened the application in terms strongly critical of the actions of the police and social services and going so far as to assert—an assertion not now maintained—that L's medical examination required the leave of the court under r. 4.18 of the Family Proceedings Rules 1991. The judge received little assistance from the father's solicitor: he supported the mother's application for discovery against the police and social services notwithstanding that no notice of the application had been served on them. Neither the mother nor the father was cross-examined on their conflicting statements which were before the judge. The judge gave a short judgment:

The sooner [the father] realises that must stop playing about with the court the better for him and for everybody. This last weekend he has gone at it like a bull at a gate. He has not bothered to find out from [the mother] what, if anything, has happened to L. He has gone off to the police without even referring to his solicitors. The police have forgotten to observe child protection procedures. The social services appear to have forgotten even the most basic lessons of child protection. Two girls have been carted off from their mother's home, without any grounds whatsoever, and medically examined, without the leave of the court, despite the pending proceedings, and [the] mother . . . persuaded that, she would have to vacate the matrimonial home, where she has lived and looked after all three children, in order that those examinations could take place.

Today I am faced with a letter from a social worker whose ability must be called severely into question, or his experience, making a recommendation that the boy, L, should remain with his father until they decide when they want to have a case conference. I have never ever before in my experience come across such outrageous conduct. I am driven to the preliminary conclusion that the whole thing is a charade, engineered by [the father] to gain some advantage in the pending hearing.

There is no statutory link between the private and public law parts of the 1989 Act, as is apparent from the judgment of this court in *Nottinghamshire County Council v P* [1993] 2 FLR 134. However, the whole philosophy behind the 1989 Act is that local authorities should, wherever possible, act in co-operation with the parents and families of children with whom they may be concerned and should only use their coercive powers when co-operation has failed. Whether or not the judge was justified in his strictures of the council's actions in the present case, it is right that I should record that at no stage have they sought to exercise any coercive powers. In the circumstances of L's complaint that he had been assaulted by his mother they had a clear duty to investigate under s. 47, while the police had their common law duty to investigate an alleged crime and could, if necessary and without any order of the court, have exercised their statutory powers to remove L to suitable accommodation under s. 46. The council could, if necessary, have applied to the court for a child assessment order under s. 43 for the medical examination of the children, but that never became necessary because they had at least the consent of the father, who could exercise sole parental responsibility under s. 2(7), for such examinations to be made. In the last resort they could have applied to the court for an emergency protection order under s. 44. None of these more stringent remedies was sought by the council in the present case because there was no necessity for them. It would only be at the time when the council first applied to the court for an order, whether under s. 43 or s. 44, or indeed for a care or supervision order under s. 31, that the court would have the opportunity to consider, vis-à-vis the council, whether their intervention in the lives of the children was justified. However, that is not to say that the court is powerless in a case such is as the present. If it were satisfied, on proper evidence, that a person with parental responsibility for a child was exercising the rights attaching to that responsibility in a way which could be detrimental to the child's welfare—eg by permitting the child to be exposed to unnecessary interviews or examinations—the court in the exercise of its private law jurisdiction could make a prohibited steps order under s. 8 restraining that person front exercising those rights. Once such an order had been made neither the council nor the police (except in exercise of their emergency powers under s. 46 so far as those extend) could have taken any step invasive of the lives of these children without first applying to the court. In the course of the hearing before us each parent offered an undertaking to the court not, pending the hearing of their cross-application, to consent to, or cause or permit, any of the children to be interviewed or subjected to any medical examination (except when such an examination was necessary for ordinary medical reasons) without the consent of the court. We accepted the undertakings thus offered.

SIR FRANCIS PURCHAS: As a result of this incident the welfare services of the council and the police became involved. These events have already been described in the judgment of Balcombe LJ and need not be repeated here. I have set out these matters at some length in order to paint a picture of a typical family dispute centred over the children in which the extended family on each side had become involved. The resolution of this multitude of allegations and counter-allegations would not have been made any easier by the disaffection which, for one reason or another, had grown up in L against his mother and her family. In her statement in support of her application for an expedited hearing dated 29 April 1993, the mother had given a detailed account of an incident on 22 April 1993 during which L had lost his temper with the mother, thrown furniture about and in which L might well have received injuries consistent with those found upon his body when he was medically examined.

Although the judge's comments about the conduct of the council and the police may be said to have been somewhat severe on the facts as presented to him by counsel, I cannot say that they were in any way objectionable; except that before making them he should have given those authorities a chance to be represented. To be fair to the judge it must be remembered that apart from causing one of their staff to write to the court recommending that L should remain with his father, the council had taken no steps to acknowledge the court's jurisdiction, nor to assist it in its task of dealing with the civil law dispute with which it was obviously concerned. By the letter from the social worker the council were attempting to persuade the judge to take a course, which it would not be open to them to seek by formal application to the court.

The judge clearly formed the view that the council were bent upon a long-term assessment of the whole family in depth which he considered, in my judgment rightly, was outside the ambit of any inquiry which they were entitled to make in the discharge of their duties under s. 47 of the Act. However, I cannot approve of the comments made by the judge about the father's conduct between 24 and 26 April 1993. Whilst he had clearly been associated with the case since the previous October, and had had plenty of opportunity to form views about the respective merits of the litigants; he had only received undertakings from the father in October 1992 and there had been no hearing at which the conflicting versions of events contained in the statements before him could be assessed. Whilst I have every sympathy with the judge in all the circumstances I have to say that in my judgment it was unwise to express himself about the father in such unqualified and intemperate terms.

After the hearing on 30 April 1993, the orders made by the court were brought to the attention of the council, who had arranged for a case conference to be held on 5 May 1993. The council wrote to the court explaining their position in a letter dated 6 May 1993. In the meanwhile they had applied to Judge Duckworth, in the absence of Judge Brown, to obtain leave to continue to hold the case conference which had been arranged. The contents of this letter have already been fully described in the judgment of Balcombe LJ and need not be repeated here. However, in the letter the council expressed its intentions in the course of acting under s. 47 of the Act in the following way:

The decision of the case conference was that L's name should be placed on the North Yorkshire child protection register under the category of physical injury. Registration under the category of emotional abuse was considered at the case conference but a decision on that was deferred pending receipt of further information and the carrying out of a comprehensive family assessment. As is usual once a child's name has been entered on the register a protection plan is formulated. The plan in connection with L included the carrying out of a comprehensive assessment of the family situation, for the continuing involvement of a child psychologist and for the social services department to discuss with [the mother] and L what resources and services were available to assist in dealing with L's difficulties.

The comprehensive assessment the social services department would wish to carry out is in line with the guidance of the Department of Health in a publication entitled 'Protecting Children: A Guide to Undertaking a Comprehensive Assessment'. *It is envisaged that such all assessment will require two visits to each parent, one visit to see each child and possibly one visit to each of the grandparents.* (Emphasis provided)

It is clear that at the time of writing this letter the council, purporting to act with the consent of the father and under the umbrella of s. 47 of the Act, were bent upon a massive intrusion into the family as a whole, including the two girls who had already been dismissed as persons in respect of whom the council had a duty of investigation under s. 47. In my judgment this was wholly outside the ambit of those duties once it was established that there was no child who was suffering significant harm or risk of harm. In order to carry out the sort of child assessment upon which the council were embarked they would have had to apply to the court for a child assessment order under s. 43 of the Act. Indeed Mr McCarthy who appeared for the council before us did not attempt to argue to the contrary, but justified the council's actions on the grounds that they were acting with the consent of a person with parental responsibility, namely the father.

With regard to the discharge of the duty placed upon them by s. 47 of the Act, Miss Mitchell submitted that no power was given to the court under the Act which would enable it to prevent the council from carrying out its duty of investigation under s. 47; nor was there any inherent jurisdiction in the county court. Miss Mitchell told the judge that the council were acting with the agreement at least of the father who had parental responsibility. As a result of the case conference the council had formulated a 'child protection plan'. It was clear that at that stage the council envisaged on-going investigations with the father's agreement. This the judge considered to be an unwarranted interference with the exercise of his own jurisdiction to deal with the cross-applications which were before him. He indicated that as a result of the interim orders he had made he had effectively withdrawn parental responsibility from the father. Miss Mitchell accepted that his order had limited the father's parental responsibility vis-à-vis the mother, but seemed to submit that the father still continued to have parental responsibility which would support the council's intentions to continue with the investigation.

From this exchange it is clear that the council were bent on an on-going assessment of the whole family which would largely duplicate the inquiries being made and decisions taken in the pre-existing proceedings with which the court was already seized. Where private proceedings under Part II of the Act are already on foot, one must of course distinguish the duty imposed by the Act upon local authorities to investigate situations of imminent risk in an emergency situation, in which the local authority have a clear duty to investigate under s. 47 of the Act notwithstanding the current private proceedings. In cases where action is required depending upon the imminence of the risk, the Act gives power to the local authority to make an emergency protection order under Part V of the Act, or other cases to apply to the court for orders under Part IV of the Act. The police have similar powers to investigate a suspected crime under quite different powers. By the time that the matter was before Judge Brown on 17 May 1993, the police had decided to take no further action, and there was clearly no need for emergency action to be taken by the council under Part V of the Act. I have therefore every sympathy with the judge in the attitude he adopted to the disinclination on the part of the council to apply to be joined as parties to the proceedings which were current before him, whilst indicating at the same time that they were bent upon a course of major assessment of the whole family without any order of the court. In my judgment this was a wholly improper attitude on the part of the council.

12.3.2   SECTION 37 INVESTIGATIONS

CHILDREN ACT 1989

37.   Powers of court in certain family proceedings

(1)   Where, in any family proceedings in which a question arises with respect to the welfare of any child, it appears to the court that it may be appropriate for a care or supervision order to be made with respect to him, the court may direct the appropriate authority to undertake an investigation of the child's circumstances.

(2)   Where the court gives a direction under this section the local authority concerned shall, when undertaking the investigation, consider whether they should—

(a)   apply for a care order or for a supervision order with respect to the child;

(b)   provide services or assistance for the child or his family; or

(c)   take any other action with respect to the child.

(3)   Where a local authority undertake an investigation under this section, and decide not to apply for a care order or supervision order with respect to the child concerned, they shall inform the court of—

(a)   their reasons for so deciding;

(b)   any service or assistance which they have provided, or intend to provide, for the child and his family; and

(c)   any other action which they have taken, or propose to take, with respect to the child.

(4)   The information shall be given to the court before the end of the period of eight weeks beginning with the date of the direction, unless the court otherwise directs.

(5)   The local authority named in a direction under subsection (1) must be—

(a)   the authority in whose area the child is ordinarily resident; or

(b)   where the child [is not ordinarily resident] in the area of a local authority, the authority within whose area any circumstances arose in consequence of which the direction is being given.

(6)   If, on the conclusion of any investigation or review under this section, the authority decide not to apply for a care order or supervision order with respect to the child—

(a)   they shall consider whether it would be appropriate to review the case at a later date; and

(b)   if they decide that it would be, they shall determine the date on which that review is to begin.

Law Commission, 'Family Law Review of Child Law Guardianship and Custody, Law Com No. 172

5.5   We therefore recommend that, where in such family proceedings it appears to the court that there are exceptional circumstances in which a care application may be appropriate, the court may direct the local authority to conduct an investigation. Having investigated, the authority should consider whether the case is more appropriate for a care or supervision order, or for the provision of services on a voluntary basis, or for some other action (such as referral for services from some other agency). If there is a case for an order, the authority will presumably be under a statutory duty to apply for one. If the authority decides not to apply for an order, it should report back to the court on the reasons for that decision and on the alternative action taken, if any.

NOTTINGHAMSHIRE COUNTY COUNCIL v P
RE P (MINORS) (LOCAL AUTHORITY: PROHIBITED STEPS ORDER) [1993]
3 WLR 637 (CA)

SIR STEPHEN BROWN P: The court has before it a series of appeals from a judgment delivered by Ward J on 27 October 1992. The judge then refused an application by the Nottinghamshire County Council for a prohibited steps order made pursuant to s. 8 of the Children Act 1989. By its application the council stated that it wished the court to order that the father should not reside in the same household as his daughters and should not have any contact with them unless they themselves wished to have contact with him and that any such contact should be supervised by the Social Services Department, such contact to be negotiated between the mother, father and the daughters with a condition that the mother should not knowingly place the daughters in a position where they come into contact or reside with the father.

. . . The judge found that the mother was weak and had no capacity to protect the children and that she was probably totally under the control of her husband. He further found that if the father were to be excluded from the home there was a real risk that the girls would run away to him. On 8 May the judge also said about the father:

I have no doubt whatever that Mr P is in need of help. He is a very disturbed and disturbing man. He bristles with aggression. Though he may be all bluster, he is nonetheless a man with a temper, who portrays himself as frightening. He has a frightening effect upon those he deals with.

He said further:

The all pervasive atmosphere of sex in this house is frightening. Given the harm already suffered, the risk of further harm that this man will not stop with M (the eldest girl) but will lay his hands upon the other two is a real risk which gives me cause for grave concern. As to the capacity of each of the parents to meet the girls' needs: their parents have demonstrated themselves quite unable to do so.

At that hearing in May 1992 the judge considered the range of powers available to the court under the 1989 Act and complained that the form of the local authority's application did not give the court power to make a supervision order. He referred to the fact that the circuit judge to whom the case had initially been remitted had asked the local authority to consider this and had then referred the matter to the local authority under the provisions of s. 37 of the 1989 Act. The Judge said in his judgment on 8 May:

I made it perfectly plain when speaking to the manager of social services that I felt it [the supervision order] would give me teeth and powers that I did not have without their application but the local authority refused to give me the opportunity to exercise any of the powers which are ancillary to a supervision order. I respect their point of view that they do not seek to remove K and E from their home not least because they could not control them if they were to take them into care. I wholly understand that dilemma. But why the local authority have concluded that a supervision order would not give the court any useful powers that it would not otherwise have, I simply do not know.

A wider question arises as to policy. We consider that this court should make it clear that the route chosen by the local authority in this case was wholly inappropriate. In cases where children are found to be at risk of suffering significant harm within the meaning of s. 31 of the 1989 Act a clear duty arises on the part of local authorities to take steps to protect them. In such circumstances a local authority is required to assume responsibility and to intervene in the family arrangements in order to protect the child. Pt IV specifically provides them with wide powers and a wide discretion. As already pointed out the Act envisages that local authorities may place children with their parents even though they may have a care order under s. 31.

A supervision order may be viewed as being less draconian but it gives the local authority a wide discretion as to how to deal with children and with the family. A prohibited steps order would not afford the local authority any authority as to how it might deal with the children. There may be situations, for example where a child is accommodated by a local authority, where it would be appropriate to seek a prohibited steps order for some particular purpose. However, it could not in any circumstances be regarded as providing a substitute for an order under Pt IV of the 1989 Act. Furthermore, it is very doubtful indeed whether a prohibited steps order could in any circumstances be used to 'oust' a father from a matrimonial home. Although counsel had prepared detailed submissions upon this aspect of the matter it has not been necessary to consider the point in order to resolve this appeal. It is a most regrettable feature of this case that the local authority having initially intervened under Pt V of the 1989 Act in order to obtain an emergency protection order did not then proceed to seek orders under s. 31 in Pt IV of the Act. This is even more regrettable after Judge Heald had directed the local authority to consider the position pursuant to a direction under s. 37 of the Act. In the trial papers there appears what is headed:

The Report of *Nottinghamshire County Council Re: Section 37 Direction Nottinghamshire County Council and P and P.* [It then states:] At a hearing before His Honour Judge Heald on 2nd March 1992, a Section 37 Direction was issued to the Local Authority. The Local Authority has since reconsidered the case and the merits of making an application under Section 37. The Local Authority does not feel it appropriate to make an application for a Care or Supervision Order as it does not believe those Orders would be effective in the protection of these children. The Local Authority has decided to continue with the application for a Prohibited Steps Order in relation to the father of K and E and would intend to offer appropriate support, services, and assistance, in the light of that Order being made or any other such Order being made. The Local Authority will review this case following the Court Proceedings on 9th and 10th April 1992.
[Signed] Peter McEntee Area Director, North Area. Social Services Director.

That clearly is not a satisfactory answer to a s. 37 direction and we agree with the judge that he was left in an intolerable situation. This local authority persistently and obstinately refused to undertake what was the appropriate course of action and it thereby deprived the judge of the ability to make a constructive order. We wish to add that it was wholly inappropriate in the first place for the local authority to apply for leave to issue an application for a prohibited steps order ex parte before a single justice of a family proceedings court. If the matter had been referred at the earliest opportunity to the county court it is likely that the application would have been refused. In our view this should have happened. In future any such application if made to a family proceedings court should be transferred to the county court.

Furthermore, no such application should be dealt with 'ex parte'. An immediate and obvious deficiency in attempting to initiate such a procedure is that there is no power under the private law provisions of the 1989 Act for the court to appoint a guardian ad litem to represent the interests of the children. It is to be hoped that a serious lesson will have been learned as a result of these proceedings and that local authorities will recognise that where children are believed to be at risk of suffering significant harm, their appropriate avenue is via Pt IV of the 1989 Act which is specifically designed to accommodate public law applications.

In the result there are now no orders in force which are capable of regulating and safeguarding the position of these children. In point of fact the elder has now reached the age of 16 but the younger is now still only 13 years of age. The situation remains that they are at risk and the local authority is under a statutory obligation to take steps to protect them and to seek to ensure their welfare. The court has been told that as a result of action taken by the regional health authority prompted by the judge, the father did in fact go to the Gracewell Clinic following the proceedings before Ward J. However the court has also now been told by his counsel that he has since left the clinic. The court has not been told the circumstances under which that occurred. Since the fact of the risk of significant harm to the children has been established and not contradicted there remains upon the local authority the clear duty to take steps to safeguard the welfare of these children. It should not shrink from taking steps under Pt IV of the Act. It appears from submissions made by all counsel in this court that the mother, the father and the children by their guardian ad litem would not resist the making of a supervision order in favour of the local authority pursuant to s. 31 of the Act. That at least would afford a basis for the local authority to take some constructive steps in order to protect these children.

This court is deeply concerned at the absence of any power to direct this authority to take steps to protect the children. In the former wardship jurisdiction it might well have been able to do so. The operation of the 1989 Act is entirely dependent upon the full co-operation of all those involved. This includes the courts, the local authorities and the social workers and all who have to deal with children. Unfortunately as appears from this case if a local authority doggedly resists taking the steps which are appropriate to the case of children at risk of suffering significant harm it appears that the court is powerless. The authority may perhaps lay itself open to an application for judicial review but in a case such as this the question arises at whose instance? The position is one which it is to be hoped will not recur and that lessons will be learnt from this unhappy catalogue of errors.

RE H (A MINOR) (SECTION 37 DIRECTION) [1993] 2 FLR 541 (FamD)

SCOTT BAKER J: The judgment I am about to deliver is being delivered in chambers, but I give leave for the judgment to be reported. However, I grant an injunction restraining anybody from publishing any information which is calculated to lead to the identification of the child, or any of the parties to the proceedings.

On 5 October 1991, H, a little girl, was born at the applicants' home. The natural mother and natural father live together and have another child who was born on 1 December 1989, and is therefore now $2\frac{1}{2}$. The applicants are A, who is 21 years old, and B, who is 25 years old. They are lesbians They have had a relationship since the summer of 1988. They live together about 5 minutes away from where the mother and the father live.

On 5 October 1991, H was born at the applicants' house. She has lived there ever since, for all the 8 months or so of her short life. On 11 October 1991—that is just a few days after her birth—the applicants wrote to the local authority asking to be recognised as approved foster-parents. It is clear, in my judgment, that what was intended was adoption by the back door.

Adoption is a very grave step for those concerned. The law provides careful safe-guards to ensure that the interests of the child are protected. In February 1990 A had been convicted of assault occasioning actual bodily harm. On the information that I have received during the hearing, it may well be that this was not the most serious case of assault. It involved an argument with another woman over a child; another woman with whom A had been having some form of relationship. The consequence of this conviction is that A is disqualified as a foster-parent unless that disqualification is overridden by the consent of the local authority [the applicants applied for a residence order] . . .

The applicants' care of H . . . has been entirely satisfactory. The concerns about H relate to the longer term . . .

It seems to me, bearing all these matters in mind, that it is desirable that the situation that presently exists should be formalised. It is in the interests of H that this should be done now, albeit if only on all interim basis. It appears to me that I am not concerned, at this juncture, with past breaches of the law with regard to fostering. My prime consideration is the welfare of this little girl. From the evidence that I have heard, there is a need to recognise that the de facto parental responsibility has been for the last 8 months with the applicants, and will continue to be with them unless and until such time as the local authority makes an application for a care order and the court rules otherwise.

That, however, is not the end of the matter, because my attention has been drawn to s. 37 of the Act. Section 37(1) provides:

> Where, in any family proceedings in which a question arises with respect to the welfare of any child, it appears to the court that it may be appropriate for a care or supervision order to be made with respect to him, the court may direct the appropriate authority to undertake all investigation of the child's circumstances.

The position that I have reached, at the conclusion of this hearing, is that I think it may be appropriate for a care or supervision order to be made, but the answer to the question is dependent upon further evidence as to the likely long-term emotional damage to H, and whether this can be, it not eliminated altogether, at least alleviated by proper counselling and/or other treatment for the applicants.

The question arises whether the words 'directing the authority to undertake an investigation of the child's circumstances' are sufficiently wide to cover obtaining the further psychiatric evidence that I would like to have.

In my judgment, the child's circumstances, as referred to in s. 37(1), should be widely construed and should include any situation which may have a bearing on the child being likely to suffer significant harm in the future, which is of course the critical factor as regards making a care order. The purposive construction of s. 37(1) leads me to this conclusion.

The effect of making an order under s. 37(1) emerges under s. 37(2):

Where the court gives a direction under this section the local authority concerned shall, when undertaking the investigation, consider whether they should—
(a)   apply for a care order or for a supervision order with respect to the child;
(b)   provide services or assistance for the child or his family; or,
(c)   take any other action will, respect to the child.

The consequence of my making an order of this kind is to force the local authority to apply its mind to the specific problem of whether a care or supervision order is necessary.

Section 37(3) goes on:

Where a local authority undertake an investigation under this section and decide not to apply for a care order or supervision order with respect to the child concerned, they shall inform the court of—
(a)   their reasons for so deciding;
(b)   any service or assistance which they have provided, or intend to provide, for the child and his family; and
(c)   any other action which they have taken, or propose to take, with respect to the child.

Under s. 37(4), that information has to be given to the court before the end of the period of 8 weeks, beginning with the date of the direction, unless the court otherwise directs.

I move on to s. 38. Section 38(1) provides that where the court gives a direction under s. 37(1), as I propose to do in this case, the court may make an interim care order or an interim supervision order with respect to the child concerned. An interim supervision or care order can only last for the period of 8 weeks unless it is extended.

I have come to the conclusion that an interim supervision order would be desirable because I think it is necessary that the local authority should, first of all, keep a close eye on the situation generally; and, secondly, keep a very close eye, in particular, on the question of any contact between the applicants and the natural mother. In all the circumstances, the order that I propose to make is as follows.

First of all, that there should be all investigation of the child's circumstances under s. 37, as I have outlined. In particular, I am concerned about the emotional and other difficulties with which H is likely to be faced as she grows up, and whether the applicants are likely to be able to cope with, or minimise, such difficulties. Secondly, I am interested to know what help of a psychiatric or counselling nature might be available to the applicants.

Thirdly, I would like to know the consequences to H of any such emotional or other difficulties that cannot be overcome with help, and how this should weigh against the possibility of removing H from her present carers. I appreciate, of course, that ultimately this is a matter for the court's decision in the light of the whole of the evidence.

I propose, in the meantime, to make an interim residence order. I make it in favour of A alone, for the reasons that I have given in this judgment. I do not think that B's mental health justifies a residence order in her favour, although I envisage that the two applicants will continue jointly to care for H.

I think it is desirable that I make a prohibited steps order in the nature of an injunction, which I think should have a penal notice attached to it, and should be fairly carefully drawn; the broad terms being that the mother and the father should not assume, or seek to assume, physical possession of, or contact with, the child in any way without the court's further order.

I make an order that under s. 37(4) the material information should be given to the local authority by the court either 8 weeks from today, or 7 days after the receipt by them of a psychiatric report, whichever is the later, provided in any event that the information is not furnished later than 15 September 1992.

12.4   Child Protection Case Conferences

12.4.1   WHAT IS THE CONFERENCE THERE FOR?

Home Office/Department of Health/Department of Education and Science/Welsh Office, 'Working Together under the Children Act 1989', HMSO, 1991

Encouragement of Participation of Children and Family Adults
6.23   There are a variety of practical ways in which the participation of adults in the family and children at conferences can be encouraged and made less difficult. For example, conferences should be held at a time and place which is convenient for the family as well as the professional workers; the family should be prepared for the conference by the professional worker with whom they have the closest relationship; they should meet the chair in advance; the parents and caring adults should be made aware of the issues to be discussed at the conference so that they can seek advice and prepare their point of view; the size of the professional group should be limited to those who really need to attend; and comfortable waiting facilities should be available. . . . Some of the advice below about the handling of conferences will also serve to ease the position of families on these occasions and thus encourage their participation.

Attendance at the Child Protection Conference
6.24   Those who attend conferences should be there because they have a contribution to make. Meetings that are unnecessarily large inhibit discussion and do not use valuable resources to the best advantage. Large numbers of professionals, some of whom make no apparent contribution, are particularly inhibiting to parents and children who will in any event probably find the conference a difficult occasion.
6.25   All the agencies which have specific responsibilities in the child protection process should be invited to send representatives. These include:

- the social services,
- the NSPCC (when operational in the area),
- the police,
- education (when the child is of school age),
- the health authority,
- the general medical practitioner,
- the health visiting service,
- the probation service,
- appropriate voluntary organisations, and
- a representative of the armed services in each case where there is a Service connection.

6.26   All those who are invited should be informed that the child, the parents and other carers have been invited. A child protection conference may be a large gathering in the early stages of work, where a number of agencies may be contributing to an investigation or an assessment for planning. However, once a long term plan has been formulated, and a group led by the key worker has been identified to work with the family, the number attending the child protection review will probably be reduced. It is the responsibility of the chair to ensure that the appropriate people are invited to the conference.
6.27   The chair must be able to call on advice from a lawyer from the local authority's legal section particularly when court action is under consideration and on other specialist advice when necessary, for example, the advice of a psychiatrist, psychologist or workers and interpreters with special knowledge either of working with people with a disability or of working with people from a particular race or culture.

6.28   On occasions it maybe useful to invite others working with the family to join in the conference, for example, volunteer workers. It will be necessary for the key worker or the person most closely involved to brief him or her about the purpose of the conference, the duty of confidentiality and the primacy of the child's interest. Issues about attendance, written contributions and substitute representation are matters to be addressed in the local child protection procedures.

12.4.2   WHEN WILL A CONFERENCE BE NEEDED?

'Working Together under the Children Act 1989', HMSO, 1991

Timing

5.15.3   The time between referral and the initial child protection conference will vary according to the needs of each individual case. The pace should not slacken once the protection of the child is ensured but sufficient time should be taken so that the conference does not result in premature or disorganised action. Initial conferences should take place within eight working days of referral unless there are special reasons why information from the investigation which will lead to a better decision is not available. Normally a maximum of 15 days should be set. If court action is underway the timing of the conference will be determined by the Court Rules.

12.4.3   WHAT DECISIONS CAN BE MADE?

'Working Together under the Children Act 1989', HMSO, 1991

5.15.4   The only *decision* to be taken at the conference is whether or not to register the child and, if registration is agreed, to allocate the key worker. The key worker must be a social worker, from either the social services department or the NSPCC. When a child is not registered there may still be a need for services. Provision of services should not be dependent on registration.

12.5   Short-term Orders

12.5.1   THE CHILD ASSESSMENT ORDER: S. 43

CHILDREN ACT 1989

43.   Child assessment orders

(1)   On the application of a local authority or authorised person for an order to be made under this section with respect to a child, the court may make the order if, but only if, it is satisfied that—

(a)   the applicant has reasonable cause to suspect that the child is suffering, or is likely to suffer, significant harm;

(b)   an assessment of the state of the child's health or development, or of the way in which he has been treated, is required to enable the applicant to determine whether or not the child is suffering, or is likely to suffer, significant harm; and

(c)   it is unlikely that such an assessment will be made, or be satisfactory, in the absence of an order under this section.

· (2)   In this Act 'a child assessment order' means an order under this section.

(3)   A court may treat an application under this section as an application for an emergency protection order.

(4)   No court shall make a child assessment order if it is satisfied—

(a)   that there are grounds for making an emergency protection order with respect to the child; and

(b)   that it ought to make such an order rather than a child assessment order.

(5)   A child assessment order shall—

(a)   specify the date by which the assessment is to begin; and

(b)   have effect for such period, not exceeding seven days beginning with that date, as may be specified in the order.

(6)   Where a child assessment order is in force with respect to a child it shall be the duty of any person who is in a position to produce the child—

(a)   to produce him to such person as may be named in the order; and

(b)   to comply with such directions relating to the assessment of the child as the court thinks fit to specify in the order.

(7)   A child assessment order authorises any person carrying out the assessment, or any part of the assessment, to do so in accordance with the terms of the order.

(8)   Regardless of subsection (7), if the child is of sufficient understanding to make an informed decision he may refuse to submit to a medical or psychiatric examination or other assessment.

(9)   The child may only be kept away from home—

(a)   in accordance with directions specified in the order;

(b)   if it is necessary for the purposes of the assessment; and

(c)   for such period or periods as may be specified in the order.

(10)   Where the child is to be kept away from home, the order shall contain such directions as the court thinks fit with regard to the contact that he must be allowed to have with other persons while away from home.

(11)   Any person making an application for a child assessment order shall take such steps as are reasonably practicable to ensure that notice of the application is given to—

(a)   the child's parents;

(b)   any person who is not a parent of his but who has parental responsibility for him;

(c)   any other person caring for the child;

(d)   any person in whose favour a contact order is in force with respect to the child;

(e)   any person who is allowed to have contact with the child by virtue of an order under section 34; and

(f)   the child, before the hearing of the application.

(12)   Rules of court may make provision as to the circumstances in which—

(a)   any of the persons mentioned in subsection (11); or

(b)   such other person as may be specified in the rules,

may apply to the court for a child assessment order to be varied or discharged.

(13)   In this section 'authorised person' means a person who is an authorised person for the purposes of section 31.

12.5.1.1   Advantages

'The Children Act 1989. Guidance and Regulations', *Volume 1, Court Orders,*
HMSO, 1991

4.9   A child assessment order will usually be most appropriate where the harm to the child is long-term and cumulative rather than sudden and severe. The circumstances may be nagging concern about a child who appears to be failing to thrive; or the parents are ignorant of or unwilling to face up to possible harm to their child because of the state of his health or development; or it appears that the child may be subject to wilful neglect or abuse but not to such an extent as to place him at serious immediate risk. Sexual abuse, which covers a wide range of behaviour, can fall in this category. The harm to the child can be long-term rather than immediate and it does not necessarily require emergency action. However, emergency action should not be avoided where disclosure of the abuse is itself likely to put the child at immediate risk of significant harm and/or where there is an urgent need to gather particular forensic evidence which would not otherwise be forthcoming in relation to the likelihood of significant harm.

4.10   One of the essential ingredients for a child assessment order is that an assessment is needed to help establish basic facts about the child's condition. Because information is lacking it is unlikely that an interim care or supervision order could be obtained and an examination or assessment arranged under those provisions: the condition for an interim order—'reasonable grounds for believing that the circumstances are as mentioned in section 31(2)'—s. 38(2) . . . is more demanding and would be difficult to satisfy. However, the applicant should know enough of the circumstances to satisfy himself that the child is not in immediate danger; if possible the child should have been seen recently by someone competent to judge this. A skilled social work practitioner would be in a position to make a judgement as to the child's emotional state and to obvious changes in the child's physical well-being. Finer judgements, particularly in relation to very young children, may require input from the child's health visitor, GP or other health professional. Refusal to allow a child about whom there is serious concern to be seen (as opposed to being examined or assessed) can be a classic sign of a potential emergency, and will require the response of an application for an emergency protection order under the 'frustrated access' condition . . .

Prior investigations

4.11   An application by a local authority should always be preceded by an investigation under s. 47 . . . . Since the order is for non-emergencies, there will be no justification for the investigation to be merely superficial. The court considering an application for a child assessment order will expect to be given details of the investigation and how it arose, including in particular details of the applicant's attempts to satisfy himself as to the welfare of the child by arrangement with the people caring for him . . . . If the court is not satisfied that all reasonable efforts were made to persuade them to co-operate and that these were resisted, the application is likely to founder on the third condition of s. 43(1).

. . .

Practice issues

4.23   A number of important practice issues arise. One is that as far as possible the child assessment order should be used sparingly. Although a lesser order than others in Parts IV and V of the Act, it still represents substantial intervention in the upbringing of the child and could lead to yet further intervention. It should be contemplated only where there is reason for serious concern for the child. It should not be used for a child whose parents are reluctant to use the normal child health services. There should have been a substantial effort to persuade those caring for the child of the need for an assessment and to persuade them to agree to suitable arrangements voluntarily. When an assessment order is obtained it will be necessary for the parents to work with professional practitioners, and their co-operation during the process is essential if there is to be a useful assessment on which to base future action. The matter should be pursued on a multi-disciplinary basis . . . , with pooling of information and consultation on handling the case. Any proposal to apply for a child assessment order and the arrangements to be discussed with the court for the assessment should be considered at a case conference convened under local child protection procedures. The authority will need to be sensitive to issues of gender, race and culture when formulating arrangements for an assessment. The parents may resist making the child available to local authority-appointed professionals but may be amenable to either the family doctor or an independent professional examining, or participating in the examination of the child. Arrangements of this kind may well provide sufficient information about the child's welfare and therefore should not be rejected by the local authority out of hand. If such arrangements were considered as satisfactory by the court hearing an application for a child assessment order this would provide the grounds for refusing the application. The emphasis on a multi-disciplinary assessment however suggests that the opinion of just one health professional will rarely be sufficient . . . .

4.24   Some parents, although willing to co-operate with the terms of a child assessment order, will have fears about the possible removal of their child as a result of the assessment. If used in the proper circumstances follow-up provision to a child assessment order will normally be by way of services to the child and his family to remedy any harm identified. The professional practitioner will need to make this clear and to stress the importance of encouraging the child's development with local authority support where necessary. There will, however, be cases where the results of the assessment dictate that the child should live away from home. The professional practitioner must not shirk from his responsibility in discussing this possibility and emphasising the benefits that will flow from the parents working in partnership with the local authority in these circumstances. Parents whose children have disabilities may be particularly worried by this kind of intervention and will require sensitive handling and reassurance that the intention is to enhance the life and abilities of their child, and that there is no intention to undermine their relationship with their child.

4.25   Although there may be occasions when the most obvious need is for a medical assessment, an assessment should always have a multi-disciplinary dimension. The difficulties and needs of the child must always be seen in the context of his social needs and the abilities and limitations of his parents, extended family and local community to meet these needs. All professional practitioners engaged in working with the family should be encouraged to contribute to a multi-disciplinary assessment both to pool information and to make proposals for future action to support the family.

4.26   A child assessment order puts the professional practitioners on notice and gives them up to seven days to conduct their assessment. This timescale was fixed with the intention of causing the least possible disruption to the child but allowing sufficient time for an assessment to produce the information required by professional workers and parents to formulate together plans for future action. In order to ensure that this work can be achieved within the timescale and that a detailed assessment programme can be presented to the court for it to be able to make the necessary directions, the professional team will need to plan in advance the matters to be covered during the assessment, the practical arrangements for doing this work, and the best way to involve parents and minimise trauma to the child. It has to be accepted that it may not always be possible within the seven days to do more than an initial assessment and obtain an indication of whether further work is necessary. Practitioners should consider ways of extending the assessment period on a voluntary basis if this becomes necessary. If the parents remain unco-operative and there is sufficient information to satisfy the grounds, an interim care or supervision order with conditions should be sought. (Where only one parent consents, no order would be required since s. 2(7) empowers one parent to act alone. However, if one parent objects it would be necessary to obtain an order to avoid the possibility of private law proceedings under s. 8 to resolve the dispute between the parents.)

4.27   Parents should always be told that a child assessment order may be applied for if they persist in refusing to co-operate, the reasons for making the application, the legal effect and detailed implications of the order, and the court procedure that would be followed. This information may be sufficient to persuade them that the authority are genuinely concerned about the child and that the parents should co-operate with the proposed voluntary arrangements. This information should be confirmed in writing backed up by easily understandable leaflets outlining local authority powers and duties and the rights and responsibilities of parents.

12.6   Emergency Protection Orders: S. 44

12.6.1   CRITERIA AND APPLICANTS

CHILDREN ACT 1989

44.   Orders for emergency protection of children

(1)   Where any person ('the applicant') applies to the court for an order to be made under this section with respect to a child, the court may make the order if, but only if, it is satisfied that—

(a)   there is reasonable cause to believe that the child is likely to suffer significant harm if—

(i)   he is not removed to accommodation provided by or on behalf of the applicant; or

(ii)   he does not remain in the place in which he is then being accommodated;

(b)   in the case of an application made by a local authority—

(i)   enquiries are being made with respect to the child under section 47(1)(b); and

(ii)   those enquiries are being frustrated by access to the child being unreasonably refused to a person authorised to seek access and that the applicant has reasonable cause to believe that access to the child is required as a matter of urgency; or

(c)   in the case of an application made by an authorised person—

(i)   the applicant has reasonable cause to suspect that a child is suffering, or is likely to suffer, significant harm;

(ii)   the applicant is making enquiries with respect to the child's welfare; and

(iii)   those enquiries are being frustrated by access to the child being unreasonably refused to a person authorised to seek access and the applicant has reasonable cause to believe that access to the child is required as a matter of urgency.

(2)   In this section—

(a)   'authorised person' means a person who is an authorised person for the purposes of section 31; and

(b)   'a person authorised to seek access', means—

(i)   in the case of an application by a local authority, an officer of the local authority or a person authorised by the authority to act on their behalf in connection with the enquiries; or

(ii)   in the case of an application by an authorised person, that person.

. . .

12.6.2   CONSEQUENCES OF MAKING THE ORDER

CHILDREN ACT 1989

44.   Orders for emergency protection of children

. . .

(4)   While an order under this section ('an emergency protection order') is in force it—

(a)   operates as a direction to any person who is in a position to do so to comply with any request to produce the child to the applicant;

(b)   authorises—

(i)   the removal of the child at any time to accommodation provided by or on behalf of the applicant and his being kept there; or

(ii)   the prevention of the child's removal from any hospital, or other place, in which he was being accommodated immediately before the making of the order; and

(c)   gives the applicant parental responsibility for the child.

(5)   Where an emergency protection order is in force with respect to a child, the applicant—

(a)   shall only exercise the power given by virtue of subsection (4)(b) in order to safeguard the welfare of the child;

(b)   shall take, and shall only take, such action in meeting his parental responsibility for the child as is reasonably required to safeguard or promote the welfare of the child (having regard in particular to the duration of the order); and

(c)   shall comply with the requirements of any regulations made by the Secretary of State for the purposes of this subsection.

(6)   Where the court makes an emergency protection order, it may give such directions (if any) as it considers appropriate with respect to—

(a)   the contact which is, or is not, to be allowed between the child and any named person;

(b)   the medical or psychiatric examination or other assessment of the child.

(7)   Where any direction is given under subsection (6)(b), the child may, if he is of sufficient understanding to make an informed decision, refuse to submit to the examination or other assessment.

(8)   A direction under subsection (6)(a) may impose conditions and one under subsection (6)(b) may be to the effect that there is to be—

(a)   no such examination or assessment; or

(b)   no such examination or assessment unless the court diracts otherwise.

(9)   A direction under subsection (6) may be—

(a)   given when the emergency protection order is made or at any time while it is in force; and

(b) varied at any time on the application of any person falling within any class of person prescribed by rules of court for the purposes of this subsection.

(10) Where an emergency protection order is in force with respect to a child and—

(a) the applicant has exercised the power given by subsection (4)(b)(i) but it appears to him that it is safe for the child to be returned; or

(b) the applicant has exercised the power given by subsection (4)(b)(ii) but it appears to him that it is safe for the child to be allowed to be removed from the place in question,

he shall return the child or (as the case may be) allow him to be removed.

(11) Where he is required by subsection (10) to return the child the applicant shall—

(a) return him to the care of the person from whose care he was removed; or

(b) if that is not reasonably practicable, return him to the care of—

(i) a parent of his;

(ii) any person who is not a parent of his but who has parental responsibility for him; or

(iii) such other person as the applicant (with the agreement of the court) considers appropriate.

(12) Where the applicant has been required by subsection (10) to return the child, or to allow him to be removed, he may again exercise his powers with respect to the child (at any time while the emergency protection order remains in force) if it appears to him that a change in the circumstances of the case makes it necessary for him to do so.

(13) Where an emergency protection order has been made with respect to a child, the applicant shall, subject to any direction given under subsection (6), allow the child reasonable contact with—

(a) his parents;

(b) any person who is not a parent of his but who has parental responsibility for him;

(c) any person with whom he was living immediately before the making of the order;

(d) any person in whose favour a contact order is in force with respect to him;

(e) any person who is allowed to have contact with the child by virtue of an order under section 34; and

(f) any person acting on behalf of any of those persons.

(14) Wherever it is reasonably practicable to do so, an emergency protection order shall name the child; and where it does not name him it shall describe him as clearly as possible.

(15) A person shall be guilty of an offence if he intentionally obstructs any person exercising the power under subsection (4)(b) to remove, or prevent the removal of, a child.

(16) A person guilty of an offence under subsection (15) shall be liable on summary conviction to a fine not exceeding level 3 on the standard scale.

45. Duration of emergency protection orders and other supplemental provisions

(1) An emergency protection order shall have effect for such period, not exceeding eight days, as may be specified in the order.

. . .

(3) Where an emergency protection order is made on an application under section 46(7), the period of eight days mentioned in subsection (1) shall begin with, the first day on which the child was taken into police protection under section 46.

(4) Any person who—

(a) has parental responsibility for a child as the result of an emergency protection order; and

(b) is entitled to apply for a care order with respect to the child,

may apply to the court for the period during which the emergency protection order is to have effect to be extended.

(5) On an application under subsection (4) the court may extend the period during which the order is to have effect by such period, not exceeding seven days, as it thinks fit, but may do so only if it has reasonable cause to believe that the child concerned is likely to suffer significant harm if the order is not extended.

(6)   An emergency protection order may only be extended once.

. . .

(8)   Any of the following may apply to the court for an emergency protection order to be discharged—

(a)   the child;

(b)   a parent of his;

(c)   any person who is not a parent of his but who has parental responsibility for him; or

(d)   any person with whom he was living immediately before the making of the order.

(9)   No application for the discharge of an emergency protection order shall be heard by the court before the expiry of the period of 72 hours beginning with the making of the order.

[(10)   No appeal may be made against—

(a)   the making of, or refusal to make, an emergency protection order;

(b)   the extension of, or refusal to extend, the period during which such an order is to have effect;

(c)   the discharge of, or refusal to discharge, such an order; or

(d)   the giving of, or refusal to give, any direction in connection with such an order.]

(11)   Subsection (8) does not apply—

(a)   where the person who would otherwise be entitled to apply for the emergency protection order to be discharged—

(i)   was given notice (in accordance with rules of court) of the hearing at which the order was made; and

(ii)   was present at that hearing; or

(b)   to any emergency protection order the effective period of which has been extended under subsection (5).

(12)   A court making an emergency protection order may direct that the applicant may, in exercising any powers which he has by virtue of the order, be accompanied by a registered medical practitioner, registered nurse or registered health visitor, if he so chooses.

12.6.2.1   Removal

FAMILY LAW ACT 1996

SCHEDULE 6

3.   After section 44 of the Children Act 1989 insert—

'44A.   Power to include exclusion requirement in emergency protection order

(1)   Where—

(a)   on being satisfied as mentioned in section 44(1)(a), (b) or (c), the court makes an emergency protection order with respect to a child, and

(b)   the conditions mentioned in subsection (2) are satisfied, the court may include an exclusion requirement in the emergency protection order.

(2)   The conditions are—

(a)   that there is reasonable cause to believe that, if a person ("the relevant person") is excluded from a dwelling-house in which the child lives, then—

(i)   in the case of an order made on the ground mentioned in section 44(1)(a), the child will not be likely to suffer significant harm, even though the child is not removed as mentioned in section 44(1)(a)(i) or does not remain as mentioned in section 44(1)(a)(ii), or

(ii)   in the case of an order made on the ground mentioned in paragraph (b) or (c) of section 44(1), the enquiries referred to in that paragraph will cease to be frustrated, and

(b)   that another person living in the dwelling-house (whether a parent of the child or some other person)—

(i)   is able and willing to give to the child the care which it would be reasonable to expect a parent to give him, and

(ii)   consents to the inclusion of the exclusion requirement.

(3)   For the purposes of this section an exclusion requirement is any one or more of the following—

(a)   a provision requiring the relevant person to leave a dwelling-house in which he is living with the child,

(b)   a provision prohibiting the relevant person from entering a dwellinghouse in which the child lives, and

(c)   a provision excluding the relevant person from a defined area in which a dwelling-house in which the child lives is situated.

(4)   The court may provide that the exclusion requirement is to have effect for a shorter period than the other provisions of the order.

(5)   Where the court makes an emergency protection order containing an exclusion requirement, the court may attach a power of arrest to the exclusion requirement.

(6)   Where the court attaches a power of arrest to an exclusion requirement of an emergency protection order, it may provide that the power of arrest is to have effect for a shorter period than the exclusion requirement.

(7)   Any period specified for the purposes of subsection (4) or (6) may be extended by the court (on one or more occasions) on an application to vary or discharge the emergency protection order.

(8)   Where a power of arrest is attached to an exclusion requirement of an emergency protection order by virtue of subsection (5), a constable may arrest without warrant any person whom he has reasonable cause to believe to be in breach of the requirement.

(9)   Sections 47(7), (11) and (12) and 48 of, and Schedule 5 to, the Family Law Act 1996 shall have effect in relation to a person arrested under subsection (8) of this section as they have effect in relation to a person arrested under section 47(6) of that Act.

(10)   If, while an emergency protection order containing an exclusion requirement is in force, the applicant has removed the child from the dwellinghouse from which the relevant person is excluded to other accommodation for a continuous period of more than 24 hours, the order shall cease to have effect in so far as it imposes the exclusion requirement.

44B.   Undertakings relating to emergency protection orders

(1)   In any case where the court has power to include an exclusion requirement in an emergency protection order, the court may accept an undertaking from the relevant person.

(2)   No power of arrest may be attached to any undertaking given under subsection (1).

(3)   An undertaking given to a court under subsection (1)—

(a)   shall be enforceable as if it were an order of the court, and

(b)   shall cease to have effect if, while it is in force, the applicant has removed the child from the dwelling-house from which the relevant person is excluded to other accommodation for a continuous period of more than 24 hours.

(4)   This section has effect without prejudice to the powers of the High Court and county court apart from this section.

(5)   In this section "exclusion requirement" and "relevant person" have the same meaning as in section 44A.'

4.   In section 45 of the Children Act 1989 (duration of emergency protection orders and other supplemental provisions), insert after subsection (8)—

'(8A)   On the application of a person who is not entitled to apply for the order to be discharged, but who is a person to whom an exclusion requirement contained in the order applies, an emergency protection order may be varied or discharged by the court in so far as it imposes the exclusion requirement.

(8B)   Where a power of arrest has been attached to an exclusion requirement of an emergency protection order, the court may, on the application of any person entitled to apply for the discharge of the order so far as it imposes the exclusion requirement, vary or discharge the order in so far as it confers a power of arrest (whether or not any application has been made to vary or discharge any other provision of the order).'

5. In section 105(1) of the Children Act 1989 (interpretation), after the definition of 'domestic premises', insert—

'dwelling-house' includes—

(a)   any building or part of a building which is occupied as a dwelling;

(b)   any caravan, house-boat or structure which is occupied as a dwelling; and any yard, garden, garage or outhouse belonging to it and occupied with it;'.

CHILDREN ACT 1989

SCHEDULE 2

5.—(1)   Where—

(a)   it appears to a local authority that a child who is living on particular premises is suffering, or is likely to suffer, ill treatment at the hands of another person who is living on those premises; and

(b)   that other person proposes to move from the premises, the authority may assist that other person to obtain alternative accommodation.

(2)   Assistance given under this paragraph may be in cash.

12.6.2.2   Parental responsibility

F v WIRRAL METROPOLITAN BOROUGH COUNCIL [1991] 2 WLR 1132 (CA)

In January 1978, the plaintiff, then suffering from depression, agreed to place her two children, born in 1975 and 1976, in voluntary care under section 1 of the Children Act 1948. She alleged that her agreement was based on assurances given by the first defendants, the local authority, that the placement was temporary and that the children would be returned to her when she recovered. On 23 March 1978, the second defendants, another local authority acting as the first defendants' agents, placed the children with long term foster parents with a view to adoption. The first defendants then passed a resolution assuming parental rights over the children under section 2 of the Act. In February 1979, they passed a second resolution that the children should remain in care, that the parental rights resolution would not be revoked and that rehabilitation with their parents was not in the children's best interests, and they informed the plaintiff of that resolution. By a writ and a statement of claim, dated 3 June 1985 and subsequently amended, the plaintiff claimed against the defendants damages for negligence and breach of duty in placing the children with long term foster parents, and for unlawfully interfering with her rights and privileges as a parent and hindering her in the enjoyment and exercise of those rights and privileges. On the defendants' application, the judge, having refused the plaintiff leave to amend her reply so as to allege that the defendants had deliberately concealed her cause of action from her, made an order striking out the statement of claim, under RSC, Ord. 18, r. 19(1)(a) and (b), on the grounds that the statement of claim disclosed no reasonable cause of action and that the claim was vexatious in that it was statute-barred.

On the plaintiff's appeal.

HELD: dismissing the appeal . . . That since the exercise by local authorities of statutory powers in relation to children was subject to both statutory control and the remedy of judicial review the plaintiff did not have (*per* Purchas LJ it was doubtful whether the plaintiff had) a cause of action against the defendants in negligence; and that, given the statutory framework within which local authorities carried out their duties in relation to children, it was not open to the court to recognise the existence of an independent tort of interference with parental rights; that (*per* Purchas and Stuart-Smith LJJ) any claim in negligence was statute-barred; and that, accordingly, the statement of claim had been properly struck out under RSC Ord. 18, r. 19(1)(a) and (b).

12.6.2.3   Appealing the order

RE P (EMERGENCY PROTECTION ORDER) [1996] 1 FLR 482 (FamD)

JOHNSON J: These proceedings relate to M who was born on 17 October 1994. On 7 and 8 December 1994, when he was just a few weeks old, he came on two occasions near to death. The reason for that has been the subject of very considerable investigation by paediatricians and others of unquestionable integrity and the highest experience and qualification. The suggestion made by the paediatricians who examined and saved M at the time was that someone had tried to suffocate him. Suspicion focused on his mother.

In these proceedings the mother has had the assistance of two consultant paediatricians. There has been also the evidence of the paediatricians who cared for M at the time and there has been evidence from Professor Southall who, with Dr Samuels, has developed a particular experience in tragedies of this kind. Those doctors have been at pains to analyse the possible causes of what happened to M and in the event a consensus has emerged that there was no medical cause for what happened. The last possible cause that the doctors wanted to eliminate was that the difficulties with M breathing on these two major occasions were caused by spasms resulting from some specific form of epilepsy. In order to eliminate that possible cause it was necessary for an appropriately experienced doctor to examine a scan of part of M's brain. Unhappily bureaucratic wrangling over who should pay the modest cost of that caused some unwarranted delay which I sought to overcome shortly before the main hearing of this case by indicating that the cost involved would be a proper legal aid disbursement, and so it was that this final possibility was only eliminated by the doctors yesterday, when the case started. The scan was described as normal. Accordingly, the medical evidence from these very distinguished and experienced men has arrived at a consensus that there is no medical cause for what happened and that the overwhelming probability is that M's mother smothered him in some way in some quick moment of time which no one can identify for sure. However, the evidence does not consist only of the opinion of the doctors. The mother has given accounts of what happened which contain inconsistencies and she has said things which were patently and obviously untrue as, for example, by asserting to the doctors that she was qualified as a nurse.

There are two matters which I think call for further comment which are really extraneous to the central issue, but I think I should not conclude this judgment without a brief mention of these two questions. After the incidents of 7 and 8 December 1994, the local authority obtained emergency protection orders which fell to be renewed on 29 December 1994. The application for renewal was made to three justices sitting in the Family Proceedings Court. They had evidence from a consultant paediatrician both in writing and orally. He was the paediatrician who had actually seen M at the material times. He said in his written report that somebody had interfered with M's breathing thereby causing his collapse. He said that wishing to have other professional opinion, he had consulted two other paediatricians who, he told the magistrates, were amongst the UK's leading experts on unusual breathing problems in small children. Their opinion, he told the magistrates, was that there was a very high possibility that M's breathing problems had been induced rather than having been caused by some medical condition. In the light of that evidence one would have expected a court to conclude that at the very least there was some risk to M that required the making of an emergency protection order, The risk was not of neglect or of abuse, but was life-threatening. The magistrates declined to extend the emergency protection order. Their reasons are brief in the extreme, but the suggestion from those who were present is that the magistrates may have been impressed by the fact that Dr Scanlon told them in his oral evidence that there had been other occasions of a far less serious nature when there had been some irregularity in M's breathing which could not possibly have been caused by his mother. That does not seem to me to bear in any way upon the opinion expressed by Dr Scanlon as to the cause of the two major episodes, supported, as his opinion was, by these two other experts.

I have chosen to refer to this point, not by way of criticism of the justices, but to draw attention to the fact, as experienced counsel before me all accept, that the justices having refused to extend the emergency protection order, the Children Act 1989 lacked any effective procedure by which the local authority could challenge that decision. Various devices have been suggested such, for example, as the immediate issue of an application for a care order coupled with an application for an interim care order to the justices who had a few minutes earlier refused to extend an emergency protection order. There was the possibility of asking the justices' clerk to refer an application for a care order to the county court, and in the event of his declining to do so, a referral to the district judge. All of that seems to me to be very cumbersome and, given the consequences that might have followed for M on that refusal to extend the emergency protection order, it does seem to me that consideration should be given to providing a mechanism for review. That mechanism would have to be one which could be operated very quickly.

12.7 The Guardian ad Litem

CHILDREN ACT 1989

41. Representation of child and his interests in certain proceedings

(1) For the purpose of any specified proceedings, the court shall appoint a guardian ad litem for the child concerned unless satisfied that it is not necessary to do so in order to safeguard his interests.

(2) The guardian ad litem shall—

(a) be appointed in accordance with rules of court; and

(b) be under a duty to safeguard the interests of the child in the manner prescribed by such rules.

(3) Where—

(a) the child concerned is not represented by a solicitor; and

(b) any of the conditions mentioned in subsection (4) is satisfied, the court may appoint a solicitor to represent him.

(4) The conditions are that—

(a) no guardian ad litem has been appointed for the child;

(b) the child has sufficient understanding to instruct a solicitor and wishes to do so;

(c) it appears to the court that it would be in the child's best interests for him to be represented by a solicitor.

. . .

(6) In this section 'specified proceedings' means any proceedings—

(a) on an application for a care order or supervision order;

(b) in which the court has given a direction under section 37(1) and has made, or is considering whether to make, an interim care order;

(c) on an application for the discharge of a care order or the variation or discharge of a supervision order;

(d) on an application under section 39(4);

(e) in which the court is considering whether to make a residence order with respect to a child who is the subject of a care order;

(f) with respect to contact between a child who is the subject of a care order and any other person;

(g) under Part V;

(h) on an appeal against—

(i) the making of, or refusal to make, a care order, supervision order or any order under section 34;

(ii) the making of, or refusal to make, a residence order with respect to a child who is the subject of a care order; or

(iii) the variation or discharge, or refusal of an application to vary or discharge, an order of a kind mentioned in subparagraph (i) or (ii);

(iv) the refusal of an application under section 39(4); or

(v) the making of, or refusal to make, an order under Part V; or

(vi) which are specified for the time being, for the purposes of this section, by rules of court.

CASE STUDY

INTRODUCTORY NOTE

Within this scenario, there is always the possibility that you may choose a different option to that in the answer. As long as you can justify your choice, and have the evidence to support it, you are unlikely to be severely marked down if this were a coursework. Throughout the scenario the notion of working in partnership and voluntary steps should be primary considerations. The key to understanding the Children Act 1989 and public law is to avoid legalistic remedies if voluntary options would work.

You should also note that this scenario is based loosely on a real child care case, and the steps taken at the various stages reflect those steps and actions taken by the local authority at those points in time.

STAGE 1

From the information given it would appear that there is no involvement of social services, and that the problem with Emma has been dealt with by the school acting alone.

Following the discovery of bruises and bite marks, the school should contact the child care department of the local authority. As you should recall, the Children Act 1989 and the associated guidance operates on a basis of inter-agency cooperation.

Once a referral has been made by the school, a social worker will review the matter, and a s. 47 investigation may be instigated. Whilst it may be possible for the social worker to visit Emma at school to view the injuries, this should not take place without the parents' consent. Any examination of the child, unless necessary in an emergency, if carried out in the absence of consent is a battery and damages may be sought in a legal action. Hence, the school should be advised to contact the parents and to seek their permission for Emma to be seen by a school doctor, or her own GP. If the parents refuse consent, it may be possible to seek an emergency protection order under s. 44, however the injuries are not really that severe so the criteria under s. 44(1)(a) are not likely to be satisfied. Failure to allow examination may also not satisfy s. 44(1)(b) since the parents may be willing to co-operate in all other matters.

In carrying out the review of the case, the social worker will check the area child protection register, and possibly other records, to establish if the family has been involved in the past with social services, or other agencies. Whilst s. 47 does not require a mandatory investigation if the local authority do not consider enquiries to be necessary, it is suggested that at least one visit needs to be made to the parents. Again, if the parents do not co-operate, or the visit heightens concern, an emergency protection order may be considered, but the situation must be one of an emergency nature. From the facts here, again this is not really looking like an emergency case.

Having started the investigation as a result of the referral from the school, a child protection case conference should be convened. Guidance suggests that this must be within the eight days following the referral. However, this does not always occur, given the number of professionals involved, and is not a legal requirement in any event.

Thus, the action to be taken after the events in Stage 1 are:
- referral by the school to the social services department;
- school to seek parental consent to have the child examined and details of the injuries recorded by medical professional;
- social worker to check existing records for previous or on-going involvement with the family;
- social worker to commence a s. 47 investigation as there is cause to believe that the child is suffering significant harm;
- social worker to visit home and endeavour to see child and to discuss injuries with the parents;
- child protection case conference to be convened.

STAGE 2

At this stage only basic information has been obtained, but it does suggest that the children are at risk with regard to their health and development. All the children in the family are not developing to the centile charts, although this information has to be assessed with the parents in mind. A child born to small parents will invariably be below average on the centile charts, equally a child born to large parents will be likely to be above the average on the charts. However, taking this developmental information together with the state of the home, some action will be needed.

The action you should be thinking of would hopefully not be to remove the children from the home. This situation is not, on the information provided, that bad. Also, the principle of non-intervention should be your primary concern. Hence, the provision of services looks to be a likely solution at this stage. Under s. 17 the local authority can provide services to children in need and their families. The range of services is widespread, and can be tailored to the individual family. However, you should recall that the provision of services is dependent upon the overall area provision and budgets in the local authority department. Also you should note that services can exceptionally be provided in cash, albeit that many local authorities will not do so if the services can be provided in kind.

Here possible services would include:-

- the provision of a fireguard for the home;
- involvement of a family aide to help Mrs P develop her parenting skills;
- the provision of day care facilities for the older toddlers to allow Mrs P time with the twins;
- dietary advice to be provided by the Health Visitor, and possibly an increased visiting schedule;
- counselling to Mr P to prevent his attitude to his wife exacerbating the situation;
- expectations as to the condition of the children regarding dress and cleanliness to be set out.

You should also have considered what action the case conference can take, whilst it can discuss and formulate a care plan as indicated above, its remit is to decide whether or not to register the children's names on the child protection register. In this situation registration is clear (or should be) under the category of neglect, and possibly physical abuse for Emma in addition to neglect.

The care plan outlined above can be incorporated into a contract to be drawn up between the parents and the social services. Contracts of this kind will often include the aims and achievements that are to be met by the various parties. The contract would not be legally binding, but in many cases do result in better co-operation between families and the social services and in improvements in care for the children.

A review date for the childrens' progress would have to be set and a key worker allocated to the family's case.

STAGE 3

As you can see from the information provided, the situation appears to have deteriorated rather than improved following the case conference.

The attendance of the school nurse to Emma's injuries should be subject to parental consent, however in this situation it may be justified as being an emergency situation.

The appointed key worker would need to be contacted and informed of Emma's condition together with her statement to the teacher. The teacher would need to make a written note of what Emma said as soon as possible since this could be used as evidence in court.

The social worker will need to witness the injuries and make a record of them. Parental consent should be obtained before this takes place, although if consent is not forthcoming legal action could be commenced. The key worker would need to see the parents to clarify how the injuries occurred and to obtain consent for an examination by a paediatrician. In this situation the injuries will warrant a referral to the police for investigation. Guidance should exist between the police and the social services with regard to joint investigation of child abuse cases.

When Emma is questioned further on the cause of her injuries, this will need to be done in such a way that Emma is not led or prompted, otherwise the evidence may be thrown out in any later court proceedings.

Given the severity of Emma's injuries and the alleged cause, a decision will need to be made quickly as to what should happen to Emma and her siblings. The action to be taken will depend on the reaction of the parents and the nature of the explanation given for the injuries, together with the medical opinion. However, from the history of this scenario, and the child's explanation of the injuries, it is unlikely that she will be allowed to return home, and there must be question marks over the safety of the other children.

Here you have two options to remove the children. The parents may agree for the children to be accommodated by the local authority on a voluntary basis under s. 20 of the 1989 Act. This would continue the theme of non-intervention but would not prevent the parents from changing their minds and removing the children at a later stage. It would not give the local authority parental responsibility except to the extent that parental responsibility for day-to-day care would be delegated by the parents.

The alternative, and more interventionist approach, would be for the local authority to seek emergency protection orders in respect of the children. It would be inappropriate to apply simply for Emma since the whole family has suffered in the past. The benefit of this route would be that the local authority would get parental responsibility, and would have a lesser chance of the children being removed, since the emergency protection orders would need to be the subject of a discharge application.

With the information you have, it would be necessary for you to outline both options (there is a third — to leave the children where they are, but hopefully none of you have taken this route) and then make a decision as to which you prefer explaining why.

If you decided to apply for an emergency protection order you should have completed the application form below. The important thing for you to have considered when completing this form is which of the criteria you select for the application. As you know, the local authority can use either s. 44(1)(a) or s. 44(1)(b), and you must select the appropriate one. It is unlikely that s. 44(1)(b) will be used in this case. Whilst the local authority are arguably still investigating the family, are the parents refusing access? It is not really clear from the information, and hence the s. 44(1)(a) criteria will be a safer selection. If you cannot remember the differences between the application criteria, return to the **Learning Text** and your notes to refresh your memory.

If this were an examination or coursework you would need to explain a little about the application process (*inter* or *ex parte* etc.) and the consequences of the order.

As stated earlier, you may have gone for either option. In reality, emergency protection orders were sought under s. 44(1)(a) with respect to all the children and successfully obtained.

Application for an order   Form C1

Children Act 1989

The court	To be completed by the court
	Date issued
	Case number
The full name(s) of the child(ren)	Child(ren)'s number(s)

1 About you (the applicant)

State   •   *your title, full name, address, telephone number, date of birth and relationship to each child above*

        •   *your solicitor's name, address, reference, telephone, FAX and DX numbers.*

2 The child(ren) and the order(s) you are applying for

For each child state   •   *the full name, date of birth and sex*

        •   *the type of order(s) you are applying for (for example, residence order, contact order, supervision order).*

C1(M)   (11.94) Printed by Satellite Press Limited

3 Other cases which concern the child(ren)

If there have ever been, or there are pending, any court cases which concern
- *a child whose name you have put in paragraph 2*
- *a full, half or step brother or sister of a child whose name you have put in paragraph 2*
- *a person in this case who is or has been, involved in caring for a child whose name you have put in paragraph 2*

attach a copy of the relevant order and give
- *the name of the court*
- *the name and **panel** address (if known) of the guardian ad litem, if appointed*
- *the name and contact address (if known) of the court welfare officer, if appointed*
- *the name and contact address (if known) of the solicitor appointed for the child(ren).*

4 The respondent(s)

Appendix 3 Family Proceedings Rules 1991; Schedule 2 Family Proceedings Courts (Children Act 1989) Rules 1991

For each respondent state
- *the title, full name and address*
- *the date of birth (if known) or the age*
- *the relationship to each child.*

C1

5 Others to whom notice is to be given

Appendix 3 Family Proceedings Rules 1991; Schedule 2 Family Proceedings Courts (Children Act 1989) Rules 1991

For each person state • *the title, full name and address*
• *the date of birth (if known) or age*
• *the relationship to each child*

6 The care of the child(ren)

For each child in paragraph 2 state
• *the child's current address and how long the child has lived there*
• *whether it is the child's usual address and who cares for the child there*
• *the child's relationship to the other children (if any).*

7 Social Services

For each child in paragraph 2 state
• *whether the child is known to the Social Services.*
   If so, give the name of the social worker and the address of the Social Services department.
• *whether the child is, or has been, on the Child Protection Register. If so, give the date of registration.*

8 The education and health of the child(ren)

For each child state
- *the name of the school, college or place of training which the child attends*
- *whether the child is in good health. Give details of any serious disabilities or ill health.*
- *whether the child has any special needs.*

9 The parents of the child(ren)

For each child state
- *the full name of the child's mother and father*
- *whether the parents are, or have been, married to each other*
- *whether the parents live together. If so, where.*
- *whether, to your knowledge, either of the parents have been involved in a court case concerning a child. If so, give the date and the name of the court.*

10 The family of the child(ren) (other children)

For any other child not already mentioned in the family (for example, a brother or a half sister) state
- *the full name and address*
- *the date of birth (if known) or age*
- *the relationship of the child to you.*

C1

11 Other adults

State • *the full name of any other adults (for example, lodgers) who live at the same address as any child named in paragraph 2*
• *whether they live there all the time*
• *whether, to your knowledge, the adult has been involved in a court case concerning a child. If so, give the date and the name of the court.*

12 Your reason(s) for applying and any plans for the child(ren)

State briefly your reasons for applying and what you want the court to order.
• *Do not give a full statement if you are applying for an order under Section 8 of Children Act 1989. You may be asked to provide a full statement later.*
• *Do not complete this section if this form is accompanied by a prescribed supplement.*

13 At the court

State • *whether you will need an interpreter at court (parties are responsible for providing their own). If so, specify the language.*
• *whether disabled facilities will be needed at court.*

Signed   Date
(Applicant)

C1

OYEZ

Supplement for an Application for an Emergency Protection Order

Form C11

(Section 44 Children Act 1989)

The Court	To be completed by the Court
	Date Issued
The full name(s) of the child(ren)	Case number
	Child(ren)'s number(s)

1. Description of the child(ren).

If a child's identity is not known, state details which will identify the child. You may enclose a recent photograph of the child, which should be dated.

2. The grounds for the application.

The grounds are:

ANY APPLICANT

A ☐ that there is reasonable cause to believe that [this] [these] child[ren] [is] [are] likely to suffer significant harm if

☐ the child[ren] [is] [are] not removed to accommodation provided by or on behalf of this Applicant

or ☐ the child[ren] [does] [do] not remain in the place where [the child] [they] [is] [are] currently being accommodated.

LOCAL AUTHORITY APPLICANTS

B ☐ that enquiries are being made about the welfare of the child[ren] under section 47(1)(b) of Children Act 1989 **and** those enquiries are being frustrated by access to the child[ren] being unreasonably refused to someone who is authorised to seek access **and** there is reasonable cause to believe that access to the child[ren] is required as a matter of urgency.

AUTHORISED PERSON APPLICANTS

C ☐ that there is reasonable cause to suspect that the child[ren] [is] [are] suffering, or [is] [are] likely to suffer, significant harm **and** enquiries are being made with respect to the welfare of the child[ren] **and** those enquiries are being frustrated by access to the child[ren] being unreasonably refused to someone who is authorised to seek access **and** there is reasonable cause to believe that access to the child[ren] is required as a matter of urgency.

[P.T.O.

3. The additional order(s) applied for.

☐ information on the whereabouts of the child[ren] (section 48(1) Children Act 1989).

☐ authorisation for entry of premises (section 48(3) Children Act 1989).

☐ authorisation to search for another child on the premises (section 48(4) Children Act 1989).

4. The Direction(s) sought.

☐ contact (section 44(6)(a) Children Act 1989).

☐ a medical or psychiatric examination or other assessment of the child[ren] (section 44(6)(b) Children Act 1989).

☐ to be accompanied by a registered medical practitioner, registered nurse or registered health visitor (section 45(12) Children Act 1989).

5. The reason(s) for the application.

If you are relying on a report or other documentary evidence, state the date(s) and author(s) and enclose a copy.

Signed   Date
(Applicant)

OYEZ The Solicitors' Law Stationery Society Ltd, Oyez House, 7 Spa Road, London SE16 3QQ   *1995 Edition*
                                                                                                     11.94 F28414
                                                                                                     5037609

Children Act—C11

PART TWO

12.8   The Criteria

CHILDREN ACT 1989

31.   Care and supervision orders

(1)   On the application of any local authority or authorised person, the court may make an order—

(a)   placing the child with respect to whom the application is made in the care of a designated local authority; or

(b)   putting him under the supervision of a designated local authority or of a probation officer.

(2)   A court may only make a care order or supervision order if it is satisfied—

(a)   that the child concerned is suffering, or is likely to suffer, significant harm; and

(b)   that the harm, or likelihood of harm, is attributable to—

(i)   the care given to the child, or likely to be given to him if the order were not made, not being what it would be reasonable to expect a parent to give to him; or

(ii)   the child's being beyond parental control.

(3)   No care order or supervision order may be made with respect to a child who has reached the age of 17 (or 16, in the case of a child who is married).

. . .

(5)   The court may—

(a)   on an application for a care order, make a supervision order;

(b)   on an application for a supervision order, make a care order.

. . .

(9)   in this section—

'authorised person' means—

(a)   the National Society for the Prevention of Cruelty to Children and any of its officers; and

(b)   any person authorised by order of the Secretary of State to bring proceedings under this section and any officer of a body which is so authorised;

'harm' means ill-treatment or the impairment of health or development;

'development' means physical, intellectual, emotional, social or behavioural development;

'health' means physical or mental health; and

'ill-treatment' includes sexual abuse and forms of ill-treatment which are not physical.

(10)   Where the question of whether harm suffered by a child is significant turns on the child's health or development, his health or development shall be compared with that which could reasonably be expected of a similar child.

12.8.1   SIGNIFICANT HARM

12.8.1.1   The meaning of significant harm

HUMBERSIDE COUNTY COUNCIL v *B* **[1993] 1 FLR 257 (FamD)**

BOOTH J: This is an appeal by the child with whom the court is concerned, a little girl, N, just 6 months of age, acting through her guardian ad litem, against an order of the Scunthorpe Family Proceedings Court made on 10 February 1992 whereby they committed her interim care to the local authority, the Humberside County Council. This was a difficult case for the justices. It has been a difficult case on appeal, and I am very grateful to counsel for the help I have received from them.

The material facts are these. The mother and the father are both parties to these proceedings. The mother is Mrs B. She is a lady now aged 37. She is a diagnosed schizophrenic and her condition is controlled by medication. As a young girl she was brought up by her aunt, Mrs W, in the company of her aunt's daughter, the mother's cousin, who is now Mrs H. Subsequently, when she attained her majority, the mother lived independently.

The father, Mr B, is a man somewhat younger than the mother. He is aged 29. He also is a diagnosed schizophrenic. His condition, too, is controlled by medication. He was brought up in the home of his mother. He was working, but for the last few years has been unemployed.

But in January 1992 events occurred which led to N leaving the care of her parents. The first such event occurred on either 1 or 2 January 1992, when it transpired that N had been left alone in the flat. What appears to have happened next is that the father went out to a social club by himself for about an hour, and the mother, who was looking after N, popped out of the flat for about 10 minutes to buy some milk. The parents made no attempt to conceal that. It came to the knowledge of the social workers who regarded it seriously, rightly so, and investigated the matter, although no harm had befallen N. At a case conference which was held on 13 January 1992 it was recommended that a comprehensive assessment of the family should take place at the Family Advice and Day Care Centre and that the assessment should take place as soon as possible.

There then followed a number of occasions when N was left overnight with members of the extended families.

On 23 January 1992 the local authority held a further case conference. The recommendation of that conference was that the local authority should seek a care order, and in the meantime an interim care order, and should pursue the family assessment which had been previously recommended. That application was filed in the family proceedings court on 27 January 1992. The guardian ad litem was appointed to represent N.

The case came on for hearing on 3 February 1992.

. . . On 10 February 1992 the interim care order was made by the bench, who gave full reasons for it. . . .

The issues in this appeal, which is of course supported by the parents, are first whether the justices were justified on the evidence before them to find that there were reasonable grounds for believing that N was likely to suffer significant harm attributable to the care that was likely to be given to her if no order was made.

The grounds of appeal are advanced by the child through her guardian ad litem, supported by the parents. It was submitted that there was not sufficient evidence on which the justices could reasonably believe that the child was likely to suffer significant harm if she were to return to her parents. The Act requires the court to be so satisfied. It does not require the court to consider whether or not any other party was so satisfied. But I do not think that for the purposes of this appeal anything turns on the expression by the justices as to their finding that the local authority had reasonable cause to believe the child was likely to suffer significant harm.

In a case such as this, it appears to me that the approach must be to consider first what happened to N when she was in the care of her parents, and then go on to consider whether in the event of her return to them she would be likely to suffer what could properly come within the category of significant harm. Significant harm was defined by Miss Black, in accordance with dictionary definitions, first as being harm that the court should consider was either considerable or noteworthy or important. Then she expressed it as harm which the court should take into account in considering a child's future. I think that is a very apt and helpful submission. There is of course in the circumstances of this case no question that N is presently suffering any harm in the care of Mrs H.

Returning to the events which occurred during the time that N was with her parents, it is accepted that she was left alone in the flat on one occasion. Neither the mother nor the father gave evidence before the justices either by means of written statements or orally. That is not in the circumstances of this case a matter of criticism at all. Much of the factual evidence was agreed. It was I think generally accepted that for a minimum period of 10 minutes and on any view a maximum period of one hour, this child was left alone. The mother's explanation was that it was a matter of 10 minutes when she was out buying milk, and that appears to be the case. It is also an accepted fact that N was placed in the care of members of the family at least for three overnight stays, with a possibility there was a fourth. It would appear that the justices were wrong on the evidence in holding, as they did, that there were five such occasions, but that I think is not material to the end result of this case. It is also accepted as a fact that N sustained the bruising seen on 19 January 1992 by Mrs H, and on 20 January 1992 by Dr Wing. Those are the matters which are chiefly relied on by the local authority.

The submission is made on behalf of the appellant that whether or not a child may be likely to suffer significant harm must be seen in the context of all the circumstances of the case and in relation to the particular child with whom the court is concerned. The child may be exceptionally vulnerable in one way or another. For example, if a child suffers from brittle bones then a push or a slap might be of great significance, whereas in the case of a child who does not so suffer it may be a minimal incident. N is not an especially vulnerable child, but she is a very young baby; she still is only 6 months of age. The matters which are advanced by the appellant, and which are matters to which the court must pay attention having regard to the circumstances of the case, are that N was a happy, healthy baby in the care of her parents and, as the justices themselves found, achieved her developmental milestones.

It is submitted also that the matters which cause concern happened within a very short space of time, between 1 and 19 January 1992, whereas N has successfully lived at home from the time she was discharged from hospital after her birth until the beginning of January 1992 when matters went awry, that being a quite considerably longer period of time.

It was pointed out to me, as indeed it was pointed out to the justices, that it is certainly not unusual for a baby to be left in the care of members of the extended family, particularly when the families are close families, and when parents are in the situation that these two parents were, coping with their first child. It is further submitted that the justices placed too great a weight on the bruising N sustained, and the fact that the parents could not offer any explanation as to how it occurred. While it is accepted by the appellant that the parents needed advice and guidance, and continuous repetition was required of that advice and guidance, it is said that the evidence showed that they responded very well and always cooperated with social workers. So it is said even if they made mistakes in regard to N's care, they were not likely to repeat them. For example, there is no suggestion that she was left alone in the flat after the one occasion which was examined in some depth with the parents, and they were told of the undesirability of that occurring again. Against that, the local authority have placed very considerable emphasis upon the incident of bruising and upon the evidence of Dr Wing.

Miss Black, on behalf of the local authority, submitted that the bruising is significant in itself. This was first because the child was immobile and could not have caused any injury to herself, secondly because there was no explanation as to how it occurred when one could have been expected, and thirdly because it is, she suggests, significant in its implications, in particular that the perpetrator may have lost control as was suggested by Dr Wing.

The local authority's submission is that these parents have required constant guidance and help, and although the situation in the home was controlled and stable until the end of December 1991, from January 1992 matters deteriorated very quickly indeed. Despite the input which was considerable by social services, these injuries occurred. In all the circumstances, it is submitted, at this stage on the evidence, there must be a reasonable belief in the likelihood of further significant harm being perpetrated on the child if she were to return home. That is, in a nutshell, the local authority case.

I am satisfied that on the evidence before the justices there were grounds on which they could be satisfied that there were reasonable grounds for believing that N would be likely to suffer significant harm attributable to the care of the parents if she were to be returned to them. I accept 'significant harm' has the meaning that Miss Black suggests, and is harm which the court should take into account in considering N's future.

BIRMINGHAM CITY COUNCIL v D; BIRMINGHAM CITY COUNCIL v M [1994] 2 FLR 502 (FamD)

THORPE J: These applications were directed to be heard together since both cases raise the same short point of law. The circumstances that give rise to the applications are not in dispute and can be shortly recorded.

In the case of the D family the court is concerned with two children aged 6 and 5. They are the children of Ms D who cohabited for a number of years with their father before her unexpected death on 5 March 1990. No testamentary guardian appointed by her will and the father of the children declined any responsibility after her death.

Accordingly, the local authority which had undertaken accommodation of the children after the breakdown of a number of placements in the extended family made application on 9 December 1993 for care orders in respect of both children.

Turning to the M family, the applications concern two boys, of Bangladeshi origin, aged 16 and 15. Their mother died shortly after their birth and thereafter they were cared for by their father and stepmother.

However, in February 1992 their father died in Bangladesh, where their stepmother remained. At the date of his father's death the younger boy was living in this country in accommodation which was subsequently made the subject of foster care approval. He was subsequently joined by his older brother.

Again, in their case the local authority apply for care orders. In both cases there is no adult holding parental responsibility for any of the children.

The essential argument for the local authority is that the absence of parental responsibility in any person or body imperils the children. They accept that existing powers are sufficient when things run smoothly, but they contend that the wider powers that would arise from parental responsibility are essential to cope with the unforeseen.

The route to such wider powers must be via a care order is their next submission, for the restrictions in s. 100 of the Children Act 1989 are too extensive to enable a local authority to meet the perceived deficiency by application to invoke the wardship jurisdiction. But in applying for care orders they still must meet and surmount the restriction contained in s. 31 of the Act.

Section 31(2), provides that:

A court may only make a care order . . . if it is satisfied—
    (a)   that the child concerned is suffering, or is likely to suffer, significant harm; and
    (b)   that the harm, or likelihood of harm, is attributable to—
       (i)   the care given to the child, or likely to be given to him if the order were not made, not being what it would be reasonable to expect a parent to give to him.

Mr McCarthy, for the local authority, concedes that none of these children is suffering from significant harm, but he says that the evidence establishes that there is a likelihood or risk of significant harm in a future in which the local authority is not fully empowered to deal with crises or emergencies.

He relies upon a decision of the Court of Appeal in the case of *Newham London Borough Council v AG* [1993] 1 FLR 281, and particularly on the passage at p. 289 in which the President said:

I very much hope that in approaching cases under the Children Act 1989 courts will not be invited to perform in every case a strict legalistic analysis of the statutory meaning of s. 31. Of course, the words of the statute must be considered, but I do not believe that Parliament intended them to be unduly restrictive when the evidence clearly indicates that a certain course should be taken in order to protect the child.

The applications are resisted by the guardians ad litem in both cases. The arguments presented by the guardians are basically similar, although embellishments reflect the different facts in the two cases. A common thread submits that the needs of orphaned children are specifically dealt with in ss. 20, 22 and 23 of the statute. It is emphasised that s. 20 requires:

Every local authority shall provide accommodation for any child in need within their area who appears to them to require accommodation as a result of—
    (a)   there being no person who has parental responsibility for him.

The duties of local authorities in relation to children looked after by them include the duty under s. 22(3):

(a)   to safeguard and promote his welfare; and

(b)   to make such use of services available for children cared for by their own parents as appears to the authority reasonable in his case.

Section 23(1) imposes duties on the local authority looking after a child:

(a)   when he is in their care, to provide accommodation for him; and

(b)   to maintain him in other respects apart from providing accommodation for him.

Furthermore, s. 24 provides ongoing responsibilities in respect of children who were accommodated under those provisions after they have ceased to be so accommodated. That duty is to assist and befriend with a view to promoting their welfare. The duty arises equally in the case of children who have been in care and children who have been simply accommodated.

Those sections, it is submitted on behalf of the guardians, provide a comprehensive and specific series of duties to enable the local authority to meet the needs of children who by virtue of the absence of parental support are dependent on local authority accommodation.

In the case of the D children it is submitted that the likely interval between this hearing and all adoption order is to be measured in months. In the case of the M children it is submitted that it is only 10 months in the case of the elder boy before the expiration of the period in which it is open to the local authority to apply for a care order.

In both cases it is submitted that their lives are well-settled and managed. It would be a plain distortion of the threshold test to find some theoretical risk of significant harm when none in reality is discernible.

I prefer the submissions of the guardians ad litem. Section 31 is plainly designed to protect families from invasive care orders unless there is a manifest need evidenced by a perceptible risk of significant harm. Of course in these cases the local authority does not seek to invade, but to protect and compensate children who have been bereft of parental support. I have every sympathy with the local authority's motives and their aims, but I must construe s. 31 sensibly and realistically. If there is some shortcoming in the statutory framework it is not for me to remedy the deficiency by a strained construction of s. 31, particularly in the light of the opposition of the guardians ad litem.

I conclude that it would be wrong to hold that on the undisputed facts in these cases the s. 31 threshold has been crossed. Obviously, if conditions were to change radically and present plans miscarry, it would be open to the local authority to renew the applications, but as things stand I conclude that it would be wrong to make care orders to meet the needs of any of these four children.

RE M (CARE ORDER: PARENTAL RESPONSIBILITY) [1996] 2 FLR 84 (FamD)

CAZALET J: On 17 February 1995 a baby boy who was only a few days old was abandoned on the steps of a health centre. He had been placed in a holdall. He was found by two clinic workers who immediately took charge of him. Nobody came forward to claim responsibility for him. Social services became involved, police and ambulance authorities were informed, and the baby was taken for a medical check-up to the local hospital.

The baby was examined by a paediatric consultant, who considered him to be medically fit. Arrangements were thereupon made for the baby to be placed that same day with highly experienced foster carers, Mr and Mrs K.

Initially the local authority accommodated M pursuant to s. 20 of the Children Act 1989. However, as time passed and it was realised that medical intervention might be necessary, the local authority became increasingly concerned about intrusive medical testing of the child, in particular in the absence of having parental responsibility for M. For this reason the local authority found itself in a difficult position and sought clarification of its powers by instituting care proceedings under s. 31 of the Children Act 1989.

In my view the very fact of abandonment establishes that M was suffering from significant harm immediately before the rescue operation was carried out by the two workers from the clinic. To leave a child a few days old, alone and abandoned as occurred here, with all the risks that such entails, shows in the clear terms a complete dereliction of parental responsibility. 'Harm' means 'ill-treatment or the impairment of health or development' (see s. 31(9) of the Children Act 1989). To abandon a child in the manner in which M was abandoned must constitute ill-treatment. Accordingly I consider that M was suffering from significant harm immediately prior to being found by the clinic workers on 7 February 1995.

Counsel for the local authority and for the guardian both contend that at the time of abandonment M was likely to suffer significant harm. The guardian is of the opinion that it is likely that M will suffer significant harm in the future because he will have no knowledge of his background since there is no way of establishing this. The guardian referred to a body of expert opinion about the need for children who are adopted to know about their origins. He referred to the fact that adoption agencies now collect a great deal of information, including photographs and details of a child's birth parents, so that such information can be given to the child in the future.

This knowledge enables children to have a sense of belonging and a sense of why they have been adopted. He maintained that children will accept the most unpleasant facts about their parents' past or the way in which they were conceived and other like details. What children say is that it is not knowing anything about their parentage that is the worst. They build up fantasies and these can become unbearable. He pointed out that research indicates that these fantasies are harder to bear than the awful truth that children sometimes have to face. Unless one of M's parents, or someone who knows them, gets in touch—which can now be excluded as a realistic possibility—M will never know anything of his background. There is nothing anyone can do to change this. Furthermore, there is no doubt that M is a child with special needs both in regard to his health and education. He will require continuing medical supervision with a distinct possibility of medical intervention, as well as requiring highly experienced care in order to redress the marked developmental delay from which he suffers.

I also consider that as a result of his abandonment he was likely to suffer significant harm.

For these reasons I am satisfied that the threshold criteria are here established and that within the meaning of s. 31, M is suffering and is likely to suffer significant harm if a care order is not made.

12.8.1.2 When will significant harm need to be proved?

IN RE M (A MINOR) (CARE ORDER: THRESHOLD CONDITIONS) (1994)

The child concerned is G who was born on 28 June 1991 and is now two years old. He is the son of J ('the mother'), a woman whose family came from Jamaica but who was herself born in England on 28 May 1959. The mother had three children before G: a son, L, born on 27 March 1984 now aged nine and twins, born on 12 June 1987 and now aged six. The father of the twins was a different man from L's father. Neither of these fathers retained contact with their children. In January 1990 the mother married, in this country, a Nigerian, ('the father') and G was the son of this marriage. After G's birth he lived with his mother, his half-brothers and his half-sister in a home which was visited by the father, who had retained his own accommodation.

On 12 October 1991 the father murdered the mother at her home in the presence of all four children; G was four months old at the time. It was a very brutal and violent murder in which the father used a meat cleaver and a knife. He also assaulted the mother's boyfriend. The police immediately obtained a place of safety order and the four children were accommodated by the local authority, Greenwich London Borough. After a week the three elder children went to live with the mother's maternal cousin, Mrs W. Mrs W who is also of Jamaican origin, was born on 29 March 1938 and so is now aged 55. She lives in a three-bedroomed council maisonette in Roehampton, south-west London. She is separated from her husband, by whom she had two teenage children. The mother's three elder children have since lived with Mrs W and it is common ground that they have thrived under her care. On 11 August 1992 a residence order in respect of the three children was made in her favour.

At the time of the mother's death, Mrs W did not feel able to look after G, because he was so young and because of the attention which the three elder children would require to help them cope with their mother's violent death. So G stayed with a short-term foster mother, a Mrs C with whom he was living at the time of the appeal. He had, however, retained regular contact with Mrs W and his half-siblings. The place of safety order was not renewed and G remained with Mrs C on a voluntary basis and with her he thrived. However as a short-term foster parent she could not look after him indefinitely.

On 15 May 1992 the local authority applied for a care order in respect of G. At that time the father was still awaiting trial for the murder of the mother and his position was unclear, while Mrs W had not then told the local authority that there had been a change in her initial reluctance to care for G. Between the date of the local authority's application and the date of the hearing before the judge a number of events occurred. First, on 7 June 1992 the father was found guilty of the murder of the mother and of causing grievous bodily harm to the mother's boyfriend.

. . . Secondly, a guardian ad litem was appointed for G in the care proceedings. Thirdly, two members of the father's family, G's paternal aunts, both resident in the United States of America, as well as Mrs W, all separately applied for residence orders in respect of G. . . .

By the time the case came before the judge, the two American paternal aunts were no longer pursuing their applications for residence orders. The local authority no longer pursued their application for a care order, but supported Mrs W's application for a residence order. The father and the guardian ad litem both supported the making of a care order in respect of G with a view to an adoptive placement outside his natural family. Thus there were three main issues before the judge. (1) Were the 'threshold criteria' for the making of a care order under section 31 of the Act of 1989 satisfied? (2) If so, should a care or supervision order be made? (3) Should a residence order be made in favour of Mrs W?

The judge decided that the threshold conditions were satisfied, that there should be a care order, with a view to adoption outside the family, and that Mrs W's application for a residence order should be dismissed; her order of 12 February 1993 reflects those decisions. From that order Mrs W supported by the local authority, appealed; the guardian ad litem and the father sought to uphold the judge's order.

The use of the present tense in the first of these alternatives—'is suffering'—makes it clear that the harm must be being suffered at the relevant time, which is when the court has to be satisfied of the fulfilment of the threshold conditions, i.e. when it decides whether or not to make a care order. This is clear from the language used; it is also consistent with other areas of the law relating to children. Thus, under s. 16 of the Adoption Act 1976 the court may make an adoption order, notwithstanding the absence of a parent's consent, if it is satisfied that the parent is withholding his agreement unreasonably. It is well established that the test is whether *at the time of the hearing* the consent is being withheld unreasonably; see *In re W (An Infant)* [1971] AC 682, 698, 716, 723, 725. Of course, this does not mean that the child must be suffering significant harm at the precise moment when the court is considering whether the threshold conditions are satisfied; it is sufficient if there is a continuum in existence at that time. One of the threshold conditions under s. 1(2) of the Children and Young Persons Act 1969—which was replaced by s. 31 of the Children Act 1989—was if the child's 'proper development is being avoidably prevented or neglected or his health is being avoidably impaired or neglected or he is being ill-treated.' In relation to that provision Lord Goff of Chieveley said in *In re D (A Minor)* [1987] AC 317, 350:

The words 'is being' are in the continuous present. So there has to be a continuum in existence at the relevant time, which is when the magistrates consider whether to make a place of safety order. In cases under the subsection, this may not be established by proof of events actually happening at the relevant time. In the nature of things, it may well have to be established, as continuing at that time, by evidence that (1) the relevant state of affairs had existed in the past, and (2) there is a likelihood that it will continue into the future. So it can be said that a child is being ill-treated if it has been cruelly beaten in the past, and there is a likelihood that it will continue to be cruelly beaten in the future. It is not enough that something has avoidably been done or omitted to be done in relation to the child in the past which has, for example, impaired its health, and that the symptoms or effects still persist at the relevant time; for it cannot be said in such circumstances that, at the relevant time, the child's health is *being* avoidably impaired—all that can be said is that its health has been avoidably impaired in the past.

Thus it is not enough that something happened in the past which caused the child to suffer harm of the relevant kind if before the hearing the child has ceased to suffer such harm. Of course, that would still leave it open to the court to be satisfied that the child is *likely to suffer* significant harm of the relevant kind.

In our judgment that finding is wrong in each of its two limbs. Each limb refers to the past event of the father's murder of the mother. The second limb also artificially looks only to the care given by the father, even though for the 16 months prior to the hearing the father, being in prison, was in no position to give care to G, and it ignores the care actually given to G by the foster mother. Neither limb refers to the circumstances existing as at the date of the hearing. In our judgment, on the facts as we have stated them, there was no material before the judge which entitled her to find that, as at the date of the hearing G was suffering significant harm of the relevant kind.

The judge also dealt with the second of the threshold conditions—'likely to suffer significant harm'—as follows:

I am also satisfied that if an order were not made the child would be likely to suffer significant harm in that he is a small child with special needs, has no permanent home, and the only person with parental responsibility is the father who is unable to exercise it appropriately or fully in that he is serving a life sentence with an order of deportation upon release.

If the position at the date of the hearing had been that G was no longer able to stay with Mrs C (as was the case) and that there was no other suitable home it may well have been open to the judge to find that G was likely to suffer significant harm of the relevant kind. But there was another family home available to G—that offered by Mrs W where he would be with his half brothers and sister. If G went to live with Mrs W, there was nothing to suggest that he would be likely to suffer *significant* harm, attributable to the care likely to be given to him by Mrs W if the (care) order were not made, not being what it would be reasonable to expect a parent to give to him. Admittedly the judge, after deciding that she could make a care order, came down on balance against Mrs W and in favour of unknown adoptive parents. But the judge herself found it a very difficult case, and the professional witnesses were evenly divided; one of them said 'the decision hangs on a knife edge and one does not know which way to go.' In the end the judge came to the view that Mrs W might not be able to give G the quality of emotional care which he, with his particular background, was likely to require. This is a thousand miles away from saying that if G were to live with Mrs W he was likely to suffer significant harm of the relevant kind and, having been taken by counsel through the material evidence, we are satisfied that there was no evidence before the judge which would have entitled her to find that the second threshold condition was fulfilled. We would observe that, on the way in which the judge held that the second threshold condition was satisfied, if G's parents had both been killed in a motor accident, but there was an aunt or uncle willing to take him into his or her family and bring him up with his siblings and cousins, it would nevertheless be open to the court to say that the second threshold condition was satisfied and make a care order. This would amount to a form of social engineering which we are satisfied is wholly outside the intention of the Act of 1989.

As we are satisfied that the threshold conditions were not satisfied we do not need to consider whether the judge's exercise of her discretion to make a care order could have been successfully challenged.

IN RE M (A MINOR) (CARE ORDERS: THRESHOLD CONDITIONS) (1994)

FIRST EXTRACT: The matter in issue between the parties . . . was the proper construction of section 31 of the Children Act 1989 and its application to the facts of the present case. So far as relevant it is in these terms:

(1) On the application of any local authority or authorised person, the court may make in order—(a) placing the child with respect to whom the application is made in the care of a designated local authority; or (b) putting him under the supervision of a designated local authority or of a probation officer. (2) A court may only make a care order or supervision order if it is satisfied—(a) that the child concerned is suffering, or is likely to suffer, significant harm; and (b) that the harm, or likelihood of harm, is attributable to—(i) the care given to the child, or likely to be given to him if the order were not made, not being what it would be reasonable to expect a parent to give to him; or (ii) the child's being beyond parental control. . . . (4) An application under this section may be made on its own or in any other family proceedings. . . . (9) In this section . . . 'harm' means ill-treatment or the impairment of health or development; 'development' means physical, intellectual, emotional, social or behavioural development; 'health' means physical or mental health; and 'ill-treatment' includes sexual abuse and forms of ill-treatment which are not physical. . . . (11) In this Act—'a care order' means (subject to section 105(1)) an order under subsection (1)(a) and (except where express provision to the contrary is made) includes an interim care order made under section 38; and 'a supervision order' means an order made under subsection (1)(b) and (except where express provision to the contrary is made) includes an interim supervision order made under section 38.

In my opinion the opening words of s. 31 link the making of an order by the court very closely with the application to the court by a local authority or authorised person. Section 31(2) then goes on to specify the conditions which are necessary to be satisfied before the court can make a care order or supervision order, but it is plain from this and the statute as a whole that even if these conditions are satisfied the court is not bound to make an order but must go through the full procedure particularly set out in section 1 of the statute. It is also clear that Parliament expected these cases to proceed with reasonable expedition and in particular I refer to s. 32 in which the hearing by the court is not regarded only as taking place at the time when the applications are disposed of. Indeed, I think there is much to be said for the view that the hearing that Parliament contemplated was one which extended from the time the jurisdiction of the court is first invoked until the case is disposed of and that was required to be done in the light of the general principle that any delay in determining the question is likely to prejudice the welfare of the child. There is nothing in s. 31(2) which in my opinion requires that the conditions to be satisfied are disassociated from the time of the making of the application by the local authority. I would conclude that the natural construction of the conditions in s. 31(2) is that where, at the time the application is to be disposed of, there are in place arrangements for the protection of the child by the local authority on an interim basis which protection has been continuously in place for some time, the relevant date with respect to which the court must be satisfied is the date at which the local authority initiated the procedure for protection under the Act from which these arrangements followed. If after a local authority had initiated protective arrangements the need for these had terminated, because the child's welfare had been satisfactorily provided for otherwise, in any subsequent proceedings, it would not be possible to found jurisdiction on the situation at the time of initiation of these arrangements. It is permissible only to look back from the date of disposal to the date of initiation of protection as a result of which local authority arrangements had been continuously in place thereafter to the date of disposal.

SECOND EXTRACT: [This] preoccupation with the present tense involves the proposition that if a child suffers harm and is rescued by a local authority, a care order cannot be made in favour of the local authority because it can no longer be said that the child is suffering harm and if the parent who has caused the child harm is dead or in prison or disclaims any further interest it cannot be said that the child is likely to suffer harm. I cannot accept this approach. Restrictions on the right of a local authority to apply for a care order were imposed by s. 31 to prevent a local authority interfering too readily with the rights and responsibility of parents. A local authority cannot apply for a care order unless at the date of the application the child is suffering or is likely to suffer significant harm. Once the local authority has grounds for making an application, the court has jurisdiction to grant that application. If between the date of the application and the date of the judgment of the court, circumstances arise which make a care order unnecessary or undesirable, the local authority can withdraw its application for a care order or the court can refuse to make a care order. If the court is faced with an application for a residence order and an application for a care order then the court must decide, as Bracewell J decided, whether the welfare of the child will be best safeguarded by making a residence order under section 8 or a care order under s. 31.

12.8.2   PAST, PRESENT OR FUTURE HARM?

RE D (A MINOR) (CARE OR SUPERVISION ORDER) [1993] 2 FLR 423 (FamD)

EWBANK J: Nine years ago the father in this case was living with his wife and two children. One of those children was injured at the age of 4. The wife had a baby by the father in 1983 and when the baby was 2 months old the baby died. The father was thought to have killed the baby. The baby had a fractured skull and many other injuries. The other children were put into care and the father served a sentence of imprisonment for cruelty, although he was acquitted of more serious charges.

Time moved on. The father went back to his wife when he came out of prison, but then left and in due course he started living with another woman and they had a baby that was born in January 1992. The position now is that the father is living with the mother and the baby under an interim supervision order. The risks for the baby are recognised by all the professionals involved. It is conceded that the threshold conditions of s. 31 of the Children Act are met and the question before the court today is whether there should be a care order or whether a supervision order should be made.

The history of the matter is this. The father is now 35. He started living with his wife, D, in 1978. Their daughter, A, was born in 1978. The following year there was concern about injuries caused to A. In 1981 their son, P, was born. In 1982 place of safety orders were taken in relation to both those children because of injuries on A. It was asserted that the father was responsible, but he denied causing injuries. There was an application for care orders in relation to both those children, but that application was dismissed and the children accordingly returned home. The following year the baby, I, was born. When he was 2 months old he died. He had a fractured skull and twenty-eight fractures, some of which were healing and various bruises. Both the parents denied injuring the child at any time. The father gave a false alibi relating to a time just before the child was found dead. He gave an explanation of why he gave a false alibi. He said that he had been in bed all morning and did not want people to know about it because it sounded like neglect.

The father was charged with murder and stood his trial. He was acquitted of murder and found guilty of cruelty and sentenced to 18 months' imprisonment. Care orders were made in relation to A and P and they went into long-term fostering.

In October 1984 the father was released from prison and went back to live with D. They had not been married up to this stage, but in 1988 they were to get married. In May 1990 they separated. The wife, sadly, is suffering from Huntington's Chorea, which is an hereditary complaint.

In 1990 the father started living with L, who is the mother of the child I am now dealing with. She was 16 at the time and he was 33. R was born on 18 January 1992. The local authority were concerned. The view of the local authority has modified as time has passed. In due course they issued an application for a care or supervision order. The application was dated 21 May 1992. The grounds were put in this way: 'The local authority will be applying for in interim care order, subject to a level of co-operation from the parents. The local authority wish to ensure R's safety by preventing the father living in the same household, at least until the local authority's assessment is fully completed', and they asked for leave to refer the child to a consultant psychiatrist. There have been four consultant psychiatrists involved altogether in this case.

Matters came to a head in November 1992 when, at the instigation of and with pressure from the mother, the local authority agreed to the father and mother living together with the child. The child, R, has always been with the mother. The local authority prepared a draft contract on 6 November 1992 between the mother and the father and the social services department. The purpose was said to have been to enable R to live with his parents. It refers to the risk that the father posed to children in his care and points out that safeguards will have to continue. It says that the social services will be seeking a supervision order for one year.

The local authority asked for Doctor S to be called. He said that in the current situation the risks involved were acceptable, but the major point is the prediction of whether violence will occur and the steps which can be taken to protect R. He said that the anti-social personality disorder which he had diagnosed in the father was much less severe now but there were still traces. There was a lack of concern for other people and a lack of empathy shown on the part of the father. His behaviour has improved but his psychiatric difficulties remain. He was concerned at the father's continual deceitfulness and his refusal to acknowledge any responsibility for the injuries which the children of his first family suffered. Because of his refusal, therapeutic work was impossible with him and, moreover, it was impossible to assess his motivation and the stress factors which might have led to his violence. So he said there was a degree of risk in letting him bring up a child now and he pointed out that the father not only is not acknowledging any responsibility for the injuries to the children to others, he is not acknowledging them to himself. At the end he said that the risks were high. The father was the dominant partner and he was concerned that the father showed no emotion concerning the tragic events which have occurred and that he had more concern about the father than Doctor B had.

Mr H has been the social worker involved. He has been impressed with the co-operation of the father and impressed with the care given by the father and the mother to R, but he says he agrees there is a high risk and he feels he does not have a trusting relationship with the mother and father. He does not think they would confide with the local authority and he does not think that the local authority would be informed about early stages of concern if there were any. He told me that in relation to the original draft contract, which is talking about a supervision order for one year, after a year the local authority might move to a voluntary agreement with the father and mother. He pointed out that the mother does not see the father as any risk to R.

The mother and father for their part do not see any need for local authority intervention of any sort, although they will co-operate.

The father, as I have mentioned, has denied that he has ever caused an injury to any child. Children in his care, however, have been injured, and one baby has been killed, and he has been found guilty of wilful cruelty to that child. The local authority and all the professionals in this case have approached the case on the basis that it is likely that the father did kill the baby and I approach the case on the same basis. It appears likely that at some stage he lost control of himself and caused injuries to these children. His denial of causing injury means that his motivation cannot be considered and if there is a trigger which causes such loss of control it cannot be established. The life of this family is harmonious. The child is thriving and much loved by his mother and father. But the protection of the child, in my judgment, is the most important aspect of this case and the decisive point in coming to a decision whether there should be a supervision order or a care order is that, in my judgment, if there is to be a lifting of the safeguards surrounding this child that lifting ought to be done by the court on consideration of the evidence and the lifting of the safeguards ought not to be left to the responsibility of individuals.

RE H AND OTHERS (MINORS) (SEXUAL ABUSE: STANDARD OF PROOF)
[1996] 1 All ER 1 (HL)

LORD NICHOLLS OF BIRKENHEAD: The facts are set out in the judgment of Sir Stephen Brown P sitting in the Court of Appeal ([1995] 1 FLR 643). For present purposes I can summarise them shortly. The mother has four children, all girls. D1 and D2 were children of her marriage to Mr H in 1979. D1 was born in June 1978 and D2 in August 1981. Mr H and the mother then separated. In 1984 she commenced living with Mr R and they had two children: D3, born in March 1985, and D4, born in April 1992.

In September 1993, when she was 15, D1 made a statement to the police. She said she had been sexually abused by Mr R ever since she was 7 or 8 years old. She was then accommodated with foster-parents, and Mr R was charged with having raped her. In February 1994 the local authority applied for care orders in respect of the three younger girls. Interim care orders were made, followed by interim supervision orders.

In October 1994 Mr R was tried on an indictment containing four counts of rape of D1. D1 was the principal witness for the Crown. The jury acquitted Mr R on all counts after a very short retirement. Despite this the local authority proceeded with the applications for care orders in respect of D2, D3 and D4. These girls were then aged 13, 8 and 2 years. The local authority's case, and this is an important feature of these proceedings, was based solely on the alleged sexual abuse of D1 by Mr R. Relying on the different standard of proof applicable in civil and criminal matters, the local authority asked the judge still to find that Mr R had sexually abused D1, or at least that there was a substantial risk he had done so, thereby, so it was said, satisfying the s. 31(2) conditions for the making of a care order in respect of the three younger girls.

The applications were heard by Judge Davidson QC sitting in the Nottingham County Court. On 23 November, after a hearing lasting seven days, he dismissed the applications. He was not impressed by the evidence of Mr R or of the mother. Nevertheless he concluded he could not be sure 'to the requisite high standard of proof' that D1's allegations were true. He added:

> It must follow that the statutory criteria for the making of a care order are not made out. This is far from saying that I am satisfied the child's complaints are untrue. I do not brush them aside as the jury seem to have done. I am, at the least, more than a little suspicious that [Mr R] has abused her as she says. If it were relevant, I would be prepared to hold that there is a real possibility that her statement and her evidence are true, nor has [Mr R] by his evidence and demeanour, not only throughout the hearing but the whole of this matter, done anything to dispel those suspicions, but this in the circumstances is nihil ad rem.

By a majority, comprising Sir Stephen Brown P and Millett LJ, the Court of Appeal dismissed an appeal by the local authority. Kennedy LJ disagreed.

'Likely' to suffer harm

I shall consider first the meaning of 'likely' in the expression 'likely to suffer significant harm' in s. 31. In your Lordships' House Mr Levy QC advanced an argument not open in the courts below. He submitted that 'likely' means probable, and that the decision of the Court of Appeal to the contrary in *Newham London BC* v *A-G* [1993] 1 FLR 281 was wrong. I cannot accept this contention.

In everyday usage one meaning of the word 'likely', perhaps its primary meaning, is probable, in the sense of more likely than not. This is not its only meaning. If I am going walking on Kinder Scout and ask whether it is likely to rain, I am using 'likely' in a different sense. I am inquiring whether there is a real risk of rain, a risk that ought not to be ignored. In which sense is 'likely' being used in this subsection?

In s. 31(2) Parliament has stated the prerequisites which must exist before the court has power to make a care order. These prerequisites mark the boundary line drawn by Parliament between the differing interests. On one side are the interests of parents in caring for their own child, a course which prima facie is also in the interest of the child. On the other side there will be circumstances in which the interests of the child may dictate a need for his care to be entrusted to others. In s. 31(2) Parliament has stated the minimum conditions which must be present before the court can look more widely at all the circumstances and decide whether the child's welfare requires that a local authority shall receive the child into its care and have parental responsibility for him. The court must be satisfied that the child is already suffering significant harm. Or the court must be satisfied that, looking ahead, although the child may not yet be suffering such harm, he or she is likely to do so in the future. The court may make a care order if, but only if, it is satisfied in one or other of these respects.

In this context Parliament cannot have been using 'likely' in the sense of more likely than not. If the word 'likely' were given this meaning, it would have the effect of leaving outside the scope of care and supervision orders cases where the court is satisfied there is a real possibility of significant harm to the child in the future but that possibility falls short of being more likely than not. Strictly, if this were the correct reading of the Act, a care or supervision order would not be available even in a case where the risk of significant harm is as likely as not. Nothing would suffice short of proof that the child will probably suffer significant harm.

The difficulty with this interpretation of s. 31(2)(a) is that it would draw the boundary line at an altogether inapposite point. What is in issue is the prospect, or risk, of the child suffering *significant* harm. When exposed to this risk a child may need protection just as much when the risk is considered to be less than fifty-fifty as when the risk is of a higher order. Conversely, so far as the parents are concerned, there is no particular magic in a threshold test based on a probability of significant harm as distinct from a real possibility. It is otherwise if there is no real possibility. It is eminently understandable that Parliament should provide that where there is no real possibility of significant harm, parental responsibility should remain solely with the parents. That makes sense as a threshold in the interests of the parents and the child in a way that a higher threshold, based on probability, would not.

In my view, therefore, the context shows that in s. 31(2)(a) 'likely' is being used in the sense of a real possibility, a possibility that cannot sensibly be ignored having regard to the nature and gravity of the feared harm in the particular case. By parity of reasoning the expression 'likely to suffer significant harm' bears the same meaning elsewhere in the Act: for instance, in ss. 43, 44 and 46. 'Likely' also bears a similar meaning, for a similar reason, in the requirement in s. 31(2)(b) that the harm or likelihood of harm must be attributable to the care given to the child or 'likely' to be given him if the order were not made.

The threshold conditions
There is no difficulty in applying this standard to the threshold conditions. The first limb of s. 31(2)(a) predicates an existing state of affairs: that the child is suffering significant harm. The relevant time for this purpose is the date of the care order application or, if temporary protective arrangements have been continuously in place from an earlier date, the date when those arrangements were initiated. This was decided by your Lordships' House in *Re M (a minor) (care order: threshold conditions)* [1994] 3 All ER 298. Whether at that time the child was suffering significant harm is an issue to be decided by the court on the basis of the facts admitted or proved before it. The balance of probability standard applies to proof of the facts.

The same approach applies to the second limb of s. 31(2)(a). This is concerned with evaluating the risk of something happening in the future: aye or no, is there a real possibility that the child will suffer significant harm? Having heard and considered the evidence, and decided any disputed questions of relevant fact upon the balance of probability, the court must reach a decision on how highly it evaluates the risk of significant harm befalling the child, always remembering upon whom the burden of proof rests.

Suspicion and the threshold conditions
This brings me to the most difficult part of the appeal. The problem is presented in stark form by the facts in this case. The local authority do not suggest that the first limb of s. 31(2)(a) is satisfied in respect of D2, D3 or D4. They do not seek a finding that any of the three younger girls is suffering harm. Their case for the making of a care order is based exclusively on the second limb. In support of the allegation that D2, D3 and D4 are likely to suffer significant harm, the local authority rely solely upon the allegation that over many years D1 was subject to repeated sexual abuse by Mr R.

The judge held that the latter allegation was not made out. Mr R did *not* establish that abuse did *not* occur. The outcome on this disputed serious allegation of fact was that the local authority, upon whom the burden of proof rested, failed to establish that abuse *did* occur. However, the judge remained suspicious and, had it been relevant, he would have held there was a reasonable possibility that D1's allegations were true. The question arising from these conclusions can be expressed thus: when a local authority assert but fail to prove past misconduct, can the judge's suspicions or lingering doubts on that issue form the basis for concluding that the second limb of s. 31(2)(a) has been established?

In many instances where misconduct is alleged but not proved this question will not arise. Other allegations may be proved. The matters proved may suffice to show a likelihood of future harm. However, the present case is not unique. *Re P (a minor) (care: evidence)* [1994] 2 FLR 751 is another instance where the same problem arose. There the only matter relied upon was the death of the child's baby brother while in the care of the parents. Douglas Brown J held that it was for the local authority to prove that the death was non-accidental and that, since they failed to do so, there was no factual basis for a finding of likelihood of harm to the surviving child.

In the Court of Appeal in the present case Sir Stephen Brown P adopted the same approach (see [1995] 1 FLR 643 at 652). Since the judge rejected the only allegation which gave rise to the applications for care orders, it was not then open to him to go on and consider the likelihood of harm to the children. Millett LJ agreed. He said (at 657):

> . . . where the risk of harm depends on the truth of disputed allegations, the court must investigate them and determine whether they are true or false. Unless it finds that they are true, it cannot be satisfied that the child is likely to suffer significant harm if the order is not made.

Kennedy LJ reached a different conclusion. To satisfy the second limb there must be acceptable evidence of a real risk that significant harm will be sustained, but he added (at 654):

> I . . . do not accept that if the evidence relates to alleged misconduct . . . that misconduct must itself be proved on a balance of probabilities before the evidence can be used to satisfy the threshold criteria in s. 31(2)(a).

A conclusion based on facts

The starting point here is that courts act on evidence. They reach their decisions on the basis of the evidence before them. When considering whether an applicant for a care order has shown that the child is suffering harm or is likely to do so, a court will have regard to the undisputed evidence. The judge will attach to that evidence such weight, or importance, as he considers appropriate. Likewise with regard to disputed evidence which the judge accepts as reliable. None of that is controversial. But the rejection of a disputed allegation as not proved on the balance of probability leaves scope for the possibility that the non-proven allegation may be true after all. There remains room for the judge to have doubts and suspicions on this score. This is the area of controversy.

In my view these unresolved judicial doubts and suspicions can no more form the basis of a conclusion that the second threshold condition in s. 31(2)(a) has been established than they can form the basis of a conclusion that the first has been established.

There are several indications in the Act that when considering the threshold conditions the court is to apply the ordinary approach, of founding its conclusion on facts, and that nothing less will do. The first pointer is the difference in the statutory language when dealing with earlier stages in the procedures which may culminate in a care order. Under Pt V of the Act a local authority are under a duty to investigate where they have 'reasonable cause to suspect' that a child is suffering or is likely to suffer harm. The court may make a child assessment order if satisfied that the applicant has 'reasonable cause to suspect' that the child is suffering or is likely to suffer harm. The police may take steps to remove or prevent the removal of a child where a constable has 'reasonable cause to believe' that the child would otherwise be likely to suffer harm. The court may make an emergency protection order only if satisfied there is 'reasonable cause to believe' that the child is likely to suffer harm in certain eventualities. Under s. 38 the court may make an interim care order or an interim supervision order if satisfied there are 'reasonable grounds for believing' that the s. 31(2) circumstances exist.

In marked contrast is the wording of s. 31(2). The earlier stages are concerned with preliminary or interim steps or orders. Reasonable cause to believe or suspect provides the test. At those stages, as in my example of an application for an interlocutory injunction, there will usually not have been a full court hearing. But when the stage is reached of making a care order, with the far-reaching consequences this may have for the child and the parents, Parliament prescribed a different and higher test: 'a court may only make a care or supervision order if it is satisfied . . . that . . . the child . . . is suffering, or is likely to suffer, significant harm.' This is the language of proof, not suspicion. At this stage more is required than suspicion, however reasonably based.

The next pointer is that the second threshold condition in para. (a) is cheek by jowl with the first. Take a case where a care order is sought in respect of a child on the ground that for some time his parents have been maltreating him. Having heard the evidence, the court finds the allegation is not proved. No maltreatment has been established. The evidence is rejected as insufficient. That being so, the first condition is not made out, because there is no factual basis from which the court could conclude that the child is suffering significant harm attributable to the care being given to him. Suspicion that there may have been maltreatment clearly will not do. It would be odd if, in respect of the selfsame non-proven allegations, the selfsame insufficient evidence could none the less be regarded as a sufficient factual basis for satisfying the court there is a real possibility of harm to the child in the future.

The third pointer is that if indeed this were the position, this would effectively reverse the burden of proof in an important respect. It would mean that once apparently credible evidence of misconduct has been given, those against whom the allegations are made must disprove them. Otherwise it would be open to a court to hold that, although the misconduct has not been proved, it has not been disproved and there is a real possibility that the misconduct did occur. Accordingly, there is a real possibility that the child will suffer harm in the future and, hence, the threshold criteria are met. I do not believe Parliament intended that s. 31(2) should work in this way.

Thus far I have concentrated on explaining that a court's conclusion that the threshold conditions are satisfied must have a factual base, and that an alleged but unproved fact, serious or trivial, is not a fact for this purpose. Nor is judicial suspicion, because that is no more than a judicial state of uncertainty about whether or not an event happened.

I must now put this into perspective by noting, and emphasising, the width of the range of facts which may be relevant when the court is considering the threshold conditions. The range of facts which may properly be taken into account is infinite. Facts include the history of members of the family, the state of relationships within a family, proposed changes within the membership of a family, parental attitudes, and omissions which might not reasonably have been expected, just as much as actual physical assaults. They include threats, and abnormal behaviour by a child, and unsatisfactory parental responses to complaints or allegations. And facts, which are minor or even trivial if considered in isolation, when taken together may suffice to satisfy the court of the likelihood of future harm. The court will attach to all the relevant facts the appropriate weight when coming to an overall conclusion on the crucial issue.

I must emphasise a further point. I have indicated that unproved allegations of maltreatment cannot form the basis for a finding by the court that either limb of s. 31(2)(a) is established. It is, of course, open to a court to conclude there is a real possibility that the child will suffer harm in the future although harm in the past has not been established. There will be cases where, although the alleged maltreatment itself is not proved, the evidence does establish a combination of profoundly worrying features affecting the care of the child within the family. In such cases it would be open to a court in appropriate circumstances to find that, although not satisfied the child is yet suffering significant harm, on *the basis of such facts as are proved* there is a likelihood that he will do so in the future.

That is not the present case. The three younger girls are not at risk unless D1 was abused by Mr R in the past. If she was not abused, there is no reason for thinking the others may be. This is not a case where Mr R has a history of abuse. Thus the one and only relevant fact is whether D1 was abused by Mr R as she says. The other surrounding facts, such as the fact that D1 made a complaint and the fact that her mother responded unsatisfactorily, lead nowhere relevant in this case if they do not lead to the conclusion that D1 was abused. To decide that the others are at risk because there is a *possibility* that D1 was abused would be to base the decision, not on fact, but on suspicion: the suspicion that D1 *may* have been abused. That would be to lower the threshold prescribed by Parliament.

Auld, R, 'Likelihood of Future Harm', [1996] Fam Law 488

Under s. 31(2)(a) of the Children Act 1989 a court may only make a care order or a supervision order if it is satisfied that the child concerned: 'is suffering, *or* is likely to suffer, significant harm . . .' (emphasis added).

The Court of Appeal and House of Lords considered the application of the second set of the alternative criteria 'or is likely to suffer significant harm' in *Re H and R (Child Sexual Abuse: Standard of Proof)* [1995] 1 FLR 643, CA; *Re H and R (Child Sexual Abuse: Standard of Proof)* [1996] 1 FLR 80, HL. The issue arising from the case is this—where the allegation that a child is 'likely to suffer significant harm' within the meaning of the second limb of s. 31(2)(a) of the 1989 Act arises solely out of alleged sexual abuse in the past, is it first necessary to prove to the appropriate standard of proof that such abuse has, in fact, occurred? By a majority of three to two (Lords Browne-Wilkinson and Lloyd dissenting), the House of Lords held that if the case for making a care order rested on an allegation of past abuse which was not proved, it was not open to the courts to make a care order merely because the facts raised a suspicion that there might have been past abuse.

THE FACTS

The eldest of four children alleged that her mother's cohabitee had sexually abused her. The cohabitee was charged with rape but acquitted. The local authority then applied for care orders in respect of the three younger children. The applications were based on the alleged sexual abuse of the eldest child. The local authority did not suggest that the first limb of s. 31(2)(a) was satisfied in respect of the three youngest children. It did not seek a finding that any of the three younger girls were suffering harm. Its case for the making of a care order was based exclusively on the second limb of s. 31(2)(a), that is, that the children were likely to suffer significant harm. In support of the allegation that the three youngest were likely to suffer significant harm, the local authority relied solely upon the allegation that over many years the eldest child was subjected to repeated sexual abuse by her stepfather.

Judge Davidson QC, at first instance, found that the mother and her cohabitee were lying. The judge expressed considerable suspicion that the alleged abuse had taken place. He held that, as the case depended solely on the eldest child's allegations and he was not satisfied on the balance of probabilities proportionate to the gravity of the offence that the allegations were true, he could not proceed to consider whether the children were likely to suffer significant harm in the terms of s. 31(2)(a). He, therefore, dismissed the applications. The local authority, supported by the guardian ad litem, appealed to the Court of Appeal on the ground that even if the judge was not satisfied that abuse had occurred, nevertheless the allegation itself and the judge's suspicion ought to be taken into account so as to fulfil the requirements of s. 31. The Court of Appeal held, dismissing the appeal (Kennedy LJ dissenting), that the judge had been right to adopt a two-stage approach. The two-stage approach involved:

(1) the determination of what had happened in the past, that determination being made on the balance of probabilities;

(2) if stage one yields a relevant conclusion, then, in stage two, the court can evaluate future risks on the basis of past events and other material factors.

The Court of Appeal held that the judge had rightly dismissed the applications, having fairly weighed up the matter relating to the allegations of sexual abuse and concluded that they had not been established to the requisite standard of proof, the balance of probabilities. It held that it was not open to the judge on the evidence, since he had rejected the only allegation which gave rise to the applications, to go on to a second stage and consider the likelihood of future harm to the children.

In his dissenting judgment, Kennedy LJ disagreed with the two-stage approach to assessing whether a child is likely to suffer significant harm. He said at [1995] 1 FLR 643, at p. 654G:

The issue is not whether the misconduct occurred, it is whether the child is likely to suffer significant harm, and if the court is persuaded to consider as a separate issue whether or not misconduct did, in fact, occur, then problems may well arise as they arose in this case . . . I, for my part, do not accept that if the evidence relates to alleged misconduct . . . that misconduct must itself be proved on the balance of probabilities before the evidence can be used to satisfy the threshold criteria in s. 31(2)(a).

Kennedy LJ approved what he called the one-stage approach taken by Stuart-Smith LJ in *Re H (A Minor); Re K (Minors) (Child Abuse: Evidence)* [1989] 2 FLR 313, at p. 344F:

> . . . there may be insufficient evidence upon which the judge can conclude that the father has sexually abused the children. Nevertheless there may be sufficient evidence to show that there is a real chance, possibility or probability *that he will do so in the future* if granted access.

The one-stage approach is simply the evaluation of future risks on the basis of all the evidence without making preliminary findings of fact as to past allegations.

However, Kennedy LJ agreed with the majority, at p. 654G, that *if* a preliminary issue *has been* resolved, the court cannot use evidence which it has rejected: 'It cannot make a second decision on the basis that its first decision may be wrong.' What he disputed is whether a preliminary ruling as to the past is necessary.

In their dissenting speeches, both Lord Browne-Wilkinson and Lord Lloyd agreed with the majority that a court must rely on facts, not suspicion, when considering likelihood of future harm. However, like Kennedy LJ, they doubted whether making a finding as to the truth of a past allegation is necessary for assessing future risk under the second limb of s. 31(2)(a) of the Children Act 1989. Lord Browne-Wilkinson said at [1996] 1 FLR 80, at p. 82C–E:

> . . . I agree that the judge can only act on evidence and on facts which, so far as relevant, have been proved. He has to be satisfied by the evidence before him that there is a real possibility of serious harm to the child. Where I part company is in thinking that the facts relevant to an assessment of risk ('is likely to suffer . . . harm') are not the same as the facts relevant to a decision that harm is, in fact, being suffered. In order to be satisfied that an event has occurred or is occurring the evidence has to be shown on the balance of probabilities that such an event did occur or is occurring. But in order to be satisfied that there is a risk of such an occurrence, the ambit of the relevant facts is in my view wider. The combined effect of a number of factors which suggest that a state of affairs, though not proved to exist, may well exist is the normal basis for the assessment of future risk. To be satisfied of the existence of a risk does not require proof of the occurrence of past historical events but proof of facts which are relevant to the making of a prognosis.

As Lord Lloyd said, the two bases for finding the threshold criteria met under s. 31(2)(a) are alternative, and involve different issues. Facts inadequate for finding past abuse may be adequate for establishing a real risk of future abuse. He said at p. 90E:

> The fact that the first half of s. 31(2)(a) is not satisfied on the balance of probabilities does not mean that the second half may not be satisfied.

Lord Lloyd said that where it is claimed that a child was likely to suffer significant harm, the one-stage approach sufficed. The court's approach should simply be to consider, looking at all the evidence, whether there was a real possibility of the child suffering significant harm in the future. If so, the threshold criteria were satisfied. The court did not have to be satisfied on the balance of probabilities that the child had, in fact, suffered significant harm in the past, whether by sexual abuse or otherwise, even where the allegation of abuse was the foundation of the local authority's case for a care order.

Lord Lloyd seems to have gone further than Kennedy LJ, who held that *if* a preliminary issue *has been* resolved, the court cannot use evidence which it has rejected.

Lord Nicholls did concede in his speech that *Re H and R* was an exceptional type of case. He said there might be cases where a court, although not satisfied that the child is yet suffering significant harm, might find on the basis of such facts as are proved that there was a likelihood that he will do so in the future. However, he said that *Re H and R* was not a case where that approach was possible, because: '. . . the one and only relevant fact is whether D1 was abused by Mr R as she says.' (p. 10IE)

The effect of the majority's decision in *Re H and R* seems to be that the two-stage approach must apply in cases where there is an isolated issue of fact on which the outcome alone depends. However, as Lord Lloyd said at p. 91C, that 'will seldom, if ever, be the case in practice'. A case may look as though it turns on the truth of one allegation at first sight, but on closer analysis, may not. As Lord Browne-Wilkinson pointed out in his speech, it may be superficial to conclude that only one fact, that of past misconduct, is relevant. He said at pp. 82H–83A:

> So in the present case, the major issue was whether D1 had been sexually abused (the macro fact). In the course of the hearing before the judge a number of other facts (the micro facts) were established to the judge's satisfaction by the evidence. The judge in his careful judgment summarised those micro facts: that D1 had been consistent in her story from the time of her first complaint . . . that there were opportunities for such abuse by Mr R and that he had been lying in denying that he had ever been alone either with D1 or with any of the other children . . .

It is difficult to assess whether, in similar cases, there really is *only* one fact relevant to future risk, and whether one has a case caught by the rule in *Re H and R* on hand. Given that the two-stage approach must apply in *Re H and R*-type cases, it is hard to be sure when a court must apply the two-stage test, and when the one-stage test suffices.

The decision as to which test applies could, in cases similar to *Re H and R*, make a vast difference to a child's life. An example might be a case where there is substantial (say, '45% probable') evidence of past sexual abuse to child A and such alleged abuse is the basis for an application for a care order in respect of child B, on the grounds that child B is likely to suffer future abuse. If a two-stage test applies and the past abuse is unproved, the court would not even have jurisdiction to consider a care order in respect of child B. If a one-stage test applies, child B might be permanently removed from his or her parents.

There are, therefore, likely to be inconsistent results in cases with similar facts, as a result of courts sometimes taking the one-stage, and sometimes the two-stage approach. That is the first worrying effect of *Re H and R*.

The second worrying effect of the case is that it seems to restrict the court's use of the alternative grounds for finding the threshold criteria met, which are provided by the wording of s. 31(2)(a) of the Children Act 1989. In cases where a local authority relies on the same allegations to support the alternative findings that a child is suffering or is likely to suffer significant harm, a court cannot consider future risks if it finds the allegations as to the past unproved. Consequently, local authorities may, in some cases, stop asking the court to consider both limbs of s. 31(2)(a) for fear of being estopped from raising the second limb if the court finds the first unproved. They may be better advised to ask the court to consider only the second limb, the likelihood of future harm, in the light of all the evidence.

In a recent case, *Re M and R (Child Abuse: Evidence)* noted at [1996] Fam Law 445, to be reported, the Court of Appeal established that a court facing an application for a care order and considering the matter at the welfare stage under s. 1 may not find that a child is at risk of sexual abuse in the future on the basis of a mere suspicion of sexual abuse in the past. The arguments of the minority in *Re H and R* in respect of s. 31(2)(a) apply equally in respect of s. 1(3)(e). The latter requires that a court should have regard, inter alia, to any harm which a child 'has suffered' or 'is at risk of suffering'. The same evidence may be enough to prove that a child is at risk of suffering harm, but not enough to prove that a child has suffered harm. *Re M and R* may make local authorities even more reluctant to ask the court to make findings of facts about important events in the past. Such a restriction in the flexibility of the statute does not seem to be in the interests of children.

Nothing in the statute suggests that there are any circumstances where the court should be so restricted. On the contrary, as Lord Lloyd said at p. 90E:

> The two halves of the subsection are not interlinked, logically or linguistically. They could as well have been contained in separate paragraphs.

The final worrying effect of the decisions in *Re H and R* and *Re M and R* is that they may lead to lengthy preliminary arguments over whether a one-stage or a two-stage approach should apply in a case which will lead to further delay in Children Act 1989 proceedings.

12.8.3 THE STANDARD OF CARE BY PARENTS

'Children Act 1989. Guidance and Regulations', *Volume 1, Court Orders,* **HMSO, 1991**

3.23 The second limb requires the court to be satisfied that 'the harm, or likelihood of harm, is attributable to the care given or likely to be given, to the child not being what it would be reasonable for a parent to give to the child'. Harm caused solely by a third party is therefore excluded (unless the parent has failed to prevent it) and will require other forms of intervention to safeguard the child. The care given to the child has to be compared not with what it would be reasonable to expect *the* parent to give to the child but with what it would be reasonable to expect *a* parent to give him. It follows from 'reasonable' in the text that the hypothetical parent would be a reasonable parent. The actual parents may be doing their best but are not able to meet the child's particular needs and are unwilling or incapable of making use of appropriate services. The standard of care which it would be reasonable to expect them to give may be very low. The court must compare the care being given to the child in question with what it would be reasonable to expect a reasonable parent to give him, having regard to his needs. If a child has particular difficulties relating to any aspect of his health or development this could require a higher standard of care than for the average child. The court will almost certainly expect to see professional evidence on the standard of care which could reasonably be expected of reasonable parents with support from community-wide services as appropriate where the child's needs are complex or demanding, or the lack of reasonable care is not immediately obvious. 'Care' is not defined but in the context of s. 31 must mean providing for the child's health and total development (physical, intellectual, emotional, social and behavioural) and not just having physical charge of him.

M v *BIRMINGHAM CITY COUNCIL* [1994] 2 FLR 141 (FamD)

STUART-WHITE J: This is an appeal by a mother, whom I shall call Miss M, against an order of Mr Bruce Morgan, a stipendiary magistrate for the City of Birmingham, sitting as the Birmingham Family Proceedings Court on 3 February 1994 whereby, on an application by the Birmingham City Council, he made an order committing a child, whom I shall call S, to the interim care of the city council for a period of 28 days, and at the same time made an order under s. 25 of the Children Act 1989 authorising the keeping of S in secure accommodation for 28 days.

When S was about 8 years of age, during 1989, she went to live for a period of about 5 months with Miss M's stepfamily, she initially having asked the social services to accommodate S and K following her mental breakdown.

Whilst residing with the stepfamily S made allegations of sexual abuse by her uncle. Such allegations were believed by her mother. The police ordered a medical examination which supported these allegations. There was no prosecution because of lack of evidence.

Although a referral was made to the Charles Burns Clinic for a child sexual abuse project, S was not selected. This was possibly because of her age. To date there seems to have been no fully successful guidance given at a professional level in relation to this abuse.

During 1990 S went to a junior school where the staff held that S's friendship often ended in spiteful accusations and occasional fighting.

During S's life she has made many allegations, some of which have been withdrawn. These allegations include: in June 1990 that an 11-year-old cousin had burnt her with a cigarette. This allegation was withdrawn. In September 1991 she often ran out of school telling teachers she had overdosed. At school she made a complaint in 1992/93 of bullying and teasing about her sister's misfortunes and being assaulted by taxi-drivers. All these complaints were checked and found to be unsubstantiated. When S decided she would not return to school she alleged that a boy at the school but off the school premises had forced her to have sexual intercourse. Later on, this allegation was withdrawn. She often complained of illness, mainly stomach-ache. She was seen by a doctor on three or four occasions but no illness was diagnosed. When admitted to hospital following the overdose in 1994 she told the hospital staff she was pregnant. This was untrue. She also deceived the authorities about the number of tablets taken. She made a complaint against a male resident at Athelstan House in 1993/94 who, she stated, 'had rubbed his willy on her stomach'. She withdraw this allegation but maintained that the event had occurred.

In January 1993 S took an overdose of thyroxine tablets and was admitted to hospital. After the hospital admission she was subsequently admitted to 870 unit. She was placed at 870 on a voluntary basis. There was no court order. She stated in relation to the overdose that this was done to draw attention to herself. There is a dispute as to the number of tablets taken and the court treats S's evidence of two tablets with caution and scepticism because of her other unreliable evidence.

Whilst at 870 unit the local authority assessed that S's behaviour indicated that she had experienced considerable behaviour and emotional problems and she declined the opportunity to mix with people of her own age in group therapy.

She remained at 870 from about January 1993 to May 1993. During that time the staff described her as a person unhappy about her body image and regarded herself as too thin. She had numerous tantrums when she could not get her way. On one occasion when told not to buy clothes she cut up her clothes, placing the rest in the bin.

Whilst at 870 unit she threatened to run away on numerous occasions but there is no evidence that she did. She also threatened to kill herself when made to go to school. These threats did not result in any attempts.

Also whilst at 870 unit she exhibited many types of behaviour indicative of sexual abuse. Staff felt that she had no feelings of self-respect and that she would allow herself to be used by the boys to obtain cigarettes. She often told staff she wished she were dead.

During the period at 870 unit she showed herself as somebody with little confidence, disgruntled with her appearance, and felt that staff and fellow classmates did not like her.

After leaving unit 870 and during her time at 870, S attended school on some occasions but such attendance was sporadic and whilst at school her behaviour was difficult and she truanted.

On about 20 May 1993 S was suspended from school following a serious tantrum resulting in violent behaviour. In her own words she 'beat up a school teacher'.

S's mother stated to the local authority representative at about June 1993 that S's behaviour was difficult and that she did not know how long she would be able to tolerate same.

From about 20 May 1993 to her admission to Athelstan House in about November 1993, S received no formal schooling.

On 8 October 1993, S, at her mother's request and approval, stayed at a local authority children's home following an incident whereby S broke her 3-year-old sister's finger in a door. On the day of the incident the mother stated she believed it was a deliberate assault. The next day the mother stated she believed it was not deliberate.

S was, at the request of her mother and her mother's cohabitant, accommodated in voluntary care on 12 November 1993 at Athelstan House. She remained in such care up until the date of this hearing. Agreement between all parties was that this was not the most suitable placement and S was assaulted on at least one occasion whilst a resident there.

Whilst at Athelstan House, S absconded on at least fifteen occasions in a period of about 40 days. On at least two such occasions the abscondances were overnight. She, being at the time 13 years of age, stayed with a 17-year-old boyfriend and his friends.

Whilst at Athelstan House she intimidated another female and made allegations of a sexual nature against a male resident.

She took an overdose of approximately twenty-two paracetamol tablets on 24 January 1994. She lied to the medical authorities about the number of tablets taken. As a result she was discharged and readmitted.

Whilst at the hospital she told the staff she was pregnant because she wanted more nurses. She also alleged to hospital staff that she had taken LSD, Ecstasy, cannabis, beer, sniffing-glue and gas. All these allegations she now states are untrue.

Whilst at hospital, in an agitated and aggressive mood she had to be dragged to the ward, according to M. D. Hocking, the consultant paediatrician, who also states that he has personal knowledge of over one hundred children having taken overdoses and that admissions from more than one overdose are unusual.

S had been admitted on at least two occasions and has admitted on at least seven other occasions taking tablets which have not been prescribed for her in order to draw attention to herself.

When S was admitted to the West Midlands Poison Unit on 26 January 1994 she destroyed her medical notes and attacked a member of staff. Dr Daniels, consultant psychiatrist, and Dr Rothery, a consultant in the psychiatry of adolescents, both agree that no improvement in S's behaviour can be effected without her being held in secure accommodation.

S admits that many of the allegations and false statements have been made for the purpose of drawing attention to herself.

S is a girl with learning difficulties.

Whilst at Athelstan, S, on 17 December 1993 ran away and whilst at a flat she was pushed to the floor and her eyes and hair were shaved with a razor. She refused to make a complaint. She also stated that she was picked up by a man who tried to rape her.

When at the secure accommodation unit she was asked to hand over her jewellery, January 1994. She placed the same in her mouth and threatened to swallow them.

S made allegations that whilst she was at Athelstan House an older girl wished her to shoplift and wanted to pimp for her and wanted S to take drugs.

She gave her sister E a dirty nappy to eat and on other occasions had spoken in a spiteful and unkind manner about her sister.

On the basis of these facts thus comprehensively stated, S has presented and continues to present a serious problem to anybody, be they parent or local authority, who has the duty of caring for her and to any court which has to consider what are the appropriate orders to make in respect of her.

At the hearing before the magistrate, the respondent local authority alleged that S was suffering or was likely to suffer significant harm. The magistrate unsurprisingly found no difficulty in holding that this was established on the evidence before him. Indeed, it was not and is not seriously disputed.

The local authority, in pursuance of ss. 38(2) and 31(2)(b)(ii) of the Children Act, further alleged that there were substantial grounds for believing that harm or likelihood of harm was attributable to the child's being beyond parental control. Any suggestion that there was evidence that the harm or likelihood of harm was attributable to the care given or likely to be given to the child not being what it would be reasonable to expect a parent to give was, for the purpose of that hearing, abandoned by the local authority.

The first question therefore to which the magistrate had to address himself and did address himself was whether he was satisfied that there were reasonable grounds for believing that the harm suffered or likely to be suffered by S was attributable to her being beyond parental control.

In *Re M* the Court of Appeal had to consider s. 31(2)(a) and in particular the point in time to which the words 'is suffering significant harm' relate. The Court of Appeal held, following the reasoning of Lord Goff of Chieveley in *Re D (A Minor)* [1987] AC 317 at p. 350, that the use of the present tense makes it clear that the harm must be being suffered at the time when the court decides whether or not to make a care order. The Court of Appeal overruled *Northamptonshire County Council v S and Others* [1993] Fam 136 in which Ewbank J had held, following the reasoning of Lord Brandon of Oakbrook who, in another speech in *Re D* cited with approval the decision of the Divisional Court in *M v Westminster City Council* [1985] FLR 325, that the material time was that immediately before the process of protecting the child in question was put into motion. The Court of Appeal pointed out that the provision being construed in *Re D* and in *M v Westminster City Council* was not s. 31 of the Children Act 1989 but was rather s. 1(2) of the Children and Young Persons Act 1969 where the relevant condition was met only if the child's proper development is being avoidably prevented or neglected or his health is being avoidably prevented or neglected or he is being ill-treated. The court noted the significant addition of the concept of likelihood of harm to s. 31 of the Children Act in response to the recommendation of the *Review of Child Care Law* (DHSS, 1985). Thus the

Court of Appeal in *Re M* adopted a construction of s. 31(2)(a) which did not strain the meaning of the language of the subsection but which nevertheless, because of the likelihood provision, did not give rise to the difficulty which had confronted the Divisional Court in *M* v *Westminster City Council*.

In the light of all this, it is necessary to consider the proper construction of s. 31(2)(b)(ii) which, according to the researches of counsel, is free from authority. . . .

I accept that if there are two equally possible constructions it is necessary, to consider the philosophy behind the Act, which can be derived from many sections, that children should be brought up by their families where that can occur consistently with their safety.

However, I am of the view that the analogy with *Re M* is a false analogy when the language of s. 31(2)(b)(ii) falls to be considered. Subsection (2)(a) contains a verb, in what is unquestionably the present tense (the continuous present, as referred to by Lord Goff of Chieveley in *Re D*) namely the verb 'is suffering', whereas subs (2)(b)(ii) contains no verb in the present or any other tense. It must be read together with the opening words of subs (2)(b) as follows:

. . . that the harm, or likelihood of harm, is attributable to—
   (ii)   the child's being beyond parental control.

The expression contained in subs (2)(b)(ii) is, it seems to me, plainly a substantival expression capable of describing a state of affairs in the past, in the present or in the future according to the context in which it falls to be applied. No doubt this is why the concept of likelihood finds no place at this point in the subsection.

Two other matters in relation to subs (2)(b)(ii) have been canvassed in argument. In relation to those I am prepared to assume for the purpose of this appeal, without deciding the point, that 'parental control' refers to the parent of the child in question and not to parents, or reasonable parents, in general. Moreover, in construing the word 'parental' in relation to this subsection I am prepared to hold that the control in question is that exercised, or to be exercised, not simply by the mother but by the mother in conjunction with her cohabitant Mr P.

In reaching this conclusion I am assisted by making reference to s. 1(3)(f) and to s. 2(9) and by the fact that many parents share de facto though not legal parental responsibility with cohabitants who are not related to the children and in respect of whom there is no parental responsibility order nor formal parental responsibility agreement.

To the extent to which this later view differs from that expressed by the magistrate at p. 12 of his decision, I find that he misdirected himself; but that this misdirection, if such it was, did not contribute to his ultimate decision that there were reasonable grounds for believing that S was, at all times material to his consideration, beyond parental control.

For that decision I consider that there was an abundance of evidence which was carefully reviewed. In particular the magistrate drew attention to the fact that Miss M and Mr P had, on two occasions within the 6 months which followed, S having previously been in voluntary care for some 5 months, asked the local authority to take her again into care. He further drew attention to the serious problems besetting this unfortunate child for many years and at times other than those during which she was accommodated by the local authority. He carefully considered all the matters set out in s. 1(3) of the Act, the so-called 'checklist', including the range of powers available to him. That he was correct in deciding upon an interim care order I have no doubt.

12.9   The Process

12.9.1   CARE PLANS

RE J (MINORS) (CARE: CARE PLAN) [1994] 1 FLR 253 (FamD)

WALL J: Earlier today, on the application of a local authority, I made care orders under s. 31 of the Children Act 1989 in relation to four children. The detailed family history which gave rise to the care proceedings does not, in my judgment, call for a report. The reason I have adjourned into open court is because the case raises points of general interest relating to the function of a court hearing care proceedings. Those points can be formulated in the following way:

(1)   What is the role of the court in a case where the threshold criteria under s. 31 are met and the court is satisfied that care orders are in the interests of the children concerned, but the court disagrees or is unhappy with aspects of the care plan put forward by the local authority?

(2)   In a case where the local authority's care plan is designed to cater for the long term but cannot predicate events which may occur in the short term, is it appropriate for the court to make an interim order and postpone making a final order until satisfied that the local authority's care plan is working in practice?

The care plan occupies in toto one and a half sides of A4 paper. It was clearly prepared in a hurry, consequent upon the local authority's change of stance. When I read it, I was concerned about certain aspects of it, as was the guardian ad litem. I inquired how the respective foster-placements had been selected; what knowledge the foster-parents had of the children and what introductions were proposed before the children were placed. The guardian ad litem was concerned that sufficient thought had not been given to placing K and K with J in the latter's current foster-placement. He was also concerned about the likely effect of the plan in particular on O, who was close to his mother and wished to stay with her. He also took the view that the prospect of sending O to a boarding-school with holiday periods to be spent with his mother had not been properly investigated. It also emerged that the plan had not been discussed with the children, although there had been an opportunity for the allocated social worker to discuss it with the mother outside the door of the court. . . .

Against this background the local authority urged me to make full care orders. Only by this means, it was submitted, could the full administrative machine of the local authority swing properly into action. Only by this means could the uncertainty for the children be ended and the firm planning process for their respective futures be got under way.

Furthermore, it was argued that if the court was satisfied on the threshold criteria and that it was in the interests of the children to be removed from their mother's care, that was the end of the matter; the court would no longer have the supervisory role given to it under s. 7(2) of the Family Law Reform Act 1969. Parliament had decreed that the execution of the care plan was a matter for the local authority without oversight from the court, save insofar as issues of contact were involved, or save insofar as a parent sought to discharge the care order by further application to the court.

For the guardian ad litem it was argued that the local authority's care plan remained untested and in material respects inchoate: that the responsibility for making or refusing to make a care order was laid on the court and that the court could not discharge that responsibility until satisfied that the care plan was viable. The guardian ad litem thus urged me to adjourn the applications, make interim care orders and direct that the substantive applications for full care orders be restored at a date in the future when the court would have a clearer picture and could decide on all the evidence available whether or not full care orders should be made.

These arguments, in my judgment, go to the heart of the division of responsibility between the courts and local authorities in the making and implementation of care orders and calls for an analysis of the role of the court in making or refusing to make such orders. I was referred to a number of cases touching on these issues and I hope it will be helpful if I seek to summarise the principles which can be drawn from them. They are, I think, the following:

. . .

(4)   The combination of the factors set out [under (1) and (2) above] requires the court carefully to scrutinise the care plan prepared by the local authority and to satisfy itself that the care plan is in the child's interests. Thus, if the court is not satisfied the care plan is in the best interests of the child, the court may refuse to make a care order.

(5)   It follows that the care plan prepared by the local authority is an extremely important document. In *Manchester City Council* v *F, Note* [1993] 1 FLR 419 Eastham J

stated that the care plan delivered by the local authority should accord, so far as is reasonably possible, with *The Children Act 1989 Guidance and Regulations* vol 3, chap 2, para. 2.62 (*Family Placements*), prepared by the Department of Health and published by HMSO.

(6)   The report of *Manchester City Council* v *F, Note* does not reproduce para. 2.62 of vol 3 of the *Guidance and Regulations*. In the hope, therefore, that the criteria therein referred to will become better known in the profession, I propose to read the matters listed in para. 2.62 in their entirety into this judgment. Whilst it is recognised in that paragraph that there is no prescribed format for the child care plan, the plan should be recorded in writing and contain the child's and his family's social history and the following key elements—and they are then listed:

The child's identified needs (including needs arising from race, culture, religion or language, special education or health needs).
Next:
* how those needs might be met;
* aim of plan and time-scale; the proposed placement (type and details);
* other services to be provided to child and/or family either by the local authority or other agencies;
* arrangements for contact and reunification;
* support in placement;
* likely duration of placement in the accommodation;
* contingency plan, if placement breaks down;
* arrangements for ending the placement (if made under voluntary arrangements);
* who is to be responsible for implementing the plan (specific tasks of overall plan);
* specific detail of the parents' role in day-to-day arrangements;
* the extent to which the wishes and views of the child, his parents and anyone else with sufficient interest in the child (including representatives of other agencies) have been obtained and acted upon and the reasons supporting this or explanations of why wishes/views have not been discounted;
* arrangements for input by parents, the child and others into the ongoing decision-making process;
* arrangements for notifying the responsible authority of disagreements or making representations;
* arrangements for health care (including consent to examination and treatment);
* arrangements for education; and dates of reviews.

(7)   Eastham J in *Manchester City Council* v *F, Note* (above) did not feel inclined to say that every care plan should contain evidence as to the feasibility of the long-term proposals made by the local authority. He was specifically dealing with a case in which the local authority was planning to place the child in question for adoption and was thus concerned that evidence of long-term proposals would breach the duty of confidentiality. I will return to this point in a moment.

Thus in answering the first of the two questions posed at the outset of this judgment it seems to me clear from *C* v *Solihull MBC* [1993] 1 FLR 290 and *Hounslow LBC* v *A* [1993] 1 FLR 702 that the court should only pass responsibility over to the local authority by way of final care order when all the facts are as clearly known as can be hoped. Thus, if the court having heard the evidence, is not satisfied about material aspects of the care plan, the court should decline to make a care order. Local authorities should thus be left in no doubt at all that the care plan will in each case be subject to rigorous scrutiny. Furthermore, where evidence is available in relation to material parts of the care plan, for example where it is proposed the child should be placed with identified foster-parents, evidence about these foster-carers and details of the placement should be made available and form part of the care plan.

A properly constructed care plan is not only essential to enable the court to make its decision based on all the known facts; it will or should have been compiled either in consultation with the parents and other interested parties, including where appropriate the child or children involved, or at the very least after taking their views and wishes into account. It will thus enable the other parties to focus on the relevant issues. Much court time and costs may thereby be saved.

Furthermore, whilst I fully understand Eastham J's reluctance to make a definitive statement about the desirability of providing evidence in support of the care plan, it does seem to me that wherever possible that evidence should be available. The extent and nature of the evidence will clearly vary from case to case. Thus where the issue in the case is return home against placement for adoption, a local authority may well have felt inhibited about identifying a prospective adoptive placement until such time as the principle of care leading to adoption has been established by court order. In such a case general evidence about the case or difficulty of identifying a placement for the child should suffice. On the other hand where it is proposed, as in the instant case, that the children be placed with identified foster-carers, evidence from the local authority about those carers and their suitability should be made available. This does not mean the foster-parents in question will need to be called to give evidence. Involvement of such carers in the forensic process is, in my judgment, undesirable in principle unless they have specific factual information to contribute. The local authority should, however, be in a position to put before the court in writing as part of the care plan a description of the placement and of the foster-carers by a worker who has interviewed them and knows them sufficiently to satisfy the court that the placement is suitable. That worker can then be called for cross-examination if need be.

Since in each case the evidence which requires to be called to satisfy the court as to the efficacy of the care plan will vary in substance and in degree, it is a matter for the good sense of the tribunal and the advocates appearing before it to see that a proper balance is struck between the need to satisfy the court about the appropriateness of the care plan on the one hand and the avoidance, on the other, of over-zealous investigation into matters which are properly within the administrative discretion of the local authority.

It will, I hope, be a rare case in which the court's dissatisfaction with the ultimate care plan will be such as to prevent adjudication in a case where the court is satisfied both as to the threshold criteria and that a care order is in the interests of the child. It is very much to be hoped that in the spirit of co-operation and partnership identified by Ward J in C v Solihull MBC a local authority will be sensitive to constructive criticism of its care plan from the court based on the evidence which the court has heard, or from the guardian ad litem. By like token the court will be alert to the difficulties faced by local authorities in terms of resources and manpower.

At the end of the day, however, I am in no doubt that it is the court which is charged with the heavy duty of deciding whether or not a care order should be made and that the court will only make final care orders where it is fully satisfied on both stages of the process described in para. (3) of the principles which I have set out above.

In the instant case I was urged by the guardian ad litem to make an interim care order. In my judgment, the making of interim care orders in cases which are listed as and intended to be the final hearing, and in which the court has heard all the available evidence, needs to be approached with great caution. The court must, in particular, be alert to the danger of using an interim care order as a means of exercising the now defunct supervisory role of the court. The court must also be alert to the danger of diminishing the general principle contained in s. 1(2) of the Act that 'any delay in determining the question is likely to prejudice the welfare of the child'.

RE T (A MINOR) (CARE ORDER: CONDITIONS) [1994] 2 FLR 423 (CA)

NOURSE LJ: This is the judgment of the court, to which each of its members has contributed.

This is an appeal by a local authority from the refusal of his Honour Judge Mott in the Wolverhampton County Court on 5 November 1993 to make a care order in respect of a male child T born on 31 March 1993 and thus aged just over 7 months at the date of the judge's order. The other parties to the proceedings were T's parents and his guardian ad litem, Mrs D.

The judge made a supervision order for 12 months in favour of the local authority and imposed conditions of supervision pursuant to sch. 3, para. 2(1)(b) and (c), and para.

3(1)(a) and (c) to the Children Act 1989. Those conditions are not specified in his order, but we have been shown a letter dated 23 November 1993 from the principal social worker of the local authority's children and families team dealing with the case addressed to the parents in which the specified conditions are:

(1)　attendance at a local children's day centre on 2 days a week from 9.30 am to 11.30 am;

(2)　attendance at clinic appointments as requested by the health visitor; and

(3)　notification to the supervising officer of any change in the child's address.

We think that the form of the judge's order is unsatisfactory. Where, as here, conditions are imposed under a supervision order those conditions ought to be apparent on the face of the order.

It was conceded by the parents in the court below and in this court that the threshold criteria under s. 31 of the 1989 Act were met and that a supervision order was appropriate. There was therefore an acceptance that as a consequence of the history which we shall relate hereafter there was a likelihood of T suffering significant harm attributable to the care likely to be given to him by his parents if an order under s. 31 were not made, such care not being what it would be reasonable to expect a parent to give to him.

The case for the local authority was and remains that an order requiring T's removal from the care of his parents into the care of the local authority under s. 31 with a view to his subsequent adoption outside his natural family represents the only means of protecting him from the likelihood of significant harm, and that accordingly, such an order is in his best interests. For the parents it was argued that T's best interests would be served if he were to be brought up by them, and that the issue of his protection against the likelihood of significant harm could be properly addressed by a supervision order.

Before the judge, the guardian ad litem, on balance, supported the view taken by the local authority. However, during the period between the hearing before the judge and the hearing of this appeal, her view has changed and she has filed a further report which we admitted as fresh evidence without any opposition from the other parties. In that report she acknowledges the progress which T has continued to make in the care of his parents and describes him as 'a thriving happy child who has bonded with both his parents'. Her report continues:

The attachment between parents and child is very strong and it is my opinion that it would be damaging to [T] if he was removed from their care at this stage in his life.

. . . Mr Richard Anelay QC, for the local authority, made it quite plain that if the court allowed the appeal and made a care order, the local authority's care plan remained the same: the child would be removed and placed for adoption. He submitted that the court has no power to direct the local authority as to the implementation of the care plan or to impose conditions on a care order. In particular, he submitted, the court has no power to make a care order and either impose a condition of residence on it or require the local authority to place the child at home.

Mr Allan Levy QC, for the guardian ad litem, sought to persuade us that we had such a power.

Does the court have the power to impose conditions on a care order under s. 31 of the Act: in particular can the court require a local authority (whether as a condition of the making of a care order under s. 31 or otherwise) to place a child in a given setting?

In our judgment, the answer to both these questions is 'no', the point having been authoritatively resolved by the decision of this court in *Re B (Minors) (Termination of Contact: Paramount Consideration)* [1993] Fam 301. However, in deference to Mr Levy's argument and in view of the practical importance of the point to those trying these cases at first instance we propose to give our detailed reasons for rejecting Mr Levy's contentions.

As we understood it, the essence of Mr Levy's argument was that Parliament could not have intended, in its enactment of s. 1, Part IV and s. 100 of the Children Act 1989, to create an irreconcilable tension between the duty imposed on the court by s. 1(1) to treat the child's welfare as its paramount consideration and the duty to delegate the implementation and administration of a care order made under s. 31 to the local authority concerned. If, Mr Levy argued, the welfare principle is truly paramount, the court must have the power, when initiating the placement into care, to make an order which reflects the full scope of its perception of the child's welfare. It follows, according to his argument, that if the threshold criteria under s. 31 are met and the court takes the view that the welfare of the child requires not only that he or she should be the subject of a care order, but also should live at home, then the provisions of s. 1 override any provisions of Part IV to the contrary and the court has the power so to order, either by imposing a condition on the care order or by directing the local authority to place the child at home.

Mr Levy argued that neither s. 100 of the Act nor *Re B (Minors)* (above) was fatal to his submission since the former, properly construed, did not inhibit the power of the court to impose conditions on care orders and the latter could be distinguished in that this court was not there dealing with the initiation of the child into care. He argued accordingly that the passages in the judgment of Butler-Sloss LJ which deal with the effect of the repeal of s. 7 of the Family Law Reform Act 1969 and the effect of s. 100 of the 1989 Act were obiter and thus not binding in this case.

That the tension to which Mr Levy refers exists cannot be doubted: see *Nottinghamshire County Council v P* [1994] Fam 18 at p. 43 where the President, in delivering the judgment of this court, said:

> The court is deeply concerned at the absence of any power to direct this authority to take steps to protect the children. In the former wardship jurisdiction it might well have been able to do so. The operation of the Children Act 1989 is entirely dependent upon the full co-operation of all those involved. This includes the courts, local authorities and the social workers, and all who have to deal with children. Unfortunately, as appears from this case, if a local authority doggedly resists taking the steps which are appropriate to the case of children at risk of suffering significant harm it appears that the court is powerless. The authority may perhaps lay itself open to an application for judicial review but in a case such as this the question arises, 'at whose instance?' The position is one which it is to be hoped will not recur . . .

We have no doubt that there are other circumstances in which the court's wish to impose a particular result which it perceives to be in the interests of the child will be frustrated by the restrictions on the court's powers imposed by Part IV and s. 100 of the Act. Mr Levy, however, submitted that *Nottinghamshire County Council v P* can also be distinguished. Thus, whilst he accepted that the court has no power to compel a local authority to take proceedings under Part IV, he said that quite different considerations arise once the local authority has itself invoked the jurisdiction of the court and sought a care order: in the latter instance the local authority cannot disobey an order of the court or refuse to implement a care order by which the court requires the child to be treated in a particular way.

Mr Levy's argument makes it necessary for us to look closely both at *Re B (Minors)* (above) and at *Kent County Council v C* [1993] Fam 57, a decision of Ewbank J which Mr Levy submitted was wrongly decided. In the former, at [1993] Fam 307H, Butler-Sloss LJ, with whose judgment Kennedy LJ agreed, said:

> Before the implementation of the Children Act 1989 the powers of the magistrates' court to make care orders did not extend beyond the making of the order. Thereafter the local authority took over the care of the child and was not subject to judicial control or monitoring other than by the limited remedy of judicial review: see *A v Liverpool City Council* [1982] AC 363 and *Re W (A Minor) (Wardship: jurisdiction)* [1985] AC 791. By contrast, when a child was committed to care by a judge exercising the wardship jurisdiction in the High Court, or a Matrimonial Causes Act 1973 care order in the High Court or the county court, the judge was able to make directions and require the case to return for further consideration by the court. This monitoring by the court of a child in care has been specifically excluded by the 1989 Act. The earlier provisions have all

been repealed. Section 100 excludes the wardship jurisdiction and the inherent jurisdiction of the High Court in respect of children to be placed in care or who are in care. Consequently, once a care order has been made the court can no longer monitor the administrative arrangements for the child and has no say in those arrangements, unless there is an application before the court.

In our respectful view, this is an entirely accurate statement of the law. Moreover, we do not agree with Mr Levy that the observation of Butler-Sloss LJ that 's. 100 excludes the wardship jurisdiction and the inherent jurisdiction of the High Court in respect of children to be placed in care or who are in care' is obiter. It is a critical part of her reasoning and a necessary prerequisite to the distinction which she then draws with applications for contact to a child in care under s. 34, the critical issue in that case.

The combined effect of the appeal of s. 7 of the Family Law Reform Act 1969 and of s. 100(2) of the 1989 Act is, as Mr Levy properly conceded, to make entry via s. 31 of the 1989 Act the only route into care for a child. The application for a care order can only be made by a local authority or authorised person as defined in s. 31(9). The only order the court is empowered to make under s. 31(1)(a) is an order 'placing the child with respect to whom the application is made in the care of a designated local authority'. Section 31(2) provides that the court may only make such an order if the criteria contained in that subsection are satisfied. Thus it is clear beyond peradventure that the court has no power under s. 31 to impose any conditions on a care order.

Where, therefore, does the welfare principle fit in? Section 1(5) of the Act provides that the court shall not make a care order unless it considers that doing so would be better for the child than making no order at all. Furthermore, by s. 1(3) and (4)(b) where 'the court is considering whether to make . . . an order under Part IV' (in this context, a care order), the court 'shall have regard in particular' to the matters mentioned in s. 1(3). There is in our judgment no doubt that, in carrying out this exercise, the court is applying the welfare principle contained in s. 1(1). The language of the statute is clear and unambiguous. The only care order which can be made is one which 'places' the child in care. The welfare test is applied when the court 'is considering' whether or not to make a care order. Nothing in these provisions permits the court to rely on the welfare principle in order to superimpose conditions on the care order.

Is there anything in s. 100 which is inconsistent with this approach? Mr Levy was unable to point to anything in its provisions which entitles the court to impose its concept of welfare onto the manner in which a care order is implemented. Indeed s. 100(2)(a) can only be read as prohibiting such a course.

Mr Levy referred us to a number of passages in the speeches of Lords Wilberforce and Roskill in *A v Liverpool City Council* [1982] AC 363, and Lords Scarman and Brightman in *Re W (A Minor) (Wardship: Jurisdiction)* [1985] AC 791. He sought once again to distinguish both cases on the basis that neither dealt with the vital stage at which a child was actually placed into care. In our judgment, however, the passages to which Mr Levy referred simply reinforce the correctness of *Re B (Minors)* (above). As those speeches make clear, the proposition that the court's general inherent power is always available to fill gaps or to supplement the powers of the local authority cannot be applied to a situation in which Parliament, by express enactment, has committed specific powers exclusively to the local authority.

It follows that the court does not have the power to make a care order containing either a direction or a condition that the child in question shall reside at home, and accordingly that the position for which the guardian ad litem now contends is not one which this court can impose on the local authority, assuming of course, that such a course of action is perceived to be in the best interests of the child. It also follows that *Kent County Council v C* was correctly decided. Our final observation on the law is that it is the duty of any court hearing an application for a care order carefully to scrutinise the local authority's care plan. If it does not agree with the care plan, it can refuse to make a care order: see *Re J (Minors) (Care: Care Plan)* [1994] 1 FLR 253 at p. 261C–D. The cases in which it is appropriate to take such a course will no doubt be rare.

We therefore pass to consider the actual issue, which can now be succinctly stated: was the judge's decision to make a supervision order and not a care order plainly wrong? It is only if it was that this court can interfere.

12.9.2 WHAT HAPPENS TO THE CHILD WHILST PROCEEDINGS ARE ONGOING?

CHILDREN ACT 1989

38. Interim orders

(1) Where—

(a) in any proceedings on an application for a care order or supervision order, the proceedings are adjourned; or

(b) the court gives a direction under section 37(1),

the court may make an interim care order or an interim supervision order with respect to the child concerned.

(2) A court shall not make an interim care order or interim supervision order under this section unless it is satisfied that there are reasonable grounds for believing that the circumstances with respect to the child are as mentioned in section 31(2).

(3) Where, in any proceedings on an application for a care order or supervision order, a court makes a residence order with respect to the child concerned, it shall also make an interim supervision order with respect to him unless satisfied that his welfare will be satisfactorily safeguarded without an interim order being made.

(4) An interim order made under or by virtue of this section shall have effect for such period as may be specified in the order, but shall in any event cease to have effect on whichever of the following events first occurs—

(a) the expiry of the period of eight weeks beginning with the date on which the order is made;

(b) if the order is the second or subsequent such order made with respect to the same child in the same proceedings, the expiry, of the relevant period;

(c) in a case which falls within subsection (1)(a), the disposal of the application;

(d) in a case which falls within subsection (1)(b), the disposal of an application for a care order or supervision order made by the authority with respect to the child;

(e) in a case which falls within subsection (1)(b) and in which—

(i) the court has given a direction under section 37(4), but

(ii) no application for a care order or supervision order has been made with respect to the child,

the expiry of the period fixed by that direction.

(5) In subsection (4)(b) 'the relevant period' means—

(a) the period of four weeks beginning with the date on which the order in question is made; or

(b) the period of eight weeks beginning with the date on which the first order was made if that period ends later than the period mentioned in paragraph (a).

(6) Where the court makes an interim care order, or interim supervision order, it may give such directions (if any) as it considers appropriate with regard to the medical or psychiatric examination or other assessment of the child; but if the child is of sufficient understanding to make an informed decision he may refuse to submit to the examination or other assessment.

(7) A direction under subsection (6) may be to the effect that there is to be—

(a) no such examination or assessment; or

(b) no such examination or assessment unless the court directs otherwise.

(8) A direction under subsection (6) may be—

(a) given when the interim order is made or at any time while it is in force; and

(b) varied at any time on the application of any person falling within any class of person prescribed by rules of court for the purposes of this subsection.

(9) Paragraphs 4 and 5 of Schedule 3 shall not apply in relation to an interim supervision order.

(10) Where a court makes an order under or by virtue of this section it shall, in determining the period for which the order is to be in force, consider whether any party who was, or might have been, opposed to the making of the order was in a position to argue his case against the order in full.

12.9.3 ASSESSMENTS

RE C (INTERIM CARE ORDER: RESIDENTIAL ASSESSMENT) [1997] 1 FLR 1 (HL)

LORD BROWNE-WILKINSON: My Lords, this appeal concerns a child, T, who was born on 11 June 1995. At the end of October 1995 he was taken to hospital where he was found to be suffering from serious injuries which, in the view of an experienced consultant paediatrician, were non-accidental. His parents, in whose care he had been, were young and inexperienced, the mother being 17 at the time of his birth and the father 16. They are immature and have a difficult relationship with each other. They lack family backing. They are unable to give any satisfactory explanation of how T came to suffer his injuries.

On 1 November 1995 the local authority obtained an emergency protection order. On 9 November 1995 the court made an interim care order under s. 38 of the Children Act 1989, which order has since been periodically extended from time to time. The court has appointed a guardian ad litem for T. After T's discharge from hospital, he was placed by the authority with foster-parents with whom he is still living. It is not yet known whether he has suffered permanent brain damage.

Social workers employed by the local authority conducted a prolonged investigation of T and his parents over a period of some 7 months. They reported to the court in what has been called the Orange Book assessment that, although the parents were deficient in parenting skills and their relationship was difficult, they had made progress in their caring for T, with whom they had had contact for some 4–5 hours daily from Monday to Friday in each week. They expressed the following conclusion:

> At this stage in the assessment we feel that a more in-depth assessment at a residential unit is essential and should be undertaken as soon as possible. This placement would need to be fully supervised in an attempt to test out for longer and more realistic periods of time the parents' ability to cope whilst affording T protection. The gap in the assessment so far has clearly been the lack of opportunity to assess the parents' ability to cope over long periods of time and in particular stressful situations. This will enable the parents' care to be observed at night times where there are regular occasions when T has little sleep and is difficult to settle. These situations can be demanding and stressful for carers, especially if this continues for consecutive nights as is the situation with T.

There has also been an assessment of the parents by a clinical psychologist who supported the proposal for a residential assessment of T and the parents together.

The guardian ad litem, having seen the reports of the social workers and the psychologist, reported her views to the court. She recognised that this was a very high risk case. She pointed to the severe injuries suffered by T as a baby of which there was no adequate explanation and to the youth, immaturity and unsatisfactory relationship of the parents. On the other side, she drew attention to the commitment shown by the parents in attending 5 days a week for 4–5 hours for supervised contact with T and the improvement in their parenting skills. She expressed her conclusion as follows:

> It is my view that it is inappropriate to make a final decision on T's future placement without the information which could be obtained from a residential assessment. Even if there is only a slight possibility that T could be rehabilitated with his parents I feel this possibility should, in fairness to T, be fully explored.

Despite the recommendation made by their own social workers that residential assessment would be desirable, the local authority did not agree. It was initially indicated that the refusal of the local authority to countenance a residential assessment was based on financial grounds: the proposed residential assessment would cost some £18,000–£24,000. However, the reasons put forward by the assistant director of social services to the court were not linked to money. She considered in detail what she called the crucial areas: the lack of explanation of the injuries, the lack of frankness by the parents as to the cause of the injuries, the unstable relationship between the parents, the lack of the parenting skills necessary to deal with T's special needs and the fact that the demands of those special needs would produce the stress on the parents which may have led to them injuring T. In the light of those factors, she expressed the view that any consideration of rehabilitation with his parents would expose T to an unacceptable level of risk. . . .

It was in those circumstances that the case came before Hogg J on the hearing of an application that she should make a direction under s. 38(6) of the Children Act that T and his parents should be the subject of a residential assessment at a specified place. Section 38(6) provides:

> Where the court makes an interim care order, or interim supervision order, it may give such directions (if any) as it considers appropriate with regard to the medical or psychiatric examination or other assessment of the child; but if the child is of sufficient understanding to make an informed decision he may refuse to submit to the examination or other assessment.

Before the judge, the local authority submitted that the court had no power under the subsection to direct the local authority to carry out the residential assessment proposed. The judge rejected this submission. . . .

The local authority appealed to the Court of Appeal (Butler-Sloss, Waite and Roch LJJ). The primary ground of appeal was that the judge had no jurisdiction to make the order. Butler-Sloss LJ (with whom the other Lord Justices agreed) held that the Court of Appeal was bound by its earlier decision in *Re M* and allowed the appeal. But she was plainly unhappy at the result. . . .

T's parents appeal against that decision. Your Lordships are therefore faced with a short, but important, point on the construction of s. 38(6).

Before considering the exact point at issue, it is important to put s. 38(6) in context. Before the passing of the Children Act 1989, the court, in the exercise of its wardship jurisdiction, retained a degree of control over its wards, even if the child was in the care of the local authority. Due to the decision of your Lordships' House in *A* v *Liverpool City Council* [1982] AC 363 those powers were, as a matter of practice, limited so as to be exercised only when there were gaps in the statutory regime or in support of the powers of the local authority. Apart from such cases, it was the local authority who had the power and the duty to make decisions as to the welfare of the child in its care. This approach was strengthened by the 1989 Act, which by s. 100 expressly excludes the wardship jurisdiction in certain cases.

Part IV of the Act contains a code regulating care and supervision orders (public law cases). Section 31 provides that the court may make a care or supervision order on the application of a local authority or of a very limited class of other applicants. The order, if made, places the child in the care of the local authority. But a final order can only be made if the threshold laid down by s. 31(2) is crossed, ie the court is satisfied that the child is suffering or is likely to suffer significant harm and that such harm is attributable either to the care being given to the child not being what it would be reasonable to expect a parent to give to him or to the fact that the child is beyond parental control.

There are three points to note about a final care order under s. 31. First, it is the court which has to decide whether or not to make a care order, Secondly, before the court can make an order it has to be satisfied that the harm being suffered or anticipated is attributable to the actual or anticipated care being received by the child, an issue likely to be dominated by the evidence as to the abilities and conduct of the parents and the relationship between the child and those parents. Thirdly, the threshold can be crossed where the harm is due to the child being beyond parental control, an issue on which the relationship between the child and his parents is central.

In many cases, including the present, the determination of the question whether the court should make a final care order under s. 31 requires information to be gathered as to the child's circumstances and for that information to be placed before the court to enable it to make its decision. But there are many cases where the child will be at risk in the period pending final determination of the application for a care order. To meet this need, s. 38 provides for the making of an interim care order where proceedings for a care order under s. 31 are adjourned. The threshold applicable to interim care orders is lower than that laid down by s. 31(2) for final orders: the court only has to be satisfied that 'there are reasonable grounds for believing' that the requirements of s. 31(2) are satisfied. If so satisfied, the court may make an interim care order of limited duration, initially for not more than 8 weeks and on any renewal for not more than a further 4 weeks.

The effect of a care order is laid down by s. 33. In general, this section applies as much to interim care orders as to final orders since the words 'a care order' are defined to include both: s. 31(11). When a care order is made, s. 33 requires the local authority to receive and keep the child in its care: s. 33(1). The local authority is given parental responsibility for the child and (with certain exceptions) the power to determine the extent to which parents and others having parental responsibility for the child are allowed to meet such responsibilities: s. 33(3).

Therefore the context in which s. 38(6) has to be considered is this. The child is in the care of the local authority under an interim care order pending the decision by the court whether or not to make a final care order. Under the interim care order the decision-making power as to the care, residence and general welfare of the child is vested in the local authority, not in the court. However, for the purpose of making its ultimate decision whether to grant a full care order, the court will need the help of social workers, doctors and others as to the child and his circumstances. Information and assessments from these sources are necessary not only to determine whether the s. 31 threshold has been crossed (including the cause of the existing or anticipated harm to the child from its existing circumstances) but also in exercising its discretion whether or not to make a final care order. It is the practice of the courts to require the local authority seeking a final care order to put forward a care plan for the court to consider in exercising such discretion. Section 38(6) deals with the interaction between the powers of the local authority entitled to make decisions as to the child's welfare in the interim and the needs of the court to have access to the relevant information and assessments so as to be able to make the ultimate decision. It must always be borne in mind that in exercising its jurisdiction under the Act, the court's function is investigative and non-adversarial: *Re L (Police Investigation: Privilege)* [1996] 1 FLR 731.

Against that background, I turn to consider the construction of s. 38(6) which I have already quoted. It is important also to refer to s. 38(7) which provides as follows:

A direction under subsection (6) may be to the effect that there is to be—
    (a) no such examination or assessment; or
    (b) no such examination or assessment unless the court directs otherwise.

There are two possible constructions of s. 38(6) and (7), one narrow, the other purposive and broader. The Court of Appeal in *Re M* [1996] 2 FLR 464 adopted the narrow view. They held that the words 'other assessment of the child' had to be construed as ejusdem generis with the words 'medical or psychiatric examination'. They attached decisive importance to the fact that the subsection only refers to the examination or assessment 'of the child' and makes no reference to the examination or assessment of any other person in relation to the child. They further held that for the court to order a residential assessment of the parents and child together at a specified place would involve the court in an unwarranted usurpation by the court of the local authority's power (as the authority having having parental responsibility under the interim care order) to regulate where the child is to reside. In addition to supporting the arguments of the Court of Appeal in *Re M*, Mr Harris, for the local authority in the present appeal, submitted that Parliament cannot have intended the court to have power to require the local authority against its own judgment to expend scarce resources: he submitted that the local authority is the only body which can properly assess how such resources are to be allocated as between the social services and the other services it has to provide and as between the various calls on its social services budget.

My Lords, I cannot accept this narrow construction of the subsection. The Act should be construed purposively so as to give effect to the underlying intentions of Parliament. As I have sought to demonstrate, the dividing-line between the functions of the court on the one hand and the local authority on the other is that a child in interim care is subject to control of the local authority, the court having no power to interfere with the local authority's decisions save in specified cases. The cases where, despite that overall control, the court is to have power to intervene are set out, inter alia, in s. 38(6) and (7).

The purpose of s. 38(6) is to enable the court to obtain the information necessary for its own decision, notwithstanding the control over the child which in all other respects rests with the local authority. I therefore approach the subsection on the basis that the court is to have such powers to override the views of the local authority as are necessary to enable the court to discharge properly its function of deciding whether or not to accede to the local authority's application to take the child away from its parents by obtaining a care order. To allow the local authority to decide what evidence is to go before the court at the final hearing would be in many cases, including the present, to allow the local authority by administrative decision to pre-empt the court's judicial decision.

This broad approach is supported by consideration of s. 38(7) which does not appear to have been drawn to the attention of the Court of Appeal either in *Re M* or in the present case, subsection (7) confers on the court the power to prohibit an examination or assessment which the local authority is proposing to make. It is manifestly directed to the type of conduct by social services revealed by the Cleveland Inquiry, ie repeated interviews and assessments of the child and his parents which are detrimental to the child. This negative control by the court cannot have been intended to be limited to cases where the child, and only the child, is to be assessed. If it is to be fully effective to prevent damage to the child, the power under s. 38(7) must also extend to cases where it is proposed to assess the relationship between the parents and the child.

I am not convinced by the reasons which persuaded the Court of Appeal in *Re M* to adopt the narrow construction limiting the ambit of the section to assessments of the child alone, such assessments to be of the same type as medical or psychiatric examinations. First, I can see no reason for the application of the ejusdem generis principle. What is the genus? Subsection (6) refers not to the 'medical psychiatric or other examination' of the child but to 'other assessment' of the child. Some assessments, even if confined to the child itself, may not involve any examination of that child, yet plainly such an assessment is authorised by the subsection. I can find no genus to which the principle can apply.

Next, it is true that s. 38(6) and (7) only refer to the assessment 'of the child' and not, as is proposed in the present case, a joint assessment of the child and the parents, including the parents' attitude and behaviour towards the child. But it is impossible to assess a young child divorced from his environment. The interaction between the child and his parents or other persons looking after him is an essential element in making any assessment of the child. This is shown particularly clearly by cases in which the courts have to decide whether the threshold requirements of s. 31 are satisfied because of the harm to the child that is likely to be suffered because the child is beyond parental control. How can the court determine that issue without considering the relationship between the child and the parents? The court has no power to order the parents to take part in any assessment against their wishes, any more than, as the final words of s. 38(6) show, the court can order the child to do so if the child is capable of making an informed decision. But what the interests of justice require is not a power to compel the parent to take part in such assessment but a power in the court to override the powers over the child which the local authority would otherwise enjoy under the interim care order. If the narrower construction were to be adopted the local authority could simply refuse to allow the child to take part in any assessment with his parents.

12.10 The Final Hearing: What are the Options?

12.10.1 NO ORDER

'Child abuse: finding a balance', *New Society,* **3 July 1987**

Specific worries about the events in Cleveland are difficult to answer, given the present uncertainty. The removal of so many children apparently so suddenly, on the basis of physical signs alone, in one authority has rightly aroused concern. It may have been an excess of zeal on the part of the doctors or merely the clearing of a backlog of cases following their recent appointment.

Sixteen extra social worker posts for specialists in child abuse have been created in Cleveland in the last year since the Jasmine Beckford report. This may also have something to do with it. The harder you look for abuse the more likely you are to find it.

The high proportion of children apparently showing physical signs is also remarkable. Given that most abuse—fondling, masturbation, oral sex—leaves no visible sign, this suggests what is barely credible: that the Cleveland doctors have still uncovered only the tip of the iceberg.

The sudden removal of so many children is a particular worry. In cases where there is a risk of violence or of the abuse continuing, removal may be necessary. But, setting aside the risk of a mistake, there is a danger with abusing parents that it may be interpreted as the expulsion of 'a core of moral evil' from the family. Once the child has left, the parents can cover up and deny their own emotional and sexual problems and scapegoat the child. The child is victimised in two ways: punished by being separated from its family and prevented from resolving its confusion about the abuse because this cannot be dealt with outside the family.

But the events in Cleveland raise a more general concern. The summary removal of children—in all but the most serious cases—risks turning the clock back. Child sex abuse is only just coming out of the closet. Increasing the threat of retribution—from police, doctors or social workers risks driving it back in.

In 1984 a CIBA Foundation Study Group on child abuse called for the creation of 'a non-punitive climate' which would encourage parents to come forward without the fear that family breakdown is inevitable. This requires that professionals recognise and respond to the minimal signs of sex abuse in a way which secures the safety of the child as well as initiating therapeutic work with the family. Only then do we have a chance of ending 'the years of self-sacrificial behaviour' that characterise these children. Three years later, we still have a long way to go.

This week, the National Society for the Prevention of Cruelty to Children announced a 137 per cent increase in reported cases of sexual abuse last year. The care of many of these children will require the authorisation of a court but last week the government dropped its expected bill to reform child care law from the Queen's speech on the grounds that the legislative programme was too full.

The field of child care law is a mess, with at least ten different routes into care. The main changes proposed in last January's white paper, on which there is all-party agreement, would have introduced extra safe-guards to prevent the unnecessary removal of children and strengthened the rights of parents. Had it been on the statute book today, much of the pain and anguish experienced by the families in Cleveland might have been avoided. The government's decision to drop the bill means that their suffering may not be the last.

Silberberg, N, and Silberberg, M, 'Abusing Poor Children by Trying to Protect Them',
The Haworth Press, Inc. 1982

The American Humane Association developed a list of signals by which abuse or neglect can be detected. These signals include:

—being frequently absent from or late to school
—arriving at school too early or hanging around after class without reason
—being dressed in dirty or torn clothes, being unwashed, or being dressed inappropriately for the weather
—being shy, and withdrawn
—needing, but not receiving, medical attention, such as dental work and eyeglasses
—sleeping in class
—having aggressive parents, parents who do not show up for appointments, or slovenly, or dirty parents
—having parents whom the other parents or children do not know

There is little question as to who will be accused in this diagnostic game. It is much easier to be seen as a neglectful parent if you are poor than if you are rich.

Most writers agree that child abuse occurs in all socioeconomic classes but that most intervention occurs in the lower classes. Clearly, in poor homes proper medical care is a problem; there have been tomes written on the inability of the poor to gain access to the medical care system in any meaningful way or to pay for care if they enter the system. Tardiness may mean that a child is trying to avoid an inappropriate school program (which is the responsibility of the school, not the parent) or that older siblings have to help the child get ready for school while the parent is at work. Parents whose child is not successful in school may, attempt to avoid the humiliation of returning to school to be told how bad the child is. According to this list, they must be accused of neglect for that. Even the child who dozes in class is suspect, though adults who doze through lectures are taken for granted.

The dangers in the descriptions cited above should be obvious to anyone concerned with civil liberties. Is the justified concern for a minority of children who are mistreated by their parents sufficient to allow teachers, public health nurses, school social workers, and others to make judgments about whether a family conforms to acceptable standards, especially when those standards most often represent the middle class majority? Is this not, in itself, abusive?

Are abused children better off when 'helping agencies' intervene? Usually intervention is unequally applied, often it is ineffective, sometimes it is downright harmful. As Wald (1975) suggested in a critical review of intervention techniques, many cases of public intervention are unwarranted, and often the state takes too much control over child rearing.

Too often economic considerations dictate treatment. In one state, the school district must pay for most of a disturbed child's treatment unless the child is sent out of state. Thus, there is always a great deal of pressure to institutionalize children out of state. In addition, we have heard of psychiatrists and psychologists receiving kickbacks from institutions to which they refer clients. Who investigates these stories, and what is done if they are true? The emphasis on child abuse and neglect may create jobs for middle class people with little payoff to the potential recipients.

Sometimes the abuser benefits from the abuse. A 19-year-old woman reported on in a professional journal was unable to receive any support for raising, her child, although she was poor. After she burned and lacerated her child, she received a college scholarship, day-care assistance, and other services. Had she not abused her child, she might still be living in poverty. Would it not be better if aid were provided before such serious calls for help arise?

Parents who harm their children are accused of child abuse, but if officials harm children, they can say they were rehabilitating the child. . . . Moreover, we have personally encountered the following types of abuse:

—children being removed from their 'neglectful' Indian homes and placed in 'good' Christian foster homes in areas so remote that the parents cannot visit the children, this lack of visitation then being viewed by the authorities as lack of interest! Some of these children may be placed in dozens of foster homes before they are 18. If foster homes are in short supply, we have seen brutal foster parents ignored by the watchers.
—behaviour modification techniques including time-out rooms, electro-shock, slapping, and other techniques known in the scientific jargon as 'negative'—in mental hospitals, clinics, and even schools.
—the wholesale drugging of children in order to achieve the narrow range of behavioral conformity that is tolerated in schools.
—police arbitrarily, removing a family of children from their home in the evening while the parents are out and placing them in a shelter where the staff refuses to allow access to the parent.

Why did the child abuse fighters not prevent these events? Why are they concerned mostly about abuse done by parents?

Now that state intervention has been institutionalized, it is time to introduce some checks and balances to assure that overzealous pursuit of child abuse by schools and welfare departments does not result in more harm than good being done to the children. We would propose the establishment of community review teams, consisting of con- sumers and sympathetic service providers who would have investigative or appeal functions. Presently, parents accused of child abuse find the welfare system functioning as both judge and jury. The parents find themselves lined up alone against the county social worker, the county child abuse worker, the county attorney, the county psychologist, and the county judge. The parent participates in a process that may cost $20,000 or $30,000 a case but is unable to obtain the damage deposit for an apartment! . . .

For some reason, our society is willing to spend large amounts for cure and little for prevention. We suggest that society examine the social forces and social institutions that lead to abuse and neglect rather than attempt to cure the situation on a case-by-case basis after it is too late.

12.10.2   CARE VERSUS SUPERVISION

RE D (A MINOR) [1993] 2 FLR 423 (FamD)

EWBANK J: The four psychiatrists all agree that there are risks involved with a child being with the father because of what has happened in the past. They do not really deal, nor are competent to deal, with the question whether safeguards should take the form of a supervision order or a care order. Doctor B, who is a consultant child psychiatrist, in her report which was made on behalf of the social services department, pointed out that in her opinion the father was not the nice young man that he would wish everyone to believe he is and said that it was quite probable that he has been less than truthful. However, she says:

. . . the question before the court is does he pose a significant risk to the safety of R? I have to say that in my opinion I do not believe that he does. The reasons on which I base this opinion are as follows: first, he is 9 years older and more mature; secondly, he is in the first confiding relationship which he has had and we know from research how important confiding relationships are in protecting from depression and other mental adversities; thirdly, he has given up drinking; fourthly, he is clearly attached to R and demonstrably tender towards him; fifthly, he is now partnered by a woman of a very different calibre to I's mother. I's mother was always of poor intelligence and was further handicapped by a very deprived childhood and probably was in the early stages of Huntington's Chorea when the events leading to I's death took place. For these reasons, I think the likelihood of R coming to significant harm in the care of the father is small. However, I believe that a supervision order for the maximum time allowed would allow for extra protection,

and she suggests a 3-year supervision order. In passing I remind myself that the maximum time for an initial supervision order is one year.

Doctor W was appointed by the guardian ad litem. He says:

I agree with the proposals put forward by Doctor B. I agree that an order is necessary because neither of R's parents accept the risk which the father poses. Nor do members of the extended family. [And by that he means the mother's mother and father.] An order would allow the local authority the right to supervise R's well-being. I also agree the father should not be allowed sole care of R in the initial months of his return to the care of his parents.

Then Doctor H, who is also a consultant psychiatrist, gave an opinion on behalf of the parents. He says:

This is obviously a most difficult case in which to give a firm opinion. Clearly the first cohabitation in the 1980s between the father and D was a disaster and led to much violence towards the three children and between the two partners. At the time too quite clearly the father was drinking heavily and womanising and one has to bear in mind that he was under considerable pressure from a mentally ill woman who kept leaving him.

Then he goes on to say:

This cohabitation appears to be totally different. The father has clearly matured over the last 10 years to an enormous degree and now appears, to be a hard-working reasonably upright citizen who has given up womanising and drinking and is devoting himself to set up a family life. I can of course in no way guarantee that there may not be some repetition of what happened in 1983, but the probability in my opinion is low although of course intense supervision will be necessary for the first few months if the couple were allowed to have their baby back at their home with regular visits from the health visitor and social workers.

Mr H has been the social worker involved. He has been impressed with the co-operation of the father and impressed with the care given by the father and the mother to R, but he says he agrees there is a high risk and he feels he does not have a trusting relationship with the mother and father. He does not think they would confide with the local authority and he does not think that the local authority would be informed about early stages of concern if there were any. He told me that in relation to the original draft contract, which is talking about a supervision order for one year, after a year the local authority might move to a voluntary agreement with the father and mother. He pointed out that the mother does not see the father as any risk to R.

The mother and father for their part do not see any need for local authority intervention of any sort, although they will co-operate. . . .

Before either a supervision order or a care order can be made by the court the threshold conditions of s. 31 have to be met. The first condition is that the child is suffering or is likely to suffer significant harm. Because of the evidence of the psychiatrist and because of the history of the case it is clear, in my judgment, that there is a serious risk that violence might occur on behalf of the father. So that condition, in my judgment, is met. The second condition is that the likelihood of harm is attributable to the care given to the child not being what it would be reasonable to expect a parent to give to it. Clearly, if the father were to injure the child that condition would also be met. So that it is open to the court to make a supervision order or a care order. I have to consider whether any order is needed. Clearly, in this case, to safeguard the child one or other orders will be needed. At first sight it would appear that a supervision order should be made if the child is living with the parents, a care order if the child is not living with the parents. But the statute is more flexible than that. Schedule 2, para. 14 has the heading 'Regulations as to conditions under which a child in care is allowed to live with a parent', and the paragraph provides that regulations may impose requirements in relation to a local authority allowing a child to live with his parents. So that it is open under a care order for the child to live with the parents, as in this case.

A supervision order can only be made in the first instance for one year, as provided by sch. 3, para. 6(1) to the Children Act. Paragraphs 6(3) and (4) allow an extension for a further 2 years. Schedule 3, paras 2, 3 and 4 provide for directions to be given on a supervision order. Paragraph 2 provides for directions requiring the child to comply with a variety of orders. Paragraph 3 deals with the responsible person—that will either be the mother or father in this case—and para. 4 deals with psychiatric and medical examinations. It is suggested in this case that these paragraphs and the powers given to the supervising officer would enable the child's welfare to be monitored by, regular medical examinations, by attendance at a children's centre, and directions as to where the child should live, and any other directions which seem appropriate.

If there is a breach of a supervision order the supervising officer, under s. 35(1)(c), has to consider whether to apply to the court for a variation of the supervision order or the discharge of the order. There is no direct way of enforcing the directions made under a supervision order.

The guardian ad litem in this case fears slackening of the terms of the supervision order, and indeed the withering away of the supervision order altogether, having regard to the local authority attitude towards the parents. The local authority are concerned about working with the parents. They fear that a care order might undermine the co-operation they are now receiving from the parents. And although they have spoken of a supervision order for one year, I am assured that at the end of the year there will be consideration given carefully to apply to extend the supervision order if they thought it was necessary. But the guardian ad litem says they may decide not to renew the supervision order after one year and if that was their decision the guardian ad litem would be in no position to suggest any contrary course.

The mother and father are not yet married. The father is not in a position to marry the mother because he is not yet divorced. Accordingly the mother has sole parental responsibility under s. 3 of the Children Act. But it is likely that in one way or another by marriage or under s. 4 the father will acquire parental responsibility and I approach the case on the basis that that is likely to be the case.

If a care order were made then, under s. 33(3)(a), the local authority would have parental responsibility for R and they would have the power to limit the parental responsibility of the mother and father if they thought it was necessary under s. 33(3)(b). Under reg. 9 of the Placement of Children with Parents Etc Regulations 1991 the local authority have to satisfy themselves of the welfare of a child who has been placed by them and might visit the child in any event at intervals of not more than 6 weeks during the first year of the placement and thereafter at intervals of not more than 3 months. The advantage of a care order as opposed to a supervision order, in the submission of the guardian ad litem, is that a care order is unlimited in time and can only be revoked by an application to the court and even when revoked the court can substitute a supervision order. That is under s. 39 of the Children Act.

The local authority feel that a care order is too strong an order to be made in the circumstances of this case. They feel that they are working well together with the parents and that a care order would undermine that. But my judgment that approach misses the real point in the case. The point in the case is the protection of R. In any event, the mother and father have said that they will co-operate with the local authority whatever order is made.

The father, as I have mentioned, has denied that he has ever caused an injury to any child. Children in his care, however, have been injured, and one baby has been killed, and he has been found guilty of wilful cruelty to that child. The local authority and all the professionals in this case have approached the case on the basis that it is likely that the father did kill the baby and I approach the case on the same basis.

. . . So, in my judgment, a care order should be made in this case, despite the views of the local authority. This means that the safeguards will continue and I am intending to continue them as long as is necessary, and certainly, in my judgment, it is not likely to be unnecessary before the child reaches school age at the age of 5. So I would not expect any application to revoke this order before then.

RE O (CARE OR SUPERVISION ORDER) [1996] 2 FLR 755 (FamD)

HALE J: This is an appeal against the decision of the Bradford Family Proceedings Court on 13 March 1996. The court made care orders relating to six children: M, a boy, who was born on 7 April 1987, and so is aged 9; C, a girl, who was born on 22 June 1988, and so is aged 7 years and 10 months; R, a boy, who was born on 2 April 1990, and so is aged 6; P, a boy, who was born on 28 August 1991, and so is aged 4 years and 8 months; V, a girl, who was born on 28 May 1993, and so is nearly 3; and W, a boy, who was born on 30 May 1994, and so is 23 months old. The children have always lived with their parents. They married in 1975, and have a much older child S, a boy, who is aged 17. The mother is also now pregnant again.

There have been long-standing concerns from health professionals about the children's development and certain specific health needs which have not been adequately ad-dressed in the past. The local authority were first involved with the family in 1992, but in 1993 the children were taken off the child protection register. There was a re-referral from the health visitor in late 1994, and the concerns then expressed were felt not to have been adequately addressed by the time of a case conference in May 1995. Hence, the local authority began care proceedings in June 1995. A series of interim supervision orders was made, and a comprehensive assessment was conducted.

The local authority went to the hearing seeking supervision orders. The local authority had no intention of removing the children from their home, but it wanted to maintain the progress which had already been made in working with this family, in getting them to keep appointments, and in gaining weight in the children. The guardian ad litem, on the other hand, wanted the court to make care orders. This was not so that the children

THE PUBLIC LAW RELATING TO CHILDREN

might be removed from their parents, but so that the local authority could share parental responsibility with them, and ensure therefore that the children's needs were met as and when required. The court made the care orders.

. . . one has to consider the reasons given by the justices in this case. The first point made is that they misdirected themselves in law, in that in their reasons they state that: 'In reaching our decision we have put the needs of the children as our paramount consideration'. As a matter of language that is, of course, incorrect. Once the threshold criteria have been established, the welfare of the children is the paramount consideration. It is difficult in this case to know whether the justices when they used the word 'needs' in effect meant 'welfare', in which case this would simply be a slip, or whether when using the word 'needs' they were elevating those needs above all the other aspects of the welfare of children which are referred to in s. 1 of the 1989 Act.

If this were the only reason to attack the decision reached by the justices, I would not be inclined to consider it such a material misdirection as to vitiate their decision. However, it does have to be looked at in the context of a case in which there was one main issue: that was whether, given that these children are, on any view, to remain, at least for the foreseeable future, living with their parents, their welfare will be better served by making a supervision order as asked for by the local authority, or a care order as asked for by the guardian. In relation to that choice, it is suggested that they misdirected themselves in one material particular, and also in conducting the balancing exercise, gave the wrong amount of weight to the relevant factors.

If one looks at the authorities on that particular issue, it is not surprising that all the reported cases so far concern the question of whether it is appropriate to make a care order, even though there is no present intention to remove the children from home. This is not surprising, because at first sight one would assume that if children are to remain at home the appropriate order is one for supervision of what is taking place within the home, together with a range of possible requirements which can be inserted under the Act. The authorities hold, nevertheless, that a care order may be made in such circumstances. This was held before the Children Act 1989, in the case of *M v Westminster City Council* [1985] FLR 325, and affirmed after the Act by the Court of Appeal in the case of *Re T (A Minor) (Care or Supervision Order)* [1994] 1 FLR 103. It is worth bearing in mind that the case of *Re T* was a case of extreme neglect where four previous children had been neglected and removed permanently from the home, and although it was planned that the youngest child should remain at home, the likelihood of harm to that child was such that it was considered that the local authority should be in a position to remove that child immediately. . . .

I would only point out that there must be some cases in which a supervision order is in the children's best interests. It stands to reason. Parliament provided a duty in local authorities to take reasonable steps through the provision of services under Part III of the Act to prevent children within their area suffering ill-treatment or neglect. That is in para. 4 of sch. 2 to the 1989 Act. It also provided a duty to take reasonable steps designed to reduce the need to bring proceedings for care or supervision orders with respect to children within their area, and also to reduce the need to bring any family or other proceedings with respect to such children which might lead to them being placed in the authority's care. That is in para. 7 of that Schedule. Thus local authorities have considerable duties to provide services to prevent children coming to harm, and it was Parliament's intention that those services should be offered.

Parliament also provided both a care order and a supervision order, although it is quite clear from s. 31(1), that once an application is made for an order under that section, the court is free to make a different order from the one which is asked for by the local authority. Nevertheless, if the court is to impose upon the authority an order other than that for which it asks, there should be very cogent reasons indeed to do so. It must be right to approach the question of the children's interests from the point of view which is exemplified by s. 1(5) of the Act, that when considering whether to make any order under the Act the court is not to make an order unless it considers that doing so would be better for the child than making no order at all, and by s. 1(3)(g) where it is required to consider the range of powers available under the Act in the proceedings in question. It is accepted by all the parties before this court that the court should begin with a preference for the less interventionist rather than the more interventionist approach. This should be considered to be in the better interests of the children, again unless there are cogent reasons to the contrary.

The justices in this case referred to three benefits of a care order over a supervision order, which appear to be taken from the case of *Re S (J)* [1993] 2 FLR 919. First, they say that a care order is unlimited in time, and would last until the children are 18 years old, and requires an application to be made to the court for its discharge or alteration to a supervision order. That, of course, is correct, but they go on to say: 'This, we feel, gives the court an on-going opportunity to assess the care and welfare of these children. This situation does not arise with a supervision order'. In fact, that is the reverse of the case. Under a care order, apart from questions of contact between the children and significant people in their lives, the court cedes all control over what is to happen to the children to the local authority; the court cannot assess the care and welfare of these children; it has to trust the local authority to do so. A supervision order, on the other hand, is one in which the local authority will have to return to the court for an extension, or indeed for a care order, should things not go well. That in itself is an important feature of a supervision order rather than a care order, because it has to be borne in mind that a care order gives the local authority the power to remove any or all of these children from their home without resort to a court, and in a way which can only effectively be challenged by the parents either through applications for contact with their children or by applications to discharge the care order.

Secondly, the justices say that under a care order the local authority acquires parental responsibility for the children, with power to determine the extent to which the parents might meet their parental responsibilities for their children. That is an accurate statement of the position, and it is a particularly important statement in the context of this case. In effect, what the guardian wishes to achieve is that the local authority is in a position to insist that certain aspects of the meeting of parental responsibility are carried out as and when the need arises.

The third reason mentioned by the justices is that in the event of the making of a care order the local authority are under a duty to safeguard the welfare of the children who are the subject of those orders. That is a reference to their duty under s. 22(3)(a) of the 1989 Act. It is pointed out that under s. 17(1)(a) of the 1989 Act the local authority have the general duty to safeguard and promote the welfare of children within their area who are in need. It is suggested, therefore, that there is no great distinction between the duties in s. 22 and the duties in s. 17.

There is, to my mind, a considerable distinction. The duty in s. 22 is towards the individual child who is being looked after by the authority. The duty in s. 17 is to the community of children in need within their area, and so is of a general rather than an individual nature. Nevertheless, where there are children whose needs have clearly been identified by the local authority, the local authority will obviously regard itself as being under a duty to do what it can to ensure that those needs are met, and so the distinction in a case such as this, particularly when the two other duties from Sch 2 to which I have drawn attention are borne in mind, becomes specific and clear.

As far as the balancing exercise is concerned, they appear to have given four reasons in favour of a care rather than a supervision order. The first was that neither parent gave evidence before them and they state that this aspect of the case weighed very heavily with them when deciding which type of order to make. This is a matter of considerable concern, because it had apparently been agreed between the advocates that there was no need for the parents to be called and give evidence. Had the justices been intending to attach so much weight to this in their reasons, they should, at the very least, have mentioned this and given the parents an opportunity of reconsidering their position. Without that opportunity, the parents' failure to give evidence should, in the submission of the local authority, with which I agree, have been treated quite neutrally.

The second reason that they seem to have given was that the local authority's assessment of the family was incomplete because of the parents' lack of full co-operation, and that this had some bearing on their assessment of the care plan presented by the local authority. If weight is to be attached to this factor, and I do not suggest that it is unimportant, it should be looked at in the context of what the assessment was for, the bearing which the gaps in the assessment might have on the needs of the children, and the best way in which those needs might be met. Only then can it be decided whether those gaps are material.

The third reason that they gave was that they were not satisfied that the local authority would bring the case back after a year of a supervision order if the problems remain. They may very well have been thinking of the history of the case, which was drawn very fully to their attention by the guardian ad litem. They may also have been thinking of the views of the guardian ad litem that the local authority had shown a marked reluctance to take action in response to the concerns expressed by the health professionals. The authority had closed the case on one occasion, and was now only seeking a supervision order. On the other hand, of course, the local authority had reopened the case, had considered the views of the case conference that the concerns had not been met up to May 1995, had brought proceedings, and had reached the conclusion as a result of that that they could work with the family, and that they wished to do so under the auspices of a supervision order rather than a care order. If the justices were going to reject the clear evidence of the social worker that he felt that he could work with the family under a supervision order, and also that if it did not work they would come back to court, they should have made their reasons for doing so rather clearer.

The fourth point that they appear to have relied upon is a statement in their reasons that not only did they have grave concerns about the sincerity of the parents' willingness to co-operate with anyone in authority, but that they were of the view that the parents would actively build barriers between themselves and the local authority and co-operation would be both sparingly and reluctantly given. It is one thing for families in their heart of hearts to resent the interference of the local authority and to have difficulty in accepting why the local authority has concerns. It is quite another thing for families actively to build barriers to keep the local authority out. There is evidence in this case, quite strong evidence, of the parents not accepting the need for local authority intervention, and there is evidence from time to time of their having resisted visits—in particular, a visit of the health visitor immediately after the first interim supervision order was made—but it would be going too far to say that that is actively building barriers between themselves and the local authority.

On the other hand, it can be said that set against those four reasons the justices do not appear to have given sufficient weight to other factors. These were, first, the improvements which had taken place in the course of the proceedings. The paediatrician had seen the children in August 1995 and November 1995, and there had been a demonstrable gain in weight. This did, of course, indicate that there were non-organic causes for the poor weight gain in the past, but it also indicated that it was possible for the parents to modify what they were doing in accordance with the professionals' views. There was evidence from the family centre worker that, whatever the parents had said, they had tried to co-operate with what the family centre wanted, and there had been progress in some areas, albeit quicker in some than in others. There was also, for that matter, the evidence of the guardian herself, who said that the parents had tried hard over the past few months to meet the requirements of the agencies to the best of their ability, the children's weight had significantly improved, and there has been no difficulty gaining access to the home. The parents must be given credit for this and for the physical standards in the home, but there is no indication that the justices did give the parents credit for that.

They also failed to address the issue of how best to develop and maintain a working relationship with the parents. Given that the children are to stay at home, it must always be a difficult and delicate task to seek to gain the parents' co-operation, and to work with them in understanding the children's needs and meeting those needs. There will be cases in which a care order may be the only way of achieving this; there will be other cases in which a supervision order is going to be the better approach, not least because the parents will perceive it as less heavy-handed, and this may be helpful rather than the reverse. On that particular issue the social worker's evidence was that he could work with the family, and although the guardian expressed very serious doubts about the family's approach in the light of this, the social worker was the person who knew best how he would be able to approach working with the family.

The magistrates did not have the benefit of the evidence of the parents, but, as I have already explained, I do not think the parents can be blamed for that position. Furthermore, whatever problems there had been in the past, there had been improvements both in the care of the children and in the cooperation of the parents over the period of the interim supervision orders. This, in itself, could be regarded as evidence of a parental willingness to cooperate in a statutory framework, which they would not have had in a purely voluntary, non-compulsory framework.

If one looks at all of those factors in the light of the legal considerations which I have mentioned, it does seem to me that the exercise of the justices' discretion was fundamentally flawed in this case. They should have been prepared at least to see what the effect of supervision orders would be before going straight into the most Draconian order which is permitted under the 1989 Act.

RE B (CARE OR SUPERVISION ORDER) [1996] 2 FLR 693 (FamD)

The parents had six children, two boys and four girls, the eldest now 14 and the youngest 8. The eldest, a boy, was a schizophrenic. In 1994 one of the girls revealed that the father had repeatedly sexually abused her and repeatedly beaten her and one of her sisters. When due to stand trial for indecent assault in October 1994 the father disappeared. In March 1995 full care orders were made by consent in respect of the two girls and they were placed with foster-parents. The mother was given residence orders for the other four children with an express order that there should be no contact with the father. An agreement with the local authority was scheduled to the order whereby the mother agreed to allow the authority to refer any or all of the children to experts for protection/assessment work and agreed herself to see a psychologist for assistance with parenting. Shortly before the hearing of the application by the local authority for supervision orders it was agreed that the older boy needed treatment in a residential setting and a decision as to his future was postponed. It fell to the court to deal with the remaining issue about the three youngest children, namely, whether they should be subject to care orders while remaining at home as recommended by the guardian ad litem, or to supervision orders as sought by the local authority.

HOLMAN J: . . . I am satisfied in relation to each of the three children, S, C and H, that he or she is likely to suffer significant harm and that the likelihood of harm is attributable to the care likely to be given to him or her if a care order or supervision order were not made, not being what it would be reasonable to expect a parent to give to him or her.

The legal framework

I am thus entitled to, and must, exercise a discretion whether or not to make a care order or supervision order or no order at all. In exercising that discretion I must, and do, apply the tests in s. 1 of the Children Act 1989. I must, and do, make the welfare of each child my paramount consideration, and I must, and do, have regard in particular to the matters listed in s. 1(3). I am also bound by s. 1(5) of the Act and must not make any order unless I consider that doing so would be better for each child than making no order at all.

However, it is clear that each of these children needs more protection than can be given voluntarily. To make no order is not a realistic option, nor is that suggested by the mother.

On the choice between a care order or supervision order there are now a number of authorities. It is now clear that it can be appropriate to make a full care order even although (i) all parties, including the guardian ad litem and the court itself, agree that the child should not in fact be removed from the daily care of and living with its parents; and (ii) the local authority only wish and propose that there should be a supervision order. However, it is also clear and obvious that a care order is a stronger and more serious order to make. A care order rather than a supervision order should only be made if the stronger order is necessary for the proper protection of the child.

The risks/needs

(i)   Risk from the father

Clearly, any contact between the father and any of these children would expose them to a serious risk of serious physical or sexual abuse.

For a long time the mother would not believe or accept that the father had abused R or M in the ways they describe. There is evidence that she was aware of some, at least, of the belting and physical chastisement, but she claims that it was not excessive. Of the sexual abuse the mother said in evidence that if it did occur 'it is very dangerous, very cruel and very ungodly'. But she said, and I accept, that she does not know whom to believe: her daughters or her husband, who, when she last saw him, was strongly denying the allegations.

She attended at the Crown Court on the day of the trial hoping to learn the truth. The NSPCC child protection officer, who has participated in the assessment this year, said that the mother has moved from 'disbelief' to an 'open mind' on the issue of whether the children were sexually abused. But she would still like her husband to return and the NSPCC officer does not believe that the mother accepts that the father still poses a risk to her children.

There is, as I have said, no evidence at all that the father has returned to the home or seen or been in contact with any of the children or with the mother since October 1994. It is my duty to state that I have a suspicion, not founded on evidence, that the mother knows more about the whereabouts of her husband than she will reveal. I think she does still feel loyalty towards him and I suspect that she may be in touch with him indirectly through intermediaries, if not directly, by telephone or letter. But I am also satisfied that in a physical sense he has kept well away from her and from the children. The mother and the father each know that the consequences for him and for the children are simply too great if he reappears. He is on the run and will remain on the run unless caught. If he were to return or to pay secretive visits there is no greater likelihood of the local authority learning that fact under a care order than under the proposals they make for monitoring under a supervision order. If there are supervision orders and the local authority did learn of his return, even for visits, I am satisfied that (unless, of course, the father was arrested and placed in custody) the local authority would at once seek to remove these children under emergency or interim orders.

(ii) Risks from the mother and needs of the children
However, I agree with the guardian ad litem that the risk from the father is only part of the story. In January 1995 Dr Sutton, a psychiatrist who was specifically engaged to consider the cases of R and M, concluded his report:

> I have grave concerns for all the children and would suggest that more detailed assessment is arranged in relation to the younger children as well.

This family has been dysfunctioning for many years. There is nothing to suggest that the mother personally has physically, sexually or in any deliberate way emotionally abused these children. But there is pathetic evidence from R as to her attempts to solicit her mother's help and support. The mother has participated or acquiesced in the various assessments and inquiries which have been made into this case, but she has not given active co-operation or shown that she shares the concerns for her children. She draws down barriers around her household and her children. When the NSPCC attempted to assess the children, following the order of Bracewell J in March 1995, they found it impossible to 'engage the children'. This was because of the pressure which, expressly or implicitly, she puts them under to say nothing and not to co-operate with outsiders.

A psychologist, Mrs Litwinenko, assessed all the children (except J) during 1994 and has separately assessed the mother this summer. In her report, dated 14 August 1995, Mrs Litwinenko concluded (i) that the mother herself needs professional support to 'help her cope more effectively and independently' with her children in the future (see para. 9.12); and (ii) that 'in view of the mother's total lack of acceptance of the risks to which her children have been exposed there is an urgent need for work to be undertaken with the children with regard to protection issues' (see para. 9.9).

In oral evidence she said that the younger three children need to have professional work, ideally away from home, normally individually, at least once a fortnight, and probably for as long as a year, to enable them to understand the nature of risk to themselves and how to protect themselves.

Social work input and the view of the guardian ad litem
The guardian ad litem is not confident that if there are only supervision orders the local authority will give to these children the protection that they need and the priority and

degree of social work and professional input that they require. Frankly, she has little confidence in the present social worker. She feels that, as in the cases I have quoted above, the local authority needs to be put under a positive duty to safeguard and promote the welfare of these children. She feels that that duty must endure for far longer than the year a supervision order can endure or the further 2 years over which it can be extended.

Although her confidence in the present social worker is low, she is even more concerned as to what might happen if, for any reason, the social worker, who at least knows the case well and is in some sort of relationship with the mother, were to cease to be responsible for the case. She feels that the mother needs always to be faced with the sanction that the children can be removed at once under an existing, not a possible future, care order.

In relation to the recent performance of the local authority and of the social worker, the guardian ad litem particularly criticises: (i) the failure of the social worker to know, or if she knew it, to grasp and act upon the view of Dr Dyer as long ago as April 1995 that J needs to live in a residential institution, to which I have already referred. I share that criticism; (ii) the failure of the social worker to inform herself correctly about the outcome of J's statement of educational needs. The facts stated in her care plan for J, that his statement of educational needs has now been completed and that he is receiving three sessions per week of tuition at home, are simply incorrect; and (iii) the fact that at, or in conjunction with, a review meeting held on 13 September 1995 the local authority decided that at this hearing it would seek supervision orders, not care orders, even although by then the risk assessment which the local authority itself had commissioned from the NSPCC had not been completed. The report from the NSPCC is only dated 25 September 1995. I also agree with that criticism. It does seem to me quite extraordinary that the local authority should have made up and, in effect, closed its mind before that vital information was available.

The view of the local authority
The local authority, through the social worker, have three principle objections to there being care rather than supervision orders. First, the social worker considers that they are excessive and go beyond what the circumstances require and therefore should not be made. She feels that (on the assumption that the father remains out of the picture and that she would soon learn if he reappeared) a supervision order together with the proposed schedule of agreements is sufficient to meet the remaining risks and needs in this case.

Secondly, she feels that she does now have a relationship with the mother and that the mother will feel threatened and, in fact, be less co-operative with her if there are care orders rather than supervision orders. . . .

I, of course, agree that the protection of the children is the main concern. But if they are to continue to live with their mother then her co-operation is relevant to their protection. I found her to be an intelligent but sad and oppressed lady. She is weighed down by the burden of what has happened to her children and her family. She is certainly very resentful of the role and actions of the guardian ad litem but I do consider that she is now genuinely receptive to the involvement of the social worker.

Thirdly, and I think importantly, the social worker, who knows these children well, says that she is concerned how the children would react to care orders and perceive what is happening to them. They have seen R and M removed from their home. They know that is as a result of care orders. The social worker says the children will not understand why a care order has been made in relation to them and it would not be conducive to their trust in her or to their working with her.

Conclusions
Whilst not going through it paragraph by paragraph, I have now adverted to all the factors in s. 1(3) of the Children Act 1989 relevant to this case. I now come to apply the approach set out by his Honour Judge Coningsby in *Re S (J)* [1993] 2 FLR 919 at 957B–D, which I have already quoted, but remembering that my paramount consideration is the welfare of each of these children.

In my judgment, the pressing needs of these children are, first, to be closely monitored within their home, both in relation to their progress and development generally and specifically to ensure that there is no contact with their father; and, secondly, to undertake work with professionals away from the home to teach them how to protect themselves. In my judgment, these needs can be appropriately provided within the scope of and powers under a supervision order coupled with the agreements which were scheduled to the order of Bracewell J. Whilst I have shared the criticism by the guardian ad litem about aspects of the past performance of the local authority, and of the social worker, I am quite satisfied that the local authority and the social worker do take a very serious view of the needs of these children and will not lower their guard.

In my judgment, there is real force in the view of the social worker about the likely effect on both the mother and the children if care orders are made. Since in practical terms 'responsibility' for protecting these children, whether under care or supervision orders, will lie with the local authority I consider that I should attach weight to their view as to the most effective legal framework, although, of course, that cannot be decisive. (I have deliberately put the word 'responsibility' in inverted commas in that sentence to emphasise that I have not forgotten that it is only a care order order and not a supervision order which puts the local authority under a legal duty under s. 22 of the Children Act 1989.)

In my judgment, the welfare of these children will, in fact, be better served by supervision orders coupled with the schedule of agreements than by care orders. But even if I am wrong about that, I am satisfied that there is not a sufficiently strong need for care orders (whether because of their effect as a sanction on the mother or of their effect on the duties of the local authority) so as to justify making an order of that seriousness.

The one consideration over which I have most worried and hesitated is that of duration. There is no doubt that these children will need protection for much longer than one year and probably for more than 3 years. There is no guarantee that the local authority will apply for an extension of supervision orders. But I am confident that they will, in fact, do so. I am less confident whether at the end of 3 years the local authority would apply for a fresh grant of supervision orders (although I am far from saying that I do not think they will do so) but I agree in the end with the submissions of Miss Ioannou for the mother. If a supervision order (with extensions) is the right order to make now, it is wrong on the facts of this case to make a care order simply to provide for the position as it may be after 3 years have expired.

Brasse, G, 'Supervision or Care Orders?' [1997] Fam Law 351

Before either a care or supervision order may be made, the court has to be satisfied that the child concerned is suffering, or is likely to suffer significant harm, attributable to the care given to the child, or likely to be given to him if the order were not made, not being what it would be reasonable to expect a parent to give to him (s. 31(2) of the Children Act 1989 (the Act)). Section 31(9) defines 'harm' as meaning ill-treatment or the impairment of health and development. The power to make the order is discretionary. The discretion is exercised by having regard to the principle that the paramount consideration is the welfare of the child, and to the circumstances listed in s. 1(3). Finally, the 'no order' principle applies—the court is not permitted to make any order unless it considers that doing so would be better for the child than making no order at all.

This statutory scheme begins, therefore, with the emphasis on the protection of the child who is suffering, or is at risk of suffering significant harm. However, even if it is proved that the child is a victim, or is likely to be a victim of significant harm unless an order were made, with apparent contradiction the court is not compelled to make any order. Instead, the court is required to look at the s. 1(3) checklist, which may reveal circumstances, notwithstanding the harm done, or future risk of harm, indicative that no order is necessary. In cases where it is only risk of future significant harm that gives rise to the local authority's involvement, there may be voluntary means of protecting the child in the future, such as a social work agreement or the provision of other services for the family under Part III of and Sch 2 to the Act, or simply the departure of the potentially abusing parent from the child's home. In such a case the threshold condition itself would not be satisfied. If, having gone through the statutory exercise, it appears that child protection cannot be achieved without an order involving social services intervention, the Act offers the choice of supervision or care orders.

WHICH ORDER?

Care

The principal distinction between the two orders is that the care order confers on the local authority parental responsibility (s. 33(3)(a)). Although the parents do not lose their responsibility, its exercise can be restricted by the local authority (s. 33(3)(b)). It is always hoped that the parents and local authority will work in partnership. However, the latter is most definitely the senior partner and may impose its will if satisfied that it is necessary to do so in order to safeguard and promote the child's welfare (s. 33(4)). This is in sharp contrast to the position between others who have parental responsibility, who may exercise it independently of each other (s. 2(7)).

Under s. 34 the local authority must allow the parents to have reasonable contact with the child, but until an application is made the local authority is the arbiter of what is 'reasonable'. Where the child is at risk of suffering harm as a result of contact, the local authority may refuse to allow contact for up to 7 days (s. 34(6)), and may be authorised by the court to refuse to allow contact in its discretion (s. 34(4)).

The care order requires the local authority to provide accommodation for and maintain the child (s. 22), to safeguard and promote its welfare. It has been judicially observed that that duty obliges the local authority 'to keep the child safe' (per Coningsby QC in *Re S (J) (A Minor) (Care or Supervision Order)* [1993] 2 FLR 919, at p. 948E). The local authority has a duty to plan for the child's long-term future (see s. 23). That may result in a placement with his own parents (Placement of Children with Parents etc Regulations 1991 (SI 1991/893)). Even then the local authority has intrusive powers of supervision (reg. 9), and may terminate the placement peremptorily (reg. 11). If the child cannot be placed with his parents, there is a duty to find an alternative long-term family (s. 23(6); and see the Arrangements for the Placement of Children (General) Regulations 1991 (SI 1991/890)).

SUPERVISION

The duty on the local authority is simply to advise, assist, and befriend the child concerned. It may take such steps as are reasonably necessary to give effect to the order (s. 35(1)(a) and (b)). The order may be 'tailormade' to suit the individual case by adding requirements that the child shall comply with the supervisor's directions as to where he should live, appointments he must keep, and activities in which he must take part. The 'responsible person', if he consents, may also be expressly required by the order to take all reasonable steps to ensure that the child complies with the supervisor's directions, and himself to attend appointments or participate in specified activities (sch. 3, paras 2 and 3; and see *Croydon London Borough Council v A (No. 3)* [1992] 2 FLR 350, at pp 357H and 358A, per Hollings J). The supervisor has complete discretion as to the exercise and form of the directions given (see *Re H (Supervision Order)* [1994] 2 FLR 979, at p. 980E, per Bracewell J). The court itself may impose requirements for the child to be medically or psychiatrically examined or treated (sch. 3, paras 4 and 5). The order may require the child or the 'responsible person' to keep the supervisor informed of any change of address, and to allow the supervisor to visit the child at home. If the child is living with the 'responsible person', the latter must allow the supervisor to have reasonable contact with the child (sch. 3, para. 8). On the face of it this appears to allow the local authority to set up a tightly regulated regime for the child. It has tempted at least one court into believing that this could afford almost the same protection as a care order (see *Re V (Care or Supervision Order)* [1996] 1 FLR 776). The child concerned may be a 'child in need' (defined in (s. 17(10)), but this is not necessarily the case. Although the local authority has a general duty to safeguard and promote the welfare of children in need in its area (s. 17(1)), the supervision order itself does not expressly carry with it any such duty (see *Re S(J) (A Minor)* (above)). There are no powers to remove the child from his carer. In the event of non-compliance with the order, the supervisor must 'consider whether or not to apply to the court for its variation or discharge'. If access to the child is denied to the supervisor, he may obtain a warrant to empower a constable to help him regain access (s. 102). He may also, in appropriate cases, apply for an emergency protection or child assessment order (ss. 43 and 44). All these steps require applications; there are no other powers available to the supervisor to enforce the directions he gives (see *Hereford and Worcester County Council* v *R and G* [1994] 2 FCR 981). If a care order is needed in substitution for the supervision order, the threshold conditions must be proved afresh (s. 39; and see *Re A (A Minor) (Supervision Order: Extension)* [1995] 1 FLR 335).

SUPERVISION INSUFFICIENT

Child protection — the decisive factor

Where child protection factors require the child's removal from home, a supervision order is not suitable. Thus when a mother set up home with a man who had sexually abused his daughter by a previous relationship, the local authority sought a care order to enable it to place the child with his grandmother. The Court of Appeal overturned the supervision order, with requirements attached made by the judge at first instance on the ground that when 'weighing the relative merits of a care order and a supervision order [the judge] did not . . . properly advert to the difference between the two orders . . . the requirements clearly fell some way short of the protection which had apparently weighed with the judge when he had decided that a supervision order was appropriate' (see *Re S (Care or Supervision Order)* [1996] 1 FLR 753). A child of 2 years, 7 months whose brother, aged 5, living in the same household, had suffered non-accidental injury and was himself at risk of significant physical and emotional harm if he continued to live with his mother, required the protection of an interim care order (see *Leicestershire County Council* v *G* [1994] 2 FLR 329).

Even if the local authority's plan is for the child to remain at home with a parent, the child's protection might still require a care order. Thus where there had been a history of non-accidental injury to children, culminating in the death of a child whilst in the care of the father, who was subsequently convicted of cruelty and sentenced to imprisonment, a care order rather than a supervision order was necessary in relation to a child born to the father's new partner for the child's protection and welfare. This was so even where the local authority had preferred a supervision order, fearing that a care order might undermine the mother's willingness to co-operate (see *Re D (A Minor) (Care or Supervision Order)* [1993] 2 FLR 423, and also *Re B (Care or Supervision Order)* [1996] 2 FLR 693, per Holman J's review of the relevant authorities).

Where parental co-operation is unlikely

A supervision order depends for its efficacy on the co-operation of the child's carers. If that is not forthcoming, there is no means of enforcing compliance. In one case a 17-year-old boy suffered from spastic quadriplegia and learning difficulties. He attended a specialist school as a weekly boarder. The father agreed with professionals that the placement was beneficial, but the mother opposed it on the ground that it placed too much pressure on the child. The judge declined to make a care order, lest it cause a rift between the parents. Instead, he made a supervision order with a requirement that the child continue as a weekly boarder. The Court of Appeal disagreed. A supervision order was not capable of achieving the same ends as a care order. There were no means to enforce the requirement (see *Re V (Care or Supervision Order)* (above)).

Even a written social work 'contract' drawn up between the parents and the local authority is incapable of enforcement without further proceedings; only a care order gives the local authority the necessary powers of placement, removal and regulation of contact needed (see *Re T (A Minor) (Care or Supervision Order)* [1994] 1 FLR 103). A supervision order, it has been said, 'should not in any sense be seen as a sort of watered down version of care' (see *Re S (J) (A Minor)* (above), at p. 950F–G). There is no jurisdiction, certainly in the county court, to reinforce a supervision order by obtaining undertakings from the parent in question (see *Re B (Supervision Order: Parental Undertaking)* [1996] 1 FLR 676).

SUPERVISION APPROPRIATE

Care plan rejected

There may be substantial grounds for concluding that a child is likely to suffer significant harm, such as to persuade a local authority that removal from the parents and placement in an alternative permanent family is the best means of safeguarding and promoting the child's welfare. The court may disagree. None the less, if it makes a care order the decision as regards the child's accommodation is the local authority's, not that of the court. There is no power to attach conditions to a care order (see *Re T (A Minor) (Care Order: Conditions)* [1994] 2 FLR 423). For a recent application of this principle, see *Re M (Interim Care Order: Assessment)* [1996] 2 FLR 464, in which it was held that even the question of whether a residential assessment is required is for the local authority, not the court, to resolve (per Swinton Thomas LJ, at p. 469H, and per Butler-Sloss LJ at p. 471A–B). Since that decision the House of Lords has decided that under (s. 38(6) the court may, in an appropriate case, order the assessment of a child with its parent in a residential unit (see *Re C (Interim Care Order: Residential Assessment)* [1997] 1 FLR 1). If, notwithstanding the risks involved, the view of the court is that the child should stay with the parents, supervision is probably in the child's best interests (see *Re B (Supervision Order: Parental Undertaking)* (above)).

INDIVIDUALISED PROGRAMMES OF ASSESSMENT/TREATMENT/SOCIAL WORK

Provided the parent consents, a supervision order may be made subject to a requirement that the parent and supervised child should reside for a period at a family rehabilitation centre (see *Croydon London Borough Council v A (No. 3)* (above), and *Solihull Metropolitan Borough Council v C* [1993] 1 FLR 290). Strictly, it is for the supervisor, not the court, to direct the supervised child and, if he consents to the requirement being included in the order, the person responsible for the child, to reside at such a centre (see *Re H (Supervision Order)* (above)). Once the direction has been given by the supervisor, the local authority must defray the expense of the placement (sch. 3, para. 11(2)). This will act as a constraint on such directions being given. However, in the case of an interim order, (s. 38(6) empowers a court to direct that a medical, psychiatric, or other assessment of the child be carried out. It may do this whether or not the local authority wishes it; the local authority must, notwithstanding, bear the cost (see *Re C (Interim Care Order: Residential Assessment)* (above)). As assessments may take many months to complete, the final decision would be considerably delayed with the court retaining control of the case in the meantime. Furthermore, now that it is clear that in suitable cases the court may insist upon lengthy residential assessments, the number of such cases is likely to increase. Thus *Re C (Interim Care Order: Residential Assessment)* (above) may well have given the concept of 'planned and purposeful delay' developed in *Solihull Metropolitan Borough Council v C* (above), and *Hounslow London Borough Council v A* [1993] 1 FLR 702 a new lease of life.

In *Re B (Care or Supervision Order)* (above) Holman J made a supervision order where the pressing needs of the children were for them to be closely monitored at home, and to participate in a programme of social work aimed at enabling them to protect themselves from sexual or other abusive behaviours. Where the mother was willing to cooperate whilst she retained parental responsibility, but was likely to resent local authority intervention if it were backed by a care order, supervision was deemed to be more appropriate.

CONTINUING INVOLVEMENT OF THE COURT

Once a care order has been made, the role of the court ceases unless or until a further application is made for discharge of the order, or for contact under s. 34. A supervision order, in contrast, allows the court the opportunity to assist in shaping plans for the child's future. The initial order may be made for a maximum of 12 months. The local authority must apply to the court for an extension, or for a care order if things go badly (see *Re O (Care or Supervision Orders)* [1996] 2 FLR 755, at p. 760B–E per Hale J).

LIMITATIONS OF THE PRESENT CARE/SUPERVISION ORDER CHOICE

A care order puts the local authority in control of the child's welfare; a supervision order leaves parental responsibility entirely in the hands of the parents. If the latter withdraw their compliance with its demands, the supervisor is powerless to enforce the order. Although supervision orders lack 'teeth', courts have, nevertheless, often been loath to make care orders. Instead, the courts have resorted to various devices in an attempt to construct what is missing from the Children Act 1989, namely an order available on application by the local authority which, whilst not depriving the parents of parental responsibility, enables the court rather than the local authority to direct them how to exercise it in the best interests of the child. The Court of Appeal has consistently refused to uphold either 'beefed up' supervision orders (for example fortified with undertakings extracted from the responsible adult as in *Re B (Supervision Order: Parental Undertaking)* (above)), or 'watered down' care orders, circumscribing the local authority's discretion to act as it considers to be in the best interests of the child (for example by imposing a condition of residence in a particular place, or compelling the local authority to place the child at a particular establishment (see *Re T (A Minor) (Care Order: Conditions)* (above)).

The very fact that these attempts have been made indicates the need for such an order, midway between care and supervision orders, in the scope of control it would allow over the child's care. This need will perhaps find its outlet in an increase in the number of interim orders with s. 38(6) directions attached.

12.11 The Consequences of the Orders

12.11.1 CARE ORDERS

CHILDREN ACT 1989

33. Effect of care order

(1) Where a care order is made with respect to a child it shall be the duty of the local authority designated by the order to receive the child into their care and to keep him in their care while the order remains in force.

(2) Where—

(a) a care order has been made with respect to a child on the application of an authorised person; but

(b) the local authority designated by the order was not informed that that person proposed to make the application,

the child may be kept in the care of that person until received into the care of the authority.

(3) While a care order is in force with respect to a child, the local authority designated by the order shall—

(a) have parental responsibility for the child; and

(b) have the power (subject to the following provisions of this section) to determine the extent to which a parent or guardian of the child may meet his parental responsibility for him.

(4) The authority may not exercise the power in subsection (3)(b) unless they are satisfied that it is necessary to do so in order to safeguard or promote the child's welfare.

(5) Nothing in subsection (3)(b) shall prevent a parent or guardian of the child who has care of him from doing what is reasonable in all the circumstances of the case for the purpose of safeguarding or promoting his welfare.

(6) While a care order is in force with respect to a child, the local authority designated by the order shall not—

(a) cause the child to be brought up in any religious persuasion other than that in which he would have been brought up if the order had not been made; or

(b) have the right—

(i)   to consent or refuse to consent to the making of an application with respect to the child under section 18 of the Adoption Act 1976;

(ii)   to agree or refuse to agree to the making of an adoption order, or an order under section 55 of the Act of 1976, with respect to the child; or

(iii)   to appoint a guardian for the child.

(7) While a care order is in force with respect to a child, no person may—

(a) cause the child to be known by a new surname; or

(b) remove him from the United Kingdom, without either the written consent of every person who has parental responsibility for the child or the leave of the court.

(8)   Subsection 7(b) does not—

(a)   prevent the removal of such a child, for a period of less than one month, by the authority in whose care he is; or

(b)   apply to arrangements for such a child to live outside England and Wales (which are governed by paragraph 19 of Schedule 2).

(9)   The power in subsection (3)(b) is subject (in addition to being subject to the provisions of this section) to any right, duty, power, responsibility or authority which a parent or guardian of the child has in relation to the child and his property by virtue of any other enactment.

34.   Parental contact, etc., with children in care

(1)   Where a child is in the care of a local authority, the authority shall (subject to the provisions of this section) allow the child reasonable contact with—

(a)   his parents;

(b)   any guardian of his;

(c)   where there was a residence order in force with respect to the child immediately before the care order was made, the person in whose favour the order was made; and

(d)   where, immediately before the care order was made, a person had care of the child by virtue of an order made in the exercise of the High Court's inherent jurisdiction with respect to children, that person.

(2)   On an application made by the authority or the child, the court may make such order as it considers appropriate with respect to the contact which is to be allowed between the child and any named person.

(3)   On an application made by—

(a)   any person mentioned in paragraphs (a) to (d) of subsection (1); or

(b)   any person who has obtained the leave of the court to make the application, the court may make such order as it considers appropriate with respect to the contact which is to be allowed between the child and that person.

(4)   On an application made by the authority or the child, the court may make an order authorising the authority to refuse to allow contact between the child and any person who is mentioned in paragraphs (a) to (d) of subsection (1) and named in the order.

(5)   When making a care order with respect to a child, or in any family proceedings in connection with a child who is in the care of a local authority, the court may make an order under this section, even though no application for such an order has been made with respect to the child, if it considers that the order should be made.

(6)   An authority may refuse to allow the contact that would otherwise be required by virtue of subsection (1) or an order under this section if—

(a)   they are satisfied that it is necessary to do so in order to safeguard or promote the child's welfare; and

(b)   the refusal—

(i)   is decided upon as a matter of urgency; and

(ii)   does not last for more than seven days.

(7)   An order under this section may impose such conditions as the court considers appropriate.

(8)   The Secretary of State may by regulations make provision as to—

(a)   the steps to be taken by a local authority who have exercised their powers under subsection (6);

(b)   the circumstances in which, and conditions subject to which, the terms of any order under this section may be departed from by agreement between the local authority and the person in relation to whom the order is made;

(c)   notification by a local authority of any variation or suspension of arrangements made (otherwise than under an order under this section) with a view to affording any person contact with a child to whom this section applies.

(9)   The court may vary or discharge any order made under this section on the application of the authority, the child concerned or the person named in the order.

(10)   An order under this section may be made either at the same time as the care order itself or later.

(11)   Before making a care order with respect to any child the court shall—

(a) consider the arrangements which the authority have made, or propose to make, for affording any person contact with a child to whom this section applies; and

(b) invite the parties to the proceedings to comment on those arrangements.

12.11.1.1 Section 34: reasonable contact

RE B (MINORS) CARE: CONTACT: LOCAL AUTHORITY'S PLANS)
[1993] 1 FLR 543 (CA)

BUTLER-SLOSS LJ: This is an appeal from the decision of his Honour Judge Gosling in the Birmingham County Court on 18 September 1992 to authorise the local authority to refuse to allow contact between two children and their mother. The appellant is the guardian ad litem of the two children and of their younger half-brother. The guardian ad litem is supported on this appeal by the natural mother of the three children. The local authority, which has a care order in respect of the three children, opposes the appeal.

From about March 1992 the mother was seeing the two girls regularly and has had frequent unsupervised contact with them, collecting them from their foster-mother and taking them to her flat in the home. She has shown in the last few months determination and commitment to these contact visits, which has not been easy with two girls on two buses across a big city. She has cared for them on these visits very successfully, the girls have enjoyed them and the contact with their baby brother. Since the hearing before the judge the twice-weekly contact has continued at the mother's home.

At the hearing before the judge there were three applications. The first, by the local authority, was for a care order in respect of S. It was agreed by everyone, including the guardian ad litem, that there should be a care order but that he should continue to live with his mother. The second application was made by the mother to discharge the care order in respect of the two girls. There was no realistic chance of the girls going immediately to their mother and the application to discharge was dismissed, despite the request of the guardian to have it adjourned. The third application was by the local authority to authorise them to refuse to allow contact between the two girls and their mother under s. 34(4) of the Children Act 1989 in order to be able to place them with prospective adopters. The mother opposed that application and asked for the contact to continue and to be increased. The underlying reason for the continuing contact was the hope of the mother that it might lead to rehabilitation and the return of the girls to her. The contact already taking place was incompatible with placing the children with prospective adopters. The local authority accepted that they had never attempted to assess the mother's ability to care for three children. Their view was and is, that the mother has made significant strides in her ability to care for S but to expect her to care for three children is too much and will probably lead to the breakdown of all three placements, including the placement for S. They were concerned about the length of time the girls had lived with the short-term foster-mother and the delay in placing them permanently. They considered that the children would not miss the contact with their mother, which the judge found to be true since their primary carer remains the foster-mother. But they accepted that the contact visits had been successful and enjoyable for the children. The local authority had identified particularly suitable potential adopters who were, like the children, of mixed race and who would not be willing to accept continuing contact with the mother.

Contact is another example. Once a child was in care, by whatever route, before the Children Act 1989 the decision as to continuing contact between the parent and the child in care was an administrative decision for the local authority which, before January 1984, a parent had no right to challenge. By the amendment to s. 12 of the Child Care Act 1980, taking effect in 1984, a parent had the right to challenge a termination of access by a local authority after service of notice upon him. He had no right to challenge a reduction in access even to minimal levels. There is a dramatic shift in the philosophy of the legislation. By s. 34(1) of the 1989 Act:

Where a child is in the care of a local authority the authority shall (subject to the provisions of this section) allow the child reasonable contact with—

(a) his parents: . . .

There is a presumption of continuing reasonable contact between the parent and the child in care unless or until a court order under s. 34(4):

On an application made by the authority or the child, the court may make an order authorising the authority to refuse to allow contact between the child and any person who is mentioned in paragraphs (a) to (d) of subsection (1) and named in the order.

The only power over contact left to the local authority in the absence of a court order is the emergency refusal of contact for a maximum of 7 days (s. 34(6)). Even on the making of an emergency protection order (s. 44) there is a presumption of continuing contact (s. 44(13)).

The present position of a child whose welfare is being considered under Part IV of the Act appears to me to be that he will not be placed in care unless a court has been satisfied that the threshold conditions in s. 31 have been met and that it is better to make a care order than not to do so. After the care order is made, the court has no continuing role in the future welfare of the child. The local authority has parental responsibility for the child by s. 33(3). However, issues relating to the child may come before the court, for instance on applications for contact or leave to refuse contact, to discharge the care order or by an application for a s. 8 residence order. The making of a residence order discharges the care order (s. 91(1)).

At the moment that an application comes before the court, at whichever tier, the court has a duty to apply s. 1, which states that when a court determines any question with respect to the upbringing of a child, the child's welfare shall be the court's paramount consideration. The court has to have regard to the prejudicial effect of delay, to the checklist including the range of orders available to the court and whether to make an order. On a s. 34 application, therefore, the court has a duty to consider and apply the welfare section.

Contact applications generally fall into two main categories, those which ask for contact as such, and those which are attempts to set aside the care order itself. In the first category, there is no suggestion that the applicant wishes to take over the care of the child and the issue of contact often depends on whether contact would frustrate long-term plans for the child in a substitute home, such as adoption where continuing contact may not be for the long-term welfare of the child. The presumption of contact, which has to be for the benefit of the child, has always to be balanced against the long-term welfare of the child and particularly where he will live in the future. Contact must not be allowed to destabilise or endanger the arrangements for the child and in many cases the plans for the child will be decisive of the contact application. There may also be cases where the parent is having satisfactory contact with the child and there are no long-term plans or those plans do not appear to the court to preclude some future contact. The proposals of the local authority, based on their appreciation of the best interests of the child, must command the greatest respect and consideration from the court, but Parliament has given to the court, and not to the local authority, the duty to decide on contact between the child and those named in s. 34(1). Consequently the court may have the task of requiring the local authority to justify their long-term plans to the extent only that those plans exclude contact between parent and child.

In the second category, contact applications may be made by parents by way of another attempt to obtain the return of the children. In such a case the court is obviously entitled to take into account the failure to apply to discharge the care order, and in the majority of cases the court will have little difficulty in coming to the conclusion that the applicant cannot demonstrate that contact with a view to rehabilitation with the parent is a viable proposition at that stage, particularly if it had already been rejected at the earlier hearing when the child was placed in care. The task for the parents will be too great and the court would be entitled to assume that the plans of the local authority to terminate contact are for the welfare of the child and are not to be frustrated by inappropriate contact with a view to the remote possibility, at some future date, of rehabilitation. But in all cases the welfare section has to be considered, and the local authority has the task of justifying the cessation of contact. There may also be unusual cases where either the local authority has not made effective plans or there has been considerable delay in implementing them and a parent, who had previously been found by a court unable or unwilling to care for the child so that a care order had been made, comes back upon the scene as a possible future primary caretaker. If the local authority with a care order decides not to consider that parent on the new facts, Mr Munby, counsel for the guardian ad litem argued that it is for the court, with the enhanced jurisdiction of the Children Act 1989, to consider whether even at this late stage there should be some investigation of the proposals of the parent, with the possibility of reconsidering the local authority plans. Mr Horrocks, counsel for the local authority, argued that the court cannot go behind the long-term plans of the local authority unless they were acting capriciously or were otherwise open to scrutiny by way of judicial review. I unhesitatingly reject the local authority argument. As I have already said, their plan has to be given the greatest possible consideration by the court and it is only in the unusual case that a parent will be able to convince the court, the onus being firmly on the parent, that there has been such a change of circumstances as to require further investigation and reconsideration of the local authority plan. If, however, a court was unable to intervene, it would make a nonsense of the paramountcy of the welfare of the child, which is the bedrock of the Act, and would subordinate it to the administrative decision of the local authority in a situation where the court is seized of the contact issue. That cannot be right.

But I would emphasise that this is not an open door to courts reviewing the plans of local authorities. Generally, where parties choose not to pursue applications, they are well advised not to do so. But there is now a flexibility in the approach of the court to the problems of the child before it, and occasionally the court may wish to invoke s. 10(1)(b) which provides that a court may, in any family proceedings, which includes care proceedings, make a s. 8 order with respect to a child if the court considers that the order should be made, even though no application has been made. A court may also make a contact or an interim contact order and impose such conditions as it considers appropriate (s. 34(7)).

In my view the judge was in error in not appreciating that he was able, if he thought it right, to have another look at the mother as a possible future carer and give appropriate directions for assessments to be made. He did not look at the relevant issues of possible rehabilitation and delay and came to conclusions adverse to the mother. But those decisions are very much influenced by his belief that he had no right to interfere in any way with the plans put forward by the local authority. His conclusion that his hands were tied, in my view, vitiated his exercise of discretion and his decision cannot stand.

BERKSHIRE COUNTY COUNCIL v B [1997] 1 FLR 171 (FamD)

HALE J: This is a local authority's appeal against the decision of the Maidenhead Family Proceedings Court on 8 March 1996. It concerned J, a little boy who was born on 18 April 1989 and so he was then aged nearly, 7 and is now $7\frac{1}{2}$. The court's orders placed him in the care of the local authority, but also provided that he should have contact with his mother for a minimum period of 2 hours at least twice a week.

The mother originally cross-appealed against the care order, but at the outset of this hearing she sought leave to withdraw her appeal. She recognises, no doubt with great reluctance, that the magistrates were bound to regard a care order as the lesser of two evils in this case. I am left, therefore, with the local authority's appeal against the magistrates' decision as to contact.

The court acknowledged the necessity of making a care order because J needed to remain in local authority accommodation and, although the mother said that she would leave him there without the pressure of court proceedings she might seek to remove him. But they were disappointed at the local authority's refusal to reconsider the care plan. They preferred Dr Heller's evidence in contrast to that of the other witnesses, and the reason that they gave for that was that he was much better qualified to form these opinions than the other witnesses before the court.

The local authority first put forward this appeal on the basis that the court could not interfere with the care plan. The well-known cases of *Re J (Minors) (Care: Care Plan)* [1994] 1 FLR 253, a decision of Will J, *Re T (A Minor) (Care Order: Conditions)* [1994] 2 FLR 423, a decision of the Court of Appeal, and *Re S and D (Children: Powers of Court)* [1995] 2 FLR 456, another decision of the Court of Appeal, were cited. It is clear from those decisions that the court cannot impose its own conditions upon a care order or direct the local authority how to look after a child in their care. The court cannot direct a particular type of placement, whether it be at home or in foster care or in a residential home or anywhere else. The court cannot direct that particular services be provided for a child. This means inevitably that, before passing responsibility to a local authority, the court must scrutinise the care plan with considerable care. The court has to be satisfied that giving parental responsibility to the local authority will not do more harm than good to the welfare the child. That is why in *Re S and D* reference was made to the lesser of two evils.

But none of those cases concerned the matter that was in issue in this case, the choice essentially between severing the legal relationship between child and parent and reducing their factual relationship to such a low level of two visits a year and post-box contact on the one hand, and maintaining the legal relationship between mother and child and also maintaining their real relationship at a much more important and sustainable level on the other.

Nor do those cases suggest that the court is powerless once a child is placed in care. The relationship between a child and his parents is still within the court's jurisdiction. The Children Act 1989 deliberately gave the court wide powers over the contact that there was to be between children in care, their parents and, indeed, other people. It made that contact subject to the paramount consideration of the child's welfare, together with the checklist and other considerations set out in s. 1 of the 1989 Act. . . .

It is worth while recalling that both *Re B* [1993] 1 FLR 543 and *Re L* [1994] 1 FLR 146 were appeals from decisions in which the court below had considered that it was unable to exercise its jurisdiction over contact in a way which was inconsistent with the local authority's long-term plan for the child. In each case the Court of Appeal said that that was the wrong approach. That does not, of course mean to say that the local authority's long-term plan for the child is irrelevant.

The question, therefore, becomes one of balancing the respective factors in the welfare of the child. At one end of the spectrum there must be cases where the child clearly needs a new family for life and contact with his family of birth will bring little or no benefit and is likely to impede this. At the other end of the spectrum are cases where the child is likely to return home in the short to medium term and contact is essential to enable this to take place.

There are also many cases in the middle where the child is unlikely to be able to return home in the short to medium term and so needs a long-term stable placement but where the relationships with his family of origin are so important to him that they must be maintained. One reason for this may well be that adoption is unlikely to succeed so that a child must not be deprived of his existing relationships which matter to him for the sake of putative ones which may never be found.

In these very difficult cases the court has to balance these various advantages against the difficulties that contact is likely to cause in finding and sustaining an appropriate placement for the child. Obviously contact, however important, cannot be pursued to a level which makes a successful placement impossible to find because the child needs a home and to be properly looked after, and that must be the first priority.

The local authority are not entitled to approach the case in a 'take it or leave it' manner, for two reasons: first, because, as I have already explained, the court retains control over the relationship between the child and his parents through the issues of contact and adoption. The court therefore has to balance the various factors and so must the local authority. Secondly, while I accept that local authorities are entitled to have a general approach based on their appreciation of what is in general best for children—and we are all aware of the many reasons why adoption may well provide the best solution for most young children who have to be looked after for a long time away from their family of birth—they have a statutory duty to make decisions in the interest of the individual child in their care. They cannot approach decision-making in any particular case as if it were governed by general principles alone. It is trite law that those exercising a statutory discretion are not entitled to fetter their discretion by a reference to a general policy of which they will not admit departures in appropriate cases.

For all those reasons, I do not think that it is possible to fault the magistrates in this case on their general approach. It is obvious that they took enormous care and thought very deeply about the case. Their decision was supported by the evidence of Dr Heller, which they were entitled to accept, and also by the evidence of the guardian, which they were equally entitled to accept.

12.11.1.2 Duration of the order

CHILDREN ACT 1989

39. Discharge and variation etc. of care orders and supervision orders

(1) A care order may be discharged by the court on the application of—

(a) any person who has parental responsibility for the child;

(b) the child himself; or

(c) the local authority designated by the order.

(2) A supervision order may be varied or discharged by the court on the application of—

(a) any person who has parental responsibility for the child;

(b) the child himself; or

(c) the supervisor.

(3) On the application of a person who is not entitled to apply for the order to be discharged, but who is a person with whom the child is living, a supervision order may be varied by the court in so far as it imposes a requirement which affects that person.

(4) Where a care order is in force with respect to a child the court may, on the application of any person entitled to apply for the order to be discharged, substitute a supervision order for the care order.

(5) When a court is considering whether to substitute one order for another under subsection (4) any provision of this Act which would otherwise require section 31(2) to be satisfied at the time when the proposed order is substituted or made shall be disregarded.

91. Effect and duration of orders, etc

(1) The making of a residence order with respect to a child who is the subject of a care order discharges the care order.

(2) The making of a care order with respect to a child who is the subject of any section 8 order discharges that order.

(3) The making of a care order with respect to a child who is the subject of a supervision order discharges that other order.

(4) The making of a care order with respect to a child who is a ward of court brings that wardship to an end.

. . .

(12) Any care order, other than an interim care order, shall continue in force until the child reaches the age of eighteen, unless it is brought to an end earlier.

12.11.2 SUPERVISION ORDERS

12.11.2.1 Consequences

CHILDREN ACT 1989

35. Supervision orders

(1) While a supervision order is in force it shall be the duty of the supervisor—

(a) to advise, assist and befriend the supervised child;

(b) to take such steps as are reasonably necessary to give effect to the order; and

(c) where—

(i) the order is not wholly complied with; or

(ii) the supervisor considers that the order may no longer be necessary,

to consider whether or not to apply to the court for its variation or discharge.

(2) Parts I and II of Schedule 3 make further provision with respect to supervision orders.

Sections 35 and 36   SCHEDULE 3
                                          SUPERVISION ORDERS

                                        PART I   GENERAL

Meaning of 'responsible person'

1. In this Schedule, 'the responsible person,' in relation to a supervised child, means—
    (a)   any person who has parental responsibility for the child; and
    (b)   any other person with whom the child is living.

Power of supervisor to give directions to supervised child

2.—(1) A supervision order may require the supervised child to comply with any directions given from time to time by the supervisor which require him to do all or any of the following things—
    (a)   to live at a place or places specified in the directions for a period or periods so specified;
    (b)   to present himself to a person or persons specified in the directions at a place or places and on a day or days so specified;
    (c)   to participate in activities specified in the directions on a day or days so specified.

(2) It shall be for the supervisor to decide whether, and to what extent, he exercises his power to give directions and to decide the form of any directions which he gives.

(3) Sub-paragraph (1) does not confer on a supervisor power to give directions in respect of any medical or psychiatric examination or treatment (which are matters dealt with in paragraphs 4 and 5).

Imposition of obligations on responsible person

3.—(1) With the consent of any responsible person, a supervision order may include a requirement—
    (a)   that he take all reasonable steps to ensure that the supervised child complies with any direction given by the supervisor under paragraph 2;
    (b)   that he take all reasonable steps to ensure that the supervised child complies with any requirement included in the order under paragraph 4 or 5;
    (c)   that he comply with any directions given by the supervisor requiring him to attend at a place specified in the directions for the purpose of taking part in activities so specified.

(2) A direction given under sub-paragraph (1)(c) may specify the time at which the responsible person is to attend and whether or not the supervised child is required to attend with him.

(3) A supervision order may require any person who is a responsible person in relation to the supervised child to keep the supervisor informed of his address, if it differs from the child's.

Psychiatric and medical examinations

4.—(1) A supervision order may require the supervised child—
    (a)   to submit to a medical or psychiatric examination; or
    (b)   to submit to any such examination from time to time as directed by the supervisor.

(2) Any such examination shall be required to be conducted—
    (a)   by, or under the direction of, such registered medical practitioner as may be specified in the order;
    (b)   at a place specified in the order and at which the supervised child is to attend as a non-resident patient; or
    (c)   at—

(i)   a health service hospital; or

(ii)   in the case of a psychiatric examination, a hospital or mental nursing home, at which the supervised child is, or is to attend as, a resident patient.

(3)   A requirement of a kind mentioned in sub-paragraph (2)(c) shall not be included unless the court is satisfied, on the evidence of a registered medical practitioner, that—

(a)   the child may be suffering from a physical or mental condition that requires, and may be susceptible to, treatment; and

(b)   a period as a resident patient is necessary if the examination is to be carried out properly.

(4)   No court shall include a requirement under this paragraph in a supervision order unless it is satisfied that—

(a)   where the child has sufficient understanding to make an informed decision, he consents to its inclusion; and

(b)   satisfactory arrangements have been, or can be, made for the examination.

Psychiatric and medical treatment

5.—(1)   Where court which proposes to make or vary a supervision order is satisfied, on the evidence of a registered medical practitioner approved for the purposes of section 12 of the Mental Health Act 1983, that the mental condition of the supervised child—

(a)   is such as requires, and may be susceptible to, treatment; but

(b)   is not such as to warrant his detention in pursuance of a hospital order under Part III of that Act,

the court may include in the order a requirement that the supervised child shall, for a period specified in the order, submit to such treatment as is so specified.

(2)   The treatment specified in accordance with sub-paragraph (1) must be—

(a)   by, or under the direction of, such registered medical practitioner as may be specified in the order;

(b)   as a non-resident patient at such a place as may be so specified; or

(c)   as a resident patient in a hospital or mental nursing home.

(3)   Where a court which proposes to make or vary a supervision order is satisfied, on the evidence of a registered medical practitioner, that the physical condition of the supervised child is such as requires, and may be susceptible to, treatment, the court may include in the order a requirement that the supervised child shall, for a period specified in the order, submit to such treatment as is so specified.

(4)   The treatment specified in accordance with sub-paragraph (3) must be—

(a)   by, or under the direction of, such registered medical practitioner as may be specified in the order;

(b)   as a non-resident patient at such place as may be so specified; or

(c)   as a resident patient in a health service hospital.

(5)   No court shall include a requirement under this paragraph in a supervision order unless it is satisfied—

(a)   where the child has sufficient understanding to make an informed decision, that he consents to its inclusion; and

(b)   that satisfactory arrangements have been, or can be, made for the treatment.

(6)   If a medical practitioner by whom or under whose direction a supervised person is being treated in pursuance of a requirement included in a supervision order by virtue of this paragraph is unwilling to continue to treat or direct the treatment of the supervised child or is of the opinion that—

(a)   the treatment should be continued beyond the period specified in the order;

(b)   the supervised child needs different treatment;

(c)   he is not susceptible to treatment; or

(d)   he does not require further treatment,

the practitioner shall make a report in writing to that effect to the supervisor.

(7)   On receiving a report under this paragraph the supervisor shall refer it to the court, and on such a reference the court may make an order cancelling or varying the requirement.

CASE STUDY

STAGE 4

As you know, an emergency protection order is only a short-term option, and the local authority must decide what will happen to these children on a long-term basis. Any decision needs to be made reasonably quickly after the emergency protection order has been granted, since it is not possible to extend the order more than once.

In this scenario, the local authority is in a good position to make longer-term decisions since they have been working with the family for several months. By now they should have a good idea of the parents' capabilities and prospects for change.

The options that the local authority can choose are probably as follows:

- Let the emergency protection orders expire and return the children to their parents, with possible ongoing support under s. 17 of the Children Act 1989.
- Try to negotiate with the parents to allow the local authority to accommodate the children under s. 20 of the 1989 Act.
- Seek supervision orders under s. 31 of the 1989 Act.
- Seek care orders under s. 31 with either the long-term aim of rehabilitating the children (or some of them) with the parents or for long-term fostering/adoption.

The options are set out with the least interventionist first through to the most draconian.

It is suggested that the first two options are unlikely to be pursued by the local authority due to the background of the case. The parents have not appeared to be very capable of change, despite an extensive input into the family.

If the latter two options are viable, the local authority must make an application under s. 31 to the family proceedings court. You should note that the local authority may apply for one order, but the court decide that this is not appropriate and then make the other s. 31 order.

Discuss the application process and the progression of the case, i.e.:

- the application must be on notice;
- the appointment of a guardian ad litem to represent the childrens' interests;
- the likelihood of interim care orders being made since the case will be subject to some element of delay;
- the possibility of further assessment of the parents' skills being ordered by the court at the local authority's expense (*Re C*).

When discussing the final hearing, explain the criteria which have to be satisfied by the local authority before the court can consider the making of an order under s. 31, i.e. that the child is suffering or is likely to suffer significant harm and that that harm is attributable to the care being given (or likely to be given if the order is not made) not being what it would be reasonable to expect a parent to give.

The children here are not beyond the control of the parents and hence s. 31(2)(b)(ii) is not relevant.

Go on to explain that once these threshold criteria have been met (noting the timing as per *Re M*) the court must then consider the factors in s. 1 of the 1989 Act — the welfare of the child being paramount, the welfare checklist and the question of whether an order is necessary at all. Part of this includes the evaluation by the court of all other possible orders under the 1989 Act — for example the making of s. 8 residence orders to the wider family.

The court is guided in this task by the expert reports by the guardian ad litem and the local authority's care plan, which must be produced for the final hearing.

Decide which order is suitable in this case — the facts given do not suggest the possibility of the wider family as alternative carers. The poor history of the local authority's intervention may also move the emphasis onto a care order rather than the supervision order. Do not forget that the local authority could place the children back into the care of their parents under a care order.

The care plan should indicate whether rehabilitation is considered possible or if long-term fostering/adoption is preferred. Post-order contact is another matter that needs to be included within the care plan. Mention should be made to the dilemma that exists if the court believes that a care order is in the best interests of the child, and yet disagrees with the care plan, since the court cannot place conditions on the local authority post-care order.

If possible, identify the most likely outcome, and then explain the consequences. So, if you feel that a supervision order is best, refer to s. 35 and sch. 3 of the 1989 Act. If you feel that a care order is the better outcome, the effect of ss. 33 and 34 need to be discussed. Whilst you may have mentioned the possibility of adoption in the long term, you would not be required to do more than refer to it in this way. In other words, you should not start to discuss the legal criteria for obtaining an adoption order.

From the four stages to this scenario you have hopefully been able to put the public law relating to children into a practical context. This is a typical case scenario. However, not all cases commence with a s. 47 investigation or go through to a s. 31 care order. Many will start with an emergency protection order, and may even end there. It all depends on the facts. What you need to develop is the ability to make choices regarding the direction of a case, and justify your choice with reference to the facts and the law applicable.

CHAPTER THIRTEEN

ADOPTION

13.1 What is Adoption?

13.1.1 A DECLINING PHENOMENON?

Judicial Statistics, Lord Chancellor's Department, 1995

Table 5.4 Adoption of Children: Summary of Proceedings, 1995

Nature of proceedings	High Court	County Courts	Family proceedings courts[1]	Total
Applications:				
by step-parents	38	2,465	725	3,228
by others	219	2,001	161	2,381
Total	**257**	**4,466**	**886**	**5,609**
Orders made:				
to step-parents	37	2,270	570	2,877
to others	212	2,115	113	2,440
Total	**249**	**4,385**	**683**	**5,317**

[1] Contains imputed data

13.2 What are the Effects of Adoption?

ADOPTION ACT 1976

12. Adoption orders

(1) An adoption order is an order giving parental responsibility for a child to the adopters, made on their application by an authorised court.

(2) The order does not affect parental responsibility so far as it relates to any period before the making of the order.

(3) The making of an adoption order operates to extinguish—

(a) the parental responsibility which any person has for the child immediately before the making of the order.

(aa) any order under the Children Act 1989;

(b) any duty arising by virtue of an agreement or the order of a court to make payments, so far as the payments are in respect of the child's maintenance or upbringing for any period after the making of the order.

(4) Subsection (3)(b) does not apply to a duty arising by virtue of an agreement—

(a) which constitutes a trust, or

(b) which expressly provides that the duty is not to be extinguished by the making of an adoption order.

(5) An adoption order may not be made in relation to a child who is or has been married.

(6) An adoption order may contain such terms and conditions as the court thinks fit.

(7) An adoption order may be made notwithstanding that the child is already an adopted child.

39. Status conferred by adoption

(1) An adopted child shall be treated in law—

(a) where the adopters are a married couple, as if he had been born as a child of the marriage (whether or not he was in fact born after the marriage was solemnized);

(b) in any other case, as if he had been born to the adopter in wedlock (but not as a child of any actual marriage of the adopter).

(2) An adopted child shall, subject to subsection (3), be treated in law as if he were not the child of any person other than the adopters or adopter.

(3) In the case of a child adopted by one of its natural parents as sole adoptive parent, subsection (2) has no effect as respects entitlement to property depending on relationship to that parent, or as respects anything else depending on that relationship.

(4) It is hereby declared that this section prevents an adopted child from being illegitimate.

(5) This section has effect—

(a) in the case of an adoption before 1st January 1976, from that date, and

(b) in the case of any other adoption, from the date of the adoption.

(6) Subject to the provisions of this Part, this section—

(a) applies to the construction of enactments or instruments passed or made before the adoption or later, and so applies subject to any contrary indication; and

(b) has effect as respects things done, or events occurring, after the adoption, or after 31st December 1975, whichever is the later.

42. Rules of construction for instruments concerning property

(1) Subject to any contrary indication, the rules of construction contained in this section apply to any instrument, other than an existing instrument, so far as it contains a disposition of property.

(2) In applying section 39(1) to a disposition which depends on the date of birth of a child or children of the adoptive parent or parents, the disposition shall be construed as if—

(a) the adopted child had been born on the date of adoption,

(b) two or more children adopted on the same date had been born on that date in the order of their actual births,

but this does not affect any reference to the age of a child.

(3) Examples of phrases in wills on which subsection (2) can operate are—

1. Children of A 'living at my death or born afterwards.'

2. Children of A 'living at my death or born afterwards before any one of such children for the time being in existence attains a vested interest and who attain the age of 21 years.'

3. As in example 1 or 2, but referring to grandchildren of A instead of children of A.

4. A for life 'until he has a child,' and then to his child or children.

Note. Subsection (2) will not affect the reference to the age of 21 years in example 2.

(4) Section 39(2) does not prejudice any interest vested in possession in the adopted child before the adoption, or any interest expectant (whether immediately or not) upon an interest so vested.

(5) Where it is necessary to determine for the purposes of a disposition of property effected by an instrument whether a woman can have a child, it shall be presumed that once a woman has attained the age of 55 years she will not adopt a child after execution of the instrument, and, notwithstanding section 39, if she does so that child shall not be treated as her child or as the child of her spouse (if any) for the purposes of the instrument.

(6)   In this section, 'instrument' includes a private Act settling property, but not any other enactment.

44.   Property devolving with peerages etc.

(1)   An adoption does not affect the descent of any peerage or dignity or title of honour.

(2)   An adoption shall not affect the devolution of any property limited (expressly or not) to devolve (as nearly as the law permits) along with any peerage or dignity or title of honour.

(3)   Subsection (2) applies only if and so far as a contrary intention is not expressed in the instrument, and shall have effect subject to the terms of the instrument.

47.   Miscellaneous enactments

(1)   Section 39 does not apply for the purposes of the table of kindred and affinity in Schedule 1 to the Marriage Act 1949 or sections 10 and 11 (incest) of the Sexual Offences Act 1956.

(2)   Section 39 does not apply for the purposes of any provision of—

(a)   the British Nationality Act 1981,

(b)   the Immigration Act 1971,

(c)   any instrument having effect under an enactment within paragraph (a) or (b), or

(d)   any other provision of the law for the time being in force which determines British citizenship, British Dependent Territories citizenship, the status of a British National (Overseas) or British Overseas citizenship.

13.3   Who can be Adopted?

ADOPTION ACT 1976

13.   Child to live with adopters before order made

(1)   Where—

(a)   the applicant, or one of the applicants, is a parent, step-parent or relative of the child, or

(b)   the child was placed with the applicants by an adoption agency or in pursuance of an order of the High Court,

an adoption order shall not be made unless the child is at least 19 weeks old and at all times during the preceding 13 weeks had his home with the applicants or one of them.

(2)   Where subsection (1) does not apply, an adoption order shall not be made unless the child is at least 12 months old and at all times during the preceding 12 months had his home with the applicants or one of them.

13.4   Who can Adopt?

ADOPTION ACT 1976

14.   Adoption by married couple

(1)   An adoption order shall not be made on the application of more than one person except in the circumstances specified in subsections (1A) and (1B).

(1A)   An adoption order may be made on the application of a married couple where both the husband and the wife have attained the age of 21 years.

(1B)   An adoption order may be made on the application of a married couple where—

(a)   the husband or the wife—

(i)   is the father or mother of the child; and

(ii)   has attained the age of 18 years;

and

(b)   his or her spouse has attained the age of 21 years.

(2) An adoption order shall not be made on the application of a married couple unless—

(a) at least one of them is domiciled in a part of the United Kingdom, or in the Channel Islands or the Isle of Man, or

(b) the application is for a Convention adoption order and section 17 is complied with.

15. Adoption by one person

(1) An adoption order may be made on the application of one person where he has attained the age of 21 years and

(a) is not married, or

(b) is married and the court is satisfied that—

(i) his spouse cannot be found, or

(ii) the spouses have separated and are living apart, and the separation is likely to be permanent, or

(iii) his spouse is by reason of ill-health, whether physical or mental, incapable of making an application for an adoption order.

(2) An adoption order shall not be made on the application of one person unless—

(a) he is domiciled in a part of the United Kingdom, or in the Channel Islands or the Isle of Man, or

(b) the application is for a Convention adoption order and section 17 is complied with.

(3) An adoption order shall not be made on the application of the mother or father of the child alone unless the court is satisfied that—

(a) the other natural parent is dead or cannot be found or, by virtue of section 28 of the Human Fertilisation and Embryology Act 1990, there is no other parent, or

(b) there is some other reason justifying the exclusion of the other natural parent, and where such an order is made the reason justifying the exclusion of the other natural parent shall be recorded by the court.

IN RE D (AN INFANT) ADOPTION: PARENT'S CONSENT) [1977] 2 WLR 79 (HL)

LORD WILBERFORCE: . . . There only remains—the crucial—point (3). As to this, it seems to me that the judge faced the essential issue: whether to refuse the adoption order and let things go on as they were, with the likelihood of longer periods of access by the father, and the boy finding out about his father and his father's way of life and meeting his partners, or whether to bring down the curtain now and foreclose these problems. He looked at this question through the eyes of a reasonable father who he said, surely rightly, would want the boy to stay with him and would realise that the boy would then come into contact with homosexuals. The reasonable father—meaning a father placed in the circumstances of the actual father—would, said the judge, say, 'I must protect my boy even if it means parting from him for ever.' I think that all of this necessarily involves, though it is not explicitly said, a decision that it would not be reasonable to leave the future relationship of the boy and his father to be dealt with by the matrimonial court: either the boy would suffer and be at risk, if association with his father were to be continued, since before very long the boy would be able, whatever the provisions about access might be, to make his own decisions, or if this risk were to be avoided and association with the father were to be cut off, the father would have nothing to offer his son. This was reflected in the judge's own words, added it seems in his own writing, to the transcript: 'The father has nothing to offer his son at any time in the future.' This destroys at once the main argument, which is so strong in normal cases (e.g. *In re B* [1975] Fam 127) that the maintenance of the tie with the possibility of parental influence is valuable to a child and should not be cut off. On the facts of the case it was, in my view, an entirely justifiable and, indeed, a right decision.

My Lords, I would add two observations in this difficult and painful case. First, as I have already said, there is nothing in the present decision which would warrant or support a general principle of dispensing with a parent's consent on the ground of homosexual conduct alone. The courts in these cases are not concerned to condemn, or tolerate, the way in which adults choose, legally, to live. This case has to be decided as it does, for reasons which are individual to it and to these parents. These reasons must reflect, in my opinion, and in this I would qualify the judgment of Sir Gordon Willmer, the different attitude which courts must take where children are concerned from those cases which only affect adults. Whatever new attitudes Parliament, or public tolerance, may have chosen to take as regards the behaviour of consenting adults over 21 inter se, these should not entitle the courts to relax, in any degree, the vigilance and severity with which they should regard the risk of children, at critical ages, being exposed or introduced to ways of life which, as this case illustrates, may lead to severance from normal society, to psychological stresses and unhappiness and possibly even to physical experiences which may scar them for life. (I say this with all the qualifications which are brought out in the valuable discussion in *Reg* v *Willis (Peter)* [1975] 1 WLR 292 per Lawton LJ). I think that the reasonable parent in the circumstances here shown would inevitably want to protect his boy from these dangers . . .

LORD KILBRANDON: First, it could easily be productive of injustice if one were to attempt any hard and fast rule as to the attitude which the courts ought to adopt, in custody, access or adoption matters, towards those whose sexual abnormalities have denied them the possibility of a normal family life. This is because it is not possible to generalise about homosexuals, or fair to treat them as other than personalities demanding the assessment appropriate to their several individualities in exactly the same way as each heterosexual member of society must be regarded as a person, not as a member of a class or herd. Naturally, in a family law context, the fact of homosexual conduct cannot be ignored, but no more can the consequences of taking it into account be standardised. The kind of influence, in this type of problem, which the fact may have will be infinitely variable. I can see no trace, in the present case, of the learned judge's having tried to make any rule about what view the court should take about the position of a homosexual spouse in an application for adoption; on the contrary the decision at which he arrived plainly rests upon a careful and detailed examination of the problem as it affected this father, this child, and this family. Any other approach would have been wrong. . . .

AMT (KNOWN AS AC) (PETITIONERS FOR AUTHORITY TO ADOPT SR)
[1994] Fam Law 225 (CS)

A disabled boy was taken into care in England immediately after birth and was placed with fosterparents. The mother thereafter had no contact with the boy. The local authority attempted to secure a permanent placement with a view to adoption, but this proved unusually difficult due to the boy's special needs and disabilities. Over 3 years later the petitioner was identified as a suitable placement. Following a favourable report from the guardian ad litem the High Court granted permission for the boy to be moved to Scotland and placed with the petitioner with a view to his adoption. The petitioner, a homosexual, had worked for many years as a nurse. He was unmarried and had lived in a stable relationship with his male partner for 10 years. The couple enjoyed a quiet lifestyle, were supported by their families, and experienced no prejudice from the local community. The child became very well settled in their home. The Lord Ordinary refused the application for adoption on two grounds: (1) that the natural mother had not consented to the adoption and that he was not persuaded that her consent was withheld unreasonably; and (2) that the application raised a fundamental question of principle, namely whether adoption should be sanctioned in circumstances where a single male prospective adopter proposed to bring up the child jointly with a male partner with whom he was cohabiting in a homosexual relationship. On a reclaiming motion—
HELD:

(1)   The objective test of whether the mother's consent was withheld unreasonably was fully satisfied. A mother who had had no contact with the boy since birth and was unable or unwilling to care for him herself in view of his disabilities would not hesitate to give consent to this adoption if she gave first consideration to the child's welfare.

(2)   There was no fundamental objection in principle to adoption in these circumstances. The Adoption (Scotland) Act 1978 (the 1978 Act) does not expressly prohibit the making of an adoption order on the application of a single person who is homosexual

and proposes to bring up a child jointly with a homosexual cohabitant. Part III of the Children Act (Scotland) 1995 contains no provisions relating to homosexual adoptions or to adoptions by unmarried couples. Section 6 of the 1978 Act requires the court to have regard to all the circumstances, first consideration being given to the child's welfare. Issues relating to sexual orientation, lifestyle, race, religion, or other characteristics of the parties involved are to be taken into account as part of the circumstances, but they cannot prevail over what is in the best interests of the child.

Per curiam: if the court had held that the petitioner's application was not permitted by the 1978 Act, there would have been no conflict with the Convention for the Protection of Human Rights and Fundamental Freedoms. Refusal of the petitioner's application to adopt would, on the authorities, be unlikely to be held to contravene Arts 8.1, 12 or 14.

COMMENT

This much publicised case is of interest south as well as north of the Border, since the adoption provisions are identical in not expressly prohibiting adoptions in these circumstances (see Adoption Act 1976, especially ss. 14 and 15). Nor would the Adoption Bill 1996 have changed the situation. As Chris Barton has observed:

The minimum statutory requirements for adopters do not include heterosexuality; Parliament has been content merely to limit eligibility either to both . . . parties to a marriage or to one unmarried person. ('The Homosexual in the Family' [1996] Fam Law 626, at p. 627)

The approach of the Court of Session is enlightened in stressing that the capacity of a particular adoptive placement to promote a particular child's welfare must be assessed without resort to stereotypical preconceptions about categories of families and of prospective parents. The court took judicial notice of the absence of systematic evidence (as opposed to preconception) that homosexual relationships are less stable or caring than heterosexual relationships; that homosexuals have lesser capacity to care for children than heterosexuals; that there is an increased incidence of homosexuality amongst children of homosexual parents; and that children brought up in homosexual relationships suffer stigmatisation.

Whether this decision will have much impact in practice is another question. Its facts were unusual, as were earlier cases of placements for adoption or residence with homosexuals (see *Re E (Adoption: Freeing Order)* [1995] 1 FLR 382). It is too early to view the decision as a significant step for the recognition of homosexual rights in family law. Moreover, it is not inconceivable (although, it is submitted, would be regrettable) that in the current climate of emphasis on traditional family values Parliament might at a future date move in the other direction and expressly restrict the eligibility of prospective adopters on either side of the Border to those of conventional sexual orientation.

(See also the report by Alastair Bissett-Johnson at [1997] Fam Law 8.)

13.5 Who can Arrange Adoptions?

ADOPTION ACT 1976

11. Restriction on arranging adoptions and placing of children

(1) A person other than an adoption agency shall not make arrangements for the adoption of a child, or place a child for adoption, unless—

(a) the proposed adopter is a relative of the child, or

(b) he is acting in pursuance of an order of the High Court.

(2) An adoption society which is—

(a) approved as respects Scotland under section 3 of the Adoption (Scotland) Act 1978; or

(b) registered as respects Northern Ireland under Article 4 of the Adoption (Northern Ireland) Order 1987,

but which is not approved under section 3 of this Act, shall not act as an adoption society in England and Wales except to the extent that the society considers it necessary to do so in the interests of a person mentioned in section 1 of the Act of 1978 or Article 3 of the Order of 1987.

(3) A person who—

(a) takes part in the management or control of a body of persons which exists wholly or partly for the purpose of making arrangements for the adoption of children and which is not an adoption agency; or

(b) contravenes subsection (1); or

(c) receives a child placed with him in contravention of subsection (1),

shall be guilty of an offence and liable on summary conviction to imprisonment for a term not exceeding 3 months or to a fine not exceeding level 5 on the standard scale or to both.

(4) In any proceedings for an offence under paragraph (a) of subsection (3), proof of things done or of words written, spoken or published (whether or not in the presence of any party to the proceedings) by any person taking part in the management or control of a body of persons, or in making arrangements for the adoption of children on behalf of the body, shall be admissible as evidence of the purpose for which that body exists.

72. Interpretation

(1) In this Act, unless the context otherwise requires—

. . .

'relative' in relation to a child means a grandparent, brother, sister, uncle or aunt, whether of the full blood or half-blood or by affinity and includes, where the child is illegitimate, the father of the child and any person who would be a relative within the meaning of this definition if the child were the legitimate child of his mother and father; . . .

RE WM (ADOPTION: NON-PATRIAL) [1997] 1 FLR 132 (FamD)

JOHNSON J: This adoption application has given rise to the kind of technical problem that all too often arises when English couples seek to adopt a child from a country overseas without taking proper professional advice.

The factual background to the application is that the child concerned, W, was born in El Salvador on 7 November 1992. He was the third child of a young mother whose situation appears from a letter written by Her Majesty's then ambassador to El Salvador in 1993. She lives in a one-room brick-built house with her grandmother and an 11-year-old daughter. The house is in a community built by the occupants themselves who previously lived in dwellings of wood, cardboard and plastic. The property has electricity. Water is obtained from a communal tap nearby. The mother has irregular work producing material of crochet.

The father of the child abandoned her and, for economic reasons, she decided that she would give it up for adoption. As a result of discussing her plight with another woman, she was put in contact with a lawyer who told her that there were foreign families willing to adopt her son. He arranged the completion of all the necessary documents.

The applicants are an English married couple, he now 45 and she 41. They married in 1983 and had a son, T, born in 1985. Being unable to have more children and being of an age when adoption was not available to them in England, they decided to seek to adopt a child overseas. So it was that they were put in touch with the lawyer in El Salvador previously mentioned.

They went to El Salvador and paid the lawyer £5000. They were introduced to this young woman and to W. The lawyer arranged for them to adopt W under the law of El Salvador. I have copies of the documents involved which show that W was adopted by the applicants on 28 October 1993, the order being made in the civil court there. At that time W was not quite a year old. A few days later the applicants brought him to England and he has lived with them here ever since.

On 6 January 1994 the applicants notified the local authority of their intention to apply to adopt W here in England. Their application for adoption is dated 30 March 1995. It is an unusual feature of the factual background of the application that since that application was made the applicants have separated. Their application having been made on 30 March 1995, the usual inquiries were made. In a report dated 9 May 1995 a social worker reported that the marriage of the applicants seemed happy and there was no cause for concern. The social worker reported:

I believe the marriage is stable and have sought advice from their referees in this respect. Their marriage is based on trust, loyalty and friendship and there is evidence of mutual support.

It is therefore surprising that the separation took place just a few weeks later, in July 1995. W is now living with the female applicant but has regular visiting and staying contact with the male applicant.

As, in my experience, is too often the case where the court is asked to consider an application for the adoption of a foreign child where the arrangements were made informally in a way such as this, there are reservations about the suitability of the placement of the child. I need not refer to those in any detail—they relate to the background of the applicants.

In considering whether the making of an adoption order would advance and promote the welfare of young W during his childhood, I must look at his situation as it is now. It will be apparent from the history, as I have related it, that there is really no option available to W that would not involve subjecting him to the risk of considerable harm. It is clear from the documents which I have read about his natural mother that there is no prospect at all of him being able to make a home with her. The only other option would be for me to take steps that would result in his being found a home elsewhere in England, with the intention that he be adopted into another family. I hold myself satisfied that the making of an adoption order is very much in W's interest.

I turn now to consider individually the points of law that have arisen and, in doing so, I express my appreciation for the assistance which I have received from both counsel.

Breach of s. 11 of the Adoption Act 1976
The section reads, so far as is material:

A person other than an adoption agency shall not make arrangements for the adoption of a child, or place a child for adoption, unless—
(a) the proposed adopter is a relative of the child, or
(b) he is acting in pursuance of an order of the High Court.

The placement of W with the applicants was therefore contrary to s. 11, but I am satisfied that that does not prevent the court from making an adoption order. There is here no power to authorise such a placement retrospectively, but none the less the statutory prohibition does not prevent the High Court from making an adoption order.

In this regard, the situation is different from that where a financial payment is made. The matter fell for consideration by the Court of Appeal in *Re G (Adoption: Illegal Placement)* [1995] 1 FLR 403 where, at 405, Balcombe LJ said:

It is apparent that, whereas in the case of an inegal placement under s. 11 the Act makes no express provision as to what is to happen in relation to an adoption order, in relation to an illegal payment under s. 57 s. 24(2) does make express provision.

Accordingly, I hold that the breach of s. 11 does not here prevent the court from making the adoption order sought.

13.6 The Process of Adoption

13.6.1 THE STANDARD ROUTE

13.6.1.1 The matters for the court

6. Duty to promote welfare of child
In reaching any decision relating to the adoption of a child a court or adoption agency shall have regard to all the circumstances, first consideration being given to the need to safeguard and promote the welfare of the child throughout his childhood; and shall so

far as practicable ascertain the wishes and feelings of the child regarding the decision and give due consideration to them, having regard to his age and understanding.

'Adoption — A Service for Children', Consultative Document, Department of Health/Welsh Office 1996

4.1   Under the 1976 Act the need to safeguard and protect the welfare of the child throughout his childhood is the first consideration. The Bill provides that the paramount consideration of the court or adoption agency is to be the child's welfare, in childhood and later. This brings the welfare test into line with the Children Act. In determining what is in the interests of a child the court or agency must apply the welfare checklist. The court may only make a placement order or adoption order if the parent or guardian consents to the making of an order or the court dispenses with their consent. The principal ground for dispensing with consent is that the court is satisfied that the welfare of the child requires the consent to be dispensed with. In coming to any decision the court will need to have regard in particular to clause 1(4)(f). It is however true to say that as this is a decision relating to the adoption of a child, the welfare checklist would need to be considered by the court in any event, and there is a danger that making welfare the principal ground for dispensing with consent does not add much to this.

Comments are invited, in particular in relation to the new ground for dispensing with parental consent (see clauses 1 and 46).

DRAFT BILL

1.   Considerations applicable to the exercise of powers

(1)   This section applies whenever a court or adoption agency is coming to a decision relating to the adoption of a child.

(2)   The paramount consideration of the court or adoption agency must be the child's welfare, in childhood and later.

(3)   The court or adoption agency must at all times bear in mind that any delay in coming to the decision is likely to prejudice the child's welfare.

(4)   The court or adoption agency must have regard to the following matters (among others)—

(a)   the child's ascertainable wishes and feelings regarding the decision (considered in the light of the child's age and understanding),

(b)   the child's particular needs,

(c)   the likely effect on the child (during childhood or later) of having ceased to be a member of the original family and become an adopted person.

(d)   the child's age, sex, background and any of the child's characteristics which the court or agency considers relevant,

(e)   any harm which the child has suffered or is at risk of suffering, and

(f)   the relationship which the child has with relatives, and with any other person In relation to whom the court or agency considers the question to be relevant, including—

(i)   the value to the child of any such relationship continuing,

(ii)   the ability and willingness of any of the child's relatives, or of any such person, to provide the child with a secure environment in which the child can develop, and otherwise to meet the child's needs,

(iii)   the wishes and feelings of any of the child's relatives, or of any such person, about the child.

(5)   The court or adoption agency must always consider the whole range of powers available to them in the child's case (whether under this Act or the Children Act 1989) and, if it exercises any power, must only exercise the most appropriate one; and the court must not make any order under this Act unless it considers that making the order would be better for the child than not doing so.

(6)   In this section—

'coming to a decision relating to the adoption of a child', in relation to a court, includes (among other things)—

(a) coming to a decision in any proceedings where the orders that might be made by the court include an adoption order or the making or revocation of a placement order, or

(b) coming to a decision about granting leave in respect of any action (other than the initiation of proceedings in any court) which may be taken by an adoption agency or individual under this Part,

but does not include coming to a decision about granting leave in any other circumstances, and

'relative', in relation to a child, includes any adoptive relative and the mother and father (including an adoptive mother or father);

and references to making an order include dispensing with parental consent.

Adoption: The Future, HMSO, 1993

5.18   Given its nature and purpose, the process of adoption is necessarily complex for all concerned, and can seem intrusive.

5.19   The Government therefore intends through the new legislation to introduce a wider range of simpler alternatives enabling people already caring for a child in various capacities to confirm and strengthen the legal basis of their relationship.

5.20   The first will be a *new and simpler alternative to 'step-parent adoptions'*—that is the adoption by a husband and wife of the child of one of them born into a former marriage or relationship. At present if they wish legally to establish their joint parental role vis-à-vis the child, they need to go through the full legal adoption procedure. The birth parent in the new marriage—in most cases the wife—is thus obliged jointly with her husband to adopt her own child. Another consequence is that the child's relationship with his other birth parent and the relatives on that side of the family is legally severed.

5.21   The Government intend that the new legislation will make available a new *Parental Responsibility Agreement*. This could be entered into by the birth parent with her new spouse, though it would create a new relationship only for the step-parent. It would thus create a joint parental responsibility to be exercised by both, but would not legally sever links with the other birth parent. In cases where the other birth parent registered consent, the agreement would simply be registered with the court. No court hearing and no assessment of suitability or any local authority or adoption agency involvement would be necessary. Even in cases where the other birth parent's consent was not forthcoming and the court needed to judge the issue and decide whether or not to make the order, the process would be simpler and less intrusive than adoption. Children in respect of whom such an agreement or order had been made would not have the same rights under intestacy law as adopted children or children born of the marriage but would retain normal rights of inheritance to the estates of both their birth parents. The new agreement or order would be an alternative to adoption. Many parents are likely to see it as meeting their objectives more simply.

5.22   For those who nevertheless prefer adoption, the form of the adoption order will be altered in such cases so that the birth parent is not obliged to adopt her own child.

5.23   The second alternative will be a new *guardianship order* intended to allow relatives or others caring for a child including long-term foster parents to obtain legal recognition of their role, and without going as far as adoption to put their relationship with the child onto a more permanent and clearer basis.

5.24   The order would be available to supplement the residence order that the courts already make in such cases which normally defines the child's residence until the age of 16. But the guardianship order would extend until the age of 18 when the legal concept of childhood ends, and would entitle the guardian to appoint another in the event of his own death before the child became 18. To emphasise the permanence of the relationship created by this order, no application to dissolve it could be made except with prior leave of the court. The order would not sever any legal links with birth parents. The legal term for such an order would be 'Inter-Vivos Guardianship'. Foster parents who obtained it might regard it as giving them 'Foster-plus' status.

5.25   These two new orders would add to the range of legal instruments available to reflect and reinforce the various different long-term relationships that children may have with those who care for them in different capacities. They would not sever the legal relationships with a child's birth family or involve the deep scrutiny process required for adoption.

ADOPTION ACT 1976

16. Parental agreement
  (1)   An adoption order shall not be made unless—
    (a)   the child is free for adoption by virtue of an order made—
      (i)   in England and Wales, under section 18;
      (ii)   in Scotland, under section 18 of the Adoption (Scotland) Act 1978; or
      (iii)   in Northern Ireland, under Article 17(1) or 18(1) of the Adoption (Northern Ireland) Order 1987; or
    (b)   in the case of each parent or guardian of the child the court is satisfied that—
      (i)   he freely, and with full understanding of what is involved, agrees unconditionally to the making of an adoption order (whether or not he knows the identity of the applicants) . . .

RE T (ADOPTION: CONTACT) [1995] 2 FLR 251 (CA)

BUTLER-SLOSS LJ: This is an appeal by the adoptive parents against an order for contact by, the natural mother, the former parent, made by his Honour Judge Heald on 29 April 1994 in Nottingham, which is side by side with all adoption order made to the appellants. The actual adoption was consented to by the mother. It is a somewhat unusual case where the only issue is whether there should be an order enforcing the once a year contact, which has always been agreed to by the adopters. The child concerned is a little girl called C who is now 10, having been born on 11 December 1984. Her parents never married. . . . Secondly, [the judge] said, and I quote:

> The advantage of having an order under s. 8 is that the matter can come back to the court if there are disputes. Otherwise there are all sorts of difficulties of obtaining leave and other problems.

What the judge was referring to there was the requirement under s. 10 of the Children Act, that the mother, a former parent, would not have a right to make an application for contact under s. 8, because as a former parent she requires leave.
The judge went on to say:

> I [the court] take the view I have to deal with this problem [that is the problem of contact] . . . The parties are not agreed as to what should happen. Therefore, notwithstanding the arguments by all the parties, I do not agree that the no order principle can apply because contact is not agreed. The best thing for C is that I do make an order.

In this case the only argument, really, that remains is whether the once a year, which was agreed to by the adopters and was found to be the right amount of contact by the judge, should be imposed upon these adopters, or whether it should be left to their good sense so that they could be trusted to do what they believe to be in the best interest of their daughter.
Mr Singleton for the mother has one point which he has put to us very effectively, that the mother has consented to adoption, but that her consent to adoption, although it was unconditional, none the less recognised that she would expect to see the child at least once a year, and had hoped to see the child rather more, and that such consent was in the context of this continuing contact in an open adoption. What the judge was doing by making an order was to give her some degree of security. Mr Karsten says, it seems to me with great force, that that sort of security called for by the mother is inconsistent with the unconditional element of the agreement that she gave under the Adoption Act 1976 and conflicts with the principle that consent to adoption must be, and is certainly seen, in the way in which the mother put her case, to be unconditional. One cannot but recognise, however, that the mother in this case, having consented to her daughter going to to be part of a family whom she admires and respects, none the less wishes to have some degree of certainty that she will continue to be in touch with her daughter.

It seems to me that that degree of security that she seeks has to be found in the trust that she must have in these adopters. That is a trust which is undoubtedly held by the local authority and the guardian ad litem because those experts in this field all believe that at this stage of this child's life it is right for her sake that she should continue to see her mother once a year. They have chosen this family on the basis that they also would recognise it was in the interests of this child that she should continue, certainly for the time being, to see her natural mother. These adopters themselves accept that this is right. This is all in the interests of the child, and, of course, an order under s. 8 for contact is made with the welfare of the child of the primary consideration. Nobody is suggesting that if this order is not made then the welfare of this child would not continue to be the primary consideration of these adopters in relation to her continuing contact with her natural mother.

She does have a remedy. Judge Heald thought that that need for leave to apply, and all sorts of problems like that, would be met by a s. 8 order. It seems to me that the requirement of leave is a valuable protection, both for the adopters and for the child, and it is one that is very properly in place for that protection in the case of a former parent. If the adopters act unreasonably and that becomes clear to the court, then no doubt the mother would get an order which is appropriate for the time at which this matter comes before the court, bearing in mind the age of the child. Perhaps one matter that I should refer to is in *Re C (A Minor) (Adopted Child: Contact)* [1993] Fam 210, a decision of Thorpe J, which was a very different case from this, where a mother who had not seen a child for a considerable number of years was applying for contact. Thorpe J proposed a procedure which would, first, require the case to be transferred to the Family Division of the High Court and to involve the Official Solicitor at the leave stage, together with the local authority, before the adopters were troubled with such an application.

That, of course, was a case very different from the present. If the mother does apply for leave her application for leave would be likely to go to the district judge of the local registry and would be considered by the district judge for directions. It may be that in a case such as this, depending entirely on what the facts are at this time, the district judge might think that the procedure provided by Thorpe J in *Re C (A Minor) (Adopted Child: Contact)* (above) was not necessarily appropriate to this case. It would be entirely, of course, within the discretion of the district judge as to how he dealt with it, but he might not feel bound to follow the general propositions put forward by Thorpe J in a rather different type of case.

But in my judgment the prevalence and finality of adoption and the importance of letting the new family find its own feet ought not to be threatened in any way by an order in this case.

RE B (A MINOR) (ADOPTION) [1991] Fam Law 136 (CA)

This was an application by the natural father of a child for leave to appeal against the refusal of a county court judge to allow him to be joined as a party to an adoption application by the natural mother and her husband. The mother was married but had an affair with the applicant which resulted in the child's birth. The mother and her husband were subsequently reconciled, since which time the child had lived with them as part of their family with no access by his natural father.

BALCOMBE LJ said that proper affidavit evidence of matters of fact relied on by an applicant was a pre-requisite to any application of that nature. Subject to the court's discretion to join any person or body to the adoption process, the unmarried biological father had no formal automatic right under the Adoption Rules 1984, r. 15(3) to prevent an adoption unless he had an order giving him parental rights under the Family Law Reform Act 1987 or custody or care and control under some other court order. As the natural parents were not married to each other, the applicant stood in the position of a prospective guardian whose rights could only be conferred by the court. He would not interfere with the exercise of the judicial discretion below as he was not satisfied that such discretion was based on wrong principles. There was no presumption that the natural father ought to be allowed to become a party on application. The application would, therefore, be dismissed.

COMMENT

It is well established (see *Re M (An Infant)* [1955] 2 QB 479) that, unless he has a custody or parental rights and duties order in his favour, or is otherwise a formally appointed guardian, an unmarried father's agreement to an adoption order is not required. What this case further establishes is that such fathers (unless they are liable to contribute to their child's maintenance) have no *right* to be named as a party to the adoption proceedings. Instead, this is a matter for the court's discretion under the Adoption Rules 1984, r. 15(3).

When this decision is taken in conjunction with *Re L (A Minor) (Adoption: Procedure)* [1991] 1 FLR 171, in which the Court of Appeal ruled that it is a matter for the local authority's discretion whether or not to include the particulars of the natural father in the Schedule II report it will be seen how weak the unmarried man's position is. For this reason, the unmarried father might be well advised to counter the adoption application (assuming he is aware of it) by seeking a custody, access or a parental rights and duties order. Given that it is established that a custody or access application should be heard together with that for adoption (see *Re O (An Infant)* [1965] Ch 27: and *Re G (A Minor) (Adoption and Access Applications)* (1980) 1 FLR 109), and assuming the same to be true when applying for a parental rights and duties order, then even if the application fails, the father will, at least, have had his day in court. Applying for a parental rights and duties order can certainly be effective in the context or application to free the child for adoption. In this latter respect, it might be noted that an order can be made even where the inevitable decision is that he is unreasonably withholding his agreement to his child being freed for adoption: *Re H (Illegitimate Children: Father: Parental Rights) (No. 2)* [1991] 1 FLR 214.

RE L (A MINOR) (ADOPTION: PROCEDURE) [1991] 1 FLR 171 (CA)

BALCOMBE LJ: J was placed for adoption within 6 days of her birth, on 27 July 1989. On 18 October 1989 she was placed with Mr and Mrs E, who are now applying for her adoption, by the Mid-Glamorgan County Council who are the relevant adoption agency. By the order under appeal the judge ordered that the Form 6, the originating application for an adoption order, be amended so as to show the man who is said to be the father of the child, namely F, and directed that F be discreetly interviewed by the council's social worker, 'to ascertain his wishes and feelings in relation to adoption and the application'. From that order the council appealed with the leave of the judge, since they feared that M might withdraw her consent to the adoption if F had to be told of J's existence, while they were satisfied that the proposed adoption was in J's best interests. Since there was no respondent to the appeal we asked for, and were granted, the assistance of an *amicus curiae*, and we are much indebted to Mr Roderic Wood for his able submissions.

The father of an illegitimate child is not a 'parent' within the meaning of that word as used in s. 16 or elsewhere in the Act—see *Re M (An Infant)* [1955] 2 QB 479—but he may be a 'guardian' if he has a parental rights order under s. 4 of the Family Law Reform Act 1987, or has a custody order under some other Act—see s. 72(1) of the 1976 Act as amended.

Section 66 of the 1976 Act gives a rule-making power to the Lord Chancellor. It is material to observe that s. 66(3)(a) provides that, in the case of an application for an adoption order in relation to a child who is not free for adoption, rules shall require every person who can be found *and whose agreement or consent to the making of an order is required under this Act* (our emphasis) to be notified of a date and place where he will be heard on the application and of the fact that, unless he wishes or the court requires, he need not attend. No such notification need be given to the father of an illegitimate child unless he comes within the definition of a 'guardian' as above. No new rules have been made under s. 66, but the Adoption Rules 1984 (SI 1984 No. 265) remain in force under the transitional provisions (1976 Act, s. 73(1), sch. 2, para. 1).

. . . Each parent or guardian (not being an applicant) of the child must be a respondent, unless the child is free for adoption: for the reasons already given this will not include the father of an illegitimate child unless he comes within the meaning of a guardian. However, if the putative father is liable by virtue of any order or agreement to contribute to the maintenance of the child, r. 15(2)(h) requires that he be made a respondent. . . .

Rule 22(1) of the 1984 rules provides that where (as here) the child was placed for adoption with the applicant by an adoption agency (the council), that agency shall supply a report in writing covering the matters specified in sch. 2 to the rules. Schedule 2 provides that, so far as is practicable, the report supplied by the adoption agency shall include all the following particulars. The schedule is then divided into seven main paragraphs headed respectively 'The Child' (para. 1), 'Guardian' (para. 3), 'Prospective Adopter' (para. 4), 'Actions of the adoption agency supplying the report' (para. 5), 'General' (para. 6) and 'Conclusions' (para. 7). Paragraph 2, which is the relevant paragraph in the present case, is headed 'Each Natural Parent, including where appropriate the father who was not married to the child's mother at the time of his birth'. There then follow subparas (a)–(l), giving the particulars to be supplied concerning each natural parent defined as aforesaid. The judge held that the words 'where appropriate' in the heading to para. 2 in effect added nothing to the meaning of this provision. He said:

> The main submission on this matter of Mr Evans is that the words 'where appropriate' mean that if the local authority doesn't think it is a good idea to ask the father about his wishes and feelings then they needn't do so. That does not seem to me to be the natural construction of the words, and I think that the words 'where appropriate' are there only because provision is being made specifically for requiring the information concerning the father of an illegitimate child, and that if the words were omitted the meaning might not be very different, but it is thought, for the sake of clarity, desirable to say 'where appropriate' by way of recognition that the child may not be illegitimate.

In our judgment, the judge here fell into two errors. In the first place, the words 'where appropriate' are highly significant. It will be recalled that, prima facie, the father of an illegitimate child is not a parent of that child, where the word 'parent' is used in the course of the statutes relating to adoption or the rules made thereunder. Thus there is here an extension of the meaning of the word 'parent'. If it had been intended to include the father of an illegitimate child in every case, the words 'where appropriate' are wholly superfluous. In our judgment, the words 'where appropriate' were clearly intended to confer a discretion upon the adoption agency preparing the report whether or not to include particulars of the father of an illegitimate child. Secondly, the discretion was in any event that of the adoption agency. The judge had no power to interfere with the exercise of that discretion unless it had been improperly exercised. The judge thought that no discretion existed but if, as we hold, there was such a discretion, then it is impossible to say that it was improperly exercised. The council, being convinced that adoption was here in J's best interests, was concerned that it should not fall through because of an approach, unwanted by the mother, to a putative father who was not even aware of J's existence.

ADOPTION ACT 1976

18. Freeing child for adoption

(7) Before making an order under this section in the case of a child whose father does not have parental responsibility for him, the court shall satisfy itself in relation to any person claiming to be the father that—

  (a) he has no intention of applying for—

   (i) an order under section 4(1) of the Children Act 1989, or

   (ii) a residence order under section 10 of that Act, or

  (b) if he did make any such application, it would be likely to be refused.

16. Parental agreement

  (1) . . .

   (b) . . .

   (ii) his agreement to the making of the adoption order should be dispensed with on a ground specified in subsection (2).

  (2) The grounds mentioned in subsection (1)(b)(ii) are that the parent or guardian—

  (a) cannot be found or is incapable of giving agreement;

(b) is withholding his agreement unreasonably;

(c) has persistently failed without reasonable cause to discharge his parental responsibility for the child;

(d) has abandoned or neglected the child;

(e) has persistently ill-treated the child;

(f) has seriously ill-treated the child (subject to subsection (5)).

RE W (AN INFANT) [1971] 2 All ER 49 (HL)

LORD HAILSHAM OF SAINT MARYLEBONE LC: My Lords, this appeal concerns the future of a male child, W, who was born on 28th March 1968. Like all cases in which the contest is between foster parents and a natural parent, all perfectly sincere in their motives, of which there have been quite a number in recent years, the decision is one which must cause pain in whichever direction the dispute is resolved and in any tribunal charged with the decision must cause anxiety and a deep sense of responsibility. I feel constrained to express my sympathy with the parties and to say that one of the pleasanter features of this case has been that each has treated the other with a measure of consideration and compassion and behaved with a respect for the interests of the child not universally shown in cases of this kind. I must add that at the conclusion of the hearing before the committee both leading counsel expressed a desire that members of your Lordships' committee hearing the case should disclose the nature of the decision they had it in mind to recommend to the House and in order to put an end to the period of uncertainty and distress the parties must necessarily suffer whilst awaiting the final result of these protracted proceedings my noble and learned friends and I thought fit as an exceptional procedure to accede to this request. I am sure your Lordships will endorse the course we thought fit to take.

The case falls to be decided under the terms of the Adoption Act 1958. It is a proposal for the adoption of W by the foster parents, the present appellants, with whom W has resided since a few days after his birth, and it is resisted by the infant's mother, the respondent to the present appeal.

The relevant test prescribed by the Act of 1958 is that the withholding of consent by the parent must be 'unreasonable'. Sachs LJ interpreted this word as involving necessarily a degree of what he described as 'culpability'. Counsel for the appellants had no difficulty in establishing that much of Sachs LJ's judgment is based on this interpretation. He said: 'Only if there is culpable conduct by the true parents can they [ie the foster parents] step in without the consent of the latter.' In his view the test is whether the mother has been 'guilty of conduct culpable to quite a high degree' . . .

In my view, there is no reason for interpreting the word 'unreasonably' where it occurs in the statute as importing necessarily any element of culpability.

. . . Section 5(1)(b) lays down a test of reasonableness. It does not lay down a test of culpability or of callous or self-indulgent indifference or of failure or probable failure of parental duty. As the last words in sub-s. 5(2) make quite clear, the tests in s. 5(1)(b) are quite independent of the test in s. 5(2), on which counsel has to some extent plainly modelled his submission. It is not for the courts to embellish, alter, subtract from, or add to words which, for once at least Parliament has employed without any ambiguity at all. I must add that if the test had involved me in a criticism of the respondent involving culpability or callous or self-indulgent indifference, I might well have come to the same conclusion on the facts as did Sachs and Cross LJJ. But since the test imposed on me by the Act is reasonableness and not culpability I have come to the opposite conclusion.

The question then remains as to how to apply the correct test. The test is whether at the time of the hearing the consent is being withheld unreasonably. As Lord Denning MR said in *Re L* (1962) 106 Sol Jo 611:

In considering the matter I quite agree that: (1) the question whether she is unreasonably withholding her consent is to be judged at the date of the hearing; and (2) the welfare of the child is not the sole consideration; and (3) the one question is whether she is unreasonably withholding her consent. But I must say that in considering whether she is reasonable or unreasonable we must take into account the welfare of the child. A reasonable mother surely gives great weight to what is better for the child.

Her anguish of mind is quite understandable; but still it may be unreasonable for her to withhold consent. We must look and see whether it is reasonable or unreasonable according to what a reasonable woman in her place would do in all the circumstances of the case.

From this it is clear that the test is reasonableness and not anything else. It is not culpability. It is not indifference. It is not failure to discharge parental duties. It is reasonableness, and reasonableness in the context of the totality of the circumstances. But, although welfare per se is not the test, the fact that a reasonable parent does pay regard to the welfare of his child must enter into the question of reasonableness as a relevant factor. It is relevant in all cases if and to the extent that a reasonable parent did take it into account. It is decisive in those cases where a reasonable parent must so regard it.

I do not understand *Re K (an infant)* [1952] 2 All ER 877 as deciding anything different from what I have said. I specifically endorse the often quoted passage from Jenkins LJ, in which he said:

Prima facie it would seem to me eminently reasonable for any parent to withhold his or her consent to an order [for adoption] thus completely and irrevocably destroying the parental relationship. One can imagine cases short of such misconduct or dereliction of duty is is mentioned in s. 3(1)(a) [i.e. of the Adoption Act 1950] in which a parent's withholding of consent to an adoption might properly be held to be unreasonable, but such cases must, in our view, be exceptional.

Exceptional, yes. But the test is still reasonableness, or its opposite, and reasonableness, or its opposite, must be judged, as Russell LJ observed in the instant case, and as both counsel agreed, by an objective (as distinct from a subjective) test. Indeed, I cannot myself readily visualise circumstances in which the words 'reason', 'reasonable' or 'unreasonable' can be applied otherwise than objectively. And, be it observed, 'reasonableness' or 'unreasonableness' where either word is employed in English law, is normally a question of fact and degree, and not a question of law, so long as there is evidence to support the finding of the court. It seems to me that the passage in Jenkins LJ's judgment in *Re K (an infant)* immediately following that which I have quoted above is too often forgotten and deserves to be better remembered. He said:

It is unnecessary, undesirable and, indeed, impracticable to attempt a definition covering all possible cases of that kind. Each case must depend on its own facts and circumstances.

In my opinion, besides culpability unreasonableness can include anything which can objectively be adjudged to be unreasonable. It is not confined to culpability or callous indifference. It can include, where carried to excess, sentimentality, romanticism, bigotry, wild prejudice, caprice, fatuousness, or excessive lack of common sense.

This means that, in an adoption case, a county court judge applying the test of reasonableness must be entitled to come to his own conclusions, on the totality of the facts, and a revising court should only dispute his decision where it feels reasonably confident that he has erred in law, or acted without adequate evidence, or where it feels that his judgment of the witnesses and their demeanour has played so little part in his reasoning that the revising court is in a position as good as that of the trial judge to form an opinion. In my view, by imposing the necessity for a clear prognosis of lasting damage to the child Russell LJ was falling into the same error as the other Lords Justices in applying to the Act a criterion of construction different from that which the language of the Act in fact prescribes.

RE E (A MINOR) (ADOPTION) [1989] 1 FLR 126 (CA)

BALCOMBE LJ: This is an appeal from an order of his Honour Judge Wootton sitting in the Birmingham County Court on 4 February 1988. By that order the judge directed that the consent of the appellant (the natural mother of E, born on 10 June 1984) be dispensed with on the grounds that she was withholding her consent unreasonably, and made an order in favour of the respondents, the Birmingham City Council, freeing E for adoption.

Nevertheless, the evidence before the judge that it was not in E's best interest that the mother should resume his care was cogent, and the judge was clearly entitled to find, as he did, that there was no prospect of that happening and that it was inevitable in the circumstances of the case to find that adoption was in E's best interests. Ms Dodson, for the mother, makes no complaint of that finding. The gravamen of her case is that the judge could not properly find that the mother was unreasonably withholding her consent to E being freed for adoption.

It is common ground that this is the test which the court must apply, in deciding whether an order freeing a child for adoption is in the best interests of the child. This question must be answered first, before considering the next question: whether to dispense with the parents' consent on the ground that it is being unreasonably withheld, see *Re B (A Minor) (Adoption by Parent)* [1975] Fam 127, 137. It has also been decided by this court that this test—under s. 6—does not apply to the question whether a parent is unreasonably withholding consent to an adoption order, see *Re P (An Infant)* [1977] Fam 25.

The provision for dispensing with the consent of a parent to an adoption order is contained in s. 16(1)(b)(ii) of the Adoption Act 1976, and the grounds for such dispensation are contained in s. 16(2) including that contained in para. (b)—that the parent is withholding his consent unreasonably. . . .

Then, after a careful judgment in which he made the finding that adoption was in E's best interests, he concluded:

> As regards the mother's consent to the freeing order, I have very little doubt that no reasonable parent in possession of all the relevant facts would refuse. Of course he or she would have much sympathy for the mother in that the present situation has largely arisen from the ill-treatment she herself received as a child. But I believe the reasonable parent would inevitably say that the welfare of E requires the freeing order for adoption and to refuse consent would in effect be to penalise him for the ill-treatment his mother received. Let us at least give him the opportunity of a decent and stable family life—so would all the hypothetical reasonable parents say.

Ms Dodson's case is that, notwithstanding his careful direction, the judge fell into the very trap against which he had warned himself, and substituted his own views for that of the hypothetical reasonable parent. In my judgment she has successfully made out that case. The requirement that the court must look at the case from the point of view of the hypothetical reasonable parent often requires the court to indulge in feats of mental gymnastics, but it cannot be gainsaid that the hypothetical reasonable parent who has a number of children, one of whom is the subject of an adoption application, will have in contemplation, when she (or he) makes her (or his) decision, the needs and feelings of the other children. Mrs Macur for the respondent council, fairly conceded this, although she added the qualification that such a parent must never lose sight of the fact that all the children deserve equal consideration: she cannot postpone the needs of the subject child to those of the other children or of her his own. I accept this qualification; the reasonable parent must here perform a balancing exercise. But it does not appear from the judgment that, in considering this case from the point of view of the reasonable parent, the judge gave any weight to the point that a reasonable parent would take into account M's interests. . . .

Nor does his finding, that it would be better for M that there should be a clean break in his relationship with E, appear to give any weight to the obvious distress that would be occasioned to M if E were to be removed altogether, and finally, from the family unit. However, so far as these findings were relevant to the judge's decision that adoption was in E's best interests, they were findings which he was entitled to make. Nevertheless, in my judgment Ms Dodson is justified in her criticism that, neither in this passage nor elsewhere in his judgment, does the judge indicate that he gave any thought to the question: what weight could the hypothetical reasonable parent properly give to M's interests? In my judgment this failure on the part of the judge entitles the court to review the judge's decision on this issue.

Apart from the question of M's interests, there were other considerations which the hypothetical reasonable parent was entitled to take into account. Although the judge came to the decision, as he was entitled to do, that there was no prospect of the mother resuming care of E, this was far from a foregone conclusion. The mother had the support of her former social worker, and her friend Mrs L, a teacher, and although the judge rejected the views of Mrs L, as being too partisan, and of the social worker, as being based on an inadequate and out of date assessment of the facts, in my judgment the fact that these two witnesses, in particular the social worker, held the view that the mother was now capable of caring for E, was something that the reasonable mother was entitled to take into account in reaching her decision. Ms Dodson also took us to those passages in the evidence of the other witnesses where they were in favour of the mother, but I do not think it helps to consider that evidence in detail; it is sufficient to say that although these witnesses were of the view that E could not safely be returned to the mother, they recognized that there were a number of positive factors in the mother's favour.

In addition to the other factors already mentioned, there is also the fact that, although the council had in mind prospective adopters for E, this was an untested placement. It was accepted that E could not stay with Mr and Mrs F. So the hypothetical reasonable mother could also take into account, although I doubt whether she could properly place much weight on this factor, that the choice lay between the family unit, with all its known deficiencies, with which E had never lost contact, and a new and untried (although carefully vetted) placement with adopters. . . .

In my judgment, for the reasons I have endeavoured to give above, on the facts of this case the mother's refusal to consent to the adoption order in respect of E was within the band of possible reasonable decisions. She may have been wrong, she may have been mistaken, but she was not unreasonable. Accordingly, I would allow this appeal and set aside the order freeing E for adoption.

RE P (ADOPTION: FREEING ORDER) [1994] 2 FLR 1000 (CA)

BUTLER-SLOSS LJ: This is an appeal by a mother from the order of his Honour Judge Wigmore sitting in Plymouth on Friday, 14 January 1994 when he made an order to dispense with the agreement of the mother in a freeing for adoption application under s. 16(2)(b) in line with s. 18 of the Adoption Act 1976. He also made an order tied to the freeing for adoption that there should be contact by the mother to the children four times a year.

The children concerned are twins of 5, nearly 6, being born on 23 September 1988. The mother suffers from schizophrenia and has so suffered for a number of years. The children have been in and out of care and have been in care, as far as I can see, permanently since about May 1992. . . . The judge said that he had little doubt:

. . . that the welfare of these children demands now the security and stability that an adoptive placement can give them, so if the matter were to go no further than that, it seems to me that I would certainly be saying, 'Yes, these children should be freed for adoption'.

Consequently, in line with s. 6 of the Adoption Act, he found that adoption would promote the welfare of the children throughout their childhood.

He then considered the second issue which was whether it was proper for the court to dispense with the agreement of the parent to the making of the adoption order. He said:

I have been so impressed in this case by the description of the happy relationship between the mother and the children on contact visits, and very obvious love that the mother has for the children, her great concern for them and, as far as I can tell from the second- and sometimes third-hand evidence, the love that the children exhibit for their mother . . . Given all these matters, it seems to me that there is a very strong argument . . . that the continuity in the lives of these children can really only be supplied by their mother. If this were a case where there was a stark choice between an adoption with no contact in future with the mother or no adoption, I think I would be constrained to say in this case—and I think I have to make this clear in case this matter goes further that I would not hold that the mother was unreasonably withholding her consent because, it seems to me, that quite apart from the obvious interest that she has, she can reasonably say, even on the rather stringent test which I shall come to in a moment, that for the good of the children there ought to be continuing contact.

Consequently, it appears to me from that passage of the judge's judgment (and it is fair to say it was a judgment given extempore at the end of case, but it is clearly set out by the judge that) if there is to be adoption, there is a precondition that there should be continuing contact; if there is not to be continuing contact, it would not be unreasonable for the mother to withhold her agreement.

Consequently he made both orders, continuing contact and holding that she had unreasonably withheld her agreement.

The judge therefore found that contact was a necessary part of the future life of the children and was to be built into the adoption. He recognised, of course, he could not make an order on freeing which bound the prospective adoptive parents at the moment of the adoption or thereafter, but he sought to make such contact a precondition. He believed that he could ensure that the mother's position on contact could adequately be protected in future adoption proceedings in a number of ways.

The appeal by the mother is on the short ground that the judge ought not to have dispensed with her agreement. It is a ground which, in my view, has to succeed. The judge would not have dispensed with agreement if there has to be no contact as part of a condition of the adoption. But despite all his valiant efforts to protect the mother, he cannot guarantee that there will be an adoption order with contact.

. . . In this case, the judge has said that he ought not to dispense with the agreement of the party if there was not to be contact post adoption; otherwise, as I have already said, the precondition.

This presents for the adoption agency major problems, in my view, because these children are not entirely easy to place. We all know that children rising 6 can be placed. It is not just a question of babies; we also know that more than one child can be placed together, but there are two potential impediments to these children being placed. The major impediment is that of the real risk that these children (or one of them) may suffer from schizophrenia in teenage or early adulthood. That is not a risk lightly to be considered because not only the mother, but I believe the mother's father and undoubtedly the eldest son of the mother by another relationship, all suffer from schizophrenia. Not only is it a real impediment, potentially, it has turned out in actuality to be an impediment because a family—which had been identified at the time that the case came before the judge—has withdrawn on the basis of their concern about the potential medical condition of these children. And, although the local authority has identified, I believe, five other families, all of them willing to consider continuing contact after adoption, so far none of them has proved acceptable. Seven months on from the judge's order, these children are still waiting to find a suitable family. It would not be unrealistic to say that there may come a time when a family is identified which is prepared to take children with potential medical problems of a serious kind which might cast a shadow over their childhood, but is not prepared to deal with a mother who is schizophrenic and a mother who they would feel might be intrusive to their family. At this moment the local authority is not looking for such a family, but as an adoption agency they may have to cast more widely, if they are not able to find a family within the conditions laid down by the judge.

The future of these children and the future of the adoption proceedings is inevitably uncertain. No guarantee can be given to the mother that there will be an adoption with continuing contact, and in the absence of such certainty, why was the mother unreasonable in saying no? In my view, the judge was not justified in the position in which he found himself on a freeing application to say that she was unreasonably withholding her agreement when he also held that there was to be contact after the adoption, and it was only on the basis of contact after the adoption that it was reasonable for her to have her consent dispensed with.

In my view, this judge should have been more robust. Either he should have refused the application and said, 'This is a matter to be dealt with on adoption', or he should have said, as in *Re A* to which I have already referred, that 'adoption is more important than contact', and the reasonable, hypothetical parent would find it to be so. Or he might have said 'contact is so important that if suitable adopters cannot be found to agree to adoption, then these children will have to be fostered long term', but, in any event, as in the first of the three premises that I have suggested, refusing to make the freeing order.

As I see it, he has fallen between two stools in not saying either, 'adoption in any event although contact is highly desirable', or leave it to the adoption application when the mother can fight her corner as to whether or not at that stage the adopters should be accepting contact or there should not be an adoption order. But the mother must, on the basis of the judge's findings, have the right to be heard on the condition to be attached or not attached (as the case may be) to the actual adoption order. . . .

Consequently, the judge should not have dispensed with the agreement of the mother under s. 16(2)(b) and the local authority should be free to make such arrangements as are best for the children, bearing in mind that the guardian ad litem's approach to this matter is that continuing contact with the mother after adoption is desirable but not imperative, as I understand the guardian's stance in this case. Therefore, I would set aside the judge's order dispensing with consent.

13.6.2 FREEING

13.6.2.1 When can freeing be used?

ADOPTION ACT 1976

18. Freeing child for adoption

(1) Where, on an application by an adoption agency, an authorised court is satisfied in the case of each parent or guardian of the child that—

(a) he freely, and with full understanding of what is involved, agrees generally and unconditionally to the making of an adoption order, or

(b) his agreement to the making of an adoption order should be dispensed with on a ground specified in section 16(2),

the court shall make an order declaring the child free for adoption.

(2) No application shall be made under subsection (1) unless—

(a) it is made with the consent of a parent or guardian of a child, or

(b) the adoption agency is applying for dispensation under subsection (1)(b) of the agreement of each parent or guardian of the child, and the child is in the care of the adoption agency.

(2A) For the purposes of subsection (2) a child is in the care of an adoption agency if the adoption agency is a local authority and he is in their care.

(3) No agreement required under subsection (1)(a) shall be dispensed with under subsection (1)(b) unless the child is already placed for adoption or the court is satisfied that it is likely that the child will be placed for adoption.

13.6.2.2 What does freeing achieve?

RE A (A MINOR) (ADOPTION: CONTACT ORDER) [1993] 2 FLR 645 (CA)

BUTLER-SLOSS LJ: This is an appeal by the mother of a little boy, A, now 3, born on 7 March 1990. She appeals from the order of his Honour Judge Batterbury made on 28 September 1992 in the Medway County Court. The parties before the court were the local authority in whose care A is, his mother, his father and his guardian ad litem. The judge held that it was in A's interests that he should be adopted, he dispensed with the agreement of both his mother and his father; he freed A for adoption; he terminated contact between him and his father and made an order for contact with his mother under s. 8 of the Children Act 1989 to continue until the making of the adoption order. The contact was for 1½ hours once a month. The mother appeals against the making of the freeing order. The father does not appeal and has played no part in the appeal.

The judge found that there was no prospect of rehabilitation with the natural family and long-term fostering was a less suitable option for this little boy than adoption.

However, he accepted the evidence of the guardian ad litem and ordered monthly contact until the adoption hearing took place. He took into account the possibility that there might be contact after adoption, but left that decision to be made by another court.

We have been told that the local authority have sought prospective adopters who would agree to open adoption, and have not found any. They are also unable to place the child with prospective adopters while the present contact arrangements are in place. They intend, therefore, to apply to reduce contact very substantially and hope to find adopters who would agree to very limited contact between the child and his natural family.

Miss Walker, on behalf of the mother, raised a number of issues under two headings: that the judge erred in finding that A's welfare required him to be freed for adoption, and he erred in finding that the mother unreasonably withheld her agreement to the proposed adoption at the freeing stage. She accepted, however, that she could not argue against the judge's findings that there was no prospect of rehabilitation and that adoption was in the child's best interests. Her submission centred upon the unsuitability of making a monthly contact order side by side with dispensing with the consent of the parent enjoying that degree of contact. It was premature to make a freeing order at a time when the mother continued to have a part to play in the child's life and when the extent, if any, to which she would have a future role was entirely uncertain. The mother ought to have the opportunity to be heard at the time of adoption on the unresolved issue of future long-term contact. In those circumstances it was neither in the child's interests to make the order nor was the mother unreasonably withholding her agreement to adoption.

The effect of an order freeing a child for adoption is to extinguish parental responsibility of those previously endowed with it and thus to bring to an end the relationship between the child and his natural family (see Adoption Act 1976, s. 12(3)). The child is in a sort of adoptive limbo and parental responsibility is assumed by the adoption agency, in this case, the local authority (s. 18(5)). The parents become former parents, ss. 18(5), 19 and have no right to make an application under s. 8 of the Children Act 1989. The finding by the judge that the welfare of A requires him to be adopted is not challenged and on the evidence is unassailable. Consequently, the consideration as to whether the freeing application prematurely curtailed the mother's right to oppose the adoption of her son has to take into account that, on the first test of welfare, the case for adoption is very strong and is likely to remain so on the subsequent adoption proceedings. Insofar as there may be a conflict between two concepts, the benefits of adoption and the benefits of continuing contact with the mother, I infer from the judge's reasoning that adoption would still be in the child's best interests even if the adopters chosen for him could not tolerate any contact with the mother. Such a placement might be less good for the boy but would not tip the balance against adoption on the welfare test. In my judgment, although he did not spell it out, the judge clearly had in mind the possibility of adoption with no contact.

He went on to consider the mother's refusal to agree to the adoption in the light of his finding on welfare. There was no prospect of rehabilitation. The judge accurately assessed the fragility of the relationship between the mother and B, who has now left. He dismissed the alternative of long-term fostering and held that a reasonable mother would recognise that adoption was the right decision for her son.

The only issue which remains arises from the unusually high degree of contact ordered by the judge and the exclusion of the mother from taking any part in the adoption hearing. Does that exclusion make her refusal to agree at the freeing stage reasonable, although it might be unreasonable at the adoption hearing?

Miss Walker suggested that two decisions of this court supported her argument that continuing contact of a substantial amount by the mother was incompatible with a freeing order. Both cases were decided before the implementation of the Children Act 1989.

Mr Karsten QC for the guardian ad litem has submitted that these two cases are no longer applicable since the coming into force of the Children Act 1989. In my judgment he is right. At the time of the judgment of Balcombe LJ it was not possible to attach a condition of access to a freeing order although it could be attached to an adoption order. The effect of the freeing order was to terminate any earlier access order without the power in the court to continue contact during the limbo period prior to adoption. Since the Children Act, as is shown in the present case, a judge has the opportunity both to free but also to preserve contact between the child and the natural family pending adoption. The wider jurisdiction of the court now exists since a s. 8 application, including a contact application, can be made in any family proceedings, and by s. 8(4)(d) this includes proceedings under the Adoption Act 1976. Although a former parent, this mother retains the right to be heard on contact. She will have the right to respond to the local authority's application to vary the existing contact order and to apply herself to vary it. The contact order cannot survive the adoption order, but a contact order can (in theory at least) now be imposed upon adopters after the making of the adoption order as the alternative to the making of an adoption order with conditions.

. . . the mother can be heard on the only issue which remains: whether she can have continuing contact after an adoption order is made. Applying the test of the reasonable parent, she would recognise that A should be adopted and that she retains the opportunity to take part in any decision on her future relationship with him. In those circumstances I do not see how this court can properly interfere with the decision of the judge, made in the exercise of his discretion, that the mother was unreasonably withholding her agreement under s. 16(2)(b) of the Adoption Act.

Hayes and Williams, *Family Law: Principles, Policy and Practice*, **Butterworths, 1995**

. . . Indeed the contact order appears to have been positively counter-productive in furthering the adoption plans for the child. The general principle enshrined in section 1(2) of the Children Act 1989 is that any delay in determining a question about a child's upbringing is likely to prejudice the welfare of the child. In the case of a young child who needs to form permanent attachments as soon as possible, such delay may be extremely damaging. Yet eight months after the freeing order a suitable adoptive family had not been found for the child, and evidence was given that this was because of the effect of the contact order on the willingness of prospective adopters to put themselves forward. Sections 18(5) and 12(3)(a) of the Adoption Act 1976 state that parental responsibility is given to the adoption agency on a freeing order being made, and that the order operates to extinguish the parental responsibility which any person has for the child immediately before the order was made. It is suggested that for a court to free a child for adoption and at the same time to make a contact order under section 8 should normally be regarded as being inconsistent with these provisions unless it knows that there are adopters who are willing to accept the child on these terms.

. . . it is clear from *Re P (Adoption: Freeing Order)* [1994] 2 FLR 1000 that a court should not free a child for adoption against the wishes of the parent where it takes the view that adoption should only be authorised on the condition that contact with the parent continues to take place.

. . . But, in a case of this kind, unless a court makes an unconditional freeing order, the decision whether contact is more important than adoption is delayed until the application to adopt is made. This in itself may make it difficult to obtain prospective adopters for children who are continuing to have contact with their natural parents. Adopters may not be prepared to put themselves forward unless they are satisfied that questions relating to consent, and to contact, have been resolved. Yet, at the same time, it may be in the interests of the children to have contact with their natural mother until an alternative family is found, and perhaps after it has been found. And a parent may not be unreasonable in withholding her agreement to adoption unless and until such an alternative family is found. Thus the problem can become circular, and identifying at which point the circle should be broken may be an extremely difficult decision to make. Stating that the welfare of the child should be treated as paramount is easy. Determining how to give effect to that principle can sometimes demand a degree of wisdom and foresight with which the best-intentioned of decision-makers are not necessarily endowed.

13.6.2.3   How long does it last?

ADOPTION ACT 1976

20.   Revocation of s. 18 order

(1)   The former parent, at any time more than 12 months after the making of the order under section 18 when—

(a)   no adoption order has been made in respect of the child, and

(b)   the child does not have his home with a person with whom he has been placed for adoption,

may apply to the court which made the order for a further order revoking it on the ground that he wishes to resume parental responsibility.

(2)   While the application is pending the adoption agency having parental responsibility shall not place the child for adoption without the leave of the court.

(3)   The revocation of an order under section 18 ('a section 18 order') operates—

(a)   to extinguish the parental responsibility given to the adoption agency under the section 18 order;

(b)   to give parental responsibility for the child to—

(i)   the child's mother; and

(ii)   where the child's father and mother were married to each other at the time of his birth, the father; and

(c)   to revive—

(i)   any parental responsibility agreement,

(ii)   any order under section 4(1) of the Children Act 1989, and

(iii)   any appointment of a guardian in respect of the child (whether made by a court or otherwise),

extinguished by the making of the section 18 order.

(3A)   Subject to subsection (3)(c), the revocation does not—

(a)   operate to revive—

(i)   any order under the Children Act 1989, or

(ii)   any duty referred to in section 12(3)(b), extinguished by the making of the section 18 order; or

(b)   affect any person's parental responsibility so far as it relates to the period between the making of the section 18 order and the date of revocation of that order.

(4)   Subject to subsection (5), if the application is dismissed on the ground that to allow it would contravene the principle embodied in section 6—

(a)   the former parent who made the application shall not be entitled to make any further application under subsection (1) in respect of the child, and

(b)   the adoption agency is released from the duty of complying further with section 19(3) as respects that parent.

(5)   Subsection (4)(a) shall not apply where the court which dismissed the application gives leave to the former parent to make a further application under subsection (1), but such leave shall not be given unless it appears to the court that because of a change in circumstances or for any other reason it is proper to allow the application to be made.

IN RE G (A MINOR) (ADOPTION: FREEING ORDER) [1997] 2 WLR 747 (CA)

In 1993 M, a child aged three with severe emotional and behavioural difficulties, was taken into care. The local authority later applied for an order under s. 18 of the Adoption Act 1976 freeing him for adoption. The judge granted the freeing order, thereby discharging the existing care order and vesting sole parental responsibility in the local authority as adoption agency. Subsequently the prospective adopters decided not to proceed and M became a boarder at a special school. The local authority still wished to place M for adoption but accepted that such event might never occur. Twelve months after the making of the freeing order the authority was obliged under s. 19(2) of the Act to notify the mother of its failure to place M for adoption, whereupon the mother applied under s. 20 of the Act to revoke the freeing order. The judge dismissed the application. On appeal, the Court of Appeal held that, notwithstanding the mother's consent, a revocation order under s. 20 could not be made conditional upon the local authority obtaining a fresh care order but operated so as to vest sole parental responsibility in the former parent and, since that was not appropriate, the freeing order would continue in force.

On the mother's appeal:

HELD: allowing the appeal, that the Adoption Act 1976 operated alongside and as part of the general legislation regulating powers over children; that where an application had been made under s. 20 of the Act of 1976 for the revocation of a freeing order but it was inappropriate for the former parent to have sole and unfettered responsibility, the court could make the order provided that the welfare of the child could be protected by making the revocation conditional upon such consequential orders as were appropriate under the Children Act 1989 or under the court's inherent jurisdiction or in some other way; and that, accordingly, since there was no justification for keeping the freeing order relating to M in force at a time when no adoption might ever take place, the order would be revoked upon the making of a care order relating to him under s. 31 of the Act of 1989.

Decision of the Court of Appeal [1996] 2 FLR 398 reversed.

13.7 Post-adoption Issues

13.7.1 REVOCATION

RE K (ADOPTION AND WARDSHIP) [1997] 2 FLR 221 (CA)

BUTLER-SLOSS LJ: This is an application by a guardian, supported by the grandfather, to extend time for appeal against the adoption order made by a county court judge in January 1994. This court has given leave to extend the time.

Turning now therefore to the appeal, the appeal is technically by the guardian, but he is doing it on behalf of the grandfather whom we have made an intervener to these proceedings. The child adopted is a little girl called E, born on 21 March 1992 in Bosnia, a citizen of Bosnia and a member of a Muslim family. I will repeat the direction we gave yesterday that there should be no identification of this child or any member of the family with whom she lives, or her natural family so as to lead to the identification of E.

A very shortened version of her very complicated history, considering she is only 4 years old, is as follows. She is a victim of the conflict in Bosnia. In the summer of 1992 she was found with another baby, her cousin, under the bodies of a number of adults. It was first said that she was found in a field and then the facts emerged that it was in fact a garage in a village near where she comes from. From the facts which have subsequently been ascertained, several members of her family, including her mother and her small brother, were murdered in this village near her home. Her father is missing and so far nobody knows anything about him. Her grandfather and other members of the family were taken by Serb soldiers and placed in camps from where eventually, after much suffering, they were released. Some of the family are now in Switzerland, including the grandfather, others in Slovenia, and others remain in Bosnia. The grandfather in Switzerland, the head of the family, is trying to bring together the surviving members of his family after this dreadful atrocity.

E and her cousin M were rescued both wounded, together with another cousin who died. They went to hospital and E went on to the orphanage in Banja Luca. Her story was taken up by a journalist and came to the attention of the adopters ('the respondents'). With the help of a charitable organisation, they arranged for the child to come to England, primarily for medical treatment and to be cared for by them. They obtained Home Office permission for the child to remain in England. They are a family who have already adopted a Romanian child in addition to their own natural family, and they wished to make a personal contribution to helping child victims of the Bosnian conflict. The injuries to E turned out to be far less serious than feared, although she has still some three pellets lodged in her head and she requires careful medical supervision for the future. From hospital, E returned to live with the respondents where she has become one of the family, speaks only English and has been baptised a Christian.

The information available to the respondents about E's circumstances was sketchy and inaccurate. Since she was found under the bodies of a man and a woman, it was assumed that they were her mother and father. It is now known that it was indeed her mother who was killed and her father, as I have already said, has never been traced. Her cousin M was believed to be her sister. It was also believed that she has no other family. What was clear, however, was that the Bosnian government had not washed their hands of her, but had given express permission for her to come to England and had provided for her a guardian, who was not a relative, but head of the Bosnian Red Cross at that time.

Further there was a letter, which appears to have been translated on 13 January 1993, which says as follows:

> The office of Republic of Bosnia and Herzegovina in the Republic of Croatia, Zagreb is informing you that on the base of the law during the war all the adoptions (complete and incomplete) are to be stopped.
>
> The presidency of the Red Cross of Bosnia and Herzegovina in Croatia, Zagreb represented by [the guardian] will take over the care of the children E [and the other child] till the end of the war.
>
> This document puts all the procedure of adoption out of law.

It is then signed by somebody and I do not know who that may be. That letter makes it entirely clear to me at least the opposition of the Bosnian government to the adopting of any of its children who might leave the Republic of Bosnia. There was a letter written by the respondents before this child came into their care to a person who was instrumental in helping this little girl to come to England, and the letter said (dated 14 October 1992):

> This letter is to confirm that we will foster E during her stay in England for medical treatment. This will include pastoral care while she is in hospital and thereafter our home is hers during her recuperation.
>
> While we know E has been orphaned, we understand some members of her family have been traced. Therefore we fully recognise that once the current hostilities are over, it may well be appropriate for E to return to her remaining family in former Yugoslavia.

The letter sets out the way in which they will look after this little girl while she was in England.

The respondents decided to adopt E. They had made informal and unsuccessful attempts to gain more information about her background. They were under the erroneous impression that she had no surviving immediate family, although they knew of the wider family. They made an informal and unsuccessful attempt to be in touch with the Bosnian guardian. Their adoption application was made to the county court on 19 August 1993 by a local solicitor, without much experience, I suspect, of possible contested adoptions. They changed solicitors at a later stage to solicitors far more conversant with family matters but too late in fact to put the matter right. The adoption application did not specify that there was a guardian who was relevant for the purposes of giving or withholding agreement to the proposed adoption under s. 16 of the Adoption Act 1976. The Sch 2 report of the social worker sets out the situation at the English end and what she was told by the respondents about the Bosnian end, but did not investigate further. At a directions hearing on 7 December 1993 the respondents informed the court of the existence of the guardian and the judge who had charge of the adoption gave the directions. The directions that he made were that the applicants do file a further affidavit dealing with service of a letter to various people; exhibiting a copy of the decision appointing the guardian; a letter was to be sent to the guardian seeking his agreement to the adoption and, if a reply was received, the matter be restored for further directions; if no reply was received to the letter referred to in para. 2 within 28 days, the case would be listed for hearing on the first open date thereafter, reserved to the same judge.

The respondents filed an affidavit giving all the information which they had at the time and their efforts personally to inform the guardian. The judge directed it was not necessary in this case for a guardian ad litem to be appointed for the child under the provisions of the Adoption Rules.

In the adoption file there was provided to the court the written permission of the Bosnian government for E to leave Bosnia and the prohibition on the adoption of Bosnian children. In January 1994 the judge dispensed with the consent of the guardian without any further information about the guardian, and made the adoption order without requiring any further formalities. In an uncontested adoption hearing, it is not surprising there was no judgment, but we have two pieces of paper, one of them a note provided by the judge as to his recollection, and secondly of findings from the evidence. The findings said that the child had been portrayed in a film and was the same child known as E in the care of the respondents, but on the best information available, it was believed that her parents were dead. Soldiers were believed to have found the child and taken her to hospital. The person who did so was not her father and he was not a parent or guardian. In fact that information was erroneous from start to finish. It appears that there had been a change of guardian but the guardian who was to give his consent was the one who was purportedly served; under subpara. (5) all reasonable steps had been taken to obtain the consent of the guardian and the said guardian had been unable to give his consent. It was not in the interests of E for an adoption order to be delayed any further. E was a child of special needs requiring medical supervision for the possible need for urgent medical treatment at any time during her minority, and possibly requiring special educational provisions or facilities.

The grandfather, who is the true motivating force for this appeal, seeks the return of his grandchild to the family and as the first step he seeks the setting aside of the adoption order. . . .

There is undoubtedly a strong merits argument in respect of the welfare of the child brought up for the first years of her life with this devoted family, who have spent much time, a great deal of money and effort to transform her from a wounded victim of conflict to a happy and obviously delightful child who is a valued member of a large and loving family. The issue to be faced, and not to be faced by this court, is where does her long-term welfare lie?—with the stability and continuity of this loving substitute family, or within the natural family against whom there is no criticism but whose family solidarity has been cruelly shattered by war and atrocity but where there remain many members anxious to have her returned to them?

We are grateful to the Official Solicitor for agreeing to act as amicus and to Mr Stern on his behalf for his admirably succinct but comprehensive skeleton argument which is a devastating indictment of the inept handling by the county court of the entire adoption process. I shall deal first with what went wrong and then how the court should approach the consequences. . . .

These were serious omissions and the court accepted inadequate evidence and failures of procedure and the judge appears to have considered that the welfare of the child and her special needs obviated the necessity to comply with the requirements of the Adoption Rules. In taking that course he was plainly wrong.

What should this court do? Mr Jackson has argued and has argued with cogency that we should not at this late stage interfere with the status and settled life of this little girl and such an interference would not be consistent with her welfare. He has suggested that the prospects of success by the grandfather to oppose an adoption order if there is a rehearing are not strong.

However, the procedural irregularities go far beyond the cosmetic. The guardian was appointed by the Bosnian government to protect the interests of a Bosnian child in England and the English system of justice has failed to give him the notice he was entitled to about the intentions of the respondents to make the child a member of their family and to cut the link with her natural family and with the country of her birth. Proper service upon the guardian would have elicited the whereabouts of members of E's family and would have enabled the court—clearly it should have been the High Court—to consider the undoubted opposition of the natural family to the adoption proposed. Further, the edict of the Bosnian government prohibiting adoption of Bosnian nationals was actually before the court in the adoption file and was not taken into account. The welfare of the child herself dictated that proper steps should be taken to balance the natural family with the prospective adoptive family, at the very least.

We were asked to look at three decisions of this court. In *Re F (R) (An Infant)* [1970] 1 QB 385, this court indicated the inherent jurisdiction of the court to set aside an adoption order in a somewhat similar case and did so. In *Re F (Infants) (Adoption Order: Validity)* [1977] Fam 165, there was no party aggrieved by the adoption order and the adoption order was not set aside, and the observations made by Ormrod LJ in rather different circumstances do not seem to me to apply to this case. In *Re B (Adoption: Jurisdiction to Set Aside)* [1995] Fam 239, Swinton Thomas LJ in his judgment at 245 set out those earlier cases and the circumstances in which an adoption order might be set aside. The law seems to me to be clear that there are cases where a fundamental breach of natural justice will require a court to set an adoption order aside.

I am satisfied that a fundamental injustice occurred to the guardian and, through him, to the natural family, and indeed to E herself since the wider considerations of her welfare were not considered. There was no proper hearing of the adoption application in January 1994, and in my judgment the order cannot stand. The delay, although unfortunate, cannot be laid at the door of those seeking to set the adoption order aside and, balancing the importance of the status of an adoption order against the plethora of procedural irregularities going to the root of the adoption process, the balance tips strongly in favour of setting the order aside. The procedure in this case displays all the characteristics of a fundamental breach of natural justice which, on the facts of this case, cannot be overlooked.

RE B (ADOPTION: JURISDICTION TO SET ASIDE) [1995] 2 FLR 1 (CA)

SWINTON THOMAS LJ: The appellant was born on 8 March 1959, and is now aged 36. His natural mother is now married. She is English and at the material time she was a Roman Catholic. The father was and is an Arab from Kuwait and by religion Muslim. The mother and the father were not married, and in 1959 he knew nothing of the adoption or indeed of the pregnancy. Nothing turns on his ignorance. The prospective adoptors were both Jewish, the woman having been born on 4 January 1911 and the man on 25 October 1913. They married on 7 November 1948.

After the appellant's birth on 8 March 1959, his mother wished to place him for adoption. In 1959 the attitude of society generally towards unmarried mothers and illegitimacy was somewhat different from the general attitude today. The mother was, for natural reasons, anxious that the arrangements for the adoption should take place in a part of the country where she was not known and, insofar as it was possible, anonymously. . . .

In an affidavit sworn on 17 June 1993, the appellant's mother said that she told the nursing home that the child's father came from the Persian Gulf area, and that he may have come from a Gulf State. She says that she did not give them the name of the father, and never indicated that the father was Jewish. She says that if she had known that the appellant was to be placed with a Jewish family she would have had serious reservations. She says that she would also have had reservations if she had known that he was to be placed with working-class parents. She had been led to believe that he was going to middle-class parents and she wanted him placed with an educated family. She says that she would also have had reservations about the placement had she known of the age of the adopters. She thought they were in their 30s. She feels that she was misled. It is, perhaps, relevant to note that in that affidavit the mother states that she would have had a number or reservations in relation to this particular placement. She says that she did not say that the father was of Syrian/Jewish stock. . . .

On 20 July 1959, his Honour Judge Fraser-Hanson made the adoption order in favour of the adoptive parents, the subject matter of the present application. . . .

Having been received into the Jewish faith on 31 March 1970, the appellant continued to be brought up in that faith. In 1983 he graduated with a degree in Semitic languages and literature. In 1978 he began to make some inquiries about his background. In 1986 he decided to emigrate to Israel, and he at once ran into difficulty. People in Israel assumed that he was an Arab. He was suspected of being a spy. He was asked to leave and return to this country. He was then told that he was persona non grata in Israel. He continued his researches into his background. On 13 April 1988 the adoptive father died, and the adoptive mother died on 28 February 1991. On the death of his adoptive mother he was bequeathed a legacy, of £10,000, In about 1989 the appellent traced his natural mother. He then made contact with his father, who, as I have said, is a Kuwaiti national living in Kuwait. The present position undoubtedly causes the appellant very considerable hardship, as he says in his affirmations. He wants to work in the Middle East and is qualified to do so. It is extremely difficult, if not impossible, for him in his present position to obtain work or even visit Israel or any Arab country. He feels this acutely and feels that he does not belong now to either the Jewish or the Arab community. It is in those circumstances that he applied to set aside the adoption order of 27 July 1959.

In my judgment such an application faces insuperable hurdles. An adoption order has a quite different standing to almost every other order made by a court. It provides the status of the adopted child and of the adoptive parents. The effect of an adoption order is to extinguish any parental responsibility of the natural parents. Once an adoption order has been made, the adoptive parents stand to one another and the child in precisely the same relationship as if they were his legitimate parents, and the child stands in the same relationship to them as to legitimate parents. Once an adoption order has been made the adopted child ceases to be the child of his previous parent and becomes the child for all purposes of the adopters is though he were their legitimate child.

There are certain specific statutory provisions for the revocation of an **adoption** order. Section 52 of the Adoption Act 1976 provides for the revocation of an adoption on legitimation. Section 53 provides for the annulment of overseas adoptions. Those exceptions provide for specific cases. Unlike certain other jurisdictions, there are no other statutory provisions for revoking a validly made adoption order. Parliament could have so provided if it had wished to do so. Accordingly Mr Levy is compelled to submit that the court has an inherent power to set aside an adoption order made in circumstances such as these where, as he puts it, the order was made under a fundamental mistake of fact.

There are cases where an adoption order has been set aside by reason of what is known as a procedural irregularity. See *Re F (R) (An Infant)* [1970] 1 QB 385, *Re RA (Minors)* (1974) Fam Law 182 and *Re F (Infants) (Adoption Order: Validity)* [1977] Fam 165. Those cases concern a failure to effect proper service of the adoption proceedings on a natural parent or ignorance of the parent of the existence of the adoption proceedings. In each case the application to set aside the order was made reasonably expeditiously. It is fundamental to the making of an adoption order that the natural parent should be informed of the application so that she can give or withhold her consent. If she has no knowledge at all of the application then, obviously, a fundamental injustice is perpetrated. I would prefer myself to regard those cases not as cases where the order has been set aside by reason of a procedural irregularity, although that has certainly occurred, but as cases where natural justice has been denied because the natural parent, who may wish to challenge the adoption, has never been told that it is going to happen. Whether in adoption order call be set aside by reason of fraud which is unrelated to a natural parent's ignorance of the proceedings was not a subject which was relevant to the present appeal. . . .

In giving his judgment in this case ([1995] 1 FLR 1), the President said at p. 7:

In my judgment the adoption was regularly made in accordance with the procedure of the court. It was then acted upon in the sense that the child was accepted into the adoptive family and brought up throughout his minority. I do not believe that the court in these circumstances has any power to set aside or to purport to nullify the order which was made on 20 July 1959.

There is no case which has been brought to our attention in which it has been held that the court has an inherent power to set aside an adoption order by reason of a misapprehension or mistake. To allow considerations such as those put forward in this case to invalidate an otherwise properly made adoption order would, in my view, undermine the whole basis on which adoption orders are made, namely that they are final and for life as regards the adopters, the natural parents, and the child. In my judgment Mr Holman QC, who appeared as amicus curiae, is right when he submits that it would gravely damage the lifelong commitment of adopters to their adoptive children if there is a possibility of the child, or indeed the parents, subsequently challenging the order. I am satisfied that there is no inherent power in the courts in circumstances such as arise in this case to set aside an adoption order. Nobody could have other than the greatest sympathy with the applicant but, in my judgment, the circumstances of this case do not provide any ground for setting aside an adoption order which was regularly made. Accordingly I would dismiss this appeal.

13.8   End of Chapter Assessment Question

Why are adoption applications from step-parents and relatives seen with some disquiet?
What problems can arise from this sort of application, and what alternatives exist?

13.9   End of Chapter Assessment Outline Answer

In this question you are looking at the category of individuals who adopt in approximately half the adoptions made in England and Wales. However, as you will recall from
the extracts from the report *Adoption — a service for children*, the number of adoptions
made in favour of step-parents is of concern.

You should identify that placements with relatives are one of the three ways in which
a placement is legal under the Adoption Act 1976 (s. 11), the other two being by order
of the High Court, or where the placement is made by an adoption agency. Given that
a placement with relatives is legal, you should then identify why these types of
placement are questionable. The difficulties that arise depend on whether it is a
step-parent applying to adopt jointly with a natural parent, or a relative of the child, say
for example a grandparent or aunt/uncle.

Taking the situation of a joint adoption application by a step-parent and natural parent
first, the perceived difficulties arise by virtue of the consequences of the adoption order.
The effect of the order will be to terminate all the legal links between the birth parents
and to recreate them with the adoptive parents. In a step-parent adoption this will mean
that one birth parent (normally the father) will lose all rights and responsibilities with
respect to the child. The question has to be whether it is right for this to happen, whether
the making of the order is in the interests of the child — albeit that s. 6 of the Adoption
Act 1976 does not require the court to consider the child's welfare as paramount but only
as the first consideration amongst others.

One of the major criticisms of step-parent adoptions is that it does sever the legal links
between the child and the one birth parent, and this is seen as detrimental to both child
and parent. This is more so if the child has had some form of relationship with that
parent. The need to know about one's origins is currently perceived as very important
(and hence the ability to trace birth parents being made available to adopted children),
and is something that may be lost on adoption.

The reasons behind the step-parent seeking to adopt can also be criticised. In some
cases the adoption is predicated by a wish to change the surname of the child (officially)
since this is not easy to achieve under the Children Act 1989. The adoption may be
sought (and agreed to by the birth parent) in order to avoid the intervention of the Child
Support Agency or simply to exclude the birth parent from the new family. However,
this should not suggest that all step-parent applications are based on inappropriate
reasons; many are sought to cement the new family unit, and to highlight the step
parent's commitment to the family.

Whilst the first three reasons mentioned, are in themselves, seen to be problematic, the
more 'beneficial reasons' are still not viewed as being totally acceptable. Many second
marriages break down with the result that the children will lose yet another parent. This
loss arises regardless of the adoption order, but is often deemed more serious since there
may have been no contact with the birth parent since adoption. You may not agree that
this is a valid concern sufficient to justify restrictions on step-parent adoptions. Also, it
is stated that the security of the family unit can be created and maintained by use of
other orders.

Those other orders will be the s. 8 residence order, and possibly a s. 8 contact order
to the non-caring birth parent. You should discuss the effect of these orders and also
highlight the differences between them and the adoption order, to illustrate why they
may not be utilised fully. Such differences include the fact that parental responsibility is
not exclusive to the adoptive parents, that the order will only last until the child is 16,
whilst adoption is for life etc.

Turning to relative adoptions, the major criticism that is levelled at these, is the potential distortion of the family structure post adoption. When there was a greater stigma on illegitimacy, situations would arise where grandparents would adopt an illegitimate grandchild. This would then result with the child's mother becoming the child's sister — a situation that is not viewed favourably. In addition, if the relatives adopting the child are somewhat older, there is the risk that the child will be left without a full-time carer in the future (this being one of the reasons why adoption agencies place a maximum age limit on prospective adopters). Other criticisms that can be made concern contact with the birth parents(s). If the birth parent was a poor carer, or even an abuser, the adoption by a relative may raise further concerns over contact. Will a relative be sufficiently strict to ensure that no harm will arise from continued contact? An advantage of relative adoptions over stranger adoptions is that the child will remain within the wider birth family, and hence have (potentially) greater knowledge of their origins.

The alternatives to adoption where a relative is involved again are to be found in s. 8 of the 1989 Act. You would not be expected to go through another explanation of the orders if you have already done so with regard to step parents. You should however point out that the problems with s. 8 may be the same.

You could usefully conclude this answer by mentioning the review of adoption and the White Paper produced in 1996, and the possible changes to step-parent adoptions.

CHAPTER FOURTEEN

THE INHERENT JURISDICTION

14.1 What is the Inherent Jurisdiction?

Venn diagram

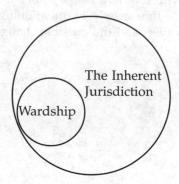

14.2 Injunctive or Declarative Orders

RE R (A MINOR) (BLOOD TRANSFUSION) [1993] 2 FLR 757 (FamD)

BOOTH J: This is a sad case and one which, tragically, is not uncommon. The application, which is made by the local authority, is for an order which will enable a child to receive blood transfusions. Her parents, who are baptised members of the faith of Jehovah's Witnesses, are not able to compromise their beliefs to give their consent to this treatment. The application raises a point of procedural importance and for this reason I am giving judgment in open court; but it is also of importance that the child and her family are not identified.

The little girl with whom I am concerned is 10 months old, the only child of her parents, Mr and Mrs R. She suffers from B-cell lymphoblastic leukaemia and is presently in hospital receiving treatment. She has already been given blood products as a life-saving measure at the time of her admission but she is likely to need more in the future. The evidence is that blood products could be necessary at any time over the next 2 years, which is the length of time during which she will need treatment. The medical consultants responsible for her believe that this is the only treatment likely to maximise the little girl's chances of being successfully treated.

The parents are extremely anxious that their daughter should receive the best possible medical care. Their primary objection to the proposed medical procedure is one of scriptural conscience. But the parents are also aware of the known hazards of blood transfusions and are anxious on this account. They further make the telling point that advances in medical science are so rapid that alternative blood management becomes possible in many procedures and as parents they want to be able to argue for their use whenever possible. If the court authorises the use of blood the parents are concerned to ensure that it is not a blanket authority to the doctors to do whatever they wish without consultation with them.

To obtain the court's authorisation for the use of blood products the local authority applied for a specific issue order under s. 8 of the Children Act 1989. By definition a specific issue order means an order giving directions for the purpose of determining a specific question which has arisen, or which may arise, in connection with any aspect of parental responsibility for a child. Such an order is made under the private law provisions of the 1989 Act and a local authority requires leave to make the application. This the authority obtained from District Judge Segal on 19 May 1993 and thus they made the application to me the next day. But as a preliminary point of procedure, Mr Daniel, for the parents, submitted that in a case of such gravity as this where the court was asked to override the parents' wishes based upon their profound beliefs, the local authority should have instead applied to invoke the inherent jurisdiction of the High Court, seeking leave to do so under s. 100 of the Act. In support of this submission Mr Daniel relied principally upon dicta of Johnson J in *Re O (A Minor) (Medical Treatment)* [1993] 2 FLR 149.

Section 100(3) of the Act provides that no application for any exercise of the court's inherent jurisdiction with respect to children be made by a local authority unless the authority has obtained leave of the court. But such leave may only be granted if the court is satisfied that the result which the authority wishes to achieve could not be achieved through the making of any other order which the local authority is entitled to apply for and that there is reasonable cause to believe that if the court's inherent jurisdiction is not exercised with respect to the child he is likely to suffer significant harm. Without the use of blood products, the evidence is that the child is likely to suffer harm, but Mrs Dangor, for the authority, submits that since a specific issue order under s. 8 can provide the remedy which the authority seeks and is an order for which it is entitled to apply, the exercise of the court's inherent jurisdiction is not appropriate.

It is, therefore, important to consider the judgment of Johnson J in the case of *Re O* (above). The situation with which he was dealing was similar in many respects to the present one. He had before him an application for an order authorising the use of blood products in the treatment of a child for which the parents, again Jehovah's Witnesses, could not give consent. But in that case the local authority concerned had adopted procedures very different from those taken by the authority in the present case. They applied to the local family proceedings court for an emergency protection order which they obtained. That was done without notice to the parents. That order vested parental responsibility for the child in the local authority and thus they were able to authorise the blood transfusions to which the parents were refusing their consent. Thereafter an interim care order was made by the justices before the case was transferred upward to the High Court. Johnson J was then asked to determine not only whether the court should, on the facts, override the sincerely held beliefs of the parents, but also to determine the legal framework within which that question was best decided. The procedure followed in that case was markedly different from that adopted by this authority who do not seek parental responsibility for the little girl but only an order in relation to the use of blood products. It is also noteworthy that this authority applied directly to the High Court as they were able to do under the private law provisions of the Act.

It was in the context of the public law procedures that Johnson J considered the legal framework most suited for these difficult and anxious cases.

. . . In his judgment he went on to say this (at p. 155A):

> They should ordinarily be made under the inherent jurisdiction of the court, but if made under the provisions of the Children Act should be transferred to the Family Division as a matter of urgency.

It is that dictum which provides the foundation for the submission made by Mr Daniel that the order which I make should be made in the exercise of the court's inherent jurisdiction and not by way of any order made under the Children Act.

I am in complete agreement with the essential premise of the conclusions reached by Johnson J. Such issues are of the utmost gravity and are of particular anxiety since the decision of the court may run counter to the most profound and sincerely held beliefs of the parents. For these reasons the most strenuous efforts should always be made to achieve an inter partes hearing. Such issues should also be determined, wherever possible, by a High Court judge and this is of particular importance in those exceptional circumstances where an application must be made ex parte so that the parents cannot be heard. But in my judgment these prerequisites can be as well met by an application for a specific issue order under s. 8 as by an application for the exercise of the court's inherent jurisdiction. A s. 8 application can, and in circumstances such as these undoubtedly should, be made to the High Court. When leave to make it is sought by a local authority, or other appropriate body or person, the district judge, as in this case, can give all necessary directions for a speedy hearing. It will then be heard by a High Court judge. Although there is yet no reported decision as to whether or not a specific issue order can be made ex parte, I should be very surprised if the words of the statute had to be interpreted so narrowly as to deny the court power to give such relief where it was otherwise justified and the circumstances compelled an ex parte hearing. But if such an issue were to come before a judge of the Family Division who was constrained to find the court's jurisdiction to be so limited, the power to invoke the exercise of the inherent jurisdiction of the court would be immediately available and appropriate.

In the present case I am in no doubt that the application is well-founded under s. 8 of the Act. The result which the local authority wishes to achieve, namely, the court's authorisation for the use of blood products, can clearly be achieved by the means of such an order. There is no need for the court otherwise to intervene to safeguard the little girl, so that I am satisfied that it is unnecessary and inappropriate for the court to exercise its inherent jurisdiction.

RE R (A MINOR) (WARDSHIP: MEDICAL TREATMENT) [1991] 4 All ER 177 (CA)

LORD DONALDSON OF LYMINGTON MR: This appeal from an order of Waite J on 9 July 1991 involves a consideration of the power of the court to override a refusal by its ward, a 15-year-old girl, to undergo medical treatment involving the taking of medication. So far as is known such a question has arisen on only one previous occasion, namely in *Re E (a minor)* (21 September 1990, unreported), decided by, Ward J, a 15-year-old boy who had religious objections, supported by his parents, to being given a life-saving blood transfusion. Possibly in that case, and certainly in this, the judge accepted that the effect of *Gillick* v *West Norfolk and Wisbech Area Health Authority* [1985] 3 All ER 402 was that, if a child had achieved a sufficient understanding and intelligence to enable him or her to understand fully what was proposed and to be capable of making up his own mind on the matter, the parental right (and the court's right) to give or refuse consent yielded to the child's right to make his own decisions (see [1985] 3 All ER 402 at 422, per Lord Scarman) and that this applied as much to a situation in which the child was refusing consent (this case and *Re E*) as to the case in which the child was consenting (the assumed position in *Gillick's* case). However, in *Re E*, as in this case, the judge held that the child had not achieved the required degree of understanding.

There was some urgency and at the conclusion of the hearing we announced that the appeal would be dismissed. We could at the same time have given reasons for agreeing with the judge's decision on the facts as to the child's degree of understanding, which would have been determinative of this appeal on any view of the law. However, the Official Solicitor had asked us to give guidance on the extent of the court's powers in such situations and we therefore took time to put our reasons into writing. In dismissing the appeal we made an order that in reporting these proceedings there be no publication of the identity or whereabouts of the child, her parents, her carers or any institution in which the child was resident or being treated or educated. . . .

In the instant appeal Mr James Munby QC, appearing for the Official Solicitor, submits that (a) if the child has the right to give consent to medical treatment, the parents' right to give or refuse consent is terminated and (b) the court in the exercise of its wardship jurisdiction is only entitled to step into the shoes of the parents and thus itself has no right to give or refuse consent.

The wardship jurisdiction

In considering the wardship jurisdiction of the court, no assistance is to be derived from *Gillick's* case, where this simply was not in issue. Nor, I think, is any assistance to be derived from considering whether it is theoretically limitless if the exercise of such a jurisdiction in a particular way and in particular circumstances would be contrary to established practice. It is, however, clear that the practical jurisdiction of the court is wider than that of parents. The court can, for example, forbid the publication of information about the ward or the ward's family circumstances. It is also clear that this jurisdiction is not derivative from the parents' rights and responsibilities, but derives from, or is, the delegated performance of the duties of the Crown to protect its subjects and particularly children who are the generations of the future (see *Re C (a minor) (wardship: medical treatment) (No. 2)* [1989] 2 All ER 791 at 793).

Whilst it is no doubt true to say, as Lord Upjohn did say in *J v C* [1969] 1 All ER 788 at 831, that the function of the court is to 'act as the judicial reasonable parent', all that, in context, he was saying was that the court should exercise its jurisdiction in the interests of the children 'reflecting and adopting the changing views, as the years go by, of reasonable men and women, the parents of children, on the proper treatment and methods of bringing up children'. This is very far from saying that the wardship jurisdiction is derived from, or in any way limited by, that of the parents. In many cases of wardship the parents or other guardians will be left to make decisions for the child, subject only to standing instructions to refer reserved matters to the court, eg the taking of a serious step in the upbringing or medical treatment of a child, and to the court's right and, in appropriate cases, duty to override the decision of the parents or other guardians. If it can override such consents, as it undoubtedly can, I see no reason whatsoever why it should not be able, and in an appropriate case willing, to override decisions by 'Gillick competent' children who are its wards or in respect of whom applications are made for, for example, s. 8 orders under the Children Act 1989.

RE W (WARDSHIP: DISCHARGE: PUBLICITY) [1995] 2 FLR 466 (CA)

BALCOMBE LJ: . . . On 5 December 1991 the mother left her house, together with the four boys, and went to live in a women's refuge. She alleged that the reason for this move was that the father had assaulted her. . . .

There followed cross ex parte applications by the parents: the mother in the county court for a non-molestation injunction, to be followed by divorce proceedings; the father in the High Court in wardship, for an injunction to restrain the mother from taking the children out of the jurisdiction and to return them to their former home. It is not now necessary to describe in detail the exact progress of the subsequent court proceedings. For present purposes it is sufficient to say that the father's wardship action became the forum for the determination of the issues concerning the boys and that by early January 1992 the mother (still living in the women's refuge) had interim care and control of the boys with supervised visiting access to the father. The Official Solicitor was then appointed guardian ad litem of the boys. By April 1992 all four boys who had previously been reluctant to make a choice between their parents, were expressing a clear preference to live with the father, and their behaviour with their mother was becoming out of her control. During the summer of 1992 they all, either together or in different combinations, ran away from the mother to the father, on a number of occasions, and were all (but in particular the elder two) alleging that the mother had assaulted them. By the end of August 1992 it had become plain that the mother could not manage the boys, and on 27 August 1992 the district judge made an order by consent to the effect that the boys should stay with the father but with access to the mother. However, even access to the mother did not work, as by then the boys were saying that they did not wish to see her.

This was the position when the matter came before Connell J in November 1992. . . .

The order that the judge made was to continue the wardship, to give care and control of the boys to the father, to make detailed provision for access by the mother and to direct a review in June 1993 unless otherwise agreed. Connell J reserved the matter to himself if available. He also made a family assistance order under s. 16(4) of the Children Act 1989.

Unfortunately matters proceeded far from smoothly. In January 1993 the mother discovered that the father was using his home, which was also the home of the boys, as a 'refuge for men'. She applied for an injunction and on 29 January 1993, before Booth J, the father gave an undertaking to the court not to use his house as a refuge for men, or for a similar purpose, at any time when the property was occupied by the boys as their home.

In April 1993 the father, without notice to anyone, changed the boys' school. On 4 May 1993 he was ordered by Connell J to return the boys to their original school; that did not happen. However, on 12 May 1993 there was a consent order that the boys should remain at their new school. They are still there.

Also on 12 May 1993 all four boys made applications to terminate the appointment of the Official Solicitor as their guardian ad litem and to be represented by a solicitor of their choice. Among the reasons given for the applications were that they were 'forced to see mother to be persecuted' and 'forced to be wards of court'. The applications were dismissed on 8 June 1993.

As will be apparent from the reasons stated in the applications, access with the mother has not worked as the judge had hoped. Contact ceased in June 1993 and the mother has not seen her sons since then.

In September 1993 the father applied to have the wardship discharged. This application came before Connell J, who, on 24 September 1993, dismissed it, but directed that the matter be reviewed in July 1994.

On 27 April 1994 an article appeared in the *Independent* newspaper entitled 'Our fight to stay with Dad'. Although the names used in the article were changed, the four boys were shown in silhouette in a photograph, and it seems at least possible that anyone who knew the family could identify them. More significantly, the father does not deny that he allowed the boys to speak to the newspaper reporter, expressing their strong dislike of their mother and their dissatisfaction with their representation by the Official Solicitor. The Official Solicitor then applied to the court for directions and on 19 May 1994 Connell J ordered that:

(1)   the plaintiff [the father] be restrained from giving information or interviews concerning the issues in these wardship proceedings to the media;

(2)   that plaintiff [the father] be restrained from causing or permitting such information or interviews to be given to the media by the children [S, P, B and M] or any other third party concerning the issues in the wardship proceedings.

This order shall remain in force until further order.

The order was endorsed with a penal notice.

In July 1994 the father again applied to have the wardship discharged. Connell J was not available, and the application came before Miss M.C. Hogg QC sitting as a deputy High Court judge, who on 8 July 1994 dismissed it.

The appeals before us are both by the father. In the first he appeals against the order of 8 July 1994. In the second, with leave granted by this court, he appeals against the order of 19 May 1994. . . .

It was common ground before us that this wardship should not be continued unless it offered advantages to the boys which could not be secured by use of the orders available under the Children Act 1989. A similar approach appears to have been taken before the deputy judge, although there is no reference in her judgment to the case of *Re T* [1994] Fam 49. After setting out the history of the matter, and referring to the judgment of Connell J of 12 November 1992 and to the number of unusual applications since November 1992, she concluded:

This is a father who, in my opinion, having read of the activities in the papers, believes he has the sole right to care for these children. In his view he has the right to care for the children and sometimes, in my opinion, his view has not been the right way to deal with it. It cannot be right, as was decided and which he accepted, with regard to the use of the home as a refuge. Nor can it be right for the publicity, but I will say no more, because the matter is under appeal.

It is disquieting and I think this court needs to retain oversight of these four boys. They do not see their mother and there have been these unusual applications. I have the distinct feeling that the father might continue imposing his will in a way that may not be to the advantage and benefit of these children. Moreover, I share the Official Solicitor's view that there has been insufficient change in the last 5 months to justify any alteration of what Connell J said in September 1993 and this was the judge, of course, who knew this case intimately.

I therefore dismiss the application.

Miss Hoyal, for the father, repeated before us the submissions that had been made on his behalf below, to the effect that the prolongation of litigation when there are no live issues between the parties, and the father and the children are vehemently opposed to it, is harmful to the paramount welfare of the children. Apart altogether from the fact that the prolongation of the litigation appears to be largely due to the actions of the father, rather than those of the mother or the Official Solicitor, in my judgment there are the following reasons why the welfare of these boys will be protected by the continuation of the wardship, where comparable protection could not be achieved by orders under the Children Act:

(1) The status of wardship requires that the father cannot make any major changes in the boys' lives without the leave of the court. His previous behaviour, outlined above, indicates that he is often unable to consider objectively what is in their best interest. It is not possible to frame a prohibited steps order under s. 8 of the Children Act which could anticipate every way in which he might act—as he has in the past—in an unpredictable or publicity-seeking way which could be harmful to the boys. Thus wardship can afford the boys some degree of protection from the father's actions.

(2) Each boy will remain a ward of court until he attains his majority, unless the wardship is previously discharged. The continuing nature of the wardship proceedings means that the Official Solicitor remains in office as guardian ad litem of the boys unless and until he is removed from that office. This is in contradistinction to the position under the Children Act where there are no continuing proceedings, and every application is separate and discrete. The advantage of the continuing nature of wardship is not only that the Official Solicitor remains in office, and is available to give assistance to the boys and their parents, whenever required; it is also that the case can be reserved to one judge who has a knowledge of its history and all its ramifications.

(3) The presence of the Official Solicitor as guardian ad litem of the boys, and his ability to take action when the boys' interests so require—as in the case of the article in the *Independent*—means that the mother need not herself make the necessary application. If the mother had to make these applications, the dislike of her by the boys, already sufficiently intense, would only be increased. The Official Solicitor has a useful role to play as a buffer between the mother and the father.

(4) It is by no means clear that a prohibited steps order under s. 8 of the Children Act would be effective to restrain the father from seeking publicity of the kind that appeared in the article in the *Independent*. The prohibition under such an order relates only to a 'step which could be taken by a parent in meeting his parental responsibility for a child'. 'Parental responsibility' is defined by s. 3(1) as '. . . all the rights, powers, responsibilities and authority which by law a parent of a child has in relation to the child and his property'. It is at least arguable that a prohibited steps order may not be used to prevent some non-parental activity such as publishing information about the child, because this is not a step in meeting parental responsibility: see Hershman and McFarlane *Children Law and Practice* (Family Law, loose-leaf), vol. 1, para. C[322].

These reasons do not differ in substance from those given by the deputy judge in refusing to discharge the wardship. In my judgment there is no basis on which this court could properly interfere with her decision; in any event I am satisfied that she was right. I would dismiss the appeal against her order of 8 July 1994.

14.3 Wardship

14.3.1 WHEN DOES WARDSHIP BECOME EFFECTIVE?

RE K (ADOPTION AND WARDSHIP) [1997] 2 FLR 221 (FamD)

At the commencement of the hearing, counsel for Mr and Mrs F indicated that they wished to withdraw their application, and I formally refused it. That could not be the end of the story, however, for E is presently in this jurisdiction in the de facto care of Mr and Mrs F. She has been there since November 1992. It is the only family she has ever known and she regards Mr and Mrs F in effect as her parents. Dr Cameron uses the phrase 'psychological parents'.

With the consent of all the parties the court proceeded to order that E should become a ward of court. A formal application was made to issue an originating summons by Mr and Mrs F. This was done with the consent of all the parties and accordingly E became and is now a ward of this court which assumes the responsibility for her welfare.

The court must consider, in the light of the representations of all the parties and the whole of the circumstances attending this tragic story, how the best interests of E may be secured in the immediate and foreseeable future.

The K family want E to be restored to their care as soon as possible. They had not of course seen her since the tragic events of May 1992 when she was a little baby. Arrangements were made by the Official Solicitor for the grandfather together with the uncle, R, and his wife to visit Mr and Mrs F's home between 9 and 11 January 1997. There they met E. . . .

Both Mr and Mrs F have expressed regret to the K family and have said that they are very sorry for what they have done. I am nevertheless left with the impression that either they do not fully appreciate or are unwilling to acknowledge the gravity of the consequences of their behaviour. In the field of adoption, particularly of international adoption, trust is absolutely vital. In this instance the trust of the K family and of the Bosnian Red Cross and the Bosnian Government has been seriously undermined and damaged.

The Court of Appeal has since reversed the adoption order made by the county court and, as a result of ordering a rehearing, the adoption application has finally been refused. There is now no question of E being adopted by Mr and Mrs F. She is and must be regarded by everyone as a K. She is, however, still in the care of Mr and Mrs F who have looked after her for practically the whole of her young life.

I have heard the evidence of the grandfather and of E's uncle and of his wife. I have heard from Dr Cameron of the circumstances in which they live in Switzerland. I was greatly impressed by the dignified bearing of each one of them. They were, if I may say so, first-class witnesses, not exaggerating anything, and giving their answers frankly and directly. They have all been through a terrible time. The grandfather and uncle in particular have been casualties of war interned in a concentration camp, having seen their home village destroyed. They are very conscious of their family links and they have a large extended family not only in Bosnia but in other parts of the world. The grandfather, I am told, keeps a frieze of the village in his room and is sentimentally very attached to his home village in which he cannot presently live. It means a very great deal to them that E has survived.

Their circumstances have been carefully described to the court. Their proposal is that as soon as it is possible E should make her home with her uncle and his wife. They have a little boy, who is 2 years of age, and they have M, the little girl who was injured with her cousin E in the garage in Bosnia. She is now 5. They also have in their family the 13-year-old son from the uncle's wife's former marriage.

I have no doubt at all of their good faith and their very genuine wish to have E as a member of their family as well as their sincere belief that they could overcome the difficulties involved. As Dr Cameron has pointed out, they have a very strong sense of having been betrayed. They speak of E having been stolen.

E's present physical circumstances have been described as being wholly excellent from the standpoint of a little girl, She has a wonderful country home with a loving caring family albeit a substitute family. The care which has been given to her has not, however, been overdone. It has been sensible care and her medical needs have been responsibly addressed. She attends a good private school where she is being given good tuition to meet her needs and certain difficulties which she has. She is described as being a happy, outgoing child with an excellent personality. She enjoys a family life with the two boys C and D. It is possible that she might know that D is an adopted child, but I very much doubt whether any such considerations enter her mind.

Dr Cameron has described the 'exceptional' looking after parenting of E over the past 4 years. . . .

He says that Mr and Mrs F have shown themselves willing and able to voice tenaciously what they perceive to be in E's welfare and best interests. Secondly, he says that now they are confidently able to promote open contact with E's natural family as she grows up. He adds his comment that these two factors are significantly protective towards a child's developmental well-being when being brought up in a substitute family. The disadvantage of her remaining with Mr and Mrs F is that of being brought up largely out of contact with her Bosnian culture, her Muslim religion and the Bosnian language and the knowledge of all her extended family as she grows up. Dr Cameron notes what he describes as a further disadvantage if it is considered that Mr and Mrs F have been involved in a subterfuge in holding her in England away from her natural family.

I have to say that I find that they have been involved in such a subterfuge. . . . He sums up the welfare consideration in the following terms:

While the [K] family's right to have [E] returned to them is completely accepted, and from [E's] point of view she has been deeply wronged by this being denied her, the question is how best to promote [E's] welfare now, 2 months short of her fifth birthday, after she has grown up for the past $4\frac{1}{2}$ years of her life within the same settled English country family.

[E] is more vulnerable to emotional/behavioural disorder than the average child. Her vulnerability arises from three causes:

(1) Serious brain injury at 9 weeks, with three metal fragments retained within her brain.
(2) Institutional (dietary, medical and emotional) neglect during 5 important formative months in her first year of life.
(3) Death of her mother, and her father missing, in her first year of life.

A child without such a history of harm and losses would be likely to be psychologically more resilient. [E] is emotionally attached; she is not an emotionally free child as she was when abandoned to the care of the orphanage. [E] has a deep long-lasting emotional attachment to the [F] family continuously from 7 months onwards. [E's] primary psychological attachment now to the [F] family includes sharing in family experiences with all of them for the past 4.2 years of her 4.9 years of life. The little girl's trust in the [F] family is absolute. Removing [E], even very skilfully, would cause in her the unavoidable reaction of protest, despair and detachment, the universal anger/depressive response seen in happy young children when removed forcibly from the only home and family they have ever known. This response varies in severity. [E's] vulnerability makes her likely to have a more profound reaction than most.

Dr Cameron points to the problems which would be likely to be encountered if she were to return to her K family. He points to what he describes as protest, despair and detachment. She would feel herself to have lost her primary family and she would pine for them and in consequence show depression and physical/emotional withdrawal. What he describes as oppositional and defiant behaviour: non-communication and reluctance to speak; regression in behaviour by possibly starting wetting and maybe soiling as well.

From a welfare point of view there is a high risk of injury and serious disturbance if she were now to be moved to Switzerland. She might regard it as punishment, but it would be punishment not for her actions but punishment for the adults' past mistakes. . . .

I believe that Mr and Mrs F, notwithstanding the appalling irresponsibility of their past behaviour, are nevertheless capable of acting in E's interests now that the whole situation has been revealed. It will require very great strength of character on their part. It will require an almost superhuman effort on their part to gain the confidence of the K family.

On the part of the grandfather and the uncle and step-aunt it will require an equally difficult and strenuous effort to act in what I believe to be E's interests. They feel angry and cheated. It is appropriate that the court should recognise and make clear that it recognises the wrong which they have suffered. But the court has now to consider first and foremost the interests of E. The court will keep control of E as its ward and will endeavour to ensure that those who have responsibility for her act in her interests. It is essential for E's well-being that there should be stability and security in her young life.

I shall order that the wardship shall continue during her minority or until further order. I shall order that the Official Solicitor shall continue to act as E's guardian ad litem until further order. I shall order that E be in the care and control of the plaintiffs, Mr and Mrs F. I shall order that there shall be access or contact to the K family as follows. First, at least four visits in each year including a period of between 7 and 10 days at the plaintiffs' home and a period of 7 to 10 days at the home of either the grandfather or of the uncle and his wife in Switzerland. In addition two weekends at the homes of the grandfather and/or of the uncle and his wife. There will be unlimited indirect contact by means of letters, cards and gifts. The Official Solicitor has indicated that he or his representative would be prepared to supervise the first and second periods of contact and if possible Dr Cameron should be concerned in those matters too.

14.3.2 CONSEQUENCES OF WARDSHIP

RE S (MINORS) (WARDSHIP: EDUCATION) [1988] 1 FLR 128 (FamD)

WAITE J: In these wardship proceedings the court is concerned with the future of four children: J, now very nearly 13; H, aged just 8; and twins, R and J, aged 7. They were made wards of court at the suit of the borough council because of grave concerns regarding the conditions under which they were living in the home and their lack of development at school. The body of evidence filed by the local authority in support of the wardship proceedings includes affidavits from Mrs Y, a teacher in charge of the special school for maladjusted children currently being attended by H, and from Mrs R, who is an educational psychologist employed by the county council, dealing with the psychological development of all the children.

The case is typical of many others in that the children's development at school is closely linked with the quality of home care they have been receiving, and is thus bound to play an important part in any decision eventually reached by the court. To that end, on 20 September 1986 Eastham J gave leave for all four children to be examined by a consultant clinical psychologist. So far as I am aware—and I am sure Mr Orford will correct me if I am wrong—there was no opposition to that order by the council.

The case has now taken in some respects a fortunate turn in that a good deal of the controversy has been removed, largely as a result of the withdrawal from the children's lives of a man who was thought to represent the threat of a very serious and dangerous influence. So the parties have come to court today ready to ask me to make, by consent, an order that the children should continue to enjoy the protection of wardship, but that they, should all remain in the care and control of their mother, subject to the safeguard of continuing supervision by the council and an undertaking by, the mother to use her best endeavours to ensure that the children have no contact at all with the man in question.

The only issue remaining for decision and still in dispute between the parties is the one of education. The mother asks, with the support in principle of a recent report from the consultant clinical psychologist, Mrs M, that H should, at a suitable moment, leave his special school and transfer to the general system. She asks also—though this is not a matter dealt with in any detail by Mrs M—that the twins should cease to receive the special nursery nurse assistance and tuition which they are presently receiving in their normal school. There is no controversy about the future of J. The mother's views are supported by her former husband, the father of the three younger children, who has come to court today—acting in person—to tell me his views.

At a preliminary stage, the local authority has objected to the wardship jurisdiction being exercised at all. Mr Orford submits on the authority's behalf that there is a clear statutory code laid down by the Education Acts, in particular the Education Act 1981, which makes it the statutory duty of a local authority to assess the special educational needs of a child and to provide for him or her in a suitable case by special schooling. The 1981 Act contains machinery for consultation of parents and a right of objection and appeal all the way up, if need be, to the Secretary of Stare. The court should therefore decline, says Mr Orford (tactfully but firmly), to interfere with decisions about the general or special education of the children who are its wards. The child population generally has been placed under this special educational code, and the mere fact that particular children happen to be wards of court should not make any difference.

In opposition to that submission, Miss Kushner, for the mother, says that the local authority have seen fit at their own request to surrender their statutory powers under the Children Act 1975 and have invited the court to become a judicial parent. What is good for the Children Act is good, she says, for the Education Act, and once the jurisdiction has been invoked, it has been invoked for all purposes. She points out, moreover, that here issues of custody and education are closely entwined—as witness the fact that Mrs R was brought into the case as a witness at a very early stage.

On this matter of jurisdiction I have no hesitation in preferring the submissions of Miss Kushner. Once the local authority have decided to entrust a decision as to the future of these children to the High Court, it is no longer open to them to pick and choose and say to the judge: 'You can deal with this aspect or the other of the children's future, but we reserve our statutory right to a monopoly opinion on certain matters.' Once wards of court, these children are 'in for a penny, in for a pound', and I hold that I have just as full and unfettered a jurisdiction to decide their educational future—notwithstanding the statutory code—as I have to determine any other step that requires to be taken in their lives with the appropriate authority of the court whose wards they remain.

That is my ruling. We can proceed now to evidence and argument on merits.

14.4 The Local Authority and the Inherent Jurisdiction

14.4.1 RESTRICTIONS

CHILDREN ACT 1989

100. Restrictions on use of wardship jurisdiction

(1)   Section 7 of the Family Law Reform Act 1969 (which gives the High Court power to place a ward of court in the care, or under the supervision, of a local authority) shall cease to have effect.

(2)   No court shall exercise the High Court's inherent jurisdiction with respect to children—

(a)   so as to require a child to be placed in the care, or put under the supervision, of a local authority;

(b)   so as to require a child to be accommodated by or on behalf of a local authority;

(c)   so as to make a child who is the subject of a care order a ward of court; or

(d)   for the purpose of conferring on any local authority power to determine any question which has arisen, or which may arise, in connection with any aspect of parental responsibility for a child.

(3)   No application for any exercise of the court's inherent jurisdiction with respect to children may be made by a local authority unless the authority have obtained the leave of the court.

(4)   The court may only grant leave if it is satisfied that—

(a)   the result which the authority wish to achieve could not be achieved through the making of any order of a kind to which subsection (5) applies; and

(b)   there is reasonable cause to believe that if the court's inherent jurisdiction is not exercised with respect to the child he is likely to suffer significant harm.

(5)   This subsection applies to any order—

(a)   made otherwise than in the exercise of the court's inherent jurisdiction; and

(b)   which the local authority is entitled to apply for (assuming, in the case of any application which may only be made with leave, that leave is granted).

Parry, M, 'The Children Act 1989: Local Authorities, Wardship and the Revival of the Inherent Jurisdiction', (1992) 3 *Journal of Social Welfare and Family Law* 212

The new and exhaustive statutory code for the making of care and supervision orders, in particular the prospective nature of the criteria in s. 31(2) and the concurrent jurisdiction extending to the High Court in s. 92, are matched by major limitations in s. 100 upon the use by local authorities of the inherent jurisdiction and in particular wardship.

Thus, s. 100(1) abolishes the power in the Family Law Reform Act 1969, s. 7, whereby the High Court in exceptional circumstances could place a ward in the care, or under the supervision, of a local authority. A child is only to be subject to a care or supervision order as a result of an application by a local authority, or the NSPCC as authorised person, to that effect. The court must then be satisfied as to the criteria in s. 31(2) and, additionally, that the child's welfare, as the paramount consideration, requires the making of such an order in accordance with s. 1. As proceedings under the inherent jurisdiction (which includes wardship proceedings) are within the Act's definition of 'family proceedings' (s. 8), if a court exercising the wardship jurisdiction considers that it may be appropriate for a care or supervision order to be made it cannot make such all order, but may direct the local authority to undertake a s. 37 investigation of the child's circumstances. The decision whether or not to apply, for a care or supervision order is, however, for the local authority to make.

Section 100(2) then goes on to provide that:

> No court shall exercise the High Court's inherent jurisdiction with respect to children—
>   (a)   so as to require a child to be placed in the care, or put under the supervision, of a local authority;
>   (b)   so as to require a child to be accommodated by or on behalf of a local authority;
>   (c)   so as to make a child who is the subject of a care order a ward of court; or
>   (d)   for the purpose of conferring on any local authority power to determine any question which has arisen, or which may arise, in connection with any aspect of parental responsibility for a child.

It needs to be stressed that the first, second and fourth of the above restrictions relate to the *inherent* jurisdiction, which includes but is not limited to wardship, whilst the third relates specifically to the *wardship* part of the inherent jurisdiction. The nature and extent of each restriction calls for further analysis.

The High Court's inherent jurisdiction, including wardship, is not to be used to place a child in the care, or put under the supervision of a local authority
Section 100(2)(a) corresponds to the repeal of s. 7 of the Family Law Reform Act 1969. A child call only be placed in the care or under the supervision of a local authority after an application under s. 31 and proof of the relevant criteria in s. 31(2) *and* s. 1; not, as prior to the Act, of the High Court's own motion on the sole basis of the paramountcy of the child's welfare. The Act removed wardship as a local authority 'safety net' because:

> Such a discretion, guided by the principle of child's best interests, may be appropriate and defensible where a court is deciding a dispute between warring members of a family. However once the court become(s) involved in intervention from outside the family, and especially where State intervention is proposed, I do not believe that a broad discretion without defined minimum criteria, whatever its guiding principle can be justified. (Mackay, 1989, p. 508).

The High Court's inherent jurisdiction, including wardship, is not to be used to accommodate a child by or on behalf of a local authority
The provision of accommodation by local authorities is an important part of their support duties for children and their families under Part III of the Act. These duties have replaced the former mis-named 'voluntary care' where a child was received into care under s. 2 of the Child Care Act 1980. As with committal of a child into care a child may be provided with accommodation only in accordance with the Act and not under the inherent jurisdiction.

The High Court's inherent jurisdiction is not to be used to make a child who is the subject of a care order a ward of court
This restriction corresponds with that in s. 91(4) that if a ward of court is committed to the care of a local authority the wardship is terminated. So too a child who is the subject

THE INHERENT JURISDICTION

of a care order cannot be warded and such a child does not become a ward on the making of an application in wardship (Supreme Court Act 1981, s. 41(2A) as inserted), as would otherwise be the case. Section 100(2)(c) of the Act thereby gives statutory effect to *A* v *Liverpool City Council* [1982] AC 363 and *Re W (a minor)* [1985] AC 791 regarding the use of wardship against a local authority in whose favour there is a care order. It goes further, however, by preventing local authorities from not opposing a third party's initiation of wardship regarding a child who is the subject of a care order.

Section 100(2)(c) relates to the use of wardship and not the wider inheritance jurisdiction. It is possible for a local authority to apply for the exercise of the the High Court's wider inherent jurisdiction, for example to obtain all injunction regarding a child who is the subject of a care order without the child being made a ward of court if, as will be discussed later, the court has granted leave under s. 100(3).

The High Court's inherent jurisdiction, including wardship, is not to be used to confer power on a local authority to determine any question in connection with any aspect of parental responsibility

Section 100(2)(d) relates to the case where a local authority which does not have parental responsibility, as it would by virtue of a care order, seeks to determine an issue regarding a child's upbringing. It cannot invoke the inherent jurisdiction so as to authorise *it*, for example, to determine whether the child should undergo particular medical treatment. The restriction is a further example of the principle in the Act that a local authority should only have power to determine issues arising in connection with parental responsibility if there is a care order in its favour. Where there is, the local authority will have parental responsibility and be able to determine such questions. As the child is 'looked after' by the local authority in the terms of s. 22, the authority must consult as appropriate, with the child, his or her parents and others concerned regarding the matter to be decided (s. 22(4)).

Where the child is not in care and the local authority wish to seek the court's guidance on such issues, it is submitted that they will usually be expected to apply for 'a specific issue order' or 'a prohibited steps order' under s. 8. If the court decides to exercise its powers to make such an order it must not do so in any way which circumvents s. 100(2) (s. 9(5)), for example so as to require the child to be accommodated by or on behalf of a local authority. The Act thus operates to restrict, rather than as Freeman (1990, p. 167) argues, to prohibit the local authority from seeking a specific issue order. Conversely if a local authority wishes to use the inherent jurisdiction as a form of 'specific issue' or 'prohibited steps' order it can do so only within the narrow confines of s. 100(3).

Local authority applications under the inherent jurisdiction
The restrictions in s. 100:

> only prevent the inherent jurisdiction being used as an alternative to a care or supervision order or otherwise to confer compulsory powers on local authorities in respect of children. However, subject to that limitation, and to obtaining the leave of the court . . . the High Court will continue to be able to exercise its inherent powers at the instance of a local authority, whether the child is in care or not.' (Mackay 1989, p. 507).

There is thus some limited scope for a local authority to seek the exercise of the inherent jurisdiction, particularly if the child is in care as the authority is then disqualified from seeking a specific issue or prohibited steps order (s. 9(1)). The local authority might wish to do so, for example, so as to seek the court's direction with regard to a specific and sensitive or urgent issue concerning a child which cannot satisfactorily be dealt with under the Act. Examples might relate to undesirable publicity (as in *Re M (minors) (wardship: publication of information)* [1989] 3 WLR 1136); or significant medical treatment such as abortion (as in *Re B (wardship: abortion)* [1991] 2 FLR 426), sterilisation (as in *Re B (a minor) (wardship: sterilisation)* [1988] AC 199), where Lord Templeman opined that any sterilisation of a girl under 18 should *only* be carried out with leave of a High Court judge or an operation to preserve (as in *Re B (a minor) (wardship: medical treatment)* [1981] 1 WLR 1421) or prolong (as in *Re J (a minor) (wardship: medical treatment)* [1990] 3 All ER 930) the child's life, provided in any such case, however, that the leave criteria are satisfied. The point has been well made that 'While such an issue is obviously crucial to the child concerned, it must not be assumed that leave will always be given.' (White, Carr and Lowe 1990, p. 133.)

Section 100(3) provides, that: 'No application for any exercise of the court's inherent jurisdiction with respect to children may be made by a local authority unless the authority have obtained the leave of the court.' This leave requirement is potentially a formidable hurdle because the court's discretion to grant leave can only be exercised if it is satisfied as follows. First, that the result which the authority wish to achieve could not be achieved through the making of an order (which the authority is entitled to for assuming in the case of any application which may only be made with leave, that leave is granted) other than under the inherent jurisdiction, i.e. under the statutory jurisdiction. Secondly, that there is reasonable cause to believe that if the court's inherent jurisdiction is not exercised the child is likely to suffer significant harm (s. 100(4) and (5)).

The local authority, in seeking such leave, thus has the considerable burden of proving how the child protection legislation available to it is, in the circumstances inadequate, (so if the child is not in care, why is a care or supervision order unavailable or inappropriate) *and* that there is reasonable cause to believe that the child is likely to suffer significant harm if the High Court does not exercise the inherent jurisdiction. The narrowness of this second part of the criteria for leave has rightly been questioned (Lowe 1989, p. 88; Eekelaar and Dingwall 1989, p. 218) in view of the fact that the local authority is not seeking parental responsibility to be vested either in itself or the court, but merely for the court to be able to determine a particular issue. The effect of these leave qualifications is such as to limit considerably the use of the inherent jurisdiction by local authorities, particularly where the child is not in care, as the local authority is not then disqualified, as it is where the child is in care (s. 9(1)), from seeking a specific issue or prohibited steps order.

Even if the leave requirement is satisfied, *and* the court decides to exercise its discretion in favour of allowing the application to be made, the local authority will still have to establish its case for the grant of the relief sought. If the relief is an injunction, then reference has already been made to the possible need for the applicant, on his own or the child's behalf, to establish a legal or equitable right sufficient to support the injunction. The better view, it is suggested, is that the court is not being asked to grant an injunction within the framework of s. 37 of the Supreme Court Act 1981, but within the wider *parens patriae* jurisdiction, under which the court should have power to grant an injunction where it is necessary in order to protect the child. The test to be applied at this stage depends upon the nature of the issue in question. If it relates to the upbringing of the child, including, it is submitted, medical treatment, or the administration of the child's property, then in accordance with s. 1(1) of the Act, the court must regard the child's welfare as the paramount consideration. Where, however, the proceedings relate not to the exercise of this 'upbringing jurisdiction' that is what, under the pre Act law, Lowe and White called the 'custodial jurisdiction' (1986, p. 145), but to what Lowe and White classified as 'the protective jurisdiction' where the court's concern is to protect the child from harm, for example from the effects of publicity, the child's interests are not necessarily paramount (see *Re X (a minor) (wardship: jurisdiction)* [1975] Fam 47). The court's function is to balance the protection of the child against the rights of others and, notwithstanding that some harm to the child may be foreseen, some other interest, in particular the public interest, may on balance, prevail. In this way the rights of third parties can adequately be protected without the need for the applicant or the child to have a proprietary interest capable of being supported by an injunction in the way suggested in *Richards* v *Richards* [1984] AC 174.

14.4.2   WHY S. 100?

Lord Mackay of Clashfern, 'Perceptions of the Children Bill and beyond',
***New Law Journal*, 14 April 1989**

Restrictions on wardship

I now turn to one of the more controversial and, I believe most misunderstood provisions in the Bill, the restrictions on wardship, about which there has been a good deal of comment. Most of it has expressed reservations, some of it, very grave in tone. This is not, perhaps, surprising. The wardship jurisdiction has come to be relied on as the judicial 'fail-safe' where children are concerned and great importance has rightly become attached to it. What has made matters more difficult is that the Government's decision to restrict its use was taken late in the day, partly in the context of its decision to provide a concurrent jurisdiction for care cases. Accordingly, there has been little opportunity to explain what the effect of the Bill is on wardship and why the Government thinks some restriction is called for. I hope that this evening I can make our purpose and the effect of the Bill clear.

As I understand the concern, it centres on a belief that restrictions in the Bill on local authority resort to wardship will remove wardship as a safety net and, secondly, prevent or hinder the more difficult or complex local authority cases coming before a superior court and, in particular, the High Court.

As regards removing wardship as a safety net, I should begin by saying that in the Government's view wardship is only one use of the High Court's inherent *parens patriae* jurisdiction. We believe therefore, that it is open to the High Court to make orders under its inherent jurisdiction in respect of children otherwise than through wardship.

Bearing that in mind, the next thing I should explain is that the restrictions in the Bill only prevent the inherent jurisdiction being used as an alternative to a care or supervision order or otherwise to confer compulsory powers on local authorities in respect of children. However, subject to that limitation, and to obtaining the leave of the court, to which I will return in a minute, the High Court will continue to be able to exercise its inherent powers at the instance of a local authority, whether the child is in care or not. Thus, for example, if injunction relief is needed to protect a child in care from harm or there is a particularly difficult issue, such as an irreversible medical procedure, the High Court's inherent powers will remain available to deal with it, subject to leave.

As regards local authorities needing leave, in the Government's view the inherent jurisdiction should not be invoked in a matter covered by statute. Further, as I explained earlier, there should be no state intervention in families save where, as a minimum, there is a likelihood of significant harm to the child. The grounds for local authority leave reflect that policy. However, those grounds would not prevent the High Court, for example, exercising its inherent power to sanction or forbid an abortion being carried out on a child under a care order, there being no statutory means of seeking a court order and the decision, if wrong, plainly being likely to cause significant harm to the child.

Reasons for restrictions

As to the reasons why restrictions on the inherent jurisdiction are thought desirable, there are three. First, as I explained earlier, conditions under the Bill provide in effect that compulsory powers by the state over a child are not even to be contemplated unless it is shown that the child is at least likely to suffer significant harm as a result of a lack of reasonable parenting. To put a child in compulsory care or under supervision or otherwise to give local authorities compulsory powers in other circumstances could not be justified in the Government's view.

I realise, of course, that it will be said that there will be difficult borderline cases where at present wardship, which can be invoked simply on the basis of the child's best interests, would offer a remedy. In my view, however, that argument underlines the need for the restrictions in the Bill and I say so for this reason. Wherever rules of law apply there will always be borderline cases where it may be difficult both as a matter of law and on the merits to say whether a case falls or indeed should fall, within or without a rule. The only means of avoiding borderline cases is to avoid rules and to operate a discretion. Such a discretion, guided by the principle of child's best interests, may be appropriate and defensible where a court is deciding a dispute between warring members of a family. However, once the court become involved in intervention from outside the family, and especially where State intervention is proposed, I do not believe that a broad discretion without defined minimum criteria, whatever its guiding principle, can be justified.

The integrity and independence of the family is the basic building block of a free and democratic society and the need to defend it should be clearly perceivable in the law. Accordingly, unless there is evidence that a child is being or is likely to be positively harmed because of a failure in the family, the state, whether in the guise of a local authority or a court, should not interfere. To provide otherwise would make it lawful for children to be removed from their families simply on the basis that a court considered that the State could do better for the child than his family. The threat to the poor and to minority groups, whose views of what is good for a child may not coincide closely with that of the majority, is all too apparent, and it is one which the Bill takes steps to remove by precluding the broad inherent jurisdiction being used as an alternative to orders for local authority care and supervision under the Bill.

The second reason for the restriction on the inherent jurisdiction is that we have not thought it appropriate or practicable for the responsibility for a child in the care of a public authority which is statutorily charged with looking after him to be subject to the detailed directions of another public authority, namely the courts. In such circumstances, we have only thought it essential that everyone, and not least the local authority itself, should be clear that the authority is responsible for the child and his welfare. Again, we are back to perception. Accordingly, provided that the authority does not exceed the limits of what is reasonable (and expose itself to judicial review) it should not be subject to mandatory directions from outside about how to discharge its duties towards the child. Perhaps I should add, however, that the Bill will require local authorities to set up machinery with an independent element to hear complaints and representations about their care of a child.

Finally, as I have already explained, the Bill will enable the Government to set up a concurrent jurisdiction in care related cases which will match the weight and complexity of the case to the tier of court, with the most complex or difficult cases coming to the High Court. That rational system, which aims amongst other things to ensure that the scarce expertise of the High Court is reserved for the most complex or difficult cases, would be disrupted if a local authority could secure a High Court hearing simply by choosing to invoke the inherent jurisdiction rather than seeking an order under the Bill.

Turning briefly to concern about the risk of hindering High Court hearings of the most complex or difficult care cases, that is the exact opposite of what the Government believes will be the result of the Bill, for as I have explained earlier we are setting up machinery to ensure that such cases are identified and channelled expeditiously up to a county court or the High Court.